LONDON

AND THE LIFE OF LITERATURE

IN LATE VICTORIAN ENGLAND

The Diary of George Gissing,
Novelist

GEORGE GISSING

September 1888

LONDON
AND THE LIFE OF
LITERATURE
IN LATE VICTORIAN
ENGLAND

The Diary of George Gissing, Novelist

EDITED BY

PIERRE COUSTILLAS

Director, Centre for Victorian Studies, University of Lille

LEWISBURG
BUCKNELL UNIVERSITY PRESS

First American edition published 1978 by
ASSOCIATED UNIVERSITY PRESSES, INC.
Cranbury, N.J. 08512

Library of Congress Catalog Card Number 77-72970

ISBN 0-8387-2145-1

Typesetting by
Cold Composition Ltd
220 Vale Road, Tonbridge, Kent

Printed in Great Britain
Redwood Burn Limited, Trowbridge, Wiltshire

Contents

Introduction 1
1887 PRELUDE 17
1888 RELEASE AND ESCAPE.................................... 18
1889 GREECE GLORIOUS AND INGLORIOUS.................... 115
1890 THE SEARCH FOR A WIFE 190
1891 MARRIAGE AND MEDITATION............................ 235
1892 DOWN IN DEVON... 266
1893 THE LURE OF LONDON 294
1894 PRIVATE AND PUBLIC 326
1895 A LEAP FORWARD.. 359
1896 SHADOWS OF THE PAST 399
1897 DOMESTIC TROUBLES AND FLIGHT TO ITALY........... 432
1898 THE UNATTAINABLE WITHIN REACH 479
1899 THE IDEAL TESTED 510
1900 WORK AND WORRIES..................................... 523
1901 DISEASE AND DEPRESSION 535
1902 A LIFE'S EVENING.. 540

Notes.. 551
Who's Who in Gissing's Diary 567
Index of Gissing's Writings 591
Index of Persons 595

Acknowledgements

FOR the privilege of editing the diary of George Gissing I am grateful to the late Alfred Gissing, the author's younger son, to the Henry W. and Albert A. Berg Collection of the New York Public Library, and particularly to its curator, Lola L. Szladits; also to John Spiers of the Harvester Press. Without their kind permissions and generous assistance publication would have been impossible.

I am also indebted to a number of friends and correspondents for helping me to clarify difficult points: Francesco Badolato, Vittorio Bartocetti, Alan Clodd, C.S. Collinson, John Coombes, Chris and Michèle Kohler, Jacob Korg, Piet Kropholler, Michel Krzak, Sylvère Monod, Padre Rulli, S.J., Gillian Tindall, Martha Vogeler, and H. Whittleston.

Special thanks are due to Denise Le Mallier who, with her usual efficiency and generosity, threw invaluable light on some persons mentioned by Gissing during the years he stayed in France, and to Hubert Le Bourdellès and René Leclerq whose familiarity with Latin and Greek helped me to solve several thorny questions.

P.C.

Editor's Note

FOOTNOTES, indicated by an asterisk, have been used only in exceptional cases: (1) to supply information which was required immediately for understanding the passage and which, for stylistic reasons, could not be given in square brackets in the text; (2) whenever Gissing himself appended a note to an entry. If the authorship of the footnote is not made obvious by the context, "Gissing's note" is added.

Editorial square brackets have been used when the information supplied is very short and is more conveniently inserted in the text than in a note at the end of the book: thus unusual or obscure abbreviations have been expanded and publication data have been given. Also any brief explanation which clarifies a statement or helps to identify a person without rendering the text less comfortably legible. Similarly words inadvertently omitted by Gissing have been supplied in square brackets. Round brackets in the diary proper are always Gissing's.

The notes at the end of the book are intended to elucidate points on which it was impossible to throw light in a brief statement in square brackets. In these notes information is provided about such persons as appear once in the Diary and whose identification matters only in connection with the passage concerned. They may also contain relevant bibliographical details or refer the reader to a particular entry or another note. "Who is Who in Gissing's Diary" records the names of persons who play a significant part in the Diary, or at least who appear a number of times.

Titles of newspapers and periodicals have been systematically italicized for clarity's sake. The titles of books, poems, articles etc. have been left in inverted commas. Foreign quotations have been translated only when the meaning was not obvious, or when the sense, as distinguished from the phrasing or style, was particularly important for the understanding of the passage.

Introduction

THE private life and personal habits of novelists have been an attractive subject for journalists and the reading public at large since the establishment of the popular press. They may or may not be of interest. A description of the study of Mr. So-and-So, the author of this or that celebrated novel, will only appeal to people who are concerned with the futile accessories of literature, but when we happen to lay hands on a document which enables us to visualise an author at work year in year out over a period of fifteen years, we can claim to possess a document of exceptional value. Such is Gissing's diary. The man in the street invests the writing of fiction with the glamour of independence and abundant royalties. In fact a novelist has a good many masters besides his own wayward self, and a plentiful financial return is a rare (and, as often as not, dangerous) blessing. Gissing's diary, if we brush aside Malagrida's warning that speech was given to man that he might conceal his thought, reads like a deflationary enterprise. It shows us, better than any writer's diary I know of, what it is like to be a novelist—"a trade of the damned", he himself said to Austin Harrison. By any standard the present diary would be valuable since very few novelists have ever had the taste or the staying power to keep a diary, but seen against the background of the late Victorian period, it stands by itself—a mirror of late Victorian life as well as of a distinguished intellect cast in the mould of a fragile body. It throws light on a number of cultural, historical, aesthetic and biographical questions, it enables us to watch the process of literary creation from the conception of a story in the novelist's brain to the receipt of the publisher's cheque, and it certainly disposes of the ludicrous charge that Gissing had no inspiration but his own biography. As we read on, our mind receives a myriad impressions—the dramatic account of a woman's death in the eighties, a comment on some historic occurrence, a pathetic self-questioning or qualm of conscience, the sarcastic account of a literary gathering—and we form an image of a past world such as no literary historian or chronicler of historical events can give us.

I

Gissing's productive years coincide with qualitative and accelerated changes in the field of culture and his own particular case enables one to witness these changes from an interesting angle. Fraught as it is with reflections on the intellectual context of the period, his journal provides material for, and invites a fresh discussion of, some of the historical and sociological issues dealt with by Raymond Williams, Richard D. Altick and Guinevere L. Griest among others.

1

What Williams set out to write in *The Long Revolution* is "a critical history of ideas and values" from the 1780s, that is from the outset of the Industrial Revolution to the mid-twentieth century. He brilliantly analyses the spread of democracy during that period, disentangling the political, social (educational in particular) and economic factors. His aim, more or less clearly acknowledged, was to review the evolution and diversification of the notion of culture, through a careful consideration of the development of education and of the popular press. And in his discussion Williams attempts to demolish the view that the year 1870, with the passing of Forster's Education Act, is a watershed in the history of Britain's cultural expansion. Now, if some of his arguments are sound and cogent, some others seem to me to be invalidated rather than confirmed by Gissing's career as it appears in his diary. The point is all the more relevant as Williams himself involves Gissing and *New Grub Street* in his discussion[1]. It is quite true that popular education did not start abruptly in 1870, nor does R.C. Ensor, the object of Williams' attack, ignore the findings of Llewellyn Woodward in the previous volume of the Oxford History of England. There was in the 1830s and 1840s a widespread if disorderly movement for the education of the illiterate masses. The *Penny Magazine,* launched by the Society for the Diffusion of Useful Knowledge, had reached a circulation of 200,000. Thanks to the removal of the taxes on newspapers, both daily and Sunday press expanded notably before 1870. Furthermore a number of popular weeklies were founded and flourished before the creation of Board Schools. Yet, it is clear enough that 1870 was a crucial date and that Williams' tendency to play down the importance of Forster's Act must be resisted. He himself, after fighting Ensor's view, adopts a number of Ensor's arguments, admitting that "the forces making for cheap newspapers gathered strength as the press moved into the 1870s and 1880s"[2]. Anyone reading in turn popular periodicals of the 1840s and of the 1880s and 1890s is bound to feel a difference which is more fundamental than the difference of type and illustration. Before 1870 popular education was diffused in an atmosphere of philanthropy to which was attached the flavour of the Sunday School, and the human virtues lauded by Samuel Smiles. The name of the Society for the Diffusion of Useful Knowledge has markedly pro-Forster connotations; like the SPCK nowadays, it had by the last twenty years of the nineteenth century, with Northcliffe and Harmsworth in the fray, an old-fashioned air. The number of weeklies and dailies continued to increase after 1870, catering for the needs of a growing mass of readers, from those whom Gissing called the quarter-educated to upper-middle classes. A rough count shows that there were dozens which published book reviews and in which Gissing's volumes were reviewed. Book-reviewing extended remarkably between 1870 and 1900. It is impossible not to see in such a phenomenon a direct consequence of the cultural expansion triggered by Forster's Act. Besides, the popular press which, earlier in the century, had aimed at educating its readers tended more and more to please—and flatter—their tastes; instruction gave way to entertainment. Gissing watched this development and analysed it in *New Grub Street;* his testimony—indirectly confirmed

2

by the mention in his diary of many new low-brow magazines—is that of a clear-eyed observer, and it has a value which the present-day generation, not having the feel of the situation, must respect.

Gissing's life and a number of his exponent characters throw some further light on the question from another angle. English fiction up to about 1870 offers a type of hero which one may briefly describe as the model young man of lowly origin who climbs the social ladder through his own efforts and ends his career perfectly integrated into society. Jem Wilson in *Mary Barton*, Adam Bede and Jabez Clegg in Mrs. Linnaeus Banks's *The Manchester Man* are characteristic examples. This type of character, after Forster's Education Act had roused cultural ambitions in a new generation of young men, was quickly replaced by another type of hero, many variants of which appear in Gissing's works—the lower-class young man with frustrated intellectual aspirations. Gissing lucidly expounded his views on the subject in a letter of 10 February 1895 to Morley Roberts: "The most characteristic, the most important part of my work is that which deals with a class of young men distinctive of our time— well educated, fairly bred, but *without money*"[3]. Arthur Golding in *Workers in the Dawn*, Osmond Waymark in *The Unclassed*, Bernard Kingcote in *Isabel Clarendon* are the first three in the novels, but of course *New Grub Street* and *Born in Exile* offer the classic examples[4]. Hardy in *Jude the Obscure*, Mark Rutherford and the early Wells, whose social origins were similar to those of Gissing, also depicted this type of young man. In Gissing as in those of his characters named above there prevails a feeling of alienation, of which he was exquisitely conscious. He sensed painfully the interrelation between the political, economic and cultural changes discussed by Raymond Williams.

The date of Gissing's birth made him an ideal observer of the enforcement of the 1870 Act since he belonged to the first generation that was to benefit from it. One of his father's last public actions as a municipal councillor in Wakefield had been to take the necessary steps for the creation of a local school board in pursuance of the provisions of the Act, and George could notice in his native town the materialization of the legislator's intentions. He saw around him a new generation of children accede to literacy but he did not view himself as one of them. In this he was right—he did not feel a part of the new system since he attended a private school, and he was justifiably convinced that he would anyway have carried on his formal education pretty far. His father's taste for culture and his own intellectual capacities made this certain. His own academic results encouraged him to consider himself as a member of the intellectual élite, by whose side the literate masses were swelling. His open letter about his novel *Workers in the Dawn*[5] shows him stepping aside from the masses, deliberately choosing the longest path to success. The difficulties of all sorts which he experienced as a man and as a writer reinforced his aloofness. Because he was so very exacting with others as well as with himself, he tended to regard any mass phenomenon more and more critically. Pride and disenchantment (apt to turn into bitterness) are two variants of one fundamental attitude—the refusal to conform culturally (I do not say

3

socially). His determination to distinguish himself from the masses emerges repeatedly—he writes novels which are sharply critical of these very masses, even though compassion is at times stronger than condemnation; he refuses to be interviewed by Frederick Dolman because he will not stoop to communicate with the public except through his own finished artistic products; he declines a tempting offer from the London *Figaro* to publish a front-page article on his career; he will not hear of Heinemann, a publisher with many second-rate authors on his list, when the question of a collected edition of his works is made desirable by the dissolution of the Lawrence & Bullen partnership.

Yet Gissing did not hold aloof to the extent of defeating himself. For one thing he needed contact with the masses, at least as long as his work would be concerned with the lower classes—and just in the same way he needed contact with the upper classes. Both sections of the community became to him nothing more than material from the late eighties onwards. His favourite approach was anonymous: he would attend a meeting of his own free will, but decline an invitation to a party; he would observe, but feel ill-at-ease in a circle where he was sure to be observed. When outside his own study, his deep-rooted class consciousness was sure to betray itself by and by; things, people and situations he naturally considered in social terms, unless his judgement was primarily literary. Social class and literature were two inevitable dimensions of his mental framework, and if this developed into an idiosyncrasy which makes Gissing an extreme and typical case in English literature (such phrases as "born outsider" and "permanent stranger" are other ways of describing the same reality), the social and educational conditions of his time were a highly favourable hotbed for the growth of such an idiosyncrasy.

The speeding-up of the cultural evolution in the last two decades of the century, especially in the nineties, is clearly reflected in Gissing's diary, all the more so as the development of his career is almost patterned on the changes in the cultural climate (that is, in the main, the growth of the reading public and the popular press, the liberalisation of publishers and the greater permissiveness of society). He himself was fully conscious of the near coincidence. His ironical preface to the second edition of *The Unclassed,* published in 1895, eleven years after the first, is an example of his awareness. In the early eighties, his relations with publishers were difficult doubtless because his merits were not yet widely acknowledged and he had chosen to deal with solidly established firms of the old school like Smith, Elder, Chapman & Hall, and Bentley, but no less because of the publishers' firm stand against harsh realism and against a candid treatment of human problems which ignored moral and/or religious considerations. Of course his pessimistic outlook was thought to be an additional sin. The liberalisation of publishers and the multiplication of publishing houses in the nineties appeared manifest to Gissing at a time when his own reputation was making serious headway. Lawrence & Bullen came to him and behaved with liberality and intelligence. If some difficulty occurred between author and publishers, it was solved amicably. The extension of the fiction market in the nineties, due to the increase in the number of readers and to the fall of

4

the three-decker (implying that henceforth new fiction could be bought instead of being almost invariably borrowed), changed the attitude of publishers. Cheap series were launched wherever possible, and Gissing who, ten years before, could hardly find a publisher for his work, was swamped with requests for one-volume novels. The cheap book had won the day. Yet, although publishers like Fisher Unwin, Cassell and Methuen were pleased to have him on their lists, he was no truly profitable author. Except when he happened to catch the public fancy (as was the case with *The Private Papers of Henry Ryecroft*) or when publishers reissued his novels in sixpenny or sevenpenny series (mainly after his death), there were only a few thousand people prepared to buy his books in England. He complained that he was a victim of the library system, which is true. The vast majority of fiction readers, for whom the novel was essentially an amusement, would not hear of an author who offered a serious criticism of life and invited his public to think. The suburbanite who bought an inexpensive novel at the railway stall to pass away the tedium of the journey did not wish to read an author who had a consistently pessimistic view of existence. Yet the fact remains that Gissing benefited from the advent of a new class of readers. Not all of them were averse to earnest fiction: some found his analysis of British society strangely consonant with their own findings and apprehensions; they found in characters like Gilbert Grail or Godwin Peak a poignant analysis of their own frustrations—and not a few readers of this type wrote to the author to express their admiration and respect, which was but another way of saying that he had helped them better to understand their own social predicament[6].

The revolution in publishing brought about by the fall of the three-volume novel—a mode of publication which favoured the social class that could afford a guinea's subscription to a circulating library—was part of another upheaval concerning the press in general. Gissing examined the latter problem in *New Grub Street,* which implies that the movement which spread in so spectacular a manner in the nineties was clearly noticeable in the previous decades. For a writer who chose to live by his pen the number of weeklies and monthlies likely to accept short fiction and popular articles on literary, historical and geographical subjects was considerable, and certainly greater than today when radio and television encroach on the time which was formerly devoted to reading.[7] Although Gissing refused to stoop to journalism of the type he attempted for the *Pall Mall Gazette* in 1880, and though the names of journals and reviews carrying such contributions scarcely appear in his diary, we can appreciate the development of such periodicals from the mention of those which published short stories from his pen. For indeed, the popularity of that medium was characteristic of the turn of the century. Gissing's case shows that even an author who appealed to a small body of readers could place some of his writings in publications which were obviously intended for the masses. C.K. Shorter and Jerome K. Jerome were not the only editors who welcomed and invited contributions from him to their low-brow magazines. If he had chosen to compile articles on literary or historical subjects of the kind which Andrew Lang and F.W. Robinson turned out by the score, the columns of dozens of periodicals would have been open to him. In fact, he did make concessions in the nineties, not infrequently complying with an editor's request for his views on a topical or literary question—his diary records only a small portion of these ephemeral writings. Confronted with the rapid evolution of the literary market and the collapse of the three-volume novel he wondered how he himself would be affected. The answer was that his situation remained very much the same—he obtained larger advances for his later books, but with the notable exception of *Henry Ryecroft* his publishers' accounts pointed to unearned royalties at the time of his death. In the course of twenty-three years his public had grown appreciably but slowly, and if, financially, his peak year was 1895 it was only because he agreed to write two short novels for publishers who were celebrating loudly the emancipation from the three-volume bondage. He later blamed himself for having yielded to these requests from Fisher Unwin and Cassell, but he truly rejoiced at the spread of education and its consequences with regard to literature. Only—witness *Henry Ryecroft*—he had very moderate expectations. Intellectual progress, he thought, might as often as not lead to mere personal frustration. Many young people to-day could testify to the accuracy of his predictions.

Gissing's diary, even if considered apart from his correspondence with William Morris Colles and James B. Pinker, throws interesting light on the question of the literary agent. His business abilities being by his own admission rather short, he was tempted to try the services of A.P. Watt for 'Godwin Peak' (retitled *Born in Exile*) in 1891. Coming after the success of *New Grub Street,* Gissing's decision was not dictated by despair. Irritated by the asininity of James Payn, who had read his manuscripts for Smith, Elder, he was in a mood for experiments. The experiment with Watt was a valuable though chastening one which proved that very few publishers were prepared to take the moderate risks Smith, Elder had been taking with five titles from *Demos* to *New Grub Street.* That Watt lacked imagination is certain, yet the repeated refusal of well-established firms to accept Gissing's price (£200 for all rights) shows the limits of an agent's power. Disappointed by the ultimate results, Gissing sought the services of Colles, but as he came at the same time upon publishers who were in genuine sympathy with his work, namely Lawrence & Bullen, Colles was really given no chance of showing that he was more capable than Watt. Colles placed a number of Gissing's short stories and tried very hard, with scant success, to lure him further on the road to commercialism. He was suspicious of Lawrence & Bullen and would have liked Gissing to give them up for the benefit of larger, more active firms like Ward, Lock or Methuen, whose concern for literature pure and simple was doubtless more questionable. Colles finally got a novel to sell, *The Town Traveller,* which unfortunately Gissing had grown to dislike even before it was printed. The agent's failure to serialise the story, which does not say much for his industriousness, led to his disgrace—the tasks he was afterwards entrusted with were minor ones, consisting essentially of the inevitable sequels of their former relations. Pinker was more active, got better prices for his client, achieved greater success with regard to serialisation, but failed to collect all Gissing's works under one publisher's imprint, largely because Bullen's demand of £500 for the goodwill and stock of his eight Gissing titles was unreasonable. Both agent and author allowed their prejudices against Heinemann, who was prepared to pay this sum, to overrule their business acumen, and time has proved them wrong. On balance there is no doubt that both Colles and Pinker helped substantially to promote Gissing's fame, and they would have obtained better terms for him had they been given more time to negotiate agreements. This applies in particular to serialisation, which could always be arranged, even in the case of an author who was by no means popular. But both agents mortgaged the future by thinking exclusively of the present—they aimed at getting the best possible prices within the time limits they were granted and this naturally involved the scattering of Gissing's works among a number of firms; the prospect of a collected edition receding accordingly. In *New Grub Street* Whelpdale is one of the tradesmen of literature; his job, like that of Colles and Pinker, is a patent sign of the commercialisation of literature. By the end of the century it was quite certain that the writer who had no turn for business, yet was determined not to let himself be exploited by his publishers, was sure to profit by the services of an agent. Gissing's career illustrates the concurrent notion that the relations between authors and publishers were becoming less personal: he had known George Chapman and George Smith personally, he was a friend of Bullen and Lawrence, but he only carried on an impersonal correspondence with Methuen and Constable, and not primarily because he no longer lived in London. The age of specialisation was only starting.

As early as 1877 when he returned from America Gissing realised that the choice of a residence (necessarily a garret or a cellar at the time) mattered much for an aspirant to literary glory. His choice was readily made then between the city and the country but the old alternative was nonetheless to inform his life and works. Some statements of his on the subject have been collected and discussed briefly by Asa Briggs in *Victorian Cities*, but the question has not yet been examined thoroughly. Here again Gissing's diary provides valuable material to the potential student of the subject. The author's relationship with the city was largely a love-hate one. Immediately after his chastening experiences in the States, he thought of London as a refuge. The Manchester affair was still fresh in the minds of all who knew him in England and the anonymity of life in a large city was a soothing prospect to a hypersensitive young man. Besides only London could supply the material he needed for his projected multi-volume study of working-class life. Neither *Workers in the Dawn, Thyrza* nor *The Nether World* would have been written if he had not been a slum-dweller in London for half a dozen years. Surely he detested the life he was living, but he was often in that state of exaltation which Henry Ryecroft was to look back upon glowingly from middle age. His knowledge and rendering of London settings, of the London atmosphere, of the mental attitudes and speech of its lower-class inhabitants has a permanent as well as an historic value. The organic link between city life and his work is too obvious to require stressing. The destroyed portion of the diary would certainly have made a demonstration even more superfluous. The city also meant culture to young Gissing, culture in the form of free and circulating libraries, lectures and newspaper reading-rooms. Publishers and editors were near at hand. If the value of his work was acknowledged, invitations would follow more naturally than in the country, where the density of literary-minded people was notably inferior. London was Grub Street and "the valley of the shadow of books". However, loneliness combined with disillusions often drove him to despair. After some thirteen years' incessant toil and undernourishment, he went to live in Devon and thought he had hitherto existed in absolute ignorance of all that gives life its value. The experiment (did he ever cease experimenting as regards abodes?) was of short duration. Far from cultural centres, he felt his intellectual faculties benumbed and realised after writing *The Odd Women* that he was getting short of material. His stay in Birmingham in the autumn of 1892 clearly indicates where his real home was. For once he and his wife Edith seem to have agreed—life in the country was very dull, they had had their fill of trees and meadows. The lure of a recently founded library brought him back to the London area. Exeter was to suit Henry Ryecroft better than it did George Gissing, who could not forget a casual remark of *The Times* about *Born in Exile* to the effect that the book had a provincial atmosphere.

Significantly, the return to the London area coincided with a new phase in his career—the writing of short stories, the renewal of inspiration apparent in *In the Year of Jubilee* and prolonged in *The Paying Guest* and *The Whirlpool,* the many contacts with literary men, publishers, editors during the period 1893-97. Simultaneously, Gissing, whom newspapermen and critics had so far ignored consistently except when he had a new book out, became a man whose contributions were sought, whose portrait was wanted and whose opinion was requested on a variety of subjects, literary, political and even dietary. Characteristically, he did not trouble to write down the most futile of these requests in his diary. It is arguable to a certain extent that this change would anyway have occurred sooner or later, but I am convinced that Gissing's residence near London and his resolve to live henceforth in lesser seclusion hastened critical recognition. The appearance of paragraphs about his doings and of surveys of his works can be dated from that very period. Jasper Milvain, the prototype of the drawing-room *littérateur* in *New Grub Street,* may be cynical, but he is no fool. Conversely, once Gissing, for domestic and health reasons, left England and went to live in Paris, then in provincial France, the paragraphs about him in the English press became fewer, fewer also his portraits, and if assessments of his writings continued to appear occasionally, he complained not without reason that he was being forgotten. The city, or more accurately London, was, if I may say so, the residence best suited to his reputation. But it was evident throughout his life that he could be fully happy nowhere. This was due to his fundamental restlessness, but also, towards the end of his life, to the disease which made each new change of climate beneficent at first, then tragically vain. The countryside, especially the foreign countryside, was synonymous for him with cultural starvation.

Thus, as always with Gissing, one comes up against a dilemma, a conflict of values. He is indignant at social injustice but fears that progress will lead to a levelling down, instead of a levelling up of human values; he writes a remarkable series of novels of modern English life, but dreams all the time of ancient civilisations on the shores of the Mediterranean; he wishes he had been born French, but once in France, longs for a cottage in Devon. Any balanced appreciation of him has of necessity to take into account what he might have been as much as what he was, what he might have done as much as what he did.

II

An historical and sociological document, Gissing's diary is also a window into his own mental universe. Its existence has been known for many years but only a handful of individuals, mainly scholars, have ever been able to see the original and read it through. The author's friends were aware that he kept a diary and some of them—Morley Roberts and Clara Collet for instance—must have wondered how they figured in this intriguing document. Algernon Gissing, the novelist's impecunious brother, doubtless realised early enough that his own recurrent sponging habits would be recorded in George's account of his melancholy journey through life. But the present diary was read by no one in his lifetime, not even by his intimates. With typical Victorian reticence, Gissing thought there should be a well-defined frontier between a novelist's public life, which was to be strictly limited to his literary production and opinions on intellectual matters, and his private existence, which in his own case he always tried to protect from the prying glances of interviewers and busybodies. Six months before his death he significantly wrote about the controversy over the 'secrets' in Carlyle's life that the affair was "grossly indecent" and that, if it was "inevitable that the external facts of his domestic life" should be commented upon, no one had "any business to go beneath the surface in such a matter"[8]. One may therefore rest assured that he would have shared the anxiety of Gabrielle Fleury—the Frenchwoman with whom he spent the last years of his life but could not marry—when she feared that his diary might be entrusted to strangers—as was to happen to his letters to Bertz and to Clara Collet[9]. She herself regarded George's diary as an "explosive" document, a mirror in which not a few contemporaries would not like to see themselves. Indeed it is true that his exacting views with regard to human nature and his high artistic standards (a motive for frequent dissatisfaction with his own work) prompted hypercritical and disenchanted judgments on a host of people. For a quarter of a century, the publication of letters to his family was postponed because of the many susceptibilities to be humoured, and the result was a volume which gave an incomplete and misleading picture of the man's life. Substantial extracts from the diary were included—mainly passages showing Gissing in Italy and Greece—but the choice was as clearly indicative of the editors' reverence for Mrs. Grundy as of Gissing's culture. None of the questions raised by Morley Roberts' fictionalised biography was given an answer. Private life was as good as banished from the book even though both correspondence and diary threw abundant light on it. It was assuredly easier to print brief references to the weather than interesting comments on a leading contemporary, dead or in his eighties. Yet it must be acknowledged that the position of the family was not an easy one, and time alone could smooth down the difficulties, real and imaginary, which still prevailed in the inter-war period. Fortunately, things began to change in the 1940s, when the diary was sold to the Berg Collection of the New York Public Library. A manuscript vital to research into the life and work of a representative, if neglected Victorian writer, was now available. The huge gaps left by Algernon and Ellen Gissing in editing their brother's letters and personal papers could now be filled. Scholars visited the Berg Collection, they read this impressive record of the novelist's life and quoted from it in biographies and collections of letters— leaving aside the hottest bits either through self-denial or because there were still restrictions attached to quoting. Yet again some obstacles remained in the way of publication. Up to about 1960, Gissing's name was apt to frighten nineteen out of twenty publishers, all of whom would anyway have considered it more legitimate to reprint the novels than to publish a diary which, being neither by Pepys, John Evelyn nor Fanny Burney, could not be expected to appeal to the general public. Also the editing, which involved a struggle with Gissing's microscopic handwriting on poor paper, and with such languages as Latin, ancient and modern Greek, German, Italian and French, was a daunting prospect if added to the difficulties involved in the identification of hundreds of persons of various nationalities and the authorship of numberless books.

In the early seventies all the obstacles and objections to publication were at long last overcome or bypassed. No one in this permissive age of ours is likely to carp at the frankness of Gissing's confessions when he dips below the surface of his existence, that is below writing and reading, below his occasional meetings with professionals of literature. What if his chronic amorousness, mainly apparent in the months or years between his spells of married life, is more obvious than ever? It makes tepid reading when compared with the self-advertising exhibitionism of some modern autobiographies. Could he help it if he had a strong sexual instinct? Nor are his severe judgments on a number of contemporaries likely to hurt anyone, since those who appear in the diary are now dead. Time, moreover, has more often than not confirmed his views of predictions. The more spectacular mushroom reputations of the nineties, the best selling authors of fervid fiction, the jingoism of the turn of the century as well as the cultivation of aestheticism and decadence are now seen in a proper perspective. Sometimes, however, Gissing let himself be misled in his literary appreciations by his basically sensible deflation of a writer's pose. We concur with his severe remarks on George Moore's personality—that of a vain and vulgar individual—but we demur at his summary dismissal of *Esther Waters*, a novel which deserves to rank with Gissing's best. In the same way, Arthur Morrison's approach to realism may have been a narrow one, dictated by personal motives on which criticism is only beginning to throw light, but we do not think that Gissing is in the least doing justice to *A*

Child of the Jago when he waves it aside as "poor stuff". But these are exceptions, and he could go out of his way to acknowledge the merits of a book by Mrs. Henry Wood or Rhoda Broughton or even Hall Caine, whose limitations appeared clearly to the more responsible critics of the time. He could also admire the genius of Kipling and at the same time detest his nefarious appeal to the least creditable instincts of the masses. On the whole, his judgments on contemporary works are few; he was usually content to record what he had read and was as chary of praise as of blame; his opinion, when expressed at all, is to be sought in his correspondence, most of which is still unpublished[10]. Here we see Gissing at work often under adverse circumstances, writing a few pages on Monday which he partly rewrites on Tuesday, and on the average, destroying more than he produces. We see him almost invariably making a series of false starts over his new story, but of his aims in it, of the notes preparatory to writing proper, the diary shows us next to nothing. We see him on holiday, complaining about his loneliness or an unsuitable companion, but except when he is travelling abroad (especially in Greece and Southern Italy, with future books in mind as he goes about), his jottings must be completed by other sources—some notebook or loose sheet which has found its way to an institutional Library.

Each reader will naturally have his own opinion as to what is more striking and characteristic. The impressions of one who is familiar with the contents are difficult to analyse. Novelty blunted and blurred by many years' reference to the material concerned is the antithesis of novelty. Yet read and re-read as one may, some aspects lose nothing of their vividness. The innumerable references to the weather and the mood of the sky stress Gissing's extreme sensitiveness; though a part of himself was always living in the past and near the Mediterranean, he could not overlook the present and reacted to his environment—visual, auditive and emotional—with the sensitivity of a seismograph. The admission made in *By the Ionian Sea* and the *Ryecroft Papers*, when his health was shattered, holds good for the eighties as well. A beam of sunshine would fill his mind with joy, but it soon enhanced the wretchedness of life around him. Poverty, domestic worries, then ill-health, compelled him to roam over the world in imagination more often than bodily. Fortunately his was a capacious imagination and he compensated by reading for his inability to undertake long journeys. From his early days at Wakefield he used to dream of the sites of ancient civilizations, the literature of which he so intensely visualised, and he would lament his failure to read some Latin or Greek author at a given time more bitterly than his temporary neglect of recently published literature. It would be easy to picture on a map the limits of his world. For the northern countries he cared but moderately. He saw them through men whose works he admired, like Ibsen and Jacobsen, or through the books of acquaintances like Edmund Gosse and C.F. Keary. Russia he regarded as a land of living contrasts—political oppression and spiritual generosity, censorship and pioneer works in literature. Germany ceased to interest him when unified; he felt out of sympathy with its modern writers and looked back longingly to the Romantic time of Goethe. His visit to his friend Bertz in April 1898 confirmed him in his detestation of militarism—a scourge he had found in milder or more picturesque forms in France, Italy and Greece. America, where he had been brought to the verge of starvation, meant to him a doubtful development of democracy, the collusion of big business and political power, and there were few American writers whom he held in unmitigated esteem. France, like Russia, had a host of distinguished writers, but the French bourgeois observed at close quarters were rather trying. As for Italy, his Calabrian notes make it plain that if it was the cradle of the civilization which most appealed to him, the late nineteenth-century evolution of the country filled him with apprehensions. So, as some sort of disappointment always awaited him in the present, he perpetually sought a refuge in the past (a man like Wells failed to understand Gissing's reaction though he himself would constantly fly away from the present into the future) and in out-of-the-way countries. In this connection, one is surprised to see him read so many narratives of travel in the Middle East. Surprised because this aspect of Gissing's cultural interests has not been emphasized so far, also because his novels, which so faithfully mirror his own attitudes and concerns, reflect nothing of this[11].

Despite this escapism, Gissing kept in close touch with some realities of his time. He was, until his reputation was made, inclined to keep off, to watch and act from an entrenched camp; yet he was remarkably informed about the literary life around him, not only in England, but also in countries whose literatures had an acknowledged international status. His diary is, among many other things, a sort of directory to contemporary literature. It bristles with the names of contemporary writers, and his correspondence and personal papers show that he read many books about which his diary is silent. His great interest in the classics did not blind him to the merits of current literature. A checklist of the works he read or purchased (being no collector, he never seems to have bought books which he failed to read) would show the catholicity of his reading and the eclecticism of his taste. More than once he forced himself to read pretty worthless current fiction with a view to determining whether the praise he had come across in journals and magazines was justified. One wonders whether, in some cases, what was originally at once curiosity and the fulfilment of an intellectual duty did not degenerate into fascination by sheer mediocrity. If not, why did he read so much Marion Crawford, so much Grant Allen? He moaned over the time he wasted on "such trash as this", but went on reading. Clearly, Percy Dunn, the melancholy hero of his short story "Spellbound", has an autobiographical dimension.

Full of facts though it may be, Gissing's diary inevitably strikes its reader by its omissions or its tantalizing hints. To the former belongs his affair with Mrs. Williams—the widowed sister of Beatrice Webb, afterwards Mrs Dobbs. She is mentioned occasionally in 1898, but neither the first description of her—"loud; bullies waiters; forces herself into our conversations"—nor the detached, ironical references to her in the letters to Gabrielle Fleury would lead one to suspect the ghost of a romance between them before Gabrielle appeared in his life. The role played by Mrs. Williams in the spring of 1898 is comparable to that of Miss Curtis,

12

Edith Sichel and Connie Ash in the interval between the death of Marianne Helen Harrison, his first wife, and the courtship of Edith Underwood, who was to be his second. In like fashion, the muted, though recurrent allusions to Gabrielle are hardly suggestive of the tumultuous passion poured into his letters to her. Unfortunately, complementary documents do not always compensate for the silence or discretion of the diary concerning a given relationship. One would like to know more about his ties with an old school mate like A.J. Smith, a former pupil like Walter Grahame, a friend like Mrs. Henry Norman, or even such acquaintances as the Traverses of Weybridge. Sometimes, one cannot even establish a link between outside information and the diary. If, as may well be the case, Noel Ainslie, a Lawrence & Bullen author who obviously came to know Gissing well in 1898, is a pseudonym, which name in the diary pairs off with it best? An invaluable source of information, the diary is also a potential starting-point for further research.

Why did Gissing write a diary? The answer to this question is not a simple one. That his diary was at first essentially meant to be a record of his life for self-consumption is certain. Although the past had been very dark, he experienced a savage pleasure in leafing through the daily account of his struggles with solitude, physical and/or mental, and with the blank page. The entry for 7 April 1902 is significant. Gissing's realism was largely inverted idealism and a realistic record of fifteen years' work, when taken in at a glance, roused in him a romantic vision of his life. Each entry is a very selective record of his activities on a given day. He noted his progress in his current work, but his reading and correspondence are not set down systematically. Some minor contributions to periodicals, some letters to editors which achieved publication, were skipped through indifference or carelessness. Yet, there is no doubt that the diary was in Gissing's lifetime his best memento: for instance he could easily check in it when he had sent a certain manuscript to a lazy literary agent, or how much he used to receive for a 4,000 word short story when he began to try his hand at this medium.

It is no less certain that he also conceived his diary to be a document for the scholars of generations yet unborn who would study his life and works. Just as he thought that his stories would have great relevance for posterity, he regarded his journal as an object which would testify in his favour, and against his time of which he was by his own estimation a victim. From the very cover of the first of the three copy-books he used, we see him anxious to preserve a bit of the past which, by tearing off a number of pages, he has obliterated. The dramatic account of Nell's death, which was to stimulate him to write *The Nether World,* his strongest arraignment of Victorian society, was assuredly intended to be an act of self-vindication, and some complaints against, and scenes with, Edith were admittedly recorded for the enlightenment of his biographers. His motivation, however, varied with time, and he ultimately grew tired of chronicling not only "the wasted days", as he often depressedly called them, but the days of fruitful production. From the moment he settled in France, the entries, with a few exceptions for days when he travelled geographically into the past, become more and more meagre. That by 1902 he no longer had the energy to write every evening the two or three lines which would have summed up his activities of the day testifies not only to his weariness but to the detachment with which he then viewed himself. The man who was projecting to write further historical novels, another volume in the manner of *Ryecroft* and a book on Wakefield in his father's lifetime had lost too much of his interest in the present to go on translating into a personal language the dreary figures of the calendar. What he had often yearned for with characteristic lassitude as "the happy finis" was now looming ahead.

Notes

1 *The Long Revolution,* Harmondsworth, Penguin Books, 1971, p. 196.
2 *Ibid.,* p. 220.
3 Pierre Coustillas and Colin Partridge (eds.), *Gissing: The Critical Heritage,* London & Boston: Routledge & Kegan Paul, 1972, p. 244.
4 This type of character also appears in his short stories, and it has a female counterpart—Emily Hood in *A Life's Morning* for instance.
5 *Gissing: The Critical Heritage,* Item I.
6 A striking observation in this respect is the proportion of second-hand copies of Gissing books which have been studied and lovingly annotated, with cross references, and for *Henry Ryecroft,* supplied with a more satisfactory index and biographical details.
7 Incidentally, the latest edition of the *Cambridge Bibliography of English Literature* lists only a selection of these new periodicals and magazines.
8 Letter to Edward Clodd, 16 June 1903. *The Letters of George Gissing to Edward Clodd,* ed. P. Coustillas, London, Enitharmon Press, 1973, p. 92.
9 Gabrielle voiced her fears in her unpublished letters to Clara Collet in the mid-1900s.
10 The following volumes have been published: *Letters of George Gissing to Members of his Family,* ed. Algernon and Ellen Gissing (1927); *George Gissing and H.G. Wells, Their Friendship and Correspondence,* ed. Royal A. Gettmann (1961); *The Letters of George Gissing to Eduard Bertz, 1887-1903,* ed. Arthur C. Young (1961); *The Letters of George Gissing to Gabrielle Fleury,* ed. Pierre Coustillas (1964); *Henry Hick's Recollections of George Gissing, Together with Gissing's Letters to Hick,* ed. P. Coustillas (1973); *The Letters of George Gissing to Edward Clodd,* ed. P. Coustillas (1973). A few letters to C.K. Shorter were printed privately in 1915 under the title *Letters to an Editor.*
      The unpublished correspondence is widely scattered. The three main collections are in the Berg Collection of the New York Public Library, the Yale University Library, and the Carl H. Pforzheimer Library.
11 Stanley Alden remarked in his perceptive article on Gissing as a humanist that "his characters have a way of going off suddenly to Odessa, St Jean de Luz, Honolulu, Tasmania or the Bahamas" which is quite astounding. "Someone", he notes, "has always returned from a trip round the world, or is setting forth for Egypt or Queensland. All his chief characters are citizens of the world and by preference of that part of the world distant from main-travelled roads." This is perfectly true. A long line of characters from Arthur Golding to Will Warburton corroborate this view, but there remains the double fact that this extensive travelling of his well-to-do characters never seems essential in the novels, never projecting a shadow of exoticism, and that the Middle East does not receive more than a few casual mentions in the novels.

14

On inside cover

July-Sept 1885   Wrote "Isabel Clarendon"
Sept-Nov 1885   Wrote "A Life's Morning"
Dec-March 1885-6   Wrote "Demos"

During the same months, I first studied Italian, and read through the whole of the "Divina Commedia".- Also, it should be noted, I earned my living by teaching, which generally took all the morning.-

"The Nether World" (Cornwall Mansions) March 19-July 22 1888 (17 weeks)

1887

(living at 7K Cornwall Mansions, Clarence Gate, Regent's Park - which I occupied for six years in all.)

Tuesd. Dec. 27. Heard from Miss Crum* of Mr. Grahame's death at Cannes. Walter was to have joined his father there a fortnight hence. Our work thus broken off — (from today.)

After a fortnight's break in writing (chiefly occasioned by having to give some lessons in the evening to Bernard Harrison,) resume "The Insurgents". Have reached middle of 3d vol., but I see that much must be re-written. Began it last July, and have toiled ever since. To-day returned to Chap. I, which I must have written six times, and again re-wrote it. But to-morrow it will once more be cancelled, I see. Cannot hit the right tone.- Wrote 4 to 10.

Thursd. Dec. 29. Wrote from 2 to 10, a good spell. Finished Chap. I, revised II, and did something at III. Curious similarity bet. Chap. II and the opening of Mrs. Woods's "A Village Tragedy", but mine was written long before I read her book.- Have been obliged to ask mother to lend me £10, to pay my rent; the first time I lacked it since coming hither, three years ago. I had expected that Smith would pay the £50 for "A Life's Morning" [serialised in *Cornhill Magazine,* January-December 1888].- Thucyd[ides] IV, 11-13.

Frid. Dec. 30. Proofs of "A Life's Morning" for the March number.- £10 from mother to pay rent.- Wrote from 2.30 to 8, and got clear nearly to end of Chap. V. Reads tolerably well.- Thucyd. IV, 14-18.

Sat. Dec. 31. Recd £15 from F[rederic] Harrison, for my short coaching of Bernard. Also arrives cheque for £50 from Smith, so that I need not have written to mother after all.- Went into book-market and purchased: Beaumont & Fletcher and Dekker, (Mermaid Series) two vols. of the small Thackeray, and "Great Expectations" in the small Dickens.- Corrected proofs of "Life's M.", Chaps. V & VI.- No writing.

*Walter Grahame's aunt.

1888

Sunday Jan. 1. Thucyd. 19-21 (IV).- Reading "Great Expectations".- Went to [Morley] Roberts at 4 Danvers St. Chelsea, and was led to remonstrate with him on his choice of morbid subjects for stories.

Mond. Jan. 2. Gave Bernard last lesson.- Read idly at "Great Expectations", and thought over my story.- Wrote nothing.- In one of my fits of expensiveness, went and bought a good travelling bag.

Tuesd. Jan. 3. Profitless day. Finished "Great Expectations". Walked about town in evening.- Wrote nothing.

Wed. Jan. 4. Resumed writing. From 3 to 9.30 did six pages, bringing me into Chap. VI of Vol. I. Note from Walter Grahame, asking me to resume work to-morrow. Nothing read.

Thursd. Jan. 5. Grahame from 10 to 12.30. Then dinner in Edgware Rd., at the usual eating-house, where I get meat and two vegetables for 8d, and really of very decent quality. Then a walk round the park, resuming my wholesome habit of last spring and summer. Wrote from 3 to 9.30, and did my 6 pages, bringing me into Chap. VII. I am almost satisfied with vol. I so far. The construction, I think, is neater than anything I have done yet.- Must get to bed about 10 each night. I find that plenty of sleep keeps me up to the mark in imagination and composition.- Sent to Nelly [Ellen Gissing, his sister] a parcel containing: "Æneid" Bk I, Bohn's Vergil, and Tourguéneff's "Väter u. Söhne".

Frid. Jan. 6. Wrote from 3 to 9, but with no result; it must all be cancelled. Never mind; have recast the chapter in my thought, and will go at it again to-morrow. My patience is inexhaustible.

Sat. Jan. 7. Finished, thank heaven, the Chapt. of Peake's antecedents, chap. VII. Wrote 9 to 11, and 4 to 8.- Bought Murger's "Les Vacances de Camille", and George Sand's "La dernière Aldini".- Headache.

Sund. Jan. 8. Reading Murger's "Vacances de Camille".- Roberts.

Mond. Jan. 9. Hideous fog; bad cold. None the less a good day. Wrote 4.30 to 10, and finished Chap. VIII, 6 pages. In good vein, thank heaven!

Tuesd. Jan. 10. Fog still; cold worse. Nevertheless wrought well. Finished off Chap. IX and X, re-writing some six pages. Finished "Vacances de Camille", charming story! Began "La dernière Aldini".-

Wed. Jan. 11. Fog denser than ever. Cold so much worse, had to lie up in house. Little writing done, but dismissed Chap. XI.-

Thursd. Jan. 12. A terrible day; the fourth that we have not seen the sky. Happily began to clear in the evening. My cold too bad to let me go forth. In morning read, finishing "Dernière Aldini". In afternoon Alexander Grahame [Walter's brother] called, to inquire after me. Wonderfully handsome fellow that, and voice astonishingly like his sister's at times.- Began to write at 4.30, and went on till 9.30, with effort. Did nearly 5 pages, however, bringing me to 75 of Vol. I.

Frid. Jan. 13. Fog hanging about still, until 3 in afternoon,then clearing. Got up at 10; cold almost gone, but did not go to Grahame. Began to write at 4, and went on till 9.30. Did nearly 7 pages, getting into Chap. XIII.

Sat. Jan. 14. Black fog at noon, then cleared, and at night thanked heaven for showing its stars once more. Shopping in morning. Began to write at 4, finished 11. Wrote my 6 pages.

Sund. Jan. 15. Didn't venture to go to Roberts, on account of my cold. Wrote, for the first time on Sunday for about a year. As a rule, the Sunday atmosphere renders me unable, but I am resolute to get the book finished as soon as possible. Did 5 pages. Finished "François le Champi", and began "Pauline", one of G. Sand's early tales.- Fog gone at last; a wind occasionally.

Mond. Jan. 16. Wrought from 4 to 10.30 and finished vol. I. Began "Le Péché de M. Antoine" [by George Sand]. Looking through Baedeker's Paris, in preparation for a visit as soon as I am free. Terribly cold day; east wind.- Went to Grahame again as usual.

Tuesd. Jan. 17. Wrote 5 pages; worked from 4 to 10. See that I must re-write a chapter of vol.I, eheu! Read a little of "M. Antoine". East wind. New moon just visible; very red 8 o'clock.

Wed. Jan. 18. Recd cheque for £38.18 from Mr Grahame's executors,- for last quarter. Read at "M. Antoine". Wrote from 4 to 10.45, and did 7 pages.- Still the east wind.- Shall send the cheque to mother to-morrow to bank for me.

Thursd. Jan. 19. Sent cheque to mother. Walked to Tott[enham] C[our]t Rd for tobacco etc.- Wrote 3 pages to finish the difficult Chap.II, and passed Chap. III as it stood. This brings me to p.23.- Cold and cloudy. Must be several weeks since there was a single gleam of sunlight.

19

Frid. Jan. 20. Letter from Alg[ernon] [his brother] saying that Hurst & Blackett have accepted his novel [*Joy Cometh in the Morning,* 2 vols., 1888]. They offer royalty of 4/- after 280 copies sold.- Wrote not quite 6 pages.- Troubled by sleeplessness these last nights.

Sat. Jan. 21. Not quite 6 pages. Bought some bottled ale, thinking it might help me to sleep if I drank some before going to bed.

Sun. Jan. 22. Roberts'.- Bottled ale has given me a headache. Clearly I can't use it. Shall try a glass of hot water at bedtime. Still reading "M. Antoine".

Mond. Jan 23. A wasted day. That sudden inability to work which often comes upon me, and is almost certain to do so just before any change in the ordering of my ways (Grahame's last lesson to-morrow.) Gave up attempt to write as soon as I had sat down. Must leave off tea; I verily believe it accounts for my sluggish digestion, constipation, etc. Have an idea for a division of the day to begin on Wednesday.- Read in Forster's Dickens, a book I constantly take up for impulse, when work at a standstill.- Weather exquisite all day; warm and sunny. Observed buds on the branches of trees as I walked round park last Sunday afternoon.- Pains in the back; doubtless result of taking a bath last night. Dare not go out for a bath, yet at home I always catch cold.- Made bilious also by having Irish stew for dinner. There are few things now that I can eat with impunity.

Tuesd. Jan. 24. Grahame's last lesson. In afternoon walked about, also in evening. Bought Balzac's "Pierrette", and began to read. Made all arrangements for beginning work at 9.30 to-morrow and writing throughout the day. Bought cocoa; I believe it will greatly help my indigestion.

Wed. Jan. 25. A terrible day. Got up with a headache, and from 9.30 to 2 wrote - or rather struggled to write, - achieving not quite 2 pages. Suffered anguish worse than any I remember in the effort to compose. Ate nothing at 2, but started and walked to Hampstead and back. Head a little better. Dined at a café, extravagantly spending 1/9; a bottle of seltzer benefited my head, I think. At 7 tried to write again, and by 9.30 finished 1 page. However, this completes Chap.5.- Alg. sends an account of Hurst & Blackett's attempt to swindle him. They have inserted a clause in the agreement by which said agreement is limited to twelve months; after that they claim to sell off remnant copies on their own account. These publishers' meanness surpasses belief. I have advised him to resist.

Frid. Jan. 27. After a hopeless struggle with illness, went off to Broadway, departing, as usual, half an hour after getting the idea. Could not let Alg. know in time, so passed the night at Evesham, staying at "Rose and Crown". Was awoke by the "chimes at midnight", the first time I ever heard them; made me feel I was in Shakspere's country.

Sat. Jan. 28. Walked on to Broadway, six miles. Alg. met me half-way on the road, with his little dog. Delighted with their cottage; daintily furnished. An excellent young servant called Sarah.

Sat. Feb. 4. Returned to London, after enjoying myself much, though the last few days were spoilt by Kate being unwell. An invitation to dine from the Cookson Crackanthorpes forwarded to me; of course had to decline. Lane, the manager of Corn[wall] Resid[ences] wrote requesting me to have my windows cleaned, as the appearance was disreputable! Walked a little during the week, but not further than to Chipping Campden, some 5 miles. Talked of Alg's book, for which agreement with Blackett is signed. Much improved in health. Thought carefully over the remaining portion of my book, and got it clearly arranged.- Take the new evening paper, *The Star*, - furious radicalism, and useful to me.- Have had a good deal of frost, and some snow, but tolerable weather on the whole.

Sund. Feb. 5. Bad headache, traceable, I suppose, to a bottle of Bass I drank last night. In afternoon walked to Child's Hill. Evening spent in Clerkenwell, wandering. Finished Balzac's "Célibataires" vol. I, and took up "The Tatler" again. The latter very refreshing. To bed at 11, in hope of work to-morrow.

Tuesd. Feb. 7. Two days of blank misery; incapable of work; feeling almost ready for suicide. This evening a little light comes to me. Will it be credited, that I must begin a new novel? I am wholly dissatisfied with the plan of what I have been writing. This terrible waste of time. I dare not tell anyone the truth; shall merely say that I am getting on very slowly.

Wed. Feb. 8. Did actually begin a new story; to be called, I think, "Marian Dane". What is more, wrote the whole of Chap. I, 8 pages. Sat from 9-12, and from 3 to 9. Had a good walk, round by Kilburn.

Thursd. Feb. 9. Wrote 4 more pages, but decided that I must begin over again. This work has only been preliminary. Go this evening to the Edgar Harrisons' [the previous occupants of his flat]: at 29 Arlington Park Gardens, Gunnersbury.

Mond. Feb. 13. After days more of misery, gave it up and came to Eastbourne. Took two rooms at 27 Brightland Road, 10/- a week. No one in the house but the landlady, a poor old single woman. Bad cold weather.

Tuesd. Feb. 14. Got to work in evening, and wrote 5 pages of the first chapter again. In low spirits, and sleeping poorly.

Wed. Feb. 29. Am still at Eastbourne, but have long since given up the idea of doing any work here. Perhaps it is as well to rest merely. Roberts has been with me for a week. The weather terrible, much snow and incessant east wind of deadly coldness. My sitting-room is very draughty and I can seldom get warm save by a sharp walk. The occasional talk of foolish Miss Brown, my landlady, is rather trying.

Have subscribed to Gowland's Library, and during the last fortnight have read a lot of recent novels. "The Deemster" by Hall Caine is better than I anticipated; there is, I think, some really strong romantic writing in it. But the characterization is feeble when one thinks of Scott. First vol. of Mrs Lynn Linton's "Ione" [1883]; terrible twaddle, and could get no further. I marvel how this woman has got her reputation. Then went for refreshment to "Martin Chuzzlewit". Incomprehensible weakness of story in this book. Next, Miss Broughton's "Second Thoughts", which I enjoyed; the woman has a style of wonderful freshness, - if it were not for her damnable historical present. Marie Corelli's "Romance of Two Worlds", a queer piece of juvenile fanaticism. Don't know whether she is in earnest, though.

Think a good deal of my novel - the *old* novel once more, upon which I have no doubt I shall resettle when I get back to 7K. Have got tolerably full notes for vol. I, story substantially the same as before, but details a good deal altered. . .

I broke off this writing to go to Lewes, where I spent a snowy afternoon. At 5.30 I was home again. A telegram waited for me. "Mrs Gissing is dead. Come at once." I caught the 7.45 train, and was at 7K by a quarter to 11. Had telegraphed to Roberts who met me at the door, and stayed through the night with me.

Thursd. March 1. At 8.30 Roberts and I started for Lambeth. I felt an uncertainty about the truth of the telegram, and Roberts offered to go alone to 16 Lucretia Street, Lower Marsh, to make inquiries. I waited for him, walking up and down by Waterloo Station. He came back and told me that she was indeed dead. Thereupon we both went to the house; a wretched, wretched place. The name of the landlady, Sherlock. She told us that M[arianne] H[elen] G[issing] died at about 9.30 yesterday morning, the last struggle beginning at 6 o'clock. They found my Eastbourne address on an envelope in a drawer. I went upstairs to see the body; then Roberts accompanied me to the doctor who had been called in, name McCarthy, West[minster] Bridge Road. He gave us a certificate. Immediate cause of death, acute laryngitis. Roberts took his leave, and I returned to the house. Then a married daughter of Mrs. Sherlock went with me to see the undertaker, of whom a coffin had already been ordered, - a man called Stevens, whom we found in a small beer-shop which he keeps, 99 Princes Rd, Lambeth. Arranged for a plain burial which is to cost 6 guineas. Leaving him, we went to the Registry Office, Lambeth Square, and registered the death. Thence to Lucretia Street again, where I arranged with the Sherlocks that they should attend the funeral; I am to give them £3, to buy mourning and pay their trouble and various expenses of late. After discussing these things, I went up to the room, to collect such things as I desired to take away.

Let me describe this room. It was the first floor back; so small that the bed left little room to move. She took it unfurnished, for 2/9 a week; the furniture she brought was: the bed, one chair, a chest of drawers, and a broken deal table. On some shelves were a few plates, cups, etc. Over the mantelpiece hung several pictures, which she had preserved from old days. There were three engravings: a landscape, a piece by Landseer, and a Madonna of Raphael. There was a portrait of Byron, and one of Tennyson. There was a photograph of myself, taken 12 years ago, - to which, the landlady tells me, she attached special value, strangely enough. Then there were several cards with Biblical texts, and three cards such as are signed by those who "take the pledge", - all bearing date during the last six months.

On the door hung a poor miserable dress and a worn out ulster; under the bed was a pair of boots. Linen she had none; the very covering of the bed had gone save one sheet and one blanket. I found a number of pawn tickets, showing that she had pledged these things during last summer, - when it was warm, poor creature! All the money she received went in drink; she used to spend my weekly 15/- the first day or two that she had it. Her associates were women of so low a kind that even Mrs. Sherlock did not consider them respectable enough to visit her house.

I drew out the drawers. In one I found a little bit of butter and a crust of bread, - most pitiful sight my eyes ever looked upon. There was no other food anywhere. The other drawers contained a disorderly lot of papers: there I found all my letters, away back to the American time. In a cupboard were several heaps of dirty rags; at the bottom there had been coals, but none were left. Lying about here and there were medicine bottles, and hospital prescriptions.

She lay on the bed covered with a sheet. I looked long, long at her face, but could not recognize it. It is more than three years, I think, since I saw her, and she had changed horribly. Her teeth all remained, white and perfect as formerly.

I took away very few things, just a little parcel: my letters, my portrait, her rent-book, a certificate of life-assurance which had lapsed, a copy of my Father's "Margaret"[1] which she had preserved, and a little workbox, the only thing that contained traces of womanly occupation.

Came home to a bad, wretched night. In nothing am I to blame; I did my utmost; again and again I had her back to me. Fate was too strong. But as I stood beside that bed, I felt that my life henceforth had a firmer purpose. Henceforth I never cease to bear testimony against the accursed social order that brings about things of this kind. I feel that she will help me more in her death than she balked me during her life. Poor, poor thing!

Friday, March 2. In morning arranged my books roughly on the shelves; during papering etc. they have been lying in a great heap on the floor. In afternoon went to Lucretia Street, and saw her in her coffin. The face seemed more familiar to me. Gave Mrs. Sherlock the promised £3; funeral will be on Monday at 2 o'clock. A daughter accompanied me to a low public house, where the landlady had a pawn-ticket for H[elen]'s wedding-ring, security for a debt of 1/9. I paid the debt, and redeemed the ring, from the broker's.- Cut a little hair from the poor head, - I scarcely know why, alas!

Sat. March 3. Had note from Nelly, offering to come for a week. Wrote accepting at once.

Sund. March 4. Went to Roberts.

Mond. March 5. Nelly arrived at 1 o'clock. We went and had dinner at the Café in Chapel Street.

Wed. March 7. Went with Nelly to the Ballad Concert at St James's Hall.

Sat. March 10. Have had a violent cold since Wed. night. Better today. Nelly returned to Wakefield by the 1.30. Came back from King's Cross and read in the newspapers about the death of the Emperor William, etc. Of course in low spirits. Have begun to take Cod Liver Oil. My rooms are now once more in order; all the books arranged. On Monday, please the Fates, I begin work.- Read Heine's "Enleitung zu Kahldorf : über den Adel", "Vorrede zum ersten Band des Salon", "Ueber den Denunzianten".

Wed. March 14. Still wasting time. Ill and in wretched spirits. To-night a letter from a certain Fanny Le Breton, 50 rue de Bourgogne, Paris, who writes wishing to translate "Demos". She is also reading "A Life's Morning". I have always imagined it the most unlikely thing for a new English writer to find readers in Paris.

Thursd. March 15. Went to the Grosvenor Library, and took a year's subscription. The librarian, on receiving my name, said "Ah, a very familiar name to us". Got out Hardy's "Woodlanders", and began to read it with much delight. Am feeling a little better, I think. Some ideas have been coming to me to-day. There is a little sunshine, happily.

Sund. March 18. Finished "The Woodlanders". There is some exquisite woodland painting in it, but the human part is on the whole painfully unsatisfactory. Hardy cannot deal with anything above the humours of the rustics. Therein he is admirable. Read "Problems of a Great City", by Arnold White, and got some hints out of it. Went to Roberts.

Mond. March 19. Felt greatly better, in body and mind. Believe the Cod Liver Oil is helping me. Began a novel to be called "The Nether World", and wrote six pages, which satisfy me.

Tuesd. March 20. Thick snow on the ground this morning, a vile day. Wrote from 5 to 10.30, five pp. Went to Grosvenor, and got [Walter] Besant's "Fifty Years Ago", and a Life of Phelps.[2]

Wed. March 21. In afternoon visit from Plitt and a friend of his who has recently been with Walt Whitman at Philadelphia. Nothing of particular interest to be gathered, however.- Sat down at 6, and wrote 4pp.

Thursd. March 22. Wrote 1 page. Feeling ill again.

Frid. March 23. Still miserable. In evening visited Plitt, who lodges at Rock Villa, by Gunnersbury Station. Pleasant evening. Drank a bottle of Australian wine.

Sat. March 24. See that Hurst & Blackett advertize Alg's novel [*Joy Cometh in the Morning*] in the daily papers with the headline "Mr. Gissing's New Novel". Wrote a line to [George] Smith about this, begging him to observe that the book was not mine. In afternoon came [Charles] Anderson [Vicar of St John's, Limehouse]. Evening wrote 4pp. Feeling much better once more, and see my book very clear before me. Reading Bourget's "Mensonges".

Sund. March 25. Foggy, cold, rainy. Roberts came.

Mond. March 26. Alg's novel arrived; I read it carefully and wrote a criticism. It seems to me to promise much, but of course is *young.*- With E[dgar] Harrison went over a die-sinker's place in Oxendon Street. Got useful ideas for "Nether World". In afternoon with Harrison to Bethnal Green Museum. Cold, foggy, rainy. Suffering much from rheumatism in shoulders. At night came two letters: one from young George Smith, saying that they have written to H[urst] & B[lackett] about the lying headline; the other, forwarded by S[mith] & E[lder] from a Miss E.F. Scott, 61 Avenue Wagram, Paris, praising "Life's Morning", and asking me to write to her.[3] An odd letter, but it interests me. Wrote a reply, in very moderate tone.

Tuesd. March 27. Still reading "Mensonges". Wrote 4pp.

Wed. March 28. To National Gallery with Plitt.- In evening had to go back to beg. of 3d chapter. Did 5pp.

Thursd. March 29. Morning spent in Clerkenwell. Arrange now not to have dinner before 2, so that I am ready to sit down to work at 4, and do not need tea, which was always an unwholesome necessity. I take a cup of coffee on coming home from dinner. Wrote 4pp.

Frid. March 30. Good Friday. Morning in Clerkenwell.- Finished "Mensonges".- Sat down at 3.30, and wrote till 10.30, doing 7pp. Good work this!

Sat. March 31. Got Daudet's "Trente Ans de Paris", and Ruskin's "Hortus Inclusus". Impossible to see why the latter should be pubd.[4]- Wrote 4pp.

Sund. Ap.1. To Roberts'. Weather windy and cold still. My thrice accursed chimney smoking as badly as ever.

Mond. Ap. 2. Spent day at Crystal Palace, and brought back a lot of good notes.- Bought *Murray's Mag.* for this month,which has an article by Edith Sichel on Besant and myself[5].- No writing.

Tuesd. Ap. 3. Had to re-write what I did on Saturday. Suffering much from rheumatism in the shoulders. Sent Nelly (it being her 21st birthday to-morrow) a little book called "Literary Landmarks of London" [by Laurence Hutton, 1885].- Another letter from Miss Scott. Shall not write again.

Wed. Ap. 4. Re-writing. Got [John William] Horsley's "Jottings from Jail" [notes and papers on prison matters], a most useful book, and Emily Pfeiffer's "Women and Work".[6]

Thursd. Ap. 5. Re-writing. First fine day, but cold wind.

Frid. Ap. 6. Re-wrote, and got two new pages done. Think I shall get ahead now.- A letter from one W.C. Sowerby[7], 58, Upper Bainbryp St., Derby, asking if Dunfield in "A Life's Morning" be not Wakefield, and saying that, as a boy, he knew my Father. Replied.

Sat. Ap. 7. Got from library Dostoievsky's "La Femme d'un Autre".- Letter from Miss Crum, asking me to resume work with Walter Grahame on Monday.- Wrote 4 pages.

Sund. Ap. 8. Roberts and Plitt came.

Mond. Ap. 9. Grahame recommenced lessons. Going to read with him: Thucyd[ides] IV; Eurip[ides] "Andromache"; Sallust's "Jugurtha", and Horace "Od[es]" IV.- Four pages.

Tuesd. Ap. 10. Frosty and bitter weather. East wind.- Reading Gogol's "Taras Bulba".- Wrote 4 pages.

Wed. Ap. 11. Raining, cold.- Wrote my 4 pages. I go to Grahame at 10 and leave him at 12.30. Then have dinner in Edgware Road, and read the *Star.* Then a walk of an hour, generally round the Park. A cup of coffee follows, and work till about 7.30. Then cocoa and bread and butter, and work again till 10.- A miserable letter from Roberts to-night. Rejections, discouragements. I know not how to help him. Wrote a reply, urging him to work still.- Another letter from Sowerby this morning.

Thursd. Ap. 12. Some home-made cakes from Broadway. Foresee indigestions. Wrote my 4pp.

Frid. Ap. 13. Four pages.

Sat. Ap. 14. In doubt about last pages. Tried to alter, but only ended in doing nothing. Perhaps the Broadway cakes to blame.

Mond. Ap. 16. Re-wrote last 4 pages, and half another page. Fine weather at last; sunny and warm.- Sent Roberts 10/- yesterday; a thing I cannot afford, and have no business whatever to do. But he seems in dire straits.

Thursd. Ap. 19. Went to see the E[dgar] Harrisons last night. Been getting on very poorly with work. Re-reading "Le Nabab" [by Alphonse Daudet], and running through (it is not worth reading) Baring-Gould's "Red Spider".- Letter and flowers from E[lla] G[aussen] yesterday. 3pp. to-day.

Mond. Ap. 23. Nothing done since last Thursday. A vile change in the weather again; rain and fog. To-day took a sudden idea to go down to Eastbourne,- solely to look in at 13 Church Street. Got there at 3.30, and left again by the 5.30. A long talk with Miss Curtis.

Tuesd. Ap. 24. Sent "Thyrza" to Eastbourne, and wrote a letter to Mrs. Thornborough [Miss Curtis's aunt], explaining.

Wed. Ap. 25. From the library: George Moore's "Confessions of a Young Man",- interesting but disgusting book, and Bourget's "André Cornélis", which seems poor.

Thursd. Ap. 26. Two lines from Miss Curtis, acknowledging "Thyrza". Put me into a good humour. Got to work again, by heaven's mercy, and re-wrote four pages.

Frid. Ap. 27. Four pages. A little sunshine, and change to a violent west wind. Never anything in moderation.

Sat. Ap. 28. Four pp.- Finished "André Cornélis".

Mond. Ap. 30. Five pp.- A sunny, warm, inspiriting day.

Tuesd. May 1. Five pp. Tremendous wind again. Bad night, last; awake for four hours. Did not affect me to-day, however, for a wonder. Reading nothing at present.

Wed. May 2. Wind continues.- Did 4pp.- No letters whatever coming for me just now. I notice that there is periodicity in the arrival of my letters.- Finished vol.1, and 2 pp. of next.

Thursd. May 3. Higher wind than ever. Furious rain at times.- Five pp.

Frid. May 4. Feeling out of sorts. Wrote a page, then broke down.- Got from library: Vernon Lee's "Juvenilia", and "Eastern Scenes" by Mrs. Walker[8], whom Miss Curtis mentioned to me as being her aunt.

Sat. May 5. I see a 2/- edn of "Demos" announced this morning. Also interesting announcement of a new review, called the *Universal* [*Review*], ed by [Harry] Quilter, which is to have a novel by Daudet [*One of the Forty,* i.e. *L'Immortel,* translated by Verrall].- Wrote from 3 to 10, and did 5pp.

Mond. May 7. Grahame ill, so that I spent the morning in mere idleness. Only 3 pp. at night.

Tuesd. May 8. A day of blankest idleness and misery. In morning to Bank of Engd, to change notes, mother having sent me £20*. Afternoon to Grosvenor, where I got vol. I of Hardy's "Wessex Tales", and vol. II of Vernon Lee's "Juvenilia". Read them both in an hour and a half, then paced my rooms in agony of loneliness. This becomes intolerable; in absolute truth,I am now and then on the verge of madness. Thought of Miss Curtis, and longed, longed that she too might have thought of me. This life I *cannot* live much longer; it is hideous.

Wed. May. 9. To Eastbourne - and back. All gone off in smoke. Never mind; the better perhaps.

Thursd. May 10. A day of wretchedness, of course. Trying to read "The Virginians" [by Thackeray]. Went to the Temple Bar news rooms, and saw that in Gladstone's article on "Robert Elsmere" (*Nineteenth Centy,* May) there is a reference to "The Unclassed", the only modern novel he mentions. The oddest thing that Gladstone should be the man to revive mention of that book. He calls it "A novel of the speculative and didactic class." This is justice at all events.[9]

Frid. May 11. Forced myself to work, and did 5 pages, pretty well. Wrote 3.30 to 10. Grahame been ill all this week.

Sat. May 12. Got from library 2nd volume of Hardy's "Wessex Tales", and Daudet's "Sapho".- Wrote 5 pp., and at 10 o'clock went out for ramble among the streets. Got back at 12.30.

Mond. May 14. 5pp.- Grahame still unable to work. In the mornings I walk about the park.

Tuesd. May 15. Have asked Lane [the manager of the block of flats called Cornwall Residences] to get me a tenant for 7K. if possible. Cannot hold out here much longer, if only on score of expense.- 3pp. only. Fearful difficulties in Chap. VI of 2nd vol.

Wed. May 16. To library, and got: Journal des Goncourt vol. I, and "The Academician", by Henry Erroll [a novel in three vols., 1888], vol. I. Latter, poor stuff.- In afternoon visited Miss Hand [a friend of the Gaussens'], and

*That is to say, of my own money. At this time, I kept money, in her name, at Wakefield Bank (1902).-(Gissing's note)

in evening, to the [Edgar] Harrisons at Gunnersbury. They advise me to warehouse my furniture, and I think this will be the plan.

Thursd. May 17. Inquired terms at Tilbury's Warehouse.- Wrote nothing.

Frid. May 18. Some re-writing of last few pages; but had again to cancel. In an evil frame of mind.

Sat. May 19. Re-wrote again; and managed a clear 3pp.- Grahame going away for next week. This will make three weeks out of my pocket.

Sund. May 20. This morning beheld an idiotic experiment. I rose at 5.30 (glorious sunshine), made a cup of cocoa, at 6 o'clock and sat down — to write! The result was that by 7 o'clock I had written five words, and had fretted myself into a headache. This has solved decisively the question of Walter Scottian work in my case; it is wholly out of the question.

Mond. May 21. Whit Monday. Went to the Telegraph office, and inserted advt of 7K, to be let at Midsummer. Cost 3/-, and I suppose will not bring a single reply. Wrote from 2.30 to 9.30, and did 4 pages. About 2pp. of this terrible Chapter VII remain.

Tuesd. May 22. A hard day. Finished my Chap. VII, and 2pp. of next; 5 in all. Wrote an hour in the morning, and then from 3 to 11.- In morning called a man in reply to my Advt. Afraid he won't take the rooms.

Wed. May 23. Note from man in Wilts, asking particulars of the flat.- Replied to Fanny Le Breton, who has begun translating "Demos".- Wrote 4 pages, bringing me to 50 of vol. II. Ça marche!

Thursd. May 24. From 9 to 11 in the morning wrote a page, finishing chap. VIII. The next chapter begins a new section of the book, and must be thought over for a day.- Got from library vol. 2 of the Goncourts' Journal. The personality of these men is repugnant to me; and much of the journal loathsome, but I read the book with extreme interest. In their writings I can feel no kind of interest; never read a page, and probably never shall. Contrast this with the passionate personal delight I have in Daudet and all that is his.

Frid. May 25. Four pages.

Sat. May 26. Wrote from 3 to 11, but only did 2½ pages. Very difficult, the beginning of Chap. X.

Sund. May 27. Roberts came as usual, and at 10 o'clock we sallied forth to have supper together. In a day or two he is going to Cornwall, for long holiday. Went to Reggiori's in Chapel Street, and enjoyed ourselves,—bill

7/2. Drank bottle of Médoc and ½ bottle Chianti. One hour wrested from fate.

Mond. May 28. Headache, of course. Grahame recommenced. Told them of my intention to let 7K. and go away. Read 3rd vol. of the Goncourts' Journal, terribly depressing. Wrote nothing. So cold, I had to light the fire. Have not yet been able to see the 2/- "Demos" which came out on Saturday.

Tuesd. May 29 - Sat. June 2. Did as good as nothing. Had to rearrange some of the details of the story and to make myself clearer about the close. On Sat. went to Hyde Park to see the demonstration against compensating the brewers and publicans.[10] Weather begun to be warm. On Thursd. Roberts departed for Cornwall, sending me his will to take care of. Recd proofs to the end of "Life's Morning".

Sund. June 3. Spent the morning in putting away letters, which accumulate in the drawer of my writing-table, and in pasting into a book the reviews of my early books.[11] After "Demos" I have preserved no press notices.- Wrote from 4 to 8, re-writing part of chapter VIII; Roberts being away, my Sundays will henceforth be free.- A very hot day; my old misery of excessive perspiration is beginning again.- Wrote to Nelly, and at dusk went for a walk.- Have just re-read "The Blithedale Romance" [by Hawthorne].

Strange how sternly I am possessed of the idea that I shall not live much longer. Not a personal thought but is coloured with this conviction. I never look forward more than a year at the utmost; it is the habit of my mind, in utter sincerity, to expect no longer tenure of life than that. I don't know how this has come about; perhaps my absolute loneliness has something to do with it. Then I am haunted with the idea that I am consumptive. I never cough without putting a finger to my tongue, to see if there be a sign of blood. Morbidness — is it? I only know that these forecasts are the most essential feature of my mental and moral life at present. Death, if it came now, would rob me of not one hope, for hopes I simply have not.

Mond. June 4. Had to go back to beginning of Chap. X. Did 4 pages, finishing at 11.- In afternoon went to Ludgate Hill, to buy note-paper and order certain plays of Ibsen at Trübner's.

Tuesd. June 5. Some lettuce and radishes from Broadway, the first fruits of their cottage garden.- Wrote from 3.30 to 11.30, doing 4 pages. See my way clear to end of 2nd vol.- Reading Hawthorne's "American Note-Books" again.

Wed. June 6. Half a page short of 4. At 10 o'clock a rush of blood to the head — due, I suppose, to indigestion, brought work to an end for this night.

Thursd. June 7. Letter from Madge [his sister], who is suffering from vaccinated arm.- Walk round the park from 2 to 3. Got to work at 4, made up what I couldn't finish last night, and did 4 more pages. A good evening; finished at 10.

Last year I was constantly reading Greek; this, I shall probably read none at all, except the little I do with Grahame. Could I have foreseen the future, I would have written nothing last year, after my futile "Clement Dorricott". Let me note here the history of "Clement". I wrote it from February to May, immediately after finishing "Thyrza". Then I took it to Bentley and offered it for "Temple Bar". For that purpose he declined to use it, but was willing to publish it in vols. I declined — thinking it unworthy to succeed "Thyrza"—and threw it aside, wrapped as it came from Bentley. Will it ever come out, I wonder?[12]

Frid. June 8. A hard job to get my 4 pages done to-night, but succeeded, reaching p.73. A few days now will finish vol. II.- Have taken up "Elle et Lui" [by George Sand] for odd moments. Do other people re-read books to the same extent as I do?- Dull, cloudy, cool days, these last; a drop of rain at times. Not at all like June.

Sat. June 9. In the morning walked out along Finchley Road; cloudy, slowly clearing, — warm.- Evening, did 3½ pages, unable to finish the 4. My weariness weighs heavily on me.

Sund. June 10. Corrected the last proof-sheets of "A Life's Morning". Thank heaven! A great trial to me, this re-reading of a weak production. Yesterday recd from Germany four of Ibsen's plays, in Reclam's translations. Read to-day "Die Stützen der Gesellschaft" [*Pillars of Society*] with much enjoyment on the whole.- Wrote to Roberts at Mevagissey, Cornwall.- In evening read "Rosmersholm" [also by Ibsen], a strange piece, which I don't quite understand. Walked down Harley Street and back.

Mond. June 11. No letter.- In afternoon to Tott[enham] Ct. Rd for tobacco. Could not write, as I am again at a standstill for clear ideas. Just as I had made an attempt, note comes from Miss Crum, asking me to go to Oxford to-morrow, to see a Mr. Smith, with regard to a tutor for Walter Grahame. Telegraphed to said Smith.- Read half Ibsen's "Die Wildente" [*The Wild Duck*].- A magnificent day, but cannot enjoy it. I never enjoy anything now—*never anything.*

Tuesd. June 12. Went by 10 o'clock train to Oxford, and saw Smith at his rooms at Balliol. Then lunched with him at his house, 7 Orick Road; arrived there by myself at appointed hour, and had to introduce myself to Mrs Smith. At same moment another man presented himself for lunch, also unexpectedly. An odd household. Three little children. Young lad lodging there. Smith himself a man of eight and thirty, I suppose, but may be older; rather a childish fellow, and dry; looks like a clerk in a house of business, exactly.- Being my first visit to Oxford, I rambled about High Street in afternoon and looked into several of the colleges. Got ideas for a chapter in my next novel. Returned by 4.5 express.- No letter.

Wed. June 13. Had to go back four pages; did this re-writing and no more. Terribly wearisome this Chap. XII; it is poor stuff, all this idealism; I'll never go in for it again.- Began Ibsen's "Gespenster" [*Ghosts*].- No letter.

Thursd. June 14. Re-wrote last page of yesterday, and did nearly 5 more, a good evening's work, from 3 to 11. In a little better mood about it.- Finished "Gespenster".- No letter.

Frid. June 15. Clouded rainy day; so cold that I had to light a fire in the evening. At 7.30 a letter from Nelly. Did my 4pp. by 9 o'clock, and went out to buy a newspaper, for I had heard that the Emperor Frederick died this morning.[13] It has given me a slight feeling of sadness, and I lament that a young savage has come to the throne.
　By the bye, at Oxford Station I saw a copy of "Demos" in a form unknown to me. It is the 6/-edn, with a different binding, with my name on title-page, and sold at 3/6.[14]

Sat. June 16. A foolish day. In morning went to Grosvenor and got vol. I of "The New Antigone" [an anonymous romance in 3 vols., 1887], which had a success in the spring. Find it poor, amateurish, without any force of characterization. In afternoon read and, as I thought, prepared for work; but when I sat down at 3 the attempt was abortive. This often happens just when I particularly wish to finish anything; I had only 5 pages to complete vol. II; now it goes on into a new week.- Miserable, and so cold I could scarcely sit, (rain and cloud all day, and temperature of late like January,) I went off to Terry's theatre and saw [A.W.] Pinero's "Sweet Lavender", getting a place in the pit, when I had meant to go to the gallery, and so spending 2/6 when even 1/- would have been extravagance. Ye gods, what a play! Sentimental farce; conventionality gone mad; acting the feeblest I ever witnessed, excepting Terry's extravagant part. Came home in frightful state of hunger, and ate a quarter of a loaf of bread, washing it down with cold tea and water. Luxurious times, these! - Letters from Alg and his wife.

Sund. June 17. I have lived in London ten years, and now, on a day like this when I am very lonely and depressed, there is not one single house in which I should be welcome if I presented myself, not one family — nay, not one person—who would certainly receive me with good will. I wonder whether any other man would make such a statement as this with such absolute truth.- Thought I might have written to-day, but found it impossible. No gleam of sunshine, and still very cold. In morning wrote letters to the girls and to mother, who is still at Broadway. In evening went to the Bermondsey Gladstone Club, Grange Road, Bermondsey, to hear the parson [Stewart] Headlam[15] lecture on Christian Socialism. The man's appearance rather suprised me: a shrewd face and very fluent speech. Every

32

point of lecture of course unanswerable in theory. It is well to go to these clubs occasionally, to remind myself that I am not giving way to prejudice merely in despising the intellectual qualities of their frequenters. The speakers after Headlam were contemptible in a degree not to be expressed by words, - with perhaps one exception.- Went and returned by train; Monument Station.- Nothing else done to-day, except read a little Greek for Grahame to-morrow; think over my next chapters, and read a few chapters of "Villette".

Mond. June 18. Again not a ray of sunlight, and as cold as if we were in January. Ordered a cwt of coals, and lighted a fire. At Grahame's this morning we had a fire also. Wrote from 3.30 to 10.45, and <u>finished vol. II.</u> Gloria! - No letter.

Tuesd. June 19. No sunlight. Wrote 3.30 to 9.45 and did a little more than 4 pages, hard, close writing; embodying many notes. How easily I used to write when I never used notes at all, but improvised straight on! I think I may congratulate myself on an advance in artistic method.- No letter.

Wed. June 20. Much rain, very cold.- In afternoon to Grosvenor, thence to Oxenham's Auction-rooms, to look in at sale of the properties of St James's Theatre, (dissolution of Hare-Kendal partnership). Nothing much to note.- Home, and sat down with Henry James's "Partial Portraits", foreseeing that it would take up my evening; impossible to resist articles on Daudet, Tourguéneff, and so on. A paper on Stevenson I cannot read; my prejudice against the man is insuperable, inexplicable, painful; I hate to see his name, and certainly shall never bring myself to read one of his books. Don't quite understand the source of this feeling*.- Having finished the "Portraits" turned to Maupassant's "Pierre et Jean", the first of this author's books that I have seen, though I remember a disgusting story of his in the "Figaro"—really and truly disgusting.- Moon visible this evening amid the clouds.- No letter.

Thursd. June 21. The longest day, Grahame tells me, and as far as its appearance goes we might be in November. I woke up at 4.30 in the morning, and saw the sun shining till about 6, (the first time for a week,) then came cloud and rain, which lasted all day long.- Good evening's work; 3.30 to 10, and did 4 pages.- No letter.- Surprises me much that I have heard nothing from the Gaussens, who were to be in town at the end of May.

Frid. June 22. Reading Maupassant's "Pierre et Jean".- Wrote from 3.30 to 10, four pages.- At two o'clock the sun once more showed itself, and shone till seven, a noteworthy fact.- No letter.

Sat. June 23. Fine day, getting warm at last. In morning, read *Spectator* as usual, and went to Grosvenor. Got Daudet's "L'Evangéliste", and "Savage

*Was this mere jealousy? Of course I have long ceased to be capable of such feeling. (1902) (Gissing's note)

London" by man called King[16].-Wrote only 2 pages. Out of sorts and in some doubt about details.- No letter.

Sund. June 24. Fine day; hot. Reading "L'Evangéliste". Wrote to mother, asking her to send me £10 as soon as she gets back to Wakefield. Also, long letter to Bertz.- In evening to Clerkenwell Green.

Mond. June 25. As I rose in morning, felt all at once that it behoved me to go and see if the Gaussens were at Craven Hill. Did so, at 4 o'clock, and stayed half an hour; had to accept invitation for Wednesday afternoon. Only got to work at 6 o'clock; did 2 pages. On Wednesday I shall of course write nothing. What would become of me if I had regular social intercourse?—A tremendously hot day.- No letter.

Tuesd. June 26. Day of fog and sweltering heat and thunderstorms.- Wrote 3 to 10, did 4 pages.- Letter from one H. Latham,[17] of Wakefield, who says he is a writer of stories and begs me (his grandfather having known my father) to help him to an editor. I am "in the magic circle". That phrase alarms me; indeed the whole letter is painfully of the common stamp. Must write a grave reply.

Wed. June 27. First thing in afternoon replied to Latham. At 4 to Mrs. Gaussen's, and had a not unpleasant couple of hours. Miss Agaby sang, and of course invited me to her pupils' concert next Wednesday, - another day to be sacrificed.- Got to work at 6.30 and wrote drearily till 9, re-writing last page, and doing only one more.- Heavy rain, and fog. Feeling headachey.- No letter.

Thursd. June 28. Letter from Alg.- Cool, fine day; thunder and rain in after-part. Worked 3.30 to 10.45, and did 4 pages. Sent off letter to Roberts, Falmouth, written last night.- With what terrific reluctance I sit down to work every afternoon! Weariness and ill health have much to do with it, I suppose. It takes me always two hours before I am really progressing, and two hours of sheer agony, renewed each day. Ah, when the end comes!

Frid. June 29. Cloudy day.- Insufficient work, only 3pp.; not in good cue.- Letter from Latham, thanking me for my hard advice. Letter from E[lla] G[aussen], asking me to lend her MS of "Clement Dorricott". Replied in negative. Have taken up the "Tatler" again for my reading at odd moments.

Sat. June 30. Letter from Miss Carter of Ripon. She says that "The Unclassed" has been asked for there, but is not allowed to be circulated, and takes upon her foolish self to reprove me for writing such a book.Rec. £10 from mother. Went and paid my rent to Lane. To library: got [John Pentland] Mahaffy's "Greek Life and Thought" and Selections from Swinburne. Fine breezy day.- Work from 3.30 to 10, but only 2½ pages. At this rate I shall finish by about next Christmas. Can't understand why I find it so difficult to get on.

Sund. July 1. A day as thoroughly wasted as any in my life. Took a pill last night, and I suppose that accounts for headache. An hour in the Park in the morning; the rest of the day did not stir. Doing what? Absolutely nothing; not even reading. Took up a vol. now and then, but could not attend to it. Walked from one room to the other. Lonely, lonely, lonely. Weather bright, but almost cold.- To bed at nine.

Mond. July 2. Ceaseless rain all day long, and again so cold that I am obliged to light a fire. This in July! Worked 3 to 10.45, with a break of an hour or two for thinking over difficult points. Wrote rather more than 3 pages. No letter.

Tuesd. July 3. Letter from Nelly. Bright day, but cool.- Work 3.30 to 9.45, and did rather more than 4 pages; in smoother water now.- Wrote reply to Nelly, about our projected visit to seaside in August.

Wed. July 4. At 3 o'clock to Miss Agaby's concert at Steinway Hall. Two hours and a half of mortal ennui. Mrs Gaussen there; also spoke to Miss Bagram, and after concert went downstairs to have cup of tea. The whole affair very painful; the people so deadly commonplace.- On returning, of course unable to work. Replied to Miss Carter's letter, then went to the Royal Music Hall, as a needful relief. Reading Tourguéneff's "Punin und Baburin". No letter.- Rain in morning, but very fine later; still cool.

Thursd. July 5. Heavy rain all day; cold.- Wrote 3.45 to 9.15, and did a little more than 4 pages. The worst is over now, I am at the middle of the last vol., and the rest will be straightforward. Extraordinary letter from Roberts, from Falmouth.

Frid. July 6. Cold, rainy, some thunder.- Took my walk round the park in afternoon, as generally of late. Wrote 3.30 to 9.45, four pages.- No letter.

Sat. July 7. Rainy, no sun; had to light a fire in evening.- Got from library Daudet's "Lettres de mon Moulin", and Maupassant's "Mont-Oriol".- Wrote from 3.30 to 9.15, and did my 4 pages.- No letter.

Sund. July 8. In morning to Mile End Waste, for a strike meeting of Bryant & May's match girls.[18] Very few of the girls themselves present. Speeches from Mrs. Besant, Burrows, John Burns, Cunninghame Graham, Clementina Black, Stewart Headlam etc.- Gave 1/- at collection.- Dinner in Holborn, with unwonted pint of stout.- Afternoon, wrote to Roberts.- Evening, into Regent's Park, where again attended the strike meeting, and again gave 1/-,- rather, I'm afraid, because I was ashamed to give nothing, in my bourgeois costume. On the way home had an experience familiar enough and horribly distressing; of a sudden, like the snapping of a cord, I became aware that the plot of my story, as arranged for the next few days, would not do. Sat late, brooding, and had a troubled night.

Mond. July 9. Woke to the most miserable distress; striving vainly to see my way in the story. Seldom have I suffered keener mental pain. Thought, thought, at the rate of a hundred thousand miles an hour. Dressed in a suicidal mood. Fortunately a bright morning, or it would have been worse with me. In afternoon, still thinking, and at length reconciled myself to a scheme. But could not write; brain too much fagged.- Weather almost cold and since noon very cloudy.- No letter.

Tuesd. July 10. To get story in order, had to go back and re-write 2pp. at end of vol. II, and 4 early in vol. III. Finished both places, so that to-morrow my work is clear before me again. I think I can go on to the end now.- Letter from Nelly, about proposed seaside holiday. Sunshine for an hour or two in morning, then dull and very cold. Suffering from rheumatism in shoulders. Reading "Mont-Oriol".

Wed. July 11. Bitterly cold. Paper says there was 6 in. of snow on the Grampians yesterday. Letters from Alg, Bertz and Miss Carter,- a surprising batch for me.- Sent "Joy Cometh [in the Morning]" [by Algernon Gissing] and "Western Avernus" [by Morley Roberts] to Bertz.- Wrote from 2.45 to 10 and did 5 pages. Satisfactory. Of course had to light a fire.

Thursd. July 12. There were slight falls of snow yesterday morning in London, and in several parts of England. To-day so bitterly cold that I had to put on an overcoat, and of course to light a fire. Wrote 3.30 to 10, and did 5 pages.- Much rain and no sunshine.- No letter.

Frid. July 13. Fine, warm day, thank heaven! Wrote only from 3.30 to 6. Did 2 pages, the capture of Bob Hewett and the excitement of them made me so ill that I could do no more. A disappointment this. Walked about the streets till 9.30.- No letter.

Sat July 14. To library and got Tolstoi's "Polikouchka".- Fine day, dull at evening.- Letter from Nelly, proposing Seascale[19]. Wrote from 3 to 9. Had to go back and insert a new chapter; did only 3 new pages, with a lot of copying and botching besides.- At 9.30 went out and had a walk.

Sund. July 15. Ceaseless rain from morning to night. Thought I might work, but as usual, the Sunday effect was too strong, so contented myself with planning the 3 chapters that remain to end of book. In these wish to emphasize that the idealistic social reformer is of far less use than the humble discharger of human duty.- In afternoon lit the fire, and passed quite a pleasant winter evening—absolutely indistinguishable from an evening of December.- Read Tolstoi's "Polikouchka" and "Une Tourmente de Neige". Cannot like him so much as either Tourguéneff or Dostoievsky, but I acknowledge his wonderful literary instinct.- Read also in Lockhart,[20] and scraps of "David Copperfield". Wrote to Alg, and to Madge and Nell.- Finished "Mont-Oriol" on Saturday. Seems to me essentially a commonplace book. Have no kind of pleasure in it—neither in subject nor style.

Mond. July 16. Much thunder last night; it woke me.- This morning Miss Crum asked me for the account. Grahame's last day will be next Tuesday.- Ordered [R.C.] Jebb's "Antigone" [1887], as a present for Grahame.- Dull, cold day.- Worked 3 to 9, in excellent humour, doing my 5 pages. Only 20 remain. After 9 went out for a walk, and concocted what is to be the closing sentence of the book—a good one I think.- No letter.- Made out account, and posted to Miss Crum.

Tuesd. July 17. Dark morning, and in afternoon furious storm.- A little talk with Miss Crum at 12.30; said good-bye and took cheque for £31.10.6.- Went to tailor's and ordered a suit.- Wrote 3 to 10, and did 5pp. Am finishing the book in my good vein.- Letter from Nelly.- No reading of any kind.- Got the "Antigone", a superb edition.

Wed. July 18. Heavy rain.- To tailor's to be fitted, and of course they were not ready, so had my walk in rain for nothing.- Wrote 3 to 9.30; did 4pp., but am dissatisfied; think they must be done again, confound it!—No letter.

Thursd. July 19. Fine day, but cloudy; warm, To tailor's and got fitted.- Worked 3 to 9, re-writing last five pp.- Sent note to Smith, Elder, telling them the new novel is ready, and informing them that I wish it to appear before "A Life's Morning".- Letter from Alg, lamenting a review of "Joy Cometh" in last *Spectator*.

Frid. July 20. Cloudy and rain.- Wrote 3 to 8, doing only 4pp., which leaves one chapter still.- Reply from [James] Payn, saying it would be unjudicious to publish two books at same time. Who proposed it? Cannot send the MS till Monday.

Sat. July 21. Fair day. To library; got [Hector Malot's] "Sans Famille" and Tolstoi's "A la Recherche du Bonheur". Clothes from tailor's.- Wrote 3 to 10, doing nearly 5pp.. Thus have 2½ to finish to-morrow. To think that I should write these words at last!- No letter.

Sund. July 22. Wrote from 8.30 to 11 in the morning and from 6 to 8 at night, so long did it take me to finish the last 2½ pages. However, I can write here: Finished "The Nether World".- Fine day; very close at night. Reading "Sans Famille".- Wrote note to Payn.

Mond. July 23. Fine weather; day of tumult.- Grahame in morning; thence to leave "Nether World" at S[mith] & E[lder]'s.- Dinner at Wilkinson's, Fleet Street.- Bought Daudet's new book, "L'Immortel", and glory in thought of reading it.- To the vegetn Rest in St Martin's Lane to try and meet E[dgar] E. Harrison; had a talk with him.- Bought hat a Heath's, and socks and tie at Baker's. Home by 4; shaved and went to the Gaussens', to say good-bye, having decided to go to Wak[efiel]d to-morrow instead of Wedy.- Had to wait couple of hours before Mrs. Gaussen and Ella returned. Pleasant chat.- Home, supper, and packing.- Peeps into "L'Immortel".- Letter from Alg, saying he and Katie will come here during August.

Tuesd. July 24. Said good-bye to Grahame, and gave him the Antigone. To Wakefield by 3.20 train; "home" at 7.30. Evening of talk.- Fine day.- Read at "L'Immortel" in train.

Wed. July 25. Rain all day. Did nothing; at night a few pages of "L'Immortel". Short walk with Nelly and talk of "style" in novels.

Sat. July 28. Alg and wife arrived at 7K.

Sund. July 29. Have finished "L'Immortel". about which I have my private doubts. Am reading George Sand's "Lettres d'un Voyageur". Since last Friday night almost incessant rain.

Mond. July 30. Rain nearly all day. In afternoon met Nelly's friend Dora Carter [a cousin of Mary Carter of Ripon]. In evening all together to Mrs. Hall's.[21] Alg has sent *Spectator* and the *Star*. Writes a letter, with account of meetings in Regent's Park yesterday. Am reading Latin with Nelly.

Frid. Aug. 3. Left Kirkgate Station at 8.13 and reached Seascale at 4 o'clock, having travelled via Preston. Fine day till 5 o'clock, then rain. Short walk in evening; uncomfortable. Lodgings at 2 Scale Villas, facing sea. Miss Hodgson, landlady. Party: Mother, Madge, Nelly and self; have two bedrooms and a sitting room at £2.14.6 a week.

Sat. Aug. 4. Rain and high wind ceaselessly all day long. Hour's walk in morning; came back drenched. Girls and I bought sand-shoes. Some nineteen years ago.[22] when I was here last, there was not a shop in the place; now there are three or four.- Alg sends me the *Star* from London.- Sent off her 5/- to Mrs King [his charwoman], whose payment I continue.- Read in a desultory way. We have brought "Vanity Fair", Selections from Browning. "Golden Treasury", Irving's "Sketch Book", "Vicar of Wakefield", "The Newcomes" and "Sartor Resartus". Did half an hour of Latin with Nelly.- Thought out a short story of which scene to be laid here. Have an idea of a story to be laid in a place like Sowerby Bridge, where there are factories immediately surrounded with hills and moorland. Should have to live there for a while.

Sund. Aug. 5. From early morning, fine; at noon, warm; but windy and many clouds. Mother and girls went to an iron church, which—as well as a chapel of sandstone—has got itself built here[23]. I walked meantime to Gosforth and back. Afternoon we spent together on sands. Evening mother and girls again to iron church.- Read in "Golden Treasury", Irving's "Sketch Book", and "Sartor".- Feel tolerably well in body, and at some ease in mind, though with no genuine contentment or gladness. Scarcely ever give a thought to "The Nether World".

Mond. Aug. 6. Rain all day; no sunshine.

Tuesd. Aug. 7. Rain nearly all day; no sunshine. Walked a good deal, getting wet.- Alg sends A.J. Smith's card, left at 7K.- Recd *Spectator.-* The surf very loud to-night.

Wed. Aug. 8. A fine day. Mother and Madge joined a public conveyance at Beach House, and drove to Wastwater. Nelly and I went by train to Boot, at end of Eskdale Railway, and thence walked up the Burmoor Beck, to Burmoor Tarn, and so over the pass into Wastdale. Just as we reached the lake, mother and Madge who were strolling about, encountered us. We all talked for a few minutes, then Nelly and I trudged on to Strands. There had tea, at the Strands Inn. A party of young girls in light dresses, walking about the village; Nelly thought it a marriage party. After an hour's rest, we walked on to Gosforth and Seascale, getting home at 7.45. The others had arrived ten minutes before, having driven home by way of Drigg.

Thursd. Aug. 9. Letter from Roberts, announcing his return to Chelsea.- Fine day, mild, cloudy at times.- Loitered about the shore. Madge suffering from scorched face.

Frid. Aug. 10. Hot, misty day. Wandered about or sat on shore. Nelly miserable with tooth-ache. Not at all sure whether this way of spending a holiday is not mere waste of time.

Sat. Aug. 11. Fine day.- Walk in morning with Madge and Nell to Calder Bridge. Afternoon on sands.

Sund. Aug. 12. Fine day.- Mountains wonderfully clear.- Church-going by mother and girls.

Mond. Aug. 13. Last night, terrifically windy; the blasts woke me. Wind continued all to-day. Walk inland with Nelly, and gathered flowers. Heavy breakers. Mountains clear. An angry sunset.- Our lodgings abound in earwigs.

Tuesd. Aug. 14. Alg leaves 7K for Broadway.- A glorious day; clear view of Isle of Man and mountains cloudless. At 12.15 Madge and Nell and I took train for Sellafield, then walked to Calder Abbey, and back by road to Seascale. In evening strolls by seashore. The place over-run by an excursion of 500 children from Whitehaven.- Reading frequently in the "Golden Treasury".

Wed. Aug. 15. Train from Seascale to Egremont at 8.45 and walked (alone) from Egremont to Ennerdale through Cleator. Dinner at Fox and Hounds, Ennerdale Bridge, then over the moors to Calder Bridge, and good road, about six miles. Back to Seascale through Sellafield. Fine day and hot. Isle of Man very distinct.

Thursd. Aug. 16. Fine day, warm,. Two excursions flooded the place. Day spent idly in reading by the shore. At evening, a walk along Gosforth road, to have last look at mountains in evening light.

Frid. Aug. 17. Left Seascale by the 11.45 train, and reached Wakefield by way of Bolton and the L[ancashire] & Y[orkshire] R[ailway]. Home at about 6.30.

Wed. Aug. 22. Nelly left for a fortnight at Scarborough, with Dora Carter.- Days spent of late worse than idly. Reading a little, however; "Hermann u. Dorothea" [by Goethe] and "Odyssey".- Walk to-day with Madge to New Miller Dam. Weather fine. Have been sitting for portrait at Hall's, several positions[24]. . .

Sund. Sept. 2. Time has been wearing on; I wait here for Nelly's return, but shall be glad to resume some kind of movement. A walk by myself yesterday round by Stanley, Altofts and Normanton. No news yet from Payn. The *Star* and the *Spectator* are sent to me. Frame of mind nervous and discontented. On the whole have determined to go to Paris whether 7K be let or not.- Have been reading a great deal of Crabbe,[25] whom I recognize as a predecessor of our realistic school of fiction. Six books of the "Odyssey", translated aloud to Madge. Hawthorne's "Seven Gables", Wordsworth's "Prelude". Find it impossible even to think about my next book. The atmosphere of Wakefield would soon make the completest dullard of me.

Wed. Sept. 5. Lena Maddison [a friend of the Gissing sisters] comes on a visit of two days. Good figure; good profile; good-natured; but childish minded and untaught.

Thursd. Sept. 6. Nelly returns from Scarborough.- Reading Pepys's Diary, and by way of contrast, the "Pilgrim's Progress". The latter I have never yet read through.

Sund. Sept. 9. Preparing for departure to-morrow. Have never been so long away from London since I first went to live there in 1877. Weather cold and still frequent rain, but endurable. Determined to go very shortly to Paris.

Mond. Sept. 10. Left early for Broadway. Evesham at 2.37, and Alg met me at Station. A fine evening. All going well at Smallbrook Cottage.- Nelly went to-day to stay with an acquaintance at Bradford—delightful sojourn.-

Tuesd. Sept. 11. Fine day. In morning came Mrs Shailer, whom our family call "aunt", though I know not why, and Mary Bedford, to call and meet me for the first time. In afternoon after walk with Alg, Katie and I go to tea with the same two in Broadway. A pleasant little house they live in, looking on the street of Broadway; their former house (Russell House), which belongs to Mary's brother Tom, is let to the American artists Millet and Abbey.[26] Home by moonlight-setting. Alg keeps at his work; is writing "A Lion of Cotswold".

Wed. Sept. 12. Walked to Honeybourne Station, and thence by train to Stratford-on-Avon, my first visit. Cannot say that I found any pleasure in going over the Shakspere House. Half a dozen other visitors, and the cackle of the old women demonstrators made it impossible really to look at anything, or to think one's thoughts. On to the church, where paid sixpence for admission; here a little more peace, but still old woman demonstrator at hand. A ghastly thought occurring to me, I asked: "Have you many people on Bank Holidays?" Yes, they had a great many. "Scarcely the places to see in a crowd," I suggested. "No", replied the old woman, and added, with reference to Shksp's House, "the rooms are too small for that." On going to sign the visitors' book in the church, I asked if "anyone of interest" had been lately. The reply was: "No one *since the Princess Louise*".[27]

Walked over the fields to Shottery, eating my sandwiches. A perfect day; unclouded sky, and the slightest delicious breeze. From Anne's cottage ran out children holding flowers, for which money was of course expected. I bought a rosebud, looked at the cottage, and passed on, not daring to face the possibilities of admission. To me this walk about Shottery was the best of the day. Lovely pastures and cornfields; paths and hills and fine trees; all in glorious sunlight. Here I could think of W[illiam] S[hakespeare].

Walked back to Stratford Church, and for a couple of hours lay on the stone wall at the waterside of the graveyard. Smoked many pipes, ruminated much, and watched the muddy water. A rat swam right across from the other side. The words most often in my mind were

"We are such stuff
As dreams are made on, and our little life
Is rounded with a sleep."

Back to Honeybourne by the 4.55 and home at 7 o'clock. Deadly tired.- A letter to-day from Ella Gaussen, from Kingstown, Ireland. Mrs. King sends *Star* from London.

Thursd. Sept. 13. Letters from Nelly, Roberts (enclosing unmounted photograph,) and Plitt. Idle day. Wrote to people at Wakefield and to Nelly at Bradford. Also a note to Payn, asking for news of "The Nether World". Walk in afternoon to Saintbury.

Sund. Sept. 16. Long walk with Alg in the morning, through Stanton and Snowshill and round by the tower to Broadway again. Stanton, a village of great beauty; more nearly the ideal old English village than any I ever saw. The houses dated early 17th Centy. Stanton Court, an exquisite old

41

residence, with lawn open along the highroad.- Read Bk 9 of "Odyssey" aloud. In evening came Tom Bedford.

Mond. Sept. 17. To tea at Mrs Shailer's; previously a walk with Tom and Mary Bedford.- In mid-fields encountered one Austin Williams, to whom, I am given to understand, Mary has for some years been practically engaged. The thought a very painful one; for he is apparently a man of no education, of no refinement, and labours on a farm.

Tuesd. Sept. 18. Note from James Payn, from Scarborough, saying that he has not yet begun to read "The Nether World" and fears he cannot report on it for some weeks yet. Got up to-day with bad rheumatism in shoulders, which grew so bad that after dinner I had to bestow myself in bed.

Wed. Sept. 19. Rheumatism kept me in bed till 12 o'clock. Mrs Shailer and the Bedfords to tea. Alg kept at his desk and did not see them; the necessities of his work compel him to this, which of course seems inexplicable to the relatives.

Thursd. Sept. 20. Rheumatism a good deal better. To dinner at Mrs. Shailer's. A glorious day. No rain since my coming here. After dinner, Mary set off to take part in the Broadway School-feast. I then walked with Tom to look at the old church. Leave-takings, in view of my departure to-morrow.- No reading done these last days.

Frid. Sept. 21. Left Smallbrook cottage and to town by the 11.51. Fine weather still. Shortly after arrival at the lonely 7K received letters from Nelly and Madge. To bed early.

Sat. Sept. 22. To Roberts at 10 o'clock and had dinner with him in the Strand. To the station to inquire about trains for my journey. Got a man to pack my Raphael cartoons, to be sent to Wakefield. In afternoon a letter from editor of the *Weekly Dispatch*, asking me to contribute stories. Am very doubtful; must talk with Roberts about it to-morrow. Working at a multitude of preparations for departure. Sent to Nelly a Latin Grammar and "Wahrheit u. Dichtung" [by Goethe]; to Madge, [Charles] Waterton's "Wanderings [in South America]" [1825]. Decided to go to Paris by Newhaven and Dieppe, next Wednesday.

Sund. Sept. 23. Roberts came in afternoon. No good talk; both dull.

Mond. Sept. 24. A letter from a stranger, Rev. George Bainton, of Coventry, who says he is going to deliver a lecture on art of composition, and is writing to one or two "well-known authors" requesting them to give him hints as to their own methods of study in such matters. Wrote a rather long, and I think good, reply.- Took books back to Grosvenor; must lose the second half year of my subscription;- how many things have I lost for lack of foresight!- Very long preparing for departure. In afternoon to Plitt at Gunnersbury; he makes up his mind to go with me, and we shall live together in Paris.- Letters to Madge, Nelly and Alg.- Bought tin kettle, saucepan, frying-pan and spirit lamp, for use in Paris.- Oct. *Cornhill* arrived [containing the tenth instalment of "A Life's Morning"]; sent it on to Wakefield without opening, as usual.- In good spirits, though a little over-excited. Wish it were Wednesday evening.

Tuesd. Sept. 25. Went at 11 to see Edr of *Dispatch* (W.A. Hunter) at 2 Brick Court, Temple. Owing to his not having recd my letter, he was not there. A deluge of rain all morning, and got wet through. Then telegram from Hunter, asking if he could come here this evening. At 9 he comes, and we had an hour's talk. A slow, commonplace, and—in matters of literature— very stupid Scotchman. He wants a tale from me, to run 10 weeks; offers 5 guas. a week. Has merely heard of me through Mrs Ashton Dilke[28]; knows nothing of my books. My doubts are stronger than ever.- Letter of thanks from Rev. Bainton, who asks to be allowed to print my letter in his lecture.

Wed. Sept. 26. Left for Paris by the 7.50 from Victoria. Before starting, a telegram of farewell from Alg.- At Victoria, [Edgar] Harrison and Roberts both met us. A smooth crossing to Dieppe, but for me disagreeable, as I had started with a sore throat, and it got worse during night. Had to desert the deck, and pay the extra 2/- for a berth below.

Thursd. Sept. 27. Paris at 9.30; throat very bad. Took a cab and ordered to drive to the Hôtel Cujas, Rue Cujas. Behold, the place was pulled down! A wretched driving about to several places for rooms, and at last put up at the Hôtel Atlantique, Rue Jean-Jacques Rousseau. Double-bedded room. Went to bed almost immediately and in extreme wretchedness; throat worse than ever, nothing to eat or drink, no light even till 9 o'clock. Plitt might have helped, but he was in a foolish drowsy state, and indeed is just as little practical as all other Germans I have known. He hums and ha's for an hour over every proposal.

Frid. Sept. 28. Throat no better, but so hated the room in which I had tossed ill all night, that I got up at 7 and went out with Plitt for breakfast. Very fine day. Excellent *basin* of coffee at a Crémerie in the Rue de Rivoli. Thence in search of permanent lodgings. Plitt bent on an impossible cheapness, and gravely considered many rooms not fit for kennels. Everywhere evil odours. At last I made a desperate effort to fix him to some rooms in the Hôtel Londres, Rue Linné, near the Jardin des Plantes; tolerably clean, and decent people. He decided for one on the 5th floor, I for one on the 2nd; his rent 25fr. a month, mine 35. But in order to make him contented, I had to offer to pay 5fr. of his rent; he accepted at once, without a hint of delicacy, or indeed of obligation! And yet the man is a good and honest fellow, only stupid, very stupid; I have never known intimately so stupid a man.- We moved our goods in a cab at noon. Have with us a set of cooking utensils for spirit lamp, so can make coffee, etc. But as yet I see small prospect of work. Plitt wants to study flower and fruit painting; of course in a painfully conventional way, but yet I daresay with chance of selling his drawings.- Dined for 1.20 in the Rue de Rivoli, and after it a bottle of white wine between us. Early to bed, with absolutely no voice left, though throat not feeling very sore.

Sat. Sept. 29. Paid in advance, by our own desire, the first half of our month, and made a few arrangements for comfort, such as getting a large can of water for room, in addition to the pint or so which the jug holds. My room is really two, a little cabinet de toilette leading out of it. The whole hotel just been cleaned and painted, thank Heaven! Must get a wash-hand basin; the thing I have at present under that name is of course only a moderate sized slop-basin.- Postcards to mother, Alg and Bertz.- Throat still very bad, but can speak a little; fever and perspirations. My room not uncomfortable. By great good chance it happens to contain a little writing-table. Looks on to the court, and so is not very noisy.- This morning heavy rain, clearing towards noon. Plitt has got to his painting already; I of course can do nothing yet.- Read *Le Soleil,* royalist paper.- Dined at a place I used to go to, Rue S. Jacques.

Sund. Sept. 30. Sent address to Mrs King. Throat much better. Rainy morning, and w. wind. Passed an hour in Notre-Dame, during mass; a boy's voice singing, pleasant to hear. Strolled through Jardin des Plantes. Weather cleared at noon. Déjeuner at home, then for a long walk in west end. Place de la Concorde beautiful in clear sunlight. Wearing my old clothes, and with boots made muddy, this morning, I felt an outcast among the endimanchés of the boulevards. Bought and read *Le Petit Moniteur* (ed. by Ernest Daudet), and *La Nation.* A good dramatic critic in the latter. Towers of N[otre] D[ame] beautiful against deep blue sky as I came home. Wind cold. My room made disagreeable to-day by the voices of neighbours—voices hard and rude and violent, showing the low class of people who live in this hotel. Indeed it is a sad mistake to be here at all. Poor Plitt is not the man for my companion in Paris; but on n'y peut rien!

Mond. Oct. 1. Fine day, though not very bright. Left home at 9 o'clock, and walked until 4 in afternoon. Round the boulevards. To the Salle de lecture at the Bibl[iothèque] Nationale. To the reading room in the Passage de l'Opéra. Read many papers. Déj[euner] at Rue du Temple—my favourite place for "tripes à la mode de Caen".- Sent letter to Rev. G[eorge] Bainton, replying to his request to be permitted to use my letter in his lecture when he prints it.- Throat almost well.- Noticed a revolting illustration of a paper called *La Diane*; a decapitated head of poor Bazaine[29], (who is just dead,) held by an executioner's fist, by the ear; underneath is written: "Français, regarde la face d'un traître, et souviens-toi!" A despicable thing, this.- Noticed portrait of George Ohnet[30]; surely the most ignoble face ever owned by a man of letters.-Portrait of the centenarian [chemist] Chevreul; rather painful to look at.- George Sand's "François le Champi" just revived at the Français; most of the papers speak of the piece with Parisian superciliousness; yet one or two are wise enough to regret the idealism it embodies.- Bought for Nelly an interlinear French translation of [Cicero's] "De Senectute" and "Aeneid" III; think they will be of great use to her.- Dined Rue Saint Jacques.- To circulating library 6, rue de la Sorbonne, and got Catulle Mendès' "La Première Maîtresse"[31].- Throat all but well; had a good sleep last night.

Tuesd. Oct. 2. Rain all day; nevertheless wandered about.- To the Galleries of the Odéon, where as usual was sorely tempted to spend money, resisted however. Excellent déjeuner for 1.10 at a rest. in B[oulevard] St Michel. Compare the following meal with any English dinner procurable under 5/-: half-bottle wine, vermicelli soup, noix de veaux au chicorée [sic], macaroni au gratin, 2 pears.- Walked about the Palais Royal, thence to Madeleine to buy the *Standard*, in order to read of the two new .murders in Whitechapel,[32]-these making six, seemingly by same man.- Read *Petit Journal*.- Vast crowds of people at the Magasins du Louvre where the exhibition of nouveautés d'hier is just on. Throat quite recovered; feel particularly well at last.

Apropos of the Whitechapel murders, the *Petit Journal* says: "Les Anglais, quand ils parlent de la France, affectent une pruderie telle qu'il semblerait que notre pays est maudit. Or, nous l'avons démontré cent fois, les Anglais ont renié toute pudeur et sont d'ignobles exploitants de chair humaine. Voici une preuve de plus." [When speaking of France the English affect such prudery that it would seem this country is cursed. But as we have demonstrated time and again, the English have no decency left; they are ignoble exploiters of human flesh. This is new evidence of it.] This is the kind of trash a paper of great circulation gives to ignorant reader.

To-night on the Boulevards men are crying: "Voilà les mémoires de Frédéric III; quinze centimes!" A reprint, I suppose, of the extracts of F.'s journal just pubd in the *Deutsche Rundschau*, and making such an uproar.

Went to the Salle des Conférences, 39 Boulev[ard] des Capucines at 8 o'clock, and heard Louise Michel[33] on "Le Rôle des femmes dans l'Humanité". I had expected to see a face with more refinement in it; she looks painfully like a fishwife. Dressed with excessive plainness, in black, and wearing an ugly bonnet. Much fluency, of course, and signs of intellect. Demanded absolute equality of women with men in education and rights. At one place she raised indignant protest, by describing, to illustrate her own courage, the artistic beauties of les incendies—"comme une aurore"— during the Commune outbreak; cries and hisses interrupted her. I had to reflect a moment to enter into the feeling of these people. We English have no fresh memories to stir us in this way.

On returning home, find letter from Roberts, and one from Nelly, who by a strange mistake has put only a penny stamp; cost me 80c.

Wed. Oct. 3. Nelly sends letter from Smith & Elder, (again only 1d stamp, so again pay 8d). They begin by saying that my books as yet do not sell at all ("Thyrza" only 400 copies) and offer £150 for "The Nether World". I accept. This will enable me to go to Italy with Plitt.

(See Oct. 12th) Spent morning at Père La Chaise, gloriously bright. In afternoon with Plitt to the west end, and saw the Tour d'Eiffel, which has already risen about 400ft.[34] Of course did not impress me; mere artificial bulk cannot do so. Rain came on. Dined in B[oulevard] St Michel, and home to talk of Italian journey, having bought Baedeker's "Italie Méridionale" on the way.- Letter from Katie.

Thursd. Oct. 4. Bright, cool, sky gloriously blue.- A *décret* has just been issued by the President, requiring all foreigners really resident in France to present themselves to the authorities with establishment of identity. English and German papers make an outcry, but, all things considered, the new arrangement seems not unreasonable. Of course does not affect those who like myself are merely en voyage.- In morning went to see the animals in the Jardin des Plantes; poor collection, compared with Zoological Gardens.- Déjeuner at home; a bloater and some marmalade. The washing up, which generally falls to me, is anything but pleasant.- In afternoon to Cook's office, to make inquiries about routes to Naples. Plitt seems almost to repent of his project; I heartily wish he would do so altogether, then I should go to Florence and Rome. The odd thing is that I have not yet been able to make him understand my interest in Rome; he keeps repeating that the town is "not at all nice, you know". But indeed he is intellectually borné to a painful degree; I wish we might part in some friendly way.-

In evening to hear Francisque Sarcey on Daudet's "L'Immortel" at the Salle des Conférences. A great treat. He objected strongly to Daudet's *personal* pictures, but soon put aside that subject and went through the novel, reading passages, and bestowing rapturous praise on the style, the peculiarities of which he discussed. Inspiriting to hear work thus dealt with. Delightfully dramatic manner of reading.

Frid. Oct. 5. Letter from S[mith] & E[lder], promising to send cheque to address I shall indicate, and agreeing to publish "The Nether World" next spring.- To the Louvre for an hour.- Bought firewood, (100 kilos for 3fr. 50) and for the first time sat down by a wood fire in a hearth of French fashion.- Bright, cold day.

Sat. Oct. 6. Cloudy, but some sunshine. Two hours in morning among the antiques at the Louvre.- Wrote to Mrs Gaussen, and sent her my portrait.- Evening to see adaption of Dostoïevsky's "Crime et Châtiment" at the Odéon. Effective here and there, but on the whole a poor play—inevitably so and poorly acted. Paul Mounet played Rodion; made him too much a melodramatic Hamlet. One of the two murders is cut out; alas! how much else also, from D's marvellous book! Sonia very poor.- Post-card from Nelly.-

Sund. Oct. 7. Bright day, but bitterly cold wind. Rose in astonishing health and spirits. The knowledge that I am safe from penury for a year has helped me wonderfully.- Working hard at Italian.- Afternoon, two hours among the Italian pictures and Renaissance sculpture at Louvre.- Saw the new monument to [Léon] Gambetta [the French politician who died in 1882] in the Place du Carrousel; a winged lion at top; rather pretentious and *noisy* affair.- A "Grande Kermesse" going on where Tuileries once stood; five or six huge balloons getting inflated; watched some of them rise, with men in the cars. Observed how very ignoble on the whole is the appearance of a French crowd,- little, ugly men and women.- Dined amid uproar at a very cheap restaurant in Rue St Jacques. Drank cider instead of bad wine, for cheapness' sake. Déjeuner at home to-day; purchased from a charcutier's.- Wrote to Bertz, and post-card to Smith & Elder, telling them to send my cheque to Wakefield.- Plitt amazed me to-day by going into raptures over a wretched painted bill in a grocer's shop, a miserably conventional cluster of flowers; he asked leave to take it away and copy it! At the Louvre he said of one of Da Vinci's pictures that it was very nice, but wanted cleaning and brightening up!

Mon. Oct. 8. Wasted day. Got information about steamers from Marseille to Naples. Third class (sur le pont) only 17fr.; I wonder whether I can stand that; voyage is only 24hrs, but it won't do to arrive with a bad cold, as when I got to Paris.

Tuesd. Oct. 9. Post-card to Roberts. Plitt has bought the placard advertizing soap; gave 2fr.!- Roamed about the Odéon. Bought "Notre patron Alphonse Daudet", by Hugues Le Roux; "Athalie" in Bibl[iothèque] Nat[ionale]; and a cheap copy of Goethe's "Italienische Reise". Got Bottin[35] at a café and looked up Daudet's address, 31 Rue de Bellechasse.

Wed. Oct. 10. Wrote letters to mother, Madge and Nelly; received none.- Walked to 31 Rue de Bellechasse, and looked at Daudet's house, or rather the house of which, I suppose, he occupies a part. A large, plain, dignified stone building, with usual porte cochère; windows of first floor all shuttered; perhaps Daudet is away? Stood and looked and thought. Could Daudet know of me, assuredly I should not need to stand in the street.- A rainy, warm, English day.- Plitt much astonished that I object to dine in a dirty little eating-house solely frequented by working-people; cries out against my prejudices.- "I don't understand", he says, "how you ever got any knowledge of workpeople!" Suppose I had answered: "I am studying the type at this moment"?- I had recommended Gaboriau's "Petit Vieux des Batignolles"[36] to him as an example of extreme ingenuity; he reads it, and tells me he doesn't care for murder stories, and that he cannot see that it is any better than the run of such.- Sent a letter to Hachette, asking for Fanny Le Breton's address, which I have forgotten.- Saw for the first time the huge church of St Sulpice, but had not time to go in.- Evening at home, reading Italian.- Bought Baedeker's "Northern Italy", so that now I have all 3 vols., French edition.

Thursd. Oct. 11. Letter from Bertz, greatly to Plitt's disgust—he being terrified lest we be seized as German spies; strange mania. Then a note from

Hachette, giving me Mlle Le Breton's address—50 Rue de Bourgogne. In evening, letter from Nelly, enclosing S[mith] & E[lder]'s form of receipt.- Wrote to Bertz, on Plitt's account, telling him to send his letters to England—bah!—Two hours at Louvre in morning, in Salon Carré. N° 410 Rembrandt's Holy Family at Nazareth, the homeliness of it. How the patches of yellow sunlight grow upon one! They touch the mother's breast, the child, and the floor in front; elsewhere the room deliciously gloomy. The splendid old high fireplace.- 121 Gerard Dow's dropsical woman. Touching effect of the thin spring sunshine—so airy, blue, healthful—at the window, and the leafy sprig hanging through into the room.- Turned aside to look again at Ingres' two pictures in the Salle des Fresques: La Source and Oedipus. Why is it that the face of the former seems incongruous with the nude body? Does it seem so to everyone? Perhaps it is because we expect a classical, ideal face on the nude, and not a modern portrait, as this is.- Apropos of that, Baedeker's guide says of some picture: "The faces evidently portraits". Think over this. *Ought* they not to seem portraits in any case—if human beings? Virgins etc are another matter. Of course I understand all about the idealized countenance.-

Remarked one of the English "guides" going round with young man and woman—just such a pair as would adopt such a proceeding. But Heavens! the pronunciation and the general intelligence of that guide! "There's a Alleghery"—pointing to a picture which bore on the frame "Antonio Allegri, dit Corregio".

Afternoon to St Etienne du Mont; beautiful interior; numerous rich points of view. On to St Sulpice, a church in wholly different style; chapels are painted in fresco. Looked at the large shells made into bénitiers, — presents from Venice to François I.- Back to Italian.-

Evening to Sarcey's lecture on "François le Champi, le Roman et la Pièce". It is being played at present at the Français and is rather a failure. S[arcey] blamed the actors; too old; compared them disadvantageously with those who first played the piece ("je m'en souviens comme si c'était hier") at the Odéon. Very curious to hear this old gentleman discoursing in his pétillant way of the charms of actrices. Curious altogether the manner in which he discussed to a mixed audience the motif of the novel. George Sand, he remarked, found nothing unnatural in the mixture of maternal and womanly love; it was thus she loved De Musset and Chopin- "comme maîtresse et comme mère".- At the theatre, the great fault is that all the adequate preparation for the change is omitted. G[eorge] S[and] manages it "Avec une infinité de préparations charmantes . . ." Read passage from the preface, autumn evening; cp. her method of painting landscape with the modern. Hers was method of Jean-Jacques [Rousseau] and of Chateaubriand—she gives you the *sentiment* of the scène. "François" superior to "La Mare au Diable" in language.- Traced growth of love in François, beginning with his obscure desire "d'être embrassé". Sarcey had noticed that women are not shocked at the theatre by the change of relations in the same way that men are. There was a very small audience at this lecture.

On way home, bought [Daudet's] "Trente Ans de Paris"—couldn't resist any longer. Hope to learn a page by heart every day. All my feeling spoilt by having to sit the rest of evening with Plitt, who is arranging trumpery scraps that he has bought. I understand the man now; he is not an *artist*, but an *artisan*,- that's all. He aims merely at decorative house-painting. Asked me: "Wasn't George Sand a woman?" I try not to speak to him of things that interest me, but often foolishly break my resolve.

Frid. Oct. 12. Fine day. Walked to St Eustache and looked in. Thence along Rue du Faubourg Montmartre, where a market was in full swing on both sides of the street. The people certainly more wholesome to look at than those in a corresponding English scene; the blouses and blue aprons give a clean air, and the women's dresses, however poor, are always kept in good repair. The large market-baskets tell of homely carefulness; the English are slovenly in their methods of buying.- On to cemetery of Montmartre, passing through the famous Rue des Martyrs, the quarter of the Murger Group. In cemetery graves most interesting are in the Avenue Cordier (Gautier, Murger) and Avenue de la Cloche (Heine). *Murger*: pedestal with bust in relief on the front, not very clearly cut. On left side of the block is "A l'ami", on the right "A l'écrivain". Above a statue of youth, a graceful girl, holding roses in her left hand, and about to drop one from her raised right hand.- *Théophile Gautier*: a pedestal, surmounted by statue of seated Calliope, against whom leans a medallion of G. with flowing hair. On front of pedestal: "A Théophile Gautier, 1811-1872 Ses Amis". On right side:

> "Priez Dieu pour son âme et par des fleurs nouvelles
> Remplacez en pleurant les pâles immortelles
> Et les bouquets anciens."

[Pray God for his soul and with tears in your eyes Put fresh flowers in the place of faded wreaths and pallid immortelles.]

On the left side:

> "L'oiseau s'en va, la feuille tombe,
> L'amour s'éteint, car c'est l'hiver;
> Petit oiseau, viens sur ma tombe
> Chanter quand l'arbre sera vert."

[The bird flies away, the leaf falls to the ground Love fades away, for winter has come; Little bird come and sing Over my grave when trees are green again.]

At the back:

> "Où retrouverez le temps sacrifié
> Et ce qu'a de votre âme emporté sur son aile
> Des révolutions la tempête éternelle?"

[Where will you recover the wasted hours And that part of your soul Which the everlasting storm of revolutions Has carried away on its wing.]

The medallion, by the bye, rests on two volumes, one of which is lettered "Emaux et Camées".-*Heine*: a plain iron-railed gravestone, hung round with bead-wreaths, and with a plant growing in a pot at the head. Very plain marble headstone, surmounted by a small urn. Inscription, in plain, clear, black letters: "Henri Heine", underneath which "Madame Henri Heine". No date, no word.-

Déjeuner in the Rue Lepelletier, a rest. crowded with shopmen and girls. Near me sat two young shop-boys, who took the ordinaire at f. 1.15, and went through it from soup to coffee and cigar,- evidently their habit. Imagine English shop-boys lunching thus! Then to Louvre, and spent an hour in the Salle des Dessins (I, II, III). In room II noted 389 and 391, two marvellous studies of drapery by Da Vinci,- examples of his search after perfection. 386: a head by Da Vinci, used as a frontispiece to [Walter] Pater's "Renaissance".

Note from Mlle Le Breton, asking me to come and see her. Shall go to-morrow.- Bought "Candide".

By the bye, I forgot to note the other day some particulars from Père La Chaise. *Michelet's* monument. Painful subject. Half draped dead body lying at full length, with a genius standing over it, pointing to the words: "L'histoire est une résurrection". A mistake, I think, the whole idea. *Balzac*. A simple bust on a square pedestal; below it, a volume with pen on the top, and inscribed "La Comédie Humaine". On left side of pedestal, inscription to his wife. In front: "Honoré de Balzac, né à Tours le 20 mai 1795, mort à Paris le 18 août 1850". This is under a plain urn carved in relief. Note the massive head.- *Chopin*. A statue of a muse bent sorrowing over a lyre. In front of pedestal the bust of Ch[opin] in relief. "A Frédéric Chopin, ses amis".- *Rachel*. In Jewish Cemetery, close to entrance. Plain vault tomb of the ordinary kind; over the front, in plain letters, "Rachel". The stone all scribbled over with pencilled names, and on the floor inside several visiting cards, which had been dropped through the grating.

Sat. Oct. 13. Rainy morning. To the Pantheon, where frescoes are still far from finished. To left hand, on entering, a picture which seems to be both disgusting and ludicrous. I suppose it is the beheading of St. Denis. The head has just fallen off, and the saint reaches forward and grasps it like a football; from his severed neck spirts light *exactly like that of a fusee*. Two other headless bodies lie near, the necks dripping blood, horrible.- At 1.30 to Mlle Le Breton, 50 Rue de Bourgogne, just behind the Chambre des Députés. Found her an oldish and very plain woman, living with her sister, who is older and still plainer. All French talk—je m'en tirai tant bien que mal. They have just finished "Demos". Asked me what I demanded for "Thyrza" and of course I told them I shouldn't ask anything. Hachette will publish "Demos" presently. It was found "trop sérieux" for the [*Journal des*] *Débats*. Stayed an hour and a half.

In evening to the Odéon. [Racine's] "Athalie", with Mendelssohn's music. Athalie by Mme Aimée Tessandier. Well, I did not greatly care for her. It is the first time I have seen one of these great classical pieces, and I have read so much about Rachel that I am easily disappointed. The dream in Act II was well delivered, and the dialogue with Joas excellent on both sides. But the last act was hurried enormously, and poor. Is it necessary, by the bye, for personages, even in this statuesque style of drama, to come forward and speak directly to the audience? I disliked it.- Noteworthy that the one piece of scenery which serves all through was of extreme plainness; no extravagance of decoration here.- Of the music, I most enjoyed beginning of Chorus to Act II, end of Chorus to Act III, and the familiar march at beginning of Act IV.- Fine line, the first of Athalie's dream "C'était pendant l'horreur d'une profonde nuit".- As for the recitation of verse, I find that there are *four* distinct beats in each line, *not* six. Thus:

C'est des mi<u>ni</u>stres <u>saints</u> la de<u>meu</u>re sa<u>crée</u>;
Les <u>lois</u> à tout pro<u>fane</u> en dé<u>fen</u>dent l'en<u>trée</u>.

For the first time I was near "la claque" [hired clappers]. Plitt and I took seats in 3rd Gallery. We were early, but on entering the attendant would not allow us to sit in front row. "C'est pour *le service"*, he said! And indeed there shortly entered the noble army of claqueurs,- looked like broken-down medical students.-

On returning home, Plitt talked of drama, and made this profound remark: "English is a good language for business and science and comic plays—but it's no good for pathos. An English tragedy is impossible."

We looked into the foyer, which is surrounded with busts of Murger, Gautier, Bouilhet, etc. Murger's face is wholly unlike what I should have expected. He reminds one a little of Garibaldi.

Sund. Oct. 14. Strange thing that I, all whose joys and sorrows come from excess of individuality, should be remarkable among men for my yieldingness to everyone and anyone in daily affairs. No man I ever met *habitually* sacrifices his own pleasure, habits, intentions to those of a companion, purely out of fear to annoy the latter. It must be a sign of extreme weakness, and it makes me the slave of men unspeakably my inferiors. Now, here is Plitt. It would take an hour to write down all the things I do and say in one day, just to suit his variable moods and temper. Why do I regularly wash up all the things after meals? Why do I catch a bad cold waiting for him outside a shop where he is purchasing follies? Why do I stint myself of butter, that there may seem more for him? Not out of affection, most surely, but mere cowardice. I never dare say what I think, for fear of offending him, or causing a misunderstanding. And this has so often been the case in the course of my life.- Therefore it is that I am never at peace save when alone.

This morning went to High Mass at St Eustache. Déjeuner in Rue Jacques. Plitt home, and I to the Louvre. Salle des Dessins V—497 an exquisite study of drapery by A. Dürer. Approaching Da Vinci, and especially reminding one of him after the rough work of Annibale Carracci in Salle IV.- 501, Dürer, a strange sort of caricature of the Da Vinci smile.- 509, Van Dyck, a fine head.- 565, splendid copy by Rubens of horsemen fighting, by Da Vinci. (Why is not this scene horrible to me, like, *e.g.* the war scenes of De Neuville? Is it not because the costumes are antique, and war can be accepted as an accompaniment of earlier civilization, but is revolting in connection with the present?)—Salle XI. Splendid horses by Géricault—just walked through the most modern French Gallery. Thomas Couture's large picture "Les Romains de la Décadence", gives me pleasure. The central woman's face—noble, satiated, self-dissatisfied—pleases me much.- Looked at Greuze's "La Cruche Cassée"; one of those pictures of which I cannot say anything definite at once.- Coming down, turned into the Sculptures. The Venus of Melos gleams very pale at the end of a long gallery—against a dark background, and contrasting with the yellow marble of the Borghese Mars in the foreground.

In evening came two copies of *Les Débats* from Mlle Le Breton, containing articles by Jules Lemaître on "L'Immortel".

I copy following from paper of to-day: "La Société anonyme, créée en vue de la mise en exploitation de la tour Eiffel vient de se constituer définitivement au capital de 5,100,000 francs. Sur ce capital, 5 mill. seront payés à M. Eiffel pour l'indemniser de ses frais de construction, et les 100,000 qui resteront disponibles seront consacrés aux frais d'exploitation".

[A Limited liability company, which is to run the Eiffel Tower, has just been established with a capital of 5,100,000 francs. Out of this capital five million francs will be paid to M. Eiffel to cover the building expenses, and the remaining 100,000 will be devoted to running expenses.]

Mond. Oct. 15. Cold day, but sunshine as usual. Louvre unfortunately closed every Monday. An hour in the Luxembourg Gardens from 3-4. Curious, the crowd of maid-servants with their infants, in sheltered sunny place near central basin. Their bare heads and white aprons. Large family party.- Read a little of the "Italienische Reise" [by Goethe].- At night to the Français, to see Mounet-Sully in "Oedipe Roi", translated by Lacroix in verses. Preceded very foolishly, by a farcical little piece called "Un Mari qui Pleure" [by Jules Prével, 1869]. The tragedy impressed me much; Mounet-Sully I thought, on the whole, noble, self-restrained, pathetic,- a great figure. Plain, but good, scene, dresses careful. Again I thought how this would be "got up" at the Lyceum! The first three acts were only divided by music, which played whilst a single member of the chorus recited the verses which should have been sung; then curtain fell before last 2 acts. This was the one thing that annoyed me, perhaps an unfortunate necessity. I could see how splendidly the interest would have culminated, without this breach. Very notable was the perfection of the minor actors; the two Shepherds excellent, especially the one who speaks the final revelation of Oedipus's identity. The King hurls him to the ground, and he—shaking with age, and terror and anguish,—remains there; his lines were nobly spoken. Great Apollo! What would this become in an English theatre! I fancy I see the wretched lout trying to be *old* and at the same time to be *dignified*.- The last act, where Oedipus comes forward with blood-stained eye-sockets, seemed a little long. We feel it so in the Greek, I am sure. We do not wish to linger over this wretched spectacle.- Well, it was delightful. I never expected to see Oedipus acted.-

On coming home, found letter from Alg, saying he has with great difficulty finished "A Lion of Cotswold" [published as *Both of this Parish* in 1889]. In despair of continuing work, he even went for two days to 7K.

Tuesd. Oct. 16. Returned the *Débats* to Mlle Le Breton, and wrote to Roberts, from whom I have a letter this morning. Uneasy sore throat—as usual. I do hope I shan't be troubled thus in Italy.- Should note that yesterday— the rentrée des Chambres—the walls all about the Chambre des Députés were placarded with "A bas les voleurs!"[37] Said to be the work of the editor of *La Cocarde*, a Boulangiste journal. The police tore the posters down.- In afternoon to Louvre. Again wonderful study of drapery by Leonardo in the upper Room of Drawings (1641). Also noticed there an autograph letter of Raphael.- In reading the "Italienische Reise" I notice the curious coincidence that the summer preceding G[oethe]'s departure for Italy had been strangely wet and cold in Germany—just like our summer this year.- Alg writes that weather with him is now fine but cold.

Wed. Oct. 17. Last night, bad night; had to make hot water at 1 o'clock and inhale steam. All to-day (weather glorious) suffering from influenza and throat. Went out in morning; rest of day sitting by a fire, reading "Italienische Reise".- Letter from Nelly enclosing the returned letter of Bertz, which the latter, in consequence of Plitt's craze, had sent to Wakefield.- Find the *Figaro* by far the most fruitful of Parisian newspapers. To-day, having a supplement, it cost 20c. Really, newspapers are very dear here; 15 and 20c. are common prices. The *Petit Journal* is only 5c., and so are a few other somewhat paltry sheets. On the whole, I remark much dearness in many things which I have been accustomed to buy cheaply in London. Condensed milk is generally 90c. a tin; tea and coffee fabulous prices; lamp-oil dear.- I remark in the "Italienische Reise" that Goethe had got into exactly my own state with regard to Italy before his visit there; he says he could not bear to read a Latin book, or to look at a picture of Italian scenery. Again and again I have felt and expressed that, these last few years.- Wrote to Nelly, asking her to send £10.

Thursd. Oct. 18. Wonderful weather, but unable to go out all day; severe cold. Of course it happens that Mlle Le Breton sends a ticket for the Chambre des Députés, for today. Gave it to Plitt, who naturally had not the slightest interest in the matter, and made a merit of looking in for 10m. in the afternoon.- Read at Goethe, and Baedeker's introductions to Italy, the articles on Art. Taking a little ammonia in hot water; seems to do good.- Writing in French to Alg.-

Frid. Oct. 19. Beautiful day, but cold wind. Letter from Walter Grahame, sent by S[mith] & E[lder]. Out in the morning and déjeuner Rue St Jacques.- Glancing at the advts in the *Figaro*; curious, the habit of abbreviating words, scarcely ever used in English papers. Thus, under the heading "Correspondances Personnelles", I find: "Georges A.A. ne vis pl. dep. v. dép. meurs d'env. de v. rev. éprou. prof. chag. suis t. l. j. marche du nav. att. impt de v. nouv. bien trist. donnez. adr. et détls du voy."[38] So also in advts of lodgings etc.-

I experience at present a profound dislike for everything that concerns the life of the people. Paris has even become distasteful to me because I am living in this quarter, in a house thronged with workpeople, and where, to get away, I must always pass through dirty and swarming streets. All my interest in such things I have left behind in London. On crossing the Channel, I have become a poet pure and simple, or perhaps it would be better to say an idealist student of art. Imagine then how it jars on my nerves to be perpetually in contact with Plitt. From head to foot the man belongs to the working class. Every day I have a new indication of it. He suffers much from dyspepsia, and in the fits, shows himself intolerably coarse of nature, cannot control his temper or his words, talks with childish inconsistency and irresoluteness etc. During our walk to-day, we passed the "Nouveau Cirque", somewhere or other. "Ah!" he exclaimed, "I'd much rather see that than the Oedipe Roi!" Again, he has the mania of stopping before every paltry shop where very cheap articles of clothing and the like, are exposed; he cannot resist something very cheap, even if he have no need of it. He bought a binocle the other day, and said to me "I think I could get more than that for it, if I tried to sell it again." The things he admires in the way of designs on adverts etc. are not to be imagined, the paltriest scrawl on a soap-box delights him. He is the artisan, the mechanic, pure and simple. Yes, he will spoil my Italy for me, but I must be content to learn how to live and travel there this time. And perhaps he may go from Naples to Australia, in which case I have Rome and Florence alone.-

Replied to Walter Grahame's letter. Plitt rather more endurable this evening, soothed by a purchase he has made of some execrable chromos.- A vulgar nature notably reveals itself in the want of suavity where trifles are concerned. E.g., Plitt exclaims to-night that some preserve I had bought was bad. I look at it, and say with a smile "Oh, I think not". At once he is clownishly ill-humoured, and goes to the fire to spit out what he has in his mouth. Imagine Alg, or any decent man, with me under such circumstances,- the laughter and joke that would accompany such a discussion. But the vulgar man is incapable of taking good-humouredly anything that seems disadvantageous to his pocket, or his stomach, or anything that is his. You cannot differ in opinion with him; he takes coarse umbrage immediately. Which is only another way of saying that the vulgar man cannot converse.

Sat. Oct. 20. Zola has just pubd a new novel "Le Rêve". It is absolutely inoffensive, they say; more, it is even "écrit pour les jeunes filles". The papers are joking much.-

Very fine day again. My cold all but gone. Went to Louvre in the morning, and took the Netherlandish schools. Sect. VII of Gde Galerie, 408 and 409, two little Rembrandts, each representing a philosopher musing in a fine old mediaeval chamber. In each a broad winding staircase,- perhaps typical. Light of course from window. In 408 a famulus is keeping up a fire, just a little gleam on the floor of the right hand corner.- 462 Rubens's Flemish

Fair. Exquisite arrangement of colours, marvellous life; but a gross and bestial scene.-Sect. VI. 690 Picture of a hanging carcase of beef, by Rembrandt; a skinned and opened carcase. Woman looks in at door. Odd subject surely for R.- 392 Van Ostade, an interior just like one of Rembrandt's. I wish I had the skill to distinguish the two masters. Homely scene; mother nursing child by big fireplace, father opposite. Rich litter all over, and in foreground a hen pecking. Beautiful light falls through lattice, onto a cradle. Fairy-tale impression, which delights me.- Cannot care much for the Marie de Medici series of Rubens.

In afternoon went to the exhibition of models for the statue of Danton, just opened at the Gde Salle des Fêtes of the Hôtel de Ville. Considerable number of competitors. Without any doubt I select one as the best, and shall be curious to hear whether it is chosen; it is by a certain Baffier[39]. Danton stands on a pedestal, on either side of which a flight of steps runs up to his back; he is planted very solidly on both legs, extends right arm almost straight, body straight, head level. His look is fine; brutal, bull-doggish, triumphant, just a little grotesque, as should be. I like it.

The others mostly conventional. Ludicrous how universal is the extended arm, the thrown back head, the melodramatic pose of body. A very common inscription is the "De l'audace, encore de l'audace, toujours de l'audace!" [Boldness, more boldness, perpetual boldness!]. I noted two absurd instances of a winged genius of some kind *poising* on Danton's shoulder,- a monstrous effect in sculpture. Also two instances of dwarfing the figure by putting a high column behind it.- There was one very simple figure, not bad, by a certain Bourèt[40]. Danton stands with hands tied behind him, underneath written: "Tu montreras ma tête au peuple, il n'en voit pas souvent de pareille." [Show my head to the people, they rarely see the like of it] Impression, however, too tame and flattering.- Incident that befell me. In taking notes, I had thrust my stick under my arm; an *agent* comes up to me: "La canne à la main, s'il vous plaît, monsieur!" Now in England an attendant would never have thought of such a request.-

Bought a small photograph of "La Cruche Cassée" [by Greuze] to send Madge on her birthday.

Sund. Oct. 21. Is it not a ludicrous thing that, after coming abroad for my pleasure and profit, I should allow myself to suffer ceaselessly, and lose nearly all the benefit of my holiday, owing to a quite voluntary association with Plitt? Seriously he embitters a great deal of each day for me. To-day the weather has been wonderful, but the first part of it was wasted in a walk to the Bois with Plitt. He remarked on that end of the town that he didn't like it so much as our quarter: "You feel so cosy in the east". Of course! Got rid of him at 3 o'clock and fled to the Louvre.

Delightful coup d'oeil of the Salle d'Auguste. It occupies a corner of the rez-de-chaussée, compact in itself. The setting sun gleamed through the windows, and its reflection from the Seine made flickering light upon the rich gilding of the ceiling. Fell on one or two busts, and made them dazzling. The cold marble of busts and statues in beautiful contrast with the colours of the painted ceiling, the gilding, and the coloured marbles of the floor. Down the middle are two noticeable great busts: that of Antinous as an Assyrian god (hole in head where the lotus flower was stuck, and eyes vacant of the jewels once set there; pensive expression and fine hair) and that of Rome personified. The hall occupied with the Julian emperors. At the far end, in an alcove before which is a platform of mosaic, stands Augustus.-

Dinner spoiled by Plitt's bad temper over a tough cutlet. Banged plates about and swore. I dread to dine with him.

Note the laudable habit of French newspapers in giving only the initials of people concerned in accidents and petty police cases.- Reading on at the "Italienische Reise". Find absolutely no time for any French lit[erature] except the newspapers.-

On coming out from my calm enjoyment in the Louvre, clash with a great crowd in the Place du Carrousel, gaping at a lot of balloons going up.

Mond. Oct. 22. Still wonderful weather. Morning to shipping office in Rue Rougemont, B[oulevard] Montmartre. Also to change a cheque—bank cheque, which I recd from Nelly last night; £10. Did this at an agency in the Place de l'Opéra. This will be the best way to have money sent me, for there are agencies in Italy, and it avoids registering of letters.- Afternoon to call on Mlle Le Breton and her sister Mme Xavier Raymond. Several other people came in. For the first time saw an example (off the stage) of the jeune fille,- rather an aristocratic one too, I suppose, for her father was referred to as "le Général", and she spoke of being fond of riding.- In walking back along the Quai d'Orsay looked at the ruins of the old Conseil d'Etat, left untouched since 1871. All the interior burnt out, but walls perfect.

Surely if ever there was a good omen for a journey, it was one when I came across this cheap little copy of the "Italienische Reise". One sees very few German books on the stalls. I noted this book one morning, and, after hesitating, did *not* buy it. Two days later, though I did not remember the place, I again came across it, and by that time I knew the book was necessary to me.-

Plitt has been telling me of the very cheap route to Florence by the English G[reat] E[astern] R[ailway]. You go from Harwich to Rotterdam, and thence direct by rail, through Cologne, Bâle, the St Gothard, and Milan. Must try and bring Nelly this way some time next year.

Tuesd. Oct. 23. Fine, but foggy; by night quite thick in the streets.- Morning occupied with business. Sent off parcel of books to Wakefield. Sold for 3fr. an excellent pair of boots that are too small for me.- Afternoon to New York Herald reading-room. Bought Sarcey's "Siège de Paris".- Couple of hours at Louvre. Is there not a noticeable resemblance between the attitude of one of the figures on the Borghese vase in the Salle des Cariatides and that of Bacchus in Titian's "Ariadne"?- How well one gets to know the face of the Madonna in And[rea] del Sarto's pictures! Lucrezia, I suppose.- Dined cheaply and badly. At the ordinary restaurants of Paris it is impossible to get either beef or mutton, both are incredibly bad, mere bits

56

of leather; raw, to begin with, and seemingly the poorest possible meat. The veal is a little better, but still very badly cooked.-

Am getting very impatient with these last days. To-night letters from Alg and from Roberts.

Wed. Oct. 24. Day of no account. Fine weather still. In morning, hour at Louvre; afternoon walk in Jardin des Plantes. There, by the bye, I made a strange discovery; Bertz has twice asked me to look for an allegorical group of statuary—the soul combating with the flesh and vainly trying to escape its clutch,- nymph in hands of a satyr, I supposed, or something of that kind. Now the group proves to be, *tout bonnement,* a hunter struggling in the grip of a bear; that there may be no mistake, the hunter is carrying one of the bear's cubs, which he has just killed. Now it seems incredible that Bertz should thus have deceived himself, (he says he often looked at the group, and with much spiritual satisfaction,) but there seems no kind of doubt that he was blinded by the Germanic tendency to see more than the subject contains!- Reading Sarcey's "Siège de Paris". He is delightfully severe at the expense of the Parisians, and indeed his whole story reads amazingly.

Thursd. Oct. 25. In morning to look at the Place des Vosges; an interesting quarter. Glorious day, as if midsummer. Afternoon to Louvre. Looked long at the Van Dyck in the last section of the Gde Galerie; a burgher and his wife kneeling before the Madonna and child; the man kisses the child's hand. The couple have good, honest faces; the husband oldish and world-worn, something pathetic in his look and attitude. The madonna's face very beautiful, and the kind of beauty that I like; of course not describable. Pensive and calm.- Passing the entrance of the Beaux-Arts on the Quai Malaquais, turned in to the public exhibition of the Prix de Rome. The first prize for sculpture was "Orestes at the Tomb of Agamemnon"; fine, I thought.

To-day happened just what I have all along anticipated. At the last moment P[litt] declared he wanted to stay a fortnight longer in Paris,-had found matchless studies of flowers, etc. Of course such a proposal was to me impossible; I *could* not stay, should be ill if I tried. I plainly told him so, for once in my life (the rarest of things) taking a reasonable stand on my own will. Very well, "then he must go to the expense of buying the copies instead of hiring them." He grumbled, and, as I—in my soft, foolish way— tried to excuse myself for a selfishness of which I was not guilty,- he knew perfectly well how eager I am to be gone and all the arrangements I have made about letters etc.- all at once a bright idea came to him. "Suppose we *split the difference!* You shall give me 5fr. towards the cost of the copies, and if I can sell them again I'll give it you back".- Like an ass, I agreed at once, and he was content. Now a question arises. Was this calculated, foreseen, on Mr. P's part? It is not impossible, though I don't like to charge him with it. But in any case, the terrible ignobleness of the fellow! Well, well, I have a strange companion for my first journey to Italy!-

57

Sent Roberts yesterday's *Figaro* which contains the opinions of several French men of letters on the Censorship question. From S[mith] & E[lder] comes *Cornhill.* and I sent it at once to mother. I see it contains advt of "A Life's Morning", in 3 vols., for 15th Nov. I wrote the book in 2 vols. only; I fancy the vols. will be small.

Frid. Oct. 26. I am really writing this on Tuesd. Nov. 1st, but it is better to note the days; for the first time I can sit down to copy out my rough notes of this journey. Indeed it is the first time since I left England that I sit down with any pleasure to write; for at least I am in comfortable surroundings.- Before leaving Paris, P[litt] amused me by purchasing a few numbers of the Bib[liothèque] Nat[ionale]—choosing those of which the names sounded stiffest. Thus, he bought Condorcet, Pascal, etc, and said to me rather scornfully: "Well, you see, *my* reading must be deep, for I have only a little time to give to it." This was clearly the outcome of pique because he saw that I had noticed his utter lack of interest in books. In fact, he cannot read: *ten minutes* at the very most can he persevere with book or newspaper.

Left the Gare de Lyon at 10 o'clock, by 3rd class. Fare to Marseille f.58.45. Of course slept little in carriage. At Lyon a little after 9 next morning, and thence onwards I began to understand what is meant by the South; by sunlight and air! The valley of the Rhône marvellous in autumn foliage. The poplars a sort of old gold, flashed upon by the sun; such a colour I never beheld and it cannot be described. Noticed the strange way in which the hill-sides are terraced for vineyards. The dead vine leaves sometimes lying in patches of crimson. Lyon seems to be on a hill, and the railway to pass by a long tunnel under it, from Lyon-Vaise to Lyon-Perrache. Rather foggy. At Perrache stayed 15m.- At Valence, 25m. South of this the hills began to be rougher in aspect, less terraced. Poplars if anything richer in hue. Odd little haystacks, conical, with a pole coming out at the top. Rocks all limestone; the roads very white. Little white-shining towns perched on top of hills; old castles. Just before Avignon noticed the first olive-trees. Cypresses beginning to abound.

Sat. Oct. 27. Marseille at about 7; dark. At Station pestered by men wanting to direct us to a hotel. Left our luggage en dépôt, and went to the Hôtel National, by Station. Decent, moderate place. Sent postcards to Alg and mother. Plitt had of course eaten too much on journey and became very ill; vomiting all night. As he was also in a terrific temper (I find him to be one of the worst-tempered men I ever knew,) I went out for a walk. Up and down the Rue Canebière; think I never saw so many brilliant cafés in so short a space.- Bought paper, in which I read of a China vessel that morning boarded in the harbour by the loafers of the port, on pretence of carrying luggage; they insulted the captain and officers, and with difficulty were beaten off.- A wretched night with Plitt.

Sund. Oct.28. Plitt of course declared he couldn't, or wouldn't proceed; talking of giving up Italy altogether. Did my best to persuade him that sea air would be good for him. He set off at last making me as uncomfortable as possible. On board the Durance, Compie Fraissinet (4 Pl[ace]de la Bourse, Marseille) at 9 o'clock,- Quai de la Joliette, just under the cathedral. A poor boat, much stinking. Came on board about 100 Italian labourers who were returning to Italy from America; had come across Continent from Antwerp. Plitt took 3rd class passage (deck and no food), for 17fr.; I of course took 2nd, which allowed a berth and good meals, for 70fr.- Cloudless sky.- In afternoon Plitt transferred self to 2nd class, owing to filthiness of the Italian crowd, and so did a young American, named Orf, from Missouri, a fellow of 20 who is going to Rome to be for 5 years at an American College—I suppose Rom. Catholic. We three henceforth ate together in the saloon. Good meals but only two a day, at 9 and 5. South French cooking, vastly greasy. Stinks on board intolerable.- Mediterranean a huge delight to me. Noted the white-grey barrenness of the limestone rocks just outside Marseille. Effects of shadow. Odd shapes also of these rocks. At 11 a.m. the last quarter of the moon visible in the blue sky. Merest speck of white cloud here and there. Saw two young Italian girls dressing their mother's hair on the deck, taking it in turn to use the comb in search of lice. Dazzling white specks of houses along the coast. Toulon, wonderfully situated; huge hills behind, called the Montagnes des Maures.

In talk with the man from Mizzouri (as he of course calls it) noticed his frankness: "Wine, now, why, I don't taste it once in a year!"

Mond. Oct. 29. Up early; close to Corsica. Snow on peaks. The multitude of gorges, wonderfully shadowed. 8.30 a.m. Capraja, on left hand, and Elba showing in distance, a warm grey. 10.45, first sight of Italy, the Maremma Coast, beyond Elba. Snowy heights of Corsica glorious behind.- 12.45, between Elba and Pianosa, a convict station on latter, flat small island. Monte Cristo drawing near, high rock.-

I note, as another of the characteristics of P[litt]'s mind his inability to understand an abstract judgment. If I condemn this or that thing in the Italians on the boat, he at once triumphs in the idea that I shall be disgusted with most things in Italy, which all along he has prophesied. He cannot understand that I can enjoy the study of things which I yet condemn.

2.5 Giglio in sight; Elba, a great island, retiring. We go very slowly.-

The man from Mizzouri rather dense. "Did you ever read", he asked, "the book called Don Quixote? Well, I've begun it over and over again, but never could get on with it." Valuable this, for I always take D.Q. as a test of people's minds. Plitt put in: "Well, it's a book I don't care for myself; you can't read it unless you know all about Spanish life and customs."

4.45 Sun setting; it makes Giglio a glorious rose-colour. Corsica very faint in the west, behind the translucent mass of Monte Cristo. Elba still well in sight. Sharks leaping about the boat. The sun impossible to regard steadily, even when on horizon.- Sun gone behind Corsica, which is now very dark and clearly defined, though scarcely to be seen half an hour ago.

Tuesd. Oct. 30. On deck just in time to see sun rise, we going straight towards it. Now among the Isole Ponzie.- 10.15 off Gaeta, a great mass of high mountains, with a few white clouds on them.- 12, the mass of Ischia full in front; very high, the top touched with clouds. It conceals all beyond.- 12.30 Vesuvius becomes very dimly visible. Dark summit just to be distinguished, mist below. The smoke blows towards Capri, a sign of fine weather. It is not black, the smoke, but like an ordinary rose-tinted cloud.-

An intelligent Italian, who comes out from the 3rd class passengers, tells us that the emigrants are of the people known as Assassini di Calabria, being the children of a brigandish race. Eight days ago there was a mutiny of such fellows on this ship; they demanded food etc, and the captain turned hot-water pipes onto them.

In the Port of Naples at 4 o'clock. There followed an indescribable scene. As soon as the ship approached, there came forth dozens of little boats, the boatmen roaring out the name of hotels which they represented, of course in language quite unintelligible to me. The uproar was deafening. Fortunately P[litt] had made acquaintance with two Italians on board, who were able to undertake the bargaining for a boat; at length eight or nine of us got into one, with a great quantity of luggage. P.'s and my luggage amounted to nine articles - a terrible job to keep an eye on them. As we pulled towards the custom house, the sun was setting, and I never saw anything so glorious as Vesuvius; the sails in the harbour were red. At custom house began a yet more terrific struggle. First of all we had to fight with porters to keep our luggage; then when it was once on the table, we were crushed in a roaring, struggling crowd. No attempt at order; I suppose this scene could only have taken place with an emigrant ship. Providentially, we yielded ourselves to the directions of a shabby but lively little fellow who seemed to speak every language. The wild and grotesque gesticulations all about us. Baggage strictly examined, as we came from France, and the abolition of the commercial treaty[41] is just now giving so much trouble. P.'s tobacco-pouch and two packets of tea sent off to an inner office, but eventually returned to us. Then again a fight between the porters authorised by our little fellow and all the others about. At last, out we went in procession, after our truck, and—going we knew not whither— were lèd to the Albergo New York, Str[ada] Piliero, just opposite the lighthouse. With much difficulty we got settled about a room for two nights and paid all charges, which in the end did not exceed some 4fr. apiece. The little fellow shook hands with us all effusively, though we gave him nothing.

Dinner, and a walk about the Via Roma, then friend Orf took his leave, and went by the 10.40 to Rome.

Wed. Oct. 31. Searched for lodgings, and decided for some recommended by Baedeker,- Frau Häberle, Vico Brancaccio, 8, 3° piano. Very good room and excellent position, but rather dear,- P.'s 35fr. a month and mine 45fr. The landlady a very decent German woman. Of course a tiled floor and no fireplace. My window looks west, and only sees the prom[enade] of Posillipo; it is on the 4° piano. But extremely quiet, owing to the impossibility of traffic in the precipitous streets all round. Have a good writing-table, and very decent bedroom accommodation.- Spent the rest of the day idly.

Thursd. Nov.1. Removed luggage, and with difficulty, as usual, for the police made our porters go all round by the Sa Lucia. A terrific work for them, up the Rampe Brancaccio, in blazing sun.- Rest of day, sky rather heavy. I see that the bay of Naples is by no means always blue.- Found a decent eating-place, the Trattoria Fieramosca, 11 Strada Carlo Berio. Convenient that there are English grocery stores in the Piazza dei Martiri. Bought spirit for boiling water, which is always needful.- Did little else.

Frid. Nov. 2. Jour des Morts. Should like to go to the cemeteries, but this morning feel rather unwell. Was feverish in the night and scarcely slept. Believe I drank too much wine yesterday. This morning had coffee and then went to the druggist's (Kernst) in the Str[ada] San Carlo, where I bought some quinine, and also got the address of an English doctor, in case of need.

Let me see if I can put down some of the points which seem most characteristic of Naples to one who has just arrived. The amount of buying and selling, especially in poor streets; the fanciful harness of horses; the multitudes of donkeys; the hard and excellent paving, squares placed diamond-wise; the enormous houses, vast doorways, great rooms, thick walls; the madonna faces among the lower classes; the elegant appearance of officers; the abundance of clerics in the street and their leisurely walk,- including monks of mediaeval appearance; the gradoni; the soft note of the street-organs; the saints with lamps before them; the long musical cry of sellers going about the streets at night.

Last night my first view of the fire of Vesuvius; the two previous nights the mountain was veiled with cloud. The best view is from the S. Lucia. The fire was like a red leaping beacon, very small, without reflex on the smoke.

In restaurants, I notice the grated Parmesan cheese brought to put in soup, and the water always brought with coffee.

A very cloudy day. Scarcely any blue sky visible.- It was well I had my Mediterranean voyage just when I did, for the weather is turning very boisterous.

Sat. Nov. 3. At midnight, last, a tremendous storm; I was awakened by the thunder, which did not rumble, but went off in great claps like artillery. Wind roaring and furious rain, incessant lightning. The sea was already very rough when I looked at it about four o'clock. I find it was scirocco yesterday; I have speedily come to know what this means. All day I could scarcely drag one limb after another. This morning a splendid N.W. wind, and very clear sky. Felt well again and ready for a long walk. To my grief, P. proposed to go out with me, but the fact of going through the *grotta nuova* soon made him churlish, and at Fuorigrotta he turned back, much to my satisfaction. Then I began to enjoy myself. From Fuorigrotta to Bagnoli, a walk of about a couple of miles, a long straight road between vast vineyards, pines also growing on either hand. The autumn tints are little noticeable, nothing like that wonderful Rhône Valley. Saw great numbers of little lizards darting about the banks. The vineyards are not hedged, nor walled, but protected by great trenches. At Bagnoli found the sea breaking in great waves on the rocky shore. The sky in the S.W. black as night, but all the rest blue and laughing. Tempted onwards, and soon came to Pozzuoli, where I had to face a combat with swarms of guides and carriage-drivers who swarm before the gate by which you enter the town. A happy lie saved me. "Ho già tutto veduto!" [I have already seen everything!] I cried, and my trouble was at an end. But a scrubby little naked-legged boy stuck to me through the street. I was looking for a wine shop (having already eaten two rolls and two pears which I had put in my pocket) and he, observing this, kept recommending a place. In vain the attempt to throw him off; I yielded at last, and let him guide me into a paltry little osteria. There I had a half-bottle of wine, and the ragged boy, very good-tempered, sat by me. When I had finished, I poured out half a glass, and, with a soldo, gave it to him to drink, saying "Non seguite più." [Now stop following me] He obeyed me.

Glorious little town Pozzuoli, richly Italian, full of colour. Remember the little square, with fountain and two statues, the delightful little port (best of all) and the little public garden, with its streets, where I sat and smoked a pipe, and looked at the ships, and over towards Baja. One of the soft Italian organs played the while. I felt happy, and more than happy.

Decided not to trouble about the Amphitheatre this visit, but walked on, through the disagreeable factory quarter (if anything can be disagreeable under such a sky) and soon came to the Lago Lucrino. Its smallness astonished me, but I suppose the rising up of Monte Nuovo greatly lessened it. A branch road opposite the Hôtel de Russie (where the landlady called to me in vain to come in and eat *ostriche* [oysters]) led me in about ten minutes to another lake, blue amid hills. An old boatman, the only man in sight, came up to me, and pointing to the water said: "Lago Averno!" So I actually stood by Avernus! Gathered some flowers, wild thyme, I think, and from the old man bought four shells, which he advised me to have made into cuff-links. He wanted to take me to the Sibyl's cave, but it did not come into my scope to-day. Went back to the shore, and picked up a lot of pretty shells; some for mother. Sketched the form of Capri, which was right in front:

[Sketch of Capri]

Day got brighter still as I went on. I stopped a little short of the Baths of Nero, reserving Baja itself for another day.- The sea indescribable greens and blues. The sand on the shore is a very dark brown; no strand to speak of.

I do very well for my breakfast now at a little place in the Strada della Pace, where I have a caffé latte and two rolls for 2d 1/2 ; if butter, 10c. extra. This morning a little girl came in to take away a cup of coffee in one of the odd little tin vessels, with a cap, which are common here for that purpose; her hair was a perfect black and very curly, whilst her face was exactly that of an angel in one of Botticelli's pictures which I remember but cannot indicate.

Among other characteristics of Naples, I must note the cows and goats led about the street to be milked anywhere; the cows almost always with a calf, the goats very pretty; both with tinkling bells.- Then, the singular cry of

62

drivers urging on their horses "a-a-ah!" in a note of comically fierce remonstrance, too often with a fierce blow added.- Few streets where you do not smell roasted chestnuts.

Bought two lemons (just off the tree, the outside and inside both green) for 5c., and quench my constant thirst with water into which I have squeezed the juice. The water, by the bye, I first boil, and make a rule nowhere to drink a drop of water in the simple state. Perhaps this is needless precaution since they have the acqua di Serino here, but it makes me more comfortable. Rather expensive, however, as I have to give 3fr. a litre for the spirit for my cooking lamp.- Bought a bottle of vino da pasto [table-wine] from the "English Grocery Stores" in the Chiaja; cost 60c.!

Very boisterous again to-night.

In the little country towns I notice nearly all the upper windows are hung round with clusters of fruit, either put there for ripening, or merely as a convenient way of storing. The waiter at my trattoria tells me they are pomidori and sorbe [tomatoes and sorb-apples]. The former make splendid red patches on the walls. Sometimes melons (cocomeri) are also seen. These things add to the singular and lively effect produced by the painting of the houses all colours. The general tone, I think, is a dark yellow; there are often blue stripes. I noticed the flat roofs more particularly than hitherto.

Sund. Nov. 4. An excessive weariness always comes upon me in the evening. For one thing, to walk about Naples is to be constantly climbing, a severe exercise. This morning went to the Museo, which is free on Sunday, and just looked round. Must go when there are fewer people. Bought pomidori and figs,- the first time I have eaten the latter fresh. Also bought one of the pine-cones which are so common here, and found, after much difficulty, that the only eatable part of it is a little nut at the root of each section; the cone seems to have been roasted, or something of the kind. Fruit is wonderfully cheap; a soldo will generally buy all one wants of one kind. The Strada di Porto a great fruit market. Grapes of course in vast abundance; pomegranates; at least three kinds of tomatoes; sorbe; figs; lemons; apples and pears; and a lot of fruits of which I do not know the names. I see lemons and figs still thick on the trees. For 2 soldi I bought 13 figs!

There is a custom here of showing raw meat and fish to customers in the restaurants, that they may choose before it is cooked.- Notice the vast number of places called "Banco Lotto". A drawing of the public lottery every week, and the winning numbers always exposed.- Salt and tobacco sold together: "Sale e Tabacchi".- We are not troubled here with bulletins to fill up at hotels and lodgings. In every way I prefer the life and customs to those of France. Singular that I even feel a sort of pleasure in being under a monarchy once more!

Mond. Nov. 5. The date reminds me of Bonfire day; how far I am from such associations!- Started early for a walk about the east part of the town. Turned from the port up the Strada del Duomo, and explored several by-streets, the Strada Anticaglia especially, where traces of the theatre in which Nero performed are still to be seen. Entered the Duomo, sacred to St Januarius,- whose blood I hope to see liquefied on Dec. 16th next. For the first time saw the confessional at work; little open boxes down each aisle; the priest very stolid (occasionally letting his eye wander to people walking by). The confessing women chattering quickly and loudly.- Thence along the Via Tribunali, to the Castello Capuano, where are the Tribunali themselves. An extraordinary place. The large room with fading frescoes, full of tables at which men are writing—I know not what. The extreme informality of everything. The "money-changers" and cigar-sellers about rooms and staircases—the former with their regular piles of coppers. The tumble-down state of all the premises, which indeed are scaffolded at present for repairs, but seem quite past anything of the kind; long, narrow passages; thick walls; air of mediaevalism.- On to the Porta Capuana, and Porta Nolana, to the Carmine.

Other characteristics of streets: the public writers at their tables under the gallery of San Carlo. The extreme care with which the decently dressed people keep themselves warm; at present it is no uncommon thing to see furs, yet the weather is very hot.- Bit of touch-rope hanging out of tobacconist's door, for convenience of lighting cigars.-

Had lunch at a trattoria near the Carmine, and then took tram for Portici, whence walked to Torre del Greco. Very uninteresting ride and walk; nothing to be seen for the high houses in unbroken line all the way; scarcely an occasional glimpse of Vesuvius, capped with great black cloud. At Torre del Greco wandered down to the port. Passed through the Piazza del Plebiscito, where is a column with foll. inscription: "Sarà perpetua la gratitudine di questi abitanti verso i fratelli di tutta l' Italia, nei quali fu tanto viva la carità della commune pàtria recentemente unita, che, quando, il dì VIII di Dicembre del MDCCCLXI, un cròllo del soprastante Vesuvio ruinò quanto era murato, accorsero da ogni parte con ajuti si generosi che ne furono alleviate le miserie presenti e ne avanzò da fondare un asilo d'infanzia." [The inhabitants of this city will be eternally grateful to their brothers throughout Italy, whose love for their recently united country was so strong that when, on the eighth of December 1861, a tremor from towering Vesuvius destroyed all the buildings, there came from all the provinces such generous assistance that the misfortunes of the occasion were relieved, and there remained enough to found an orphanage]. On the walls I observed placards announcing the opening of the "Scuola d'incisione sul corrallo". Every year a fleet goes to Sicily and Africa for coral from here.- The sea breaking heavily down at the shore, which consisted of black scoriae, remarkable to observe,- huge black burnt ugly masses. I broke off some bits. Wherever the soil is burned up, it is like that of a coal-pit,- like I observed it where men were digging on the side of Monte Nuovo on Saturday.-

Fine sunset. Vesuvius crowned with enormous clouds of glorious colour. Ten minutes after sunset, these clouds had dispersed, the peak was clear, and below it wreathed a ghostly grey mist. Wind from N.W., I think. No rain to-day.

Should have mentioned that in the morning I bought several books: Leopardi's "Poesie e Prose", "Le Mie Prigioni" ["My Prisons", by Silvio Pellico, 1832], "Canti Popolari Toscani", and lectures by Mariani[42] on Ital[ian] Lit[erature] in 18th and 19th Cents.

Tuesd. Nov. 6. Getting anxious to have a letter from England, in a day or two, I suppose.- Much oppressed to-day by the heat, and by P[litt]'s company. Did nothing much but read Italian. Continuing experiments, I bought some *fiori di latte,* a sort of cream-cheese, sold, the best, at 1.75 the kilo. Rather tasteless. Eat more and more fruit; to-day had three very large bunches of grapes for 2 soldi.-

It is well that I have seen Naples now, for in the newspapers I read a great deal about proposed changes, widening of streets etc, spoken of as "lo sventramento".* Even the Chiaja is threatened. And indeed to see it at 5.30 of an evening when all the carriages are returning from the Corso is a thing to remember. But such changes will make quite a different Naples. I see that the old University buildings are to be abandoned, and new built,- if the money can be got, which is spoken of as doubtful. The University session opened yesterday, with an address by Prof. Alberto Marghieri, on "Le scienze morali e le carriere che vi si attengono" [Moral Sciences and the careers related to them]. It is noted that great numbers of ladies were present.-

Remember the incessant braying of donkeys in Naples.

Wed. Nov. 7. Missed my newspaper to-day, it is so hard to get everything in. Generally read the *Corriere di Napoli* in morning, and the *Piccolo* evening.- Showery morning, but soon gloriously fine. Walked round the Strada Nuova di Posillipo, and down to Bagnoli. About the highest point of the road is a marble slab with foll. inscription: "Napoli ridenta in questo loco, trepidante, angosciosa, l'ultimo affettuoso vale donava a Giuseppe Garibaldi, liberatore. I superstiti, le associazioni liberali unanimi all'immortale eroe sacramo questa pietra. Il Giugno MDCCCLXXXIII." [Liberated Naples, quivering and apprehensive, gave in this place the last affectionate farewell to Giuseppe Garibaldi, Liberator. We, the survivors, and the unanimous liberal associations, dedicate this tablet to the immortal hero. 2 June 1883]- After passing the top of the hill, the road descends, passes through a deep cutting, and then comes to a sort of rond-point where is a marvellous view over the bay of Pozzuoli, and inland of Camaldoli. Glorious as are the prospects of Naples before the top is reached, the view towards Baja has more charm for me. A N.W. wind, and the sea rolling in splendidly. Ah, what colours! Often shall I take this walk, I trust. Pozzuoli, there in mid-distance,- Monte Nuovo, half hidden, Baja ! There are no words for it. The little island of Nisida, now brutalized by a bagno, is just below. Baedeker says that here Brutus came after the assassination of Caesar, to a villa of the son of Lucullus, and here Cicero visited him. Here, too, Brutus parted with Porcia when he set forth for

*this word, and 'il risanamento' constantly repeated [Gissing's note]

Philippi.- Only glanced at the Grotto of Sejanus, in passing. I cannot afford to pay every entrance fees and must lose much that I should like to see.-

Had lunch at Bagnoli, after rambling along the shore and gathering shells. Shared my salami with two fine cats. Then walked along the straight road, between palms and vineyards, to Fuorigrotta, and on home.- The new moon is getting bright; will be beautiful before long. Fine sunset to-night; my window just faces it.

Thursd. Nov. 8. Walked to Camaldoli, and only after much straying reached the monastery. At the last moment had to ask a fellow to guide me. On reaching the top of the hill, where the village is, you go through the white gate, through a place which is a sort of farmyard, and thence leads a path up to the monastery. The view from the garden was perfect; not a speck of cloud on Vesuvius. Most respectable middle-aged monk conducted me; scrupulously clean; spoke the Italian of an educated man. No refreshment was offered.- On leaving, I noticed foll. inscription at a spot just before entrance: "Non possono passar questo termine le femine sotto pena d'escomunica latae sententiae." [Women are forbidden to go any further under penalty of excommunication *latae sententiae.*]-

Struck down the side of the hill and after a very hard walk got to Pianura. Thence round to Soccavo. Foll. inscription in the street: "Comune di Soccavo, Circondario di Pozzuoli, Collegio ellettorale di Chiaja, distretto di Pozzuoli, provincia di Napoli" [Commune of Soccavo, division of Pozzuoli, constituency of Chiaja, district of Pozzuoli, province of Naples]- sufficiently comprehensive. Being very tired and thirsty, I turned into a place which was Banco Lotto and Caffé combined. Here found a notable landlord, a young man, married, with child of two months old, - very decent fellow, of some education. His Italian was quite intelligible. Told me he was the president of the local "Società del mutuo soccorso", and was evidently proud of his distinction. Oddest thing of all, when he knew I was an Englishman, he brought out three English books of which he had somehow become possessed, they were: "Verdant Green" [by Cuthbert Bede, 1853], an Eng. transln of "Paul et Virginie", and an odd vol. of Hannah More's works. The first was illustrated, and my friend had ʿdiscovered that the subject was - buffo, molto buffo [very funny]!- He had even found out that it dealt with the adventures of a university student. The picture of V. Green at the beginning he pointed out to me as that of "il protagonista!"—surely the first time Verdant was ever so dignified.- One of his specialities is the inventing of liquori; he showed me some bottles of such. Well, the wine he gave me (and of which indeed he boasted) proved to be about the strongest I ever drank; the walk from Soccavo home was a strange muddle with me. I wonder I got home at all, and did not rather break my neck whilst I was making an unauthorized footpath through gardens down a hill into the Via Tasso.

At home, found letters from Bertz and Roberts, both with good news of articles accepted etc. Wrote to Roberts.

I copy the foll. notable piece of literary criticism from a leader on American affairs in the *Corriere di Napoli* of to-day. "I pochissimi poeti che

66

quel gran paeso ha prodotto, ó sono degli spiriti latini, come Longfellow, ó torbide effervescenze alcooliche, come Edgardo Poe, ó la voce del sangue barbaro e della selvaggia natura, non ancora in tutto dominate, come Nataniele Hawthorne." [The very few poets whom that great country has produced, either are Latin spirits, such as Longfellow, or turbid effervescent alcoholics, such as Edgar Poe, or the voice of barbaric blood and wild nature, not yet completely tamed, such as Nathaniel Hawthorne.]

Frid. Nov. 9. A day of rest. Wrote letters to Nelly and Bertz. Weather very heavy; S.W.wind, I suspect.- Went and had a warm bath; or what, it seems, is called such at Naples; in reality is was barely lukewarm, and probably would have done me harm had it been warmer. The attendant, in closing the door, said "buono bagno, signore!"

Whilst we were at dinner to-night, at the Fieramosca, there came in two young fellows of picturesque aspect, very decently dressed, and one with long black hair; seemed to be Germans, but stood and begged in Italian. My astonishment was great. Plitt says they were wandering "Kraftsburschen", and that this practice is called "fechten" in Germany. Notices, he says, are put up in villages : "Das Betteln und Fechten verboten [begging and soliciting prohibited]"! I repented all through dinner that I had sent them empty away.- Letters from mother, Nelly and Madge.

Sat. Nov. 10. Last night was awoke by furious firing of a gun or pistol (explosive bomb, I discover later) in the street below. No shouts of alarm; don't know what it meant. Then came a great thunderstorm, which lasted for an hour or more.- To-day a clouded sky, much rain, and very cold east wind.

In the morning took my overcoat to have the lining of one of the sleeves mended, to a tailor in the Strada di Ponte di Chiaia, just by here. Of course I had to bargain hard about the price. At first he said he couldn't do it for less than 5 lire, but came down to 2½. The job was not worth more than 2; this I offered, and, when he refused, resolutely walked away. I had already got into the next street, when I felt a tap on my arm; it was the tailor; he beckoned and raced off back to his shop. I followed, and then he agreed to my price. It was finished at mid-day.

In the afternoon a marvellous view of Vesuvius and all the Sorrento promontory. The east wind seemed to have cleared the air in that direction; the mountains were indescribably near, so that they looked much smaller than usual. Somma, with its cut, jagged ridge, was of red-brown colour, up to the top. Vesuvius had its deep black cone. But strangest of all was the way in which the wind blew the smoke; it *lay* all down the side of the mountain, to Torre del Greco, perfectly white in colour, almost like a great train of snow, and only at the bottom broke away into flying mist. I walked all along the Via Caracciolo, and could not take my eyes from the sight. A wild, stormy sunset, with strangely twisted clouds.

Fine moon to-night; its reflection on the sea is perfectly blue.- Replied to Madge's letter, and sent postcard to Walter Grahame.

Sund. Nov. 11. A severe tramontana. They say here that it never lasts more than three days. Smoke of Vesuvius still blowing white down the side. Fine sunshine for all that.

Left Naples by 10.25 train for Pompeii, choosing today because admission to the ruins is free. Took with me a wallet of provisions. Of the visit itself little can be said; like everything else here, it exceeded my expectations. I will jot down points that interested me.- The lizards running about the sunny old walls.- The huge, irregular blocks of lava of which the paving consists, with the deep ruts of wheels;- how long wearing this must prove!- The high narrow pavements; that approaching the theatres is worn quite hollow.- The little barber's shop in the Strada di Mercurio, with its block of stone in the middle for customers. I gathered some ferns there.- The fine face and figure of the wounded Adonis in No. 18 of same street.- I understand now, of course, vastly better the arrangement of Roman houses. The streets are certainly very narrow.- The theatres rejoiced me. Remember the deep cutting for the curtain, and the three doors on to the stage.

A superb view from the top of the Temple of Jupiter. A good deal of snow on the Apennines. Surely few towns are more exquisitely situated.

The extraordinary and delicate care with which the place is preserved. Whenever a piece of stucco has been loose, there is a little iron clamp to hold it. Wooden beams often inserted above doors, showing that a process of rebuilding has at times been carried out. What a place of stucco it was! Delightful perfection of the division into *regiones* and *insulae* and streets and numbered houses.

A pretty Italian girl, with her parents, was looking about her in a pleased but rather worried way and I heard her say, in very sweet and clear tones: "C'è ancora cosa che non abbiamo visto?" [Is there anything else we haven't seen?]—The young girl and the old, old town!

As I had no train back until 6.14, and it was impossible to wait after sunset in the cold, I set out at 4.30 and walked to Torre Annunziata. There waited a little and caught a train which took me without stopping to Naples—a Castellammare train I suspect.- To dinner at the Fieramosca, where I am on good terms with a queer old waiter,- at least I don't know whether he be old or young, but his face looks very aged, and pathetically worn. I delight him by a *mancia* [tip] of 15c. or 20c., I suspect others give him 5c.

To-day the festa of San Martino. Also the birthday of the Principe di Napoli, Vittore Emmanuele, son of Humbert. The Municipio brilliantly illuminated with gas.

Detestable spirit just now between France and Italy. Constant talk of war. But what I see of the Italian papers are nothing like as bad as the French, which become hateful on questions of international politics.-

Have practically decided to go to Rome at the end of this month. Shall be very glad to be free of Plitt, who himself seems anxious to get rid of me. He has been to visit an acquaintance here, a schoolmaster, who is going to recommend him as tutor to the son of the Portuguese ambassador. What may be required, I cannot divine. P. said to me, with a nodding of the head,

"Well, you see, they want a man who is fluent in the four languages, and who can represent the *dignity of the family*. Not everybody would do."- And this in perfectly good faith.

Mond. Nov. 12. Bright day, with soft S.W. wind. Tired, after yesterday's excursion. In afternoon, walk with P. to Posillipo, and had oysters (at extravagant price) at the Trattoria della Sirena, with a bottle of vino di Posillipo. Home, and read a good deal of [Silvio Pellico's] "Le Mie Prigioni".

Tuesd. Nov. 13. A day just like many a warm sunless autumn day I have known in England. Not a ray of sunshine from morning to night; densely clouded sky. In the morning read; in afternoon (after much annoyance from P., who at first wished to go, and at last turned back in disgust) walked to the Campo Santo, in the Strada Nuova di Poggio Reale. From the Porta Capuana the road leads through the most disagreeable part of Naples, made especially oppressive by the lowering sky. Great blocks of working class lodgings are being built here; if one or two points were lost sight of, one might be in the East End of London, for the buildings are exactly like the model lodging-blocks. The smaller houses indescribably filthy. A little further on, and you reach the place where all the dirt-carts of Naples seem to shoot their loads; there is a horrible stench for about a mile of road. On either side, market-gardens which appear to use the filth of the town as manure. The ugliness of the district cannot be described. Vesuvius is in front, but of Naples itself, in the proper sense, nothing can be seen, and only a few plane-trees on either side of the road remind one of Italy. Take away Vesuvius, and one might be in a wretched part of Lancashire.- But then, the weather had, I doubt not, very much to do with this impression.

The Campo Santo occupied me for an hour and a half. It is quite unlike the Parisian cemeteries, for instance. First of all, the foliage is extraordinarily rich and thick; everywhere an abundance of evergreens, of palms, of garden flowers,- like a closely planted garden. In one part, orange-trees heavy with fruit. Here and there, yew-trees are cut into the shape of canopies, over tombs, or trimmed, Dutch-like, along the walks. As for the tombs, the multitude of large edifices first of all strike one, and then prove to be mostly the common burial places of societies; over the front one reads, for instance, "arciconfraternita di S. Barbara", and so on. Looking through the iron gate, one sees that the interior is arranged as a chapel, often very large, and that round the walls are niches—the separate tombs—enclosed with a marble slab, each one—in the fashion of the Roman Columbarium. Some of these edifices are enormous. The exact meaning of the word "*Arci*confraternita"—often contracted "Arcta"—I don't know[43]. Some of the buildings are splendid with marble columns, etc, but the taste is poor in general. Here and there is a marble pedestal with a religious painting on it, a lamp in front.- (See, Sat. Nov. 24th).

Most curious the custom of burying in niches. Here and there great walls stand constructed for this purpose—apart, I mean, from the tombs just spoken of, with six or more niches one above the other, and any number

69

lengthwise. At first I supposed that the oblong marbles were merely commemorative, and that the graves were in the ground below, but one or two open niches showed the fact. At each end of the marble covering is a keyhole, and other orifices just enable one to look into the interior; in one case I distinguished a skeleton so that it would seem coffins are not used. And I don't see how they can be, for the holes are very small, yet on many of them one reads an inscription like this: "Lorenzo S.—per se e suoi".

The only name I recognized was that of Thalberg. On the front of a great building, large enough to be a church, was written "Sigismondo Thalberg".

Very noticeable is the common custom of putting a portrait bust on the tomb, however insignificant the man. These busts are well executed, and obviously good likenesses; the realism is perfect, even collar, tie, waistcoat, etc, being carefully carved. In a few cases, I saw a painting, or even a photograph, inserted under glass in the front of the stone. But the most astonishing of such things was the grave of a certain "Giuseppe Manensi", near the main entrance, below. An elaborate marble pedestal, with stairs, etc, is crowned by a bust of a military looking man, with imperial moustache and the kind of beard called "goatee". Below the bust stands a life-size group of four persons,-the wife and three children. The lady rests, on her right arm, against the pedestal of the bust; she is most elegantly dressed, with much lace about her garments. Two little girls are before her, one holding flowers, the other clinging to her hand; and near is a little boy holding his hat. All are patent likenesses, and the effect is most ludicrous,- a hideously commonplace representation of modern grief. Who on earth suggested this thing? It is very recent; I suppose a speculative sculptor proposed it to the widow.Oh, the expression of that wretched boy, who is holding his hat!

The inscriptions are absurdly effusive, as a rule. Take the following, which, by the bye, is on a great pile of marble: "In questo modesto avello, eretto dalla pietà dei mesti genitori, reposano ad eterna pace la maggior parte dei discendenti del Cav. Emilio Marrullier, dei quali la sorte rìa con spietata falce non rispettò nè etade nè virtude." [In this modest tomb, erected by the piety of his mourning parents, rest in eternal peace most of the descendants of Emilio Marrullier Esq. Cruel fate with its relentless scythe respected neither their age nor their virtue.]

Turning from that, my eyes fell on a flat rough stone, with the single words: "A notre chère Maman—C—S—Née—Décédée—". French, yes, and how beautifully earnest it seemed after the other. Thus does my mood change, now preferring the Italian, now the French.

Wed. Nov. 14. Again an English day; no sun, and almost ceaseless rain. Went to the Museo and spent all the afternoon there. Looked in at the "Raccòlta Pornogràfica"; astonishing collection, certainly. Unfortunately, a disreputable old attendant (who watches the closed door to see that no woman enters,) bores you with his remarks and guidance.-

With regard to the Farnese Bull, it seems to me to stand on too high a pedestal. There is, in fact, no good point of view for seeing it.

70

Noteworthy that everywhere the statues are provided with fig-leaves,- even little statuettes. Gross absurdity, and I did not expect it here. Of course nothing of the kind at the Louvre.

Delightful things in the room of *Capolavori*. That exquisite Orestes and Electra, at right hand as you enter; the delightful simplicity of the archaistic style. Electra has her arm round her brother's neck, and both smile.- What a sweet and noble head is that of Euripides, seen so often here, with his long hair hanging down on each side of the face!- And poor old stumpy-nosed Socrates!-

A wonderful collection of coins; I had not supposed that so many existed from classical times. Of course could only glance along a few of the cases.-

The "Comestibili" from Pompeii. I note the foll. things: eggs (scarcely discoloured); chicken-bones; knuckle-bones (for games, I suppose); dates; plums; wallnuts in perfect preservation, only black like all the other things; rice and grains in quantities; figs; loaves of bread—one with the baker's name stamped on it; bottles of oil; rope; soles of shoes; half-burnt purses, with coins sticking to them; a curtain tassel.-

Fine bust of Dante (bronze) in the "Stampe" room.- I notice that the artists who go to the Museum to copy have the habit of exposing their work there, for sale. Of a landscape of Claude Lorrain, no less than six copies were standing all together. Another favourite was the Danae of Titian.-

Why is it that I *never* see any English people here but such as are of the Cook's tourist type? As surely as the English language falls on my ear, so surely do I hear an ignorant or an idiotic remark.

My dinner to-night disagreed with me; upset.

Thursd. Nov. 15. Feeling far from well, after bad night. In morning down to the Via Caracciolo, and watched fishermen dragging in their nets. This they do from enormous distances, with ropes; an operation of an hour or more; eight or ten men haul in leisurely, one behind other, and coil the rope. When the net is near land, small boats take it up. The bronzed legs of the men.- Also watched the oyster-fishing. A man anchors his boat, and then dredges the bottom of the sea with a net at the end of a pole some 20ft long.- Scirocco to-day, I am afraid; musty and hot, with a little sunshine however.

See in the paper (I read the "Corriere di Napoli" every morning) that the ten public scriveners under the corridor of the San Carlo have notice to move at the end of the present year. Indeed it was high time that I saw Naples.

To-day is pubd in 3 vols. "A Life's Morning". I rejoice unspeakably that I am out of the way.

Frid. Nov. 16. Postcard from Nelly in which she mentions that a daughter [Enid] was born to Alg and Katie on Nov. 11th.

Fortunate change in the weather. Brilliant day, and very warm, but tempered on the whole by a pleasant tramontana. Went with P[litt] to Pozzuoli by tram, thence walked to Baia. Went half round the Lago Averno, and examined the ruins of baths. Inside grow lemon trees, with plenty of fruit on them; no one to prevent you gathering. A peaceful spot, this. The old boatman at end of highroad is the only man of the guide species that one has to encounter, and he is easily dismissed. The lake is enclosed all round with stone; very clear and deep at edge. Everywhere abundance of wild thyme; it scents the air.

At Baia went to the Albergo della Vittoria and had dinner; prices not extravagant, and civility. Amusing to see plates of willow-pattern (English manufacture) and knives from Sheffield. A few ships in the little harbour; waiter said they came chiefly for the Pozzuolian earth that makes specially good mortar.- Bargained with a driver, and so got back to Pozzuoli in time for the 4 o'clock tram. The bay of Baia is lined with Roman brickwork; not a yard where you don't see traces of the old villas. Much quarrying going on. New roads—shorter cuts, of course—being made from Pozzuoli.- Old fellow at Baia, a guide, who astonished me by speaking very good and connected English. Remarkable how the people about here pick up scraps of foreign languages. I think I didn't note that, on the evening of our arrival here, just as we were entering the Hotel, an old reprobate shouted in my ear- "Bad hotel, bad hotel!"

At Fuorigrotta left the tram, and walked over the hill to the Via Tasso. Splendid views first over Pozzuoli, then over Naples. The latter about the finest of Naples I have yet seen, - full moon just rising.- From Fuorigrotta rose in the evening stillness an incredible uproar, characteristically Italian.

Glorious moonlight to-night.

I note from the paper, that to-day *fox-hunting* begins in the Roman Campagna!—The foll. formalities at beginning and end of an ordinary letter to the editor of the "Corriere" are noteworthy : "Gentilissimo Signor direttore . . . Gradisca i miei migliori atti di grazia, ed i sensi del mio perfetto ossequio." [Most kind Mr. Editor . . . Please accept my best thanks and the expression of my perfect homage] And a vice-sindaco begins a letter to the editor as follows: "Egregio signor direttore, Le sarei grato se V[ostra] S[ignoria] Ill[ustrissima] con quella gentilezza che la distingue, volesse usarmi la cortesia di pubblicare nel suo accreditato giornale, ciò che segue." [Distinguished Mr Editor, I should be grateful if your most illustrious lordship, with that kindness which distinguishes you, would do me the courtesy to publish what follows in your eminent newspaper.]

Sat. Nov. 17. A day of rest, made disagreeable towards evening by a touch of diarrhea,—somewhat alarming in Naples. Seems to be gone, however. Wonderful moonlight. At the window of the corridor, where the moonbeams fall, I have just read with ease a page of the "Golden Treasury". The sky is a dark blue, with clear stars.

Sund. Nov. 18. After some doubt whether I was quite well enough to go, I started by the 10.25 train for Salerno, purposing an excursion of some days. Glorious view of Salerno from the railway at Vietri and between the tunnels by which S[alerno] is approached. On arriving, had a meal, and, without stopping to see the town, took a "carrozza" for Amalfi: 5*l.* and *mancia.* As soon as we got to Vietri on the road, up drove two other carriages, and the three rascals attempted to make me change, on pretext of a fresh horse being needed. Easy to imagine the fix in which I should have been had I yielded. "Questo è mìo fratello," said my lying driver, pointing to one of the others not the least like him. A brief "non voglio" put an end to the matter, and on we went. An astonishing road, made 30 yrs ago, by sheer mining, along the coast. Sometimes very high above the sea, sometimes making great bends into the gorges; all along, indescribable views. Vine terraces. On the side of the sea the road is walled, and in places the wall descends like a huge bastion. The terraces also laboriously built up with blocks of stone. The villages stand wherever a gorge occurs ; many are far up on the heights, and communication must be a terrible business. We passed the solid castles, built under Charles V, against pirates. A fine sunset. Far away, the hills of Calabria became a dark blue. The hills above me gradually covered with white thick clouds, threatening rain. Passed Vietri, Cetara, then round the Capo d'Orso, where I said good-bye to Salerno, and began to see the Amalfi side; then Majori (where stood an eccentric studio, painted with figures and bearing inscription: "Sole oriente orior, sole cadente cado" [I rise with the rising sun and go to bed with the setting sun]), Minori, Atrani. Dark by when we reached Amalfi, and drove straight to the Albergo d'Italia. Incessant begging all along the way, and it seemed to me, no very good spirit in the country people,- tendency to mock unkindly.

Got a room for 1,25 l.; had dinner. Only other person a German lady who read a book all the time. We exchanged a very few words.- Then for a walk down to the little port. Splendid full moon. Amalfi gleaming white in the huge cleft of grey, clouded mountains. Boats all drawn up on the strand. Gentle waves breaking. In the piazza a band playing, because Sunday. Air very warm.- The town lighted (and very badly) with oil-lamps, mostly those belonging to the shops and houses. In the piazza, a large fountain with image of S. Andrea; always a crowd of women about it.- At 9.30, when I was going to bed, began a furious uproar of squibs and crackers, at first much to my alarm. The Italians enjoy every kind of noise, childishly; fireworks always going off.- In the night noticed for the first time the custom whereby Italian clocks strike the past hour after sounding each quarter. My room just under the Campanile, so that I scarcely slept at all.- Then at 4 a.m. a vehicle of some kind clattered down the street, with blowing of a horn ; post, or something of the kind, I suppose. Everybody in the town seemed to be up very shortly after.

Mond. Nov. 19. A day of hard and incessant rain; landlord tells me the weather changed at midnight. A very decent fellow, the landlord, who had the sense to speak Italian slowly and clearly to me. Made a few attempts to see the town and neighbourhood.- At the central fountain, always a crowd, with strange variety of occupations: washing, both clothes and vegetables, drawing water, chattering. Beautiful shapes of the vessels.- Afternoon went up the Valle de' Molini. Though it is the only road that leads straight up the glen, to follow it is enormously difficult; incessantly one strays into inextricable passages, slums, staircases, to right or left. The number of soldi I had to give away, surprising. Men, women and children,- all begged, and seldom one that showed good will, that did not laugh jeeringly.- I note here that the Italian people have the *vices of poverty;* that explains all.- The valley has its name from the number of paper mills working here; all turned by the stream that comes down from the mountains. The women and children, bending under huge bales of rags. Of course a rich view on either hand; wild, lofty crags. Gathered some maidenhair from one of the beautiful little clefts.- Still, could not quite enjoy myself; partly because of rain; more because of pestering by beggars. Not professional beggars; here *everybody* asks "un sord'".- Note, by the bye, the change of *l* to *r* in the Neap[olitan] dialect. Amalfi is Amarfi; lapilli are rapilli; soldo is sordo, etc.

Made two sketches from my window; one of a round tower, that stands clear against the sky on a height; the other of the Campanile.

[Under the sketch of the Tower:]

In cathedral, saw the inscription: "Hic intus homo verus certus optumus recumbo, Publius Octavius Rufus, decurio"
[Herein I lie, a truthful, reliable and virtuous man, Publius Octavius Rufus, decurion]

[Under the sketch of the Campanile:]

The dome and intersecting lines are of red and yellow tiles. The inner brickwork of tower of parallel alternating red and blue. The rest a cold grey stucco,- I think.

This evening the German lady proved much more talkative; we got on very pleasantly and I found my German went better than I should have expected.

Tuesd. Nov. 20. Started early and drove back to Salerno; weather again calm and sunny. Many butterflies flitting about. At Salerno just caught the train southwards, and at 12.45 was at Pesto. Train full of peasants; most of them had good handsome faces, and by their talk seemed good fellows. All along rare views of the Apennines. As we neared Pesto, passed a few herds of buffaloes; but they are practically the same as cattle, and graze placidly and unalarmed by the train. The land getting rapidly cultivated all along route of railway. At Paestum, for a delightful change, there is no pestering by guides. I walked straight to the Temple of Ceres in peace. Only one party of three or four Germans had come down by same train. Here discovered, for first time, mistake in Baedeker; he says the guardian's house is by the Temple of Ceres, whilst it stands by that of Neptune. Before entering latter bought four sols of cheese at a vile little osteria, the only one in the place, and was cheated shamelessly—a piece of one inch solid. Paid a lira for admission to the space where the two main temples stand; guardian very decent fellow, speaking good French. When I had entered, two women came up, and asked me if I wished to buy refreshments,- but did it respectfully and quietly, and accepted my request for a mere ½ bottle of

74

wine without the least pestering. Perhaps wife of the guardian. So I ate my bread and cheese in the Temple of Neptune, and drank the wine, which was very sweet; Calabrian, the woman told me.

Owing to necessity of taking train back northwards, had only 2 hrs altogether—grossly inadequate, of course. The stone of the temples has become honeycombed wonderfully; here and there incrusted with what seems to be petrified fungi. In every crevice are pretty coloured snails; I brought away several. Many lizards. The ground all about thick with a rank vegetation. Everywhere quantities of what I had hitherto taken for wild thyme, but which a note from Alg tells me is peppermint. The Temple of Neptune, a golden brown; contrasting strongly with the white of the so-called Basilica, next to it. I picked a fragment of marble, and, at same time a bit of the travertine; the one quite cold in the hand, the other warm.

Exquisite views all round. Blue line of sea, with Capri and the Sorrento peninsula. But the most striking is to stand in the middle of the temple of Neptune, and then glance towards both ends. At the one, a very narrow strip of the bluest possible sea,- only that; the other way, a splendid valley, rising upwards on the mountains;- both these seen between the grand Doric columns.- Think that these columns have echoed to the Greek speech!- It was intensely still. A carter going by uttered the peculiar wailing song, so commonly heard about here; his horse's bells tinkled. Between the two temples a donkey, laden with a sack, was grazing.- Clouds began to thicken; the rays of the westering sun came through them, making the other clouds on the mountains a rich colour. The ordinary colour of the crags in sunshine I cannot express; I mean it is a peculiar tint for which I know no name.-

A few farm houses stand in the neighbourhood. The fields, where fine oxen were turning up the black earth, are marked with stones which once built Paestum—the ruins of a great city! The remains of the city wall very vast and impressive.

At Battipaglia (as in coming) had to change, and there decided to stop at Pompeii for Vesuvius to-morrow.- At Nocera station, women crying, "Uova fresche! (pronounced *fresh-che*) Mele! Pere!"- The porters, when the train is ready to start, first cry "Partenza!" then a moment after, "Pron-ti!" By the bye, I find the Italian officials everywhere polite and intelligent. My experiences with them are much pleasanter than with the French.

As I walked from Pompeii station to the inn, the moon rising, right in front. On my left hand, the dead town in darkness, and behind it the bulk of Vesuvius, with an angry glow. On either side of road, plane-trees.- Put up at the "Sole", a capital place. Found a lot of Germans there, good fellows. The amusing waiter, Giuseppe. Paintings on walls of the eating-room. My bedroom in a little outhouse built at back of garden into which my door opened straight.-

Here made the acquaintance of John Wood Shortridge. At dinner, he was talking German,- very fluently, but in a way that betrayed him as a foreigner. Something in his accent reminded me strangely of—I knew not what; of something very familiar. After dinner it came out he was a Yorkshireman, and with a strong Yorkshire accent: there was the secret.

Related to old Dr. Wood of Wakefield and to Towlson White. Was delighted to hear I knew the people. He has been in Italy 17 years; is married to a Capri woman, and lives at Massa Lubrense.

Wed. November 21. Ascent of Vesuvius. Started at 8.30, on horseback, guide also on a horse. Fine day on the whole, but rather too misty for a good view, a spot of rain once or twice. At Boscoreale stopped and had bottle of white Vesuvian wine; tastes very like cider. I had fears about my horsemanship; however, I stuck on without difficulty, even when we galloped, but the bruising and abrading was awful. The ascent at first through vineyards, some of Lacrima Christi. At point where the climb begins, we left our horses, and also the food. Found it impossible to get rid of the two "ajuti", who, at expense of 3 l. apiece, insisted on lugging me up the steep parts, by means of a cord. The pleasure greatly spoilt by this needless nonsense; nowhere is the climb difficult; the only thing is, it means the ruin of a pair of boots. As you get to the top, it is difficult to avoid taking the sea for sky, especially with a little mist on it; Capri I constantly took for a high cloud. until I corrected myself. At one point much suffering from sulphur fumes; but soon got through this.- Did not venture onto the inner cone; it smoked furiously and looked red hot; I should have had no boots left at all. Ground covered with bright yellow sulphur; collected a lot of pieces. Much activity of volcano; vast volumes of smoke, and constant vomiting of small stones; the smoke a dark rose colour at times. Inside, the incessant noise as of a foundry—a throbbing, beating, with a huge burst now and then.

Down again to the horses. A lad, who had taken care of them, I found was called Raffaello; and my guide's name I found afterwards to be Michelangelo! We ate our lunch, I sharing mine with guide. Should have mentioned that a man met us with wine up above; had one bottle going and one returning, at cost of 2 l. a bottle. One bottle we had brought with us from Boscoreale, and this we now drank.

At Boscoreale, in the little inn, found an American lady, who with strong accent, instantly cried out to me, "*Can* you speak any Italian?" - She said her husband and daughters had gone up the mountain, and she was waiting their return; in a state of exhaustion, and couldn't speak a word of anything but English, to ask for food. I ordered for her a beefsteak with potatoes and raw tomatoes. Much gratitude, and she came to the door to see me off.

Heavens, the state in which I reached home! Knees and backside and bottom of spine seriously abraded; also knuckles, with occasional clinging to pummel. Not a bone that didn't ache. It would have been nothing, but for the riding.-

Pleasant evening with Shortridge and the Germans. One of the latter an interesting fellow who talked in rather an eccentric way and made much use of the word "faktisch" [really]. I learnt afterwards that these fellows all got drunk by the fire (there actually was a fireplace) and at one o'clock a.m. all sallied forth to the Amphitheatre, dragging Giuseppe with them. One of them rolled down to the bottom, and all but injured himself; next morning he had a stomach ache.

Going to my bedroom, through the dark garden, I met a little lad belonging to the house.- "Buona sera, signore", he said, and I replied "Buona sera".- Then "Va bene, signore?" "Va benissimo!" "E una buona parola !" ['Good night, sir', he said, and I replied 'Good night'. Then, 'All right, sir?' 'Quite all right!' 'Those are good words!'] Curious reply that.

Thursd. Nov. 22. Little thought, last year, where I should spend my next birthday. Decided to run over to Naples, and back again at night in order to go with Shortridge to Massa to-morrow. Walk in morning with S. to Scafati and back. Home to Vico Brancaccio, where letters waiting,- Nelly, and Walter Grahame.- Changed clothes, dined at Giardini di Torino (the best and cheapest place in Naples, I have found it out too late,) and took 7.30 train back to Pompeii.

Frid. Nov. 23. Set out walking with Shortridge. Little short of Castellammare overtaken by two of our Germans, in carriage, they persuaded us to mount. Had wine, and took, all together, another carriage for Sorrento. Through Vico Equense. This side of the peninsula very different from the other; for most part a long slope upwards, richly covered with olives and *agrume* (the general name for oranges and lemons). The first glimpse of the Piano di Sorrento, delightful. Not really a plain, but a gently rising wide and deep lap, surrounded by mountains, and with a sheer line of high cliffs all along the sea front—a singular effect. Through Meta—then pulled up at Sorrento. The Town of Tasso. In a piazza, a statue thus inscribed: "A S. Antonino Abbate, che nel secolo VI, fuggendo le devastazioni dei Longobardi qui riparò e visse e indi, beato in cielo, questa sua seconda patria, incessantemente protesse e conservò il comune e i cittadini.- A documento di votiva gratitudine e di fede perenne, con danaro collettizio, questa statua P.P.- A. MDCCCLXXIX" [To St. Antonino Abbate, who in the sixth century, fleeing the ravages wrought by the Lombards, sought refuge and lived here, then blessed in heaven, his second homeland, incessantly protected and preserved the commune and its inhabitants. In token of devout gratitude and eternal faith, with the money collected, this statue P.P.-1879.]

Had a capital dinner at the Trattoria del Leone. In the yard, a plain marble fountain, with this inscription:
"Sordibus abstersis, instructo marmore, priscus
Fons nitet ; et manat gratior unda tibi."
[Cleaned and with its marble restored, the old fountain
shines again, and the water flows more pleasantly for you.]

Here the Germans remained for the Capri boat, and Shortridge and I walked on to Massa. Wonderful walk. Half-way, one of the richest views I have yet seen. Vesuvius right opposite, perfectly cloudless; right, Piano di Sorrento, with its upward sloping olive-hills. Far below my feet, the little Marina of Sorrento, with its boats drawn up. All around, gleaming limestone hills. In far distance, Naples,—the long salmon-coloured line of houses, from Posillipo to Torre Annunziata, and Camaldoli rising up behind. Capri and Ischia both in sight. The sea foaming under the tramontana, which was strong. Over all, sunlight from the west.

Reached Shortridge's house,- Villa Cozzolino. He is building an addition to it, and things all in disorder. Poor wife (of whose jealousy he complains,) enceinte, pretty once, but no more. Four children: Jessie, Nannie, Kate and Jack. All speak the local dialect of Italian, and no English; wife the same. A brother living with Shortridge, Herbert, by name. Educated at Edinburgh, and has passed all but final medical exams; now a hopeless drunkard. All round house a big garden, thick with loaded lemon-trees.- No w.c. existing yet! A garret hung with pomidori, sorbe, pumpkins, and a few of the common bell-shaped cheeses. Had a strange dinner, chiefly consisting of sausages, home-made, villainously flavoured with anise. After dinner sat round a brazier, which was fitted into a moveable circular form of wood. At seven o'clock to bed, down in a room below level of rest of house, a large vaulted room, where the brother sleeps. I found him in bed; he told me that he *always* goes to bed at this hour, as also the rest of the family. Servant brought down a bottle of wine, and we talked. In his drunkenness, the man could scarcely speak English; always mixing it up with his dialect Italian,- constantly bringing in *cosi* and other like words. Frequently used the phrase "A thing impos-sible", and so on. Tried to defend himself against charge of idleness. Has got a pile of medical books from England, and pretends he wishes to study, but is prevented by a thousand things. His quarrels with the people of Massa; his doctoring the peasants, etc.- At his bedside was bread and salame; told me he ate this at 1a.m.; the only time he had any appetite. And indeed he did so, for I awoke at that hour.- In the morning he was a different man, and spoke rather refined English, no touch of dialect. Once had plenty of brains, I doubt not, but is now past all help. Altogether one of the strangest households I have yet known.

Sat. Nov. 24. Walk with Shortridge up to the castle of Santa Maria. Splendid view of Capri, close at hand. Brilliant sun; much snow on the Apennines. S[hortridge] talking gloomily of his affairs; wishes to take children to England. I should have mentioned that the father and mother of the wife also live in the house; sheer peasants, and doing servants' work, but excellently treated by S[hortridge]. The old man he addressed as Raffaello.- Much information on our walk. All the comuni about here compelled by government to keep, under penalty, a supply of snow from end of April to end of Sept., for use in typhus etc.; it is sold to the people at 4 soldi a kilo.- Learnt that the dead at Naples are buried for 18 months in ground, and only then their bones are put into the wall-sepulchres I saw; S[hortridge]'s tale of the man he saw scraping his father's bones. The quail nets along the shore; birds come from Africa, in spring and autumn, and are caught in nets. Many fall a prey to the abundant hawks of Capri.- The clock of Santa Maria struck the hours in the old Italian way.- We passed the house where Murat lived, and whence he viewed the capture of Capri by French. His rooms still kept as he left them, precisely. Astonishing stories about the English people who from time to time have made Capri their home; a strange lot of blackguards.

With S[hortridge] made acquaintance of a young fellow called Giacomo Gargiulo, who has learnt from S. to speak very decent English. He went down with me to the Capri boat in afternoon. Here I learnt that, on the boats, a difference is made between natives and forestieri; for latter there are special high charges!

Reached Capri in the dark, and walked up from the Marina Grande to the town. The lights of Naples very clear across the bay. Had note of recommendn from S[hortridge] to one Busselli, landlord of the Hôtel Tiberio; there put up. Room for 2.50 for two nights.

Sund. Nov. 25. Festa in Capri. Found the diminutive piazza swarming with people. Walked first of all to the Piccola Marina, on opp. side of island, to see S.'s old house as I had promised. Was guided by a decent lad called Alfonso, who claimed to be relative of S.'s. A German, living at Rome, said to have bought the house for 12,000l. Garden full of geraniums and other English flowers,- S.'s favourites. A fine morning. The limestone crags gleaming agst intense blue of sky. Wonderfully rich vegetation. Baedeker says the flora has 800 species. Vesuvius cloudless; wind from west. From Piccola Marina over to the M[arina] Grande, and thence in boat to Grotta Azzurra; a little difficulty in entering, owing to swell on sea. The blue of the water indescribable, but only near entrance; I expected to see the rocks all round blue with reflection, but it was not so; perhaps insufficient sunlight. The silver gleam when the oar was moved in the water. A splendid view of the sheer crags as we rowed by, going and returning. Corals on the rock just below water-mark; boatman said they were too hard for use. The pellucid green water near, and in the harbour almost as wonderful as the Grotta; the weed at the bottom—at great depth—green beyond expression.

Made a sketch of the kind of lock common about here on outside doors. a-b is door-post, into which runs end of padlock, passing through the staples c,d,e, which are fast in the door, f is the lock working round on the iron.

[Sketch]

In the afternoon found my way up to the Villa of Tiberius. The Salto di Tiberio an awful height; a stone seemed to be a whole minute or more in reaching the bottom. Baedeker says the height is 738ft, and that the highest cliffs at the E. are 1,000ft sheer! Drank a glass of white wine at the little osteria by the Salto, and took a rose (blooming in garden) from the woman there; also wrote my name in the visitors' book. Then on, a little higher to the ruins of the Villa. A talkative old woman presented herself as guide; she said the place was the property of herself and two or three brothers and sisters. A fine, peaceful cow stabled and ruminating in part of the ruins. A very few traces of mosaic, all else gone,—except indeed the beginning of a paved roadway, which seemed to run downward to the sea, and which had a double track for wheels, as if vehicles used to be hauled up. The lower part covered with earth; the ground of a peasant who refuses to excavate. Brought away a little bit of mosaic stone. Talk with the hermit who lives here by his chapel. Lightning is constantly striking the place; he showed me the marks of the last bolt, which fell in Sept. last. The hermit happened to be absent in Capri; his bed-chamber riven down the wall. Gave him 50c., and wrote my name again in visitors' book. (*Fulmini* called *furmini* by old woman).

Rich afternoon. Big bees humming everywhere, and flies frequent. Many daisies growing on the way. View of Capo Minerva (Capo della Campanella). In descending turned aside to see the Arco Naturale, an immense arch. Then homewards. Oleanders and lentiscs. Gave a soldo to woman, and she begged for "un altro baiocco" [tenth part of a paolo; a farthing].- first time I have heard the word used.-

Not very comfortable in Busselli's place. Much better if I had gone to the Pagano, where the painters live.- At night a short stroll. Vesuvius across the water, now obscured, now flashing an angry glow.

Mond. Nov. 26. Cheapest way of getting to Naples is by the boat which leaves at 6.30 in the morning. With the long walk down to the Marina, this seemed too early and I decided to take the dearer boat at 2.30. If I had been at the Pagano, could have slept at the Succursale it has down on the shore.- Cloudy and threatening morning; in much fear lest the boat in which I departed should not come from Naples. Walked up the tremendous Anacapri road to the turning point of the cliffs, and at last, at 11o'clock, saw the smoke of the steamer coming over from Sorrento, where it touches.- Home to dinner, and paid a bill much dearer than it should have been; then down to steamer. Here again the fare for forestieri fixed at higher rate than for natives; only one ticket, 5*l.*-

On walk towards Anacapri, passed numbers of women, many barefooted, coming down heavily laden with wine-casks, great bundles of hay, sacks, etc. On road bet. Capri and the Marina noticed a villa with "Rest" carved over doorway.

Evening darkened as we sailed towards Naples. A fierce red sunset between black clouds. Vesuvius veiled. Beautiful view of the Piano di Sorrento,- its peculiar shape, cliffs, etc. A cold wind, but sea calm. Landed at the Santa Lucia, and to dine at the Giardini di Torino.- Found letters from Nelly (with cheque for £10), Bertz, Alg and [Edgar] Harrison.

Tuesd. Nov. 27. Day of letter writing and journalizing. Postcard to Nelly, acknowledging cheque. Letter to Shortridge. Postcard to [Edgar] Harrison, who is trying to let 7K for me.- To dine at the Giardini di Torino, a restaurant up a dark street on left hand side of the Via Roma, a most excellent place which I wish I had known of sooner. The only drawback is absence of carte, but the choice is great, the dishes plentiful, the company agreeable. Electric light; and a swarm of most respectable waiters; many of them in their evening dress, with their Italian faces, remind one ludicrously of tenors and baritones. The prices are incredibly low; for 1,50*l.* I make a banquet. Half a bottle of excellent wine is 20c. About six o'clock we have music in the shape of volunteers, who collect halfpennies at intervals. Here I have for the first time felt kindly towards soldiers. Numbers of officers come every evening,- fine, well-fed fellows, and it amuses me to see them enter in their sweeping cloaks, with clanging swords by their sides.-

The Neapolitans are fond of driving a team of three in their carts. I have several times seen, yoked side by side, a horse, a big white ox, and a little donkey!

In newspaper to-day I read extracts from new regulations just issued with regard to building in Naples—minute directions to a sanitary end. They are pushing ahead greatly in this matter. The w.c. question (one of *the* questions in Italy) seriously dealt with.

The foll. from to-day's *Corriere* is delightful; from a leader dealing with municipal corruption, which is very rife in the town: "La base della coscienza napoletana è—questo è per noi un articolo di fede sul quale non ammettiamo discussione—la virtù; ma la base del carattere napoletano è la *rassegnazione*. Questo maraviglioso popolo *si rassegna con eccessiva facilità al male;* e, quando accoglie con favore il bene, pare ancora che vi si rassegni." [The base of the Neapolitan conscience—this is an article of faith about which we are not prepared to admit of any discussion— is virtue; but the base of the Neapolitan character is resignation. This marvellous people resigns itself too easily to evil; and when it welcomes good, it still seems to do so with resignation.] The italics are mine.-

I note that, in reply to a "Grazie", the well-disposed of the lower orders reply either "Padrone!" or "Niente!"

Found Plitt in evil humour. Oh, for the day that sees me free of him!

Note here the address of a sister of Shortridge, on whom I have promised to call: Mrs. Jolly, 19 Goldsmith Gardens, Acton, London.

Wed. Nov. 28. Dull day; did nothing particular, except write letters to Walter Grahame and Katie to be posted in Rome.

Thursd. Nov. 29. Decided to leave for Rome by the 10.40 to-night. Day of packing. With many sighs of relief, got at last really clear of Plitt, and, after a great struggle at the ticket office,- no queue, or anything of the kind at Naples, not even a barricade,- found myself with a ticket for Rome. Carriage full; I was too late to get a corner, so of course did not rest the whole night. Some good fellows and amusing. One lad, lithe and good-looking, amused us particularly. First he played some airs on a little wooden whistle; then he stowed himself away on the top of the rack for luggage, and slept there comfortably; on getting up, he said comically once or twice- "Farò un poco di ginnastica!"- Not a Neapolitan, from his language.- As often as he woke, he tickled me greatly by shouting to a companion "Bosco! Bosco!" A good, frank lad, I think.- Another phrase, used by another passenger, struck me through the strangeness of its sound; he said he was going, not to Rome, but to "la penultima stazione."- All night long, a hundred times, one or other was using the phrase "a Roma". It rang in my ears strangely enough. Century after century has this name

"Roma" been used, and pronounced doubtless in much the same way.- An odd, and dangerous, thing was the examination of tickets whilst the train was at full speed,- the collector going along from door to door outside.- At about 7, Rome was reached. It was too dark to see anything before the aqueducts.-

But I had forgotten to note that last evening-this Thursday that is,- was a fine sunset, and I went up for a last view of Naples to the Vomero. From there I sketched Vesuvius; then went over to the other side of the hill, and sketched the Pozzuoli gulf,- that, as always, pleased me better. I copy these sketches here,- poor enough but souvenirs. Again I noticed the astonishing noise that rose in the evening stillness from Fuorigrotta.

[Sketches of Vesuvius and Pozzuoli Gulf]
Underneath the latter Gissing wrote:
"Nullus in orbe sinus Baiis praelucet amoenis".
[No bay in the world outshines pleasant Baiae.]

Frid. Nov. 30. Had breakfast, and, guided by Baedeker, hunted for a room. Speedily decided on two little ones on 4th floor, 59, via Margutta;- very comfortable indeed, though as much at 50l. the month. A decent landlady. Paid rent in advance. Very sunny, and indeed remarkably well furnished. I am rather far from the old city, but at all events the position is very healthy.- Sent off cards to Roberts, Bertz and Plitt, and posted my letters to W[alter] Grahame and Katie. In spite of intense weariness, could not resist the Forum and Colosseum in the afternoon.- The astonishing difference between Rome and Naples! They are not the same nation. Here no noise, no pestering to buy, etc.—all grave and quiet and dignified. In that respect a change vastly for the better.

Sat. Dec. 1. I notice already that the type of Roman face is much better than that of the Neapolitan,- vastly more dignity. In Naples I never saw beautiful girls; their faces are very round, and immensely stupid. Here it is quite different; beauty seems common. I miss my fruit very much. None to be had here at Naples prices; no stalls in the streets.

A day of wandering. First thing, it rained hard; but cleared up at 10. Went to Piale's Lib., and got their card of the week's diary in Rome,- very useful. Then on to the Pincian and enjoyed the view. Then to Pantheon, where closing time came before I had seen much. I copied, however, the inscripts. on tombs of Raphael and Annibale Carracci who lie separated only by a chapel.

"Raphaeli Sanctio Joann. F. Urbinati
Pictori eminentiss. veterumq. aemulo
Cujus spirantes prope imagines si
Contemplere naturae atq. artis foedus
Facile inspexeris
Julii II et Leonis X Pontt. Maxx. Picturae
Et architect. operibus gloriam auxit

Vix annos XXXVII integr. integros*
Quo die natus est eo esse desiit
VIII Id. Aprilis MDXX
Ille hic est Raphael timuit quo sospite vinci
Rerum magna parens et moriente mori."

"[To Raphael Sanzio, son of Giovanni, of the city of Urbino, most eminent painter, who emulated the ancients. Those who behold the images he produced, which almost breathe the breath of life, will see nature and art combined. He enhanced the glory of Popes Julius II and Leo X by his pictorial and architectural work. Whole, he lived thirty-seven whole years, dying on his birthday on the eighth of the Ides of April 1520. He is the famous Raphael by whom Nature feared to be defeated while he lived and to be deprived of life when he died.]"

"D.O.M.
Hannibal Caraccius Bononiensis
Hic est
Raphaeli Sanctio Urbinati
Ut arte ingenio fama sic tumulo proximus
Par utrique funus et gloria
Dispar. Fortuna(m)*
Aequam virtuti Raphael tulit
Hannibal iniquam
Decessit die XV Julii An. MDCIX aet. XXXXIX
Carolus Marattus summi pictoris
Nomen et studia colens p. an. MDCLXXIV
Arte mea vivit natura et vivit in arte
Mens decus et nomen caetera mortis erant."

"[Deo Optimo Maximo, Here is Annibale Caracci, very close to Raphael Sanzio, of Urbino, in his art, talent and fame as well as in his tomb. They were equal in death though not in glory. Raphael's fate matched his merit, Annibale's did not. He died on the 15th of July 1609, aged 49. In 1674 Carlo Maratta had this put up to keep alive the name and study of this great artist. My art brings nature to life and she lives through my art. Intelligence, honour, fame, all else was destined to pass.]"

Then had dinner, and walked up to the Capitol. In the old café on the left hand of steps, a wolf is no longer kept,- a policeman smiled when I asked, and said it was many years since there had been one. But my Baedeker (1880) taught me to expect it.- Curious that, viewed from front, the heads of the two horse-tamers seemed too large,- just as I have often noticed in the cast of Michelangelo's David at S[outh]Kensington.-

* i.e. he died on his birthday. One might transl. "Whole, he lived XXXVII whole years."
*Surely this should be acc.; the stone reads *fortuna*.
[G.G.'s notes.]

83

It still keeping fine, I walked right on to the Porta di San Paolo (Porta Ostiensis), getting clear ideas of the topography of the hills. Then entered the Protestant Cemetery and walked up to Shelley's grave, which is right at the top under the Aurelian Wall. The inscription, on a plain flat marble, is this:

"Percy Bysshe Shelley.
Cor Cordium
Natus IV Aug. MDCCXXCII
Obiit VIII Jul. MDCCCXXII
Nothing of him that doth fade
But doth suffer a sea-change
Into something rich and strange."

The enclosed space just round the stone is covered with violets.- of course not now in flower. On the left hand is a precisely similar stone to Trelawny, who died in England, and, it seems, was buried here.[44]

The old cemetery is quite distinct, at a few paces distance; you first pass through a wooden gate, then over a field, then through a locked door, which leads you over the deep trench (walled on both sides) which surrounds the little graveyard. The key of the door I found, by guardian's direction, in a hole in the wall. Very few graves here. A few pines and cypresses and some roses in bloom. Keats' grave just by the entrance; the marble slab with his bust is placed against a wall close at hand. Inscript.:

"This grave
Contains all that was mortal
of a
Young English Poet
who
on his deathbed
In the bitterness of his heart
At the malicious power of his enemies
Desired
These words to be engraven on his tombstone
'Here lies one
Whose name was writ in water.'
Feb. 24th 1821"

This is a simple upright marble, which I sketched.- since there is a danger that the old graveyard may be destroyed to make a railway.

[Sketch]

The carving, except the roll at the bottom and the oblong on it, is in very low relief.

The inscription on the other slab to Keats is become at present all but illegible, the black of half the letters quite gone.

The grave itself is covered with weeds. Next to it on the same plot of ground which is all enclosed with iron rails and a thick low hedge of some common shrub which I ought to know the name of, lies Severn. Over Keats, from left hand corner, grows a laurel, now with black berries.

Severn's inscript.:

To the Memory of
Joseph Severn
Devoted friend and death-bed companion
of
John Keats
Whom he lived to see numbered among
The Immortal Poets of England.
An Artist eminent for his representations
Of Italian life and nature.
British Consul at Rome from 1861 to 1872
And Officer of the Crown of Italy
In recognition of his services to
Freedom and Humanity
Died 3 Aug. 1879 aged 85

The only difference between appearance of the two stones is that Severn has a pallet instead of the lyre. A very small stone by the foot of this grave is to the child Arthur Severn, of whom it is mentioned that Wordsworth was present at his baptism in Rome.- I also found the gravestone of Augustus William Hare, Late Fellow of New College, Ox. and Rector of Alton Barnes, Wilts.

Leaving the cemetery, I walked on to the Monte Testaccio, and looked long at the view.- The origin of the hill is obvious, as you walk up it,- everywhere potsherds.- I noticed that the size of St Peter's dome can only be appreciated from some distance; from here it seemed immense, looming above the horizon; this morning from the Pincian, rather small. With delight, distinguished Mt. Soracte in the N.W.-

Home tired to death, and without appetite; so made a dinner of buns and pears.

Sund. Dec. 2. In one respect, an Englishman like myself is badly off in Italy. Everywhere I meet swarms of Germans, I find German restaurants, etc., but never one of my own countrymen,- I mean at mealtimes, etc. The fact is, the English who stay here for a longer time are rich, and of course live in good quarters; the poorer English here are mere tourists. Yet there must be a few decent fellows abiding in Rome, if only one could find them.

Was disappointed this morning. It being Sunday, the Kircherian Museum and the Palatine ought to be open free; but a stupid election business of some kind was made an excuse for closing them,- as also the Forum; I suppose to enable the custodians to vote, and yet that is no reason for such an amazing proceeding.- However, the Capitoline Museum was open from 10-12, and thither I went.

The splendid majesty of that great sea-god (I think the shell in his hand proves him of the sea, and not river, as Baedeker believes,) in the Cortile! Calm rest in blessed sunshine, in an enchanted land.- The interesting little case of ivory *stili* in Room VII.- The Venus of Praxiteles revolves on its pedestal—a very sensible arrangement, standing as it does in a niche; a custodian turns it round now and then.- Busts of Euripides; again my delight, as at Naples. That one numbered 42 has, I noticed, a singular resemblance to Tennyson.- Very interesting are the sepulchral inscriptions set into the walls all over the Museum. I copied one or two.

"D.M.
Festibae Libertae
Quae vixit ann. XXV
Ippolytus Patronus
B.M.F."

"[To the Manes. To Festiba, the freedwoman who lived 25 years, her former master Ippolytus.]"

One imagines here a tender story.

Again:

"Licinius L.L. Felix
Sibi et suis."

"[Licinius L.L.Felix, for himself and his family]."
The form is exactly preserved in many of the inscripts. on the tombs at Naples—"per se e suoi". Here is a poor little stone:

"Symphanus
Vixit Ann. I
Menses VIII."

"[Symphanus, who lived one year and eight months.]"

And here a voice from far off:

"D.M.
Obelliae Fortunatae
Conjugi carissimae
C. Julius Magnion
Et sibi."

"[To the Manes. For Obellia Fortunata, beloved wife of C. Julius Magnion and for himself]"

In the afternoon went to Forum of Trajan, thence to the Ponte di Quattro-Capi and on to the Isola Tiberina. The colour of the Tiber is indeed remarkable; Horace's "flavus" is exactly the word; where the sun gleams on it, it is a deep tawny hue, and seems thick with substance.- Then through the Ghetto, and so home.- Dined at Tratt[oria] degli Artisti on the Via della Vite, and found it a purely German place. I don't take kindly to this.- A gloriously fine day, with cloudless sky.

Mond. Dec. 3. To St Peter's. The bronze seated statue of St Peter, with the toes worn away and white-shining with kisses. Much display of devotion in this business; saw woman kiss the foot several times, and then press her face against it.- The confessionals for all languages: Pro Lingua Gallica, Pro Lingua Anglica, etc. In a chapel just on right hand after entering, a service of some kind was going on, only clericals being present; one in a bishop's mitre—or something of the same shape,—intoned from a great book, and all the rest kept up a ceaseless droning. The air was dense with fumes of incense, and candles had to be held to read by. Indeed a piece of the middle-ages. I turned away from the gloom and incense and found myself in a great stream of sunlight through the windows of the church.-

The weather very fine, and warm in middle of day; but first thing in the morning almost frosty,- my hands are pinched when I go out.-

At 12 o'clock to the Borghese Palace. Asking permission is a mere formality; you apply to a clerk, and sign your name. Went through all the rooms.- Towards sunset up onto the Pincian, where were many carriages and a great number of young priests taking an airing. St Peter's dome shows well from here, standing directly against the sky.-

Strange to see everywhere about the streets—on public proclamations, offices, even dust-carts, the letters "S.P.Q.R." [Senatus Populusque Romanus, i.e. The Roman State]. Another curious thing of the kind is the printed formula "Est Locanda" stuck up on houses etc. to let. Is this of old use, I wonder?-

I suppose it is in great measure due to my improved health, and the great amount of exercise I take, that I have had moments of strange peace lately. If I awake in the night, I lie thinking of only the pleasantest things, and experience a strange revival of some of the feelings of my boyhood—the peculiar love of art, etc.

In evening, went to the Biblioteca Alessandrina, just behind the Pantheon. Could not obtain a book at once, but applied to have Vasari ready for me to-morrow evening.

Tuesd. Dec. 4, To S. Pietro in Vincoli, and gazed long at Michelangelo's *Moses.* Thence to Colosseum, and walked about it for an hour. On to the Forum, where I made the acquaintance of an American, a good sort of fellow, without education. He began by addressing me: 'Well, can you locate it?' Unable to speak any language but English, he was getting along in strange fashion, of course being swindled everywhere. Had Cook's Hotel Coupons (which he called *cewpons*) and naturally always found that extras made up almost as much as he would have paid in any case. We walked about the Forum, then had lunch, then turned southwards to the Porta San Sebastiano, and out onto the Appian Way, as far as the tomb of Caecilia Metella. I overtaxed myself, and got back in extreme exhaustion.- For all that, went to the Biblioteca, just because I had ordered the book, and at 10 o'clock got home in state of utter deadness.

Wed. Dec. 5. Very tired this morning.- Wanted to have a bath, but was told at the place that all Rome was without water, owing to a sudden failing of the Aqua Marcia somewhere. That "Aqua Marcia" had an antique sound!- Went to the Rospigliosi Gallery, and gazed my fill at Guido's

Aurora.- Thence to the Church of Sta Maria Maggiore.- After that, on to the Forum, where I met one of the Germans who accompanied Shortridge and myself to Sorrento. Not an educated man, unfortunately.-

The Forum itself strikes one as strangely small. Nothing like what we call a great open-air meeting could be held in it; at least so it seems to me, after studying the boundaries with Murray and Baedeker.- The paving of the Via Sacra and Vicus Tuscus and Clivus Capitolinus is very rude. The best piece is to be seen immediately in front of the Temple of Saturn; here the slabs of stone are of quite irregular shape, but fit well like a puzzle. Why didn't they save trouble by cutting stones of same size? It is the same at Pompeii.- Looked into the Cloaca Maxima, which is open just at S. end of the Basilica Julia,- smelling badly, too. Ferns growing down there.- One or two inscriptions took me. On a broken bit of entablature: "Dominis Omnium Gratiano Valentiniano et Theodosio Imperatorib. Aug." (Theodosus was Eastern emperor at same time that others were in the West.) Again, on a broken pedestal: "Toto orbe Victori D.N. Constantio Max. Triumfatori Semper Aug."- Gathered a bit of maidenhair from base of pillar of Phocas.- Have now got the topography clearly enough.- Round by the Colosseum, looking at the Meta Sudano, base of Nero's colossal statue, and the Arch of Titus. Sculptures on inside of arch very well preserved and interesting; the golden candlestick and silver trumpets being carried out of Jerusalem, and Titus entering Rome in triumph.

Have arranged my living on a tolerably economical plan. Breakfast, in the Via di Ripetta, costs me 30c. (which allows 2 cups of coffee); lunch I take at home, or in my pocket,- salami, bread, apples. My dinner I get at a Cucine opposite the Palazzo Borghese, and manage it for l. 1.35 at most, with ½ litre of white wine, soup, a dish, and fruit. The occasional expenses are the wash,- gratuities, etc.

Thursd. Dec. 6. In morning a letter from Alg, and in evening one from Bertz.- Wished to visit the Spada Gallery but found it was closed for some time. Went on, across the river, by the Ponte Sisto (old Janiculan Bridge) to the Palazzo Corsini, where I spent three or four hours. Made the foll. notes: *Madonna and child by Michelangelo Caravaggio;* singular realism. The Virgin has an aureole, the child none, and there is no background. Really a portrait-picture of modern woman and baby; both dressed very plainly, the child in a cloth frock. Face of mother very homely.- Interesting to compare this with the *Presepe of Vandyck*, which hangs next to it,- which also is realistic, (no aureoles,) but in quite a different way. It is poetical in feeling, and suggestive of more than the vulgar domesticity of Caravaggio. Mother is a peasant, but deeply and rather sadly thoughtful, as she draws away the veil from sleeping child.- *John the Baptist, Carlo Maratta*, a good example of degradation. A pretty infant lies on the ground, on a red cloth, and holds a toy cross. Above are two cherubs,- chubby heads, merely, with wings,- a paltry affair.- Then, close together, come three Ecce Homos. (1) *Carlo Dolci.* His favourite effeminate face, with long soft hair. The blood trickling down is peculiarly offensive,- a very realistic colour, whilst the rest of the picture is anything but real.

Take all else away, and the face is that of a downward looking lover in despondency. (2) *Guercino*. Realistic, even painful. Blood-shot eyes and mouth open in pain. The drops of blood made glistening in a curious bit of trickery, and surely an error. The face itself, I fancy, is a good bit of painting. (3) *Guido*. No realism in the blood-drops. The whole idealistic, in a truer way, of course, than Dolci. However, there is nothing more than a refined sadness in the upturned face,- a tenderly pious man, in rather sad prayer.- Another "Ecce Homo" of Guido's comes later. No aureole, and no realism of blood; an older man, and more pain in the face. But these heads of Guido's are monotonous.-

I notice a *"Madonna with child and Angels" by Carlo Maratta*, in which, at the back, is a face which is obviously a portrait. Astonishing how this stands out as a bit of reality against all the other insipidities.-

Salvator Rosa's "Prometheus". Now, here is realism! A wretch bound down to a rock,- his bowels protruding beneath the tearing vulture; and blood pouring down; his *mouth wide* in a yell of agony.- Well, why not? the story implies all this.- And yet of course it is as wrong as it could be, in art. Here is a mere galley-slave under torture, no Prometheus.- The various battle-pieces of Rosa interested me. I understand now the phrase "Ce damné Salvator", which Ruskin quotes.

Home for a little while, then on to the Barberini where I had about an hour.- Of course examined carefully the *Beatrice Cenci,* and the *Fornarina.* The fine "Schiava", either by Titian or Palma Vecchio, delighted me as a piece of painting. The portrait of Andrea del Sarto's wife, by himself. Also a good Holy Family by Andrea.

Then up onto the Pincian, where band was playing. A rich sunset, ending in an ambre sky, against which St Peter's stood up nobly.

Frid. Dec. 7. To the Doria Gallery, where there are greater numbers of uninteresting pictures than I have yet found anywhere. The *"Susanna and Elders" by Annib. Carracci* (Room II). The subject nobly treated, and it is a very difficult one to manage. Contrast this with the loathsome "Susanna" of Domenichino which I saw in the Corsini yesterday, where the woman props herself on her back in shallow water, and is a mere prostitute at play.- In Room IV is a grand half length *St. Joseph by Guercino.*- In Gallery II a fine *Quentin Matsys*. Two fiercely cunning old money-lenders, and two countrymen pleading with them; half lengths. The faces magnificent.- Looked long at the "Mulino" of Claude, and of course with prejudice enough. Wish I had sufficient knowledge of nature to judge such things independently. Indeed, I might say that of all paintings.- The Galleria de' Specchi, a wonderfully gorgeous effect. Down each side, between the windows (which here and there are red-draped, making rich light enter,) are mirrors set in deep and richly moulded frames. In front of each window is an antique statue,- these of no great mark, but still antique. The floor is patterned with coloured marble; the ceiling is painted in every inch with subjects and figures and ornament. Three glass lustres hang down. Murray says that the Ball-room is the most splendid room; I should rather like to see it.- In the midst of the Gallery I speak of stands an antique Odysseus hanging under the ram.

Walked through Forum, and spent half an hour in the Colosseum. Gathered a flower for Bertz. Returning home, finished Bertz's letter, and posted.- A letter this morning from Roberts.

Sat. Dec. 8. Most of the day spent in Forum and Colosseum. The latter irritates me. I can't understand the arrangements, and have access to no good book. The guide-books are futile. Again and again I try to distinguish clearly the various rows of seats, and cannot determine their exact position.

The weather is still brilliant. I notice the blueness of the sky far more than at Naples; I suppose because I always see it from between houses.- Letters to-day from mother and Nelly.

Grubbed about the Temple of Julius Caesar, and from the basement picked out some bits of pottery, which must be very old, seeing that the digging out of the basement only has exposed them. Also found a number of curious snails, and brought away.- Walked through the Velabrum, to the site of the Forum Boarium. Turned aside to look at the Cloaca Maxima. Saw the church called Bocca della Verità; the round temple formerly called of Vesta; and the Temple of Fortuna Virilis, with its fine columns and basement.—The Ponte Rotto is stopped; a new bridge seems to be building there. The whole locality in state of ruin,- indeed that applies to the greater part of modern Rome just now; everywhere new streets are being made.-

As I ascend homewards from the Forum, I always hear singing in my head;

"Dum Capitolium
Scandet cum tacita virgine pontifex."

[So long as with the silent virgin the pontiff shall ascend the Capitol]

After dinner, home and read Horace's First Epistle.- At nine o'clock went out, to see for the first time the aspect of Rome at night. It being the Immac. Conception, there was flaring illumination on the top of the Church of Trinità de' Monti, up between the turrets. The effect from the Via de' Condotti was very striking; the lights seemed to shine on the summit of an impossibly high building.- The main streets all but empty. The electric light is frequent (four lamps gleam round the column of Augustus) but one doesn't see whom they are for. In search of a little life I went into the Caffè Venezia, and had coffee; few people there, and those not at all enlivened by some music that was going on.- Nowhere saw a single haunter of the pavement. In the Caffè were some women, but oldish and plain; if hetairai, then of the dullest species.- Tempted into one of the numerous Pasticceria shops, and bought some delicious cakes. The wonderful things of that kind that one sees in the windows.- Home by the Piazza del Popolo, duller and duller.

Sund. Dec. 9. To the Kircher Museum, and found very little there that interested me. It being a free day, many of the best rooms seemed to be closed.- Away speedily to the Palazzo de' Conservatori. Here found rich matter. The well preserved half length of Commodus is interesting; for my own part, I am not sorry that all the best marble statues have lost their polish, to judge from the effect on this one.- The Wolf of the Capitol; good to see this with one's eyes.- The Boy extracting thorn; is this the original of all the existing duplicates?-

Found some good things in the Pinacoteca. Sala I. *A Holy Family, attributed to Giorgione.* Very striking. The mother has a large illuminated Bible open before her, and with one hand she points to a text she has just found. Her look of awe at the Child shows that the text has some reference to the Messiah, and perhaps to his fate. The Child is raised towards her by Joseph, and it stretches its arms to her. The colouring rich, the grouping admirable. Expecially fine, the Virgin's attitude. Sala II. *Portrait of Michelangelo,* supposed to be by himself. Seems to be the original of the engraving I have at home. If so, the expression is blander here; has an awakened look, almost of happiness. Sala IV. *Veronese's Europa.* What a distance between this treatment of the subject, and that we find in antiques! To begin with, the picture combines three different times. The main group at left of canvas, shows Europa just seating herself on bull, the animal is kissing her foot. Loves fly in the air. To the right of that, she is seen riding away, her maidens beside her. And lastly, in the distance, the bull is swimming with her over the sea; the maidens crying out. An odd feature is that two animals, on the left a dog, on the right a cow, are looking on with clearly expressed astonishment.- I can see that the grouping and colouring are fine, but the picture is one of those that give me no real pleasure. It would be so, even if that repugnant blending of three actions were not there. In such a subject one wants more simplicity—in fact, one wants the antique. *Guercino's St. Petronilla.* I don't know the story. The saint is being raised out of her tomb, to be shown to her lover, who stands by. A grand picture, I think. Of enormous size, occupying all one end of the hall. More than I thought Guercino capable of.- *Guido's Sebastian.* Here is the culmination of Sebastianish sweetness. Take the head alone, and it belongs to a very charming girl.-

The Sale dei Conservatori were open, I am glad to see. With delight I saw the fragmentary *Fasti Consulares* which are set in the wall, with blanks left where they are imperfect. Many a familiar name I read here, with the mention of triumphs after them.- "De Poeneis", and "De Siculis" caught my eye several times. In one room, the funeral wreaths of Garibaldi are preserved.-

Went next to the Palatine, and by degrees got an idea of the plan of the Palaces. It was a good idea to set up board with appropriate quotations from Latin authors.- In the gardens between the Palace of Caligula and that of Tiberius, large pink roses are in bloom, and several trees heavy with oranges. Warm sunshine. From the hilltop, I remarked well the situation of the Circus Maximus. Of the seven hills, the Capitoline, Palatine, Aventine and Quirinal are still well distinguishable; the others scarcely rise as distinct hills. Of course the Janiculus is plain enough.-

The Romans of to-day are a very orderly people, but they have the bad habit of scribbling their names on objects of interest. Some statues and busts on the Palatine are completely disfigured with pencilling.-

Happened to read in Murray, Byron's stanza on the Palatine. What poor stuff it is! And I am afraid the same applies to the greater part of "Childe Harold". I seldom see a quotation but it strikes me as feeble.

Thence to the Pincio, to hear the band and see the sunset. There is absolutely no rowdy element in public gatherings here, though the working classes are well represented. The Romans are generally grave, and always rather silent. I looked for beautiful faces, and could find hardly any. Some pretty ones, but these with a tendency to be coarse and stupid. Now and then a very pure contour, and these generally of grave expression.- The picturesque costumes of the nurses carrying babies; much white, and brilliant head-dresses. The head-dress of plain black lace common in lower classes.- The elegant soldiery of course strongly represented; but they look best in their mantelli at night.-

Desperately hungry. Tried a new ristorante also near the Borghese, and did very well. Soup, fish, cignale, apple, and ½ litre of wine for 42 soldi.- Anglici 1/9! The cignale done in the kind of sauce called agrodolce, which I can't say I like.- I notice that most Italians lay the napkin on their knees, in this, as in costume, imitating the English. The costume is perfectly English at present. It was so at Naples.

Saw the *Daily News* to-night at the Caffè Venezia, and it tells me that they are having summer heat at present in England.

Mond. Dec. 10. To the Vatican, for the first time, and spent the morning in merely *orienteering* myself. Impossible to look at anything, what with the excitement of being on such ground, and the agitation which invariably disturbs me amid unfamiliar surroundings. The procedure is simple. Entering by the Portone di Bronzo, at the top of the right colonnade of Peter's, you go up the first staircase to the right, and there sign your name on two papers, one for the Paintings, the other for the Museum. Having got these, you come down again, and ascend by the Scala Regia, which leads from the Portone di Bronzo right up to the door of the Sistine Chapel. It is a little red door, with "Capella Sistina" written on it. There you knock. Coming forth again, another flight of stairs conducts to the Stanze di Raphaello. There you traverse, and come out by the same door as you entered at. Almost opposite you then, on same landing, is the entrance to the Loggia of Raphael. Again you come out by the door of entrance, and a short walk along the loggia at right angles brings you to the staircase which leads up to the loggia above, in which is the door of the Gallerìa, where you ring.- That is all that one has to see in this part of the palace.- Stay, I have forgotten that, out of the *last* of the Stanze, you go through a little door into the Chapel where the Beato Angelico's frescoes are.

To reach the Museum, you go back to the front of St Peter's, and, by the left side of the *perron*, pass right round the whole building, and finally, through some stable-regions, reach the entrance to the Sala della Croce Greca. All the other rooms go in a straight course before you, and to leave you have to come back the same way.

The impression I brought away was, that it is a good thing only *old* men are elected Pope. A young man, finding himself in possession of such a palace, would surely go mad.- Came away at 1 o'clock, exhausted, and had a lunch at a trattoria hard by. Then home and read a little. On my way to dinner looked in, in the dusk, at Santa Maria Sopra Minerva, which is the only Gothic church in Rome, and moreover contains Michelangelo's Christ, and at the church of Gesù. Both these I must see in daylight, if possible.

My dinner last night was a little too expensive. Went to-day to the Trattoria del Giardino, on the Via delle Botteghe Oscure, out of the Via d'Ara-Coeli. Have been there before; dirty, but cheap and satisfying. Dined for 1.30.

A strange sunset, which I saw from the Capitol. The west was crimson, and just above the place where the sun had set rose a distinct *column* of deeper crimson than the surrounding,- a column of parallel sides, not very high, breaking the lines of a few dark horizontal clouds,- which could be seen fairly through it. I never saw anything like it before.

A clouded half-moon. After dinner walked over to the Forum. It is awful at night. Looked with strange feelings at those few heaps of rubble which represent Caesar's Temple. That especially takes me. There the Dictator's body was burnt, and there Tiberius delivered the funeral oration over Augustus.

Bitterly cold all to-day. Braziers distributed through the Vatican. In the Capitoline Museum on Sunday I saw one which was kept glowing with a key, precisely as Goethe describes the thing, when he first saw it at Naples [on February 26, 1787]. Strange thing that there are no book-shops in Rome,- I mean no old bookshops of the kind I expected to see, where one could pick up old copies of the classics. The few stalls I have come across show only some ecclesiastical works, and paltry modern things,- seldom even the Italian classics.

Tuesd. Dec. 11. There are no street organs in Rome, and, by the bye, there were none in Paris. I regret it. In Naples the monotony of tunes was astonishing, but I preferred that to none.- An interesting feature of the by-streets are the splendid teams of oxen bringing in loads of straw etc. from the country. These fine beasts, with their immense horns, always make me think of the antique. Such animals Virgil saw, and Homer, I suppose. The oxen at Naples were of larger size—marvellous beasts—but they hadn't the same long horns.

On my way to Vatican, crossed the Bridge at Ripetta. All the district on the other side, bet. that and the Castle St. Angelo, marked on the maps as occupied by the Villa Salonge and Villa Altoviti, is now being built upon, and great square ugly barrack-like houses are rising thick. Indeed modern Rome is extremely ugly.

Find I can use my *permessi* for successive days, by just asking for them back again as I go away. This will save trouble. I noticed a curious thing as soon as I had entered the Sist[ine] Chapel; there is evidently a system whereby visitors are kept out of the Chapel, if a little discouragement will do it. When a knock comes at the door, the attendant does not at once go, but waits to see if the knocker will persevere. In one or two cases, no second attempt was made, and then a distinct look of satisfaction came to the man's face. I don't understand this. Is it connected with the fact—also to me inexplicable—that visitors to the Chapel seem never to give gratuities?

For an hour gave good attention to the *Last Judgment* and the *ceiling*. How it enrages one to see the coarse drapery that has been daubed on to some of the finest figures,- thus defeating M[ichael] A[ngelo]'s very purpose, for they are always figures seen in some strange position, with wonderful foreshortenings! In revenge, one chuckles over the portrait of Messer Biagio di Asena, with his ass's ears.- When I began to examine the painting, at about 9.30, the light was poor; with difficulty I made out details; between 10 and 11 everything was much clearer, and that seems to be the best time.

I suppose few people notice the face of Satan (is it not?), which looks out from the cave at the bottom. A terrible face, with white eyes and white teeth; throwing upwards a look of fearful rage and hatred.

What impressed me most to-day was the left-hand bottom group,- the dead rising from their graves. It is awful beyond words to see those skeletons re-assuming flesh: some but half transformed, indescribable things between corruption and life. In foreground at bottom is a fearful face, half putrid, just awaking from death—with a sort of nameless horror in its look. Then the man who just turns in his grave. The awed hope on some of the faces.

I turned to the ceiling.- What are the exquisite figures seated on the beams which divide the nine spaces? I don't find them mentioned either in Murray or Baedeker. One of them—on the last beam but one at farther end—is obliterated all but hand and foot. The guardian told me it was the result of the explosion of the powder mag[azine] at St Angelo. The ruin seems to have been whitewashed over. Of the Sibyls I suppose the Delphic is my favourite.—By the bye, it would be very difficult to decide whether the architectural shaping of the roof were actual or merely painted; the illusion constantly troubles me.- All the pictures of the ceiling have to be seen with one's face towards the Last Judgement.-

What defence can anyone contrive of the monstrous practice of putting fine pictures on high ceilings—or on ceilings at all?

Went to the *Loggia*. Yes, I like these Bible pictures better than anything else of Raphael's that I know. They fill me with keenest joy. The clear colouring, the sweet, idyllic treatment, the exquisite landscape; it is the Bible made into a fairy-tale, of the most touching kind.- That lovely picture of Jacob with his flocks meeting Rachel and Leah at the well.- Those that have suffered most by damp are naturally the squares on the *outer* side all along. But most are nobly preserved, the colours gem-like in their freshness.- What a sweet and gentle idealism there is here! Take the Joseph and Putiphar's wife; why it suggests nothing more than that she is asking for a kiss.- They bring back to me the early longings of the days when I copied several of them from outline engravings that father possessed.-

Had lunch, and went round to the Museum. (Not feeling quite well; my

94

old complaint tormenting me much, so that I had constantly to sit down. Indeed it has never left me quite free since I quitted England).- Went carefully through a few halls: the Sala delle Muse, the Sala degli Animali, the four Cabinets round the Cortile di Belvedere (how pleasant the constant splashing of the fountain is!) and the three rooms that follow (Meleager, the Rotondo—with its fine view, and the Torso.) This was all I could manage.- The animals are wonderful, but there seems to be a doubt about their periods.

Wed. Dec. 12. From 9 to 2 at the Vatican.- There was rain in the night, and this morning the air is wonderfully clear. Cold, but invigorating.

First to the Chapel, to get the good light. Attended to the frescoes round the walls. I notice that all but three of them contain several subjects in one—various *times* treated in same frame.- I then made sketch-plans of the roof and sides of the Chapel. The length is 146ft, the breadth 50: thus, nearly 3 times as broad as long.

[Two sketches of "Main Entrance" and "Plan of the Side Walls"]

The end of the main entrance consists of two sections of the side,- only that the windows are not real but painted, and the door stands below. The opposite end is occupied by Last Judgment, which does not reach to the ground; below it, in one corner, is the door by which visitors enter.

Went round to the Museum, and there ate a lunch of bread and cheese, with a quinto of Velletri, which I carried in my pocket.

The Sala Rotonda. All round are glorious busts. If the eye suddenly falls on that of Antinous, from a little distance, one no longer wonders that so many likenesses of the man were made; a divine profile.- Two Jupiters. that called of Otricoli and the Jupiter Serapis. The former the more majestic; the latter remarkable for a divine placidity. The former has one deep line across his forehead; one might almost attribute to him something of the care of rule, or something of pity for mankind; he might be repeating:

$$"ου \; μὲν \; γάρ \; τί \; που \; εστιν \; οἰζυρώτερον$$

[There is nothing more pitiable than man, Iliad, 1, 447] etc". The Serapis is above care of all kinds: a sublime and passionless reverie holds him; the face is unutterably bland.

Sala delle Muse. Some interesting inscriptions on old Hermoe of philosophers.
Thus:

ΣΟΛΩΝ
ΕΞΗΚΕΣΤΙΔΟΥ
ΑΘΗΝΑΙΟΣ
ΜΗΔΕΝ ΑΤΑΝ

"[Solon, son of Exekestides, Athenian: "Nothing in excess".]"
Of this the head is missing.—Again:

ΒΙΑΣ
ΠΡΗΝΕΥΣ
ΟΙ ΠΛΕΙΣΤΟΙ
ΑΝΔΡΩΝ ΟΙ
ΚΑΚΟΙ

"[Bias of Priene: "The bad are the majority of mankind".]"
A Pittacus, also with head lost stands:

ΠΙΤΤΑΚΟΣ
VPPA
ΜΥΤΙΛΗΝΑΙΟΣ
ΚΑΙΡΟΝ ΤΝΩΘΙ

"[Pittacus, son of Hyrradius, of Mytelene: "Know the opportunity".]"
Another, also headless:

ΚΛΕΟΒΟΥΛΟΣ
ΛΙΝΔΙΟΣ
ΜΕΤΡΟΝ ΑΡΙΣ
ΤΟΝ

"[Cleobulus of Lindus: "Moderation is best".]"

There is a bust representing Epimenides asleep. Why?- Epicurus is remarkable for his large nose. From the Belvedere window—the middle one in the Vestibule of the Belvedere Cortile,- there was a glorious view to-day. Much snow to be seen on the further Apennines. The colour of the hills recalling Naples. Just in front of the window, on the balcony, is a fine old dial, with the names of the winds in Greek and Latin all round it.

Gallerìa delle Statue. The two seated statues of Poseilippos and Menandros. One sees that it was the custom to throw large cushions across the marble Greek chairs. Baedeker says that these two were long worshipped as Saints at San Lorenzo in Panisperna. One chuckles to think of it.

Sala dei Busti. The beautiful sepulchral busts of a Roman and his wife. Her left hand rests on his shoulder, and her right is clasped in his left. The man is ugly, but true-looking; the woman intelligent and gentle.-

Museo Chiaramonti. What a vast number of sepulchral inscriptions remain! I am always tempted to copy some.- "Junia Torquatae V.V.L. Alce Fecit Sibi et Carissimo C. Junio Epepho Contiberto et Viro Optimo." They have such a sincere sound.-

As I walked in the long gallery among the statues and busts, there came by a young priest mumbling out of a missal, or something of the kind; learning by heart. What a place to use for such study!

After dinner, as there was a fine moon, walked along the Forum and looked into the Colosseum.- Back by the Fontana di Treví, which I saw for the first time.-

Letter from Shortridge to-day. Wrote to Roberts.- Reading a lot of Stornelli in my "Canti Popolari Toscani." Also an Epistle of Horace, as I often do.

Thursd. Dec. 13. Resolved to have a day off from the Vatican, and started to go out on the Via Appia. But my old trouble began to affect me, and I only got as far as the Arch of Constantine. Turned back and visited two churches, which I had yet only seen imperfectly. First the Gesù, which is celebrated for its richness of decoration. But there is a sad lot of tinsel about it. I looked at the columns and globe of lapis lazuli in one of the chapels; think it is the first time I have seen that stone.—Then on to Maria Sopra Minerva, the one Gothic church in Rome. On the left of the altar is Michelangelo's Christ, absurdly disfigured by a loin-cloth of bronze and a metal aureole. That the right foot may not be kissed away, it also is enclosed in a bronze shoe, which of course is much worn. The effect of the whole is painful. Near at hand is the tomb of Fra Angelico, with an upright image of him in stone, beneath this inscription: "Hic jacet Vene. Picto Fr. Jo. de Flo. Ordis Pdicato 27. 14LV." Also these lines:
> "Non mihi sit laudi quod eram velut alter Apelles,
> Sed quod lucra tuis omnia, Christe, dabam.
> Altera nam terris opera extant, altera coelo
> Urbs me Joannem Flos tulit Etruriae."

[God send I may not be praised for having been another Apelles But for having given to thine own, O Christ, all that I earned, For there are works which live on earth, and others in heaven. My name is John; the town in which I lived is the Flower of Etruria.]

Thence home to lunch, and read some Horace. Feeling better, and it being much too cold to sit indoors, I started out again and walked over the Ponte Sisto up to the church of San Pietro in Montorio. Very sorry I have not been here before; the panorama is indescribable. It fills one with many thoughts. As I let my eyes wander from the glimpse of the Volscian hills between the Alban hills and the Sabine away to Soracte I thought of all that happened bet. the time when the Romans were fighting with the Volsci, and that when Horace wrote: "Vides ut alta stet nive candidum, Soracte." [You see how Soracte stands there covered with white snow?] A history in itself, and yet how little compared with what has happened since!- Frascati is clear on the side of the Alban hills, and close by there was Tusculum. I must return more than once.- On this site the legend says that St Peter was crucified. I looked at the old dilapidated Via Crucis which winds up one side of the hill to the church.

Walked past the Fontana Paola to the Porta San Pancrazio, and, by Baedeker's advice, followed the road thence, outside the walls, down to the Porta Portese. The lower part of the descent affords a fine view of the Campagna.

When I got to the Capitol there was a beautiful effect of evening light. The afterglow of sunset was mingling with the moon, which stood three quarters, high in the sky. I have never yet seen the Forum in such a delicious aspect.

Dined at the Trattoria del Giardino in the Via delle Botteghe Oscure. The place is rather dirty, but I get a good dinner, with ½ litre of bianco, for 1.30. The people, too, are very decent.

The more I see of the working-class Romans, the more I admire their temper. Scarcely yet have I seen a man or woman in ill humour, and never have I heard violent language,- a remarkable thing in a large city.

Frid. Dec. 14. Still suffering much, and begin to fear I shall have to seek out a doctor.- However, went to the Vatican. The Chapel for an hour, studying the Prophets and Sibyls; then to the Loggia, where my delight increases. By the bye, the painting of these frescoes was done by pupils, Giulio Romano, etc.; but of course the designs are Raphael's. Wonderful how the pupils in those days could be trusted to carry out a master's ideas. I think the "Abraham and Melchisedek" is about the finest of all for colour, perhaps also for grouping; the fine effect of the large jars in front. "Joseph telling his Dream" is exquisite; the grouping splendid.- Back home by 1 o'clock, and passed afternoon in reading Poynter's "Italian Painting".-

Each morning at breakfast I see the *Popolo Romano*. There is a meteorological column, with the rising and setting of sun and moon. Now I have noticed, all through this month, that the sun is stated to rise at 7.35 and set at 4.4.; the moon to rise at something a.m., and set at 3.23pm. A huge joke, morning after morning the same. I wonder whose fault it is?

Woke early this morning and enjoyed wonderful happiness of mind. It occurs to me—is not this partly due to the fact that I spend my days solely in the consideration of beautiful things, wholly undisturbed by base necessities and considerations? In any case the experience is most remarkable.-

Weather continues splendidly bright, but most severely cold every day. This evening bought some Roman new year's cards to send to England when the time comes.—Read Horace Ep. I VII.

Sat. Dec. 15. Had waited anxiously for to-day; it is the only chance I shall have of seeing Raphael's frescoes in the Farnesina, which are open to the public only on the 1st and 15th of each month. Got to the place at 10, and enjoyed myself for an hour and a half. Of course considerable numbers of people there, and many with whose appearance I have become familiar during the last fortnight, from seeing them at this and that gallery. A red-haired man near me remarked to his friend: "All these things are awfully pretty, but I don't think they're good architectural decoration,- do you?"Again I remark the commonplace character of the English people here; it is a very rare thing to hear a remark that encourages one to look at the speaker.

There are two rooms to be visited in the Villa. The first contains the Psyche paintings. The pictures are ranged round the four sides of the ceiling, in pendentives, and the two last occupy the whole of the ceiling itself. Between the pendentives are cupids carrying the symbols of the gods they have subdued. The ground of all is a deep blue, much faded, and between all the pictures are borders of flowers and fruit and leaves, the work of Giovanni da Udine,- also painted stucco-work of which it is easy to believe that it deceived Leonardo da Vinci. The paintings were executed by Giulio Romano and Francesco Penni, after Raphael's designs; they have unfortunately been restored by Maratta. The best preserved is the 2d picture, in which Cupid points out Psyche to the Graces. The colour is beautiful, and Cupid's head a delight. But my favourite of all is one of the last, that where Mercury is leading Psyche up to Olympus; Psyche's face has a heavenly sweetness and humility.- By the bye, why is Mercury, alone of all the figures, shown in flagrant nudity? Must be some reason for this.-

The succeeding room contains, on the wall, Raphael's "Galatea". It has much faded, and on the whole it did not interest me as strongly as the Psyche series. On the ceiling are two pictures by Baldassare Peruzzi (the architect of the Villa), one of Perseus beheading Medusa, and the other Diana drawn by oxen. I think I distinguished the Sienese school in the style of these works. But the most interesting, to me, of the decorations, after "Galatea", was a head in black and white in one of the lunettes,- just drawn on the rough plaster, which is left untouched,- said to be by Michael Angelo, but doubtful. A fine bit of work.-

Home to lunch. No sunshine to-day, and bitterly cold. Ought to have mentioned that, on the way to the Farnesina, I looked in S. Maria della Pace, and saw Raphael's Sibyls. The sacristan draws back a curtain to show you them, and under such circumstances I never can examine a work to any purpose.

In afternoon walked out to the Castro Pretorio. By following the Via Sistina and Via delle Quattro Fontane, on to the Railway Station, one crosses, first the Quirinal, then the Viminal, then goes on to the Esquiline,- the ups and downs being quite distinguishable. From the Pretorio, which to-day also is occupied with barracks, walked round by the Via Quattro Settembre, into the Via Nazionale. At the foot of the latter street is a piece of the old wall, enclosed in railings in the middle of the street. Near at hand I bought some socks in a large English shop called "Old England", a useful place. Then bought at a bookseller's Melani's "Pittura Italiana" (Pts 2 and 3) 4 lire—which seems a capital little handbook. Home by the Sistina, where I was tempted into a shop to buy photographs. Got some views of Rome, some of Raphael's frescoes, and some better photos from the Sistine Chapel,- altogether 7.50.- Dined in the Botteghe Oscure, and coming home bought four coloured photos of Forum etc. for presents for people at home.-

Sund. Dec. 16. Spent the morning in the Capitoline Museum, looking again at my favourites. In the Hall of the Philosophers: the magnificent bust of Cicero, larger than all the others. The two busts of Julian the Apostate; a curiously ignoble profile, not so bad in full face; the beard knotted in a singular way under the chin,- the beard which Gibbon speaks of as "populous". Again noticed the remarkable resemblance between the Euripides and Tennyson.

The Venus. It is the Venus of Cnidus, and by Praxiteles. The Venus de' Medici has the same attitude, but different accessories. This one has at her side a vase, on which is thrown fringed drapery; it reaches exactly as high as her lower hand.

Went thence to the Palatine, and saw it much more thoroughly than before. Distinguished the Flavian, Tiberian and Caligulan palaces; that of Augustus is covered by the Villa Mills. It makes one wretched to see the multitudinous fragments of beautiful marble,- the scraps of coloured marble pavement, etc. Lingered in the vast atrium of the Flavian Palace, and in the Imperial Basilica, beside it; in the latter, the tribune where the emperor sat is clearly distinguished, and even a bit of beautiful marble trellis-work remains in front of it. How men have trembled in front of this bar! And I stand here and smile sadly.-

Enjoyed the view from the Belvedere. The Circus Maximus is occupied with huge gas-works. Then round to the Paedagogium, and looked at the Graffiti. Then the fine bit of tufa wall, said to belong to the Roma Quadrata, and the cave said to be the Lupercal.-

A cold and sunless day again. A good deal of rain. After dinner in the evening, strolled back along the Via Nazionale, and was of course tempted into a confectioner's shop. Home, eating cakes, etc, by way of the Quattro Fontane, and passed a Cucina I mean to try to-morrow. The moon nearly full, but clouded.- Read at Melani.

Mond. Dec. 17. A fine change in the weather; like summer again, except for frost in morning. Set off early, and walked to San Paolo fuori le Mura. The interior is magnificent—a modern magnificence of course; but the white and painted outside reminds one of a very large mechanics' institute, or something of the kind. The campanile does not strike me as noteworthy.

Thence took the Via delle Sètte Chiese,- the pilgrim's road,- and through a great deal of mud came out at the church of San Sebastiano. From there a magnificent walk to the VIth stone (modern) on the Via Appia. Just past the tomb of Caecil. Metella is an osteria called "Ristorante della Passegiata Archeologica"; an amusing name. Passed many yokes of oxen, and admired them, as always. I see that a ring is put through their nose, and a single rope attached to this goes up between the horns and serves for a rein. The yoke is very heavy and ancient-looking. Strange to hear the sound of a train going across the Campagna, where the intense stillness is so remarkable; the voices of birds and nibbling of sheep are almost all one hears generally. Got my first good view of the aqueducts,- the long, broken Aqua Claudia. The wonderful light on the hills; beyond the Sabine and Alban, gleaming snowy peaks of the Apennines. From this distance a good view of Rome; one sees how it just rises out of the surrounding plain; it shines, very white. What a delightful view of the city there must have been from Tusculum, which was up by Frascati!

I sat down and ate my bread and cheese on someone's tomb,- ruined, forgotten. Whose may it have been? The busts in relief on a few of the tombs are interesting; portraits looking out at you after these centuries. The general attitude is for one hand to be resting on the bosom of the toga.-

Hard to believe that the rude traces of paving left here and there date from the best times. Rugged blocks, like the Via Sacra. Yet I suppose a good pavement would have worn into this. Traces of wheels. The narrowness of the road impresses one.

An inscription I copied: on left hand of road, just after (or before) the huge skeleton pyramid with mushroom base. The second word in 3d line I can't understand, though I copy the letters exactly. Notice archaic spelling:

"Hoc est factum monumentum
Maarco Caecilio.
Hospes gratum est quom apud
Meas restitistei (?) seedes
Bene rem geras et valeas
Dormias sine qura."

[Gissing translated as follows in a letter to his sister Margaret: This monument is erected to Marcus Caecilius. Stranger, I am grateful when you sit down by my resting-place. May you prosper in business and in health, and may your sleep be without care!]

In evening to see the Forum and Colosseum by moonlight.

Tuesd. Dec. 18. Posted letters to Madge and Nelly, with some Christmas cards.- Letter from Mlle Le Breton, in which she says she has lately seen Mr and Mrs Henry Reeve (edr, I understand, of the *Ed[inburgh] Review,* is it so?[45]) who declare themselves great admirers of my novels. The French transln of "Demos" still delayed; is to be put to press immediately after Jan. lst.-

In morning to the Vatican, where I gave attention only to the Gallery of Paintings. Looked long at the Transfiguration, which is in a room with the Madonna del Foligno and the St Jerome of Domenichino, and those three alone. In the Transfig. the lower group is pyramidal. On the left, two arms pointing upwards make a continuous line, and on the right a converging line is made by another upward arm; that of the boy tends also in same direction. This effect of course directs attention to the scene above. Within the lower group, attention is strongly turned towards the boy; faces directed towards him, and some hands pointing. Goethe notes that the open book signifies that the disciples have been looking in vain for remedies; the scene above indicates the only help left.- The eyes of the boy are not easily seen aright. Looking closely, one finds that they do not regard the ascending figure, as at first they seem to, but are wrenched in different directions; the left eye really looks downwards.- Fine expression of appealing misery on the face of the father.

Came home to lunch, then walked out to the Ponte Molle, and thence by the fields to the site of Antemnae. Again a wonderful day, quite hot. Recognized that wonderful effect of light, of which Goethe speaks. The scene itself—that is, the foreground—is miserable enough. From the Porta del Popolo to the Ponte Molle mostly a squalid street; the immediate vicinity of Italian towns seems to be always squalid. The Tiber flows through a district which is obviously subject to inundations; the waste tracts on each side, up to the bases of the hills, look withered and miserable, as if recently deluged and left dry. Everything enhances the wretched effect. On the N. side of the river is a great factory of some kind, with a high ugly chimney; on the hither side some miserable huts. Thick mud forms the banks. At the foot of the hill on which stood Antemnae,- it is in the angle between Tiber and Anio (Teverone)—the ground is occupied by a place for musketry practice. The only relief to the eye is in looking far away to the Sabine Hills, with the peak of Monte Gennaro said to be Lucretilis—wonderful in sunlight.

At the junction of Tiber and Anio gathered some heads of reeds which I mean to take home for them at Agbrigg. Back by train from Ponte Molle,- the Pons Milvius. Dinner at a new Cucina in the Via Sistina, on the right hand just before ascent of Quirinal, a much cleaner and pleasanter place than that in the Botteghe Oscure. After dinner yielded to temptation and bought pastry.-

The Roman newspapers are miserable rags. I find myself falling back on the *Corriere di Napoli,* which really has a lot of interesting matter, and is well conducted. It seems to sell greatly in Rome.

Bought Dante's "Vita Nuova", and a couple of vols. of the Biblioteca Universale.-

Wed. Dec. 19. To-day I have been at Veii. I had thought it too far for a walk, but managed it, with a good deal of weariness at the end. Took the tram to Ponte Molle, and thence tramped up into the Campagna by the Via Cassia, which is the left-hand road, that on right being Via Flaminia. It has modern milestones, made in imitation of the old Roman. Here and there, on either side of it, one sees the strata of tufa etc, where a cutting has been made. From the 6th milestone, the road is paved like the streets of Rome, with small diamonds of lava, bordered with diamonds of larger size; on either side is a broad walk unpaved. I wonder how far the paving extends; it seems a remarkable work.- The views along the walk are magnificent. The best of all is at a wide opening on the East side, about 200 yds after the 7th milestone; a vast extent of barren plain, spreading from a little valley in the foreground. In the farthest distance stands Soracte; to the right of it are the Sabine hills. The colour of the Campagna at this season is that of dead grass, here and there a little greener or browner. Rarely a pine-tree, and very few other trees,- save in the clefts and valleys which intersect all the country. The shapes of the hills are very softly rounded, often with strange folds and carvings. As I returned the sun was hidden; the sky a limpid blue-grey; and under this light the effect of desolation was marvellous.

On the road I passed numbers of the old-fashioned vetture,- the very same that were used for travelling before railway. Of course along the road there is still no rail communication. They carry luggage on the top and behind and invariably look a century old,- weather-beaten, patched, dirty, drawn by poor horses, generally with bells.

Not far after La Storta,—which used to be the last relay before Rome—the road parts; left hand to Bracciano, right to Viterbo. I followed the latter, and, at a short distance, by the first road off to the right was led to

Isola Farnese. This is supposed to have been the Arx of Veii. In middle ages was a stronghold. Doubtless called Isola because a high crag surrounded by ravines. Very picturesque, but in summer desolated by malaria; population 100. I spoke to the priest, who was walking up and down the street; the shabbiest priest I have yet seen, and evidently quite uneducated. He found a guide for me to the ruins, which are on the property of a farmer, who keeps a key to the Painted Tomb,- called here "La Grotta". A lad set out with me, and we had a long difficult walk; impossible to find the way alone; wild tracks over brushwood and moor and hill. Saw the Ponte Sodo, the stream believed to be the Cremera, the Columbarium, and the Tomb. The last very interesting. The guide lit a candle, which was insufficient, but I just made out the paintings, on the walls, and the fine great Etruscan vases, which have been left just as when the tomb was found. On the tufa walls the chisel marks are distinct. Brought away a bit of tufa from inside.

On the way there passed through a field full of magnificent long-horned cattle. Madge would have been slightly alarmed.

Paid the guide 2 lire (he had asked 2.50, but at once agreed to my reduction,- how different from Naples!) and had a glass of white wine in the osteria at Isola,- a clean place, with a wood fire burning on the huge hearth. Walked back to the main road, and noticed how the approach to Isola was a deep cutting in the tufa,- a strong position for defence. Passed a man tending cattle in the road; his legs were wrapped with rough goat-skins. Later I saw another shepherd with sheep-skins on his legs; I suppose the damp renders this necessary.

I find in Murray['s Guide Book] that during late years nearly all the ruins of Veii have been destroyed; there used to be traces of walls and gates, etc.,- now nothing but what I have mentioned. Still, I noticed that all over the fields lay scraps of pottery and brick and cut stone; I suppose they must all be remains of one period or another.

Got back to Ponte Molle at 5 o'clock—a dull evening.- Read at Melani's Hist[ory] of Nat[ional] Painting.

Thursd. Dec. 20. A day of cloud and rain.- Postcard from Nelly.- Made a parcel of a lot of books I don't need, and dispatched them to Agbrigg, through some agents here. This will lighten my luggage.- Went to Station to inquire about trains for Florence. Most of the day read at Melani.- Dinner at a Cucina Toscana, at top of the Via Nazionale; had excellent dish of haricot beans in oil.- Noticed a custom of advertising to friends by means of placard on the walls the death of private individuals. A black-bordered bill, headed with cross, stated, for instance, that a certain man, described as "uomo onesto e laborioso", died yesterday, the 19th, "nei conforti della Santa Religione", and will to-day, 20th, be buried; friends invited to attend.-

A curious relic of Latin phrase struck me in the Corso. A man stood at a shop-door, shouting: "Vendita *all' asta pubblica*! Ingresso libero!"

Every day I hear someone or other in the house here calling out the name of a certain "Amalia!" I wonder who this Amalia may be, who is in such constant request?

103

Frid. Dec. 21. Note from Walter Grahame, in which he tells me that Mrs [Margaret L.] Woods has printed a vol. of poems for private circulation [*Lyrics and Ballads*], and that her sister, Miss Bradley, has a copy for me.- Also short letter from Roberts, from Birmingham, in which, as usual, he has strange adventures to announce. Speaks of writing a book on Bohemian life in London, to be called "In Clay and Colour". [Published as *In Low Relief: A Bohemian Transcript,* 2 vols., 1890.]

This morning a second visit to the Borghese Gallery, taking [Edward] Poynter's little "Ital. Painting" with me, and seriously studying the first three rooms. Room I is mostly the Milanese school, influence of Lionardo. Sodoma's "Leda" has the Lionardo face precisely; I believe it is all but exactly the head of that strange dark picture in the Louvre, called I forget what; also that of the St Anne.- Francia's pictures. His female faces are long, and gently melancholy.

Room II. Contains 14 Garofalos; also several Giulio Romanos. Influence of Raphael predominates. Here too is Raphael's "Entombment", a picture in his second, or Florentine manner.- Two pretty fountains in this room, for drinking; the water flows out of a metal spout in such a way as to form a perfect cone, from the source down into the basin.

Room III. Again 6 Garofalos,- pictures quite uninteresting to me. Take no.52, a Flagellation; the colour is more than poor, and Christ's head, meant I suppose to express perfect resignation, expresses nothing at all; it is that of a man in rather melancholy thought about trifles.- Here is *Correggio's "Danae",* one of the celebrated pictures that give me very little pleasure. The colour is cold,- perhaps has faded. Danae's face is insipid, to me even ugly, and her attitude disagreeable. A winged Love draws away the sheet that covers her, (her figure good) and from above descends a lateral golden cloud. The two little cupids sharpening an arrow are delightful—the best of the picture.- In the room are 6 pictures said to be Andrea del Sarto's.-

Remember the German man and wife, of rather more than middle age, whom I have so frequently met of late. They are evidently doing Rome with much zeal. The husband constantly exclaims "Herrlich!" [splendid!] and so on; the wife seems to be the more intelligent. To-day I heard her exclaim: "Das muss ein Carlo Dolci sein!" [It must be a Carlo Dolci!]—and, on referring to the catalogue, she cried: "Wahrhaftig!" [Quite true!] Her delight at identifying the picture was extreme.-

In afternoon to the Vatican Museum, eating bread and salame as I walked along. Lounged with delight in my favourite Sala Rotonda. Three heads of women I studied: *Julia Domna,* the wife of Septimius Severus; *Plotina,* the wife of Trajan; and *Faustina,* the wife of Antoninus Pius. All fine busts, and very different.- Julia Domna is the most pleasing. A notably Patrician face; about the fine lips, something like a touch of idle scorn and pride—not ill-natured, of rather slow understanding, one would say. A woman to humour and to be friends with. Would take her dignity as a matter of course,- but might easily fall below it.- Plotina is anything but beautiful, and scarcely Patrician; one sees that the bust is idealized, for all that. Very heavy features, high cheek-bones, big mouth and chin. A dull homely woman, but conscientious; a touch of anxiety on her forehead. Looks like a careful housewife, and one to be trusted in all things.- Faustina, an intensely aristocratic type of beauty. The good nature of Julia Domna is lacking here; a cold pride on her lips and forehead. Splendid coronet of woven hair. A woman to be afraid of, unsubduable. Leaving the Museum, turned into St Peter's and was in time to hear Vespers sung in the Choir-chapel, the first on the left. Good voices.

To dinner in the Botteghe Oscure again, which is cheaper than all the other places.- All day heavy rain, and warmer than of late. Streets in a frightful state of mud. In the night a thunderstorm.

Sat. Dec.22. Printed form from Bertz, announcing his election as Secretary of the Deutscher Schrifsteller-Verband [The German Society of Authors].- My old evil troubling me to-day; wanted to go to the Borghese Casino, but did not feel equal to it. Spent most of the day at home. In morning just looked in at S. Maria del Popolo, and glanced at Pintoricchio's frescoes. But I get little profit from churches. The light is always bad—often no light at all; and then I am not at my ease, can't sit down and gaze and think like in a gallery; feel I must be moving on.- Afternoon to the Forum and back.- After dinner, walked through Trajan's Forum. That tremendous fragment of granite column, which lies on the road, by the side of the enclosure; it is at least 4 feet in diameter and some 15 feet long—or longer. I suppose, from the numerous fragments in the enclosure, that the forum was enclosed with such pillars.- Note from Murray that the Column is exactly the height of the neck of land joining Capitol and Quirinal, which was cut away when this Forum was made as a link with the new quater in the Campus Martius.- Cloudy day, but fine on the whole. Read some Epistles of Horace.

At 9.30 a little walk about the streets—dull as usual. Moon rising in a misty sky. Rather fine effect at Ripetta, with moon and other lights. The river rushing loudly, swollen by recent rains. Several small ships moored here have converted themselves into wine-shops, with a signboard up on the mast, announcing Sicilian wines, and that there is "ingresso libero" [free entrance]. I suppose this is usual.

Sund. Dec. 23. Still raining, with intermittent sunshine. Noticed a strange announcement on the walls, issued by the Sindaco of Rome. It referred to the fact that considerable numbers of new buildings remain in a state of suspended work, with scaffolding etc. all round them; this is pointed out as a danger and inconvenience to the public, and it is ordered that by a certain day all such scaffolding etc. shall be removed. This must be rather significant of financial affairs here.

In morning to the Palazzo de' Conservatori.- In the *Protomoteca:* the fine features of Marcantonio Raimondi; a little like Albrecht Dürer.- Characterless, poor face of Domenichino.- The attenuated little head of Leopardi is a shock.- The *Gallery:* The Cumaean Sibyl by Domenichino (repetition of that in the Borghese,) and the Persic Sibyl by Guercino; how durst these men take such subjects? The latter is simply a pensive lady engaged in letter-writing. The former always reminds me of somebody by Sir Joshua [Reynolds].- The series of Apollo and the Muses, by the Umbrian La Spagna. Pure Perugino. Here too, as in Raphael's Parnassus, Apollo plays on a fiddle.

To Vespers at Trinità de' Monti, and only wish I had been before. Exquisite singing by the nuns; a solo and a duet that enraptured me. The church is attached to the Convent of the Sacré-Coeur,- establishment for education of girls. In one of the chapels is Daniele da Volterra's masterpiece, "The Descent", but of this I couldn't get a sight.

Read some Horace, then for a walk round by Via Nazionale. The confectioners' shops a terrible temptation,- but resisted. The windows were full of "Panettone di Milano", round cakes, some of them about a foot in diameter, or more. It is easy to understand why the Italians are not more intellectual. The bodily temptations are too strong. The confectioner's altogether outrivals the bookseller's.- Feeling very lonely to-day.

A curious habit the cocks have of crowing between 10 and 11 at night. I notice it nightly. Makes one think, just now, of Shakspere's "Tis said that ever gainst that season comes" etc. [*Hamlet,* I, i, 158. "Some say that. . ."]

Mond. Dec. 24. The *Corriere di Napoli* to-day begins an enthusiastic article on Gladstone, who is staying at Posillipo, with the words "Sir Guglièlmo Gladstone".-

A rainy morning. Not feeling very well. Went to St Peter's, and found it resounding with carpenters, who, it seems, are putting up tribunes etc. for the great function of next sunday, when the Pope will appear. It will be just a day too late for me. Copied the inscription on the tomb of the Stuarts which is on the left hand near the entrance; a handsome piece of sculpture by Canova, with three portrait-busts at the head.

"Jacobo III
Jacobi II Magnae Brit. Regis filio
Karolo Edoardo
Et Henrico decano patrum Cardinalium
Jacobi III filiis
Regiae Stirpis Stuardiae postremis
Anno MDCCCXIX
Beati Mortui
Qui in Domino Moriuntur."

"[To James III, son of James II, King of Great Britain. To Charles Edward and Henry, dean of the Sacred College, sons of James III. The last scions of the Stuart Kings. In the year 1819. Blessed are the dead who die in the Lord.]"
I was astonished to learn from Baedeker that the mosaic copy of the "Transfiguration" is four times the size of the original. In St Peter's one loses all idea of size.

Proved an exquisite afternoon, clouded, but with soft rays of sunlight, and warm. Climbed some stairs on the S.E. end of the Colosseum, and sat there looking over the arch of Constantine, whilst soldiers were drilling on the ground just below me. The Colosseum is a ruin, but soldiers and slaughter still thrive.

Went down into the *Mamertine Prisons,-* a terrible place. Stairs have been made down into the lower hole, to which originally only the round hole in the upper floor led. The upper prison made into an oratory; in that below is a spring, shown as having miraculously arisen when Peter and Paul were here.- Thought of Jugurtha, of the Catilinarian conspirators, etc.

Thence to San Giovanni in Laterano, and examined the church, which pleased me. The façade is beautiful, and the view from it one of the most charming I know in Rome. Better still from the steps which go up to the so-called Triclinium Leo III, just opposite. In front the Sabine and Alban Hills, with just a tip of the Volscian between. In the foreground the fine arcaded city wall, with the gate of San Giovanni, and the older Roman gate hidden by trees. Beyond the walls, the long stretch of the Aqua Claudia.- The faint sunlight gave a singular white gleam to the top of the Sabine Hills; I thought at first there was snow on them.

In the church heard a choral service—Vespers—at 3 o'clock. It was held in the Cappella del Coro; and a procession of priests went thence, first to the Altar of the Sacrament, then to the high altar, performing many genuflections etc. at each. Some good singing, but the whole affair impressed me as paltry. A swarm of curious foreigners pressing about the entrance to the chapel, and hemming in the procession; the thing became a mere exhibition. No worshipping congregation. The offices of the Rom. Cath. Church seem to be performed for the entertainment of the clerics alone; I suppose it all rests on the vicarious theory. But the result is an air of sham and foolishness. Walked across, by the Via Merulana, to Santa Maria Maggiore, and thence all the way down the Esquiline, by the Via Urbana, Via Baccina, and Via Bonella, to the Forum. This part of Rome thickly populated with working class; the streets to-day one continuous market; reminded me of Naples a little. A good deal of merriment going on, and, as always in Rome, much good temper. In the Piazza di Spagna a lot of holly with berries is for sale, but I fancy this is mostly for the forestieri.

Saw for the first time the three remaining columns of the Temple of Mars Ultor, which stood in the Forum of Augustus. It makes one's heart sink to look at these remnants of glorious buildings, wedged into mean streets.

Tuesd. Dec. 25. Christmas Day. Bright sunshine the first thing, but soon darkened, and at 10 o'clock a severe thunderstorm. I was then in St Peter's, where I remained from 9.30 to 12, hearing service after service in the Cappella del Coro. Masses were going on in nearly all the chapels, and I suppose the business is unbroken all to-day and perhaps all last night. Again the crowd of curious foreigners, but also great numbers of Italians, with much kissing of Peter's toe. A pontifical mass at 11. The singing was spoiled for me by the sight of a male soprano,- a disgusting spectacle. And then the fact of service being held in a chapel which is only a fragment of the church takes away from the impressiveness. It seems that there is no organ in the central part of St Peter's. Again a strange effect produced by listening for a long time to these resonant voices chanting their psalms etc., and watching the richly clad priests go about their wonderful ritual. At one moment contempt for them all, at another reverence, seeing that they represent a system which was once so powerful, and embodies so much human intellect. By the bye, it must be a great undertaking to learn the routine of these offices.

Walked much about the church.- Surely the ugliest tomb ever designed is that of Alexander VII, by Bernini, in the left aisle—where the bronze skeleton, holding a timeglass, pokes itself up beneath a mass of marble drapery.

In going out, noticed the all but incredible fact that grass grows everywhere on the paving of the approach to the church. This would seem impossible. Is a proof of the vast size of the façade.

Thunder had cleared the air, and the day had become like summer,- very sunny and warm. Underfoot terrible mud. Modern Rome seems to me more and more ugly. To live in it is like occupying a house which is being reconstructed. Walked up to San Pietro in Montorio, and there ate bread and salame. Distance very misty.

Walked across to S. Maria Maggiore, again up the Esquiline. This is certainly the one picturesque part of inhabited Rome. The glimpse of the temple of Mars Ultor from the middle of the Via Baccina is very fine indeed; it almost looks like a temple now existing, and no ruin.- S. Maria was lighted up with vast number of candles, and a fine choral vesper-service went on from 3 to 4.30,-this time the real choir of the church being used. But again the music was spoiled for me by those male sopranos.

In the Borghese Chapel (a magnificent place) met the Missouri man, Orf, in his dress of ecclesiastical student. We remained together all the time. He told me that the Roman lower classes invariably insult him and his companions in the street and behave in the same way to most clerics; it is the young generation only that behaves thus. Government officials also disrespectful, he says. In return, the students never salute the king or prince when his carriage passes.- I asked him about the tonsure. It is received 3 years before priesthood: the first of the minor orders. A bishop gives it, by cutting off little locks in the presumed form of a cross.- One curious observance I saw in operation. In each confessional-box, the priest sat with a long rod, and with this he tapped the heads of such as knelt before him for the purpose. Symbolical of humiliation, I suppose?-

All day the vessel containing the Culla (bits of wood of the Manger) had been exposed on the high altar; a large gold casket, with crystal sides and surmounted with figure of child. At five o'clock a great procession was formed, and this was carried down the nave, with singing. Great crowd of people, but no kneeling or other sign of reverence; mere curiosity.

Quitted Orf, and went to dine at the Fagiano in Piazza Colonna. Bad dinner. At home found letter from Bertz. Brought home some pastry,- eheu! Out at 9.30 to have a glass of vino caldo. Newsboys shouting "La Riforma! Unico giornale di stasera!" [*The Reform*! The only paper this evening!] A wet, miserable night; the streets wretched.

108

I have noticed much lately the gross cruelty with which fowls for the market are treated here. Every day I see them being carried about the streets by the legs, heads hanging down; and they are often packed so closely together in crates that they can scarcely flutter a feather. Horses don't seem to be much ill-used. There is little or none of the "Ah-h-h!" which used to be so incessant in Naples. The oddly matched teams (donkey, horses, mules, oxen) are never seen in Rome.-

I should have noted about Orf, that he attends classes at the College of the Propaganda, where the lectures *are in Latin*. A great variety of nationalities there: Arabs, Abyssinians, negroes, etc. I should like to know for certain what kind of Latin such men speak.- Letter from Bertz.

Wed. Dec. 26. The *Corriere* contains reports of numerous injuries to people at Naples by the explosion of dynamite bombs,- a very common amusement there just now. No doubt that was what caused the terrific explosions in the street below my lodgings, which used to alarm me at night.-

In the morning to S. Maria della Vittoria, but office was going on, and I could not see Bernini's sculpture, of which, I hear, Taine speaks with much praise. In the Via di Venti Settembre saw—or half saw—the king, who was driving a drag, three other men with him. I hear he often drives himself.- A miserable day; not a gleam of sunshine, and thick mud everywhere.-

Then to the Vatican Museum, where I lingered long in the Sala Rotonda and Sala delle Muse. Tried hard to grasp the two busts—Tragedy and Comedy—which are on each side of the passage from former to latter room. There is by no means the marked difference bet. their faces that one unreflectingly expects. Melpomene is crowned with ivy and vine; Thalia has plain hair, filletted low behind, and with two curious bands over the forehead. Both are in stern abstraction, and I have not yet been able to express—though trying hard—the difference between their expressions.- In the Sala delle Muse, the same two are to me more impressive. In fact all the Muses here are finely individualized, and in exquisite attitudes. Thalia is crowned with ivy, Melpomene with vine. The face of the latter is stamped with silent pain. Thalia,- a sweet and noble face—shows a weary sadness, with deep, far-looking eyes.- Calliope, who leans forward in eagerness, has a joyously inspired face.- I note that Euterpe is always represented with a little sort of flute in her hand, or rather a pipe. Terpsichore and Erato hold lyres of different shapes. Polyhymnia wraps herself in her robe,- in splendid inspiration.

The Antinous of the Rotonda (divine in profile, not so good in ¾ face,) has his hair in ringlets all round the back of his head.

It was bitterly cold, and I could not stay as long as I wished.- Came home and found letter from Nelly enclosing cheque for £10; also line from mother, and a short letter from man called Bradleigh Swan, of Farnham, lauding "A Life's Morning".- Went into the Via dei Condotti and bought some more photographs—very fine ones.- Afterwards walked round to Trajan's Forum. Whilst I leaned over the parapet, an old decent woman came and threw down a paper of food-scraps, whereupon five remarkably fine cats ran forward out of holes and corners, and pawed the food over. But they were not hungry, and the woman, laughing in a very good-hearted way, turned to me and said "Sono tutto grassi!" Then she told me that great numbers of cats were always found in this Forum, and the people fed them.- Thence round by Forum Romanum to the church of Ara Coeli, where a great crowd of poor class people was coming out. I was just too late to be able to examine the church, for darkness had come on; but a strange impressive thing happened. Two priests came through a cluster of people in front of a chapel in left aisle, and opened sliding doors, which seem to be fitted in a wall of natural rock. There was exposed what I take to be the Presepe scene, but only one priest held a candle and I could see little. However, one of the two took up from the darkness a quaint image of the Bambino, doubtless the sacred image, and held it on high. The people knelt, as did also the second priest. Then they carried off the image to some other part of the church. It was a striking little procedure, in the gloom. Several altars lighted with candles.- On the stairs, a good deal of toy-selling, with little Bambino images.- Dinner at Botteghe Oscure.- Read two Epistles of Horace.-

Thursd. Dec. 27. Suffered so much last night from my old complaint that this morning I got up very late. It rained hard all night and until 11 to-day, then began to be dullishly fine.- Read until 2 o'clock, then went to Ara Coeli, where I saw remarkable things. The vision of last evening explained itself. The 2d chapel on the left is fitted up with a scenical representation of the adoration of the shepherds and the Magi. For framework there is a proscenium representing rock. The scene itself is most elaborate. Figures stand in various attitudes around the Madonna and child, and also there are sheep etc., made of I know not what. Above are clouds and angels, and at the top, receding, the Padre Eterno in a glory; all is lighted artistically from behind, and produces an excellent theatrical effect. The Bambino is a carved piece of wood, tapering to the feet, and richly set with jewels and ornaments.

Opposite this chapel, against the first pillar at the right of the nave, is raised a little carpet-covered platform, and on this the most wonderful recitations were delivered by children, mostly of from 6 to 10 years old. Nearly all girls; the few boys were comparative bunglers. They seemed to be the children of contadini and poor townspeople, and were much dressed for the occasion, unfortunately in the modern fashions. A few showed shyness and could not be persuaded to recite, but for the most part there was astonishing self-confidence. They began and ended with a bow, and knelt when repeating a prayer. Some children repeated their piece several times, enjoying it. The best of all I heard was a sort of little miracle-play acted by two raggazine. They represented shepherds; one leaned against the pillar and pretended to be asleep; the other expressed astonishment at sight of star and angels, and soon awoke her companion; then, after long speeches, they went together to find the "bambinello". The verses were in short lines of 4 trochees, $-\cup|-\cup|-\cup|-\cup|$ and "bambinello" often ended the line. The way in which the children recited and acted was most remarkable. I wonder who taught them. The mere act of memory was noteworthy, and they had an excellent articulation.- All around stood a great crowd of mostly contadini, the women with fazzoletti [kerchiefs] on their heads; children swarming, and making considerable noise.- At 3 o'clock vespers with music began in the church, but that made no difference to the recitation. I came away at 4. On the steps a great fair going on, and swarms of people.- It struck me as symbolical that this, the church of the poor, should have to be reached by climbing 124 steps.

The church itself is very interesting. The columns on each side of the nave are ancient and come from all sorts of different places, so that they are all unlike each other, and even on pedestals of different heights. Much interesting old carving on the tombs of the pavement, which is thus made very rugged to walk on.- Between the 3d and 4th chapels of left aisle hang a great number of very rude little oil paintings—ex-votos—representing various escapes from risk of death. Most of them are incidents of being run over by vehicles; the drawing of horses and men very comical; also there are children falling out of windows, and a few other calamities. In each case, a top corner of the picture shows saints or madonna watching over the individual; and at the foot of each are inscribed the letters "P.G.R." The meaning of these?- (*Per Grazia Ricevuta,* I find from an inscript, at Florence).

Then to the Forum and Colosseum, where I enjoyed a delicious sunset. Home for a little reading, then to hear some music at the Caffè Venezia. Ah, if only a few organs played about the streets of Rome, what a different place it would be!

"Sir Gladstone" is several times repeated in to-day's *Corriere.*- The paper has long articles on the death of the statesman Mancini,- to me unknown. A great advocate, it seems, and the originator of abolition of death penalty in Italy.[46]

Frid. Dec. 28. A fine day, clouded in afternoon, but of summer warmth. Indeed the cold seems to have gone for the present.- In morning to St Peter's, and ascended the Cupola, going right up into the ball—where I didn't feel at all comfortable. Of course glorious view, though misty. Saw the full extent of Vatican and its gardens. Much snow on Apennines.- Then a farewell hour in the Sistine Chapel, where there were great numbers of people. Again admired the exquisite beauty of those figures between the pictures of the ceiling. Let no man say that Michelangelo is always rugged!

Thence to Mackay, Hooker and Co., bankers in the Piazza di Spagna, and changed Nelly's cheque, getting 253 lire for the £10.-

Had lunch and walked on to the Lateran Museum, which I had always postponed. Purposely confined myself to the Museo Profano.- Room II. The carved capitals, exquisite ornamental friezes, and detail in general, from Trajan's Forum, complete the idea of magnificence one derives from the larger ruins. What superb work, every inch of it!—Room V. On entering this from the corridor, one has at once a fine view of the statue of Sophocles, away at the end of a perspective.- Noticed a beautiful little cistus, carved with ivy leaves. The inscription: "L. Cecilius Isio fecit se vivo sibi arca hederacia, in quo (*sic*) se poni jubet.V.A.L." Don't quite understand the grammar, and the three letters are dark to me.- By the bye, what is the little plate that goddesses (e.g. Juno Barberini, Vatican) and sometimes Empresses, hold out in their hand?- Room IX. The sublime calm on Sophocles' face. Eyes of clear and not sad vision.- Room X. Noticed the head of a woman, from a tomb; intellectual, with closed lips; evidently a striking likeness. Curiously like Kitty Lushington [his former pupil]. Ah, who was she? We know just how she looked.- The charm of a fine relievo in chiaroscuro. Only appreciable when a good light comes from one side of it.-

How often I have been irritated by the universal fig-leaves at Rome! They are stuck even on small figures in bas-reliefs, and even occasionally on women.-

Walked round to the steps of the Triclinium Leonis III, and thence made a poor little sketch of the Porta San Giovanni and the shapes of the Alban Hills beyond. See next page.- Then to the Colosseum. Copied an inscription on a stone near the main entrance: "Decius Marius Venantius Basilius Ū.C̄. et Īnl Prāef Ūrb [Vir Clarissimus et Inlustris Praefectus Urbis] Patricius Consul Ordinarius Arenam et Podium quae abominandi terrae motus ruina prostravit sumtu proprio restituit." "[The most eminent and illustrious Decius Marius Venantius Basilius, Prefect of Rome, Patrician, ordinary Consul, restored at his own expense the arena and the podium which an abominable earthquake had destroyed.]". The date of this? Can't read the titles. And why "abominandi"?

Finished the afternoon at Ara Coeli, where again children were reciting. The most curious to-day was a long sermon (of 20m., I believe,) delivered by a girl of about 12,- hard-voiced and self-concious child. It was a justification of religion against modern disbelief, and, doubtless, taught her by the Frati,- of course in prose. I followed it pretty well, and some phrases remained with me. One period began: "O congiurati filosofanti!" She went through all the miracles that evidenced Christianity.- "E tace Dio? Dio non tace, favella!".- At the end she knelt down and addressed a prayer to the stage opposite: "Bambinello Santissimo, che tua benedizione scenda su tutti, e principalmente su miei genitori e parenti!" [O philosophizing conspirators! Is God silent? God is not silent, he speaks . . . Most Sacred Infant, may your blessing descend upon every one and particularly upon my parents and relatives] (Most of the reciters end with prayer for their parents.) The sermon was followed by loud "Brava"s from the crowd.

Dinner in the Botteghe Oscure. In giving the lad who waits a larger tip than usual, I told him I was going away. "Ah!" he exclaimed, looking towards the good-natured woman of the shop, who was in the next room, "bisogna chiamare Regina." And he called "Regina!", by which I suppose she is his sister. She shook me warmly by the hand, and asked when I should come back. We bade each other good-bye.

Sat. Dec. 29. In the morning, packed. A fine summer day, very warm. Took the 1.30 for Florence, a treno diretto, and therefore with prices increased

10%. An enjoyable journey whilst daylight lasted. The most noteworthy thing in the first part was the view of St Peter's. Just after crossing the Anio, you see it, far away, between the hill of Antemnae and Monte Mario,- a great, wonderful dome, solitary, with no trace else of the city. It must be very impressive for those who come to Rome by this route. It remained visible, high on the horizon, for five minutes. Then grand views of Soracte, which from this side stands out far more prominently; one understands why Horace, with his Sabine experiences, calls attention to it. The railway passes almost by the foot of the mountain; its jagged ascent was wonderful.

The russet Campagna showed well under a sky heavily clouded yet brilliantly sunny; it needs the cloud-shadows moving over it. The large herds of sheep and the cattle, with the herdsmen in goatskins.

The line follows the Tiber valley as far as Orvieto. At Chiusi it began to be dark, and thus it happened that we passed along the very edge of Lake Trasimenus without my being able to see anything.- Florence at 8.30. Put luggage in deposit, and walked to the Casa Nardini, 17 Borgo SS. Apostoli, to which Baedeker directed me. Took a room at once for 35 l. a month.- The journey cost (with all incidl expenses) 1.28.30. I thus begin here with 1.236.

[Sketches of the Porta San Giovanni and of "Soracte, from Railway"]

Sund. Dec. 30. Good night's rest,- an unknown thing to me in a new place. To-day fine but cloudy, and little sun. It being Sunday, resolved to reconnoitre as many of the Galleries as possible; thus saving expense. I am never able really to see the pictures at a first visit. Went to the Uffizi, the Pitti, the Museo in the Bargello, and the Belle Arti. Something like despair is the result; it is cruel to have my opportunities of study curtailed by having to pay a lira each visit. Familiarized myself with the outside of the chief buildings. Unfortunately the Campanile has got scaffolding near the top, which spoils the aspect.- Delightfully impressed by first view of Florence. A wearying day, but I am nothing like as tired after it as I should have been three months ago.- Sent postcards to Nelly, Alg and Bertz.

Whilst I think of it, I will make a note of the diet with which I became acquainted at Naples and Rome. There was not much difference between the two places, in nomenclature. *Naples.* Minestra, zuppa, and brodo used all to express "soup". One would say often, however, "in brodo",- e.g. Riso in brodo, zuppa ad erbe was common.- Fritto di pesce a frequent request. At the Giardini di Torino there were some fine dishes called Pasticcio di riso and Pasticcio di Maccheroni.- The commonest form of maccheroni was al pomodoro; also frequent, al sugo.- Manzo bollito (plain boiled beef) and manzo in umido (beef à la mode) always to be had, and the cheapest thing.- Risotto very good.- Uno stufato was stewed meat with vegetables.- Frittura mista, a good mixed fry of vegetables and, generally, sheep's brain,- done in little balls.- Una Cotolétta alla Milanese always expensive but very good; the cutlet was done in breadcrumbs, egg, etc., and a lemon brought with it.- With the soup there

113

was invariably a plate of Parmesan cheese.- A very abominable dish is an insalata cotta; it means cabbage, or broccoli, with oil and vinegar poured over it.-*Rome*. Manzo still the commonest and cheapest. Next frequent arrosto di vitèlla.- The so-called "Rosbif" a strange stuff, seemingly heated up off a cold joint and cut very thick, with gravy poured over it.- Tèsta di Vitèlla good sometimes.- Fegato not so well done as at Naples.- Una bistecca generally means a mutton chop.- Of vegetables, the commonest were broccoli (always brought with oil and vinegar over it) and spinacci. Soups were: Capellino (the slender kind of maccheroni, in brodo), minestra a verdura (a decent mess of vegetables,) a fagioli, lenticchie, and pastina (macch. in form of pellets put into soup). Spaghetti a name for various forms of maccheroni.

At Naples the cheapest wine seemed to be Posillipo; you asked for a mezza bottiglia, or a quinto. Vino del Vesuvio very like cider, and excellent drinking. Capri expensive and never genuine. At Rome the wines are advertized in the Trattorie and Magazzini, the price (of ½ litre) being given in soldi thus: "Velletri, 5,7,8". The common wines are Velletri, Zagarolo, Castelli Romani, and others. If cheap is wanted, you ask for "Romano rosso". The cheap eating-houses are called cucine. A common thing to see "Ottima Cucina" put up also. Also "Cucina Casareccia".

The charcutiers, abundant in Naples, always show "Fiore di Latte" in window; I do not find this in Rome. In Rome such shops generally called "Pizzicheria", and frequently have "Generi diversi" inscribed above.

Mond. Dec. 31. Again suffering, but did not allow it to interfere. In morning went to S. Croce, and walked round. Then lighted on an English bookseller's, on the Lungarno, and bought, to my delight, four of Ruskin's books in Lovell's (American) reprint. The American price is from 15 to 20 cents a piece; I had to give from 1 lira to 1.80; however, it seemed cheap enough. Got "Mornings in Florence", "St Mark's Rest", "Architecture and Painting", and "The Art of England". At the same time bought [J.A.] Symonds's 2 vols. of "Italian Sketches", in Tauchnitz.

In afternoon walked the length of the Viale dei Colli. Very misty over the town and distance, but yet had glorious views. Only looked up at San Miniato. Home early in evening to write letters.- At eleven o'clock wandered out into the streets, to see end of old year. In the Piazza del Duomo a male soprano singing to a guitar. Finally was tempted into the Ristorante Etruria, Via Calzaioli, and had a supper of cignale,- in vast discomfort, owing to the place being full of Italians in exuberant spirits, who were supping at table d'hôte. It made me feel wretched. At midnight they all began to shout and stamp and ring bells, etc.- a terrific uproar. I rushed out into the streets.

114

1889

Tuesd. Jan. 1. A wonderful day like a brilliant summer day in England. Walked out to Fiesole. The walk is an easy one, and the way this: by Via Cavour to Porta San Gallo; through the gate and straight along the Viale Regina Vittoria (già Pattone) till you come to the barrier and Piazza delle Cure. Hence start the trams for Fiesole, but to walk one takes the street to the left—Via Borghini—just opposite the trams. The first turn out of it to the right, and you are in the long Via Boccaccio, which goes to the Domenico. Before long fine views of Fiesole begin.

How impressive, as colour, are cypresses against the Italian blue of sky!—I had a frittata at a caffé on the Piazza, then walked up to the terrace in front of S. Alessandro. Two columns of cipollino lie there on the ground. The view marvellous, but Florence and hills thick with haze. This began to clear at 1.30, flying away in feathery scraps, and then the Val d'Arno was fully revealed. I sat for some hours: the temperature perfect; the sky blue beyond thought. Shall go up another afternoon for the sunset.-

Before the Franciscan monastery, just above Sant'Alessandro, stands a cross of this form [sketch in the middle of the page]. The right hand oblique pole has representation of sponge on it; the other is a spear; and below it just where they unite are 4 little white cubes, dotted like dice. Are they meant for dice?

Reading an account of the great ceremony at S. Peter's last Sunday, when the Pope celebrated close of year, I find it stated that, at his arrival, all the vast multitude in the church broke into *handclapping* and waving of handkerchiefs! A curious proceeding, surely.

By the bye, I had an idea that the main axis of churches always was from W. to E., at all events heading towards Palestine. Else, why the system of orientation? But I find that the churches of Rome and Florence (though S. Peter's is due E. and W.) lie in the most various directions.

To-night finished writing a long letter to Nelly. Reading at the Ruskins I bought yesterday. Have found a good Cucina for dinner in the Via Porta Rossa, near the Mercato Nuovo. I think it will represent in Florence my good old Botteghe Oscure at Rome.

Wed. Jan. 2. In the morning to the churches of San Spirito and Carmine. In the Brancacci Chapel (Carmine) the light was not good enough to allow me to examine the frescoes. On the way, looked at Casa Guidi, which is the corner house between Via Maggio and Via Mazzaretta; opposite the w. end of the Pitti. When Mrs. Browning says "Neath Casa Guidi windows, by the church", she means Santa Felice, which occupies the opposite corner of Via Mazzaretta. On the front of Casa Guidi is an inscription: "Qui scrisse e mori Elisabetta Barrett Browning, che in cuore di donna conciliava scienza di dotto e spirito di poeta, e fece del suo verso aureo anella fra Italia e Inghilterra. Poñe questa memoria Firenze grata, 1861." [Here wrote and died Elizabeth Barrett Browning who, in her woman's heart, reconciled the learning of a scholar and the soul of a poet, and made of her golden verse a link between Italy and England. This memorial was erected by Florence with gratitude, 1861.]

After lunch, to the *Uffizi*—previously dwelling with delight on the view of the Palazzo Vecchio against the blue sky at the end of the Portico.- I noticed that in Florence the fig-leaves on statues are merely hung on by a piece of wire round the haunches, instead of the sheer plastering practised at Rome.- One's enjoyment of the *Niobe Statue* is utterly ruined by the fact that all round the room, behind the row of statues, are placed (it seems recently) 13th and 14th century paintings, leaning against the walls; while higher up hang huge canvases of Rubens and some others. I thought with grief of the Museo Chiaramonti.-

In the Corridore Orientale an extraordinary picture, by Giovanni da San Giovanni, of Venus combing lice out of Cupid's head.

Ritratti dei Pittori. Strange portrait of Andrea del Sarto. A Holbeinisch face; very fat.—[G.F.] Watts, [John Everett] Millais and [Frederick] Leighton hang together on the line; fine portraits. Of course Watts is the noblest, a Titianesque head, and in the proper clothing. Millais, in something like a shooting coat, is a bluff and prosperous English squire, of most genial character. Leighton, in red gown, with decoration and white tie, as president of the Academy, is a supremely fine English gentleman.

Tribuna. The Venus de' Medici; similar in attitude to the Venus of the Capitol, has beside her a dolphin, on which two little cupids are sporting.— I look long at the splendid altar-piece of And. del Sarto—hung high, alas!—of Madonna with S. Francis and S. John the Evangelist. Exquisite head of S. John.

A bitterly cold day, though bright. Fierce East wind.- Reading Ruskin still.

Thursd. Jan. 3. Suffering much.- Stayed at home, after breakfast, till 11 o'clock, and finished my sketch of the Porta San Giovanni. Then went out and had my mid-day coffee and frittata. After that to the Boboli Gardens, which are open on Thursday. The bitter tramontana has blown the atmosphere clear; wonderful views in every direction.- Walked up to Bello Sguardo, but could not enter the grounds; a woman at the gate said to me: "Non si passa; c'è il padrone".- Down by the side of Monte Oliveto, and walked a little in the Cascine; thence home.

The number of inscriptions, on walls etc., in Florence is astonishing. One on the Lungarno is amusing; it solemnly commemorates the fact of a man having there jumped into the river to save a boy, who had fallen in!-

It is terribly cold in the wind to-day. I notice the use in shops of little porcelain braziers which look something like ornamental jars for flowers.- Wrote a post-card to [Edgar] Harrison, and a long letter to Bertz.

116

Frid. Jan. 4. As bitter a day as ever I knew. The tramontana blowing with edge like a knife. Sunshine, and even warm in shelter, but in the open unendurable.- In the morning to Santa Croce, and made a careful study of the sepulchral slabs and the Bardi chapel, guided by Ruskin. I must not pretend that the old Christian work delights me, but I get to like it better, and I see its merits.- Then to the Biblioteca Nazionale, in the Uffizi, and wasted an hour over the *Quarterly Review.* The reading-room has a good supply of periodicals from all countries.

In afternoon walked round the Viale de' Colli,- most of the way well sheltered from the terrible wind. But still suffering from old complaint. In the evening to the Marucelli Library, Via Cavour, which is open at this time of the year from 6 to 9, and read some of Vasari.

My diet does not satisfy me. This morning I tried the Caffè Alighieri, Piazza S. Croce, and found excellent milk there. Shall take it in future without coffee. Then for mid-day I have bought some butter, which I shall use with bread or bun. Then in the evening I had dinner at the Tratt[oria] del Giglio, Piazza S. Firenze, which I found a good place. Fair dinner for 1.35, beyond which I oughtn't to go.

Sat. Jan. 5. A street leading to the Duomo is called Via della Morte. I suppose the dead used to be carried along there.

Still the bitter wind, rather more north. Ice in the streets this morning. Went first of all to the Battistero, and, as well as was possible in such temperature, looked at the bronze doors. Miserably thick with dust, but glorious. Then to S. Maria Novella. In the Rucellai chapel, Cimabue's Madonna, which I know so well from engravings. In a chapel near the choir, Brunelleschi's wooden crucifix; it is framed, and with glass in front.- In the chapel of Phil. Strozzi, the frescoes of Lippino Lippi. Impossible, of course, to see them properly, but I liked what I could see.- In the chapel in left arm of transept (Strozzi) are Orcagna's (Andrea) frescoes of Last Judgment and Paradise. The faces are exquisite. In the choir, Ghirlandajo's work. Strange that his type of woman is so plain; could not find a beautiful face. His men are portraits.

Lunch of bread and butter,then to the Pitti for two hours.- From the windows of the Sala di Flora there is a splendid view of Fiesole, with the Palazzo Vecchio right in front.- A number of Carlo Dolcis; most of them terrible in their velvetyness, and some no better than Christmas cards. The Pitti is strong in Andreas. In the Sala del' Iliade a divine "Adorazione del Bambino" by Perugino; I never saw anything more beautiful than the Virgin's face.

Picked from the newspaper an odd Italian phrase. "Andare a babboriveggoti" = to die. Seems to mean (according to Barretti) "father I see thee again".

Dinner at the Giglio (an excellent fritto misto, like at Naples,) and then to the Marucelli Liby, where I read again at Vasari. To-morrow being Befana, there is blowing of horns by boys about the streets to-night. But I imagine the celebration has decayed. And then the cold is too severe to allow open air merriment.

117

Letter to-day from Nelly, enclosing a request for a story, from me, sent by Tillotsons of Bolton[1]. They offer £10 for 5,000 words. Cannot do anything for them. Also note from S[mith] & E[lder], saying they are ready to send proofs of "Nether World". Sent them my address. Also a letter from Willie Stannard, wishing to hear from me. It shows a good deal of intellect; indeed, surprises me. Wrote a reply to him.

Sund. Jan. 6. Befana [Epiphany] and therefore no galleries open. In morning wandered about, disconsolate. Still severely cold, but the wind has fallen. The *bronze* horses in the P[iazza] della Signoria have long beards of ice, where water ought to flow.- At 12 ate my bread and butter, and then took a long walk. Out through the Porta Romana, to Poggio Imperiale, and thence up to the Torre del Gallo, where Galileo had his observatory. A little museum is kept there. Two fine busts of Galileo, various autographs, and some of his instruments. Magnificent view from the top of the Tower. Thence down to Galluzzo. On the way found a sheltered place, and sat in the delicious sunshine. A peasant girl, passing, said: "Felice sera a lei!" [Happy evening to you!] Too tired to get as far as the Certosa in Val d'Ema, so back by main road to Florence.

On way to Galluzzo passed Galileo's Villa, and made a sketch of it. It was here that Milton visited him [in 1639]. On the front is a bust and long inscription in Latin.

In the evening found a lively place, Cornelio's Caffè, a little way to west of the Baptistry. Swarming with people, and a band playing dance music. Extraordinarily mixed company. Three English women, an insoluble problem; an old one, looking like a decent farmer's wife, and two who called her "Mamma", but whom at first sight I had taken for disreputable Italians,- their faces not the least English. Impossible to guess their history.- The singular feature of the crowd was the strong domestic element. Numbers of family gatherings, men, wives and children. It speaks well for the Italians, and indeed I notice that a festa is greatly made on behalf of bambini. To my table came a couple of families, and opposite me sat two little girls, whom to watch was as good as any theatrical performance. The younger about seven, very pretty, but wearing spectacles and the other about 10, of coarser type, but also interesting.

[Sketch of Galileo's Villa]

The comical womanliness of these two is indescribable,- their grave discussions of dress, their discreet laughter. They had ices, and the younger one was discontented because hers was brought without cream. In this only she showed childishness, repeating petulantly (and in comical contrast with her spectacles) "Non mi piace senza crema!" [I don't like it without cream]. She did not finish the ice, and offered remnant to her mother: "Vuoi?" [Would you like it?]. The men of the party had with them a fine big dog, who performed tricks, with sugar on his nose etc. To the dog they gave the rest of the ice-cream and when he licked it awkwardly, the little girl

118

exclaimed "Ha cascato il mezzo a terra!" [correct form: E cascato a terra! It has fallen to the ground!] And how they all laughed,- taking me into their merriment with friendly looks.- They are good creatures, these Italians; I like them more and more.

Amused at one of the waiters. Absolutely San Sebastian in evening dress! The very face of the saint! He showed much skill in rushing about with loaded trays. I took a vino caldo and a coffee. I find a common drink is ponce (punch), and there are two kinds: rosso and bianco.

Mond. Jan. 7. The suffering too much at last, so I went to Dr. Wilson, 9 Via Tornabuoni. He merely prescribed a daily aperient and bade me leave off the red wine, which is too astringent. The bitter cold makes my days wretched; every morning there is ice about the streets.- At night to the Library, and looked into [Marquis Francesco Eugenio] Guasco's "Murae Capitolini Antiquae Inscriptiones", and [Jan] Gruter's "Inscriptiones Antiquae [totius orbis Romani", Amsterdam 1707]. Guasco is a humorous fellow; here is a note of his on a stone which reads "Dis Manes". *"Dis Manibus*: sextum enim casum cum nominativo aut accusativo sociare, ebrio tantum quadratario concessum" [only a drunken carver can be expected to use the sixth case, i.e. the dative, with a nominative or an accusative].—I find there are some sep[ulchra]l monuments dedicated "Somno Aeternale".

I have found the exact meaning of *Minestra*. It includes all things made out of paste, whether dry or moist. The two species of minestra are: *Asciutta* and *in brodo*. Thus a risotto is minestra, as well as what we call soup.

Tuesd. Jan. 8. No better and, if possible, suffering still more from cold. Morning to Piazzale Michelangelo, and round by Viale. Afternoon to Natl Library. Have decided to write something for Tillotson, and choose the Ara Coeli business. Sent a note yesterday to ask if this would do.- In evening to Marucelli Liby. Again an amusing quotation from Guasco, who is commenting on some mistakes in an inscription "Graecorum Λ pro A, *benemirenti* pro *benemerenti;*- non apocryphum esse lapidem, ut sententia fuit Maffejana, sed potius multibibum fuisse quadratarium declarant" [The Greek letter Λ for A, *benemirenti* for *benemerenti* do not mean that the stone is apocryphal, as Maffei thought, but rather that the carver was a heavy drinker.]

Wed. Jan. 9. A miserable day, no sunshine, much rain and bitterly cold. Forced to have a fire. They burn wood here, and the fire is lit with *pine*— pine cones. The huge round stove does not go far towards warming the room. It being anniversary of death of Victor Emmanuel, the lib[rarie]s are closed, so I had not even that resource. The doctor's medicine is as yet wholly inoperative.- In afternoon walked to the foot of the hill of Fiesole, a very wretched trudge. Dinner early, and home to discomfort.

An interesting article in the *Corriere* on the Papal question. Here it is alleged that the Pope would come to a compromise, were it not for foreign interference, urging him to stick to his claims, and that this is the really dangerous aspect of the matter. It seems that when he became Pope, Leo XIII did not give the benediction to the people from St. Peter's.

I notice the commonness of the expletive "Perdio!"— it is printed as one word. Surely its trivial use is a strange sign of moral shallowness.

Thursd. Jan. 10. There comes to breakfast every morning a poor old fellow who has had a stroke. It takes him nearly two minutes to seat himself, and the waiter has to break up his bread for him, so that he can soak it in his coffee. This morning he said, as he came in "Ieri stavo veramente male!" [Yesterday I felt really bad!] Not long for this world, clearly!

Wrote a letter to Roberts.- Again not a glimpse of sunshine. In afternoon walked nearly to the end of the Cascine, in rain and gloom, though, thank goodness, it is a little warmer. The abundance of evergreens is a great feature of Florence.

In evening to Marucelli, and began a long letter to Walter Grahame. Feeling a little better. Instead of red wine, I take a glass of Marsala in water, a poor substitute.

Frid. Jan. 11. Again a sunless morning. Cleared a little at 4 o'clock, and from the Piazzale Michelangelo I had a fine view of sunset amid struggling clouds and thick mist.- Letter from Roberts.- Finished letter to Walter G[rahame] and posted.- Evening to Marucelli. Feeling better still, but the time is being sadly wasted. I don't know what the doctor will charge me, but I do not feel warranted in spending on the galleries in any case.

Sat. Jan. 12. All day a thick fog. The sun struggled through it for an hour at 1 o'clock, and I went for a long walk out towards Fiesole and round by the stream Affrico. Evening very thick in the streets and bitterly cold. Lit my fire and read Horace. Letter from W[illie] Stannard and from his mother. Sent postcard to Nelly, asking if the parcel I sent from Rome had ever arrived.

Evidently Florence is always foggy. Even in summer, says Baedeker, the city is hidden in mist during forenoon. I heartily wish I were out of it, but that is impossible. I suppose Venice won't be much better.

Sund. Jan. 13. In the morning sunshine, but cloudy and cold later. To the Cappella dei Principi. The walls rich with wonderful marbles and the tops of the sarcophagi seemingly set with precious stones. Next to it is the Sagrestia Nuova (of San Lorenzo). Here saw Michelangelo's tombs of Giuliano and Lorenzo de' Medici. Thence to Convent of San Marco, where the paintings did not greatly interest me—in my present state of mind—but the disposition of the cells and the relics of Savonarola did. In nearly every cell is a small mural painting. The library full of very solid divinity, and the illuminated psalters etc. exquisite.

In afternoon to Uffizi where I examined the Venetian schools. But gave more attention to the busts of the Emperors, ranged along the corridors.

There seems to be almost a perfect collection, from Augustus to Constantine; on one side, the Emperors, and opposite, either their wives or some other relative. I find that, from Augustus to Commodus, the faces of nearly all are now familiar to me; doubtful ones still, however, are: Claudius, Galba, Titus and Domitian.

Letter from Harrison (E[dgar] E.) asking if he hadn't better give up his efforts to let "7K", as he suspects that Lane dissuades every proposing tenant. I replied in affirmative. Letters also from Alg and Katie. Madge is staying with them for a month.

I note that the clocks in Florence do not strike the hour at each quarter. But several of them have only the hour-hand.

Mond. Jan. 14. At noon cleared up; till then gloomy and cold. Spent morning at Bibl[ioteca] Naz[ionale] looking over [Victor] Duruy's "Hist[oire] des Romains".- At 2.30 to Dr. Wilson, to tell him that I seem cured of my ailment. Paid him 10 fr.- 2 doz. photographs lost! Then walked by the Viale dei Colli, right round.- Dinner at a new place,- the Trattoria dell'Antica Posta, near Piazza della Signoria. Seems an improvement; cheaper, and more given.

In evening read some Horace, then, at 9 o'clock, started for a walk in the full moon. Went first of all along the river to the Porta San Niccolò, but found that the iron gates there, by which one ascends to the Piazzale Michelangelo were closed. So went all round by the Porta Romana, and the whole length of the Viale. Met not a soul, and at one of the villas was alarmed by the furious barking of huge dogs. From the Piazzale a fine view. All the buildings of the town distinct, and the hills bold against the sky. The dam in the river roaring very loud. Michelangelo's "David" a strange and awesome sight.- Interesting to see Galileo's tower, dark against the sky, as I came along the road.- To return came down the face of the hill, and, by following the walls, found an entrance not far from the grating at San Niccolò, so that I might have spared this long walk. (The Porta San Miniato, I find it is called.)

Tuesd. Jan. 15. A day spent in the house, thinking of the novel I must write when I get back home. No very good results. No proofs yet from S[mith] & E[lder], but saw at the Bibl[ioteca] Naz[ionale] this morning that "The Nether World" is advtd for March in last Saturday's *Athenaeum*.- A little sunshine at times, but mostly clouded and very cold.

Man going along the street crying: "Cenciajo!" [rag-and-bone man]— The cabdrivers here, to attract your attention as you pass, say: "Vuole?" In Naples they shouted "Lei! Lei!" -

Wed. Jan. 16. All day no sun, and rain in the afternoon. Suffering now from diarrhoea. The change of diet seems to have completely upset me. In morning to Bibl[ioteca] Naz[ionale], where I am looking through Duruy's "Hist. des Romains". The rest of the day trying to warm myself at the stove.- Began a letter to Nelly.- Read some Horace.-

Thursd. Jan. 17. A fine day at last. Warm wind,- though how it can be so, blowing hither from Fiesole, I don't understand. Clouds gradually cleared away, and a superb afternoon. Morning to Bibl[ioteca] Naz[ionale], afternoon to Fiesole, though suffering much.- As I climbed from the piazza to the monastery, a band of monks were just coming down, and they mumbled prayers or psalms, or something of the kind, in unison.- On the back of the seat in front of Sant' Alessandro, is carved "Ai suoi fratelli viaggiatori di tutti i paesi, un inglese A.D. 1872." [To his fellow travellers from all countries, an Englishman A.D. 1872] To bed at 9 o'clock in much misery.

Frid. Jan 18. There is an incredible item of news in yesterday's *Corriere*—or rather, that of day before, as I always have it a day late. In the course of a lecture delivd before the Brit[ish] Archaelog[ical] Society at Rome, by the "onorevole Bonghi" [member of the Italian Chamber of Deputies], the lecturer said what appears in the foll. passage: "Quando l'on. Bonghi ha ditto che il municipio era intenzionato di costruire un ponte di ferro attravèrso il Foro Romano, una esclamazione di maraviglia dolorosa è scoppiata unanime in tutta la sala." [When the Honourable Bonghi declared that the municipal council intended to build an iron bridge across the Roman Forum, an exclamation of painful wonder burst unanimously from the audience.] I should think so!

Again a magnificent day, finer than yesterday, only a fierce wind in unsheltered places.- In morning a letter from Nelly, announcing safe arrival of parcel. Replied to her. Then bought a dozen photographs. In afternoon a long walk, the whole length of the Viale dei Colli. I have not previously been over that part which descends beyond the P. Michelangelo. A great deal of snow on the mountains; wonderful effect in the brilliant sunshine. Along the Lungarno as I returned, found it almost too warm. In one place there sits—and probably has sat for years—crouched on the pavement against the house-wall, a blind old woman selling matches. She never looks up or speaks, and her forehead is burnt to a toast. I wonder whether she sits there in summer? Even to-day I saw her wipe off perspiration.- Watched men and women washing clothes of all kinds in the river opposite the Borsa.

Strange how little I eat now-a-days, yet without feeling hunger. At breakfast I have a glass of milk and 2 panini; at mid-day one or two panini with butter, and perhaps an apple. Then at 5 o'clock comes my one real meal, which of course is anything but sumptuous, as it seldom costs more than 1.45.—It is noticeable that I have never once met an Englishman in the places where I eat. Very rarely even a German.-

Sat. Jan. 19. Forgot to mention, a few days back, that I wrote to two Venetian lodging-houses recommended by Baedeker. To-day had a satisfactory reply from one,- saying that I can have room with stove for 35 l. Name Gründl; I think this will settle my abode there.- Also letter from Roberts, in which he tells me that at last he has got a copy of "Thyrza" to send to Mlle Le Breton.-

Again a glorious day. Suffering much unfortunately. In afternoon sat for three hours, reading, in the Cascine, in hot sunshine. Went down then onto the bank of the river, and found some flowers, blue, like small crocuses. Gathered some for pressing, and also took some of their bulbs, which perhaps will grow at Wakefield.—An hour or more after sunset a wonderful blue afterglow over the houses opposite Lungarno, with a brilliant single star amid it.- Home to read Horace.

Sund. Jan. 20. This morning came about half vol.I of "Nether World", sent directly by printers, Ballantyne & Hanson, from Edinburgh. In the afternoon I corrected the sheets and posted them at once. It reads well.

Not such a day as yesterday; towards afternoon cloudy, but still warm. In evening to Uffizi. At 4 in afternoon walked to the Cascine. Great crowds of people. Utter absence of anything corresponding to English rowdyism, male or female. Good taste in dress; quiet colours. Young girls mostly have hair "à la Thyrza". Saw a great number of beautiful faces. I notice more and more the democratic spirit of these southern people; the distinctions of the north do not exist in anything like the same trenchant way. The labouring-class girls go bareheaded, with coloured shawls on their arms; they are very fat-faced and rosy, as if their work did them good. Numbers of such go to the galleries on Sunday. No giggling, no horse-play. Much nice politeness among all.

In evening wrote a letter to Bertz, and postcard to Ballantyne (with address at Venice,) then to Cornelio's. Here a great throng. Good-humoured struggle to get seats for all newcomers. Curiously, the two little girls I noticed a fortnight ago again sat opposite me, and again had ices. I delighted in watching and listening to them. They had great white feathers in hats.

Mond. Jan. 21. Fine, but windy. A walk on Viale de' Colli, thinking of my next story. Taking medicine again.- In afternoon bought a few more photographs, finding, to my great joy, the Melpomene and Thalia of the Sala delle Muse.- Made up a collection of small pictures to send to W[illie] Stannard.- Began long letter to Katie.-

The *Corriere* surpassed itself this evening. "Molte belle ed elegante signore, sparse fra la platea, le poltrone, i palchi, ed anche un gaietto sciame di vaporose signorine"! [Many handsome and elegant ladies among the audience in the pit, in the stalls and boxes, and also a graceful bevy of gauzy young ladies.]

Tuesd. Jan. 22. Bought yet more photographs, securing copies of the Muses for Alg and Bertz. Got my three Empresses of the Sala Rotonda.- I must have lived with excessive cheapness in Florence, to be able to spend thus.- A cold and very windy day, but sunshine.- In evening took a week's subscription (3 l.) at Vieusseux' Reading-rooms.- Despatched letters to Katie and Alg.-

Wed. Jan. 23. Sunny day, but again much colder. However, I do not suffer now since, for one thing, my ailment is much better again, and then I can go always to Vieusseux'. An admirable place; well-lighted, well-warmed, with easy chairs and a great supply of periodicals. There is also a reference library with dictionaries, encyclopaedias, etc.- Read an article on John Morley, in *Quarterly [Review]*, which seems to me good as far as it goes.[2] It points out the undoubted inconsistency between the literary Morley and him of the platform. I always explain this as a mere case of unscrupulous ambition.

In afternoon to Fiesole.—Boys have a game of running down the hill there on rollers.-

A note from Nelly, mentioning card from Plitt, from Naples. Replied to him. Also wrote to Alg, asking him to send Roberts 3/6 for "Thyrza".[3]

Thursd. Jan. 24. Bright, but still bitterly cold. Spent afternoon and evening at Vieusseux'. In this weather it is impossible to walk, for you are cut to pieces, and the Galleries are impossibly cold.- Much better in body; indeed feel quite well, but don't know how long it will last.- Letter from Bertz, who has fallen into the reactionary depression I expected.- Thinking about a paper I should like to write on the *Thalia* of the Sala delle Muse, to be called "In the Hall of the Muses".[4] Also working out my new novel.- Concerning the electoral uproar in Paris—the Boulanger affair— the *Corriere* well says: "Le polemiche dei giornali diventano sempre più oscene."

Frid. Jan. 25. Postcards to Bertz, and to Signa Gründl, at Venice; latter to say I am coming on 30th.

Morning at the Uffizi, where for the first time I went along the Pitti corridor. The engravings only extend as far as the hither end of the Ponte Vecchio, and are not very numerous.- Looked carefully at the busts of the younger Faustina. Cannot make much of her; an insipid face. There is a bust of her mother which is practically the same as that in the Sala Rotonda, but less finely wrought.- By the bye, I have never yet seen a photograph of the Sala Rotonda Antinous in *profile,* and yet that is the best view, as I often saw. Of course there is a reason why it should be. The bust has no personality, but mere perfection of outline.-

From an engraving, I find that the familiar "Woman taken in Adultery" is by Titian. I did not know this.

Inscription on a cippus in the Iscrizioni: "Ti[berio] Claudio Fortunato, erepto fatis iniquissimis." Poor Fortunatus!

A day of marvellous brilliancy. Not a speck of cloud to be found on the blue, which is intense above and grows whitish all round horizon. In the Cascine are a number of big trees, perfectly bare of leaves, whose trunk and branches are a gleaming white. They have a wonderful effect against the blue; every twig distinct.- Bitter wind, but in shady places the sun very hot.

Sat. Jan. 26. Finer day than even yesterday. Quite hot, and not a cloud from morning to night. To Fiesole and sat on terrace for couple of hours.

Strange to look down on the compact little city of Florence, and try to grasp the significance of that cluster of human dwellings.- Purchased Kroker's "Archaeologie", an excellent little primer.

Sund.. Jan. 27. To-day is the election at Paris; shall be anxious to hear result.- Misty in morning, but cleared to fine sunshine. Morning at the Accademia delle Belle Arti.- Sala II contains admirable pictures. 51, the Adorazione dei Pastori of Lorenzo di Credi. Studied the detail of the foreground, which is of botanical accuracy: a great number of flowers are distinguished, each petal painted like a miniature. Under the Child's head is a sheaf of straw, and here every pipe is perfect.- Cp. this with the rougher work of Ghirlandaio next to it, 50. Same subject, and a few flowers and leaves are indicated, but slightly.- 34, a wonderfully preserved Angelico. Here too a rich foreground of botanical accuracy, but done without perspective.- 59, Four Saints by Andrea. I can never enough admire his young male faces. Something peculiar to Andrea in their beauty.- 55 Perugino's Assunzione, spoken of as a masterpiece. The individual figures delight me, and the heads are exquisite. But what about the whole?—the decorative symmetry and other conventionalities. This spoils the picture for me. I can't help it. In foreground no detail of herbage attempted; simply a flat green colour. The Peruginos in this room are all very fine.

In passing the Duomo saw two great painted inscriptions over the front doors—have lately been hung there, and I suppose have some reference to the time of year. One is: "Placate, o fideli, colle vostre preghiere l'Altissimo, empiamente vilipéso dai bestemmiatori". The other: "Festeggiamo cogli angeli Gesù Redentore. Coi supplici voti propiziamoci al giudice venturo" [O ye faithful, appease with your prayers the Most High whom blasphemers impiously despise.- We celebrate Jesus the Redeemer with the angels. With fervent vows we propitiate the judge to come].-

An hour with the Emperors at the Uffizi.- Afternoon at Vieusseux'. Strikes me something might be made of the society there; e.g. the man who turns over all the papers in despair at having read them several times.- Evening to Cornelio's. Note that a waiter, in response to a call, cries "Eccolo!"

Mond. Jan. 28. Glorious day again, better than yesterday.- Notice in Brogi's window a sheet on which is lithographed the whole of the Div[ina] Commedia, in a minute handwriting said to be done without lens. The three divisions of the poem each occupy an oblong, perhaps 8in. long and 5 deep, subdivided into columns.- In the same window is displayed this morning an astonishing collection of blackguard caricatures,- sort of Valentines; something to do with Carnival, perhaps? An English bookseller of corresponding respectability would scorn to put such things in his window.

Tuesd. Jan. 29. Took leave of Florence. A dullish day, though sun visible. Left at 10.35, and reached Bologna at 4.20. Here put up at the Tre Re, Via Rizzoli.

A wonderful railway journey, over the Apennines. The highest point of the ascent is at Pracchia, 618 metres. Up to Pracchia there are 22 tunnels. Then comes one of nearly a mile and a half, and after that 22 more tunnels before Pistoia is reached;- in all 45 tunnels. When the descent begins, the line follows the valley of the Reno, often a wild narrow gorge. The mountain streams on each side were generally frozen, and made white lines on the hills. On the peaks a good deal of snow. At the little stations, country people—handsome red-cheeked women—looked with curiosity at the train. What a life it must be in these little villages, far up on the mountains. Most of them are conglomerates of houses,- all built together in a block, as if for strength against the winds. The mountains very rocky; thin grass, and those small trees with the dead brown leaves thick on them which I have seen so often.

Bologna makes a strange impression. All the streets are arcaded on both sides. The two leaning towers, Asinelli and Garisenda. Here again heard street-organs, for first time since leaving Naples. The shops of the salumièri very rich; huge sausages, a foot in diameter, cut through, and other wonderful composts. Tins of mortadella. Superabundance of barbers' shops.- Spent evening at the Caffè Commercio, Via Ugo Bassi, where some really good playing went on. Crowds of people; livelier even than Cornelio's at Florence. The town decidedly noisy. All night long—for I could not sleep—I heard singing and shouting in the streets. The Bolognese seem to live a merry life.

Wed. Jan. 30. First thing in morning visited the Accadèmia delle Belle Arti, and saw Raphael's S. Cecilia. An attendant gave some useful help in my rapid glance over the pictures. He told me that some people believe Titian's Martyrdom of S. Peter was not burnt, but stolen. The only picture lost in the fire, it seems. Improbable story.

Left by the 11.20 express, taking 2d class. Very cold, and no sunshine. From Bologna onwards a great dreary plain,- one vast vineyard, with rice etc grown between the vines. The latter trained between trees that are cropped into shape of a fork; I know not what tree. Ferrara, a dreary view in the distance, Here the ticket-office at station inscribed "Viglietti" [instead of Biglietti]. Just after Ferrara, crossed the Po, a vast muddy river,- above level of the country. A little rain fell. Then approached the Euganian hills, most of them curiously conical,- volcanic formations.- The approach to Venice not quite what I had expected. Like going over Morecambe Bay, but at low tide. Gulls flying on the lagoons. The bridge is of stone, and very low.

By gondola from station to Palazzo Swift, S.Maria del Giglio 2467, Canal Grande. The landlady, Siga Gründl, ready for me. Found a packet of proofs [of *The Nether World*]. My window looks onto the Canal, and is opposite the Salute [the church of S. Maria della Salute]. Spent a couple of hours walking about the P[iazza] San Marco and Riva degli Schiavoni. Then home to unpack, and delighted by a vocal concert on a gondola moored in front of a house near by. Delightful female voice.-

126

The intense quietness of Venice. The dipping of oars below my window, and the slow moving lights of gondolas.- Sent postcards to Nelly, Roberts and Bertz.—The landlady tells me that [J.A.] Symonds has once or twice put up here.

Thursd. Jan. 31. A fine day, though a little misty. In morning walked much—*pour m'orienter!* Lunched at La Calcina (Fond[amenta] delle Zattere); very good, but a little too dear for me. I see that one gets beer almost everywhere in Venice, and good beer.- Before going out, corrected proofs; dispatched them; up to p.208 of Vol.I.-

The Venetian type of beauty is more distinct than anything I have yet seen; unmistakably oriental. The girls of lower classes wear long shawls.-

Unfortunately the Piazza is "up"—drain-manufacturing. S. Marco also boarded in places,- the restoration always going on. Same with Pal[azzo] Ducale.- Drank coffee in afternoon at outside table on the sunny side of the Piazza. Pleasantly warm; the shops and restaurants even think it needful to drop the curtains along the arcade.- The pigeons delightful. They are fed at 2pm, at expense of town; but also pick up crumbs from tables. Very tame, and often whizz past your ear in flying.-

Plenty of sunshine comes into my room, thank heaven!

When I asked for "una mela" [an apple] at the Trattoria to-day, the waiter absolutely did not know what I meant. Another customer cried out "Da un pomo!" But it is extraordinary that the fellow should have been utterly ignorant of the word mela.

Frid. Feb. 1. Cold and sunless. Fortunate that I can make a fire.- It appears that Venetians do not take *caffè latte*, but caffè alone; when I asked for the former it took a long time to provide. Perhaps the position of Venice explains this; I shall see.- Spent morning at Accadèmia; also looked into S. Maria della Salute. Found a good trattoria just this side of the Piazza,- Al Padiglione. Just a trifle cheaper than the Città di Firenze.

Letter this morning from Bertz. Sent on from Florence was one from W[alter] Grahame, and also note from Tillotson's, saying they will have "Christmas on the Capitol", but must hold it over till next Xmas. So I shall not trouble to write it till I get home.-

I notice the Venetians sound *c* like *s*. The dialect in the streets of course all but unintelligible to me.

My lodgings are by far the most comfortable I have yet had. There are double doors,- as seems to be the case in the other rooms; I wonder whether it is universal in Venice. The attendance is excellent. The old landlady a most decent creature, and her two servants (they seem too good to be merely servants,) are extremely respectful.- It must be very cold on the other side of the Canal; never any sun.- A walk after sunset along the Riva degli Schiavoni. A sad pearly light over everything. San Giorgio and the Salute, exquisite groups. Saw two boats with the coloured sails, which Ruskin speaks of as still lingering here and there; the sails are really painted, like banners, yellow and red, and at the mast-head is a strangely elaborate vane.—Dined well at the Città di Firenze. I find it is very common here to have pieces of 2 centimes and the like. My bill came to 1.63.- This afternoon, white gulls were flying about the Canal, under my windows.- I find, by the bye, that the tide rises and falls considerably in the canals,- some three feet.

The singers on the gondola come at 8 every evening. The woman's voice is glorious. To-night they sang "Addio a Napoli" and "Santa Lucia".-

Sat. Feb. 2. Find I can get caffè latte at the Caffè Orientale on the Riva.- After breakfast took the steamer from the Calle Valeressa to the Scalzi, and thence set out to try and walk to Madonna dell'Orto. Lost myself hopelessly, and had to give it up for to-day. Got round to the Rialto, and thence made way to S. Maria Formosa, where I had a good look at Palma Vecchio's S. Barbara. But the church was crowded; to-day is the Purificazione della B.V. [Beatissima Vérgine].

Returned to my plan of having lunch at home, bread and butter and apples. The bread here is the same as at Bologna, exquisite—a sort of white biscuit.

In afternoon got into the Piazzetta (by chance) just in time to see the weekly lottery-drawing. It takes place in the pavilion at the foot of the Campanile,- of course, as Ruskin says, a horrible desecration. There was a great crowd, but I saw no excitement whatever. The machine used is like this:-

[Sketch]

It is made of wire, and at the place indicated, has a little door. The machine was placed in the doorway of the building, full in view of the people. Behind, at tables, sit officials. A little boy in a white gown stands at one side, at the other an officer. The latter begins by holding up successively printed numbers, from 1 to 10, at the same time crying them out, and, as he drops each paper, it is put into a metal ball—I don't know how—and the ball is dropped into the wire case by the boy. When 10 are complete, another man turns the handle of the machine some half dozen times, first in one direction, then the other, so that all can see the metal balls rolling about. This process is repeated, by tens, until 90 is reached. The boy is then blindfolded, and after vigorous turning of the machine by the officer, the child dips his hand into the open hole and brings out a ball, which he drops into a glass dish held by the official. The dish is handed to the man behind, the paper is brought out, and its number shown to the people; whereupon the number is stuck up on a board. There are five drawings, and between each the boy keeps his arm held up in the air. When the fifth number is stuck on the board, all is over and the crowd disperses.

From 2 to 5 a large and good military band played in the Piazza. I walked about, listening to it and looking at the buildings. A great crowd, taking the form of a promenade on the north side. Again I feel the democratic nature of Italian society. All classes blend in the easiest way, and the workgirls in their long coloured shawls and bare heads promenade among ladies without a trace of self-consciousness. Admired the fine figures of the gondoliers. Great numbers of tables put out before the cafés.

Dinner at Città di Firenze. A most excellent zuppa di fagiuoli; but the place is really too dear. Strolled down to the Riva, and found a group of boatmen singing a sort of catch—a part-song without words. Fine voices.

Sund. Feb. 3. A wild morning. Driving rain, mixed with large snow-flakes. The Grand Canal swept into waves, and sea-gulls sweeping over it. The whistling of the wind exactly like what one hears on board ship in wild weather.- I wonder whether the gulls coming into the Canal foretells storm?

Went out in the wet, had my coffee, and then to the Palazzo Ducale, which is open free on Sunday. First visit, of course could do little but survey the rooms. I see that I have my work set with Tintoretto. In the Sala del Maggiore Consiglio, I copied a modern inscription: "L'assemblèa dei Rappresentanti dello stato di Venezia in nome di Dio e del Popolo unanimamente decreta: Venezia resistarà all' Austriaco ad ogni costo. A tale scopo il Presidente Manin è vestito di poteri illimitati. II Ap. MDCCCXLIX.—A memoria del voto qui dato, il comune pose XXII Marzo MDCCCLXXXI.".-

Home to lunch. Proofs came this morning, to end of Vol. I; began to read them. Weather had cleared; a fine cloudy sky, with sunshine.

Then to Accadèmia, but it closed at 2, and I saw little.- Walked out to the Punta della Salute, enjoying the sea-breeze. Thence to the Piazza, where the band was playing. Sat down at Quadri's, and had glass of Marsala. A shoeblack importuned me. "Ma piove!" I cried "No, no", he replied, "Non piove! Garantisco che non pioverà. Se piove, restituisco i soldi!" ['But it is raining', I cried. 'No,no', he replied. 'It isn't! I guarantee it won't rain. If it does, you shall have your soldi back!]- Then out to the Public Gardens; a splendid sky of delicate blue seawards. At the extremity is a small collection of animals; I watched two little kangaroos washing each other's faces. Heard a lion roar, but for some reason, the beasts not to be seen to-day.- The young palm-trees here are housed in wickerwork, turned to the north, for the winter; they stand like sentinels in their boxes. Those of somewhat higher growth are encased round the trunk, and have a pavilion raised above them.- At the entrance to the Gardens is what seems to me a really noble monument to Garibaldi. In the midst of a basin of water stands a pile, in shape of slender pyramid, of rugged stones. On the top is Garibaldi, an iron figure; his left hand rests on hilt of sheathed sword, and his right on an open scroll. In front of the pyramid, below, is a reposing lion, with head watchfully raised; behind, in corresponding place, one of G's soldiers, his arms folded, his bayonetted musket slung behind him, his head evenly poised and looking resolutely forward. Nothing melodramatic, nothing *French*; on the contrary, fine restraint and noble suggestion. G's costume, quite realistic, is still finely picturesque.

A great crowd on the Riva and Piazzetta. On the Riva are several shows, of a paltry kind. Noticed some magnificent heads of old boatmen and many beautiful women.

129

I note that the simple houses of Venice have front doors of the English fashion. Lack of space would naturally lead to this style of building, in most cases, rather than the court-yard plan.

Suffering much to-night. Bought a flask of purgative water to use again, as at Florence. But this cannot go on for ever. Corrected proofs.

Mond. Feb. 4. Postcard from Nelly.- Posted proofs to end of Vol. I.- Found a good deal of snow lying on the Piazza. Altogether a wretched bleak day, with a cold gleam of sunshine now and then.- In morning looked in at Maria Formosa to see Palma's S. Barbara again. Thence to S. Giovanni e Paolo, which is being made into a new church by extreme process of restoration. The sacristan took me into the former chapel of the Rosary, which remains still in its ruined state, as after the fire which destroyed Titian's picture. By the bye, a picture of Bellini's was burnt at that same time, so that my guide at Bologna was not quite accurate. Some fine bas reliefs there (much damaged) by Banazzo,—pronounced Banasso by the sacristan.

In afternoon, suffering; lit a fire and read [Ruskin's] "S. Mark's Rest".— Dined at the Padiglione, very cheaply. I think this place will suit me for good. Then went to the reading-room at the Ateneo, in the Campo S. Fantino, by the Fenice theatre. Admission 25c., and open till midnight. A large collection of periodicals.

All last night was very stormy. Loud washing of the water against the house below.

Tuesd. Feb. 5. I take my candle from the porter, at the foot of the stairs every night. He is a most reverend white-headed and white-bearded man; a fine head.

A rich red sunrise this morning, but followed by dull and bleak day again. At 4.30, however, a fine sunset began. I walked about the Molo and the Giardino Reale, watching Venetian ladies and gentlemen converse and take leave of each other, and go off in their private gondolas. All the Riva became purple with sunlight, and San Giorgio glowed magnificently.- A bright new moon after dark; promising for to-morrow.

This morning wasted because I had taken medicine—though without effect. In afternoon walked a great deal. Stood on the Rialto, and looked at the front of the Fondaco dei Tedeschi, where, between two of the top windows, is a scarcely distinguishable female figure in fresco,- the last trace of Giorgione's painting. What these house-fronts must have been!

The green-grocers' shops, in the morning, sell hot cooked turnips—they look and smell like turnips at all events.

I notice that very many of the campanili in Venice have a distinct inclination from the perpendicular, as if everywhere the ground were sinking. Inside S. Marco, the pavement is absolutely *hilly.*-

The Italian students seem to be a rowdy lot. The papers always have accounts of uproars in this and that university town.-

By the bye, why does Ruskin invariably address himself to rich people? In "S. Mark's Rest", e.g., when speaking of the Pillars, he tells you to

130

imitate the capitals by cutting "a pound of Gruyère cheese". Then again: "From the Grand Hotel, or the Swiss Pension, or the duplicate Danieli with the drawbridge, or wherever else among the palaces of resuscitated Venice you abide", etc.- This is a great fault. And, moreover, the Danieli has not a *drawbridge*. This fault of temper leads him into other errors. Speaking of the Rialto: "You will probably find it very dirty,- it may be indecently dirty,- that is modern progress, and Mr. Buckle's civilization." Absurd; old Venice was vastly dirtier, as we well know.-

Every day at 12 a gun is fired,- I think from S. Giorgio. Also at 8pm.

Wed. Feb.6. Fine day, but bitter wind. At night a dense fog.

In morning to the Palazzo Ducale, examined the Museo Archeologico—not much of interest—and went through the prisons, terrible places. In the place where executions were held, there are three round holes in the floor for blood to run down.- In afternoon by steamboat to Lido; costs 40c., return. There is a glorious strand; very thick with shells. A calm, sunny sea. I must go there often.- Evening to the Ateneo.

In going out of the room, my landlady says: "La riverisco!" This seems to be usual form of respectful leave-taking.

Thursd. Feb. 7. Suffering all night, and this morning. I wonder how all this will affect my looking back on Italy?

A walk in the Giardino Pubblico this morning, watching a great steamer being towed in through the lagoon. Sunshine, but very cold. Home to lunch, and wrote to Roberts, from whom a letter this morning,- also postcard from Nelly, saying that Alg and family arrived at Agbrigg last Saturday.

I copy the foll. from an article in the *Figaro* on Boulanger's antecedents.[5] Saying that no one foresaw his prominence, the writer adds: "Les Clubs, dédaigneux, riaient et ne pariaient pas. Quant aux femmes, elles rêvaient d'autres adultères."—On the whole this article is excellent, warning and scornfully reproving the populace from the point of view of a man of letters.

In Venetian, the *sc* is pronounced *ss*; e.g. *pesce* becomes *pesse*. The affirmative *già* becomes *ja,* the zz pronounced like in English. I have already noted *sinque* for *cinque*. Every evening I have, at the Padiglione, what the waiter calls *zuppa verse* (s like z), and I suppose he means *verde*.

The music still comes every night, just before eight.

Frid. Feb. 8. By the 11 o'clock boat to Lido, and back by the 4.30. A magnificent day, windless and warm. A slight mist.—Walked nearly the whole length of the island, stopping just in view of the Porto di Malamocco, where a sandy beach recommenced, after the long stretch of stone battlement. The sea very calm. Picked up a great many shells. Watched a great steamer coming in to Venice by way of the Porto.- perhaps from the East.

The band in the Piazza plays several afternoons a week. Unfortunately there are no concerts at the Caffès of an evening. Still, I have got into the

expensive habit of going to Quadri's, after dinner, to read the *Figaro*.—
Wrote to Nelly.-

Sat. Feb. 9. Letter from W[illie] Stannard, acknowledging photographs.-
Proofs up to p.96 of vol II.

A heavy snow storm this morning. Lasted till noon. Snow lay till night.
Spent most of the day at home, correcting proofs.—Wrote letter to
Shortridge. Also note to Mrs King, asking if she can resume work at 7K.

Am thinking out my new novel. Got some satisfactory names to-day.

Sund. Feb. 10. The snow still on the roofs, but a fine day and warm in the
Piazza. Morning at the Accadèmia. I have tried to interest myself in the S.
Ursula series of Carpaccio, but cannot. It is some defect in me, doubtless,
but the pictures absolutely make no appeal to me. I cannot feel poetry in
them. An interesting realism here and there strikes me, but not in sufficient
degree to hold my attention.- On the other hand, I was greatly interested by
two Giovanni Bellini's; one, a Madonna with S. George and S. Paul; the
other a Madonna between Magdalen and S. Catherine. They are in the
Renier Collection. The faces of all are dispassionately meditative. The
colouring is beautiful, very warm; the drapery light in a wonderful degree.
In these two pictures the figures are half-lengths. I suppose my lack of
interest in Carpaccio partly arises from utter carelessness about the
subjects—for he is a *subject* painter. The Bellinis may mean anything and
simply respond to one's ideals.

I see that there was serious rioting in Rome the other day, by *muratori*
[bricklayers] out of work. Crispi, by way of meeting the case, has forbidden
all political meetings, of whatever kind, throughout Italy. A sage measure
this!

In afternoon walked to the Fondamenta Nuove, and thence had a
wonderful view of the Alps, a long line, all white with snow. After that,
mounted S. Mark's Campanile. As no one is allowed to ascend alone, I
accepted the companionship of a fellow loitering about with this purpose,
and of course had to pay for him. And now for an illustration of a hateful
fault in my character, my lack of decision. On descending, the guide asked
me if I had seen the manufacture of Venetian glass wares. "No",- and a lot I
cared about it. And I positively allowed him to lead me across the Piazza to
a place in the Calle dei Fabbri,- knowing all the time that the matter was
absolutely uninteresting to me and that it simply meant expense. Well, we
went into the works. I saw a "Venetian pearl" blown and ornamented, then
was shown over the collection of things for sale,- inwardly cursing all the
time. Of course I had to buy: it was a paltry neck-pin, for 2 francs, and then
I had to give the workman something in return for the glass bubble. Getting
out to the Molo, I threw both pin and glass into the Canal,- making a vow
to be more manly in future. Both things were paltry and worthless. To the
guide I gave 1 franc,- and thus, the ascension of the Campanile cost me
3/6!

The view was wonderful enough, but a hard and cold wind blowing. The
Alps spreading into infinite distance; the Euganean Hills very faint. I don't

understand how [J.A.] Symonds can speak of these hills as visible from Lido and about there.

Needing something to read, I bought to-day Balzac's "Parisiens en Province", which is new to me.- To-night the wind is whistling again very keenly—just as on board ship.

Beautiful faces I saw this afternoon among the long-shawled, bare-headed work-girls, who were promenading in the Piazza.

Mond. Feb. 11. Found a new caffè, in the Ruga Vecchia, by the Rialto, where I can get my breakfast a little cheaper. I find, by the bye, that *caffè latte* is called, in Venice, *caffè bianco*. It is not as rare a thing as I at first believed; but very much less drunk than in the other towns. Small cakes are here called *pasti*.

In the afternoon went to look at the Greek lions in front of the Arsenal. I had stood before them for a moment, and was trying to read the old inscription, when the sentinel stationed here moved towards me and said: "Non si posta!" So I had to move on at once; about the most ridiculous business I have encountered in Italy.

It is amusing to read of the panic caused in Rome by the riots. A couple of jocose blackguards waved handkerchiefs in the Via Frattina and cried: "Eccoli!"—whereupon the tradesmen rushed to shut up their shops. This was the day after the row.- Among the public orders issued is one to "suburban dealers" not to sell any inflammable materials!

The deficit in the Italian budget for 1888-9 will be 192 millions of francs. The total deficit up to 30th June 1889 will be 400 mills. A nice state of things.

A sentence from the *Corriere:* "Da che mondo è mondo, non vi sono state che due specie di politica: politica conservatrice e politica revoluzionaria." [Since the beginning of things there have been only two sorts of politics: conservative politics and revolutionary politics.]

To-night have been to hear a lecture, at the Liceo Benedetto Marcello (behind the Fenice) on Zola. The room was crowded. A great number of ladies and girls, and even a troop of schoolboys, in the uniform of some establishment. The lecturer confined himself to the details of Zola's life, and the lecture was one long glorification of our friend's heroism and many other virtues. It was delivered extempore, and with extraordinary animation; to look at the man and hear him without understanding, one would have supposed he was reciting a tragedy.- I compared this with Sarcey lecturing on Daudet. The matter was poor, commonplace. "Potente", I heard it called, as I was going out.

A fine day, and warm in the sun. But still a bitter wind, and the snow lying about. The moon getting beautiful.

Tuesd. Feb. 12. Magnificent day, but for the cold wind. A long walk in morning, though at first I didn't feel very well, having been kept much awake in the night by an odd sort of swelling in the throat—not an ordinary sore throat at all. My other ailment has not troubled me for three or four days.

Set off resolved to get to Madonna dell' Orto, and did so. Saw the "Last Judgment" and the "Golden Calf" of Tintoretto, on each side of the Choir. But, as always, the seeing meant little; in fact you *cannot*—physically—see pictures in a church. I must study Tintoretto in engravings. One can do this, for it is sheer treatment of subject that distinguishes him. A charming little Madonna in one of the chapels by G. Bellini. His faces have become easily recognizable.

In returning walk about the Ghetto Nuovo and Vecchio. The former consists of high, plain-fronted houses, round a campo with its well. The windows are all fitted with wooden shutters, green—or once so; a very squalid aspect. "Calle Beruch", I noticed written up. Thought of Shylock.

By the Ponte d'Olio is an inscription: "5562. Ultimo nùmero del Sestière di S. Marco."

The Canals very beautiful this fine day. In shadow they were a cold olive green—distinctly olive. A gleam of sunshine makes them a brilliant green of the same kind. Delightful effect when sunshine slants on a Canal, a little way off, between dark houses of foreground.

Just S. of Madonna dell' Orto is the triangular little Campo dei Mori. I suppose it is so called from the coloured images of two Moors built into houses—odd figures and giving a very quaint aspect to the locality.

More observations of popular life. In the morning one sees women going about with water from the wells, in metal buckets hung by a bar over their shoulders. Thus:

[Sketch]

At the greengrocers', hot boiled potatoes (bursting out of jackets) and hot turnips are sold; the smell of the latter goes far. Also hot stewed apples.— Saw a remarkable head-dress of, I think, Jewish woman: the back of her hair positively *armed* with long bright pins, radiating from centre at the nape of her neck. The workgirls commonly have a coil of hair on the front of the crown, with an amber ornament stuck through it. Sometimes their long grey shawls are replaced by brilliant coloured wraps of wool.-

The sky grew gloomy about 3 o'clock, and then a wind rose. To-night the Canal is stormy, absolutely roaring against the houses.-

I find that, in the Piazzetta dei Leoni, there is a bath of fresh water kept for the pigeons: a square hole in the middle of the paving.-

Notes at dinner to-night. A man came in selling cooked apples. The custom is to take one out of his basket, by means of a little stick thrust through the apple, and then soak it in a glass of wine. Eat it off the stick.- A man comes every evening calling *pasti*, and his procedure has puzzled me. He gives the customer a bag containing marbles; the customer takes out three, and consults certain numbers on them; then cries out either "Ho vinto!" or "Ho perduto!" After which he chooses pastry. I asked the waiter to-night to explain. It seems that the game is for 25c. of pastry. If the numbers on your marbles amount to 100, or less than 100, you have won, and pay only 5c., if to more than 100, you pay the whole price—strange instance of Italian love of gambling.-

Some interesting things in the *Figaro* to-day. Article on a painter called Jean-François Raffaelli[6], whose subjects are taken from low life and scenery of the banlieue of Paris. Said to be very good; should like to see them. But the man is affected by the modern craze for preaching a theory as well as executing work—for acting the interpreter as well as the representer. He calls himself a *caractériste,* and boasts of having invented the word, together with *caractérisme;* writes brochures, lectures etc.- Then there is a note by Sarcey announcing the end of his conférences in the B[oulevard] des Capucines. Comical reason: says that managers have got into the habit of fixing their premières precisely for the Thursday evening when he is lecturing; and as he loves premières, he has to give up his lectures! Will perhaps give matinées—but then again these would interfere with his déjeuner, which he likes to linger over. (I wonder whether this article is a hoax?)

Wed. Feb. 13. Hurricane all night. This morning, our ground floor quite under water. The Piazza almost the same: water of some kind rushing up through holes; pavement on N. side flooded. At high tide, the sea more than level with the Piazzetta. A furious wind, and bitterly cold; a little snow.- Grew calmer towards evening; feeble sunset. Had to spend much time in caffès, and at the Ateneo. Began letter to Bertz.

The waiter at the Padiglione is called "Adone". (No, I believe this ought to be Oddone.)

By the bye, there is a marked difference in matter of ordinary honesty bet. north and s[outh] Italy. Here I am never absolutely cheated; in Naples I was never anything else. And things are really cheap in Venice,- I mean simple articles of food and drink. A cup of coffee at Quadri's, one of the best restaurants is only 25c.—At dinner I generally have a zuppa di verdure (zuppa *verze*) then some meat (vitello arrosto, manzo lesso or brasato etc) then perhaps some vegetables, then an apple; a quinto of bianco with it (16c.). Venice is strong in tripe and fagioli; the soup made out of these is excellent, and a lot of it. A favourite wine (red) is Verona.- The common cigars are Virginia (with straws.)

In the house they call me "il Signorino"—flattering! The servant who lets me in (no latch key) of an evening says "Buon riposo!" The porter salutes me with "Servo suo!" which I find is not limited to the lower classes.

A pretty sight to see girls feeding the pigeons in Piazza. The birds perch in clusters on the hand and arm.

Thursd. Feb. 14. Sunny, but colder than ever. The wind has gone, however.—In the morning first of all to San Zaccaria, and looked at G. Bellini's "Santa Conversazione." It is hung absurdly high; always something wrong with pictures in churches. Then to S. Sebastiano, and saw—or tried to see—Veronese's work: it profited me little. A poor unfortunate sacristan. Finding that he spoke hoarsely and breathed hard, I said that I feared that he had caught a cold this bad weather. "No," he replied, with a smile, "I've had it for many years; and cough too." Not many more to come for him, fortunately. I gave him half a franc, and afterwards much wished I had given a whole one. Perhaps shall see him again. He was good and patient, poor fellow.

Then walked round by the Spiàggia di S. Marta. A great deal of new building there, especially an immense cotton-mill. I thought myself in Lancashire, standing under the hideous walls and high chimney, and hearing the hum of machinery.

After to Giardini Pubblici, as usual, and tried to warm myself. Watched an Austrian Lloyd steamer go out,- slim, low boat, evidently built for speed.- Heard a decent looking girl exclaim, laughing: "Dio santissimo!"

Finished a long letter to Bertz, and posted.- A slight return of my malady to-night. Always so, as soon as I leave off the purgative.

The moon getting fine; but too much mist. Venice beautiful under it to-night.

To attract a gondolier's attention, you shout "Poppe!"-

Frid. Feb. 15. No sunlight all day; very cold, and a good deal of snow. Did little but sit wrapped up by the fire. Finished reading Balzac's "Parisiens en Province". Balzac's works become more and more unsatisfactory to me. I wish I had some of George Sand's.

Sat. Feb. 16. Letters from mother and Nelly. Proofs up to 197 vol II; letter from Plitt—proposing that we should journey home together. I thank you, no!

The most wonderful change in the weather. Not a cloud all day. At 11 went to Lido, and sat on the shore till 4 o'clock, under a black-blue sky and hot sun. A splendid view of the Alps, behind Venice. They spread over about 90° of horizon. Thought much of new book. Had short talk with a Malamocco man,- a veritable "flying Dutchman" in appearance.

At 6 o'clock took my stand on the Ponte della Pàglia, and watched the full moon rise over the houses of the Riva—a great brilliant globe, dimming the gas-lamps. The sky deep blue; blue also the water, in which San Giorgio clearly reflected. My landlady, when I came in, took me to see the view from a window at the far end of the house, looking straight out to the Giardini Pubblici and Lido; an astonishing expanse of glorious moonlight; a gondola, crossing the reflected gleam, drew it on, far along the water.

Sund. Feb. 17. A beautiful morning. Misty, but blue above. Went to Giard[ini] Pubb[lici] and saw the white line of Venice misty—splendid between blue of sky and blue of sea.- Home to correct proofs. Dispatched them, and wrote to printers, telling them to send to Agbrigg after the 21st Feb.- Letter to mother and to Nelly.-

Music on Piazza in afternoon.- Moon finer than last night. Rose, a dark yellow, below a bank of cloud. Wonderful crowd on N. and W. sides of Piazza and in Merceria. The working-classes principally, at night. Several *maschere,* grotesquely attired, running along with horse-play. Noticed especially two girls in a sort of Moorish costume—long white line[n]robes, covering the head.- Many shawls of the old Cashmere pattern; chiefly older women. The class just above the work-girls wears a head-dress of black lace, or black velvet or wool, pinned at back of head.- Drank two *pònci* at Quadri's and made myself feel in good spirits. Suffering less these latter days.

Replied to Plitt's letter.- Ah, if only I had a companion here!

A glorious track of moonlight in the water, stretching right away from Lido to my [sic] the front of this house.

I see that in 1888 there were 2108 failures in Rome, and 9110 more cases of medical assistance given to paupers than in 1887. Seems to be all the result of Crispi's attempt to over-hasten material progress.

Mond. Feb. 18. Again splendid day. Morning worked at my story in Giard[ini] Pubb[lici].- Afternoon strolled about the Zattere. Passed a yard where gondolas were being repaired; I see they are flat-bottomed.- Suffering a good deal.- The moon magnificent to-night; almost red, and throwing a narrow clearly-defined strip of light on the water. A curious thing that, should a gondola traverse the dark space of water immediately between my eye and the beginning of the gleam, the motion of the oar makes the water shine there too, as brilliantly as beyond; on the trouble subsiding, darkness comes again. The cause of this?

At the *Traghétto,* the gondolas lie with prow to shore, so that, when setting off, they first have to back out then turn round.- I notice it is very common for a man to row a small boat with two oars, the handles crossed, he standing and rowing forwards.- The gondoliers seem generally to wear big heel-less shoes; and indeed other people of the lower classes also.- A very picturesque cap is that of moleskin, without brim; sits well on a shock of fine black hair.-

I like to watch the long-shawled working-girls buying ribbons etc., in the Merceria.- Of their faces, there is a broad distinction between those that are pretty and those that are beautiful, both, however, superb in their kind, and the former of wonderful healthiness.

Tuesd. Feb. 19. At 1.30 in the night, two Germans took possession of the room next to mine, and for half an hour talked and laughed at the top of their voices, now in German, now in Italian, with like fluency;- Austrians perhaps. Every word audible in my room. They got up at 7 this morning, and shouted and stamped about without the slightest consideration for the rest of the house. This is absolutely characteristic of Germans; I know now that they are not calumniated when such grossness is attributed to them. The English rough would be more considerate, but at the same time he would not exclaim about the beauty of the sunrise, as these fellows did.

In the morning to the Scuola di San Rocco. I know not why I have delayed this visit thus long: partly I waited for a very clear morning; as Baedeker says, and very truly, that nothing can otherwise been seen. You do not enter at the front doors, but have to ring bell at a side door. Cleaning and restoration going on, but I enjoyed the pictures more than any I have yet seen in Venice. The custodian upstairs spoke to me of what "Il Professore Roskin" had written on the works.

Mainly struck by the "Nativity",- birth in the upper half of picture, in a loft under loose rafters, and shepherds in the room below;- delightfully fresh treatment;- and by the "Temptation": the Fiend a fine figure of young masculine beauty, winged, with golden hair, holding up a stone in each hand to Christ who stands above, under a pent-house. Indescribable savour of imagination.- The Christ before Pilate a noble figure.- Must go again.

There is a hand-catalogue, in the four languages. The English is rich. I copied some specimens. "The multiplication of brods and fishes". *"In the middle.* The Sin of our Fathers; *on every side*: Three kinds (i.e. *Children*) in the Oven of Babylony". *"In the middle:* Moïse who spring the water; *on every side* : The ardent wood, and the luminous column". "Daniel in the Trench of the Lions". "Eliseus dispansing brods". "The wood carvings are by *anonymous*".

In afternoon went to look at Tintoret's house. It stands in the Fondamenta dei Mori, just to the E. of the Campo dei Mori. A fine old front; inscription and bust. The first floor has pointed windows, with carving; bird cages and washed linen hung out of them. The neighbourhood a very poor one; I noticed that there are still *dyers* about there. Much linen hanging out of the windows, thus early in week.- Then walked along the Cannaregio (Mestre Canal) to discover the frescoes of which Symonds speaks. I find there is a series, on the N. side; the houses from No.927 to 933 have continuous pictures, very faint, but beautiful, between first floor windows; poor working-class homes.

Must read Th[éophile] Gautier's "Voyage en Italie", as well as Taine's. Also Stendhal's "Promenades dans Rome", and Howells's "Venetian Life".

The *Figaro* to-day has an odd blackguard phrase. "M.—a *chiffonné* une de ses demoiselles de comptoir."

A fine morning, and warm. From three o'clock, however, the sun disappeared.

Wed. Feb. 20. My landlady has a sprightly little kitten (I have only seen two or three other cats in Venice, and the dogs are all muzzled, or led, and few of them) which frequently gets into the beds.- I often hear her cry out, in the next room: "Hu! Fuori, subito!" which always impresses me comically, as if she were addressing the cat in Latin. "La cucina, subito!" she exclaims.

Warm day, but clouded at times.- Letter from Bertz, saying that Frau Steinitz has begun to translate "Demos".- Proofs up to p256 of v. II.- Morning at the *Ateneo,* where I read in the *Revue des Deux Mondes* an article on William Collins by Emile Montégut.[7] The article shows great knowledge of English literature; I suppose he is one of the very few Frenchmen who have it. And that reminds me, I must read Paul Bourget's *"Etudes et Portraits"*—I think that is title.

Last night scarcely slept; extreme suffering.

The commonest kind of cheese here is called stracchino; also eaten in Florence, and perhaps in the south. A yellow cream-cheese, with a curious taste of varnish.

Afternoon to Giard[ini] Pub[blici].- An animal-show on the Riva, with a big live snake exposed outside. Man holding forth, and constantly repeating this phrase: "Come la natura li ha creati nei suoi deserti."

A man at the trattoria, declining an offered newspaper, said "La rigrazio di cuore!"

Thursd. Feb. 21. A day of much misery. Driven to a doctor, at last.- Dr. Menzies, Palazzo Banca Veneta, S. Maria del Giglio. He prescribes an injection in the morning. His fee was 20 francs, and the medicine etc. cost a little more than 9 francs. So here is a nice day's work.

Fine weather, if I could have enjoyed it. Letter from Katie, saying Nelly is very unwell,- neuralgia and exhaustion of various kinds; obliged to be in bed.- Note from Mrs King, saying she can resume work.- Sent cards to her and to Nelly, and wrote to Postmaster of N.W. district, for letters to be sent to 7K again.

Afternoon to Ateneo.

Frid. Feb. 22. Proofs to end of 2d vol. Returned them.- Note to Nelly telling her that proofs will come to Agbrigg next week.

A bright day but sharp wind. In afternoon to Public Gardens, and there, for the first time, had a wonderful view of the Euganean Hills. Now I understand Symonds. Strange that it should never yet have been clear in that direction. The curious cones looked but four or five miles away.

I find that water can only be drawn from the public wells twice a day—in morning bet. 10 and 11 and afternoon bet. 3 and 4.

I counted the band playing in the Piazza to-day; there were 55 of them, with conductor. On certain days another and smaller band plays.

Sat. Feb. 23. Fine, but very cold. Walked to the Fond[amenta] Nuove, and looked at the Alps, which were faint and wonderfully fairy-like, absolutely without substance, transparent, aerial.- In Pub. Gardens in afternoon met Dr. Menzies, who walked back with me. Told many stories of official corruption among the Italians. Said that the island off the end of the gardens has been made quite lately, artificially.

I see that 30 fishermen of Chioggia perished in last gale! Saw to-day a funeral gondola going along Grand Canal. It is large and deep, all over gilt in patterns; the coffin stands raised in middle, with a high crucifix before it, and men standing round; the rowers had a gilt uniform. From the appearance I thought at first it had something to do with the Carnival.

In the "Paese di Cuccagna", a father addresses his daughter, who is in a fainting fit: "Creatura mia, viscere mie, corona della mia testa!" [Creature mine, sprung from my loins, crown of my head!]

Long letter from Roberts.- Wrote to A.J. Smith.- Bought some photographs of Venice.-

To read Ouida's "A Village Commune".

Sund. Feb. 24. Very fine day, but cold. The official opening of the Carnival.- In morning to the Accadèmia, and again delighted myself with the two Bellinis.- Found pleasure, too, in a picture of Cima da Conegliano's in which a John the Baptist stands on one side of a Madonna and Child; the S. John a fine conception; a young man, haggard with asceticism and spiritual trouble, with long wild hair. In contrast with him is the child, standing on mother's knee.- a sweetly graceful figure.- By the bye who is Diana? Some pictures here with his name of considerable interest, it seems to me.- [Benito Diana, early sixteenth-century Italian painter of portraits and religious subjects].- Met Dr Menzies again, and walked to Gardens. (The cold flooring of Galleries.)

In afternoon began Carnival proceedings. "S.M. Pantaleone" said to arrive at railway station, and thence conducted along Canal to the Piazza. Three steamers full of maschere, followed by hundreds of gondolas,- brilliant costumes, many of them parti-coloured. There was a regata,- race of gondolas over the same course. Two men in each gondola, in costume; they came past my window with considerable intervals bet. boats. This over, I went to the Piazza, and saw the procession. A trumpery affair, but amusing. Men on hobby-horses;- in reality walking, but with the cardboard shape of a horse attached to them, with long trappings to hide legs, and false legs hung on either side. A little boy near me kept calling out: "Quanti cavaji!"- Ven[itia]n for *cavalli.*

In the evening, the Piazza an exhibition of lunacy. Small proportion of maskers in the great crowd, but vast uproar. Cafés crammed. Nothing really good or amusing, that I saw; chiefly howling and buffoonery. No music, alas!

Sent postcard to printers, asking them, if not too late, to put as a motto to "Nether World" a passage I read to-night in the *Figaro* in Renan's speech at reception of J[ules] Clarétie at Académie [française] the other day: "La peinture d'un fumier peut être justifiée pourvu qu'il y pousse une belle fleur; sans cela, le fumier n'est que repoussant."[8]

Mond. Feb. 25. The last day in Venice. Fine, but very cold. Letter from Nelly, enclosing cheque for £10, also a letter from Shortridge with dolorous news.- Went the length of Grand Canal and back, in steamer.- Dined at the Città di Firenze, and drank 2 litri of Verona, making myself cheerful.- Bill for wood and petrolina here comes to 1. 7.05.- The *Corriere di Napoli* to-day (yesterday, that is) appears in new type and double number. Shall be sorry to lose it.- Bought Balzac's "Les Rivalités" for the journey.

The *Figaro* to-day mentions a book just pubd by Dentu: "Lettres à une horizontale; ou Traité galant de géométrie amoureuse", by Noël Kolbac.[9]

To-night I heard the music on the gondola for the last time. A longer concert than usual, as if for my behoof.

Posted as a present to Bertz, photographs of Roman Forum, and of Thalia and Melpomene in the Sala delle Muse.

Tuesd. Feb. 26. Left Venice by 9.15 train; a dull and cold morning, Luggage can be registered only to Chiasso, as, from there, one is allowed 25 kilos free.- Full tide in the lagoons, and the Alps faintly seen, touched with sun.- Had a very dim view of the Lago di Garda; misty. An Italian then pointed out to me the town of Solferino; on leaving train, he greeted me with "Stia bene!" Other men, in leaving carriage, said to all: "Buon viaggio, signori!"

Stopped at Milan, and put up at the Albergo dell' Aquila, just off Via S. Margherita. A night of suffering. Scarcely an hour of sleep. Called at 6 o'clock by a sleepy boots and caught the 7.30 train.- Of Milan had seen next to nothing: dimly, the Duomo, and, by gaslight, the long Roman Colonnade. But too miserable with bodily pain to enjoy anything.

Wed. Feb. 27. Before leaving, had a *bowl* of caffè bianco, in the Parisian fashion; very grateful. The railway carriages bore inscription: "Schweiz Centralbahn"; the 2nd class carriage well heated, by glowing coals in vessels under the seats, and contained a little lavatory. A thermometer hung for judging heat, and a handle by which warmth could be regulated.

View of Como, but very gloomy and cold. At Chiasso, examination of luggage, and registering of trunks, through to London. Change of personnel on the train; noted strong difference of physiognomy. There is here half-an-hour difference in the time, from that of Rome. At the foll. stations, all inscriptions are in both German and Italian.

The magnificent broad and flat vale stretching from the head of Lago Maggiore to Bellinzona. An indescribable line of railway; train toils up very slowly to the great S. Gotthard tunnel. Perpetual changes in the magnificent views.

At the Swiss stations, there is frankly written up: "Pissoir".

A little before Airolo, snow began to lie on ground, and it grew thicker and thicker. At Goeschenen, just after the great tunnel, it was snowing; but the weather continued sunny. My eyes soon began to suffer sensibly from glare of snow. The strange little villages, snow-buried, and without a sign of life. The landscape absolutely like a photograph, mere black and white with not a touch of colour.

The great lake of Uri, wild and desolate. A sleigh omnibus starting from Fluelen to Altdorf. A "Badhaus" [public baths] on the edge of the lake made me shiver.- At Brunnen inscriptions begin to be solely in German.- Extreme air of cosiness about the big Swiss cottages, with their long rows of windows, each row with protecting eaves. Much firewood piled against the walls. The house itself is built of wood on a substructure of stone; wooden stairs lead up to front door.

Lucerne a big ugly town; scarcely saw the lake. The Righi in view.- Decided not to stop at Basel, but to take the train there and go straight on for Brussels.

Thursd. Feb. 28. A fairly good night in train. Brussels at 7.30 in morning. Sun, but deadly cold. Sent postcard to Nelly. Can scarcely tell how I spent the day, waiting for boat-train. Walked about the hilly streets, and thought of Charlotte Brontë. Brussels is bilingual. Everywhere you hear French; but all inscriptions, including names of streets, are in French and Dutch. Fine big dogs used to drag milk-carts about; very well trained; they lie down under the cart at stoppages. French and Belgian money used indifferently. The Belg. 5 and 10c. pieces are small and of nickel.

Left by the 4.47 train which runs direct to steamer at Antwerp. A dreary evening.

Frid. March 1. Rather rough passage, but was not ill. London at 9 o'clock; snowing and streets thick with slush. Found Mrs. King cleaning rooms, which need it, with a vengeance.

Sat. March 2. By the 1.30 to Wakefield. Found Alg and Katie, with infant Enid, staying at Agbrigg.

Mond. March 4. Bought scrap-book, and arranged in it my Italian photographs.- Letter from Roberts at Birmingham. Finished proofs of "The Nether World".

Wed. March 6. Returned to London by the 5.50.

Thursd. March 7. A warm day; rain, mist, sludge unutterable. Bought boots (18/-) and several minor things. Gave Mrs. King 10/-, making her payment begin from last Monday. Wrote to invite [A.J.] Smith for next Sunday; he is at Woolwich Arsenal again, and lives at Plumstead.- My ailment is but little better. I saw a doctor here last Saturday, and must see him again.

Frid. March 8. As yet, doing nothing, and again beginning to feel the oppression of loneliness. To-day have even a slight headache.- Mist, rain and slush, but still warm.- Letter from Bertz, saying he is going for a time to Ilmenau.- Unable to read. Have resumed my dinners at the little cook-shop in Edgware Road; they now cost me 10½d:—meat, two vegetables, bread and pudding. Made oatmeal porridge this morning. It takes an hour, but I think the diet will help me. Am in doubt whether I ought to renew my subscription at the Grosvenor, which ends on the 14th. I can't afford the money, yet can't well do without the books.

In evening made a desperate beginning at my Tillotson article ["Christmas on the Capitol"]. Wrote only a few lines, and with great difficulty. It will take some time to get off the rust. To bed rather miserable.

Sat. March 9. Letter from Alg, saying that Hurst and Blackett have sent him account of "Joy cometh". They have sold 329 copies, and send him cheque for £15. Thank heaven!

A wretched visit to the doctor. He talks of operation, but it shall go hard with me before it comes to that. New remedies tried.

Sat down at 4 o'clock, and wrote the first two pages of my article. There must be seven in all. I shall now, it seems, need the money more than ever.

Sund March 10. [A.J.] Smith came in afternoon, and stayed till ten.- Reading "Antony and Cleopatra".- Dull day, but no rain.

Mond. March 11. Letters from Alg and Nelly; also from Roberts, who is at Birmingham, in some kind of relation with a troupe of actors. In morning had a walk; bright and sunny.—Evening to [Edgar] Harrisons at Gunnersbury.- No work to-day, though suffering somewhat less. Read some Pope.-

Tuesd. March 12. Letter from Aunt Lizzy [of 27 Bell Street, Ludlow], acknowledging copy of "A Life's Morning".- Suffering much all day, but better towards evening.- Wrote fairly well, from six to eleven, doing 2½ pages of article.- Of course have broken the mainspring of watch,- just when every penny is important to me.- Took it to be mended.- Dull day, but occasional sunshine.

Wed. March 13. Vastly better to-day, but no confidence. Sunshine; a long walk in morning. Evening finished my article,- practically, though I have still 2pp. to rewrite. No letters. Read some Shakespeare and Pope.

Thursd. March 14. Fine day and warm. Walk in morning. Afternoon suffering. Evening finished article: "Christmas on the Capitol"[10].- Letter from Nelly. S[mith] & E[lder] send one from a S. John Elyard, concerning "The Unclassed".

Frid. March 15. Fine day.- Sent off article to Tillotsons.- Wrote to Madge.- Unable to settle to any work. In evening walked,—for the second time to-day—round by Regent St. and Strand. Those regions grow more and more appalling to me; I stand aghast at the expenditure of such men as frequent the restaurants etc. With not one penny to spend on pleasures, I am entirely shut out from the new theatres and places that I should like to see.- Ailment grows better, I believe.

Sat. March 16. Saw Doctor; am to see him again in fortnight.- Idle walking about the town.- Grey sky, with half an hour of sunshine, but not very cold.- Reading Shakespeare and Pope still.

Sund. March 17. No sun; rain in morning; warmer.- Sunday morning occupied in strange way. Get up at 8.30, make porridge and have breakfast. Then have warm bath in front room, after laborious preparations,- struggling with the big saucepan, and so on. Then change bed-linen, look over washing, put clean things to air. Then a bit of rest and read *Dispatch*. Then time to prepare dinner. For Sunday I buy ½lb of "brisket", which costs 8d, and this last[s] for Monday dinner as well; with it eat vegetables, which I have to pare and cook.

Afternoon read at Shakespeare; suffering still. Evening walk to Charing Cross, then back to lecture by C[harles] Graham, at Percy Hall, Percy St., Tott. Ct. Rd,—on the Cradley Heath chain-makers. Got some good material, which I have noted. Home to supper of bread and butter and cup of cold tea.

Mond. March 18. Got an idea for a short story from the lecture-room last night.- Short walk in morning. In afternoon Roberts came from Birmingham. We went and had supper in Chapel Street.- Much talk, and he stayed overnight.-

Tuesd. March 19. Roberts left me at 11 o'clock. In afternoon went to Acton, and found out Mrs. Jolly, Shortridge's sister. With her living her sister Nellie, both of them refined and distinctly sympathetic. The doctor, her husband, a very decent fellow seemingly. Seem to be no children. Stayed to dinner, and left at 10 o'clock; really enjoyable evening. Miss Shortridge's comical stories of children she knows; one, a little boy who having seen his father struggle with the cork of a beer-bottle, spontaneously added to his evening prayer: "O God, please give father strength to draw out corks!" Mrs J's story of her keeping a pipe *on* for her husband, whilst he went to the surgery; thought it only would be for a minute or two; but he was detained, and she smoked the whole pipe, with terrible results.

On reaching home found title page of a new novel called "Mrs Severn" sent to me by author, Miss [Mary E.] Carter, of Ripon.

Wed. March 20. Worked mentally at novel, developing the first chapters, which I find must take place in England. Windy and rainy. Sent "Demos" to Shortridge at Massa, and "Thyrza", with note, to Mrs. Jolly. Replied to Miss Carter.

Thursd. March 21. Furious wind and ceaseless rain. Grey sky. Feeling better these days, and believe improvement has set in at last.- Worked mentally, and making notes, at novel. A walk before dinner. Letter from Nelly, and replied to her.

Frid. March 22. Note from Mrs. Jolly, acknowledging receipt of "Thyrza".- Fine spring day.- Worked at Chapter I, in evening, but find I have, as usual, begun on wrong tack.

Sat. March 23. Again a fine and warm day. Much walking and thinking, but no writing. *Decided not* to begin story in England. In afternoon a chance visit from Roberts.- Am getting my plot clearer. "The Nether World" advtd for Ap. 3d.

Sund. March 24. Fine warm day. In morning to studio of Alfred Hartley, in Chelsea, where I was to meet Roberts and see his just finished portrait. R. had not yet turned up, but I found Hudson sitting.- Hudson, the man I have wished to see for two or three years. Very striking face; gentle, sympathetic manner. Roberts's portrait a life-size ¾ length; excellent, I think.

Thence to Danvers Street and had dinner. Roberts read some of his recent verses. Home at 5 o'clock, and spent the evening over the description with which Chap. I of new novel begins;- several hours writing some 20 lines, a terrible business. But the ground is broken and I think I can get ahead now.

Mond. March 25. Dismal and rainy in morning; clear rest of day. At 4 got to work. Rewrote the description and got my two first characters introduced; also copied it all.- In body much better.- Wrote to Madge.

Tuesd. March 26. Rain and sun alternately.—Letter from Alg, saying he leaves Wakefield for Broadway shortly.- Bought Landor's "Pentameron" in the Camelot series.- No writing but a long and hard evening of mental work. Found I was not quite ready with details enough for going on. A rich flow of them this evening.

Wed. March 27. Cold and dark morning; afternoon bright. Got fairly to work in evening, and finished first 4pp.- Reading the "Pentameron".

Thursd. March 28. Letter from Ella Gaussen, asking me to come and see her in town at the Agabys'. They have left Broughton, and now live at Ellesmere, in Shropshire—I think.- Letter from Nelly who sends me £20; also some pocket-handkerchiefs.

In morning to Brit. Museum, to get some information about Naples in 1880.- On getting to work, found it better to rewrite all I have done. Did so, and improved it vastly by filling in details and transposing some paragraphs. Got to p.5.

Frid. March 29. Dull, close day; no sun. In afternoon to visit Ella Gaussen. Of course it put me out of gear, as every social obligation always does. Spent evening in fruitless muddling over my story. Wrote nothing.

Sat. March 30. Fine day on the whole. In great trouble about details of my story, but towards evening got it clear.- Read a good deal of Landor; wrote nothing.

Sund. March 31. Sunny for most part; close.- Most of Sunday morning always taken up with warm bath, which I manage to have in my study. Then I read the *Dispatch*. In afternoon, Roberts came. He is getting into much society just now.- Late in evening, read some of De Quincey's essay on "Style".

Mond. Ap. 1. Sunny and dull, intermittently. In morning began the reading of Aristophanes' "Frogs", and did 100 lines. Then a walk over Primrose Hill.- Just after I had got to work in evening, a visit from Bernard Harrison, whom at first I did not recognize. He stayed half an hour, but fortunately I was able to go on again after his departure. Says he knew from the Lushingtons I was in Italy. How the deuce did *they* know, I wonder?

Wrote to end of 1st Chapter, p. 6.

145

Tuesd. Ap. 2. Very fine day. In morning "Frogs", then a walk to Hampstead.- At 3 o'clock sat down to Chapter II and by 9.30 had written only 2½ pages. Fearful labour and worked myself into a headache. The first since I left England last October.- Letter this morning from Bertz, and replied to him.

Wed. Ap. 3. To-day is pubd "The Nether World". Wasted the day in waiting,—hoping the vols might come from S[mith] & E[lder]. No Greek, no writing. Afternoon to see Ella Gaussen again. Found idiots there.— Sunshine in morning; gloom and rain towards evening.

Thursd. Ap. 4. All day waiting for the book to come from S[mith] & E[lder]. Only ran out to dinner for half an hour whilst Mrs. King in here. Day wasted; shouldn't wonder if, in spite of my notices, the people have sent package to Wakefield.- Read some "Frogs" and a lot of Roman History; but in a profitless way. At night, wearied out and in much disgust. Work out of the question.

Frid. Ap. 5. After a miserable morning of waiting (no Greek, and only some dull reading of Rom. Hist.) the books came. Don't much care for the binding, but a glance at the pages is not unsatisfactory to me.- Sent off copy to Agbrigg, and in afternoon walked to Chelsea, to leave Roberts his. Of course no work. By heaven, I must set to, to-morrow!

A warm and generally fine day. Mist hanging about. Little to grumble about in the weather of late, for this country.

Think of calling my story "The Puritan".

Sat. Ap. 6. Fine day. In morning to see doctor for last time; not quite well, but on the way to be so.- Got to work at 3 o'clock, and wrought till 11. Had to go back to beginning of Chapter II and did 4½pp. Also rewrote last p. of Chap. I.

Note from Mrs F[rederic] Harrison, inviting me to dine next Tuesday. The deuce take these interruptions of regular work; they become very serious indeed.- No reading to-day.

Sund. Ap. 7. In morning a walk. Replied to Mrs Harrison.- To work at 6 o'clock in evening, and worked only till 10; did 2pp.- A sunny day.

Roberts cannot henceforth come on Sunday. We have agreed to change to some other day, probably Saturday.

Mond. Ap. 8. Letters from Alg, Nelly and Bertz.- Sent off Bertz's copy of "The Nether World", also Alg's.- A fine day. In the morning walked for 2 hrs. all round by Embankment.- To work by 3 o'clock, and wrote till 9.45. doing 4pp. and I think well. Thank heaven, the ship gets afloat. Got into Chap. 3.-

Tuesd. Ap. 9. Wasted day.- Roberts wrote to say he would come at 3 o'clock. At half past three there comes a disreputable fellow, with a scribbled note, asking me to go to M'bone Police Court, where Roberts was up on charge of assault. I went, and found that he had got into a squabble on the pavement, in coming to me, and had knocked a man down with his umbrella. Fine of £3 imposed,- which I had to pay. More than serious this. [For Roberts's version of this incident see his *Private Life of Henry Maitland*, Ch. IV.]

To dine at the F[rederic] Harrisons'. Usual cordiality. No one there, but a son of Prof. Beesly. They had already read "The Nether World".- Brought away with me two or three books they want me to read.

No sunshine and much rain.-

Wed. Ap. 10. Gloomy morning, and from 11.30 to 3 o'clock a very dense fog, all but night at the worst. Rain all day. Took my necessary walk in spite of everything. Read J[ohn] Morley's introduct. to the new ed. of Wordsworth [1888]. Began reading a novel called "Ideala, [a Study from Life", published anonymously in 1888, Sarah Grand's first novel], lent by Mrs. Harrison.

Wrote well, from 4 to 10. Did 4pp.

Thursd. Ap. 11. Again a bad fog from 10 to 12, then cleared up, and a little sunshine.- Finished "Ideala", on the whole an interesting book, but crude in parts and without much style.- Wrote from 3.30 to 9.30, and did 3½pp.-

Frid. Ap. 12. Bright and warm day. Rain in evening.—In morning a long walk to Westminster and Lambeth.- Wrote from 3.30 to 9.30, doing 3½pp.- Received a copy of "Mrs Severn" from Miss Carter. Began reading, and find it poor stuff. Must lie about it, I suppose. Letter from Nelly, with comments on "The Nether World", beginning "This is terrific!"

Sat. Ap. 13. Rainy and dull.- Letter from Alg, saying that Blackett offers terms for the new novel. £20 on publicn and royalty after 300 copies.- Afternoon to Roberts' where Hudson joined us. Home at 10.30, in rain.

Sund. Ap. 14. Dull and rainy. Finished reading "Mrs Severn" and wrote as well as I could about it to the author. In afternoon visit from Austin, Godfrey and René Harrison [sons of Frederic Harrison].- Did not go out all day. No work done.

Mond. Ap. 15. Fine day. In morning a long walk.- Got to work at 3.30 and had to rewrite 6 pages, 3 in Chap. II and 3 in Chap. III. Involves a considerable alteration in the story.

Tuesd. Ap. 16. Again a fine day. Finished reading "The Story of an African Farm", a very moving book, the product of a mind with which I strongly sympathize. It was pubd in 1883, and nothing has since appeared by the same writer—Olive Schreiner her real name, "Ralph Iron" the original pseudonym.- Worked from 3 to 10 and did a little more than 4pp., but these only a rewriting of what I had done in Chap. IV. To-morrow I get ahead again. Have improved all I have rewritten.

Wed. Ap. 17. Letter from mother, Madge and Miss Carter.- Sunny day. Long walk about Somers Town in morning; got some hints for a subject by the Polygon. Before going out resumed "The Frogs" and read 100 lines. Hope to be more regular henceforth. Read some Boswell and Herrick.- Work from 4 o'clock to 9.45, and did 4pp.—well, I think.

Thursd. Ap. 18. Fine morning; afternoon foggy; warm. Read 100 ll. of "Frogs".- Much shopping to do. In afternoon came Plitt who is just back from Rome. By telling me of an Italian girl who lived with him there he made me so wretched in my loneliness that work was impossible. Passed a tedious evening and to bed early.

A pair of slippers came for me from Alg.-

Frid. Ap. 19. Good Friday and a wonderful day; like fine weather in June. Needed no fire. In the morning a long walk, round City Road and back by Holborn[11].- Read 2 Acts of Ben Jonson's "Silent Woman". Did 100 ll. of "Frogs".- At 3.30 to work, and wrote well till 10; 4 pages.

Sat. Ap. 20. Gloomy morning; evening very fine, but windy. No work; a little Ben Jonson. At 3, Roberts came as usual and we had much good talk. He left at 9.30, and I walked to Piccadilly with him. Talking of Coleridge and Gillman, I hit out a comical verse, expressing a wish that I might encounter a Gillman; on way home added several other stanzas.

Sund. Ap. 21. Made 10 stanzas apropos of Gillman and sent them to Roberts[12].- Fine day, but still very windy. Did not go out till evening, then walked for a couple of hours about Oxford Street.- Thought over chapter for to-morrow and made notes. Read some Herrick and some "Tatler".

Mond. Ap. 22. Letter from Alg saying Blackett offers £25 for entire copyright of his novel; he accepts. Letter from Bertz, speaking in praise of "The Nether World".- Fine day, with showers. No reading, but to work at 3.30 and wrought till 10; did 4pp., reaching end of Chap. V.

Tuesd. Ap. 23. Fine morning, but windy. Heavy storms at evening.- The usual walk beyond Primrose Hill. Before going out read some of Cicero's first letter to Quintus.- Wrote from 3.30 to 10.30, and did 4pp.

Wed. Ap. 24. Dull day, much rain; from 5 to 6 a fog high in the air, then sunny close of day. No reading; morning spent in fretting over some details of the chapter. Walk round by Knightsbridge. Worked from 3 to 9.30 and did 4pp., also rewriting the last of yesterday.

Thursd. Ap. 25. Dull day, much rain.- Morning looked in at Museum to consult Larousse.- Worked from 3.30 to 10.15, and did 4¼pp.- A little

Boswell and "Tatler" read.- Letter from Alg and p.c. from Nelly. Replied to Nelly.

Frid. Ap. 26. A very fine day. In morning read some of Cicero's Letters. Started at 1.30 and walked to Kew Bridge, where I had to see Plitt. Spent afternoon with him in the Gardens.- Then on to the [Edgar] Harrisons' at Gunnersbury. Home late, not feeling well.- I hate this loss of time. No work, of course.

Sat. Ap. 27. No reading, no work.- In afternoon to Roberts'.- The artist [Alfred] Hartley called and we walked together to his studio. His portraits of Roberts and Hudson have been rejected by the Academy. Back to Danvers Street and sat till 10 o'clock.

Sund. Ap. 28. A very unsatisfactory day. Nothing done, nothing really read; only some mooning over Boswell. An hour's walk at mid-day. These long breaks in my writing suit me very ill; yet it is pretty clear that Friday, Sat. and Sunday will generally be barren.- Wrote to Mrs. Jolly, asking if I can call next Friday evening.- Dull day till evening; heaviness upon me. Never am well when I break off my work.

Mond. Ap. 29. Again a dire collapse. Sudden doubt about my plot and utter inability to proceed. A day and night of wretched toiling in the mind, endeavouring to make alterations. Shall have to rewrite almost all I have done.- Letter from Nellie and one from Alg.-

Tuesd. Ap. 30. Desperate walking all the morning over Hampstead way, in mist and rain, wrestling with my story. Finally got it clear, and went on with relief in body and mind. But this turn has so upset me that at night I went to the theatre, the new Garrick in Charing Cross Road, opened the other day, and saw Pinero's "The Profligate". I think I never sat through such feeble twaddle, or saw poorer acting. Was ashamed of myself for being present.

Wed. May 1. Long walk in morning; round by Camden Rd, Tufnell Park Rd, and Kentish Town Rd. Dull, but no rain. Got to work at 3 o'clock, and wrote till 10. Rewrote Chap. I, except the first page. This perpetual rewriting seems to be a necessity of my method. I always go at it with stubborn vigour. Letter from Alg, and one from Frederic Harrison, saying Bernard has just been admitted to Balliol.- Nothing read, except a few pages of "Tatler".-

Thursd. May 2. Dull and rainy morning; bad fog for half an hour at mid-day. Fine evening.- Morning to Brit. Museum, to get some Italian details. Wrote from 3 to 10, doing 4 pages of Chap. II, rewriting of a very difficult kind.

Frid. May 3. Again altering my plot, getting it into still better order.- A very fine day. No reading, no writing.- In the evening to the Jollys. Did not see Mrs Jolly, and the husband and sister were not particularly cordial. Shall not go again unless I am invited.-

Sat. May 4. No work. In afternoon Roberts.

Sund. May 5. To work again. Dismissed Chap. I. and did 5pp. of Chap. II. Wrote 4 to 10.- Fine day; very warm; a little thunder. Headache.

Mond. May 6. A very hot summer day. Walk in the morning round St. John's Wood. Got to work at 3.30 and wrote till 10, rewriting last page of yesterday and doing 4 more; the end of Chap. II. No reading.

Tuesd. May 7. Warm, but dull. Have a little cold on chest, result of hot weather. Walk in morning. Read some of Woolner's "My Beautiful Lady"[13]. The mental labour over story is at present so great that I cannot attend to any serious reading. Worked from 3.30 to 9.30 and did 5pp., being the 3d chapter.

Wed. May 8. Suffering from sore throat. No reading, except a little Boswell. Walk. Worked from 3.30 to 9.30. Rewrote 3pp. of Chap. IV, and dismissed the whole. Of Chapter V did 1p. 1/3.- A dull warm day.

Thursd. May 9. Throat and chest very bad. Began to re-read Daudet's "L'Immortel". Wrote only a couple of hours, getting on with Chap. V, but see that I have not even yet got my plot certain. Shall have at least 10pp. to rewrite.- Letter from Shortridge.

Frid. May 10. Last night did not close my eyes till 4am. A horrible anguish of clockwork thought about the novel. Must alter the whole plot again.- Thus has it been with all my other books, and doubtless will always be the same; but time goes terribly. I *must* have finished by autumn.- All day thinking incessantly. To make matters worse, it is rainy and dull. No reading. Got a few thoughts towards evening. Cold still bad. Utterly fagged out and wretched.

Sat. May 11. Again a dark rainy day. Still fagging over my changed plot. Nothing done, nothing read.- To Roberts' in afternoon. Hartley came in and we walked to his studio. Rained so hard at night that I had to come back by train.- Think I see my way through the story at last; shall begin absolutely de novo.

Sund. May 12. Dark and rainy all day. A walk round the park. Working at my story still. Wrote a letter to Bertz. Read some of [Thomas] Dekker's "The Honest Whore" [Part I, 1604; Part II, 1630].

Mond. May 13. Dark and rainy all day. In morning to buy tobacco, and MS paper. Got to work at 3.30, and wrote till 10.30, doing Chap. I, 4pp.- A letter this morning from Frau Clara Steinitz, of Berlin, who is translating

"Demos". As it is in the absurd German cursive, I can't read it. Plitt comes to-morrow, and he shall help me.

Tuesd. May 14. Dull day till afternoon, then a little sunshine. Walk to Hampstead. Plitt came at twelve, and took him to have lunch in Chapel Street. He read me the letter and I find it asks my permission to curtail "Demos" for publicn in a feuilleton. Matters nothing to me.—To work at 4. Had to begin Chap. I again, but think I have got it this time. Did nearly six pages. Still feeling dull, but better.

Wed. May 15. Sunny morning; walk. Plitt looked in, to talk over his gloomy prospects. As result, I found it impossible to get to work till past 7. Then did 3pp., finishing Chap. I. I hope and trust for the final time.- Page or two of Boswell.

Thursd. May 16. At last I feel able to say—though trembling lest it be presumption—that my way in the story is clear before me. From 3.30 to 9.30 I wrote more fluently than I have done since the days of "Demos". Did 5pp. It seems to me that I shall really go straight on now, for I have the book all mapped out. Thank heaven if this really prove the truth!
A fine sunny day. Walk about town in the morning. Letter from Nelly.

Frid. May 17. Again a brave day's work. Wrote from 4 to 9.30, and did 6pp., finishing Chap. II and getting into III. It goes at last, it goes!- Very dull weather, misty. Nothing read.

Sat. May 18. Sunshine, but cloudy. Much walking about in morning. At 3 came Roberts. Talked till 9, then went and had a half-fiasco of Chianti in Chapel Street. Talked much of a possible joint visit to Italy.

Sund. May 19. Dull and rainy day. Walk in morning. Worked from 3 to 9.45, but not very well. Only 3pp.- Reading [John] Forster's Life of Goldsmith.

Mond. May 20. An astonishing letter from Alg, who says he is abandoning Smallbrook Cottage, giving up housekeeping, and will move in a week's time to lodgings at Harbottle, Coquetdale. Selling furniture and books. This kind of thing fills me with gloomy forebodings. His inability to persevere in any course is remarkable. I fear it will be the same throughtout his life.- Wrote to him.
A dull day, very little sun. Wrote from 3 to 10. Had to rewrite last p. of yesterday, and did only 3 more. Still, it is progress.

Tuesd. May 21. Again blank discouragement. Have no heart to write details. Went to music-hall in evening.

Wed. May 22. Little better, yet towards evening saw my way clearer.- Fine, hot day.- Suffer much from lack of a library subscription. Think I shall be driven to take one.

Thursd. May 23. Hot weather. Nothing done. Wrote to Agbrigg, asking if they could have me there for a few weeks. Painters are let loose in the staircase here, and the air will shortly be poisoned. Very miserable.

Frid. May 24. Telegram from Nelly, saying they can have me at Agbrigg. Decided to go to-morrow morning. Sold a lot of my books, such as I do not need, to Westall for £3. This will pay my travelling expenses.- Again a very hot day.

Sat. May 25. To Wakefield by the 10.35. Fine in London, but gloomier as we went north.- Visit at Agbrigg from Katie [Algernon's wife], who has come over from Leeds, where she and child are staying with the Thompsons, awaiting Alg's arrival. Dreary talk with her about Alg's sale of his books. If not too late, I offered to advance money, rather than books should be sold.

Sund. May 26. Gloomy, dull, rather cold. Cheerless, as Sunday always is here.

Mond. May 27. Rain all day; cold. Worked in my room, the garret, from 9 to 1, from 4.30 to 8.30, and from 9 to 10,—some 12 hrs altogether; did 4pp. of Chapter IV. Am going to leave the changes in early chapters to be made when the vol. is finished.- In afternoon walk along Doncaster Road in pouring rain.

Tuesd. May 28. Wrote from 9 to 11, from 5 to 8.30 and from 9 to 10.30. Did 5pp.- A dull day, with half an hour of sunshine. Alg came from Leeds to dinner. He thinks it best to sell the books, and I made no more opposition.- Wrote to Walter Grahame.

Wed. May 29. Rain, sunshine, thunder. Worked 10 to 12; 5 to 8; and 9 to 10. Did 4pp.- Reading "Dombey and Son" at odd moments.

Thursd. May 30. Rain, sunshine, gloom, cold. Worked something less than the usual hours and did only 3pp., finishing Chap. V. Begin to suffer a good deal from the paltry kind of talk that always goes on at meals. Its characteristic is, that never does an abstract subject come up; only local facts, and those the meanest, are ever discussed.

Frid. May 31. No work. Depression.

June 1 Sat. Paid mother 15/- for last week's board. A fine warm day. Still no work; suffering much. Card of invitn sent from 7K from Mrs Gaussen. They are at Craven Hill again this year.

June 2 Sund. Very fine day. Did not go out. In morning read German papers containing some contributions of Bertz's [on Heine, Carlyle and

152

Herzog Ernst in the *Deutsche Presse*], and wrote him a letter about them.-
Some good new ideas for story.

Mond. June 3. Yet once again recommenced my book.- Wrote 9-11 and
4.30 to 8. Did 6pp. of Chap. I.- Letter from Roberts, saying he goes into
Sussex shortly.- Again a glorious day.

Tuesd. June 4. Fine day; rather misty. Worked 9 to 12.30; 4.30 to 8.30; and
9 to 10. Did 5¼pp. of good work.- Wrote to Roberts.-

Wed. June 5. Very fine day; almost cloudless from morning to night, and
pleasant breeze.- Worked 9 to 12.30; and 4.30 to 8.30.- Did 4¾pp.- In
afternoon my usual walk to Crofton. On my return, found that the big
Napoleon picture in the drawing-room had come down with stupendous
crash, smashing chairs and tables. Thank heaven this didn't happen at dead
of night!

Thursd. June 6. Again very fine day. Letter from Walter Grahame. Wrote
to Plitt.- Worked 9.30 to 12.30, and 5 to 8.30, doing 6pp., including some
copied from old MS. Getting on excellently.

Frid. June 7. Fine day, but much cooler, and no sunshine after noon. Letter
from Roberts.- He sends a good *Pall Mall* [*Gazette*] review of "Nether
World" [of June 4].- Worked 9 to 12.30 and 4.30 to 8, doing 6 good pages.
This brings me to end of Chap. III. Think I am in fair swing at last.- Walk
about Sandal hill in afternoon.

Sat. June 8. Clouded, doubtful. Cooler. Worked 9 to 1, and 4.30 to 8.30.
Did 6pp. So this week I have done 24pp.,—a fine advance, which gets me
nearly half through vol. I.- Letter from Edith Sichel, about the "Nether
World". Also one from A.J. Smith, who is now in Manchester; out of a
place, alas!

Sund. June 9. Gloomy day, much rain. Wrote long reply to Miss Sichel,
plainly stating the fact that my books are in no sense philanthropic, but
works of art. Replied to Smith.

Mond. June 10. Whit Monday. Nelly has holiday from her teaching. (She
teaches the children of Charles Alderson, an old schoolfellow of mine,—
eheu!) Walk with her in afternoon. Dull day and much wind. Wrote 4pp.
only.

Tuesd. June 11. Worked usual hours, and did 5pp. Fine day, but dull
at times. Nelly still [on] holiday. Walk with Madge in afternoon. Begun
Chap. V.

Wed. June 12. Dull. Worked 9 to 1 and 4.30 to 8.30, doing 5pp.

Thursd. June 13. Fine day. Worked 9.30 to 1 and 4.30 to 8.15. Did 5¼pp.-
Wrote letter to Alg, at Harbottle, where he says he is well settled.- Have at
length got clear of all the old MS of my story, and now begin to work ahead
on fresh ground. See the thing with much clearness, and write on the whole
easily. A great success, this coming to Agbrigg,- to my vast suprise.

Frid. June 14. Fine, but dull latterly. Worked 9 to 1, and 4.30 to 8. Did
4½pp.

Sat. June 15. Dull and spots of rain; little sun. Worked 9 to 1, and 4.30 to 8.
Did 5½pp., thus ending a second week of satisfactory work.- Letter from
Alg. Walk with Nelly to Sandal in afternoon. Some hours of depression.-
the old causes, which curiously seem never to suggest themselves to good
old Nelly.

Sund. June 16. Circular from Lippincotts of Philadelphia, saying they are
going to publish a supplement to "Allibone" up to end of 1888, and asking
me for biographical details.- Replied with date of birth, Owens College,
and list of books[14].- Idle walking about; a very fine day.- Reading
[William] Hepworth Dixon's Life of John Howard,- a paltry piece of
writing [*John Howard and the Prison World of Europe*, 1849]; and the
"Natural History of Enthusiasm," by I know not whom, though I think I
have heard [by Isaac Taylor, of Stanford Rivers, 1829]; a very interesting
book, with fine phrases now and them.

Mond. June 17. Very fine day, but for me an evil one. One page of writing,
then broke down. Walked to Hemsworth and back by train. Suffering
terribly from loneliness.

Tuesd. June 18. Black, black; another hideous day. Not a line of writing.
Too horrible to speak of.

Wed. June 19. Thank heaven, in my right mind once more! Worked usual
hours, and did my quantum of 5 pages. Weather gloomy and close.

Thursd. June 20. A very hot day; feeling headachy. Worked 9 to 1 and 4.30
to 7.30, doing only 4pp.

Frid. June 21. Again very fine day; hot.- Worked 9 to 1 and 5.30 to 6.30.
Rewrote the last 2pp. of yesterday, and did only 3 new. Thought I should
have finished vol. I to-day.
    Finished reading Dixon's "Life of John Howard".

Sat. June 22. Fine, but somewhat cloudy; hot.- Worked 9 to 1 and 5 to
7.30, doing 3pp. and *finishing vol. I*; 79pp. of MS. Heaven be praised! So
this has taken me just three weeks. I hope to do the others as quickly.
    Began to read Leigh Hunt's Autobiography.- Letter from Alg.-

Sund. June 23. Still very fine. Finished Hunt's Autobiography.

Mond. June 24. Midsummer Day. Very fine; breezy. Took my favourite walk by the field path from Heath Common to Crofton Station.- the most rural walk in this neighbourhood.- Worked 9 to 1, and 4.30 to 8.30. Did nearly 6pp., thus making a good entrance upon 2nd vol.- Read some lives in the English Cyclopaedia.

Tuesd. June 25. A poor day; worked long hours,—even after supper—but did only a little more than 4pp.- Sent £10 to pay rent for 7K. Long letter from Edith Sichel, in reply to mine. Not a page of reading.-

Wed. June 26. Fine, but dullish. Worked usual hours, and did 7pp., the best day yet.- Read one or two of Bacon's Essays. Letter from Roberts, from Shoreham.

Thursd. June 27. Dull and heavy day.- Worked 11 to 1 (could not begin before) and 4.30 to 8.30, doing 5pp. Read some of Bacon's Essays.

Frid. June 28. Very dull and hot; a short, heavy shower.- Letter from Bertz and some numbers of the *Deutsche Presse*[15]. Note from Thomas Hardy, asking me to go and see him in London,- thinking I am there. Note from Tillotsons of Bolton, saying they are going to publish "Christmas on the Capitol", and wish to print my autograph.
Worked 9 to 1, and 4.30 to 8; did 4 pp.

Sat. June 29. Fine day, less warm.- Worked 9 to 1, and 4.30 to 7, doing 4pp. This finishes my quantum of 30pp. for this week. Talking of going with Madge to Jersey in August.-

Sund. June 30. Fine, cloudy. Reading Burns's Letters, and Addison's papers in the *Spectator*.- Wrote to Plitt, to Roberts, and to Edith Sichel.

Mond. July 1. Fine, dull at times. Worked 10 to 1, 4.30 to 8.30 and 9 to 10, doing 5pp.—Letter from Plitt, who is about to leave England, and one from A.J. Smith, who is in Manchester still, and still without employment.

Tuesd. July 2. One of the finest days yet. Worked 9.30 to 1 and 4.30 to 7.30, doing 5pp. Letter from Alg, returning the £2. Walk in the afternoon in the fields between Heath and Crofton, which are always most delightful to me. Have decided to make my novel consist of two Parts; with some three years of interval.

Wed. July 3. Very fine day. Worked 9 to 1 and 4.30 to 8, doing 5pp. and reaching the end of Part I, middle (rather more) of vol. II. Shall have to pause to-morrow, to see my way clearly.
Romeike, the press-cutting man[16], sends from New York a review of "The Nether World" from a S. Carolina paper. Harpers are the American

publishers.—"Franklin Square Library".—Letter from Mrs. Jolly, saying she has returned "Thyrza", which I lent her. Of course no one to take it in at 7K; wrote to the Postmaster.

Still reading Burns's letters.

Thursd. July 4. Glorious day. Mostly in the open air. Postcard from Bertz, who also sends "Niels Lyhne" [by Jens Peter Jacobsen] in Reclam's edition. Began to read this. But could give little attention to anything but the difficulties of the new part of my story.

Frid. July 5. Still thinking. Fine. Read at "Niels Lyhne".

Sat. July 6. Still thinking and idling. Very fine. Read a little.

Sund. July 7. Very fine. Finished Burns's letters. Wrote long letter to Bertz.

Mond. July 8. Recommenced at the desk; worked 9 to 1, 4.30 to 8.30, and 9.30 to 10.30, doing 5pp.- Letter from Edith Sichel. Very windy, but fine. Walk in the afternoon nearly to Nostell.

Tuesd. July 9. Cloudy, a little rain.- Had to cancel all yesterday's work and, to improve matters, tore up by ill chance a newly written page, instead of an old one. For all that did 6pp., finishing Chap. I of the 2nd part.- Another American review of "The Nether World" sent by Romeike, the press-cutting man.- Read some of Addison's *Spectator.*

Wed. July 10. A day of rain, at last.- Letter from Alg, dispirited about his proofs. Worked 9 to 12.30, and 4.30 to 8.15, again doing 6pp.—Replied to Alg.

Thursd. July 11. Fine day.- Worked 9 to 1 and 4.30 to 8.30, doing 6pp.- Bought Baedeker's "Northern France". Postcard from Bertz. Wrote to Mrs. King asking her to send tobacco.

Frid. July 12. Fine, cloudy in afternoon. Nelly went to Ilkley, to stay with Aldersons till Monday. Worked 9 to 1, and 5 to 8.15, doing 5½pp.- Read a little Addison.- Mother went to York and returned, on dentist business.

Sat. July 13. Light rain most of the day. Worked 9 to 1 and 4.15 to 8, doing 6pp. But I had to rewrite the last 1½ of yesterday.- Note from Roberts who has begun to work at Mevagissey.

Sund. July 14. Some rain.- Read Addison and "Niels Lyhne"; also Goldsmith's "Traveller" and some lives in the Cyclopaedia.- Wrote to Roberts.

Mond. July 15. Heavy rain showers, and high wind. Worked only in the morning, doing 2pp. Rather out of sorts. Curious that I am always dilatory about the last few pages of a volume.- Read Addison and "Niels Lyhne".

Tuesd. July 16. Showery, but often very bright. Worked 9 to 1 and 4.30 to 6.15, doing 4pp. and *finishing vol. II.* Plitt sends some more numbers of the *Corriere di Napoli.* Read them, and some "Niels Lyhne".

Wed. July 17. Dull and cold. Struggling with the beginning of vol. III, and managed a poor three pages. Letter from Roberts.

Thursd. July 18. Very cold in morning; afternoon brighter. Wrote 9 to 1 and 4.30 to 7.30. Had to rewrite yesterday's work, and did 5pp.- Letter from Walter Grahame, saying he is off to Switzerland. Replied.

Frid. July 19. Cold and dark day; in morning so dark that I had to light gas. Much hindered in work by sundry difficulties. Wrote 2pp. in morning, but in evening cancelled them, and wrote only 1; most of the time spent in making notes for the chapter. Over-strain in mind. But think I have got things straight.

Sat. July 20. A little sunshine, but wretched, on the whole. Letter from Mrs Gaussen. Worked 9 to 1, and 4.30 to 7.30, doing 5pp.- Read some Addison and "Niels Lyhne".

Sund. July 21. Rainy often; very little sunshine. Read Canon [H.P.] Liddon's "Some Elements of Religion [Lent Lectures]". Useless to me, of course; nothing but assumptions at the bottom of it,- as what else could there be?

Mond. July 22. Fine on whole. Worked 9 to 1 and 4.30 to 8.30, doing 5pp. Read some Addison.- Sent 10/- to Mrs King which ought to have gone last Saturday.

Tuesd. July 23. A bad day. Heavy thunderstorm in morning; much rain. Worked 9 to 1 and 5.30 to 7, doing only 3½pp.

Wed. July 24. Cloudy; rain. Worked 9 to 1 and 4.30 to 8.30, doing 4pp. Had to rewrite last ½p. of yesterday. Working with that miserable sense of a clog on the brain which comes now and then; seems to be a physical obstruction to thought,- and no doubt is. About 12 o'clock had a slight relief, a sudden flow of composition for a few lines, but then a stop again. These Chaps. VIII and IX the hardest in the whole book.- A little Addison read.

Thursd. July 25. Dull and windy. Worked usual hours, but did only 4pp. again.

Frid. July 26. Not a gleam of sunshine till 2 o'clock; then rain and thunder. Had to rewrite yesterday's work. The weather oppresses me. Thank heaven I had better for the first two vols. Read some Addison.

Sat. July 27. Once more a fine day. Mother and Nelly left at 9.22 this morning for Broadway.- There arrived copies of Alg's new book, "Both of this Parish", which is announced for first time in to-day's *Spectator.-* Letter from Bertz, saying he is about to write an article on me, to serve as introduction to the German transln of "Demos".- Worked short hours, and did only 2pp.- Reading "Toilers of the Sea" [by Victor Hugo] , in preparation of Guernsey.- Madge and I left alone with the infant servant.

Sund. July 28. Dull. Wrote to Mrs Gaussen, and to Mlle Le Breton, asking if French transln of "Demos" is yet pubd.- Read a little book by one Archdeacon Smith, "Common Words with Curious Derivations". Also finished "Toilers of the Sea", and read first vol. of Alg's book. Read a little of Italian transln of French novel, "La Cocolla" [*La Corruptrice,* by Emile Goudeau. 1889].

Mond. July 29. Heavy, close, sunny on the whole. Wrote 9 to 12.30 and 4.30 to 8.30, doing 7pp.; a rare day. Letter from Plitt, saying he left Southampton yesterday for Genoa.

Tuesd. July 30. Very fine and hot day once more.- Letter from Alg, telling us how to distribute copies of his book. Wrote 9 to 12.30 and 5 to 7.30, doing 4pp.

Wed. July 31. Again very fine and hot.- Letter from Nelly.- Worked usual hours,- except that it gets too dark to write after 8.15,- and did 4½pp. Also had to rewrite last of yesterday.

Thursd. Aug. 1. Very dull and foggy day, but no rain.- Madge's school-treat.- Worked 9 to 12.30 and 4.30 to 8. In morning did 1½p., but in afternoon had to rewrite this, and did 1p. more.- Read a little Addison.

Frid. Aug. 2. Dull, close. Did only 2½pp. In unsatisfactory mood. Headache.

Sat. Aug. 3. Tolerably fine. Still headache. Morning did 1½p., and no more to-day. In afternoon went by train with Madge to Crigglestone. Mood gloomy. Wrote to Alg.

Sund. Aug. 4. Fine day. Better in mood. Read a lot of Addison. Wrote to Mlle Le Breton, Bertz and Nelly.

Monday. Aug. 5. Dull, and heavy thunderstorm. Wrote 9 to [1] and 4.15 to 7.15, doing 5½pp. Read some Addison.

Tuesd. Aug. 6. Dull, many and heavy showers. Wrote 9 to 12.30 and 4.30 to 7, doing 4pp. Had to begin, however, with rewriting yesterday's last 2½.- Read some Addison, and began to re-read [Charles Kingsley's] "Alton Locke". Letter from Grahame, from Les Avants [in Switzerland].

Wed. Aug. 7. Much rain, but fine afternoon. Worked 9 to 1, and 4.30 to 7.15, doing 4pp. Read at "Alton Locke". Wrote to mother.

Thursd. Aug. 8. Fine on the whole. Postcard from Roberts, from Padstow.- Worked 9 to 1 and 4.30 to 8, doing 4pp.,- one of them written twice.- "Alton Locke".

Frid. Aug. 9. Much rain and no sunshine. Wrote 10 to 12.30 and 4.30 to 7, doing 4pp. Only one chapter remains.- Wrote to Roberts. Finished "Alton Locke".

Sat. Aug. 10. Dull day. No writing, but thought over last chapter, still to be written.- In afternoon with Madge to call on the Langs at Thornes.- Letter from Miss Sichel, from Sunnyside, Chiddingfold, Surrey.

Sund. Aug. 11. Fine in morning; dull later. Reading nothing in particular.

Mond. Aug. 12. No sun, no rain. Worked 9 to 12.30 and 4 to 8.30, doing 4pp.- Letter from Roberts. Began to read "Hertha" by Frederika Bremer.[17]

Tuesd. Aug. 13. Fine morning; later dull. Wrote 9 to 1, and 5 to 7.45, doing 4pp. and *finishing the novel*. This makes *ten weeks and one day* for the actual writing. Quick work; of course too quick. But needs must. Am doubtful whether it will not be too "emancipated" for Bentley. We shall see.- Read at "Hertha".

Wed. Aug. 14. A day of incessant rain, or all but. In the night grew dissatisfied with the last two pages of my story. To-day destroyed them, and had to rewrite, but unsuccessfully.- Read some Shelley, and wrote some thought on Capital Punishment.[18]

Thursd. Aug. 15. Dull, but not raining. In morning succeeded in finishing the book again. It is to be called "The Emancipated".- In evening with Madge to call on the Bruces, whom I have not seen for 14 years. Sam Bruce white-headed and stricken in years, but very cordial.

Fri. Aug. 16. Postcard to Bertz, and sent back the numbers of the *Deutsche Presse*.- In a restless, excited state. Days of delay like this make me ill. To tea at the Hicks', and subsequently to the Wakefield theatre with M[atthew] B[ussey] [Hick], saw part of an unintelligible comic opera.

Sat. Aug. 17. Very fine day once more. Mother and Nelly came home, and I met them at Walton.- Read a little Lamb. In uneven spirits. Afternoon to see the Halls.[19]

Sund. Aug. 18. Fine, but cloudy.- Read in desultory way at Lamb. Packed. Wrote to Alg and postcard to Roberts.

159

Mond. Aug. 19. With Madge to London, reaching there at 1 o'clock. Dined at restaurant, and walked about streets. Bought suit of clothes for 39/6. Made preparations for starting to-morrow.

Tuesd. Aug. 20. Rain and wind, no sunshine.- Telegram from Nelly saying a reply had come at last from the Hotel du Gouffre, Guernsey. Made a lot of purchases. Left MS of "The Emancipated" at Bentley's. Looked in with Madge at the National Gallery. Dinner in Chapel Street.- In driving to Waterloo to catch the 7.25 to S'hampton, the horse in the hansom fell, we were shot forward and our luggage was flung off the top down into Endell Street. No bone broken, and luggage not much injured. At S'hampton by 10.9, and went on board the boat. Wretched night, raining, blowing, cold. Madge very sick, and I too had a turn of it at 6 o'clock next morning, when we were off the Casquets.

Wed. Aug. 21. Reached Peter Port, Guernsey, at 9.30. Took carriage and drove to Gouffre Hotel, where we took two bedrooms and sitting-room for 6/- each per diem. Tremendous gale all day, but a good deal of sunshine, and warm air. Delighted with the verdure of the place. Walked to Petit Bot Bay. In the evening was invited to go and drive with the landlord, De La Rue, who had to fetch lobsters from near Perelle Bay. A wild darkening sky; wind violent all day.

Things very satisfactory here in the hotel. Have dinner at 6.30 (in our own sitting-room, as we are the only guests at present).

Thursd. Aug.22. A wild morning. Walked (Madge and I) along the cliffs as far as Saints Bay. The sky cleared there, and it became a glorious day, so we decided to go on to Peter Port, and have lunch there. Bright and warm; the air very clear. In afternoon walked back.- Before breakfast read a little in Ovid's "Amores".-

We have decided to give up our project of going on into Brittany. Find it would be too expensive. Have decided to stay here a fortnight, and then go to Sark.

Letter from Bentleys, acknowledging receipt of "The Emancipated", and asking if I shouldn't like to effect a temporary insurance of the MS. while it is in their hands. Replied that money would be small satisfaction for loss, and that I can leave it with confidence. (Do they wish to see what value I should put on it?)

Frid. Aug. 23. Rain-clouds in morning, but on the whole a glorious day, almost windless. Walked by the coast to Pleinmont, taking with us a lunch which the hotel people made up. Fine rugged scenery all the way, and Pleinmont itself a grand, though not huge, promontory. The granite rocks show a rich variety of colour, and are spotted with bright orange lichen, often also covered with ivy. Though the sea was quite calm, the rising tide broke with a good deal of spray on the rock-islands, and among the chasms.- Walked back to dinner.- Wrote to Alg.- Read some Ovid at Pleinmont.- Cannot keep eyes open after 9 o'clock.

160

Sat. Aug. 24. Fine, but cloudy at times. Set off and walked along the coast to Jerbourg Point, then round to a place overlooking Fermain Bay, where we sat down and lunched. A very fine view over the Russel and along the shore to the north end of the island; the intense blue of sea, and the sandy colour of coast about St. Sampson's, with specks of white and light-coloured houses make a scene almost Italian.- Played with some beautiful calves tethered to the hill side.- Walked home through St Martin's, the parish chiefly inhabited by people who take houses.- Dined with two people from Nottingham, A Mr [William Scott] Hodgson (seemingly landscape painter) and his wife.

The Guernsey houses are generally of the plainest architectural type, a simple gable at each end. Built of a grey granite. The squared stones strongly outlined—sometimes yellow-washed. Often a porch, with a glass door to it and flowers on each side within. The windows always painted white, which gleams in perennial freshness—indeed all the buildings look as if finished yesterday. Generally a large hot-house, for grapes; some very large indeed. The front gardens not laid out in beds, but planted with shrubs (fuchsias common) and the grass unmown; cows and sheep sometimes grazing on the lawn.

At lunch-time read several Elegies of Ovid's "Amores". And again at night, when it rained heavily. We noticed to-day that the little red pimpernels were all but closed, which seems to foretell rain.

Sund. Aug. 25. A glorious day, warm and brilliant throughout.- Of course troubles and annoyances about church-going; fitting in of meals etc. In morning Madge went to Forest church. Afternoon we sat on the rocks, and I read Ovid,- Madge some dirty little pietistic work. Evening she went to St Martin's and I thither to meet her at eight o'clock. An exquisite evening; bats very thick in the air, and much shrilling of hedge-crickets—whatever their proper name be. An orange sky in the west, and long after-glow.

Mond. Aug. 26. Again a perfect day. Started after breakfast for Peter Port, made some inquiries there about Sark boats etc, then took the bus to S. Sampson's, where we ate lunch. Thence by public wagonette to Bordeaux Harbour, about a mile and a half north, a rocky little bay, where we saw numbers of anemones, and a variety of seaweeds.

A hateful dinner. Mrs. Hodgson proves to be an intolerable woman; at every meal she has grumbled at the food,

[Full page sketch of the Gouffre]

and to-day she refused to touch a morsel of anything, making a horrible scene, and spoiling our digestion. There she sat, vinegary and obstinate. Her husband, a mild, good-natured man, tried to converse, but could say little. In her behaviour, not a trace of common civility,—in spite of pretence of elegance and suavity. The type of creature is only too familiar to me.—It must be admitted that the dinner was bad, and that the food here is altogether indifferent. The people seem to have no idea of keeping a hotel, and, though evidently well-disposed, make no effort to supply their guests decently.

Letter from Nelly at Scarboro. Madge wrote to her; and I sent postcards to two hotels in Sark, asking terms.

Tuesd. Aug. 27. Again a perfect day. Spent it in Saints Bay, idling. On return, inquired terms etc. at several lodging-houses close by—the best part of the island. I copy down the addresses of some of them.
Mrs. Male. Rose Farm. St. Martin's. 2 bed-rooms & a sitting-room 35/-
Mrs James St. Martin's. 2 bed-rooms & a sitting-room 30/-
Goshen Villa St Martin's. 2 bed-rooms & a sitting-room 30/-

All these were clean and decent, and landladies will provide food.

Read Ovid.- The Hodgsons depart to-morrow, thoroughly disgusted.

Wed. Aug. 28. An unparalleled day; not a handbreadth of cloud visible from morning to sunset. Went to Sark alone; just to find lodgings. The boat left S. Peter Port at 9.30am., and was in the Creux at Sark an hour later. Wandered and inquired much before I could find quarters. The two hotels are Victoria and Dixcart; the former 6/- a day, but noisy; the latter 7/6 a day and seemingly very good. These being too dear for us, I succeeded at length in taking rooms at a house just in front of the post-office, Miss Massey's; 2 bedrooms and sitting-room for 30/- a week.

Went to see the Coupée and Dixcart Bay, but it was too hot to walk more than necessary. Got to S. Peter's again by 6 o'clock, and home by 7.30. Dined alone once more, thank Heaven! the Hodgsons having departed this morning.

Thursd. Aug. 29. Again not a cloud from sunrise to sunset. Very hot. Went to Saints Bay, where Madge bathed. Read some of the "Metamorphoses". In afternoon I walked alone to Peter Port, and bought some things to take with us to Sark to-morrow. Bought [Victor Hugo's] "Les Misérables" and "Ninety-three". Paid hotel bill here, which amounts to £5.11.6. Wrote to Nelly, who is still at Scarborough.

Frid. Aug. 30. Had breakfast at 7.30, and left the hotel at 8, driving down to catch the Sark boat. A very fine morning, but just a few light clouds at last. Tremendously hot when we landed. To our lodgings at Miss Massey's. Brought a fowl with us from Guernsey for to-day's dinner. Fortunately it was a day of spring tide, so that we took a guide (3/-) in afternoon, and went down to Gouliot Caves. A good deal of wading to be done. Madge was carried by the man. In late evening, a walk up to the windmill, whence many lighthouses can be seen. On the road thither, the two last houses on right hand are occupied by a party of ten Oxford men, who are reading with a tutor. Noisy merriment going on among them, just after dinner; a party out on the lawn, playing cards by lamplight; a man at the piano, singing airs from "Mikado" [comic opera by Gilbert and Sullivan, 1885]; others scattered about—talking, smoking, having coffee. The open windows and doors showed all this.

Sat. Aug. 31. In morning to the Coupée. Weather dull; a little rain at end of afternoon. After lunch descended into Derrible Bay—rather a stiff business—and went into the caverns etc. Madge bathed.- Reading "Ninety-three".- Wrote to Mother.

Sund. Sept. 1. The usual Sabbath difficulties. Early dinner, etc. But I notice that Madge is reading "Les Misérables" in spite of its being Sunday,- a remarkable thing. She went to French service in the morning, and English in afternoon. Evening the wind freshened, and we walked about the cliffs; no breakers however. Read at "Ninety-three". Far from cheerful, and look forward rather dolorously at the fortnight to be spent here. No conversation, nor the possibility of it.

Mond. Sept. 2. A dull day, with a few drops of rain. Morning to Dixcart Bay, where Madge bathed; thence to the Grève de la Ville. In afternoon, through the Seigneurie grounds, then on to the extreme point of the island. Went down into the first of the Boutique Caves. Just before reaching the small tower, which is part of the ruined fortifications, a chasm suddenly opens on the left, down to the sea; it has perpendicular sides, and in width is about twenty feet at the bottom, and at the top it is not much broader; depth, perhaps 100 feet. Perpendicular granite on each side and the low tide discloses a little beach of boulders. From the mouth of this cleft descends a pathway, steep, and difficult because it is sandy and shaly, with scarcely any foothold for a long way; you hold on to projecting granite on each hand. More than half way down, you come to a level break of the descent where is seen a tremendous cleft. That arm of it to the left is nearly a chasm; by that to the right, you enter the Boutique Caves. Here again there is difficulty. To get to the actual entrance, you climb up a crumbly path, some fifteen feet, and then find yourself on the narrow sill of a gigantic cavern, to enter which you must descend about as low as you have just climbed. Then you are in the cave. Its floor, which is covered with vast pieces of broken stone,- their sharp edges showing that the breakage is comparatively recent,- slopes rapidly down. At first you look down into mere blackness, but when the eye accustoms itself, you see that the slope is one of perhaps 60 feet, and ends at a narrow arch down below. To this we did not descend; the guide tells us that, when you reach it, daylight appears through, and you are in a great cave with outlets to the sea. However, we clambered half-way down (the cave is 50 feet high, and of same breadth) to a point where a gigantic stone seems to block the way, after which the descent becomes gloomier and steeper. There, looking to the left, we saw a narrow offshoot, a gallery which descends rapidly, and at the end of which the boulder beach was visible.- There are veins of quartz in the granite here, and also a great deal of soft, friable stone. A little water drips from the cavern roof. Samphire growing about.

A letter from Alg, forwarded from the Gouffre. Wrote to Mrs King.

Tuesd. Sept. 3. Much lightning and thunder last night. This morning very dull at first, then brilliant and hot. To Little Sark, and explored all about the extremity of the shore,- Port Gorey etc. Afternoon to the Grève de la Ville, where Madge bathed; afterwards we made our way over huge boulders covered with seaweed to the Chapelle des Mauves, and having passed through that, went into some of the great caves beyond. One of them, a long and high gallery, consists chiefly of red and green granites; the green especially beautiful, moulded by the wave into strange forms.

Letter from Nelly. Postcard from Roberts, saying he returns to town on the 7th.- Wrote to Nelly.

Wed. Sept. 4. Scarcely any sunshine, but no rain. Morning to a point whence we looked down on the Creux Harbour, and saw the steamer come in; then to the Creux du Derrible, and saw the tide high. Too calm to make any roaring. Afternoon down to the landing place at Havre Gosselin, a descent ending in ropes and a ladder, onto a little ledge of rock, where boats are moored, at all tides, in deep water.- Letter from Nelly.

Thursd. Sept. 5. An autumnal day, unclouded sunshine through a thin mist, which softened colours, and hid the sea horizons. In the morning sat by the Pilcher Monument, and went down onto the beach of Havre Gosselin; afternoon sat in the valley, leading down to Grève de la Ville, the richest and softest of the sea valleys. Read Ovid once more. In evening wrote to Bertz.

Frid. Sept. 6. Again very fine, but misty. A glorious moon, getting towards full. Morning strolling near home, afternoon to north end of the island. At eight in the evening to a concert given by certain of the visitors, in the Girls'School; tickets 1/- each. These concerts have been weekly of late, and are an old institution. The room crowded, and for the most part with as ugly people as I ever saw. A certain Hon. C. Fremantle, aged about seventy, made a fool of himself by singing a serio-comic song. Romberg's "Toy Symphony" was executed; not badly. The Oxford fellows gave some comical singing. Sark children flattening their noses ag[ain]st the windows. The room lighted with lamps and candles. The wall facing us adorned with maps and a large sheet of animals. Tickets taken at the door by M. Robin, the schoolmaster.

Sat. Sept. 7. I took the 8 o'clock boat (the "Saturday trip") and went alone to Guernsey. Fine, fresh morning, the sea whitened a little. Made a lot of purchases—Eau de Cologne, photographs, cabbage-sticks etc. Casually met De La Rue, of the Gouffre Hotel. Back by the 11 o'clock boat. In afternoon down to the Grève de la Ville, where Madge bathed; rather heavy breakers. Again glorious moon; out to the Coupée after dinner.

Sund. Sept. 8. All but cloudless day. Madge to 8 o'clock church, and again at 3 o'clock. In morning we sat and read on the hillside overlooking Port à la Jument, whence there is a fine view of the north end of island. Towards sunset walked down to the Port au Moulin. The path a delightful one, along the edge of the Seigneurie grounds, through a little wood, past the

Ecluse cottage, which is wonderfully covered with roses and giant geraniums and fuchsias. Excellent full moon.- Reading "Les Misérables".

Mond. Sept. 9. Set out in the morning with a lantern, to explore the Boutique caves again. Descended by the chasm, and down the first cave to the hole at the bottom, where light gleams at once from the large opening of the following cave onto the sea. The central cave has two openings; the tide fills it, and must roar finely at the foot of the ascending cavern, against the huge boulders. From the central cave, we went on into the gallery, which is 200 feet long, and has a good deal of shallow water in it; here we had to light our lantern. In the middle, the wind blew it out, and relighting was very difficult. Coming to the end, we found ourselves looking onto the strait (dry at low tide) between the island and la Grune, but this way is choked with impracticable rocks. We had to climb up a perpendicular wall of rough granite, on our right hand. For me alone it would have been difficult, and slightly dangerous, but I had to get the lantern (an unwieldy one) up as well, and then to help Madge, who had a terrible business of it; at the end, I had to lie flat down on a ledge of rock, and haul her up the rock by main force. Getting out of this at length, we went over onto the Grune; then home.

In afternoon to Grève de la Ville, where Madge bathed. Evening wrote to Mrs King, giving her directions

[Sketch of Miss Massey's Pantry, New Place, Sark]

with regard to our return on Saturday.- It has been a fine and hot day, but clouded for an hour in afternoon. Moon magnificent to-night. Small bright halo round it; the earth covered with delicate white mist.

Tuesd. Sept. 10. Perfect day; mist entirely gone. Took our lunch with us, and went down into the Port du Moulin. Thence, by terrific scrambling, into Saignie Bay, where we looked into the caves, but could not get into the best, as tide did not go low enough.

Rather desperate for lack of conversation.

Wed. Sept. 11. Magnificent day. Morning to Grève de la Ville; Madge bathed. Afternoon clambered down the west side of the Coupée into Grande Grève, and up again. Drenched with perspiration.—Letter from Nelly. One from Grahame, who is just returning from Switzerland. One from Bertz, with news that a German novelist, Schweichel[20], thinks of writing an article on me in the *Neue Zeit*. B. also speaks of an article called "The Nether World", by Farrar, in this month's *Contemporary* [*Review*]. Is this on my book? We shall see[21]—Wrote to Alg, and replied to Bertz.

Thursd. Sept. 12. Perfect day again; very hot. Morning to Grève de la Ville; Madge bathed. Afternoon to the Seigneurie grounds.—Read some "Metamorphoses", and got on with "Les Misérables".

Frid. Sept. 13. Perfectly fine. In morning to the north end of the island. Afternoon to get some hartstongue ferns from Baker's Valley. Evening to another concert at the Girls' School,- the last this season.

Sat. Sept. 14. Left Sark by 8 o'clock boat to Guernsey. A dull morning—of course. Just caught the S'hampton boat, and onwards. Dull still, but a calm sea. Madge not absolutely sick; out on deck all the way. A good passage, and reached Docks by 5pm. A special train had been put on, and we were in London by 9. On reaching 7K found all my directions fulfilled by Mrs King; things comfortable.

Sund. Sept. 15. A dreary and weary day. Weather dull. In morning with Madge to St Paul's. Afternoon and evening she went to M'bone Parish church alone. Read some newspapers. Headache.

Mond. Sept. 16. Very dull day, and colder; east wind. In morning to town, making purchases. Bought the *Contemporary* which has Farrar's article on "The Nether World"; written coldly and poorly. Afternoon with Madge to the Zool. Gardens. Dull evening, reading *Spectators* of last three weeks.- Letter from Alg, and note from Frau Steinitz, saying she gets on with "Demos".

Tuesd. Sept. 17. Woke up with a violent cold—of course. Notwithstanding, in morning to National Gallery, where I encountered Walter Grahame. Rest of the day sat in. Poultices etc.- Sunshine.

Wed. Sept 18. On the whole fine. Madge went to Wakefield by the 1.30 express. My cold rather worse. Sat at home, reading Dante (5 Cantos of Purgatorio) and some of the prose dialogues of Leopardi.- Note from Miss Sichel inviting me to their country house (Sunnyside, Chiddingfold, Surrey) for Friday or Saturday next week.

Thursd. Sept. 19. Rainy, vile. Cold no better. In afternoon came Walter Grahame, and stayed several hours. Read Dante and Leopardi. Note from Bentleys, saying they will be ready to talk to me about "The Emancipated" next Monday.- To bed at nine o'clock.

Frid. Sept. 20. Letter from Madge and Mother. Replied to both asking them to send me £5 from bank.- Dull day, ending in heavy rain. In morning bought an overcoat, tie, slippers etc.—a tremendous outlay in such things just now. Then to British Museum, where I read in Taine's English Literature. In evening read some [E.A.] Freeman's historical essays, at home.

Sat. Sept. 21. Sunny, but cold. At three o'clock came Roberts and stayed till 10. The usual talk and laughter.

Sund. Sept. 22. First thing in morning called Walter Grahame; asking me to dine this evening. Did not go out till then. Finished the vol. of Freeman's Essays, and took up Buckle again.[22] Sunshine, but cold.

Mond. Sept. 23. Sunny, but very cold. At 11.30 went to Bentley's, and saw Dick. He says the estimate of the book is favourable. Wanted to know how much I asked, and even expressed wish to hear how my other books were selling. Told him that of the business side of the matter I knew nothing. Asked for the copyright £250. Answer to come in a few days.- Home and at 3 o'clock to Roberts's new lodgings, 49 Redburn St. Chelsea. With him to the studios in Manresa Road, where we saw [Frank] Brangwyn[23] and McCormick. Back home at 7.30. Letter from Austin Harrison; replied. Reading Buckle. Wrote to Alg.

Tuesd. Sept. 24. Note from Miss Sichel, asking me to put off my visit till Saturday. Replied. Morning and evening at British Museum, reading Bourget's "Etudes et Portraits", and [A.H.] Buck's "[Treatise on] Hygiene" [1879]. Most of the day pouring rain. At 8 o'clock went to the Strand, and drank glass of lager. Lonely again.- Recd £5 from Agbrigg, which leaves me £5 only in the bank at Wakefield.

Wed. Sept. 25. Fine day, but cold. Morning to Museum, and read Axel Munthe's "Letters from a Mourning City". He ought to have made much more of his subject. Home at mid-day, and Roberts called. Then to Museum again, and looked into [W.B.] Carpenter's "[Principles of] Mental Physiology"; read his preface agst the Determinists. Then to the London Pavilion. Letter from Nelly.

Thursd. Sept. 26. At British Museum again.

Frid. Sept. 27. Bentley writes, offering these terms for "The Emancipated". £150 down; £50 more when 850 copies of the 3 v. edition sold, and another £50 if 1000 are sold. I shall accept. Rather miserable letter from Alg; he seems to regret giving up the cottage at Broadway.- Went to Museum and read a book called "Dolce Napoli" [1878] by one [W.J.A.] Stamer, seemingly an Irishman; a depressing and vulgar book, but containing information. Roberts came to the reading-room, and we went to Gatti's. Home at 5 o'clock, and made a poor dinner. Wrote to Mother.

Sat. Sept. 28. A fine morning. Started by the 9.30 from Waterloo, and went to Witley Station, whence walked to Chiddingfold. Found Miss Sichel living with Miss Emily Ritchie, sister-in-law of Mrs. Richmond Ritchie. Had a very pleasant day, and much gossip. The country glorious; colour of trees most wonderful. Home by 7 o'clock. Dined at Loveridge's in the Strand.- Postcard from Plitt from Pompeii.

Sund. Sept. 29. Wrote to the girls, and to Mrs Gaussen. Also to Bentley, accepting his terms. Tolerably fine day. Roberts came.

Mond. Sept. 30. In morning thought about my next novel. Replied to Plitt. Wrote to Alg. Most of day at home; read a lot of Ovid's "Tristia". In evening walked about the wet streets. Very cold. "Both of this Parish" reviewed unfavourably in last Sat.'s *Spectator*. Eheu!

*   *   *

Thursd. Oct. 3. Have grown tired of noting the monotonous and ignoble days. My solitude is a wearisome topic.- Yesterday signed agreement for "The Emancipated", and recd cheque for £150 from Bentley. Sent it to Agbrigg, as usual, to be banked for me. To-day Roberts looked in. Bought Baedeker's Greece, in the German edition. Wasted time at the Temple Bar News Rooms. Excogitated something of a short story, to be called "Manfred: a Reminiscence" [Never written].

Frid. Oct. 4. Rain all day. Reading Ovid's "Tristia", Pliny's Letters, and "La Grèce, Rome et Dante" [Etudes littéraires d'après nature] by [Jean-Jacques] Ampère. Sense of wasted time.

Sat. Oct. 5. Wet day. Did nothing. In evening the first assembly of what Roberts calls the Quadrilateral: Roberts, Hudson, Alfred Hartley and I. I gave them a scrubby sort of dinner (Hartley came later) and afterwards we sat over whisky and pipes till 10 o'clock. Vast amount of talk. A good evening.- Mother send[s] £20.

Sund. Oct. 6. Wet and dull day. In afternoon came Roberts. Evening we went together to the S[ocial] D[emocratic] F[ederation] Hall, 337 Strand, and heard Headlam on Christian Socialism. Read Ibsen's "Ghosts" and "An Enemy of Society".

Mond. Oct. 7. Did nothing, and thought nothing.

Tuesd. Oct. 8. Morning walked about City. Then to Brit. Museum. Mere pottering.

Wed. Oct. 9. Recd first sheet proofs of "Emancipated" from Clowes of Beccles. Worked at Museum. Evening to [Edgar] Harrison's at Gunnersbury.

Thursd. Oct. 10. A bright and mild day. Another sheet of proofs. In morning worked over plan of my new book, to be called, I think, "The Head Mistress". Afternoon with Roberts to Hartley's studio, where met a lot of men. Thence to the studio of Lee,[24] the sculptor. Some very interesting work.

Frid. Oct. 11. Proofs come each morning.- Dined with Roberts at a little French place in Soho, then we went to a big meeting at S. James's Hall, called to protest against the immorality of Music Halls. A thoroughly bourgeois gathering.- Wrote to Madge and Nelly.

Sat. Oct.12. In afternoon to Hudson's for the first time; Tower House, St. Luke's Road, Westbourne Park. The poor fellow is married to an old and very ugly wife, who formerly kept a boarding-house. There came in a Mr and Mrs Walker, who live in same house; remarkable pair. The husband is chaplain at—I think—Univ. College, London; the wife, a bright, pretty little woman, with big eyes, was a public singer. Walker, a dull, good-natured creature; the wife frets over her life. Inexplicable union! Hartley just looked in. Came away at 11.

Sund. Oct. 13. In evening to lecture by Prof. Wallace of Oxford at the rooms of the Ethical Society, Essex St, Strand. "Ethical theory and Moral Life". Dull, dull!

Mond. Oct. 14. To Museum. In evening Roberts looked in.

Tuesd. Oct. 15. Worked at Museum, on Woman Literature.- Wrote to Miss Sichel.- Have gone into habit of lying in bed till 9 o'clock in morning.

Wed. Oct. 16. At the Museum, as usual. In evening dined with Roberts in Soho, and then we went to the Shaftesbury to see "The Middleman" [by Arthur Henry Jones]. Bad play and bad acting, detestable conventionality of structure and dialogue.

Thursd. Oct. 17. Reply from Miss Sichel.- In morning to the Pastel Exhibition at the Grosvenor. Two pieces of Hartley's, not remarkable. Then to Museum, where read some of Bourget's psychological studies. Home and worked at my plan for "The Head Mistress".

Frid. Oct. 18. Reading still Bourget's "Essais Psychologiques".

Sat. Oct. 19. At last a proof of "Christmas on the Capitol". Corrected and returned.- Vile weather; much rain.- In afternoon came Roberts.

Sund. Oct. 20. Still raining. Wrote to Madge and Nell, to Walter Grahame, and to Bertz.- In evening to the Ethical Society where Prof. Caird lectured on "Morality and Religion"[25].

*   *   *

Thursd. Oct. 24. With Roberts to a Shaksp. Society reading at the Fenneseys', Hyde Park Mansions. An enjoyable evening; we read [Henry] Porter's "The Two Angry Women of Abington" [play first produced in 1599]. A break in the middle for refreshment, and at the end a good cold supper. After that, an hour given to discussion of the play, round a bowl of punch. Fennesey an interesting man. Also one Christie, a well-read stockbroker. Mrs Fennesey, and her sister Mrs Hamlyn.

Reading some Aristophanes. Also [F.W. Newman's] "Phases of Faith", for the first time.

Sund. Oct. 27. To the Ethical Society. [P.H.] Wicksteed lectured on "Marriage and Individuality"—jejune.- Yesterday persuaded Roberts to publish a vol. of poetry by subscription; promised to take 2 copies. Read some Aristophanes. Finished "All's Well That Ends Well", and thought about it.- Vile foggy weather. Go daily to Museum, but do little.

*   *   *

Wed. Oct. 30. A fine day, warm and autumnal. Daily to Museum. Reading Landor's "Pericles and Aspasia" again. Also Ribot's "Hérédité". At home work at "The Clouds" [by Aristophanes],with stray readings in Shakspere and Landor. Yesterday bought Philip Marston's poems [probably *Song-Tide*, in the Canterbury Poets]; they don't appeal to me.

Thursd. Oct. 31. Worked at Ribot[26].- Much proof-correcting.- Went on with "The Clouds".

Frid. Nov. 1. Moderately fine, but getting cold. Museum, read at Ribot. A good deal of Aristophanes, and some Democritus.

*   *   *

Frid. Nov. 8. A week of doing little. To-day came Roberts and Hudson, for a farewell evening.

Sat. Nov. 9. Sent Philip Marston's poems to Nelly, and Tourguenieff's "Liza" to Katie.- Purchasing odds and ends for my journey; a great deal of money dribbled away in these trifles.- Letters from Alg, Katie, Madge and Nell. Postcard from Bertz.

At 4.30 went by appointment to see Miss Sichel at 7 Barkston Mansions, Earl's Court. A luxuriously furnished flat. Waited in the dark for a minute or two till she entered; then we talked of London and its aspects. Lights and tea brought in. Much talk of my books, till at length a younger Miss Sichel with a girl friend of hers appeared, returning from the Popular Concert.- Miss Sichel interested me; for some reason her face pleased me more than when I first saw her down in Surrey. I half think she is beautiful. Left at 6.30.

Spent evening in a troubled state of mind, occasionally glancing at Darwin's "Origin of Species"—a queer jumble of thoughts.

Mond. Nov. 11. Left London by the 9 o'clock train from Victoria. A cold, uncomfortable passage to Dieppe; constant spray on deck. Reached Paris at 6.30, and drove at once to the Gare de Lyon. All my luggage consists of a travelling bag, a wallet and a packet of rugs and coats.

(The South of England from London to Newhaven, very beautiful. The trees of a pale Sienna; now and then a rich light yellow, and often dark amber. The *wasted* green of the fields. A dull, neutral sky, with flying clouds; light round the horizon.)

Dined at the buffet, Gare de Lyon, extravagantly—as to price. Ticket to Marseille, 3rd class fr.58.55. Left by the 10 o'clock express—so called. The train very long, and packed; no chance of lying down. A number of Orientals returning from the Exhibition. In our carriage, an Arab and his wife, both excellent creatures, talking French, seemed to hail from Philippeville in Algeria. The man sat, for the most part, cross-legged on the seat. The wife was elaborately dressed: a bright blue gown, with sleeves of white muslin, and over that a big cashmere shawl; on her head a cloth of yellow silk, quite covering the hair, and round it, across forehead, a broad band of red silk; from top of head round the face suspended a string of what looked like gold coins. Her hands dyed brown, and on her wrists a number of bangles. A good, childish face. She did not sit cross-legged, but frequently made and smoked cigarettes.

Tuesd. Nov. 12. A dull, cold morning. Much fog at Lyon. Weary after sleepless night. A little sunshine in the Rhone valley, where the golden trees are of course more wasted than last year. Read at [Charles Kingsley's] "Hypatia", the new 6d edn of which I bought at Victoria on starting.

At Valence an excellent lunch: un potage, une côtelette avec purée de pommes and ½ bottle of wine—altogether 2 francs.

Reached Marseille at 6.15, and went to my old hotel, the National, the first you come to out of the station. Dined, then walked out the Canebière, and at a café wrote a postcard to Agbrigg. Feeling well and cheerful. Thought much of E[dith] S[ichel]. To bed early.

Notice that the time at Marseille is ¼ hour *before* that of Paris.

Wed. Nov. 13. Hotel bill, 7 francs. To the Fraissinet boat—L'Europe—at the Quai aux Anglais, at 8.30. Boat announced to start at 9, but did not do so till 2 o'clock. Second class passage to the Piraeus, 120fr.- Of course including food. Two French-speaking Greeks on board, a Parisian young woman of the lively species, and some Frenchmen. The Greek [sic] announces that we are 13 at table.-

A glorious, warm and sunny day, with breeze.- But towards night, the breeze became a high wind; much tossing of ship. The cuisine du midi did not suit me, and I had to break off in middle of dinner. Turned in at 7 o'clock and slept well till 6 in morning.

Thursd. Nov. 14. Yesterday the best view was of yellow Marseille (a warm yellow) at the foot of its barren hills, I know not of what colour to call these hills,- perhaps a very pale slate. This morning at 6.15, saw the sun rise. A few thin clouds above it, edged with lucent gold. The ship not yet opposite

171

Savona; the crests of the Maritime Alps slightly covered with snow, which was a wonderful rose pink,- the tint I have never hitherto seen. All this part of the Riviera is a succession of barren hills; their barrenness, and susceptibility of colour, the characteristic. A succession of little yellow (or buff) towns, each close on the shore, with an amphitheatre of hills behind it.

In the port of Genoa at 2 o'clock. The bay a noble prospect. General colour of the town a pale yellow; mixed with pale reds here and there. Together with two Greeks and the Parisian girl—a poor, courageous creature, her face disfigured with eczema—took a boat and went on shore. Wrote postcard to Agbrigg and to Roberts. The Greeks went off to see the cemetery; the girl and I walked about the narrower streets, seeing little of note, then returned to the boat, in time for dinner. A beautiful sunset.

After dinner I again landed with the two Greeks, and we went to the Teatro Paganini. Saw an opera, made out of "Adrienne Lecouvreur" [the drama by Eugène Scribe and Ernest Legouvé]. A large theatre, with six tiers of seats above pit, and no baignoires; sat in the Platèa—and paid fr.1.50. Opera indifferent, but fairly successful with public. After a duo in the first act, much applauded, the female singer disappeared and returned dragging a young man in morning attire—seemed to be about 20—the composer. This was repeated many times during the opera, the shy and awkwardly-bowing young fellow appearing in the middle of scenes, without any regard to artistic effect. The overture to Act III was *bissé*, and, because the curtain had already risen, the actors—some thirty—had to stand twiddling their thumbs whilst the overture was repeated,- highly ridiculous.- Up above the proscenium was a mechanical arrangement for showing the time,- changed each 5 minutes.- Got back to the boat at 1 a.m.; the harbour marvellously calm; not a breath. But on our boat they were loading all night, the winch working above our cabin; I marvel that, for all that, I was able to sleep.

Not[e] the habit, when you help yourself to wine at table, of offering to your neighbours first. And if it is the beginning of a bottle, you first pour a drop into your own glass.

Frid. Nov. 15. Boat started at 7.45 this morning. Poor little French girl among all the men on board, a queer situation. Of Genoa she can only say that it is "infecte". Heaven knows why she is going to Athens.

Soon sailed out from shore. Unable to see Gulf of Spezzia. Fine and calm, but a good many clouds. Later, they cleared up. Sea very calm indeed. One of the officers says that the months of November and March are the worst on the Mediterranean; this weather at present is exceptional.

Am suffering from my usual inability to associate freely with foreigners. My French *dries up* when I try to talk to these two Greeks or the foolish little woman. There's nothing for it but to draw aside and be lonely.

The first island sighted, about 2 o'clock, is Gorgona, an ugly rock, appropriately used as convict station. Far away on horizon is Corsica. Presently Capraja appears beyond Gorgona, and, in the far south, Elba. The Maremma coast is pretty clear.

A wonderful sunset. High above the sun hang little diaphanous patches of glowing amber, in a sky of purple blue. From the south, just above horizon, long strips of thin cloud extend brokenly to the sun, growing warmer as they approach it and always more slender and small, until, around the sun, they become little flecks and spots of glorious resplendent gold—not to be looked at. Higher than these, one or two ragged little scraps of rose pink, exquisitely indefinite. Between the sun and the south lie at length Corsica, Capraja and Elba.

Over Maremma, as the sun disappears, the sky becomes a warm, dusky purple. The clouds between south and west lose their tint and become a sad neutral, at same time lessening and dispersing. The sea grows a cold blue-grey, glancing everywhere on its innumerable ripples.

Sun sets and in its place is a glorious tract of crimson, or of glowing rose, passing by gradation, above, into a delicate daffodil. The clouds fleck the gradation with stripes delicately pencilled as if in Indian ink, growing always blacker. Islands grow a dark neutral, at length black.-

The foll. is the shape of Capraja, which much resembles Capri.-

[Sketch of Capraja, from East]

The amusing spiritual confessions made to me by the little Parisian. "I am not devout, but I am pious. I go to church when I have time, as one ought to. If I had children, I should bring them up in the fear of God;- it's good for them to be afraid of something."

Sat. Nov. 16. Perfectly fine; hot sun at mid-day. In morning passed the Isole Ponzie, but thereafter drew away so far from land that with difficulty I discerned just the form of Vesuvius on the horizon.-

After dinner, the 1st mate took me to his cabin and gave me a glass of cognac, talking in very friendly way; also showed me his maritime maps, and told me to look out for Stromboli early in morning.- Much talk with the southern Frenchman, who is an engineer, and with both the Greeks, one of whom wishes to know my opinions about God and eternal justice.

Sund. Nov. 17. Tumbled out at 3.30, having seen the glare of Stromboli through the cabin window—a strange effect. Getting onto deck, found we were at foot of the mountain—the cave of Aeolus—which sent out a great crimson glare. The sky covered with white clouds; between them, starry spaces of profound azure; high up, the last quarter of the moon, brilliantly silver. At each eruption, the clouds above the mountain grew a deep rose-colour. Stayed on deck half an hour, then turned in again.

Rose at 7.30, being at the entrance to the Straits of Messina. On the left, the savage hills of Calabria; on the right, the strange sharp-ridged mountains of Sicily. Looking back saw the great cone of Stromboli above the horizon, summit smoke-involved. Vulcano visible away to the west. Sun rising over Calabria; a wonderful effect; the rays fell from behind a group of clouds, and came down in front of the mountains, so as to obscure them in that place.

173

Entering straits, quickly noticed the vast dry beds of torrents, on both sides, often marked off by a wall,- railway bridges spanning them. Calabria very wild, with isolated mountains and huge valleys, but a broad coast, slowly rising.- Only when you are well through the Straits, does the shape of Etna appear; it is easy to mistake some of the nearer mountains for it, they look so high. A good deal of fog, and only when we had got off Spartivento did Etna become visible in entirety. My strongest impression hitherto of a huge mountain. Is nearly three times the height of Vesuvius. Much snow towards the summit; a glorious shape, dim-shining above the blue sea.

[Sketch of Etna, from off Spartivento]

At midway, as we sailed south-east, Etna still large on horizon, but fading into invisibility; the dark became excessively hot, and the horizon misty. The broad mass of Aspromonte standing out in front.

At five o'clock a noble sunset. Sun sank in crimson, without a cloud; above it a band of glowing amber; this passing into purple blue, intense. Then did Etna become again visible, at a very great distance, but still towering above the horizon. Calabria a long line of dark hills. Stood watching for a long time, thinking unutterable things.

Mond. Nov. 18. A great change in the night. The Ionian Sea much disturbed, foaming everywhere. It did not affect me; I feel vastly better in health than a week ago. This morning no land visible. It began to be descried at 11 o'clock. At 1 o'clock the Messenian promontory was very clear, with the Oenussae islands lying before it; made out the site of Pylos, but could not distinguish Sphacteria from the line of coast. Beyond, a great mountain, crowned with snow: no other than Taygetos. The day had been clouded; now a huge storm-cloud was moving southwards before the wind; in the east, the sky was blue and sunny over Greece.

Reaching the pt. Akritas, had perfect view of the Laconian promontory; at one part, near the middle, it appears to be almost cleft in two by a great valley. As the sun descended, the effects of light became indescribable. Taygetos a marvellous vision, its summit constantly changed in shape of shifting clouds; it seemed all but transparent. Such a view is not of this earth, as *we* understand it; more wonderful, I think, than even South Italy. The astonishing barrenness of the coast is transformed into loveliness by effects of colour. This is indeed the land of Apollo. The sun set behind clouds, and the colour gradually faded from the coast, dark ascending to the peaks. At length there remained only a single peak of Taygetos illumed, but that was an exquisite rose. Afterwards, the colour of the whole range was a delicate mauve.

[Sketch of Taygetos from the Sea]

Tuesd. Nov. 19. Late last night a furious north wind began to blow, and the ship was soon tossing very heavily. Capt. says that if we had been four

174

hours later, and been caught by the storm in the Adriatic, there would have been no reaching Athens to-day. Up early in the morning, and found we were just off the island of Hydra. By nine o'clock we were well into the Saronic Gulf. The wind very fierce and cold. The sky heavily clouded, but over Attica growing fair. Wonderful glints on the Attic mountains. Presently the hill of Munychia became distinguishable, and then the height of Athens itself. Stood eagerly watching, as the details became clear. Passed Aegina, and came near to Salamis. By this time quite sunny, but very cold.

As we came to in the harbour,- which is hidden by the hill of Munychia,- strangers clambered on board. The Parisienne (who quarrelled yesterday with the Greeks, a ridiculous scene of childish anger on both sides,) was met by her Greek brother-in-law, and went off gabbling shrilly. The younger Greek, by name Constantin Parigory, discerned his father, and shouted to him with delight. These two very civilly took me with them in their boat, and, when we had got through the douane, asked me to share their carriage to Athens. We talked all the way, of course in French. The father, a very decent middle-aged man, whose French was imperfect, watched eagerly for my impressions of the road. Very sensitive about the barrenness of the soil, and eager to point out olive-trees; also to explain the impossibility of keeping down the dust, owing to sheer lack of water. We stopped at the half-way house, but didn't take anything. The entrance to Athens through mean and dirty streets; then came the modern part of the town. I was taken to the Grand Hotel, Place de la Constitution. The Greeks would not allow me to pay my share of the carriage—rather wonderful in Greeks, I thought.

I soon found that I was not in the hotel I supposed. Baedeker says that here stands the Hôtel d'Athènes, but this grand Hotel is a new place, only open for three months. The charge for room and board is 10fr. a day (gold). Certainly very cheap, for the accommodation is even luxurious, but I can only stand it for a few days; shall stay so long because Parigory said he would call. Throughout the public rooms is electric light. The landings on the staircase are curiously furnished, and carpeted, so as to make little sitting-rooms; mirrors and casts of antiques about. The dining-room large. Some twenty people at dinner: three English ladies and two Englishmen; the rest Greeks. Incident of my drinking Englishman's wine by mistake. A reading-room, with *Times, Débats* etc.

Having arrived, went and had my hair cut, then walked about Hermes Street and Stadiou Street. The sterility of the soil is certainly marvellous. The open space in front of the Royal Palace, which ought to be grass-sown, is an expanse of dust, not a blade growing; the effect astonishes one. Odd costumes in the streets. Strong military element, of course; the curse of Europe, everywhere.

My window looks up a street to Lycabettos. After dinner read, and wrote this.- Forgot to say that I went to the Post Office, and found a postcard from Plitt. Sent off letters to Mother and Miss Sichel, which I had written on the voyage. Changed £12 at Cook's office, just opened in the Constitution Place, and got for it 360fr. in paper, i.e. 30fr. to the pound.

Wed. Nov. 20. A windy and rainy morning. To-day being a fête of some kind, the Acropolis closed till 2 o'clock; much tootling of military music everywhere. First walked up to the Philopappos Mont and had good view of the country. Understand now how it might be possible for sailors off Sunium to see the top of Athena on Acropolis. Came down, and walked through ὁδός Αἰόλου, a lively street. Portraits of Constantine and Sophia, the recently married prince and his wife; as plain and vulgar a pair as one could find. Walked out to the Gare du Pirée; and thence up to the Theseion, which is glorious. But too cold and wet to study. Back to déjeuner at 12.

I notice that the Athenian populace still eat much fish. Fries everywhere sold in the streets. Very few women walking about; the girls I have seen strike me as beautiful, they have their hair platted in one cord down their backs—many at all events. Got my boots filthy with walking in the dust, moistened by rain into clay. Everywhere the same incredible barrenness of the soil. The elementary streets and roads of the environs.

Went to the Hôtel de la Couronne, and saw a good room for 3 fr. a day. Think of moving thither. Bought an Εφημερίς, and find I can read it tolerably.

In the afternoon a brilliant sun, though wind still high. Sprinkling of snow on Parnes.

General life of town very diff[eren]t from that of Naples. No one pesters you, not even the coachmen. The people seem on the whole modest. When I bought my newspaper this morning, I took hold of it to drag it out, and, as it is of tissue paper, tore it; the boy would not allow me to take this torn copy, but got out another.

Rested for a couple of hours, then went up onto the Acropolis. So in truth I have trodden this sacred soil! Made no attempt to regard details, but mused about—in spite of the terrible north wind. (The poor old guardian in the Parthenon, looking frozen to death and cursing to himself.) The declining sun, from the front of Nike Apteros; its rays streaming wildly from behind clouds, and falling athwart the Saronic Gulf, between Aegina and Salamis, against the hills of Argolis.

Thursd. Nov. 21. It is a testimony to the dustiness of Athens, that when you enter the hotel, after walking, it is the business of a waiter to brush your boots and trousers with a large brush.-

Postcard from Bertz.- Decided to take room for a month at *Io Stemma,* so sent postcards to Bertz and mother. Shall move to-morrow.- In the Pl[ace] de la Constit[ution] is Cook's office. The inscription is Θ KOUK KAI VIOS.

In the morning walked out to Kolonos, which takes about an easy hour. The hill on which stand the monuments of Muller and Lenormant is as bare as a dust heap. There certainly are olive groves in the neighbourhood, but very thin ones. The separate properties are walled in with great square blocks of compacted mud, topped with some shrub that I don't know. Continuing along the high road—along which runs a tramway—I soon came to the Kephisos, or rather to its bed, for there is absolutely not a drop of water; the bed is wide, and perhaps sometimes watered. About the bridge is a cluster of houses and a church. The churchyard extraordinary. No wall to it, and looked much like a bit of ground for rubbish by the highway; of course not a blade of grass growing. Cypresses, however. Few marble tombs; the graves generally marked thus: At the head a wooden cross, with inscription painted in white (ENΘAΔE KEITAI .... AΠEBIΩΣE THN . ;. . ETΩN . . . .) and sometimes a skull and cross-bones (alas for deterioration of old custom!) In front of the cross is a little wooden box with glass front, in which a candle or oil had burnt; behind it, two wooden sticks are thrust into the earth, and one of them transfixes a broken pot of plain baked earth. I know not the meaning of this.

[Sketch illustrating above description]

Noticed to-day the habit of which Baedeker speaks. Men carry in their hands a string of wooden beads, and keep rattling them about. Said not to be religious custom, but merely to give occupation for the hands. Surely a token of strange nervousness.

Made sketches of the Acropolis and of Lycabettos, from Kolonos. Still the same furious wind blowing and many black clouds. But much sunshine.- In afternoon gathered some flowers on Lycabettos, very like those I found last January by the Arno, bulby roots. Growing in the mere dry and stony earth, without any leaves of their own.

At dinner was a Greek lady of superb type—masses of black hair, heaped above forehead, fine eyes etc. She wore a head-dress of red silk, or something of the kind, and very picturesque clothing in general.

The English-speaking German who sits at end of table. Portentously ignorant, yet assures you that he knows everything. Gross physique. Hair cropped so as to stand up all over his head; broad flat face, which grows purple as he eats—and he eats enormously; goggle eyes. Loves dirty suggestions, and laughs apoplectically. His English very vulgar, and often absurdly bad. For instance, he repeated to-night several times the word "Posterity!" as an exclamation, and I understood at length that he meant preposterous.

In evening went to a café in the Pl[ace] de la Concorde. The coffee is brought in the little tin saucepan that it is boiled in, and poured straight into cup, with the grounds; is ready sweetened. The waiters run about with half a dozen such little saucepans.

Frid. Nov. 22. Just occurred to me that this is my birthday. Thirty-three, n'est-ce pas? Well, I have celebrated it by taking flight from the Grand Hotel, where I ought never to have gone, and establishing myself at the Stemma, where I think I shall be very comfortable. One eats à la carte. The Grand bill was fr.37.50; and as

[Sketches of the Acropolis from Colonos and of Lycabettos from Colonos, with Hymettos behind]

payment in gold is demanded I had to give fr. 45.50.- The whole affair absurdly dear, after all.

Having deposited my baggage, walked along the University Street. The University and the Academy, built of Pentelic marble, are gilded much, and painted a little, e.g. the eaves of the pediments are coloured sky-blue underneath. I don't know yet whether I like the effect or not. And did not the old Greeks carry their colouring much further? In the same street is Schliemann's house[27], a handsome building with ceiling-painted loggie, and with many statues on the roof. Over the front is written: IΛΙΟΥ ΜΕΛΑΘΡΟΝ.- Nearly opposite the big Library just being built, is the Arsakron, the girls' high school.

The lower classes seem to deal chiefly with pedlars, who are very numerous, generally having their wares on donkeys.- Walked about the New Bazaar, in Athena Street, where provisions are sold. Much fish.

Then walked up the Acropolis. Still the same intolerable wind, a serious hindrance to enjoyment; its howling never ceases. But a blue zenith; the effect of the Propylaea agst it very glorious. Terrible clouds of dust along the Piraeus road.

In the afternoon to the Central Museum. The room that most interested me was that containing the sepulchral marbles. Very beautiful and affecting, these. The departed one sits; and almost always clasps the hand of some near relative standing by. Must look at these often.

Have got petroleum for my lamp so that to-night I can see to read and write with comfort. Wrote a letter for Roberts.

Sat. Nov. 23. The wind has at last ceased. A very fine warm day, though heavy clouds about. Set out in the morning, and walked along the road to the Piraeus; thence over to the sea shore opposite Salamis, as far as Keratopurgos, which may have been the site of Xerxes' throne, rather than the little hill generally so named, but which seems too far from the position of the fleet. Saw clearly the posture of the fight. There is a lighthouse on Psyttaleia, and on Keratopurgos a powder magazine. Magnificent views over to Megara; far beyond Eleusis a great cloud-capped mountain which is perhaps Helicon, but I could not be sure. Aigaleos a low range of hills, covered with bare stones; here and there a cluster of some kind of green shrub; the colour of the mountains reddish. The sea perfectly calm, lapping on the great slabs of limestone which form the shore. The big shepherd's dogs roaming everywhere, but no savageness in them.

Back to Piraeus by 1.30. There bought two rings of bread and some figs, and ate my lunch as I climbed the hill of Munychia. The glare of the white dust in sunshine often very painful to the eyes. From the top, one of the grandest views conceivable; one of the best, I should say, for understanding Attica. The moving shadows of big clouds made wonderful changes upon the plain and mountains, seeming even to alter forms. The bay of Phaleron, and the rising plain beyond it, at foot of Hymettus, very beautiful. At New-Phaleron, a sea-bathing station,- resembling that at Lido.

Deadly tired, walked down to the station and took train for Athens; stops at Phaleron.- Piraeus is growing to be a very large and busy town. Already some dozen high mill-chimneys are belching black fumes.

To my astonishment, there was put on the dinner-table to-night the *Newcastle Weekly Chronicle*. Why this paper in particular? Must remember to tell Alg.

I see that the estates are often marked out by little structures of painted stone, in the form of an angle. I don't quite understand the system of measuring, but it is interesting to see this illustration of the "landmark". Noteworthy that ploughing scarcely at all changes the colour of the soil. At the wells, water is raised by horses, who trot round and round, turning a primitive pumping machine.

Sund. Nov. 24. Fine day, and warm. Always great clouds over the sky, but patches of splendid azure. Looked into the Cathedral. A priest intoning Greek in remarkably fine voice. Thence walked on to the Olympieion, and to the banks of the Ilissus. To my surprise I found that there was a positive little stream of water, trickling in the midst of the wide river-bed; but this sank into the earth and finally disappeared just south of the Stadion bridge. Also wonderful to tell, there is a little grass and general herbage growing on each side of the water; it refreshes one's eyes. Along the river-bed grow plane-trees, but they are all young, and I suppose have been recently planted. When Socrates sat on this spot, under the plane-tree, and discoursed the "Phoedrus", the conditions must have been very different. It was then, of course, outside the city; only in Hadrian's time did Athens extend in this direction,- as the inscription on his Arch tells. Very different must the Ilissus have been, too, when Oruthyia gathered flowers, and was carried off by Boreas. As I stood on the Stadion bridge, a great flock of sheep came driven along,- some white, some black, and a number of very young and pretty lambs. The bells round their necks tinkled, and a perpetual bleating was kept up.- the thin voices of the lambs sounding very plaintive and touching. All were very thirsty, and, just beyond the bridge, the herdsmen—clad in the strange big rough over-coat of which I know not the name—let them down to the stream. A regular scamper, the lambs leaping delightedly. And so they went on, up the bed of the Ilissus.

Went on into the Stadion, and walked round it. Returning, spent a few minutes in the Prot[estant] Cemetery.

In the afternoon went to a café and called for μαστίχα. It is a colourless liquid, which, when you add water turns milky. A sweet, pungent, pepperminty flavour.

Towards sunset, onto the Acropolis. Magnificent effects of light. From the west streamed brilliant sunlight, whilst all the north and east was covered with huge purple-black clouds. As I stood just inside the Acropolis, the Erechtheion gleamed against that cloud-background, its yellow marble wonderfully illumined, every stone distinct, its outlines seeming cut out. Beneath the dark clouds was Pentelicon; its summit hidden, itself darker than the sky, a bluish black.

179

Later, as the sun set, the eastern clouds became fiery underneath, and Pentelicon, its clefts and flanks, glowed unimaginably; such colour as one sees on imaginary mountains in the fire. One of the grandest scenes I ever witnessed.-

I notice that the Greeks represent the sound of B by μπ, and that of D by γτ. Thus, the Turkish name of place Bedéni, is written μπευτévι.

Mond. Nov. 25. Alg's Birthday.- Feeling terribly tired in body; the usual reaction after days of excitement and exertion. In morning went to Walberg's, the German booksellers, and bought a Greek-French dialogue book, and the edn of Aristophanes' Frogs in Haupt and Sauppe's series. Began to study both, loitering in sunshine about the Olympieion.

In afternoon went to look at the Lysicrates monument, the sole relic of the street of tripods. Then round the foot of the Acropolis; and, as I saw it was going to be a rare sunset, up towards Philopappos. I was well rewarded. The sky was all but cloudless, never yet have seen the mountains far and near so distinctly. Salamis was close at hand; the hill called Xerxes' throne clearly discernible. Looking east, the Acropolis stood in golden splendour; temples, bulwarks and rock, all were of the same rich warm yellow, exactly as if all were but one structure. On Pentelicon lay a huge billow of cloud, long, beautiful in shape, scarcely changing in a detail however closely I watched; its colour was rose and purple; it seemed to hide the abode of gods on the mountain summit.

As the sun grew low, the shadow of the Mouseion gradually rose on the Acropolis, which lost its glory. And when the sun had disappeared altogether, sinking splendidly behind the hills of Argolis, the cloud on Pentelicon suddenly faded to a delicate blue-grey, all its mouldings, its reliefs and depressions, exquisitely marked in degrees of tenderness; the mountain below, a deeper grey. A few minutes, and the cloud—still quite unchanged in form—was becoming a cold, cold white, snowy, chill, in strange contrast with the warm landscape below and the gradual soft flush of the sky above. Again a few minutes, and the afterglow had begun. The western sky became brilliant amber; the zenith and the east became a dark deep azure, awing the eye, whilst the great cloud again flushed softly. And this lasted for a long time, until Pentelicon had blackened into night.

After various trials, I find that the most drinkable wine here is Solon's Côtes de Parnès (blanc). I have a half-bottle at meals.

Tuesd. Nov. 26. In the morning to study the Theseion, and the Dipylon.- To the Post Office, but no letters; anxious to hear from England. Sent a postcard to Shortridge, telling him I expect to be at Naples before long.

A magnificent day. The sunlight is even trying to the eyes; I find it difficult to read in open air. Do so, however; carrying my Aristophanes about. Sat for a while reading the Frogs near the Olympieion. In afternoon climbed to the top of Lycabettos. The eastern peak is being absolutely quarried away; the stone broken up small, for making roads I suppose. Most of the breaking is done by women—poor creatures; at sunset they came running down the hill homewards. At the S. George's chapel on the top I saw a black cat, asleep. Sunset nothing like so fine as last night.

Greek for letter-box (in streets) is γραμματοχιβώτιον. - The classes on the railway are θέσις A, θέσις B etc. A general dealer's shop is παντοπωλεῖον.- One of the chief newspapers is ʽΗ Ἀκρόπολις; boys shout it about the streets in the morning: ʽΗ Ἀκρόπολι-ι-ις !

Have finished a slow reading of [Kingsley's] "Hypatia". My interest in the book is wholly gone. My pleasant recollection due only to immaturity when I first read it. In technique, its weakness is extreme. Hypatia very poorly presented. No vivification of the old life. Much might have been made of Pelagia,- and nothing is.

Wed. Nov. 27. A curious and vivid dream last night. Found myself suddenly back in London, and in a room where were present Miss Sichel, Farrar, Fred. Harrison, and others whom I forget, but whom I knew. I had no recollection of the journey home from Greece, but I was quite conscious that, for whatever reason, I had made it precipitately, and I regretted bitterly having done so. My realization of position even went so far as remembering the postcard I had sent to Shortridge, and which now was useless. I talked much with Miss Sichel and grew very intimate with her. It appeared that Farrar was a relative of hers.- How strangely this dream is composed out of recognizable materials!

Very busy with subject of Greek accent in its relation to metre. I have discovered the undoubted fact that in the *later* Greek poets the ictus and accent *generally* coincide—do so quite wonderfully in comparison with Homer. This is case in Theocritus, even; far more so in Apollonius Rhodius for instance. But I think I am beginning to be able to read all verse so as to combine accent and metre. Remember that, in English poetry, it is quite the exception for scheme of ictus to be preserved. Our ordinary way of reading Greek verse is just the same as reading English poetry without regard to the sense, but solely to the scansion.

Studied all the morning. In afternoon walked nearly to Acharnae(Menidi), striking into a side-road just beyond Patisia. Again splendid weather; rather too hot in the sun. The valley of the Cephisus is well cultivated. Olives everywhere, and any number of currant gardens; fig-trees numerous. Agaves by roadside. Some fine poplars, and other trees, in golden autumn hues; the currant bushes a very rich yellow here and there. It is obvious that formerly this plain was well irrigated; several deep and broad beds of streams. In this higher part of the Cephisus there is a little water.

Spent evening over Aristophanes.

Thursd. Nov. 28. Postcard from Plitt, who says he is going on to Rome.-

In the morning read at Aristophanes. Afternoon worked at the Acropolis. The surface evidently was never paved; the red rock (it is very red in places) was roughly smoothed where necessary; inequalities of level are frequent. In the upward walk from the Propylaea, parallel transverse ridges were cut, to give a foothold. Something fine, to my mind, in temples and statues springing thus out of the living rock, as if they grew there.

On the inner wall of the cella of Parthenon are faint pictures of saints, with aureoles; relic of Christian worship here. A strange impression they make, these Byzantine figures.- Stood on the spot where Athena Parthenos stood.- With regard to the great frieze, I cannot in the least understand how it was visible, in any true sense. It breaks one's neck to look up from inside the outer columns, and at all times it must have been very dark up there.

Looked carefully at the masses of fallen marble, distributed all about the open spaces—a vast, mournful wreck. Much wonderfully fine work, and often as fresh as if it had just come from the chisel,- the edges sharp and clean. Exquisite leaf patterns.

A very hot day, but threatening sky. All the top of Parnes hidden in dense clouds. On Hymettus they were creeping low. At sunset a high wind arose.

Frid. Nov. 29. All day furious wind again.- Spent the morning writing a long letter to Bertz. Afternoon went to the modern cemetery, out beyond the Olympieion. From here there is a fine view of the Acropolis, including beautiful the Odeion and the theatre [sic]. The monumental marbles of the cemetery in miserable taste; some very pretentious, but nothing to equal the extravagance of Naples. I noticed the relief-portrait of a man, surrounded by a wreath of gilding, and with the *shirt-stud* also carefully gilded; surely the bathos of decoration as formerly understood in Athens. The tomb of a doctor, on which were some elegiacs; I copied two lines.

πολλούς εχ χειρων στυγνου εσαωσε χαρωνος
αὐτος ὁμως αἰ αἰ ουχ υπαλυξε ρυρον.

"[He rescued many people from the hands of the dreadful Charon but alas, alas, could not escape his fate]".

I see that it is the custom to mark the head of the grave with two sticks until the slab be ready; but found no instance of the broken pots, as at the little graveyard in the country. It is also usual to put up a temporary wooden cross, with painted inscription, and, almost universally, the hateful skull and crossbones; on the ground in front of this is the veilleuse, a miniature dog-hutch with the oil lamp inside it.

A painted notice in the cemetery interested me by its having the words written without intervals, as of old.

Went thence to the Prot[estant] Cemetery. Some very fine cactuses growing here; also agaves and cypresses. Noticed a poor little wooden cross, broken off, with the name of a French woman fading from it. No grave that interested me much.

Got back to the Σύνταγμα just as, with flourish of trumpets, the king started on his drive from the palace. His carriage passed the crown-prince's house, opposite, and, as soon as it had done so, out came the young man and his princess, also driving. All the men wear hard billycocks. A little crowd waiting to see them pass. I noticed a wretched looking man in the garb of a Greek priest (the ugly high hat etc.) his coat dirty, his whole appearance mean; some accident had crippled him, and he went sprawlingly on crutches. A little dog barked furiously at him. What is this poor fellow's history? Did he come here at this hour with some hope that the royalties might notice him? The contrast between them and him.

Here, as in Italy, I see that it is usual to paste on the wall notices of people's deaths. Buried the day after death.

Sat. Nov. 30. In mod. Greek ομιλῶ = to talk. In old Greek it meant "to associate with". Cp. the parallel history of the English word "converse".

Bad weather. The wind violent, and, I think, a scirocco. Unable to walk. Sat in a café for a couple of hours in afternoon reading *Figaros*.- The dust penetrates everywhere, these windy days; in the café, every table and seat covered with it. Waiters perpetually busied in brushing it from one place to another.

Quitted my room on the 2nd floor, which had no outlook, and went up to one on the 3rd, which is to cost me only 2 francs a day; the other was 3. From the first it was agreed that I was to have a cheaper room as soon as a certain lodger vacated it.- Feeling very dull and powerless. Wrote and sent long letter to Alg. No news yet from England.

Sund. Dec. 1. Violent storm in the night; much rain, which has happily laid the dust. To-day fine and cool. A little sore throat hanging about me.

It being Sunday, swarms of soldiers are let loose upon the town. The fore-court of the Post Office, where are public tables with pen and ink, was crowded with them, all writing letters. Most of them very young fellows, and anything but imposing; of low stature, thin, badly shaped; their faces small, bony, ignoble, of dirty complexion; yet good-natured withal. Their intelligence must be very elementary. Most of them have obviously been brought up on wretched diet, and look hungry.- Music in the squares.

My room is a great improvement. I look north and west, directly towards the Sacred Way, which I see winding over the mountains. To-night I enjoy the amber sky, after sunset, beyond Aigaleos.

This morning worked at Aristophanes. This afternoon walked out in the direction of Hymettus. Immediately on leaving the town in this direction one is in the desert. The road goes along by the dry channel of the Eridanus, in places so deep and strongly rounded at sides that there must have been terrific torrents once. Had no intention of climbing Hymettus itself, but mounted a craggy little hill just at the foot of the real ascent; and thence had splendid views. Sketched Salamis; having sketched the Acropolis a short way before. On descending the back of this hill, I was sheltered from the wind, and enjoyed an exquisite half-hour. Brilliant sky; half-moon; pale on soft blue, risen above Hymettus (3 o'clock). Absolute stillness, but in the mountain far dim sounds of shepherds' voices, of barking dogs and of sheep-bells. Strong smell of some herb all about: I know not what.- The wind not fierce to-day but from this distance I could see white waves breaking on the Cynosura prom[ontory] of Salamis.

I notice that, as in Aristophanes' day, it is the men who go to market. I have not yet seen a woman purchasing in the New Bazaar.

Mond. Dec. 2. In the morning met Parigory and his father, who greeted me. Says he has called here when I was out, but I knew nothing of it. Will take me to a session of the Parliament.

A miserable day. Very anxious to have letters. Throat very bad last night, and consequently bad sleep. Reading at Aristophanes. Went nowhere.

Decidedly, I don't like the Greek people, so far as I see them. Utterly alien from my sympathies. Very different from my feeling towards the Italians.

Tuesd. Dec. 3. A fine clear morning, with sharp wind from north-east. Set out early, and started along the Sacred Way. In the mountain pass, just beyond the Daphni monastery, saw the niches cut in the rock for votive offerings; also the track of the ancient road, which in places ran differently from the present. When I reached the sea, found it foaming under the wind. Pursued road along the shore until I had a good view of Thriasian plain, and of Eleusis round the curve of the shore; then turned back. Instead of returning by the mountain pass, kept to the shore, and went all the way round the foot of Aigaleos; a delightful walk. The path obscure in places, roughly cut on rock. On the neck of the promontory where stands the Skarmanga Cloister had an exquisite view in one direction, of the Eleusis bay and in the other of Salamis. At this point there is a large farm, or something of the kind, where there seemed to have been a great festive gathering; it was just breaking up, and men, women and children, all in most picturesque costumes, were setting out, in carts and on donkeys, towards Eleusis—a strange gathering.- In the hollows of the mountain, through which runs the path, grow pines and great quantities of lentisc; the odour of the pines was strong, and mingled with fresh scent from the sea. The beautiful yellow-green of the youngest pines. When I had got round to the Salamis side, I was quite sheltered from the wind; sea calm and blue. Ate two rolls and some apples. At the Salamis ferry begins a good high road.- Met a shepherd carrying two young kids by their forelegs; the old goats, male and female, running after him. One of the kids kept up a cry just like that of a child, and the mother, with much sympathetic bleating, kept running and rubbing her nose agst the little creature.

At the hill called Xerxes' throne, a road, on the left side of it, strikes inland directly to Athens; I chose this instead of going to Piraeus.- Saw a little yellowish bird fluttering by the roadside, and picked it up; could not discover that it was hurt, yet it was unable to fly, though fully fledged. Very bright eye. Showed no signs of fear; when I laid it on its back on my hand it kept quite still seeming to look at me curiously. A specked breast, something like thrush. Left it to its fate—whatever that might be.

Fine view of Athens by this way of approach. One sees how the white mass of houses lies in the hollow between Lycabettos and the Acropolis, and spreads north onto the plain. Soon got among the olives and currant gardens. When I

[Sketch of the Acropolis from road to Hymettus.
Aigaleos and mountains of Megaris. Sacred Way to Eleusis]

was nearing Athens, and the way had become a high road, I came to a place where the road bridged a dry stream-channel, and in the middle of the bridge a great hole had just been formed, some three feet wide, evidently by the falling through of the stones. A nice place on a dark night; nobody's business, probably, to see to it. If I had been walking at dusk I should certainly have fallen through, a depth of six feet. Later on, came to another such bridge, the middle of which showed signs of giving way.

Reached home by 4.45, very tired.

Wed. Dec. 4. At last a letter from Bertz, enclosing the 3 numbers of the *Deutsche Presse* (3, 10 and 17 Nov.) in which he criticizes (or rather eulogizes) me: "George Gissing : Ein Real-Idealist".[28] Very good of the old fellow. He tells me my name is getting known to a literary circle there.

My throat very troublesome still. Feeling a little feverish now and then.

I notice that the French opera company now playing at the New Theatre is called, on the placards: ὁ γαλλιχός θιασος. [The French Troupe] Strange use of that old word! [Applying to a confraternity which solemnised the rites of a god, Dionysus in particular.]

In afternoon called Parigory, and we walked about. My throat pained me, and I felt rather miserable. He had procured tickets of admission to the Parliament, but we couldn't get [into] it; the door was kept closed agst us by porters who shouted mere gross refusals to every application of Parigory.- I ought to have asked the man to dinner, but could not face two or three hours more of talk, with this throat.

Finished "The Frogs".

Thursd. Dec. 5. The waiters have two words which one hears incessantly: ’αμέσως, [immediately]—when they are summoned, and μαλιστα [quite] when they take an order. Former word often cut down to ’μέσ’.

A cloudy day, no sunshine at all. But for me cheerful, as I have recd three letters from England. Two from Agbrigg,- one posted on 16th Nov., and other on the 26th both come together. They enclose a letter from A.J. Smith (who is settled in Manchester at Whitworth's) and tell me that Tillotson has at last sent the cheque for "Christmas on the Capitol".- Smith tells me that "Demos" is being pubd in the *Manchester Weekly Times* [July 20, 1889—February 1, 1889], and is advtd about the streets.- Wrote to Hartley, and to Smith.

Head and throat bad. Went to bed at 7.30.

Frid. Dec. 6. A second clouded day. Only half an hour of sunshine, before noon. Cold, miserable. Lay in bed till 10 o'clock and went without my usual coffee.- Wrote a letter to Hudson. In afternoon spent an hour or two in a café, reading the *Figaro*. Sad waste of time, this;- I mean the inability to walk about and see things.

Re-reading the "Frogs".

Sat. Dec. 7. Not a gleam of sun; rain all day. Went and bought at Walberg's two more of the Haupt and Sauppe series: the 1st vol. of Lucian and Plato's

"Symposion".- Spoke with a Scotchman [named Miller], who dined in our room; has recently come and is connected with the new railway line to Larissa. A strong accent; from his first words, when I greeted him, I concluded that I had been mistaken and that he was a foreigner who spoke English; I fancy this was the result of nervous shyness, generally marked in the Scotch. He said he was glad to see the rain! No doubt it reminded him of Scotland.-

Sent postcard to Nelly.

From my window watched the misty clouds creeping about Aigaleos, occasionally half revealing, but generally quite obscuring, the mountains of Megara through the Daphni valley. An even, grey, hopeless sky. Rather cold.

Sund. Dec. 8. The fourth day of gloom and rain. Morning walked as far as the Pelopn Railway Station, to look up trains. The streets in a state of extreme filth. Of course there is no public system of cleaning them. The outskirts of the town mere heaps of slush and garbage; bad odours frequent after this rain.- Cold gone at last; feel tolerably well.

Afternoon saw a few signs of clearing in the west, so went out at 2.30 though it was still raining. Walked round by the Theseion to the quarter of the three hills—the Nymphs, the Pnyx, and the Mouseion. Examined carefully this site of a great part of old Athens,—which was partly inside and partly outside the wall. The three hills make a ridge, running nearly north and south; the hill of the Nymphs (Observatory) is the lowest, that of the Mouseion (Philopappos) the highest by far; they are divided by broad clefts. On the side of the Acropolis they rise abruptly, but from the top they slope very gradually to the western plain, with many terraces and hollows. Now it is clear that the whole extent of the hills, which

[Sketch of Salamis, from the foot of Hymettos]

is very considerable, was covered with buildings of one kind or another. At present it is a vast wilderness, the surface either of barren earth, thick-sown with stones and potsherds, or of the native rock, which exposes itself to a great extent, and is a beautiful mixture of red and blue,- I suppose limestone. Of actual building one may say that nothing remains, if one excepts the scraps of the city wall on the Mouseion, and the structure of the Pnyx; but everywhere the surface rock is obviously carved for human purposes. What these were, I can't understand,- except where steps are visible. The carving is generally this: the jutting rock is squared out into right angles with perpendicular sides. Were houses built *against* these squarings? If so, the houses seem to have been without foundations; indeed, I suppose must have been, on account of the rocky ground. Here and there are oblong trenches; also deep cone-shaped cellars.- One marvels at the completeness with which every sign of the edifices themselves has been swept away. Perhaps the rubble covering the ground is the remains of them.

Examined the Pnyx. From here is, I think, the finest view of Acropolis. One sees it with the clear hill-slopes on both sides, rising boldly agst

Hymettos; to the left, low down, is the rocky Areopagus, seeming to form a part of the Acropolis itself. You get the full east front of the Parthenon; below it, the Propylaea and Nike Apteros; also below, and to the left, the Erechtheion. At the base of the hill, on right, are the tops of the ruined Odeion. Round the foot creep the agaves and trees, their various greens contrasting, and looking odd in the bare soil.

On the back of the Observatory hill runs westward a long deep chasm. This is said to be the Barathron.

About four o'clock began a right glorious sunset,- a wild and fleeting magnificence of colour, not calmly grand, like that other I saw from these hills. I had noticed for a couple of hours that there was a growing rift of light in the western sky; this grew brighter, though all the rest of the sky was dull with clouds. The white strips of ragged mist hung very low on Parnes; they reached the very foot of Hymettus, and even floated against Lycabettus. Of a sudden, the sun's rays broke forth. They showed themselves to me first in a strangely beautiful way, striking from behind the mountains thro' the Daphni pass, and illuminating the further part of Aigaleos; its rounded slopes were brilliant, and its hollows deep in contrasting shadow; meanwhile all the rest of the landscape remaining untouched. This lasted only a minute or two. The sun itself emerged below clouds into the open rift of sky, and shot glory in every direction; its shafts of light smote upwards athwart the sullen clouds and made them a wild, strange yellow. To the left of the sun, the gulf was a glory of golden mist— that yellow splendour which Turner so often tried to get; the shape of Aegina floated in it vaguely. To the right, however, over dark Salamis, there lay delicate strips of pale blue.

I turned eastwards, and there to my astonishment was a magnificent rainbow, a perfect semicircle, stretching from the foot of Parnes to that of Hymettus, framing Athens and its hills, which were ever more and more resplendent. Hymettus was of a soft misty warmth, and something tending to purple, its ridges marked by exquisitely soft and indefinite shadows—the rainbow coming right down in front of it. The Acropolis glowed—ablaze. As the sun descended, these colours grew richer, warmer; for a moment all was nearly crimson. Then suddenly the sun passed again into the lower stratum of cloud, and the glory died almost at once,- except that there remained the northern half of the rainbow, which had become double. In the west, the clouds remained magnificent for a while; there were two shaped like great expanded wings, with edges of refulgence.

I copy the foll. from a newspaper:

Μεγάλαι προετοιμασίαι ἤρχισαν γενόμεναι ἐν Λονδίνῳ πρός ὑποδοχὴν τοῦ μεγάλου ἐρευνητοῦ τῆς Ἀφρικῆς, τοῦ ἡρωϊκοῦ Στανλεϋ. Μέγα γεῦμα θ ὰ δοθῇ αὐτῶ ἐν Γουϊδ-χώλ

[Great preparations have begun in London for the reception of the great explorer of Africa, the heroic Stanley. A banquet is to be given in his honour at the Guildhall].- I surmise that the last word means "Guildhall".

Amusing to read in advertisements: ζητεῖται μαγείρισσα καλή. [Fine cook wanted]. The word καλός has come to mean merely "excellent". They use ὡραῖος for "beautiful".

Mond. Dec. 9. The rain is over and gone. A day of high summer. Fine white clouds on the mountains, but elsewhere blue and splendour. Set out at 10 o'clock and went by train to Piraeus. There made inquiries about the Florio-Rubattino boat from Patras to Brindisi. Then ate some oranges, and walked round the land side of Munychia, examining the traces of the old wall. Of the Long Walls nothing, strictly speaking, remains; a few stones in the earth, that is all. Walked on to New Phaleron. A fine sand-beach here, with hotels and bathing stations; open air theatre etc. Stopped at a little restaurant and had lunch—two boiled eggs, bread, cheese, and two glasses of resinous wine—the first of the real kind that I have tasted. It is white wine, and hugely disagreeable. Only paid 1.10.

To illustrate habitual lack of water, I saw a boy gathering the water of a deep rain puddle, filling a big pail by means of a *paper* scoop.

On to Old Phaleron. A queer little harbour here, about 20 yds square. Only ripples on the shore. Fine view all about the bay. Then turned back by the inland road to Athens. This is the favourite afternoon drive and ride for rich people, as there are no houses and the road is good. Two English girls on horseback, accompd by an aristocratic man: "Well, I too am here in Athens. You live in luxury here, and I live poorly; but I have vastly more benefit and enjoyment of Athens than you have or ever could have."

Turned off at foot of Acropolis, and once more climbed to the Pnyx. Glorious sunset. When the colour had died off Athens and its hills, the slopes of the Pentelikon became a splendid scarlet.-

The Scotchman—with whom I always sit at meals now—tells me that the books he has brought with him are:- Bible, Concordance thereto, Hymn books, and "works of religious tendency" given him by a friend.

[Sketch of Acropolis and Athenian Hills, from foot of Munychia]

Tuesd. Dec. 10. The first half of last night much suffering from my throat; choking sensations. Seems better again to-day. Walked very little. A bright, hot day again. Bought some photographs of Athens at Constant. Athanasin's, in Hermes Street. They are all rather poor compared with Italian work. Bought views of the Acropolis for Madge and Nell, and a larger one to send to Bertz. The small ones cost ½ franc each; spent 6 fr. altogether.

At lunch Parigory looked in. I asked him to dine here on Thursday evening—so my obligations will be discharged.- The Scotchman sits next to me at meals now. Another Englishman turned up; one of the young draughtsmen on the new line. Must get information about such men's work; might be useful.

Have read Lucian's "Dream" and "Charon", and half finished the

"Timon". About half through Plato's "Symposium". Read in my little anthology from time to time.

A letter from Katie.- No reply yet from Miss Sichel to the letter I sent her.

Wed. Dec. 11. Letters from Nelly, Roberts and Shortridge.- Shortridge tells me his little boy has died recently. Will be glad to see me at Massa. Wrote to Roberts.

A right glorious day; very warm, and delightful breeze here and there, a blue sky. The mountains perfectly clear. In morning walked out to Kolonos. Afternoon up onto the Acropolis. Again, impressed by the beauty of the plain red rock left to walk on, just roughly flattened for the feet. The nine steps a little to the w. front of Parthenon are also cut clear out of the rock.-

Is Ruskin right when he says the Greeks never put fine work too high to be well seen? The lofty cornices of the Erechtheion are of an exceedingly fine pattern, and one ought to have a glass to examine them. Also there is very fine work round the tops of the columns, underneath the capitals. And the old difficulty about the frieze of the Parthenon recurs.- The splendid inner doorway in the Erechtheion. The sides slope inward to the top; as also the five doors of the Propylaea, and that of the Poikile.

Can anything be more dazzling in beauty than these structures of Pentelic marble against the blue sky?

Noticed to-day several broken bits of blackguard bullet and bombshell, which are left lying about. Of what date? I suppose the fatal 1687 -

I have given the Scotchman "Hypatia". He tells me that his day of interest in romances has gone by. All very well, he says, for a man of my age but for him "the serious in life has begun".-

Forgot to note that I made an examination of the Areopagus. In the innermost recess of the great cleft among the rocks found the Eumenides' well—the scene of Æschylus play. To do so, was nearly poisoned. The whole place is a vast public ordure-ground, in reality, one would think, a centre of pest.

Thursd. Dec. 12. A dull day; at night rain. Went nowhere; in afternoon read *Figaros* at a café. Wrote to Walter Grahame and to Roberts, also postcard to Shortridge.

At 7 came Parigory, and dined with me. I gave him a decent dinner of several dishes, with a bottle of Côtes de Parnès. Afterwards we went to a café and talked. My French improves in fluency, decidedly.

Frid. Dec. 13. Paid my bill up to yesterday—which in the Greek calendar was last day of Novr. It came to dr.57.45. For the dinner of last night I was only charged 8½dr., very reasonable indeed. Room at the rate of 2 dr. a day, from the beginning.

In morning finished Lucian's "Timon". A walk round by the Temple of Zeus. Dull day, with strong n.w. wind.

Afternoon to the Central Museum, and examined the sepulchral mon[umen]ts carefully.

Every night and morning my throat still troubles me,- a soreness at the back of the palate. Seems impossible to get rid of it.

Sat. Dec. 14. Violent wind in the night. This morning sunshine, but I dare not go out, because of throat.

In to-day's Ἀκροπολίς, I notice the following instances of carelessness in the transliteration even of a familiar name. Schliemann is printed as: Σλείμαν, Σλῆμαν and Σλείμανν. Whilst Bötticher appears as Μπατιχερ, Μπαίττιχερ Μπαίτχερ, and, lastly, B'otticher.

In a list of the University officials, I find: ὁ κύριος Κυπάρισσος Στέρ ανος.

At four o'clock went with Parigory to hear a lecture at the University. It was a Greek class, the "Philoktetes". A large low room, with school-benches and desks, and an estrade; room quite full of ugly young fellows, and among them a few oldish priests. Many smoked until the moment of prof's appearance, so that the air got bad to begin with, and at end of hour was stifling. The lecturer first read about a hundred lines; then paraphrased them in modern Greek; then gave critical comment, of just the kind that would be given in England. He uttered it very slowly, allowing the students to take down word for word.- The students rather noisy. Professor wore no special dress, and put his hard billycock down on the desk before him.

For this purpose, bought "Philoktetes" in the Haupt and Sauppe edition. I think my ideas with regard to the verse were confirmed by this reading of the professor's. Still it must be noted that the line 1179: ἰωμεγ, ἰωμεν — was read as if scanned $-\upsilon\upsilon/-\upsilon\upsilon$, instead of $\upsilon-\upsilon/\upsilon-\upsilon$. And line 1170, which begins παλιν παλιν παλαιον —now this is scanned $\upsilon-/\upsilon-/\upsilon-/\upsilon$. Yet he read the παλιν not only with accent α but with a distinctly long α: pronouncing *páhlin, páhlin*. And ζέννι he pron[ounce]d *xéhni.*- Postcard from Frau Häberle, and letter from Bertz.

Sund. Dec. 15. Postcard from Nelly.- Furious wind continuing, but much sunshine. In morning finished the "Symposium", and wrote long letter to Bertz. In afternoon a walk out to the Cemetery with Miller. One of the simplest and best-hearted men I ever knew. Apropos of every striking natural feature,- the vines, palms etc.- he quotes with childish delight a verse of Scripture. No man could be less bitter in his religion, yet it seems to enter strongly into his life. Though in most respects a typical Scotchman, yet he can criticize the faults of excess in Scotch morals and religion. Shakes his head at the Greek way of spending what he calls "the Sahbath". yet laughs good-naturedly at same time. In hearing the bands play, he exclaimed: "Ah well, if I turn Greek I'll do what I can to stop the like o' that, an' they'll no like me for it." Extraordinary naïveté. Seriously talks of settling here for life, and catches at every hint of opening in any kind of import or export business. Yet he is fifty years old, his wife and family in Glasgow, and I should judge him wholly incapable of learning a foreign tongue. Was never out of England before. Quotes instances of Scotchmen who have made themselves practically natives of foreign countries; even goes on to imagine himself a member of the Greek Parliament.- in which

190

case he would alter the "Sahbath". And all this with inexhaustible geniality and honesty of heart. Utterly ignorant of ancient history; trained in nothing but accountant's work. Receives all information with utmost delight and respect. Is a teetotaller, and gravely debating just now whether it will be possible for him to continue in that course. "I'll just take a few months to turn it over". Much love of country; knowledge of birds etc. Goes to the English church on Sunday morning, and this he can get on with it [sic], as soon as he has learned how to "find his places" in the Prayer-book. Much desire to travel in Palestine. Thinks his family will come out in about nine months' time. Chuckles over the cheapness of his meals here, and is amazed at times and seasons.- In appearance a tall, bluff man, with cropped peak-beard and moustache; turning a little grey. Moralizes much on the fleeting character of life. Though shocked at the public band, yet says "Well, well, we'll just go and hear it". Has no objection to the theatre; as a prentice-lad in London, for a time, used to go every Saturday night. Expecially fond of [Samuel] Phelps [the actor]. Much gratified to see "The ladies", more frequent in the streets on Sunday.- Very characteristic of him that he has a number of gifts with honorary inscriptions: an umbrella with silver round handle, on which is engraved that it is a present from a young man in his office, on his departure for Greece; a gold watch, with inscript. inside, saying it is given by Bowling Club in recogn of his Services as Secretary, and gold seal to watch-chain, given by somebody "in testimony of his uniform courtesy".

Read 300 11. of the "Philoktetes".

Mond. Dec. 16. A very miserable day for the last. The wind still violent and colder; no sun. Did nothing much except read Sophocles.- Throat has ceased to trouble me at last. But unfortunately a few premonitions of old Italian complaint.

At night, paid my bill to to-morrow. Together with dinner it came to dr. 12.15. Gave the table-waiter, a good-natured lad, 3 drachmas. Said good-bye to Miller.

Read some 400 more lines of "Philoktetes". Wrote letter to mother, to be posted at Naples.

Tuesd. Dec. 17. Again a dark day; cold and violent wind. Left Athens by the 11.50 from Pelopn Station. Feeling far from well. Strangely bad night. Went to bed feverish, and for hours tossed about, feeling very anxious. Then came a sudden change. The fever began to decline, and, about four in the morning, there set in a violent perspiration, amid which I fell asleep.

Last view of Acropolis from the station; it looked very mournful, seen amid surroundings of modern squalor, and under this leaden sky. Parigory came to station to say good-bye, but only caught sight of me at last moment.

A cold journey, the wind violent all along. The men ploughing, here and there; a pathetic struggle with poor patches of stony ground; sometimes with oxen, sometimes with two little horses.- Came to Megara; white houses closely covering two round hills. About here, yellow pines growing all along the shore.- Just before reaching Corinth, crossed the trench of the canal, which is nearly finished; not very wide, but the depth seemed tremendous; from the middle of the bridge over it, one looked to the sea at either end.- Over against Corinth the great mountain Geraneion, capped with white storm-clouds. On leaving Corinth, Helicon came in view, a great mass of mountain with much snow; above it the sky had begun to break—a rift of pure blue; sunlight fell on the snow and the dispersing white mist.- The line, in coasting the sea, goes over endless currant-gardens (little trunks, barren now of leaves) and olive plantations; frequently crosses very deep beds of streams, with perpendicularly cloven sides.- The sky grew constantly clearer in the west, and towards sunset the snow on the hills of Lokris shone a bright rose. Parnassus did not reveal itself fully. Above it hung great crimson clouds. When the sun had set, the tops of the mountain were visible for a few minutes.

Arrived at Patras, the train boarded by shouting ruffians. Allowed two of them to carry my things to the Hotel de Patras, and there had dinner. Then took ticket at the Florio office,- 2nd for Brindisi, food included, fr. 44.15, in gold. By boat to the steamer. The night become almost calm. Having written this in the cabin, shall go to bed. Very weary.

Wed. Dec. 18. A restless night. Contrary to my expectation the sea tolerably calm. Got up in time to see the sun rise, which fortunately it *did* to-day. We were just opposite the Ambracian gulf,- I looked towards Actium. Kephallinia and Leukadia in sight, doubtful whether I could see Ithaka;- the Leukadian promontory. North, the snowy mountains of Epirus. At eleven o'clock reached Corfu, and waited there till 5 in evening. Did not go on shore. Sorry to say, the symptoms of my old complaint become more serious. Shall leave off wine, or all but.

The food on board this Italian boat nothing like so good as on Fraissinet's; and should fare badly in the berth but for my rugs etc. Some English people in 1st class, but no one companionable in 2nd.

Thursd. Dec. 19. Violent wind rose as soon as we had left Corfu, which we did at 5pm. Much rolling in the night. This morning I went up at 8 o'clock and saw land just ahead. But to my astonishment, on inquiry, I found it was the coast of Turkey! We had turned back, on account of wind, about midnight, when we must have been nearly half way over to Brindisi. At 10 o'clock entered a great bay, with an island at its mouth; on the inner shore, situated on the top of the hill, above a great gorge which descends to the shore, is a little town which I understand to be Avlona. As I have no map of this district I cannot tell exactly where this is. (This is the ancient Aulon; and the extremity of the bay was the Acroceraunian Pr[omontory]. If I had but known it!)[29]

Some amusing society in the 1st class; several Germans, of the usual coarse type. One white-haired old man who says he is close upon 80 years. Yesterday, at Corfu, he lost something, and for hours went about searching his pockets and his coat-linings, and every impossible place about him, even his shoes and the bottoms of his trousers. A tragi-comic

192

spectacle. Thinking he had suffered the loss whilst on the island, he took a boat and went back, but returned still searching his clothes. This morning he has either found the thing, or forgotten it; he seems all right.

To-day not a cloud anywhere in the sky, but wind still violent, though here we are quite sheltered. I sit on deck in the hot sun and read Sophocles. Someone plays a piano down in the saloon. A boat sent to shore to telegraph to the agency of ship. Boat came to us with natives, offering to take anyone ashore. Captain advises not to trust the people.

The inner shore is thickly wooded. Beautiful clefts and valleys. Avlona seems to have been a Venetian fortress; I gather this from chance scraps of conversation overheard in French, Italian and German.

The stewardess on board speaks French, German and Italian, yet all with a foreign accent. I don't know of what country she can be. We have also a Queen's Messenger on board. He went on land with the ship's boat, and did not return till late at night.

A beautiful sunset, soft, calm; the night crept gently into the deep hollows of the hills, which, at the inner part of the bay, became a dark green. A simple lighthouse on the shore. The wind had fallen, and in the stillness I heard the breakers murmur on the beach.

The ship's boat returning, brought a lot of provisions; live fowls and Turkish bread—flat, round cakes, ill-cooked—"cotto al sole", said the mate, but I do not know if that is literally true.

I went to bed early. At one o'clock woke up and heard the vessel in motion. A calm sea. By seven o'clock we were at Brindisi, the passage taking only *six hours*. The flat coast was a new thing for me in Italy; could see nothing beyond the line of houses round the harbour. A cloudless sky at sunrise, except for the few scraps of gold-edged cloud over the western horizon, and these were glorious; the buildings a warm yellow. Took a boat for the shore at once (1 franc) and thence to the station, which is a quarter of an hour's walk. At 9.25 there was a train to Naples. One had the choice of going via Foggia, or via Taranto and Metaponto. By the latter only there was 3rd class, so I took that way. Fare fr. 19.70. All round the gulf of Taranto the shore is sand covered with evergreen shrubs, very thick. Inland a great plain. Saw nothing noticeable at Taranto. At Metaponto,- where Pythagoras died,- bought bread and figs, for mid-day meal. Then the railway line strikes north, along the valley of the Basento. A cloudless day again. A good deal of snow even on the low hills of the Basilicata. The latter part of the journey long and tedious. Stopped at all the stations after Salerno: Vietri, Angri, Scafati etc. etc. to Naples, which we reached about 10.30pm.

Had noticed all through the journey from Patras a young Greek who travelled 2nd class on the boat, but did not take his meals at the table. On reaching Naples, I determined to speak to him, as I felt sure he knew nothing of the town and would be at a loss for a hotel. Addressed him in Italian, and he responded readily. Found he spoke a little English. I liked his face, and found his character correspondent. We went together to the Albergo d'Italia, Strada del Porto (I think) and got a double-bedded room. But of course all this happened on—

Friday Dec. 20. On landing at Brindisi, I learnt from the boatman his opinion that the captain of our ship "Il Principe Amadeo"—"è molto timido". But the passengers on board blamed the company. And indeed the stewardess told us that the ship had insufficient ballast.- very little coals and no merchandise. Doubtless it was wiser to wait at Avlona.

Sat. Dec. 21. My acquaintance, by name Alexandre Panagópoulos, is going to Buenos-Ayres, where he has a relative; simply going to "better himself". All this day we spent on the business necessary before he could arrange for his passage by a French ship from Naples. They would not give him a ticket before he produced a passport, so we had to hunt up the Greek Consul. Numerous carriages; constant going to and fro between the Porta Capuana (where the agency was) and the Riviera di Chiaia. Only by 5 o'clock was everything finished. Then we went and dined at the Giardini di Torino, which is as good and cheap as ever. As Panagópoulos cannot sail before next Saturday, I brought him to the Casa di Luca, Vico Brancaccio, and established him in my double-bedded room. I am to pay 1½ fr. a day, and he the same whilst he stays.

I find a great change in the communication between Vico Brancacc' (as the Neapolitans call it) and the Chiaia. A new descent is in process of construction: great staircases etc, in place of the old winding roads.

Sund. Dec. 22. A fine day again. In morning we took a drive up to San Martino. The view misty. Afternoon walked to Posillipo, and back by tramway. The association with Panagópoulos is not an ideal one, but he is a good fellow, and I am glad to be of some use to him during his week's stay here. Dined at the Giardini di Torino; well, as always.

The bagpipers are all about the town. They play very curious tunes, which I wish I could remember. Via Roma lined with stalls of all kinds.

Posted long letter to Mother.

Mond. Dec. 23. We went to a Caffè Turco, and fortunately Panagópoulos found some friends, with whom he spent the day. I was very glad to be free. Strolled about in the sunshine.

In the morning a thick mist hid Posillipo, but it soon cleared away. The zampognieri [bagpipers] active everywhere. They seem to have ousted the organs for the time.

The *Corriere* has just begun to publish "Addio, Amore!" by Matilde Serao[30]; I read the paper daily, as last year.- Bought a vocabulary of the Neapolitan dialect. Walked much about the Toledo inspecting the stalls and their paltry wares—the town swarms with beggars, all exposing loathsome diseases; they generally limp about in couples, one supporting the other; on their lips I frequently hear "Santa Lucia benedetta!" The steps going up to the Ponte di Chiaia exhibit a string of them.

Tuesd. Dec. 24. Bought a Germ. transn, in Reclam's series, of "Sebetia", Neapolitan sketches by Amilcare Lauria.[31]- For 6 soldi bought a couple of common earthenware lamps sold here.

Sent pictured postcards—"Ricordo di Napoli"—to Mother, Katie and Roberts. To Bertz despatched the photograph of the Acropolis.- Dined at a very good and cheap restaurant close to the railway station—Albergo del Ribecchino; cheaper then Giardini di Torino; and as good in quality.- In evening, after Panagópoulos had gone to bed, was invited to join the Häberles and some Germans in the sitting-room, where we drank mulled wine till midnight.

Wed. Dec. 25. Christmas. Yesterday was the last day of the zampognieri, and also of the stalls in the Toledo. These stalls (bancarèlle) begin at Str. Santa Brigida and extend to the Mercatello. Frequent little red-lined stalls for the sale of Bengali and the salt-petre candles, sometimes of coloured light, which the people light and hold out at the windows.

All night long a ceaseless clamour; perpetual ringing of church-bells, explosions of fireworks, and yelling. It ended about 8 o'clock this morning.

Went with P. to the Aquarium, which to-day is only 50c. Much delighted. Then to the church in P[iazza] Plebiscito, where heard some good singing.

Yesterday, a great deal of fish about the streets, especially capitoni, which were for the most part alive. The sellers kept diving their hands among the creatures, to make them wriggle.- Letters from Nelly, Alg, and W. Stannard.

Thursd. Dec. 26. Letter from Roberts, saying he is very ill,- fever etc.

A dull day; mild scirocco. Most of the uproar over, though *botte* occasionally explode. In afternoon a long walk about the dirty streets above Via Roma.

Day before yesterday strange story in the *Corriere*. For thirty years a beggar called "il beato Pollastrone" has sat by the statue of S. Peter in S. Peter's at Rome;- I remember seeing him. He alone had permission to beg in the Cathedral. Pio IX and Leo XIII had friendly relations with him; the former gave him an old dressing-gown of his own, which the beggar wore on state occasions, and always refused to sell. In private life, he dealt in fowls. The other evening, coming from S. Peter's, he had a stroke and died. He has left 50,000 lire. His dwelling was in the Palazzo Allegretti, Prati di Castello, very comfortable quarters.

Frid. Dec. 27. At midnight—last night—began a severe storm, with heavy rain, thunder and lightning. It lasted all to-day. Spent time mostly in the Caffè Turco, dull enough. Dined at the Giardini, and in coming home was almost drowned in the rain. In the little streets above the Toledo were so many rushing torrents, water came to ankles. From the house-tops fell water in tons. Every few minutes a brilliant glare of lightning and terrific roar of thunder. Grand impression in the deserted old streets, between the vast houses.

Letter from Roberts, sent from Athens, and at last the reply from Miss Sichel. Very cold and uninteresting.

Sat. Dec. 28. The storm continued till past midnight, having thus lasted 24 hrs. This morning a little sunshine, but threatening sky. Panagópoulos making purchases. Finally took leave of him at 1.30, he going to the ship's office.

At 4.30 a furious outbreak of rain and wind. Looking from my window, I saw a great body of flying mist come in from the sea, hiding Posillipo. Suddenly the rolling clouds broke in rain. But through it all there were great rents over in the west, showing green and red sky, and even great patches of far dim blue. A terribly wild half hour.

Posted letters to Roberts and W. Stannard.

La *gazzarra* (the festival) of Christmas was, it seems, much less noisy than usual this year. It is amusing to read in the papers, that, owing to exertions of police, *few if any* bombs (botte) were fired off! It must have been lively then in other years. About a dozen people went to the hospital, injured by these same bombs.

It is customary to celebrate the feast of the Christmas Vigil with Capitoni, Vermicelli alle Vongole (= arselle = [mussels]), broccoli, and vino maraniello. At night the people go to the small theatres to see the "Nascita del Verbo Umanato". But this year the play has been forbidden, owing to general scandals at the theatre. The play was popularly called "La Cantata dei Pastori". On the posters you used to read: "Il vero Lume tra le ombre" or "La Spelonca arricchita per la Nascita del Verbo Umanato". ['True light among the shadows' or 'The cave enriched by the birth of the Word incarnate'.] Always tremendous uproar in auditorium. The various parts acted in accordance with old tradition. Belfagor howled and writhed; the Madonna kept eyes on ground; Archangel Gabriel cut air with his sword; Armenzio, the old Jewish shepherd, had great beard and trembled with age. Also a comic figure, Razzullo (Pulcinella without mask) dressed like Spaniard of 2 cents. ago. He is beaten by demons and tied to a tree, liberated by Joseph, in vain tries to get something to satisfy his hunger etc. All through, perpetual interruptions of dialogue by the people. Shouts of joy when Maria spoke, and curses when the Demon blasphemed. When Joseph and Mary lie down to sleep the public cried "Buona Notte!" and "A che ora volite 'o caffè. ['Good Night!' and 'At what time would you like coffee?']

Sund. Dec. 29. Much hard rain again this morning, but afternoon sunny.

I see in the newspaper an incredible announcement that the Questura has forbidden street-organs (Pianini) in Naples. And indeed I hear none. Alas! Alas!

Dined badly at the Tratt. della Nuova Italia in the Toledo, and then, under a fine half-moon, walked all round to the Chiaia. The waves breaking loudly agst the sea-wall. Rejoiced to hear some poor fellows singing "Santa Lucia", and "Addio, bella Napoli!" in front of an hotel.- Naples without music!

Finished reading of "Sebetia". Poor as literary work, but interesting.-

In room next to me two Germans, who sing together very vilely. To-night they are chanting: "Röslein, Röslein, Röslein roth [sic], Röslein auf der 'eiden". I didn't know before that Germans dropped their h's.

Spent morning in the Museum. Whilst consulting my Baedeker, was greeted by a man who passed, in German, as "ein echt-Deutscher Bücherwurm" [a downright German bookworm]. I rather resented this, but followed the man with my eyes, and saw him begin to speak in Italian to one of the guardians. He threw his arms about, and in general behaved eccentrically. Presently he greeted me again, and I told him I was English. This surprised him. "Ihre Kleidung ist so bescheiden!" [Your clothes are so shabby!] said he with German frankness. Then he went on to say that he was a Poet from Heidelberg, and that he had just sent a volume of his verses to the Empress Friedrich—who is now staying here. In return she had sent him 15 francs,- which disgusted him much because so little. Going on with censure of her, he mentioned having seen in the paper that she had visited the Castel dell' Ovo, and there inspected the guardian's room; what monstrous indelicacy! "I am not moral; I am very immoral; I am a Poet. But for a woman to inspect a man's private room,- no, that is too much!" Whereat I laughed heartily.- A man rather past middle age; rather bald and grey.

Mond. Dec. 30. A walk out to the Reclusorio [prison-house], in Foria. An immense building. Back to Porta Capuana through filthy streets.

Tuesd. Dec. 31. This morning a postcard from Shortridge, asking me to come. Left by the 11.35 train for Castellammare. There made a bargain for carriage to Massa,- 4 francs. A wretched little horse in a beggarly carriage—tattered and crusted with the mud of ages. Before I had gone a mile I was wretched at the spectacle of the poor beast's toil, could not enjoy the landscape a bit. As always happens, the harness broke several times, and man had to mend it with string, his handkerchief, etc. Reached Villa Cozzolino at 3pm.

The house is a little better furnished than last year, but the arrangements as squalid as ever. Shortridge much pulled down by the death (by meningitis) of his "little lad", whom he called Jack. Herbert S. clearly in last stage of consumption, and, as before, drunk every night. Carmela getting stout, and always slatternly, poor creature. Eldest girl, Jessie, pale and long-faced; the others: Nannie, Kate and baby Nora all look very healthy. Kate a remarkably pretty child. The old father, Raffaele, (so addressed by S.) seems to live in the filthy little kitchen; hangs about there and in the garden; always eats alone in a corner. Is paralyzed in one leg and not long for this world. Herbert S. shouts at him from the dinner table into the kitchen "Chiudi quella porta maladetta, per Cristo!" [Shut that cursed door for Christ's sake] as often as old man moves to the door of the garden.

A vile dinner. Food bad, and piggishly thrown onto table; think I never saw such slovenly ways. A disgusting form of maccheroni, mixed with sugar, raisins, pigne, gravy etc. This is a regular Capri dish at Xmas.

Long talk with S. afterwards. Is inclined to talk incessantly of "the little lad", and loses command of his voice. Rails at his brother's scandalous behaviour. Herbert constantly abuses Carmela and children. S.'s proposal now is to leave Massa next midsummer and transplant whole family to a farm near Hartford, Connecticut. But I have no belief in his going,- unless the old man and Herbert die very soon. He is utterly irresolute; talks one moment of things as certain which in almost the next sentence he shows he does not seriously contemplate. One of his weaknesses is to imagine that all the men he has met remain his firm friends for ever. He is always promising letters of recommendation to men in all parts of the world,- "A rattling good friend of mine" is his phrase,- and often, I suspect, without justification. A really good fellow, but hot-tempered and weak, and here not likely to grow stronger.

As they could not accommodate me in the house, I had a room on the top floor but one of the higher house—so called "Palazzo"—next door. A big uncomfortable room with two beds. Violent storm of wind all night.

The lemon-trees all about here are sheltered over with straw matting. They are more delicate than the oranges, and of course a more valuable crop.

1890

Wed. Jan.1. A walk with S[hortridge] to the Punta Campanella. Fine wild coast, and splendid views of Capri all the way. At Campanella, a lighthouse and remnants of Roman buildings. Picked up a Roman coin, and a lot of pieces of vase etc. Two steep narrow staircases, one on each side of the point. Descended that on the south, which is newly repaired. Magnificent rocks. Opposite, the Calabrian hills. Waves dashing up twelve or fifteen feet.-

The myrtles are covered with their big black berries. They are good to eat.

Before going to the Point, called at the house of an old sea Captain, in Termini, and there had mid-day meal. Pork chops, cold hen, salad, fruit, and a hideous dish—which I did not touch—made out of pig's blood, cinnamon, raisins, oil, brodo etc.—In the house a lot of blinded quails in cages, which serve as decoys to wild birds.

The Captain tells as authentic a story of some unknown sailors, who landed one night at Nerano, and invited the lime-burners there to feast on food and wine they had brought from the ship; and, whilst meal going on, a number of them brought out of a boat a gagged and bound lady, richly dressed, and flung her body into the lime-kiln, where she disappeared for ever. Said to have happened some 50 years ago.

It is the law in Italy that a man who kills another in a quarrel cannot be arrested after a lapse of 24 hours. The only course then is to bring a civil suit against him.

At night looked over to the lighthouse on Cape Misenum -
"Qui nunc ab illo
Dicitur, aeternumque tenet per saecula nomen."
["Which is thus called to-day and will retain that name throughout all ages"].

Thursd. Jan. 2. Great uproar in house. Jessie let the baby fall on her head on the stone floor. Carmela cries and howls lamentably. Herbert prophesies meningitis,- and so on. A cold sunny day. There is a servant here called Assunta; Carmela calls to her "Assú!"

I happened to walk into the room when Nora was being bathed. Carmela laughed and exclaimed: "Come è bella, nuda!" How impossible for an English mother to make such a remark to a stranger!

Shortridge showed me a large number of his watercolour drawings. Some are excellent. The man is a born artist. Much talent for mechanics of all sorts. Wonderful stores of common knowledge about practical things. Says he *hates* poetry. His strange stories of his experiences when he was a

199

common sailor in all parts of the world. It seems he had a child by Carmela before their marriage.-

The house full of bric-a-brac, mostly old Italian crockery etc. Curious coloured pot vessel for holy water hanging on walls. Mandolines and other musical instruments. The only comfortable room is, of course, Herbert's; a stove there, with coal to burn.

At dinner had a dish of cignale sausages (like leather) in brodo and cabbage. For supper a porridge of semolina mixed with cauliflower and cheese. This is a Capri new-year's dish.

Frid. Jan. 3. Fine and warm. A walk with S. to the Capo di Sorrento, where are extensive Roman ruins and a strange natural sea-bath (Bagno della Regina Giovanna). The sea rushes in through a natural arch into a great round hollow.

Daffodils are out already.-In afternoon, had a carriage and went with one Ernesto Mollo, son of Massa doctor, up to church of Sant' Agata and the Deserto.

Dinner in frightful discomfort. Open door of kitchen letting in fumes of coal and wood [?] and grease. S. breaking down at night over "the little lad". It seems that Herbert often ill-used the boy, and in his illness Jack had a knife under his pillow; he showed it to his father, saying: "Ammazerò zio Herberto, quando mi faccio uomo!" [I will murder uncle Herbert when I am a man!] A pretty story, this!

Sat. Jan. 4. In the night a violent storm,- thunder, lightning, and rain in cataracts. As bad as other day at Naples.

Remember Carmela's curious wailing song over the baby's cradle.

The habit of Italians to go out and shoot all birds indiscriminately even the smallest. S. once showed a Massa man the crop of a martin full of insects, to the fellow's astonishment.

Went nowhere. A dull, weary day, now and then looking into one of S.'s books.

Sund. Jan. 5. Fine, hazy, warm. S. showed me his little machine for making maccheroni. The paste is of semolina mixed very stiffly with hot water. This is squeezed down a round tube and out at the bottom through moulds which give it its different forms.

After dinner, poor Carmela—who had just quarrelled with S.—tried to take me into her confidence. "Che vita!- Si, sono bassa, sono ignorante; còsa posso fare io?- Mio marito è buono, si, ma s'arrabbia per si piccola cosa. Egli m'a pigliata buona ragazza!" [What a life! Yes, I am low-born, I am ignorant; what can I do? My husband is a good man, yes, but he flies into a rage over such trifles. When he took me I was a respectable girl!] All in the wailing sing-song of this dialect. She says he often threatens her with knife. Laments her inability to speak English, and that she could not tell her story to S.'s sister when she was here. Her words touched me deeply. It is certain that S. is often to blame. She at least has no vices; is only a good simple untaught creature,- a Caprese!

200

Mond. Jan. 6. Rose about 5 in morning. Magnificent full moon over Ischia; sea perfectly calm. Took the posta at 7 o'clock for Castellammare, riding on the box, fare 1½fr. Curious to watch the handings in and out of post-bags (done in a very bungling way) at the different stoppages. At Sorrento we changed horses, taking three for the stiff hill that follows. Between Meta and Vico, we met the Post coming the other way, and the drivers changed seats, the Massa man and he of Castellammare thus returning to their homes.- The crowd of decently dressed (modern) loafers in each market-place. At Vico the market stalls with their great umbrella shelters.- Air very cold, but a clear sky.

Naples by 12.30. Found letters from Roberts and Bertz. Roberts been very ill with the "Influenza", and has had to go to Clapham to be nursed. Bertz sends copy of *Deutsche Presse*, in which is a reference to my work again.[1] He says he has written to Tauchnitz, asking him to print my name in future on "Demos"; Tauchnitz, in agreeing, mentioned that he has got "Nether World" for eventual publication[2].

In evening a letter from Nelly, enclosing one from James Wood. Wrote to Roberts and Shortridge and Wood.

Tuesd. Jan. 7. Magnificent weather. In morning to Holme's office to ask dates of sailing of the Orient ships. Then walked about in the Str. S. Trinita Maggiore. Bought a little Anacreon. Went into the church of S. Chiara, and looked at the sculpture on the old Gothic tombs.

In Naples it is common to see a man sitting at a street-corner with a painted board above him: "Sensale di Appartamenti" or something of the kind. He has a little book of rooms to let. They seem to be frequently consulted.

Wrote to Nelly, asking her to send me £20 on the 13th Jan.- Began to think of new novel, which probably will not be "The Head Mistress" after all.

Wed. Jan. 8. Very fine, but misty. Changed my room for one with a worse view; to please Miss Häberle, who wishes to suit another lodger.- Wrote postcard to Nelly, asking her to send Mrs King £1; ought to have been sent on the 6th of Jan.-

In morning bought a lot of Italian books: the original of "Sebetia" [by Amilcare Lauria],—"L'ultima Battaglia di Prete Agostino" by Salv[atore] Farina, "La Cieca di Sorrento", by Mastriani, and "Novelle, Scene e Racconti" by the same; and "La Napoli che Scompare", by Carlo Gaetani.[3]

We have the "Influenza" here at last; but it causes no anxiety. Hope I shall keep clear of it, however.

Last night I saw a funeral notice on the walls: "— è morto. La lega anticlericale Giordano Bruno è convocata per domani, per prendere parte" etc. ['— is dead. The Giordano Bruno Anticlerical League will meet tomorrow in order to attend".]

Lunched at home on bread and apples. Long letter to Bertz.

Thursd. Jan. 9. Cloudless day, but very misty over the sea. Walked up by Via Tasso to my old favourite view, from hill of Posillipo. Find that the plain beyond is greatly spoilt by the new Cuma railway line; and they are building big ugly houses at Fuorigrotta. As I walked, made lunch of bread and apples. Descended to the Str. N. di Posillipo by the Salita Villanova (*sic*), a descent of, I suppose, several hundred steps, very narrow, between high walls all the way. There are a few lamps, but at night it must be a cut-throat place. It issues under a little archway some distance beyond the Castle of Donna Anna.

In trying to walk back by the road, found it was blocked, because of renewed danger of the "frana" [landslip] which happened at this point last year. Workmen at the top of the hill busy sending down huge masses of stone and earth. Had to take a boat, and "fare il giro". A nice state of things, on a great high road!

At dinner had a *zuppa di vongole*—very good. Vongole seem to be cockles, but I am not sure. Risotto con vongole is also to be had, I see.

Finished Farina's "L'ultima battaglia di prète Agostino". Far more interesting than I expected; in fact, excellently written. I must see more of the man's work.

Fri. Jan. 10. In morning went at last to call on Ern[esto] Mollo, 27 Salita del Museo. He was out, but his aunt received me, in a room where two young women were sitting; don't know who they were. Got on with my Italian pretty well, then departed. In afternoon Mollo came to visit me here and stayed an hour. Invited him to dine to-morrow.

Towards evening a clouded sky.- Reading at my Italian books.

Sat.Jan. 11. Weather getting bad again. Vesuvius invisible absolutely. Rain at night.

Mollo did not turn up at the rendezvous for dinner.- In the Toledo, a funeral procession, at 6 o'clock, coming out from one of the houses. People dressed in scarlet; heads covered, and only eye-holes left.

Sund. Jan. 12. Tramontana; clear sky and sun. Spent morning at Museum.- Note the picture of Masaniello's revolt in the Mercato, Vesuvius in background. Of quite different form from present. Somma, shapèd as now, towers high above the smoking crater.

In afternoon Shortridge turned up, unexpectedly. Troubles at home, as usual. Then came Mollo, to explain that he had waited at the wrong place last night,- a stupid mistake. S. and I dined at the little rest[aurant] on the Piliero. Ate some fichi d'India for the first time.- S. takes the second bed in my room.

Influenza very bad in Naples.

Mond. Jan. 13. Cold and gloomy; tramontana. Shortridge has bad sore throat. We walked about the Strada di Porto, the far end of which is just being demolished; then through the Rua Catalana. Lunched at Tratt[oria]

202

del Falcone, on the Guantai Nuovi. For dinner went to the old Fieramosca in the Via Carlo Poerio. The place is in new hands, and very decent.

Tuesd. Jan. 14. Tramontana still, but clear sky. In the morning a walk among the streets, w. of the Toledo. Extraordinary state of this quarter; in every street are several houses blocked up with beams or brick walls. Looks as if all this hill under S. Elmo were in an unstable condition. Mere patching going on everywhere.

Note for picturesqueness the Piazzetta Rosario di Palazzo, in the Str. San Máttia. A fruit and vegetable market, backed by good church. The whole quite unspoilt by novelties.

Thence to the former Convent of S. Maria Nova, near n. end of Str. Medina. Very fine cloisters, now turned to secular uses. A splendid place to take rooms. Good gardens. The cloisters frescoed, and with fine old tombs.

Struck into the district of Pendino (Neap. Pennino) and rambled about extraordinary streets. Note the localization of crafts.- Women cutting up canes for pipe-stems.- The street of cloth-merchants, with open shops.- Carvers of images in wood, for churches. Fine effects of sun striking down narrow streets, and blue sky always at the end.

Ate at the Tratt. Mazzo di Fiori, in Largo S. Tommaso d'Aquino. Reach it by turning out of Toledo into the Vico Carrozzieri and San Tommaso, next street after Vico dei Fiorentini.

Remember the curious procession bringing the extreme unction. Umbrella over head of priest. Candles. Crowd following, which often presses into sick chamber.

Cioffi's old bookshop, under the big archway that leads to S. Chiara. Good old classics.

Note from Katie. Alg is on point of going to settle at Wickwar.

Wed. Jan. 15. Not much walking. Ate at Mazzo di Fiori. There is always music here. Two men, one with guitar, other mandoline; one sings. At night a little girl singing.

At night, Herr [Hugo] Fink looked in to my room, and we had a talk. [See January 22]

*   *   *

Frid. Jan. 17. Sant' Antonio; first day of Carnival. Horses used to be taken to be blessed by St. Antonio; still done a little, S[hortridge] tells me. The municipality has this year forbidden the bonfires that were traditional to-night. For all that, saw a few blazing here and there.-

Carmela has sent us, by the sailor Marionello, who comes daily as carrier etc. by the boat from Massa, a packet of her infernal anise sausages. We had them for breakfast this morning. Amusing that I should be pursued even here by the villa Cozzolino diet, and forced to eat it agst my stomach.

Sat. Jan. 18. Glorious weather continuing. Started this morning from the station by the new Napoli-Cumana railway line by train for Pozzuoli. There

203

visited S.'s friend, the notàio Oriani, who lives at top of a big house just within gate of the town. Found him ill in bed with influenza,as well as six members of his family. Then took a carriage and drove to Capo Miseno. At the foot of the hill,—which we didn't climb, is a military station, and a few poor houses; nothing to be had to eat. Back to the Hôtel de Russie, at Lago Lucrino, for lunch, and then on with the carriage towards Cuma. It proved a much shorter distance than I had thought; an easy walk from Pozzuoli, in fact. The road passes a height whence is a fine view over Lake Avernus,- I think painted by Turner; in the background the castle of Baia and Capo Miseno, with glimpse of Capri. A little further, passes thro' Arco Felice, an enormous Roman arch, part of aqueduct; exquisite glimpse through it of Acropolis of Cuma. Did not go to the site of the town, but lingered looking down on it. The Acropolis a vine- and shrub-covered hill, in a plain covered with wild growth. Northward a vast tract of marshy land, with great wood of quèrcie [oak-trees], where wild boars are said to be common. The sea-shore consists of hilly sand-dunes; it stretches away to vast distance, the height of Gaeta visible beyond. As yet an unspoilt scene; impressive after Paestum. But the new railway will alter all this. Again heard, as at Paestum, the wailing song of peasants.- S. made a sketch of the Acropolis.

Back to Pozzuoli, and had dinner at the house of one Stanford, an Italianized Englishman who is an overseer at Armstrong's works. He took us over these works,—a vast shed full of roaring and rattling machinery, and cannons in all stages of manufacture. Said that 1500 men are employed.Saw a monk who was waiting to get money for some saint or other from workmen, it being pay-day. This Standord married a Capri girl, who had previously been mistress of a Caprese; he has one son, a monkey-faced lad of seventeen, working at Armstrong's, speaking no English, and, as we learned, already getting dissipated. The wife I liked; she has pleasant, ladylike ways, and the excellent order of house, decency of meals, etc., testified in her favour. A very different type from poor Carmela, though her name is the same. S. tells me, however, that their life is miserable. I am disposed to think that he is unjust to the woman, through a little envious feeling.

From the garden, at sunset, a fine view over Cape Misenum and Ischia.

Back by 7 o'clock train. Found letter from Roberts.

Pozzuoli people have mostly very bad front teeth.

To-day saw green peas in flower; will very soon be ready for eating.

Sund. Jan. 19. Lutto nazionale [national mourning] for the death of Principe Amedeo. A dull day. S. and I went to some churches in morning. He goes back to-morrow. One of the causes of his leaving Massa was a quarrel with Carmela because she wished to exhume and scrape her mother's bones, who has only been buried 12 months. The legal period is 18 months.

Saw again the Viatico passing. All the people in the street either knelt down, or bent very low, bareheaded. Strange to see cocchieri [cabmen]and other blackguards thus prostrated.

Examined the great hole (60 feet across) that fell in a short time ago in the Rione Principe Amedeo, just below the Bristol. Also saw the Palazzo Sansevero, which half a year ago fell down with a crash one night.

Mond. Jan. 20. S. went back to Massa by the 2.15 train.- Dull, rainy day.- Paid my month's bill; together with charge for S. (bed and breakfasts) it comes to 87.15.- Dined at the Giardini once more.- A new song that is heard frequently, called "Malia", by Tosti.

Tuesd. Jan. 21. Museum closed these days, on account of Prince's death. Went to Holme's, and changed one of my £10 cheques; got 254 *l.*- Bought "L'Eco del Vesuvio", a large collection of Neapn songs.

Customary for the Banco Lottos to put up in front rows of numbers which are recommended. Saw one such advt to-day, with, written above: "Fatevi ricchi. Son certi" [Make a fortune. They are dead certs]. The numbers are given in twos, threes, fours and fives.

Note in a shop-window a useful book, illustd: "Usi e Costumi di Napoli", by F. De Bourcard.

Common thing to sell boiled pig's skin in streets, hot and fresh.

I see from the paper that Castel Capuano is in a most dangerous state; expected to fall—or great part of it—every day.

Had Ernest Mollo to dine with me at the Giardini. Unfortunately he wants to talk English, and so I lose practice in Italian.

A happy proverb about to-day, which is S. Sebastiano: "Fra il barbuto ed il frecciato (S. Ant[hony] and S. Sebast[ian]) l'inverno è passato" [between the bearded and the arrow-pierced saint winter has passed].

Wed. Jan. 22. Disagreeable weather. Towards night a bad cold set in, with feverish symptoms. Went to bed very early. Wrote to Madge, Alg, and p.c. to Mrs. King.- Letter from Alg, saying he is transferred to Wickwar in Gloucestershire, and that Blackett has bought his new novel, "A Village Hampden", for £40.

A certain Herr Fink, a gardener and bee-breeder,[4] comes every evening to read English. He has bought "Demos" in the Tauchnitz edn.

Thursd. Jan. 23. At home all day, and saw doctor. Slightly feverish and with headache.- Note from Shortridge, saying that his brother seems to be dying.

Frid. Jan. 24. Much better, but cannot go out. Made very comfortable by Fraülein Häberle.- I wonder what has been the expense of telegrams sent by the relatives of Principe Amedeo in reply to those of condolence from all parts of the world. In paper to-day it is stated that the telegram sent by the King to a son of Amedeo who is at Rio Janeiro cost 13,000 lire. I can hardly believe this.

Sat. Jan 25. A glorious day. In morning went to the Museum, and recd ticket of free admission to the Museum and all the local antiquities. It extends to 30th June, and of course I shall only be able to use it for a week. Lunched at Giardini. In afternoon called Mollo. Dinner at home.

Working hard at Italian, but make little progress in speaking.

Sund. Jan. 26. Gloomy again and cold. Hour's walk in morning. Lunched at Fraülein H.'s table, with Fink and two young Swiss fellows. These young Swiss abroad are an amusing study. Their dialect of German,- omitting final *n* etc. Their small round faces, pleasant-looking, of fresh complexion, boyish. Rather boisterous manners, but good, honest fellows. Fr. Häberle lives among them with extraordinary freedom; her poor old paralyzed aunt is the nearest makeshift of a chaperon. She goes into their bedrooms when they are ill etc. Much joking about love and marriage etc., but no hint at indecency.- Fraülein H., and her servant Virginia (from Siena) must have terrific daily toil. The pathos of her position.

Mond. Jan. 27. Glorious day. Feeling quite well, I went to the Museum. Entering with a permesso, you have to sign your name in a book at the pay-office, and receive a ticket to give up at turn-stile.

Spent morning among the marbles.- Note the Venuses in attitude of the Medici, with heads which are portraits. Grotesque is that representing Marciana, sister of Trajan,- a rather ugly middle-aged face.-

The full-lobed ear of the Greek ideal.

In room VI, note no.6726, a small marble bas-relief, of which I am very fond. Three figures. Bacchus, with a leopard, preceded by a faun playing pipes and dancing Bacchante. The god's head drops, as if he were overcome with wine, he holds his cone-tipped staff idly, and leopard skin hangs loosely on one shoulder; languid grace of limbs, the faun a light dancing step. But most beautiful is the girl. She throws her head back, and turns her face upwards in exultation, while she plays on a tabor; her hair flies behind, her look is rapt. One of the most beautiful things I know.

Note from Shortridge, saying child Kate and wife have influenza.

Lunch at Riticchino. Walked thence to the Mercato, and on through the narrow streets (Giudeca Grande, one of them) towards the Str. di Porto. Saw endless picturesque things. No traffic of vehicles here; streets too narrow. Vast number of the open shops for sale of "tessuti" [fabrics].

Beautiful sunset of a kind that has been repeated several times of late: my [window] looks straight towards it. The sky over Posillipo an exquisite green, and passing from that, through blue, into rich blue-purple higher up. Thin straggling clouds of the most wonderful rose-colour.

This morning Fraülein H. showed me an almond-tree, in a garden just in front of our house, which in the last day or two has become a mass of white flowers.

Tuesd. Jan. 28. Left by the 8.10 train for Pompeii, and had a long day; weather magnificent, but Vesuvius all day covered with a great cloud. Lunched at the Sole, which I find is going to the dogs. Instead of taking the afternoon train back, I foolishly decided—one of my cases of self-delusion—to stay to dinner. Found three English ladies (two young, and

206

seemingly artists, the other one of those oldish and solitary women one meets everywhere) and an American and his wife. Did not open my lips. Dinner over at 7, and had to wait till 9.20 for train. Walked miserably to the Diomede, and sat over a cup of coffee. A thick white fog over Pompeii. Home in a 3rd class carriage crowded with peasants.

Letter from Roberts, wishing me back.

* * *

Frid. Jan. 31. Feeling unwell these last few days. Loss of appetite. Been each morning to Museum.

To-day bitterly cold. I sent p.card to Shortridge, telling him that the Orient steamer "Cuzeo" is expected to sail from here on Feb.6th.

Went to see the doctor and pay him. Name is Malbranc, but a German; address 145 Via Amedeo, Chiaia. Seems to me an excellent fellow. Talks almost perfect English. Think I shall send him a book of mine when I get home. Charged me only 5 fr.

* * *

Sund. Feb. 2. Feeling really ill, and had to send again for doctor. A bad relapse. Went to bed, and stayed there till—

* * *

Thursd. Feb. 6, when I rose in a shaky condition, and for the first time ate solid food. Have had a touch of congestion of the right lung. Miss Häberle has waited on me very decently; I have wanted for nothing.

Paid bill of past fortnight. Came to f. 61.75, including medicine.

Made acquaintance of an oldish German staying here; he is waiting till one of his eyes is ripe for operation for cataract. Was a teacher for a long time in England. Is very glad, poor fellow, to have anyone to talk to.

Ship sailed to-day with which I was to have gone. By losing it, must wait another fortnight.

Frid. Feb. 7. The German with cataract is named [Alfred von]Usedom. We have three other Germans, here, on tour. One of them a great fellow of six feet at least, oldish, and with bass boice; he is called Fricke, and I hear he was once a famous singer on German stage. With him is a nephew, a painter; young sharp-faced fellow, with strong Berlin accent. They use these words ad nauseam: *colossal, riesig,* and *enorm.*

Did not go out yet. Reading German.

Sat. Feb. 8. A fine hot day. Out for the first time, for an hour. Went to Oriani's, and got some newspapers that Shortridge had sent there for me.- Letter to Mother.

Am eating in the house now, and find it very pleasant. Talk at meals all German.

Sund. Feb. 9. Tramontana, but hot sun. Walk in morning with Usedom. He is a very philosophical fellow, with Walt Whitmanish views. Sees all good in the life of the present. Says he learnt in teaching Greek history how paltry and useless it was.

Mond. Feb. 10. Walk in morning with Usedom, down to the Porto. Left newspapers at the Cantina, to be taken by Marionello to Massa. Bitter Tramontana.

Tuesd. Feb. 11. On waking at 7, astonished to see a fall of snow. Lasted only few minutes, then bright sunshine.

Wed. Feb. 12. Brighter day, but still very cold. Six or seven new Germans in the house. In the evening came Fink from Rome with his Braut [fiancée]. Remarkable face; the profile absolutely Egyptian.

Thursd. Feb. 13. Dark morning, then fine. A certain M. Walter (Swiss) has to share my room, as the house is full.

*   *   *

Wed. Feb. 19. Rather tedious days these last. Much cold, then scirocco, and now a day like midsummer. Fearful trouble about the majolica things I am to take for Shortridge. It proves to be a huge case, and the people at the office refuse to let it go as personal luggage. Must go on Saturday by freight steamer, and will cost £1. Took ticket (2nd class) by Orient. £8.8.
Visit in afternoon from Mollo, who has just returned from Massa.

Thursd. Feb. 20. Last night took leave of poor Usedom, who at last moment confided to me his fear that he will never recover eyesight. Then of Fink, who hoped I should come and stay with him and wife at Nocera some day. Then a talk with Miss Häberlin. Find this is proper spelling of her name; they have adopted Häberle only because other form was impossible for Italians. Paid bill (77 l.) and gave Virginia the servant 10 l.
Up at 6 o'clock, after bad night. Breakfast, and good-bye to L[aurence] H[äberlin]. Gave porter 2 l.
Drove down to the cantina in Via di Massa, and by appointment there met Marionello. With him took a small boat and fetched from the Capri boat a small box which Shortridge has sent to be taken to London. Then on board the "Orient". Sailed at 10 o'clock. Fine morning, but day soon clouded.
A decent lot of strangers.

Frid. Feb. 21. Feeling far from well. A violent cold, and touch of trouble in right lung. Kept my state-room all day, except at meals. Breakfast 8 o'clock; dinner at 1; tea at 6; supper of bread and cheese at 9. Violent wind, and dark sky; cold.

Better in evening. At tea-time a band played ; I know not of whom consisting.

Curious sight. A child swinging on deck; a swing purposely fitted up. This infant decidedly proof agst sea-sickness.

Distant view of S. of Sardinia first thing this morning.

Sat. Feb. 22. The meals are English with a vengeance. Dinner the longest, takes 20 minutes,- naturally, since everyone eats as hard as he can, and there is scarcely the sound of a voice all the time. It strikes me, after foreign experience, that one little morsel of bread suffices to each person; generally even this is not eaten. Food is poor. About a quarter of a pint of indifferent soup begins; then plain roast and boiled, with seethed vegetables; then pudding and apples. No cheese, and of course no coffee. And alas, how I miss the wine!

Fairly fine day. Sea perfectly smooth, but not much sun.- In evening, soft lightnings in southern sky.

Sund. Feb. 23. At 12 o'clock reached Gibraltar. The Rock is a huge promontory, precipitous on outer side, forming the east extremity of a great bay, which is surrounded by softly sloping and green hills. In the harbour lie a considerable number of old dismantled men-of-war; used for storing, they say.

A rain storm came upon us as we approached, and we saw a fine waterspout. A point of sea's surface seemed boiling, and volumes of steam rose from it, forming a great trunk in the clouds. The boiling spot moved across the front of the ship's course.

Did not go ashore. Boats came selling oranges, cigars, Florida water etc. Oranges 45 for 1/-

Started again at 2.30. Day cleared, and fine evening. The coast of Spain very beautiful in soft sunlight; gentle hills, cultivated and green. Africa opposite; huge mountains of limestone appearance. Rock of Gibraltar thickly covered with a black cloud.

Some whale spouting.

Mond. Feb. 24. Fine, very calm. Near land all day. Good view of estuary of Tagus. The ship's parson came and talked to me for a long time. Prosy and foolish old fellow, with stock idea that you must introduce into sermons "analogies of nature and grace".

In cabin with me is a Danish captain, named Hansen, who has just lost a ship on a bar near Tangiers. A good simple fellow; talks Eng[lish] well.

Tuesd. Feb. 25. Stiff N.E. wind. Getting into mouth of the Bay this morning. Sea rolling a little.

Parson came again and sat down by me: "I hear", he began, "that you are a celebrated author". He had seen my name in a book I was reading yesterday, and it seems that one Mr. Jackson, a broad-church parson travelling in the lst class, knows my doings.- This is symbolical of my life.

It is first-class people who know me, whilst I myself am always compelled to associate with the second-class.

Wed. Feb. 26. Sea much calmer. Bitterly cold.—Making the acquaintance of a young Australian doctor, who is coming to study in London, Charles Stanford Sutton. A gentleman, and with no foreign accent.- Wrote letter to Mother and finished one to Bertz.

Thursd. Feb. 27. Another bitter day. At 9am. reached Plymouth, passing the Eddystone. Stopped two hours.

Frid. Feb. 28. Tilbury Docks at 11 am. Fine sunny morning, but very cold. On landing, a fearful amount of official humbug. Recd a "baggage pass", to be filled in with one's name and the number of packages. The custom-house officer examining luggage signed this. It then had to be marked by another man with "dock charges", 6d for each package. Then had to be taken to office, money paid, and pass signed again. Armed therewith, one at last was allowed to go with luggage into railway station. Had to pay railway fare from Tilbury to London.

Travelled in carriage with Miss Harwood, an actress who is returning from 5 yrs in Australia. Two brothers of hers, one an actor, had come to meet her. They were a trifle vulgar, but the family affection between them all very good. Spoke of their mother as sure to make a great scene on daughter's reaching home; also said she had fallen into the habit of perpetual "fretting and worrying". Evidently a good bourgeois family.

London not till 5 o'clock. Cab from Fenchurch St. to Aldgate, then railway to Baker St. Had to go and find Mrs King to get key of 7K.

Sent postcards to Miss Häberlin, Alg and Roberts.

Sat. March 1. Letter from Mrs. Gaussen, proposing to me a travelling tutorship. Thank heaven, I am past that!

A frightful morning: fog, snow, slush. To Temple Bar News Rooms. No announcement yet of "The Emancipated". Wrote to Bentley, asking reason. In afternoon came Roberts. We had dinner at little French rest. near Regent St., then back, and he stayed the night here.

Sund. March 2. Letter to Nelly on money business. Have £77 left in bank. Will support me till end of September. Also wrote to Mrs. Gaussen.

Hard frost and a little snow. Began to re-read "Memoiren einer Idealistin" by Malwida von Meysenbug[5].

*   *   *

Wed. March 5. Done nothing these last days, except continue reading the "Memoiren". Vile cold weather.

This afternoon to Hudson's, with Roberts. Usual pleasant evening of talk.

Thursd. March 6. Sent copy of "The Nether World" to Dr Malbranc, with a note.

* * *

Thursd. March 13. A week of thinking over new story. It is not to be "The Head Mistress"; materials for that will lie over. To-day actually got to work, and did the first two pages,- thank heaven!

Last evening a visit from J[ames] Gaussen. Message from his mother; asking me to lend her "The Nether World". To-day sent it.

Nelly sends me £20. Talk of our proposed visit to Paris in middle of April.

Frid. March 14. Had to work over yesterday's writing. Added a very little.- Have resumed my afternoon walk right round Regent's Park. Breakfast at 8; dinner (Edgware Rd) at 12.30; cup of coffee alone at 4; supper (bread and butter with cold tea) at 7.30. Do not really have enough to eat, but no help for it.

Sat. March 15. Note from Mrs Gaussen, acknowledging "Nether World".- No writing.- Afternoon to Roberts. Suffering much from depression.

Sund. March 16. Dull day. Finished [Turgenev's] "Väter u. Söhne" for the 6th or 7th time, I suppose.- Wrote to Alfred Hartley, who is down with Influenza in Essex.

Mond. March 17. Decent weather. Letters from Alg, Madge and Nelly. Mrs. Jolly writes to say that the huge chest of majolica things has got to them safely. Bad news about Herbert Shortridge; end drawing near. Wrote to Alg, Madge and Nelly.

In afternoon got to work again. Had to go back to beginning of 2nd page, and wrote on to the 5th.

Tuesd. March 18. Began to re-read "Niels Lyhne", which I admire more than ever.- Worked morning and evening, getting onto the 9th page.- In evening came E[dgar] Harrison.

Wed. March 19. Did about 3½pp. and finished first section,- I shall not call them chapters in this book.- A dull, rainy, cold day.

Thursd. March 20. Vile day, but worked. Morning rewrote 2pp. of yesterday. Evening did 2pp. more, extending the first section.- Then unexpectedly came parcel,- "The Emancipated". There has been no advt of it yet. Went at once through 1st two vols., correcting some misprints.

Frid. March 21. In morning sent off copies of "The Emancipated" to Wakefield and Alg. Then walked over to Chelsea, to take one to Roberts.

211

In evening had doubts about what I have written of new story. Thought, and made notes. Feeling unwell, went to bed early.

Sat. March 22. No advt of "Emancipated" in *Spectator,* but see that it is announced in *Saturday* and *Daily Telegraph.* Smith Elder used to give me trumpeting for weeks ahead; Bentley seems disposed to spend the minimum..

Morning at Museum, getting notes for my story. Began to re-write the first section, and did 2½pp.

Sund. March 23. Vile weather; cold and rain. Worked morning and afternoon, doing about 2pp.- Evening read in old Boswell, *more meo.*

Mond. March 24. Vile day.- Morning, letter from Bertz, and p. cards from Nelly and Alg. Bertz encloses copy of a letter he has recd from German authoress, Frn Gabriele Reuter, of Weimar, in enthusiastic praise of "Demos".

Worked afternoon and evening, doing 3pp.- Read at "Niels Lyhne".

Tuesd. March 25. Again vile day. Worked afternoon and evening; 3pp.-

Wed. March 26. In the afternoon, sunshine. Worked usual hours, and again finished Section I. Had to rewrite one back page, and wrote 2 new.

Thursd. March 27. Bestial weather still. Morning a letter from Roberts, saying he thinks "The Emancipated" the best thing I have done yet.- Worked afternoon and evening. Did 2pp. of second section.

Frid. March 28. Warm day, with sunshine from a sky of skimmed milk.- Worked aft. and evening. Rewrote 1½p. of yesterday's and did 3pp. more; a good day.- Posted letter to Bertz at his new address: 5 Albe Strasse, Friedenau bei Berlin.

Sat. March 29. Fine day. Morning a walk to Hampstead. Afternoon came Roberts, and stayed till 9. No writing, as usual on Saturday.

Sund. March 30. Very fine. Worked morning, afternoon and night. Had to recommence Section II, but did 5pp., getting up to same point as before. Quite a new thing for me to be able to work on Sunday; a good sign.

Mond. March 31. Fine. Worked afternoon and evening, but only did 2pp.- Sent "The Emancipated" to Bertz at his new address.

Tuesd. Ap. 1. Letter from Nelly, saying she dislikes "The Emancipated" from beginning to end. Naturally. Wrote a reply of very quiet self-defence. But no use.

Worked afternoon and evening. Finished Section II. Did 4pp. in all.

Wed. Ap. 2. Letter from Alg, saying they were driven away from their new lodgings by a drunken landlady. Have gone to Norton Villa, Bredon's Norton, Tewkesbury. Wrote to him.

Worked afternoon and evening, doing 3pp.

Thursd. Ap. 3. Letter from Nelly, again about "Emancipated". Replied.- Worked only in evening, but did 3pp.- Have finished re-reading "Niels Lyhne", and taken up Heine's "Italien".

Frid. Ap. 4. Good Friday. Fine and warm. Morning to Victoria, to get table of Newhaven and Dieppe line. Had dinner before 12 at a restaurant there, paying more than I can afford 1/6. Afternoon read at Heine. Evening did not quite a page. Feeling out of the right mood; always the result upon me of these public holidays. Have a slight cold, too. Dull, dull.-

Sat. Ap. 5. Fine.- An advt of a 2/- edn of "The Nether World" for publication shortly.- Bought *The Speaker*[6], a new 6d weekly, and found it immensely dull.- In afternoon came Roberts, but only stayed till 8.30. I suspect he gets a little tired of my exclusively intellectual talk.- Postcard from Shortridge, saying his brother Herbert is dead.

Sund. Ap. 6. Dull and cold,- Cannot get on with work. Rewrote the page of Friday, but shall have to do it yet again. The familiar block of thought and fancy.- Reading Heine's "Ideen".

In afternoon short visit from Hartley, who is going to spend a month working in Constable's country.

Mond. Ap. 7. Alas! *More meo,* I shall have to abandon all I have written, and begin a new story. Am dissatisfied with the subject I have undertaken. And had finished 31pp.! Always the same, each new book.- A vile day. Did nothing but rack my brains.- Wrote to Shortridge.

Tuesd. Ap. 8. Letter from Alg.- Thought all morning and afternoon. Evening got to work at new story, to be called "A Man of Letters", and did 1½p.

Wed. Ap. 9. Dull and windy. Letter from Mlle Le Breton, saying that the French "Demos" is at last about to be pubd. Replied to her.- Worked morning, afternoon and evening; did 4½pp.

Thursd. Ap 10. Dull, cold. Worked morning, afternoon and evening. Cancelled 3½pp. of yesterday and did nearly 5pp.- Wrote to Madge.

Frid. Ap. 11. Did nothing. Out of health and spirits.

Sat. Ap. 12. Went to Roberts', and we dined at S. Kensington Museum. He has just sold his 2 vol. novel "In Low Relief"—a story literally out of his own recent life,- to Chapman, for £25 and ½ profits. Not a little elated.

Must quote the remarkable utterance of his. "How easy it is to raise oneself above the common run of literary men! And after all, what are *we*? Very commonplace fellows, in reality." The *naïveté* of this is not to be surpassed.

Sund. Ap. 13. Reading (for 20th time) [Murger's] "La Vie de Bohème". No work. Dull, dull.

Mond. Ap. 14. In afternoon came Walter Grahame. Says his aunt and sister like "The Emancipated" much.- Doing nothing. At night walked about streets.

Tuesd. Ap. 15. Fine day, but rain at night. After supper walked about streets. Nothing done or thought.

Wed. Ap. 16. The girls arrived at 6.50. Had dinner at 7K (chops and vegetables) and spent evening in talk.

Thursd. Ap. 17. In morning with girls to the British Museum.- Evening left by the 8.50 from Victoria for Paris. Of course the blackguard railway company advertizes lies; instead of starting at once on steamer, we waited for tide till 1am. A cold, rainy night, but not rough.

Frid. Ap. 18. Poor Nelly very ill all night,- (we had 2nd class tickets, but they paid extra for 1st). Madge not so bad. I suffered only from cold and general discomfort. Reached Dieppe at 7, and had to lie ¼ hour off the harbour, rolling. Tedious railway journey, veiled sky. Fruit-trees in fine white blossom all along. Paris at 11 o'clock and went to Hôtel de France, Rue Montmartre 132, just south of Bourse. Got an appartment of three rooms for 8½ francs a day, service included. Very cheap this. Had déjeuner at a Duval, and then the girls went to bed. Wrote postcards to Alg and Mother.

Sat. Ap. 19. Again rain all day. In morning to Louvre, and walked through the first floor. Déjeuner at the bouillon in Place des Pyramides. Then to Notre-Dame, Odéon, Luxembourg garden, Panthéon, and home by Les Halles. Dinner, as yesterday, at bouillon in Boulevard Montmartre. Afterwards, as it only rained slightly, a walk along boulevards. Saw the just pubd. "Demos" at a book-shop.

Sund. Ap. 20. Again rain all day; it grows desperate. Walked to the miserable little Rue d'Aguesseau, opposite British Embassy, and there the girls went to the English Church. I spent time walking about Champs Elysées in the wet. Returned and watched congregation issuing; great numbers; a long line of cabs and carriages.

Afternoon to S. Eustache; heard vespers, and a charity sermon on behalf of charitable work at Issy. Paltry preaching.- Evening walked about Place de la Concorde.

Mond. Ap. 21. Fine warm day, for a wonder. Morning to Père La Chaise. Déjeuner in Place de la République. Afternoon to Arc de l'Etoile, and went to top of it. Sitting and loitering in Champs Elysées. After dinner walked on Boulevards.

Tuesd. Ap. 22. Hard rain all day. Morning at Louvre, especially Salon Carré. Afternoon among the sculpture. At night to buy some trifles in the Bazaar Oriental.

Wed. Ap. 23. A fine day. Morning, up the towers of Notre-Dame. Afternoon to Bois de Boulogne. Walked as far as Grande Cascade.

Thursd. Ap. 24. Rain all day. Fine at evening. Morning to the Luxembourg Gallery. Afternoon to Invalides, and thence by Eiffel Tower home. Walked about Boulevards.

Frid. Ap. 25. Sunshine and rain. Morning to Louvre. Then to Luxembourg Gardens, and Odéon book gallery.

Sat. Ap. 26. Fine morning, turning to rain storms at noon. Took tram to Versailles, a ride of 2 hrs; my bad cold obliged me to go inside. Fare 70c. outside, and 1 fr. inside. Had déjeuner in the Place d'Armes, and then went over Palace, of course seeing things perfunctorily. Too rainy to see much of gardens. Back by 5.45. Evening at home suffering much from throat.

Sund. Ap. 27. Day of sun and clouds. Girls in morning to Rue d'Aguesseau, of course. I to the Louvre. Afternoon to Sainte Chapelle, which I had not seen before. Magnificent effect of the great stained-glass windows and slim columns. Thence to Notre-Dame, where we sat through a long ceremony,- a "Réunion des associations ouvrières catholiques". Archbishop officiating.- In evening to the Place de la Concorde, and saw electric light raying from top of Eiffel Tower.

Mond. Ap.28. Fine day. In morning to Montmartre cemetery. Afternoon loitered in Tuileries Gardens. Left Paris by the 8.50 from St Lazare. At Dieppe got on board steamer, but found it crammed, and a filthy little tub. Came off again at once, and at 1 a.m. took rooms at the Hôtel Albion, just opposite the landing-stage. Two rooms for 3 fr. each.

Tuesd. Ap. 29. Fine weather. Spent day about the beach. Nelly ill. At 8 in evening paid bill (23 fr.) and went on board the steamer.

Wed. Ap. 30. Steamer delayed by tide, so that we didn't start till 3am. Slow passage; very calm; reached Newhaven at 8.30. There had to wait till 10.5 till train left. Girls miserably ill. Home to wretchedness. We telegraphed to Mother from Newhaven, and decided that girls shall wait till tomorrow before going on to Wakefield.

Thursd. May 1. Fine warm day. Girls left by the 9.45. In afternoon to make purchases etc. Bought and read a trashy so called "Life" of Browning [by William Sharp], in Scott's "Great Writers".- The "Eight Hour" demonstration all over the Continent to-day; paper says huge military preparations have been made.

Frid. May 2. Fine day again. Morning to buy things. Afternoon came Walter Grahame.

Sat. May 3. Packed up, and left London, for Wakefield by the 1.30. Fine day.

Sund. May 4. Splendid day. Idled about.

Mond. May 5. In afternoon rain; no sunshine. Worked a little, but am more than doubtful whether it will stand. Recd from Alg first batch of proofs of his "A Village Hampden", which I am going to read for him.- Wrote to Rev. G. Bainton of Coventry, who has incorporated in a book of his "The Art of Authorship", just pubd, a letter of mine containing remarks on my own study of style. This he got from me last year; saying he wanted to use it in a lecture to young men. Now he sends me a few pages from his book,- the matter has grown under his hands etc.

Tuesd. May 6. Nothing done.

Wed. May 7. Made a new beginning, putting my first scene in Brit. Museum reading-room. Worked usual hours,- 9 to 1 in morning, and 4.30 to 8.30, doing 2½pp. No sunshine, but no rain.

Thursd. May 8. Dull day. Wrote 3pp. Beginning to see my way more clearly.- Another batch of Alg's proofs. This novel of his an improvement, but awkward lapses of style here and there.

Frid. May 9. Dull and windy. Rewrote 4pp. of Chap. I, and did 2½pp. of Chap. 2.- Reading Browning's "Asolando" [1889].

Sat. May 10. Dull and cold. Morning wrote 2½ pp. Afternoon rewrote the same.

Sund. May 11. Furious rain all day long. Read lives of Dion, Dionysius and Timoleon, in [John and William] Langhorne's Plutarch. Wrote to Roberts and p.c. to Alg.- Long letter from Bertz and *Deutsche Presse* [May 4], with short notice of "The Emancipated".

Mond. May 12. Sunshine, thunder, rain. In morning wrote 2pp., but cancelled them. Afternoon rebegan the 2nd Chap., and did 1p. Cannot yet get my ideas clear.

Dora Carter passes the night here. To-morrow she and her family leave Wakefield for good.- Another batch of Alg's proofs.

Tuesd. May 13. Fine day and warm. Did about 4pp.- Alg sent me Tennyson's "Demeter and other Poems" [1889] to read and return.

Wed. May 14. Fine. Worked well, and did 3pp.- Reading [Thomas] Holcroft's Memoirs⁷, for first time.

Thursd. May 15. Rain and cloud. Finished Chap. 2, and began 3, doing 4pp.

Frid. May 16. Rain and mist. Worked well, but did only 3pp. A difficult part, all description of people. Read at Holcroft. Before going to bed generally have about an hour of reading German aloud.- Letter from A.J.Smith.

Sat. May 17. Fine, but uncertain day.- Rewrote 1p of yesterday, and did about one more.- In afternoon a walk to Kirkthorpe with Nelly. Too absorbed in troublesome thought of story to talk.

Sund. May 18. Clouded mostly. Finished Holcroft, and read "Eothen" [by A.W. Kinglake, 1844].- Thinking, thinking. Not quite well.

Mond. May 19. Dull and close. Got on better with work. Left Chap. 3 to be finished presently, and began Chap. 4, doing 5pp., but shall have to rewrite the last.- Alg's proofs to end of Vol.I.- Feeling seedy still.

Tuesd. May 20. Dull, cold and high wind.- Rewrote last p. of yesterday, and did 4 more.- In afternoon a walk with Madge. Began to read Southey's Life of Cromwell.

Wed. May 21. Fine, but still windy. Worked well, doing 4pp., and finishing to end of Chap. IV (III included).

Thursd. May 22. Fine, windy. Did not quite 3pp. of Chap. V.

Frid. May 23. Fine, hot. In morning rewrote character of "Mr Solway" in Chap. III, and last 2pp. of Chap. IV. Afternoon went on again with Chap. V, and did 1½p.

Sat. May 24. Fine, hot, windy. Did 4pp.

Sund. May 25. Racking brains over story again. Unable to read anything.- Wrote to Bertz, A.J. Smith and E.E. Harrison.

Mond. May 26. Cloudy, but fine. Whit Monday. Rewrote last 2pp. of Chap. V, and did 1½ of Chap. VI.- Reading the Puritan period in [J.R.]

Green's Eng. History [Short History of the English People].

Tuesd. May 27. Dull. Cancelled last ½p. of yesterday. Wrote 4pp.- A long letter from Ella Gaussen, to which I replied. Read some Green.

Wed. May 28. Fine. Wrote 4pp., finishing Chap. VI. Then went back and rewrote 2pp. in Chap. III.- Read at Green.- A letter of depression from Alg; replied to it.

Thursd. May 29. Fine, windy. Rewrote 4pp. of Chap. IV.- Finished reading [W.H.] Edwards's Voyage up the Amazon[8], which I am making use of in my story.

Frid. May 30. Fine but cold. Did 4pp.

Sat. May 31. Fine, but colder than ever. Letter from Alg, saying he has gone to spend few days with Evans at Chelsea. Also letter from Fraülein Häberlin, at Naples.- Worked hard all day, but did only 2½pp. This Chap. VII is difficult.

Sund. June 1. So cold that fires are necessary. Dull. Wrote to Alg, asking him to get some Govt Office information for me from Evans.[9] Wrote to thank [Edgar]Harrison for tobacco, and sent Mrs King £1 for next month.- No reading.

Mond. June 2. Dull, cold. Worked 9 to 1, and 4 to 7. Destroyed last 3½pp. and did 4 instead,- the difficult point of Marian's antecedents.- Read some Plutarch.

Tuesd. June 3. Cold, windy, clouded. From 9 to 1 wrote 1p. From 4 to 8.30 went back to Chap VI, and added 1p. to it. Then rewrote 2pp. of Chap. VII.- Plutarch.

Wed. June 4. Clouded, but warm. From 9 to 1 wrote ½ a page only. From 4 to 8.30 wrote 2pp.-. Reading Bell's Lives of the Poets.

Thursd. June 5. Dull, warm. Worked 9 to 12.30 and 4 to 7, doing 4pp.

Frid. June 6. Dull, with furious wind. Worked 9 to 1 and 4 to 8, doing 4½pp. Getting on smoothly at last.

Sat. June 7. Fine, warm, less wind. Worked 9 to 1 and 4 to 7, doing 4pp.

Sund. June 8. Dull, rainy. Wasted my time reading old *Macmillan's Mags.*- Sent off the last batch of Alg's proofs. Wrote to him and to Roberts.- Nelly ill in bed.

Mond. June 9. Not a gleam of sunshine.—Nelly still in bed.—May Baseley [sister-in-law of Algernon Gissing], at the Bruces, seriously ill of rheumatic fever.- Worked 9 to 1 and 4 to 7.30. Rewrote 2pp., did 3½ more.

Tuesd. June 10. Sunny at first, then dull, then furious whirlwind and rain. In morning wrote 2pp.; afternoon rewrote them, and 1p. more. Nelly still in bed, but a little better. Reading Bell's Life of Pope.

Wed. June 11. Dull, rainy. Wrote very short hours, but did 3¼pp.- Nelly much better.

Thursd. June 12. Dull, and little rain. Nelly better, but still in bed. Wrote short hours; did 3½pp., and thus happily *finished vol. I.* It makes not quite 85pp., and so is rather longer than the vols of "The Emancipated".- Reading Craik's "[Manual of] Eng[lish] Literature [and Language]".

Frid. June 13. Not a ray of sunshine, and very cold. Morning did nothing; afternoon had to rewrite last 2pp. of yesterday.

Sat. June 14. Dull, but warmer. In morning began vol. II and wrote 1½p. Afternoon had to rewrite this, and did ½p. more.- Reading [Scott's] "Peveril of the Peak". In low spirits, and not able to work well.

Sund. June 15. Fine morning; walked for a couple of hours. Took up [Scott's] "Fortunes of Nigel", finding "Peveril" too feeble. The difference between the two books is vast. Line from Roberts. A day wasted.

Mond. June 16. High wind again, but warm. Wrote full hours, and did 4½pp., finishing Chap. I. Read at "Nigel".

Tuesd. June 17. High wind and sunshine. Worked 9 to 1 and 4 to 8, doing 4pp.

Wed. June 18. Fog, rain, wind, a wretched day. Worked with clogged mind, but did my 4pp. Last year it used always to be 5, but I can't get on with this story as with that.- Ordered the "Journal de Marie Bashkirtseff" from Hachette's; 2 vols, 6/-. Seems to be a delightful book from what I have seen of it in reviews of the English translation.

Thursd. June 19. Windy, dull. Did my 4pp.

Frid. June 20. Fine, but furious wind. Card of invitation to "at home" at Miss Sichel's. Of course must refuse, and should in any case. English society is no more for me. Letter from Roberts. Best of all, arrival of "Marie Bashkirtseff". The natural result of this was that I vainly tried to work in the morning; did a few lines, and gave it up. Then fell to at the book, and read a great deal. In afternoon, by strong self-denial, worked from 4 to 7.30, doing 3pp. Then again to Marie.

Sat. June 21. A dark clouded day; little sun towards evening. In morning did only 1 page, being interrupted because of Nellie's coming for an hour from the Hicks', where she has been staying since her illness was over. She had dinner with us, then returned for another week. I miss the music when she is away. Afternoon, in spite of a headache, did 3pp.- Read at Marie Bashkirtseff. To-day a notice of "The Emancipated" in the *Spectator,* under "Current Literature", which seems to be a deliberate insult. They are careful not to make any reference to the fact that I have previously published books.- Alg's "A Village Hampden" is to-day announced for first time.

Sund. June 22. Dull, read at Marie Bashkirtseff. Wrote to Roberts, Bertz, and a reply to Miss Sichel.

Mond. June 23. In morning all but dark for half an hour. Wretched day. Did 2pp., but must write them again.

Tuesd. June 24. Feeling stupid. Did 3pp. however, having destroyed yesterday's. Always reading Marie B. Have no confidence in this novel of mine, but must finish it, because I am all but penniless.

Wed. June 25. Dark and much rain. Miserable weather. Did 3pp., in poor spirits. Yesterday Madge went to Broadway for a fortnight, so I am alone with Mother. Nelly still at the Hicks'.

Thursd. June 26. Dull, heavy, misty. Headache. Did 3pp.

Frid. June 27. Furious wind, but sunshine. Did 3pp., finishing Chap. V. Last night finished "Marie Bashkirtseff". To-day Nelly returns to us.

Sat. June 28. Dull, as usual. Long letter from Bertz. Did my 3pp., with very little pleasure.

Sund. June 29. Fine and warm. Last night, at eleven o'clock, came to a conclusion I had not foreseen by more than an hour. Absolutely determined to abandon my story, and commence a new one, for which an idea suddenly flashed upon me. The result was an immense relief. I have still perhaps time to write a book before the end of August, that is, if I can put my heart into it.- Took up "Woodstock" [by Walter Scott].

Mond. June 30. Rain all day. In morning began my new novel, and by evening did 5pp., which ought to be my daily quantum. Heavens, the relief I feel! And not much fear in the prospect of toil either. No one could deny my courage. I had half finished the other novel.

Tuesd. July 1. Again did my 5pp. Wretched day; furious rain all last night.

Wed. July 2. Not a gleam of sunshine till afternoon, and much rain. Worked long hours, doing 5pp., including one written twice.

Thursd. July 3. After 11 o'clock, a reasonably fine day. Worked hard, but did only 4¼pp.

Frid. July 4. Fairly fine day. In morning did 3pp. In afternoon a rush of inspiration. Decided to rewrite from beginning these last days' work, to rename all my characters, and to call the book "Storm-Birds". Wrote 1½p. of Chap. I.

Sat. July 5. Fine day, but very windy again. Did 6½pp., finishing Chap. I.

Sund. July 6. Little sunshine. Reading "Woodstock", and thinking about story. Wrote to Alg.

Mond. July 7. Fine morning; in evening rain. Cold. Worked 8.45 to 1 and 3.45 to 7.30, doing 6pp. Getting on well.

Tuesd. July 8. Sunshine, but furious and insufferable wind. Worked 9 to 12.30 and 4 to 8, doing nearly 6pp.- Letter from Alg. One from Roberts, who is yachting with friends on Yorkshire coast. Replied to him.

Wed. July 9. Very fine day, but still windy. Did 5pp., finishing Chap. III. Finished "Woodstock".

Thursd. July 10. Dull, cold. Did 4¾pp. Took up "Redgauntlet" [by Walter Scott].

Frid. July 11. Having suffered much of late from weak sight, I went this morning to Leeds, and bought a pair of spectacles (6/-) at Harvey and Reynolds'. They seem likely to help me. Back at 11 o'clock but the day lost. Tried to work in evening and did a page, but shall have to destroy it. Weather like November. Never a gleam of sun.

Sat. July 12. Weather as bad as yesterday. Did my 5pp., wearing spectacles all day with ease.- Bertz has returned Alg's "Joy Cometh", and "The Western Avernus" [by Morley Roberts], which I lent him long ago.- Also sends a Tauchnitz Catalogue, in which my name is at last attached to "Demos".

Sund. July 13. A little sun, but much clouded sky and furious wind. Reading "Redgauntlet".

Mond. July 14. In the night a hurricane, and to-day scarcely less. A little sunshine and warm. Rewrote the last 4pp. In a depressed mood.

Tuesd. July 15. Warm, fine. In morning wrote a page, but had to destroy it. In afternoon went back six pages, and wrote 2 of them again. Feeling terribly wretched. The struggle to get my story clear driving me almost to madness.

Wed. July 16. Close, ending in rain. Feeling ill. Did 3pp.- Madge returns from Broadway.

Thursd. July 17. Dull. Did 4½pp.

Frid. July 18. Not a gleam of sun, and ending in rain. Did 5pp., in good trim.

Sat. July 19. Some sunshine, but cold wind. Worked well, doing 6pp., but one of them a repetition from yesterday. Still reading "Redgauntlet".- The spectacles a great relief to my eyes. I wear them all day.

Sund. July 20. Wonderfully fine morning; dull at end of day. Did nothing.

Mond. July 21. Fine, close. Wore summer suit for first time. Worked regular hours, doing 5pp., satisfactorily.- Letter from Bertz.

Tuesd. July 22. A furious gale all day, though sunshine. So bad that, for the first time since I have been here, I didn't go out in the afternoon. Wrote only 4pp.

Wed. July 23. Gale still, only ceasing at end of day. No sun. Poor work; morning wasted, and only 2½pp. in afternoon. Have to rewrite yesterday's.

Thursd. July 24. Fine, but high wind. Rewrote 5pp., and did 1 more,- Note from Roberts, who seems to have changed his abode to 15 Trafalgar Studios, Manresa Rd, Chelsea.

Frid. July 25. The wind fallen at last. Dull, no rain. Did only 3½pp.

Sat. July 26. High wind again, falling at evening. Rewrote 2pp. of yesterday, and did 1½more. Reading [Walter Scott's] "St. Ronan's Well".-

Sund. July 27. Fine, windy. In morning rewrote 2pp.- Wrote to Roberts.

Mond. July 28. Fine, windy. Rewrote 2½pp., and did 2½ more.- Getting on well, now.

Tuesd. July 29. Fine. Did 2½pp. In evening broke down with wretchedness.

Wed. July 30. No sleep at night. No work to-day. Misery.

Thursd. July 31. Fine, hot day. In better work again [sic]; did my 5pp.- Letter from Roberts.- Nelly went off to Bredon for holidays.

Frid. Aug. 1. Black day, much rain.- At a stand-still. Wrote to Smith, Elder, asking if they will buy copyright of "Thyrza". In profound misery all day and night.

Sat. Aug. 2. Fine day. Doing nothing. Wrote to Roberts.- Thinking of project for new story.

Sund. Aug. 3. Day of blank misery.

Mond. Aug. 4. Utter wretchedness, until evening, when a blessed change came, and I was able to think of my story once more. May perhaps resume to-morrow morning. Weather fine and hot.

Tuesd. Aug. 5. Fine, hot. Still unable to do any writing.- Tried to read some of Lamb's letters.

Wed. Aug. 6. Mother went for holiday to Ludlow.- Reply from Smith, Elder, saying that they have sold only 412 copies of "Thyrza", and offering £10 for copyright! Wrote back to say I will leave matter undecided until I have finished the book I am now working at.- A very miserable morning, but in evening got to work at last, and rewrote 3pp.

Thursd. Aug. 7. Abandoned work again, and shall not resume till I go to London.

Frid. Aug. 8. The finest day this summer.- Madge invited Connie Ash for the evening. A pretty girl, who sings rather well; she interests me.- Thinking of that old story "Revolt" which has been wanting to get written for so long.

Sat. Aug. 9. Blank idleness.

Sund. Aug. 10. Not a gleam of sun. Did not open a book all day, and only went out for an hour in evening.

Mond. Aug. 11. In afternoon with Madge to look at their new house in Westfield Grove [at no.8]. In passing, we left "Thyrza" for Connie Ash (I enclosed a note) and received an invitation to supper that same evening. Called at the Bruces', and saw May, who is very beautiful now. At 7 in evening went to the Ash's. Met Mr and Mrs Ash, Connie, younger sister Gertie, a pretty, dark girl, and boy Norman. Had much music. Gertie plays the mandoline. Connie sang a good deal, and beautifully. I am in love with her, and there's an end of it.- Wrote to Nelly about her.

Tuesd. Aug. 12. Idleness.

Wed. Aug. 13. Dull and rainy. Suffering much. But in evening forced myself to write for a couple of of hours. Went back to Chapter I of my story, and rewrote 3pp.

Thursd. Aug. 14. Dull weather. In morning wrote 1p. Afternoon called alone at the Ashes', and talked with the two girls for an hour.

Frid. Aug. 15. Idleness and misery, as usual. Furious hurricane all day. Read "Lazarus in London" [by F.W. Robinson, 1885], from a Wakd Library.

Sat. Aug. 16. Idleness and misery. In evening to tea with the Halls. Letter from Nelly.

*Sat. Aug. 17.*Fine day, but windy. Read [Byron's] "Maid of Athens", from Library. (Madge has a subscription at Church Institute.)

Mond. Aug. 18. In afternoon visit from Margaret Maddison [a friend of Ellen Gissing's], home for holiday from Ireland.- At six o'clock mother returned from Ludlow.

Tuesd. Aug. 19. Fine day. Left Wakefield by 8.58 for Worcester, and thence to Bredon, where Alg met me. Half an hour's walk to Bredon's Norton. Found the family in small cottage, where they occupy three rooms. Beautifully situated. Little Enid a healthy and pretty child.

Wed. Aug. 20. Fine. In morning a walk with Alg to village called Elmley,- as nearly the ideal English village as any I ever saw. The rest of the day, sauntered about.

Thursd. Aug. 21. Fine. Left Bredon's Norton at mid-day, and got to 7K about 5.30. Feeling very shaky and hopeless.

Frid. Aug. 22. Fine. Did nothing, but hope to begin to-morrow.

Sat. Aug. 23. Fine.- Made a beginning of a new novel, a jumble of the various ones I have been engaged on all the summer. Wrote 3pp., but in evening saw that they are no good.- Am on the very verge of despair and suffering more than ever in my whole life. My brain seems powerless, dried up.

Sund. Aug. 24. Very fine morning and evening; thunder and rain in afternoon. Morning walked to Battersea; rest of day spent in various rambles about here.

Mond. Aug. 25. Fine, changing to dull.- Letter from Nelly. Began yet once more my novel, to be called "Hilda Wolff". Did 6pp., mostly rewriting.

Tuesd. Aug. 26. Fine, turning to heavy rain. Wrote to Madge. Did 5pp., though against the grain.

Wed. Aug. 27. Fine, turning to rain and cold. Note from Alg. Wrote 3pp., and added 4 of the old MS.

Thursd. Aug. 28. One of the finest days this year.- Letter from mother.- In morning read some of the "Phaedo" [one of Plato's Dialogues]. I must try if I can bring my mind to something like calmness by turning to the old subjects. Afternoon and evening wrote 4pp.- Wrote to Nelly, who is now at Bridlington with the Carters.

Frid. Aug. 29. Very fine day.- Letter from Alg, enclosing advt in that Sat's *Athenaeum* ; S[mith] & E[lder] advertise "Mr George Gissing's novels. Demos, A Life's Morning, The Nether World, in limp red cloth at 2/6". Good, this; amounts to a uniform edition.- Wrote only 3pp. In evening driven madly about the streets. A magnificent full moon, but cared nothing for it.

Sat. Aug. 30. Very fine day. Feeling better. Did 6pp., which make 31 this week. If I do thirty a week I am satisfied.

Sund. Aug. 31. Very fine . In spite of Sunday influences did 2pp., writing one of them twice.

Mond. Sept. 1. Dull, but no rain. In morning did 2pp. Evening had to go back to an early chapter; rewrote 3pp., and added a fourth.

Tuesd. Sept. 2. Very dull; a little rain. Letter from Nelly, from Bridlington. Note from Roberts, asking me to join him and Hudson at Shoreham; impossible. Bought the 2/- edition of Hardy's "The Return of the Native".- Wrote 5pp.; feel headachy.

Wed. Sept. 3. Letter from poor Bertz, who says he is going to confine himself to writing for boys henceforth.- A dull warm day. Wrote my 5pp. Reading Hardy.

Thursd. Sept. 4. Tried to work, but couldn't. Ill. Finished "Return of the Native".

Frid. Sept. 5. Very fine and warm. Rewrote 3pp., and did 3 more.- In much calmer frame of mind. Worked well.

Sat. Sept. 6. Very fine. Morning did 2pp. Evening rewrote 2 some distance back.

Sund. Sept. 7. Very fine. Morning to Chelsea and Battersea. Evening walking about streets.

Mond. Sept. 8. Heard from Madge that their removal to 8 Westfield Grove is finished.- Fine, hot day. Did 5½pp.

Tuesd. Sept. 9. Still fine, but a bad day with me. Did about 1½p. Feeling ill.

Wed. Sept. 10. Very fine, hot. Did nothing.

Thursd. Sept. 11. Till 4 o'clock one of the finest days I ever knew. Very blue sky. Afterwards, clouded over. Did about 4pp.- Letter from Alg; replied to it.

Frid. Sept. 12. Day of misty sunshine. Did 4pp., one written twice.

Sat. Sept. 13. Dull.- Letter from Nelly.- Had to go back, and rewrote 1½p. Destroyed 6pp.

Sund. Sept. 14. Fine; less warm. Worked all day and did 6pp.

Monday Sept. 15. Complete breakdown again. Am at end of Vol. I, but feel it won't do. Have no pleasure in it. Wandered about in despair.

Tuesd. Sept. 16. Weather always wonderfully fine; if only I could enjoy it. Strayed about, and thought of a new story. Feel like a madman at times. I know that I shall never do any more good work till I am married.

Wed. Sept. 17. Fine still.- Began a new story, which at present I call "Victor Yule". Wrote from 3 to 11, and did a little more than 3pp. Letter from Roberts, who is still at Shoreham.

Thursd. Sept. 18. Fine morning; walked about Bloomsbury with a headache, and got rid of it. Evening gloomy and rain. Worked 3.30 to 10.30, doing 4pp.- Letter from Bertz.- Curious that I feel in good spirits about this new story. I seem to have hit the possible vein again once more.

Frid. Sept. 19. Fine, changing to dull. Walked in morning, and wrote from 3 to 9.30 doing 5pp. No reading of any kind now-a-days. A bad, bad time with me; the wasting of my life in bitterness.

Sat. Sept. 20. Rather dull. Wrote only 3pp., though I worked from 3.30 to 10.30.- Letter from Nelly.

Sund. Sept. 21. Dull weather. Did nothing; misery.

Mond. Sept. 22. Determined to resume "Hilda Wolff", and to make what I have written suffice for Vol. I.- Got [Hardy's] "The Trumpet Major" from Beeching's Library.- Fine day.

Tuesd. Sept. 23. Fine morning. Afternoon rain and thunder. Went back again to "Victor Yule", and rebegan it.

Wed. Sept. 24. Day of extreme misery. Wrote nothing. In evening to the Oxford.[10]- E[dith] U[nderwood].

Thursd. Sept. 25. Fine. A better day.- Plunged into Chap. III, without finishing I, and wrote 5pp. This is perhaps a way of getting ahead.- Reading [F. Marion] Crawford's "Marzio's Crucifix". Jejune stuff.

Frid. Sept. 26. Dull day. Worked hard, but did only about 3pp.- Reading a new novel called "Name and Fame" [by E. Lester and Adeline Sergeant].

Sat. Sept. 27. Wasted day. Misery.- Call from Walter Grahame.

Sund. Sept. 28. Fine, hot. In afternoon with Edith to Richmond; thence walked to Kew and had tea there. Back by 'bus. Exquisite sunset beyond the river from Kew Bridge; rich dusky scarlet and no clouds. Opposite, the rising of a full red moon, a wonderful sight. When we got back, Edith came to sit with me here for an hour.

Mond. Sept. 29. Wasted.- Reading for curiosity some trash by "The Author of Molly Bawn" [Mrs Hungerford].

Tuesd. Sept. 30. No work. In afternoon came Roberts, bringing his first pubd novel "In Low Relief". Read it when he had gone, and think very well of it, though style often very careless.

Wed. Oct. 1. A fresh beginning, once more. It will be "New Grub Street" after all. Did 4pp. At nine o'clock, Edith came for an hour.

Thursd. Oct. 2. Very fine day, with wonderfully blue sky. Wrote 3 to 9, doing 4pp.- Wrote to Roberts about "In Low Relief".

Frid. Oct. 3. Very fine. Like yesterday; and wonderful cloudless sky. Worked 9 to 11, and 3 to 8.30, doing 4pp.

Sat. Oct. 4. Wasted.

Sund. Oct. 5. Fine, but dull. With Edith to Putney Bridge, and thence walked over to Richmond. Edith rather tired.

Mond. Oct. 6. Recommenced "New Grub Street". Fine and warm. Wrote to Nelly, telling her I may possibly marry at end of year.- Worked 2 to 8.30, doing 5pp.

Tuesd. Oct. 7. First day of rain for a long time.- Sold a lot of my books for £6.5; the empty shelves depressing to look at.- A dolorous letter from Nelly.- Wrote 3pp.

Wed. Oct. 8. Fine day, but getting colder; I think I feel the better for it.- Wrote 5pp.- At 8.30 came Edith for an hour.

Thursd. Oct. 9. Fine, warm.- Worked 8.30 to 11.30, and 3.30 to 9, doing 5pp.

Frid. Oct. 10. Fine, warm.- Worked 8.30 to 11, and 3 to 8.30, doing 5pp. Getting on well, at last, with my new aids.- Got from library Dostoiesvsky's "The Idiot".

Sat. Oct. 11. Fine.- Wrote 5pp.- At 8.30 to Roberts, at his new address, 35 Tavistock Place.- Got back at 12.30.

Sund. Oct. 12. Misty, but a wonderfully fine and warm day. With Edith to Kew; the gardens exquisite.

Mond. Oct. 13. Dense fog, except for two hours at mid-day. Much suffering, as I walked through it to dinner. Worked 8.30 to 11.30, and 2.30 to 9, doing 5pp. as usual.- Letter from Grahame.

Tuesd. Oct. 14. Hideous fog all day. Did 3½pp, but shall have to write them again.

Wed. Oct. 15. Cold and rainy in morning. Fine afternoon. Worked 8.30 to 12, and 3 to 6.30, doing 6pp. 3½ rewritten. At 8.30 to see Edith at her home, for the first time,- 25 S. Paul's Crescent, Camden Square. Saw no one but Edith. Had supper with her.

Thursd. Oct. 16. Fine, but cold wind. Reading Mrs [Lynn] Linton's "Under Which Lord?"- surprises me by its plain-spokenness.- In morning to buy a new hat and the *Review of Reviews.*- Worked 2.30 to 8.30, doing 4pp.

Frid. Oct. 17. Bitter wind.- Letters from Madge and Nelly.- In morning did 1p., but destroyed it. In evening did 3¼, but forced to stop by bad headache.

Sat. Oct. 18. Dull day. Did 3pp. only. In evening came Roberts, who is flourishing; article of his just accepted by *Macmillan's*, and arrangement made for six papers for *Murray's.*[11]

Sund. Oct. 19. Dull, and bitter wind. At four o'clock, to Edith's where I again saw no one but herself. In evening we walked to the Roman Catholic Church of S. Joseph's on the Hill, Highgate. Saw a procession, with recitation of the Rosary. Home with her to supper. Then walked back here.

Mond. Oct. 20. Dull, but warmer. Got up in morning with a fearful lumbago. All day could not stand upright. Keen suffering. Nevertheless worked 8.30 to 12, and 2.30 to 6.30 doing 5 good pages. To bed early.

Tuesd. Oct. 21. Rain in night. To-day, dull but dry. Lumbago still very bad. Did my 5pp., heaven be thankit! Working 9 to 12, and 2.30 to 8.15.

Wed. Oct. 22. Fine, sunny. Lumbago bad. Did 5pp., and at 8 went to Edith's. Had supper with her.

Thursd. Oct. 23. Dull. Lumbago much better. Worked 9 to 12, and 2.30 to 8.30, doing 5pp. and *finishing Vol. I.*

Frid. Oct. 24. Dull. Worked all day, but did only 3 poor pages.

Sat. Oct. 25. Destroyed yesterday's work, and did no more. In evening to Roberts.

Sund. Oct. 26. Fine day, cold. Wrote to Bertz. In afternoon came Edith, and stayed till 9.

Mond. Oct. 27. Cloudless, very cold day. Wrote 1p. in morning, and 4 in evening. Reading in Wieland's transl. of Lucian.

Tuesd. Oct. 28. Dull and bitterly cold; hard frost last night. In morning [re]wrote last page of yesterday; evening worked till 10.30, doing 5pp.- Letter from Edith.

Wed. Oct. 29. Rainy, and suddenly very warm again. Did 5pp. At 8.30 to Edith.

Thursd. Oct. 30. Fine, warm, misty. Did only 2pp. Had to think much.

Frid. Oct. 31. Rainy and dark.- Last night a bad attack of diarrhoea. Made me feel ill to-day, but did my 5pp.- Wrote a short letter to Edith.

Sat. Nov. 1. Wonderfully fine sunny day.- Went to Baker's and bought 2 nightshirts (2/6 each) and pair of boots (16/10).- Did only 4pp. Roberts failed to come this evening.

Sund. Nov. 2. Showery, with a little sunshine.- Edith came at 4 o'clock. Read to her "The May Queen" [by Tennyson], and "Pied Piper of Hamelin" [by Browning].

Mond. Nov. 3. Very dull and at night rain.- Sold another lot of books, for £5.- Worked 8.30 to 11.30 and 3.30 to 8.30, doing my 5pp. Letter from Hartley praising "The Emancipated".

Tuesd. Nov. 4. Fine and warm; bright sunshine. Wrote 9 to 11.30 and 3 to 8, doing my 5pp. Am now past middle of 2nd Vol.- Reading Fenimore Cooper's "Spy",- strange revival of my boyhood.

Wed. Nov. 5. Fine, sunny. Did only 4pp., and at 8 went to Edith's. Met her father for first time.

Thursd. Nov. 6. Fine. Did no work, feeling idle.- Bought a keeper for Edith, 21/-.

Frid. Nov. 7. Bitter wind and rain; in my room, choked with smoke from the chimney .- Worked 8.30 to 11, and 2.30 to 8.30; cancelled last part of Wedy, and did 5.

Sat. Nov. 8. Beautiful day. Worked hard, but did only 3pp.- To Roberts at 8. McCormick the artist there. Stayed till 1.30.

Sund. Nov. 9. Beautiful day. Met Edith at Glo'ster Gate, and spent evening here. Read some poetry to her. Wrote to Alg.

Mond. Nov. 10. Dense fog till 3 o'clock; then an hour clear. Worked by lamplight; 8.30 to 12, and 2.30 to 8.30, doing 5pp. Letter from Nelly, enclosing new portrait of herself.[12]

Tuesd. Nov. 11. Fine, sunny. Worked all day, and did about 5pp.- Mind getting worn out.

Wed. Nov. 12. Fine. Did nothing in morning, and afternoon only 2pp.- At 8 came Edith.

Thursd. Nov. 13. Dull, rainy, muddy. No work in morning. From 2 to 8.30, 4pp.- Wrote to Edith.

Frid. Nov. 14. Fine. In morning 1p., in evening 3½.- Letter from Alg and from Edith.

Sat. Nov. 15. Dull. Did 3pp., and *finished Vol. II.* Heaven be thankit!- Bought Hardy's "A Pair of Blue Eyes".- Letter from Alg.

Sund. Nov. 16. Dull; rainy. Edith came as usual. Her father objects to my going to their house, on no grounds intelligible. She will continue to come here.

Mond. Nov. 17. Dull, but no rain; foggy. Letters from Nelly and Bertz.- Worked 2 to 8, and did 3pp.

Tuesd. Nov. 18. Dull, rain, warm. Worked from 8.30 to 11, doing 1p., and from 2.30 to 9.30, doing 4pp.

Wed. Nov. 19. Dull, but no rain. Very warm. In morning 2pp., and evening 2. At 7 came Edith.

Thursd. Nov. 20. Dull, rainy, warm. Morning did nothing. Went to Museum to get particulars of Pneumonia, for Reardon's death. Wrote from 2.30 to 9, doing 4pp.- A steamroller at work all day down in the street; maddening.

Frid. Nov. 21. Dull, rainy. Did 4pp.

Sat. Nov. 22. My wretched birthday. Sunshine in morning, changing to rain. Am 33 yrs old. Letters from Mother, Madge and Edith. Did 4pp. At 8 to Roberts.

Sund. Nov. 23. No sunshine, no rain. Edith came. Gale blowing.

Mond. Nov. 24. Sunshine, a little. High wind and colder. Worked 2.30 to 9.30, doing 3½pp.

Tuesd. Nov. 25. Cold, dull. High wind. Worked 8.30 to 11.30, and 2.30 to 9, doing 5½pp.- Letter from Alg, and invitation from Hartley to view his paintings of Constable's country at Dunthorne's.

Wed. Nov. 26. Frosty, clear. Worked 9.30 to 11, and 2 to 6, doing 3pp.- At 7 came Edith.

Thursd. Nov. 27. Bitterly cold, cloudy, a little snow. Worked 8.30 to 11.30, and 2.30 to 9, doing 3½pp. But last ½ to be destroyed.- Brain sluggish.- Letter from Ella Gaussen.

Frid. Nov. 28. A heavy fall of snow. Worked 9 to 11, rewriting last page of yesterday. Then from 3 to 10, doing 4pp.

Sat. Nov. 29. Hard frost. In morning to see an exhibition of Hartley's pictures:"Constable's Country", at Dunthorne's. Evening wrote 2pp., but badly. Not satisfied with this chapter of Reardon's death, and must do it again later.- Letter from Alg.- Roberts didn't come.

Sund. Nov. 30. Slight thaw. Cloud and fog. Edith could not come, on account of a cold.- Read some Landor.

Mond. Dec. 1. Thaw, but hideous fog. Worked 9 to 11, doing 1p., and 2.30 to 8, doing 4pp .- Letter from Edith. Replied to her

Tuesd. Dec. 2. Day of hideous fog. Black night from 9 to 10. Nevertheless, worked. Did 1p. in morning, and 4 in evening. Getting very near to the end.

Wed. Dec. 3. Fog worse than yesterday; not one hour of daylight. In morning did 1p., evening 3. At 7 came Edith. Weather had cleared; warm; changing to rain.

Thursd. Dec. 4. Much rain, warmer. In morning 1p., afternoon and evening, 4.

Frid. Dec. 5. High, cold wind and rain. Morning 1p., evening 4. At 9 o'clock, wrote "The End". But I still have the last two pages of Reardon's death to rewrite.- Invitation from Edith Sichel, to dine there on 20th, to meet the Birrells and Osborne Morgan.[13] Eheu! Of course must refuse. I have sold my dress-suit, so that I couldn't go, even if I had no other reason. But I suppose I shall never again sit at a civilized table.

Sat. Dec. 6. In morning rewrote the p. of Reardon's death, and <u>so finished</u> <u>"New Grub Street"</u>.- Sent postcard to Alg. In afternoon to British

Museum, where I began to study C[harles] Booth's "Life and Labour [of the People]".- At 8 to Roberts. Hartley looked in. Got home at 1.30.

Sund. Dec. 7. Bad bilious headache. At 3.30 met Edith as usual.- Reading Flaubert's letters.

Mond. Dec.8. Dull, cold. Wasted the day, after taking MS. to [Smith, Elder's,] Waterloo Place.

Tuesd. Dec. 9. Dull, foggy. Went to Museum, and read some more Booth.

Wed. Dec. 10. In afternoon took Edith to the Ballad Concert at St. James's Hall. A hideous fog; at 3 o'clock black as night, and so remained. The Hall so thick one could hardly see the singers.- Edith came home with me, and left about 9.

Thursd. Dec. 11. Dense fog till evening, then a cold wind cleared the streets. Went to Museum, but could not get books, because of darkness. Met Roberts there. Went home with him, then to see "The Gondoliers" [by Gilbert and Sullivan] at Savoy. On coming back, found letter from Payn, asking if he may take my MS with him to seaside.

*Frid. Dec. 12.*Dull, frosty; no fog. To Museum at 11. Read Havelock Ellis's "The New Spirit", and the Life of James Macdonnell [*James Macdonnell, Journalist,* by W. Robertson Nicoll, 1889]. Home at 7.30; copied out some notes, then read some pages of [Richard] Hooker.

Sat. Dec. 13. Thick fog in morning, then a little clearer. Hard frost. To Museum, where I began to read the "Life of Morley Punshon" [by Frederick W. Macdonald, 1887]. Roberts came at 7.30.- Later read some of Hesiod's "Theogony" and 100 ll. of the "Frogs".

Sund. Dec. 14. Foggy, and hard frost. Thousands of people skating in park. Edith came. Read 300 ll. Hesiod and some "Tatler".

Mond. Dec. 15. Hideous day again; not an hour of daylight. Thick snow fell last night. Find it useless to get up before 10 now-a-days, as I only burn oil and coal to no profit. Went to Museum at 12, and stayed till 6.30. Read [Edward] Fitzgerald's Letters. Home again to Hesiod and the "Tatler".

Tuesd. Dec. 16. Clear from fog, but wretched. Got up at 11. At Museum read at Punshon's Life. Roberts looked in at 10 o'clock in evening.- Read more Hesiod and "Tatler".

Wed. Dec. 17. In morning a call from Captain Gissing R.N., who has rooms in these buildings. A pleasant fellow.- To Museum, and read at Punshon. At 6.30 came Edith.

Thursd. Dec. 18. Up at 11. Till then a dense, tawny fog. Later cleared. To Museum. Finished Life of Punshon, and dawdled over other books. Home to read "Tatler" and the new *Review of Reviews.*

Frid. Dec. 19. Up at 11. Heavy snow. To Museum, where I wasted the time over old magazines. In very low spirits; dreading the future.- Home, to finish the "Theogony" of Hesiod. Read also [John] Conington's Introduction to the "Georgics", and some "Tatler". Get to bed about 12 each night. Have no letters, and write to no one.

Sat. Dec. 20. Snow thick; cold, dark, wretched. Up at 11. Afternoon at Museum, where read Temple's Bampton Lecture [Relations between Religion and Science, 1884,]—not for amusement.[14] Then to Roberts.— P.c. from Alg, saying his novel "Pixy" [published as *A Moorland Idyl*]is finished; and sent anonymously to Blackwood.

Sund. Dec. 21. Little clearer, but no sun. Still frost; much skating everywhere. At 4 came Edith and spent evening.

Mond. Dec. 22. Dense fog unintermittent, fog of the choking kind.- Letter from Alg.- Went to Museum, and came back at 7 from Gower Street by train. Signals invisible; trains, without order, crawling cautiously from station to station. Damnable weather.- Read 100 11. of Hesiod. Yesterday read about half of "Monsieur, Madame et Bébé" [by Gustave Droz].

Tuesd. Dec. 23. Thaw, slush, gloom. In morning came Walter Grahame, and again, to continue our talk, in the afternoon. At 8 o'clock Edith looked in for an hour; brought me a present of silk muffler.- Read 100 11. of [Hesiod's] "Works and Days". Finished "Monsieur, Madame et Bébé".

Wed. Dec. 24. Frost, gloom. Reading up geological matters for new book. Bought pair of gloves for Edith.

Thursd. Dec. 25. Frost, no fog; feeble attempt at sunlight in afternoon. At 3.30 went to Edith's and had dinner with her. Afterwards, her sister Flossie came into the room, and we had some games at cards. Walked home by the misty light of full moon.- Present from Wakefield of a pocket-flask.

Frid. Dec. 26. Thaw, gloom. Edith came at 3.30.

Sat. Dec. 27. Slush, fog, snow. In the morning was surprised by a visit from Alfred Smith. We went and had dinner together in the City. In evening came Roberts, bringing the proofs of an article on himself about to appear in the *London Figaro* [published on January 10, 1891, "Coming Men: Mr Morley Roberts"]. Some years ago the *Figaro* applied to me for my photograph, and I refused it.

Sund. Dec. 28. Frost, east wind. Must be three weeks since there was a gleam of sunlight. At 3.30 came Edith.

Mond. Dec. 29. Bitterly cold, gloom, Had a man from the Baker St. Bazaar to give me estimate of moving my furniture to Exeter. They will do it for £14.15.- At 6 came Roberts, and wanted me to come out, but I was detained by the absurd necessity of waiting for the washerwoman,- who never came after all.

Tuesd. Dec. 30. Snow; windy, terrible. Went to City, and got copies of two Exeter papers. Sent a line to Bertz. In evening came Roberts. Finished reading [J. Fenimore Cooper's] "The Prairie", and began "Wyandotte".

Wed. Dec. 31. Hard frost. No water to be had in morning. Spent day at Museum, reading [F.H.] Reusch's "Bibel und Natur", and Asa Gray on "Science and Religion".- In evening came Edith. Harrison the printer looked in. Saw the New Year in with anything but cheerful thoughts. The future full of doubt.- Letter from Nelly.

1891

Thursd. Jan. 1. A thaw. At mid-day first gleam of sunlight, the first for many weeks. Read geology at Museum. In evening came Roberts, bringing his article "The Bronze-caster" in the new *Macmillan's.*

Frid. Jan. 2. Dense fog, unchanging, all day. Read at Museum. Suffering wretchedly from suspense; no word yet from Smith, Elder.

Sat. Jan. 3. Thaw. Fog until evening. Dined with Roberts at Blanchard's. McCormick then joined us.

Sund. Jan. 4. Universal slush. Few hours' glimmer of half sunlight. Went to Edith's.

Mond. Jan. 5. Bright sunny morning. Frost again. Wasted the day at home, waiting for washerwoman. Finished [Fenimore Cooper's] "Wyandotte". Weariness of suspense.

Tuesd. Jan. 6. Again a fine day, but terribly cold. In afternoon to see McCormick at his studio. Evening to the [Edgar] Harrisons at Gunnersbury. Bright stars in frosty sky. Reading "Satanstoe [a Tale of the Colony", by Cornelius Littlepage, i.e. James Fenimore Cooper, 1860.]

Wed. Jan. 7. Again very fine morning, but clouding over later. At the Museum read Besant's paltry life of Jefferies. In evening came Edith and, by the 8.30 post, at last a letter from Smith & Elder. They think "New Grub Street" "clever and original" but fear it is too gloomy. Offer £150. I wrote at once accepting (eheu!) and asking them to add the £10 they offered for "Thyrza". Heaven be thankit!

Thursd. Jan. 8. Misty, still hard frost. Recd. £150 from S[mith] & E[lder]. They promise to let me know shortly about "Thyrza", which means, I trust, that they are ashamed of their £10 offer.- Day spent in confusion.- Went to my tailor's and ordered an ulster for £3.10.

Frid. Jan. 9. Misty, hard frost still. In evening to Edith's: saw her father, and told him that I wish Edith to come to me at Exeter in a month's time. He "would think over it", but E. says she has made up her mind. On coming home found £10 from S. & E. for "Thyrza", so that they are not ashamed after all. Card from Roberts, who has gone down to Liverpool to work up papers on steamship lines for *Murray* ['s Magazine]. Wrote to him, and sent cheque to Wakefield, where my money is always banked.

Sat. Jan. 10. Left London at 9 o'clock, and at 2 was in Exeter. Had dinner and walked to Prospect Park, where I called on C.J. Rockett, who, in reply to an advt of mine, has offered me three unfurnished rooms in his house. He himself is about to be married. Met the girl, and the landlord of the house, her brother. The rooms will suit very well. Bright sunshine nearly all day. Caught the 6.15 express back, and was at Paddington by 10.30, not very tired. On journey read "The Hand of Ethelberta", surely old Hardy's poorest book.

Sund. Jan. 11. A hideous day, black fog from morning to night. Sat reading "Ethelberta". Wrote to Edith, to Alg, and to Rockett. To bed early.

Mond. Jan. 12. Got my grand new ulster. Almost a bright morning, frost still very severe. Recd from mother, from the bank, £40. Letter from Nelly, who is gone for a week to Goole. Made arrangements for removal of my goods on Wednesday by the Baker St[reet] Bazaar people.- Call from Walter Grahame in afternoon. In evening came Edith.- Note from Roberts, Liverpool.- In evening a complete thaw.

Tuesd. Jan. 13. Slush universal. Making my final arrangements for departure. Men from Baker St. Bazaar came to pack books etc.- In evening came Edith, for good-bye. Our agreement is that we are to be married on the 10th Feb.

Wed. Jan. 14. Bright sunny morning, but cold. All my property got away by 11am. Took leave of Mrs. King, and caught the 11.45 for Exeter. On arriving, found that the people at Delamore House cannot receive me, so took a bedroom next door to them for a night or two. Spent evening in Public Reading-Room.

Thursday. Jan. 15. Brilliant day, not a cloud in sky, but bitterly cold. Walked over the hills to Stoke Canon, and there had dinner. Back by Cowley Bridge. Had again to make new arrangements for the night, and slept at the Coffee Tavern, where I am eating these days. Evening at Reading-room.

Frid. Jan. 16. Bright morning; afternoon a little snow. Furniture arrived at 10.30, and by 1 o'clock all was brought into the house.- Letter from Katie and from Edith. Former and Alg are now at Wooler [in North-umberland]. Slept at Mrs Cornish's.

Sat. Jan. 17. Sunny, a little snow. Worked to get things in order. Bought carpet, oil cloth etc. By evening had the bedroom fit for sleeping in to-night.- Went to the Registrar's Office, and gave notice for a marriage with Edith. The Registrar's Office here is the Board-Room (so written on door) of the Poor-law Guardians; at one end of the long table a raised, throne-like chair, with a little hammer on desk in front. A clerk took my information. The Registrar himself sitting at side of the long table; pleasant and chatty.

When I gave my occupation as "literary man", he said to the clerk "Put 'gentleman' ".- Recd 17/- from the Auctioneers in London to whom I gave my two big book-cases and oak chest for sale. Their charge for moving and commission came to 10/-! Have found a decent woman to wait on me, for 3/- a week.

Sund. Jan. 18. Water-pipes frozen. But a warm, unclouded sun all day. Worked at getting things into order. Put down stair-carpets and placed book-cases. Wrote to Edith. Cold still bad.

Mond. Jan. 19. Terribly cold last night. Though I had fire in bed-room, the water in jug frozen this morning. Stated in papers that at Eastbourne the sea has been frozen. At Naples men have perished of cold.- A dull day. Got my books roughly arranged on shelves. Wrote to Alg and Katie.- Reading [W.H.] Prescott's Philip II.

Tuesd. Jan. 20. A thaw and some rain. Arranged my books. A bad cold keeps me much indoors. Wrote to Nelly.

Wed. Jan. 21. Thaw still. Bright and sunny. Read some Greek history. Bought socks, sheets and other things. Wrote to Roberts and to Edith.

Thursd. Jan. 22. Mild and sunny, changing to slight rain at evening. At quarter to ten left home and walked to Dawlish, reaching there at about half past one. Beautiful view of Exeter from a high point of road in Alphington. Home by the 4.16 train. Letter from Alg.- My cold still bad.

Frid. Jan. 23. Dull and rainy. Reading little handbook of ancient Geography. Cold bad. Letter from Alg.

Sat. Jan. 24. Letters from Roberts and Edith. Wrote to Nelly and Alg. Dull, rainy, sunny in afternoon. Read papers at public library, as usual. "New Grub Street" announced as in the press.

Sund. Jan. 25. Fine sunny day. Made dinner at home of eggs and bacon. In afternoon walked out to Heavitree and on to Honiton Clyst. Reading Eng. translation of works of Emperor Julian. Cold little better. Wrote to Edith.

Mond. Jan. 26. Rain and gloom. Saw that "New Grub Street" is announced in Sat.'s *Athenaeum*. Ordered pair of trousers. Wrote to Walter Grahame. Finished Julian, and began to read a transln of Herodian.

Tuesd. Jan. 27. Bright warm day. Got in ½ ton of coals. Wrote to Edith for her birthday to-morrow. Recd letter from her. Reading Herodian.

Wed. Jan. 28. Doubtful morning, ending in rain. Walked to Topsham, and back by Heavitree.

Thursd. Jan. 29. Day of rain. Read at Gibbon. Wrote to Edith.

237

Frid. Jan. 30. Brilliant day. In morning walked up to Pennsylvania and on towards Cowley Bridge. The finest view I have yet discovered. Letter from Edith, saying she has recd one from Nellie. Wrote again to her.

Sat. Jan. 31. Fine, warm. Recd from S[mith] & E[lder] a copy of "Thyrza", for revision. I knew the cheap edn would not be long delayed after the copyright came into their hands. Reading Montaigne, to whom, for whatever reason, I have never greatly taken. But his essay "On Cruelty" conciliates me.- Heavy rain at night.

Sund. Feb. 1. A magnificent day; cloudless blue; brisk n.w. wind. In morning worked at "Thyrza", afternoon walked over hill to Cowley Bridge and back. Wrote to Edith, and to the girls.

Mond. Feb. 2. Dull and a little rain. Took up Martial. Revising "Thyrza".

Tuesd. Feb. 3. Dull, colder. Letter from Edith saying her sister is ill and wanting to put off marriage. Of course, I quite suspected this. Replied saying that I will put it off for a week till Feb. 17th, and no longer.- Martial, Gibbon and Suetonius. Finished revision of "Thyrza". Have cut out all the Emerson episode in Vol. III [ch. V], and otherwise greatly reduced the book[1].

Wed. Feb. 4. Dull. Recd first proofs of "New Grub Street" and corrected. Letter from Bertz.

Thursd. Feb. 5. Dull. Letter from Edith, making it quite uncertain when she can leave home.- Walked to Crediton, and back by train. A cold wind. Read Lucian's "Demonae" in Wieland's translm, don't possess the original. Johnson's Life of Pope. Wrote to Nelly and to Edith, telling the latter that I shall cease correspondence until she gives a final date for the marriage.

Frid. Feb. 6. More proofs. Read Johnson's Life of Milton. Some Martial.- Dull and coldish. No sun for several days.

Sat. Feb. 7. Proofs.- Read some Martial.- Posted "Thyrza" back to S. & E., requesting them henceforth to let me know when they propose a new edn of one of my books.- No letter from Edith; my last has of course given offence.

Sund. Feb. 8. Dull day, no sun. Went by train to Exmouth and thence walked to Budleigh Salterton. The furze in full yellow bloom. Had some bread and cheese, then back to Exmouth by way of E. Budleigh.- In evening read some of Pliny's Letters.

Mond. Feb. 9. No sun; at night a frost. Martial and Johnson's [Life of] Cowley.- Letter from Edith, to which I replied saying that if the marriage is not during the next fortnight, it cannot be at all.—Wrote to Alg, now in Glostershire.

Tuesd. Feb. 10. Bright, warm day. Corrected a lot of proofs. Good walk round by the Cowley Bridge Road.

Wed. Feb. 11. Hard frost last night, but to-day sunny and delightful. Corrected some proofs, then walked out to Thorverton, where I had dinner at the Dolphin. Then on to Brampford Speke, I think the most beautiful village I ever saw. Home over the hills from Cowley Bridge.- Wrote to A.J. Smith.- No reply yet from Edith.

Thursd. Feb. 12. Sunny and cheerful. Finished 1st vol. in proofs. Letter from Mrs. Bullock-Webster, of Melksham House, Wells, saying she is Hony.Sec. of a society for lending books to poor gentlewomen, and asking me to give them a copy of "A Life's Morning". Ordered one from Smith's Library (2/6) and shall send it.- Martial, Pliny.- Wrote to A.J. Smith.

Frid. Feb. 13. Such a day as occurs seldom in a lifetime. Warm, windless, brilliant. Walked from Exeter to top of Gt. Haldon, and thence descended to delightful little hamlet of Ashcombe, whence I followed the stream to Dawlish. Back by train. An exquisite walk.- Letter from Edith, saying marriage can be shortly. Replied that the day must be Feb. 25th, *or never*.- Note from Roberts.- For provender on my walk I took two twopenny porkpies, and then at Dawlish had tea and bread and butter. Of course insufficient sustenance, but can't afford more. Poverty always spoiling things that might be perfect.

Sat. Feb. 14. Misty in morning, then very fine. Got "A Life's Morning" at Smith's, and shall send to Mrs Bullock-Webster. The new *Review of Reviews.* Reading "Complete Angler" [by Isaac Walton].

Sund. Feb. 15. Headache. Made dinner at home of eggs and bacon. Reading Walton.- Wrote to Edith.

Mond. Feb. 16. Fine day again. In morning corrected proofs. Then to Free Library, where I got a ticket; the form has been signed for me by Mr Ascott and Mr Cole, two owls. Afternoon, walked out to Silverton and back. Delightful scenery all up the Exe valley.- My eyes are very bad at present; I can't read for more than half an hour without dimness and smarting.

Tuesd. Feb. 17. Frost in night, but beautiful day. In morning went to Registrar, and got certificate for marriage. Then wrote to S. Pancras Registrar, appointing the 25th, and asking if witnesses can be procured at the office. Wrote to Alg. Letters from Mother and from Edith. From the Free Library got Lyell's "[Elements of] Geology", and read a good deal of it. Also some Martial.

Wed. Feb. 18. Like an autumn day; sunshine through mist. Reading Lyell. Much misery of solitude. I rarely speak a word with Rockett or Miss Cole, and other acquaintances I have none.

Thursd. Feb. 19. Cold, but sunny. Bad headache.- Very uncivil letter from Registrar of St Pancras, saying that the lady's name in the notice sent to him was "Miss Edith Beaumont". Went to see Exeter Registrar, and by his advice sent my certificate to St Pancras. No end of these infernal obstacles, it seems.- Letter from Alg.- Seeing letter in *Times* on Greek accent in verse, wrote to the paper, giving my old views on the matter. Not likely they will print it. Finished quick reading of Lyell, for general ideas.

Frid. Feb. 20. Dull cold day. Got from the Library [Hugh] Miller's "Testimony of the Rocks" [1857]. Proofs have ceased to come for two or three days. Feeling miserable, and in complete uncertainty as to whether my marriage will take place next week (for which all arrangements are supposed to have been made) or not.

Sat. Feb. 21. Fine, but a cold wind. Letter from Pancras Registrar, acknowledging a mistake of his clerk's. Letter from Edith. Finished "Testimony of the Rocks".

Sund. Feb. 22. Exquisite day.- Letter from Alg, asking loan of £5, as he has not yet heard from Blackwood, who has had his MS about a month. Wrote to Mrs Gaussen, telling her of my coming marriage. Also to Edith. Made dinner of chops, and in afternoon walked, by Heavitree, to Sowton (beautiful sandstone lane) and back home by Pinhoe.- Dawdled over Forster's "Goldsmith".

Mond. Feb. 23. Fine. Got from library Grant Allen's "Evolutionist at Large".

Tuesd. Feb. 24. Went up to London by 10.30am. Found town buried in cold filthy fog, which has been continuous for the last fortnight. At Paddington, Edith met me; we bought the wedding-ring in Tott[enham] C[our]t Rd, and then went to St Paul's Crescent. Late at night, walked through the fog to the Bedford Head, Tott. Ct. Rd, where I took a room.

Wed. Feb. 25. Married to Edith Underwood at Registrar Office, St. Pancras. Drove in fog to Paddington, and caught the 11.45 for Exeter.- Found letters from Roberts and Alg.- Find my letter is in the *Times* to-day ["The Pronunciation of Greek"].

Thursd. Feb. 26. Back to the splendid sunshine once more. Walked over the hill towards Stoke Canon.

Frid. Feb. 27. Unprecedented weather. Went to Dawlish, and spent several hours there.

Sat. Feb. 28. Got three copies of Wed[nesday]'s *Times*; sent one to Alg, one to Roberts, and one to Bertz. Shopping with Edith. Warm sunshine and blue sky.- The proofs of "New Grub Street" are dragging on.

240

Sund. March 1. Clouded sky, at last and wind threatening rain. Short walk in the afternoon.

Mond. March 2. Dull, but very clear. Sat down in my den at the top of the house, and worked at plan of new book from 9 to 1. Arranged names.- Reading Martial again. [Half a line crossed out] Letter from Alg, saying that Blackwood refuses his story "Pixy". Alas!

Tuesd. March 3. High wind, sunny. Afternoon walked with Edith by Old Tiverton Rd to Stoke Canon and back.- Martial.

Wed. March 4. Still windy; sunny in afternoon. Worked at novel in morning; think it will be called "Raymond Peak". With Edith to the Museum.

Thursd. March 5. Windy, but glorious sun. Broken morning's work.- Wrote to Bertz.

Frid. March 6. Dull. Worked at arrangement of first chapters. Letter from Bertz.

Sat. March 7. Rain at last. Got from lib. [R.C.] Jebb's Life of [Richard] Bentley.[2] Letter from Roberts.

Sund. March 8. Rain all day; cold; no sun. Read Jebb's Bentley. Wrote to Madge and Nellie. No walk.

Mond. March 9. Bitter east wind. At mid-day began to snow; heavy fall. Wasted the morning, but at 4 o'clock sat down in den,- the old Agbrigg hour. Thought over first chapter.

Tuesd. March 10. Continuance of violent storm. Snow very deep. Worked morning and afternoon, doing first 2 pages of Chap.I.

Wed. March 11. The storm over at last. Bright sunshine; deep snow everywhere. Worked fitfully morning and evening, doing about half a page. Roberts writes to say that he is coming to Dartmouth, and will call here.

Thursd. March 12. Clouded again and more snow. Recd some proofs of the new edn of "Thyrza". No writing.

Frid. March 13. In afternoon came Roberts, calling on his way back to London. Slept at the London Hotel. Much literary talk, of course. Roberts vastly more suave than in the old days.

Sat. March 14. Fine day. In morning walk with Roberts; snow twelve feet thick and more in some of the lanes. He had dinner with us, then we all went in cab to the Cathedral, which R. wished to see; thence to station, to see him off by the 3.55 express.- Work, of course, suspended.

Sund. March 15. Dull and rainy day. Read Leslie Stephen's "Swift", and 200 lines of 24th "Odyssey". Wrote to Mother.

Mond. March 16. Showery; the snow melting fast. Got to work again, and did about a page.

Tuesd. March 17. Gloomy.- Printers have lost the last slip of "Grub Street", and printed "The End" prematurely. Wrote about it. Letter from one Harold Bateson apropos of my letter to the *Times;* sends me a pamphlet on "English Rhythms"[3].- Got Mark Pattison's [Life of] Milton [English Men of Letters Series, 1878].- Wrote about a page.

Wed. March 18. Very fine in morning; afternoon, rain. Did about 3pp. Getting on very well.

Thursd. March 19. Dull; a little sun, no rain. Did something more than 2pp. The printers have found the lost slip, thank Heaven!- Bought what I have long wanted, a decent stationery-case for my writing-table; cost 2/6.

Frid. March 20. Sunny and cloudy. Finished Ch. 1, but it must be recopied.

Sat. March 21. East wind; sun and cloud. A page in morning. Afternoon, with Edith to Cowley Bridge. Proofs of "Grub Street" finished.

Sund. March 22. Gloom and cold. Reading Thomson's "Seasons". Down to tea with the Rocketts. Wrote to Harold D. Bateson. Letters from Mother and Madge.

Mond. March 23. Gloom and cold. Did 2pp. morning and 2 evening. Getting on admirably.- Got [David] Masson's Life of De Quincey.

Tuesd. March 24. Bright spring day. Did 3pp. To reading-room, as usual, from 12 to 1, and in afternoon with Edith along Old Tiverton Road.

Wed. March 25. Sunny, showery, high wind. Did only 2pp. Got [Edmund] Gosse's Life of Gray [English Men of Letters Series, 1882].

Thursd. March 26. Sunny, stormy, blusterous day; much hail. Worked hard, revising and adding to Chap. II, which I finished.—New address from Bertz, and letter from Alg.- Wrote to Alg.

Frid. March 27. Much the same day as yesterday; wind fallen by evening. Only did 1½p.- Am trying to make my handwriting larger; "New Grub Street" was microscopic. The difficulty is that I shan't be able to calculate quantities so well.

Sat. March 28. Wind not so strong; sunny and springlike.- In morning, thought only. Afternoon beautiful walk to Brampford Speke.- Saw the first primrose.

Sund. March 29. Warm and bright. Reading XXIV "Odyssey". Some of Gray's Poems.

Mond. March 30. Very fine, but still windy. Even yet snow lies in thick masses about some of the lanes, though it is everywhere melting.- Began a complete reading of Chaucer, in the Aldine.- Letter from Nelly.- Did 3pp.

Tuesd. March 31. Fine, windy.- Letter from A.J. Smith, who talks of coming here at Whitsuntide.- Wrote to Nelly and to Roberts. Did 3pp.- Got from Library [H.D.] Traill's "Sterne" [English Men of Letters Series, 1882].

Wed. Ap. 1. Not much sun.- Wrote 2½pp.

Thursd. Ap. 2. Rain all day. No sun. Note from one Frederick Dolman asking me to be interviewed for the *Pall Mall* [*Gazette*]. Wrote telling him I lived at Exeter, and that in any case, I had nothing to tell the public.- Wrote to A.J. Smith.- Did only 1½p. in the morning; spent evening planning progress.- Chaucer. The Cookes Tale. Finished Traill's "Sterne".- Letter from Roberts saying he starts to-morrow for Lisbon and Madeira.

Frid. Ap. 3. Rain all day. Did 4pp., good work. Am in Chap. IV.—The people downstairs have—alas!—got in a piano to-day, and vigorous strumming has begun. I trust to their weakness of mind soon to tire of it.— Chaucer's Man of Lawes Tale.

Sat. Ap. 4. Rainy, with fine evening. Wrote nothing.

Sund. Ap. 5. Cloudy, but a fine day. In morning went up Old Tiv[erton] Road, and got mould for flower-pots with a few ferns. Read a portion of "Odyssey" XXIII. Chaucer's Franklin's Tale.

Mond. Ap. 6. Summerlike day.- Did 3pp.- Got from Library [Austin] Dobson's Life of Steele in "English Worthies".

Tuesd. Ap. 7. Dull; cold wind. Did 1½p., finishing Chap. IV. In evening thought over beginning of the new period in the story.

Wed. Ap. 8. Fine, but cold wind; rain towards evening. Recd 6 copies of "New Grub Street". In acknowledging to S[mith] & E[lder] told them of the "Pall Mall Gazette" man.[4] Sent a copy to Wakefield, and one to Hudson. Must keep Roberts's till he returns.—Did no writing; mused vaguely.

Thursd. Ap. 9. Dull and cold. To my astonishment saw that a little snow still lingers up on Pennsylvania Hill.- Worked morning and afternoon, doing 3pp.- Finished the Franklin's Tale.- Sent "New Grub Street" to Bertz, and a postcard.

Frid Ap. 10. Dull, but warmer. A menagerie has planted itself in a field opposite my window, and I hear the roaring of the animals. Worked all day, and did 3pp. Began Second Nonnes Priestes Tale.- Got from library Grant Allen's "Darwin".

Sat. Ap. 11. Dull, but no rain. In morning had to go back 4pp., and rewrote 2.- In afternoon walked with Edith to St Cyres, and had tea at the inn. Back by 7.30.- Good advts of "New Grub Street".

Sund. Ap. 12. Letter from Alg. Says he has given up his proposed cottage, and is on point of going to Jersey.- He and Kate both ill.- Reading Grant Allen's "Darwin".- Brilliant morning, then cloudy.

Mond. Ap. 13. Dull. Feeling unwell, and did no work.

Tuesd. Ap. 14. Rainy, but sweet and warm. Have to go back to begin[ning] of Chap. V and elaborate again; have not advanced for a week. In evening wrote 2pp.- Got [Edmund] Gosse's Life of [Sir Walter] Raleigh [in "English Worthies"].

Wed. Ap. 15. A brilliant day. S[mith] & E[lder] have sent me reviews of "New Grub Street" in the *Scotsman* and *Daily Graphic* [both published on April 13]. Wrote to stop this horror. Worked well morning and evening, doing 4½pp.

Thursd. Ap. 16. Very fine. Worked well, doing 4pp.- A letter from the old bore, Charles Anderson.

Frid. Ap. 17. Glorious day. Letter from Mother praising ["New] Grub St[reet"] highly. Did 1p. in morning, and 3 evening.

Sat. Ap. 18. Very fine. Morning began to copy Chaps. 1 and 2, which I have left rough till now. Afternoon to Pinhoe. Found white violets. In evening an unexpected visit from Edith's brother George—eheu! Letter from Bertz, enthusiastic over "Grub Street".

Sund. Ap. 19. At home all day. Dull weather. Finished Gosse's Raleigh. Some of Bacon's Essays. In morning continued the copying of my MS.

Mond. Ap. 20. Dull, and colder. Copied all day. Read nothing.

Tuesd. Ap. 21. Fine day. In morning finished copying of first 2 chapters. Evening only thought.- Letter from Mrs F[rederic] Harrison. One from Alg, announcing his arrival in Jersey and struggle to find lodgings.- Wrote to Mrs Harrison, telling her of my marriage, and that henceforth I am shut off from educated people.

Wed. Ap. 22. Rain all day. Did 3½p. Read nothing.

Thursd. Ap. 23. Dull morning; very fine afternoon. Another very kind letter from Mrs Harrison, mentioning good article on "Grub Street" in *The Speaker* [of April 18], which I must get. Wrote nearly 4pp. Have changed my afternoon hours to 5-9.

Frid. Ap. 24. Magnificent day. Did 3pp., in good mood. Wrote to Mrs. F. Harrison.

Sat. Ap. 25. Fine. Edith suffering from indigestion etc.- Got *The Speaker,* and find its review is of no importance. Morning wrote 2pp. Wrote to Madge.

Sund. Ap. 26. Walk alone in morning. Fine. Wrote to Bertz. Read close of "Odyssey" 23, and 100 ll. of 22. In evening to see Doctor, and ask him to call on Edith to-morrow.

Mond. Ap. 27. Doctor came.- Fine day, but hazy. No writing.- Got from library a book on Trees.

Tuesd. Ap. 28. Fine. Did 3pp.

Wed. Ap. 29. Cloudy in morning; fine in afternoon. Wrote only ½p., so shall not as I hoped, finished Vol. I before going to Budleigh Salterton to-morrow. About 3pp. still to do.- Letter from [Charles] Anderson, and one from Madge, with £20. Card from Roberts, announcing his return to England. Sent his copy of "New Grub Street". Wrote to Nelly, to be posted to-morrow.

Thursd. Ap. 30. Left by the 8.30 for Exmouth, and thence by coach to Budleigh Salterton, where we found two rooms looking onto the sea, at Miss Jessie Wesley's Octogon Cottage. High S.W. wind, turning to rain at evening.

Frid. May 1. Violent S.W. wind, with frequent rain. Walked up the valley of the Otter, where found abundance of Lady's Smock and Marsh Marigolds. Much walking about the exquisite lanes.

Sat. May 2. In morning to the top of West Beacon; glorious view over Exe estuary. Rain at first, then fine and warm. Left Budleigh at 4.50, and reached Exeter at 6.37. Bill at lodgings 14/2½. Found letter from Roberts in hot praise of "New Grub Street". Also circular of benevolent societies, in which my gift of "A Life's Morning" to Mrs Bullock-Webster is acknowledged.- Advt of "Thyrza" in *Athenaeum,* put down for immediate publication at 6/-. But I have not yet had all the proofs.- At Exmouth station, in Smith's bookstall library, saw "A Village Hampden" [by Algernon Gissing], and "In Low Relief" [by Morley Roberts].

Sund. May 3. Fine but cloudy. Trees all coming into leaf. Read some Odes of Horace.

Mond. May 4. Day lost in waiting for the doctor. No writing. Got [F.W.H.] Myers' Wordsworth [English Men of Letters Series, 1881] from library. Saw an article on "New Grub Street" in *Illustd Lond. News*—a whole column.[5]

Tuesd. May 5. Glorious day; very warm. Letter from girl at Edinburgh, asking my autograph. Sent it. Letter from Roberts. Wrote 2pp. Find it difficult to get into swing again.- Replied to Roberts.

Wed. May 6. Fine again. Did 2pp., finishing Vol. I. Letter from Grahame, saying he enjoys "New Grub Street".

Thursd. May 7. Fine, but growing dull; at night, heavy rain. Began Vol. II, and did 2pp. Finished Myers' Wordsworth. Replied to Grahame.

Frid. May 8. Rain all day. Got from liby [Isaac] Disraeli's "Quarrels of Authors". Wrote 4½pp.

Sat. May 9. Fine, warm. In morning wrote 2pp. Afternoon to Brampford Speke. Recd last of the proofs of "Thyrza".

Sund. May. 10. Dull. In morning worked, doing about a page.

Mond. May 11. Brilliant and very hot day; not a cloud. Wrote 2pp., in poor vein.

Tuesd. May 12. Hotter than yesterday. In morning rewrote 2nd page of yesterday. Evening did 2 more.- Letter from Bertz, saying he has sold his translation of my "Phoebe" to "Aus Fremden Zungen" for 50M. Also has found a publisher for his "Glück und Glas". Finished Disraeli's "Quarrels of Authors".

Wed. May 13. Hotter than ever. In afternoon gathered blue-bells. Wrote 3pp.

Thursd. May 14. Very fine, but cool wind. Have a slight sore throat. Did only 2pp., though working 8 hours. Get on very slowly, but I think it is solid.- Reading Ben Jonson's "Sylva".- Letter from [Charles] Anderson, saying that there have been notices of "New Grub Street" in the last two *Saturdays*.[6]

Frid. May 15. Colder, with showers. Slightly sore throat. Did 3pp., but must be re-written.

Sat. May 16. Cold, rainy. Vainly tried to work.

Sund. May 17. Cold, rainy. Wasted day. Edith ill with dyspepsia, or whatever it may be.- Constant sickness and misery.- Recd the two nos. of the *Sat[urday] Review.* And sent them to Bertz.

Mond. May 18. Cold, rainy. Wrote 1p. only. Much misery with E.'s illness.

Tuesd. May 19. Cold, and much rain, but intervals of sunshine. Wrote 3½pp.- Reading bits of De Quincey.

Wed. May 20. Have a troublesome cold. Weather improved, but rainy. Edith better. Wrote 3pp., easily. Letter from Alg, saying he returns from Jersey to-morrow, and will take the cottage in Worcestershire.- Got from lib [Isaac] Disraeli's "Calamities of Authors".- Wrote to A.J. Smith.

Thursd. May 21. Fine morning, rainy afternoon. In morning wrote 1p.; afternoon rewrote it, and added ½ more. Letters from Roberts and Nelly. Replied to former.

Frid. May 22. Rainy. Letter from [A.J.] Smith, saying he is out of employment, and so couldn't come here for Whitsuntide as he had hoped.- Am at a very difficult part of my book, Chap. XII. Wrote 2½pp.

Sat. May 23. Dull. See it announced in *Athenaeum* that a 2nd 3-vol. edition of "New Grub Street" is just published. The first time I have ever achieved this.- Wrote 3pp.

Sund. May 24. Dull, rainy.- Finished "Calamities of Authors".

Mond. May 25. Still cold and uncertain. Letter from Alg, who is at Mrs. Shailer's until he can furnish his cottage at Willersey, whither he goes after all. Letter from Roberts.- Wrote only 1p., and with difficulty.

Tuesd. May 26. Sun and rain, cold. Wrote 3½pp. Letter from Alg.

Wed. May 27. Sun and rain. Wrote 2½pp. Am past the middle of Vol. II.- Letter from Nelly.- Ordered Hardy's "Two on a Tower", which I want to re-read. Did it with a sense of extravagance,—the cost being 1/8. Look at my position, with a novel succeeding as "New Grub Street" has done. I cannot buy books, I cannot subscribe to a library; I can only just afford the necessary food from day to day; and have to toil in fear of finishing my money before another book is ready. This is monstrously unjust. Who of the public would believe that I am still in such poverty?

Thursd. May 28. Wind and rain. For some obscure reason couldn't write a line. Idle all day.

Frid. May 29. Weather improved, but still a little rain. Bought Hardy's "Two on a Tower". Wrote 4pp. Note from Bertz.

Sat. May 30. Fine, cloudy. Wrote 2pp.

Sund. May 31. Very fine and warm, dulling towards night. E. and I went to Teignmouth, thence walked to Dawlish, and home by train in evening. Small satisfaction in these conventional sea-side places.

Mond. June 1. Hot and windy. Did nothing.- Wrote to Nelly and Roberts.

Tuesd. June 2. Very fine. Did 3pp.- Took subscription at the Exeter Literary Society. Good reading room, fair circulating library.

Wed. June 3. Fine morning, dull afternoon. Did 3pp. Got from my new library [G.J.] Romanes' "Animal Intelligence".

Thursd. June 4. Fine, with showers. Wrote only 1p. Trouble in arranging the last chaps. of Vol. II.

Frid. June 5. Very fine. Wrote 3½pp.- Letter from one G.H. Knott (Common Room, Middle Temple) praising "New Grub Street". Replied to him.

Sat. June 6. Dull, rain at night. Rewrote 1½p. of yesterday. In afternoon went to Pinhoe.

Sund. June 7. East wind, but sunny. Finished Romanes' book. Letter from Alg. They are in their cottage at Willersey.

Mond. June 8. Warmer, but dull. Note from Roberts. Wrote 2pp.- Letter from Walter Grahame.

Tuesd. June 9. Fine, warm. Wrote a page and a half.- Got from liby [Alfred Russel] Wallace's "[A Narrative of Travels] On the Amazon [and Rio Negro]" [1853].

Wed.June 10. Fine. Wrote 3½pp. Work is a great struggle just at present. I am sluggish from morning to night. Possibly this Devonshire climate has something to do with it.

Thursd. June 11. Fine, but cloudy. No work.

Frid. June 12. Fine, hot. Morning did nothing, but in evening wrote 3pp. Got from liby Andersen's Autobiography. Find they have a copy of "The Nether World" there.

Sat. June 13. Fine. Wrote about 2pp.

Sund. June 14. Letter from Alg. Has decided to call his book "A Moorland Idyl". Thinks of giving lectures at popular institutions.- Went to Teignmouth, and spent day there, splendid weather.

Mond. June 15. Fine.—Wrote 5pp., finishing Vol. II. But shall have to go back to revise two chapters.

Tuesd. June 16. Very fine. Rewrote 2pp. in Vol. II.- Got from Liby Tolstoi's "Childhood". In evening did nothing but read it.

Wed. June 17. Dull, close. Wrote 1½p. in morning, and 2½ in evening. Letter from Nelly, saying that Madge is still far from well.

Thursd. June 18. Fine. In morning wrote 1p. Evening nothing.

Frid. June 19. Very hot. Quite unable to work. Note from Roberts. Afternoon by train to St Cyres, and walked back. Got from Liby "Anna Karénina". Wrote to Bentley for information about "The Emancipated".

Sat. June 20. Very hot. Did nothing. In evening gathered a lot of foxgloves.

Sund. June 21. Slight breeze, but still very hot. Wrote to Nelly. Heard from Bentley that 492 copies of "The Emancipated" have been sold. Decided to work here for another fortnight, and then finish my book at Ilfracombe.

Mond. June 22. Hotter than ever, though windy. At night, rain. Almost impossible to work up in my garret. Wrote in morning and evening, doing 3pp.

Tuesd. June 23. Clouded, close, No sun.- Wrote 3pp.- Edith bought [Hardy's] "Far from the Madding Crowd".

Wed. June 24. Hot and bright in morning; dull at night, and heavy rain. In morning wrote 1p., and nothing after. Recd from Mrs F. Harrison fine portraits of herself and Frederic—former inscribed to Edith. Wrote to thank her.

Thursd. June 25. Hot and bright. In evening a very thick mist. In morning 1p., in afternoon 2.

Frid. June 26. Fine, windy. Rain in morning.- Wrote 3½pp.- Wrote to Alg.

Sat. June 27. Furious wind, but fine.- Wrote 3pp.- Reading "Far from the Madding Crowd".

Sund. June 28. Fine in morning, rain at night. Day wasted. Decided to go not to Ilfracombe, but Clevedon.

Mond. June 29. Letter from Alg, in good spirits. His settlement at Willersey has been announced in a local paper. Wrote to Mother.- Did 3pp.- Fine but very windy day.

Tuesd. June 30. Dull, windy.- Wrote 3½pp.

Wed. July 1. Windy, rainy.- Wrote 3pp.- Alg's new book announced: "A Moorland Idyl".

Thursd. July 2. Dull, thunder-storm. In morning 1p., afterwards kept from doing anything by slight neuralgia. Wrote to Madge, who is very poorly—I know not in what way.

Frid. July 3. Cloudy, rainy, sunshiny. A hard day's work, in spite of neuralgia. Did 6pp. Read a little "Hippolytus" [by Euripides].

Sat. July 4. Brilliant day. Wrote 4pp.

Sund. July 5. Dull and windy. Packed for departure to-morrow.

Mond. July 6. Bright, but high wind. Travelled to Clevedon, and there found lodgings at Mrs Elston's, Stonington Villas, Old church Road. Cost, 16/6 a week.

Tuesd. July 7. Furious wind, with frequent showers; wretched day. Look at Coleridge's cottage, and the old church.

Wed. July 8. Morning of heavy rain; afternoon brilliant, with less wind. Tried to make a beginning at work, but failed. Have rigged up a desk in the bedroom. Evening walked to Lady Bay.

Thursd. July 9. Fine throughout. Worked from 9 to 1, and from 5 to 8.15, doing nearly 4p. Afternoon walked to Lady Bay.

*Frid. July 10.*Brilliant day. Wrote 3½pp. Reading the Hippolytus.

Sat. July 11. Very fine. Wrote 2½pp. Letter from Roberts.

Sund. July 12. Fine, hot. Walked to Strawberry Hill and Dial Hill.

Mond. July 13. Hot, misty. Wrote 4½pp. Much toil all day long, wanting to be out on the shore.

Tuesd. July 14. Fine, warm. Recd Alg's new novel: "A Moorland Idyl". Letters from Madge and Nelly. Former recovering from her illness, and going to-morrow to visit the Langs at Dunblane.- Wrote 3pp.

Wed. July 15. Fine, warm. Wrote 4pp., morning, afternoon, and evening. Hard work, but the end in sight. Letter from Bertz.

Thursd. July 16. Very hot. Much mist about. Wrote 4pp.

Frid. July 17. Fine but dull. Did 5pp. and <u>finished "Godwin Peak".</u>

Sat. July 18. Fine. Idled about. Wrote to Mother, Madge and Rockett.

Sund. July 19. Windy and dull. Wrote to Bertz and Roberts.

Mond. July 20. Day of dulness and rain. Sent off "Godwin Peak" to S[mith] & E[lder], with a letter asking £250 for English and American copyright.- Got from library Mark Pattison's "[Isaac] Casaubon", a book I was astonished to find on the shelves.

Tuesd. July 21. Dull, and a little rain. In evening along shore to Walton. Letter from Mother, saying she goes for a month to Broadway. One from Roberts.

Wed. July 22. Finished "Casaubon", and got [Henry] Frith's Autobiography. Acknowledgt from S[mith] & E[lder] of receipt of "Godwin Peak". In afternoon went to Cheddar. Frequent blue sky, but high wind and lashing rain from time to time. Surprised by the grandeur of the Cliffs. On way back spent an hour at Axbridge—delightful, sleepy old town.

Thursd. July 23. Dull, windy. In afternoon to see gardens at Clevedon Court. They rise in terraces up the hill behind the house. The topmost an exquisite platform of sward with beds and espaliers on the bounding wall.

Frid. July 24. Mostly dull, but some sun. Left by 8 o'clock excursion train for Minehead, getting there at 11.30. A blackguard assembly for some races. Walked to the Blue Anchor, a lonely spot with two or three houses, and thence by train to Watchet, a rather dirty little seaport. Finding the excursion train would hardly be back at Clevedon before midnight. I returned by a regular train, leaving Watchet at 6.17, changing three times, and getting home at 11 o'clock—a terrific experience.

Sat. July 25. Very fine day. Got from liby Darwin's Voyage in the Beagle. Letter from Harpers, to whom I had written to ask what books of mine they have repubd. Only "Demos" and "Nether World" they tell me. For former they gave £10 to S[mith] & E[lder], for latter £15.[7] Letter from Alg.

Sund. July 26. Very fine and hot. Reading Darwin.

Mond. July 27. Left Clevedon early, and went to Burnham. Got lodgings at a shop in Princess St., kept by one Miss Press; two poor little rooms, only 12/- a week.

*　　　*　　　*

Frid. July 31. Several days of wretched weather. Cold northerly winds, and frequent rain. To-day I went by myself to Glastonbury, which is about 12m. from Burnham. Spent some pleasant hours, as the weather was better. First of all, climbed the Tor. On the top is the high tower of a very old church, nothing of the body of the building left. The entrance is open, but the rear archway built up.- Then to Wirrall Hill, where a high thorn tree is growing on the spot of the miraculous tree. From here an admirable view of Glastonbury. The red-roofed little town stretches along the base of a small wooded ridge, which rises gradually to an abrupt culmination in the Tor. The Abbey hidden amid trees, but the two towers of St Benedict and John the Baptist rise greyly above the tiled roofs. Beyond is the Mendip range, Cheddar Gorge visible.- From the Tor one notices the long white roadways stretching over the levels. Wells clearly seen at the foot of the Mendips.- Much peat-cutting round about; the turfs are piled into heaps which look, in shape and colour, just like the top-halves of gigantic fir-cones.- Saw the Abbott's Barn, and noted three cottages opposite, which may serve me in a story. Very small, only one upper story, and of course no passage. Front gardens full of hollyhocks, very tall sunflowers, lilies, roses etc. Fronts overtrained by a large vine.

Enjoyed the Abbey, which lies peacefully in a park, amid great chestnuts and other trees. Black-faced sheep grazing about.- Remember the George Hotel, the Old Pilgrim's Inn, in High Street.

Sat. Aug. 1. Still gloomy and doubtful weather, with coldish wind.- Letter from Mother, who is gone to Broadway for a month whilst the girls are staying with the Langs in Scotland.

Sund. Aug. 2. Windy and gloomy. Have read [F. Marion] Crawford's "Paul Patoff". I am now going through [Mrs Humphry Ward's] "Robert Elsmere", this book having never yet fallen into my hands.

Mond. Aug. 3. Strong wind, but a day of sunshine. Furious rain last night. Crowds of people here to-day—Bank Holiday.

*   *   *

Thursd. Aug. 6. Weather a very little improved, but could not hold out longer at Burnham, which is deadly dull. Got back to Exeter at mid-day. In our first interview with Mrs Rockett we were informed that, before winter, she will need these rooms of ours. So here is the end of Exeter life! Shall probably go to Bristol, if decent quarters can be found.

Bentley sends the Aug. number of *Temple Bar,* which contains my story "Letty Coe", written, accepted and paid for about six or seven years ago.— Parcel from Harper contains three copies of "Demos" and "Nether World"—the latter a good page. Letter from Bertz.

Frid. Aug. 7. An illegible letter from [James] Payn, in which I understand him to say that the reading of my MS will be suspended for a month by his holiday. He goes on to inform me that S[mith] & E[lder] cannot possibly give £250, seeing that "New Grub Street" was a financial failure!- I replied, saying that if they will give £150 at once, I will take it, but that if even that sum is contingent upon his opinion when he has finished the MS, I must withdraw and go elsewhere.- Postcard from Bertz, telling me that "New Grub Street" is in Tauchnitz.- Wrote to him; also to Alg and Roberts, who has sent me a batch of the proofs of his poems [*Songs of Energy,* Lawrence & Bullen, 1891].- A day of dull misery, due to Payn's damned communication. If only I could really read what the man writes! His handwriting alone is an insult.- Read a few pages of [Henry] Hallam's "[View of the State of Europe during the] Middle Ages" [1818], and went to the reading-room. Weather bright, but windy and depressing.

Sat. Aug. 8. Dull, rainy day. Saw by the advt of *The Author* for August that they are still writing about "New Grub Street".[8]

Sund. Aug. 9. Dull, warm, showery. Letter from Payn; he returns the MS, saying that if I like to send it back in a month's time, he will then finish it, but could not advise Smith to give more than £150. Adds that my "pessimism" is the cause of my failure. Forthwith wrote to A.P. Watt, the literary agent, asking if he would do business for me.- Letter from Alg, and from Roberts the final proofs of his poems.

Mond. Aug. 10. Replied to Payn, and returned Roberts's proofs.- Have an idea for a short book, in which the Rocketts and all their kin will figure.

Tuesd. Aug. 11. Dull and rainy. Wrote to A.P. Watt, saying I think he ought to get £200 for "Godwin Peak". Sent him MS by registd Parcel Post.- My advt for unfurnished rooms appeared in the Bristol paper.- Got the Aug. *Author.*- Got from Free Liby the Life of B[enjamin] R[obert] Haydon [edited by Tom Taylor, 3 vols., 1853].

Wed. Aug. 12. Some answers to my advt.- Letter from Nelly, with account of delightful day at Trossachs etc.- Reading Haydon, otherwise completely idle. Sunshine and rain.

Thursd. Aug. 13. Dull, warm.- Watt acknowledges MS, and says he has sent it to Chatto & Windus, asking £200 for British Copyright.

*   *   *

Sat. Aug. 15. Fine days, but rendered utterly miserable by vile squabbles here in the house. The Rockett people behaving with every kind of vulgar malice. It makes me ill; I pass the time in sick, trembling rage unable either to read or think.- Yet I do think in a way; there has come across me, out of these miseries, an idea for a vol. of short stories, to illustrate the

253

wretchedness of life in lodgings, to be called "At a Week's Notice".-
Yesterday we had a beautiful walk by the lanes to Pinhoe. To-day went
nowhere and did nothing, suffering horridly.

*   *   *

Mond. Aug. 17. Set off by the 10.30 to Bristol, to look at the rooms offered
by people who have replied to my advts in the *Western Daily Press*. Got
there at 12 o'clock, and took a room at the Vegetarian Rest in High Street.
A day of pouring rain, from morning to night. After having looked at the
situation of the Central Free Library (there is a branch in each quarter of
the town) went to the places of which I had heard—Ashley Road and
Ashley Hill. Wretched disappointment; vulgar and dirty people, and
impossible localities. Spent the evening in the reading-room of the North
District Library, King Square. Saw by the Catalogue that they have
"Demos" and "The Nether World".- For supper a basin of bread and milk,
and to bed wet through, weary and miserable.

Tuesd. Aug. 18. Brilliant day. Went by train to Clifton; just looked at
Suspension Bridge, but too tired and wretched to notice much. Went to a
house-agent's in Whiteladies Road, and asked if he had unfurnished
rooms. He offered me some in a big house he was going to occupy himself;
wanted £30 for four rooms. Wouldn't do at all. Gave it up, and loitered
about till the 5.41 express for Exeter. Edith met me, and we talked dolefully
of failure. Decided to take a house in Exeter.

Wed. Aug. 19. Fine, with showers and a little thunder. In morning, set off
to explore Mt Radford, and there found a house which suited
marvellously—No 1 St Leonard's Terrace, Wonford Road. Eight rooms,
good bath, little strip of garden in front; rent, to my astonishment, only
£19.10. Undoubtedly the best house in all Exeter for my needs. Took Edith
at one o'clock to look over it, then in the evening went to talk again with
landlord, Mr. Bryan, living in same terrace. He agreed to let me have the
house from quarter to quarter, and was willing to do a little necessary
papering etc. Place is to be ready for us at beginning of next week. The best
day's work I have done for many a long day! Now for peace and comfort.

Thursd. Aug. 20. Unable, of course, to do anything. Fine day.

Frid. Aug. 21. Showery. Got from liby [T.H.] Huxley's "Science and
Culture".- Recd from mother £30.- In evening went to St Leonard's, and
signed lease with Bryan. Wrote to mother.

Sat. Aug. 22. Showery. Busy about purchases and arrangements for
removal.

*   *   *

254

Sat. Aug. 29. A week of horrors. Weather wretched, ceaseless rain. On Tuesday got the moving over; left 24 Prospect Park with profound thanksgiving. Not a word to the people of the house, who had proved intolerable. On Wed. morning came letter from Watt, saying that Chatto & Windus will only give £120 for the British rights; he has passed the MS on to Longman.- Letters from Walter Grahame and Roberts; wrote to Bertz.- To-day am feeling comfortable in my study; the best I have ever had for convenience, internal and external. Have had to spend nearly ten pounds in furnishing. We have a servant, one Nelly Edwards, at £9 a year; thus far she promises well.- The neighbourhood purely delightful. Gathered some marigolds from our garden.

Sund. Aug. 30. Fine day, dull at even. Wrote to Roberts and to Alg. Read 100pp. of Macaulay's History. Thought over possibilities for short stories. Letter from Bertz, with Advt of his "Glück und Glas".

Mond. Aug. 31. Rain and wind. Sat down to a short story: "A Conspiracy of Kindness".

Tuesd. Sept. 1. A day of howling wind and frequent rain. Worked 2 hours in morning and evening. Wrote about a page of my story.

Wed. Sept. 2. Vile weather still. Gale and rain. Crops all going to ruin. Worked morning and evening, but did very little. Paid Parish Rates—4/2 being the proportion due of present half year; whole rate for half year 25/-.

Thursd. Sept. 3. A fine day; no rain. Worked at my short story, but had no real heart for it. To inspire me, I need a large canvas. In evening began to think of a serious book.

Frid. Sept. 4. Fine, warm. Worked at the plan of my new novel, which promises. Shall open it at Clevedon. Trying to hit on a name. In afternoon walked to Ide, and back home by Countess Weir. Reading Macaulay.

Sat. Sept. 5. Dull. Planning first chapter of book.

Sund. Sept. 6. No sunshine, but no rain. High wind. Read at Macaulay and a couple of sermons by Jeremy Taylor.

Mond. Sept. 7. Dull, drizzly. Letter from Nelly, who is at Bridlington with the Carters, and one from Bertz, enclosing his likeness. Poor old fellow! Worked away at plan of book; getting it clear.

Tuesd. Sept. 8. Fine and warm. Working still in same way, and reading Macaulay.- Letter from Grahame.

Wed. Sept. 9. Magnificent, cloudless day. In afternoon had long walk by myself up Old Tiv[erton] Road, and back by Pinhoe. Pocketful of blackberries.- Thinking.

Thursd. Sept. 10. Cloudless again. Long walk by myself in afternoon.

Frid. Sept. 11. Just the same weather as yesterday. Finished Macaulay up to close of Revolution, and don't care for the politics that follow.- Read Park I of "Hudibras" and some Martial. Edith out blackberrying.

Sat. Sept. 12. The fourth, if not the fifth, quite cloudless day. Very hot. Recd through Williams and Norgate the six Tauchnitz copies of "New Grub Street".—Read some "Hudibras" and Book XI of Martial.

Sund. Sept. 13. Fine on the whole; but clouded, and a shower or two. Didn't go out; long day of reading. Read some more "Hudibras", and some Rabelais. In evening, "The Flight of the Duchess" [by Robert Browning].

Mond. Sept. 14. Dull, rainy, windy. Read Gibbon on monasticism.- Jotted down several ideas for book.

Tuesd. Sept 15. Dull, some rain.- Read part of Ibsen's "Die Wildente" [The Wild Duck].

Wed. Sept. 16. Dull. In afternoon a long walk. Finished "Die Wildente". Letter from A.J. Smith, to whom I posted a Tauchnitz copy of "New Grub Street".- All these days racking my brain to find a title for my new book.

Thursd. Sept. 17. Dull, rain. Thinking and reading idly.

Frid. Sept. 18. Dull, rain. Recd. from Bertz his "Glück und Glas", and began to read it. Bought Carlyle's ["Oliver] Cromwell['s Letters and Speeches", 1845], which I have never yet read.

Sat. Sept. 19. Rain all day. Read at "Glück u. Glas" and Cromwell.- Letter from Nelly, in which she mentions that her music lessons now bring her more than £60 a year. Good news this.

Sund. Sept. 20. Dull and rainy. Finished Bertz's book, and read on at Cromwell.- Wrote to Alg and Roberts.

Mond. Sept. 21. A day of wild rain and wind, cold. Letter from Roberts, from Shoreham. Wrote to Bertz about his book.- Cromwell.

Tuesd. Sept. 22. Fine day, warmer. Reading at Cromwell, and little else. Getting very impatient to hear from Watt. In afternoon gathered a lot of blackberries about Wonford.

Wed. Sept. 23. Dull morning, fine afternoon. Reading Cromwell. Sent Tauchnitz "N[ew] G[rub] S[treet]" to Nelly and copy for Mr. Hick.

Thursd. Sept. 24. Dull morning, fine later. Cromwell. Letter from Alg.

Frid. Sept. 25. Dull, close. Got from liby Guizot's English Revolution and from Pub. Lib. the life of F[rederick] W[illiam] Robertson [the Brighton preacher, 1816-1853].

Sat. Sept. 26. Clouded. Read Robertson's life.- Letter from Lawrence & Bullen, the new publishers, saying that Roberts had told them that I am engaged on a 1-vol. story, and offering to publish it for me at 6/-, giving me 1/- on each copy; also willing to pay £100 on account.- Note from Roberts, who is near Corfe Castle.- The *Illustd London News* of to-day, in an article called "London in Fiction", has this passage: "In such a book no inconsiderable part would be played by the Temple, which has been the happy hunting ground of so many of our novelists, from Sir Walter Scott to Mr. George Gissing".- The mention is good, but I have never made use of the Temple.

Sund. Sept. 27. Guizot, and thought of new story. Cannot use that at which I have been working.- Fine day.

Mond. Sept. 28. Beautiful day. In afternoon walked round by Sowton. Thinking.

Tuesd. Sept. 29. Fine morning, dull afternoon. Note of acknowledgment from Lawrence & Bullen. Got first number of *The Bookman*—interesting. "A Moorland Idyl" mentioned among books much inquired for at library. Postcard from Bertz.- Recd from Williams and Norgate seven numbers of the Universal Bibliothek. Read Ibsen's "Nora", and began Jonas Lee's "Lebenslänglich verurtheilt" [*Life Sentence*].- Got names for my new story—to be called "The Radical Candidate".

Wed. Sept. 30. Bright day. Finished Jonas Lee's story. Quite unable to get to my new book until I have heard from Watt.

Thursd. Oct. 1. Rainy. Read Ibsen's "Die Frau vom Meer" [*The Lady from the Sea*]. Wrote to Walter Grahame.

Frid. Oct. 2. Fine, but cold. In morning took a long walk. Read at Guizot.

Sat. Oct. 3. Dull and cold. Got from libs [Henry] James's "The American" and [Edward Dowden's] Southey in Engl. Men of Letters.

Sund. Oct. 4. Wrote to Watt, asking news of "Godwin Peak". Read "The American" and the Southey.

Mond. Oct. 5. Fine. Long walk with Edith in afternoon. Dr. Henderson called for first time.

Tuesd. Oct. 6. Reply from Watt. Longman won't make an offer; MS sent on to Bentley. Wrote answer, saying I couldn't wait after October, but on second thoughts decided not to send it, as I still possess £27.- From Willersey came a basket of fine pears, addressed to Edith.- Last night a furious gale, with heavy rain, and rain all to-day. In evening got the first page of new novel written.

Wed. Oct. 7. Much rain.- What I wrote yesterday will have to serve for a later chapter. Made a new beginning to-day, and wrote 3pp.- Reading Ouida's "A Village Commune".

Thursd. Oct. 8. Fine morning; afternoon and evening much rain. Wrote from 9 to 1, and from 5.30 to 8.15, doing 4pp. Postcard from Roberts and letter from Alg. Wrote to Roberts.

Frid. Oct. 9. Fine day. Recd Roberts's "Songs of Energy". Wrote 4pp. Suffering from a sort of neuralgia.- Wrote to Editor of P[all] M[all] G[azette], asking if he would let me review Roberts's book.

Sat. Oct. 10. Dark all day, much rain. Neuralgia worse. Only got up at 11, and did nothing.

Sund. Oct. 11. Day of furious wind and rain. Got up at dinner-time, suffering much. Edith has discovered that our servant's hair swarms with lice; the devil to pay. Reading Ibsen's "Ein Volksfeind" [*An Enemy of the People*]. Letter from Roberts.

Mond. Oct. 12. Bright day. My tooth all right again. Wrote 4pp. Letter from Bertz. He sends a copy of Germ. periodical, *Aus Fremden Zungen,* with his translation of my "Phoebe". Also the 1st no. of *The Tauchnitz Magazine*, which has a very laudatory notice of "New Grub Street".

Tuesd. Oct. 13. Furious storm.- Worked long hours, doing 3½pp.

Wed. Oct. 14. Tremendous gale all night, and most of to-day. Then changed to fine. Wrote 5pp.- Letter from Grahame.- Got from liby "Neaera [: a Tale of Ancient Rome", by John William Graham, 1886].- Paid rates till next Lady day—£1-1-10½.

Thursd. Oct. 15. Again gale in the night. Wretched morning, wind furious. Bright afternoon. Wrote 4½pp.

Frid. Oct. 16. In the night again a furious storm. We thought at times the windows would be burst in. To-day gusty and rainy, but fine at night with brilliant moon. Wrote 4pp.

Sat. Oct. 17. Tolerably fair. Did 4pp. Wonderful moon this evening. Finished "Neaera"; poor rubbish. The *Saturday* of to-day reviews "Thyrza" as a new production, and blames my rose-water optimism.[9]

Sund. Oct. 18. Glorious morning, but dull the rest of day. Wrote to Mother, Grahame, Bertz and Roberts. Began a regular reading of [Robert Burton's] "Anatomy of Melancholy".- Thinking about a Greek story I shall some day write.

Mond. Oct. 19. Much rain. Storm again last night. Wrote only 3pp., as I broke off at 7 to take Edith to a concert at Barnfield Hall.

Tuesd. Oct. 20. Rain all day. When will it cease?- Worked well, doing 3pp. in morning, and 2 in evening. Am writing with extraordinary ease just now. Scarcely remember a like period. Means vastly improved health, I suppose.- Read a few pages of Burton.

Wed. Oct. 21. Rain nearly all day. Wrote 4pp.- Letter from Mr [Matthew Bussey] Hick [of Wakefield], with present of grapes. Replied.

Thursd. Oct. 22. Heavy rain all day long. Letters from Mother and Nelly. Postcard from Roberts.- Wrote 4pp.

Frid. Oct. 23. A fine day, with only one little shower. Got from liby [Christopher] Wordsworth's "Greece [Pictorial, Descriptive and Historical]".- Read part of Plutarch's Lysander.- Wrote 4pp.

Sat. Oct. 24. Fine day, coldish. Did 5pp.

Sund. Oct. 25. Gloom, cold and at last rain. Spent whole day in study, busy with Greek antiquities.- At last a note from the *P[all] M[all] G[azette]*, saying they have received no copy of Roberts's book, and can only notice such as they do receive.

Mond. Oct. 26. Gloom, and in evening heavy rain. Wrote 4pp.

Tuesd. Oct. 27. Third day without gleam of sunshine. In morning wrote 1p., but no more. Suffering from rheumat. in shoulders.- Read Aristophanes.

Wed. Oct. 28. Dull morning, rest of day very fine. Wrote 5pp. Letter from Bertz.- Aristophanes.

Thursd. Oct. 29. Beautiful day, coldish. Did 5pp.- Copy from S[mith] & E[lder] of 6/- "New Grub Street".- Note from Nelly. In the Nov. *Bookman* is a paragraph: "Mr George Gissing will very soon have a new novel ready. He has chosen his subject from the political world."- I suppose the information has come from Lawrence & Bullen.

Frid. Oct. 30. Fine day, with east wind. Wrote 5pp.

Sat. Oct. 31. Fine, Bitterly cold. Did 4pp.- Read a little "[Anatomy of] Melancholy".

Sund. Nov. 1. Fine, Walk for two hours in morning. The rest of the day worked at Greek antiquities.

Mond. Nov. 2. Fine again. Recd from Bertz Ibsen's "Hedda Gabler" and "Frau Inger". Began to read former. Wrote 3pp., then went back and rewrote 2, adding 1 more to them.

Tuesd. Nov. 3. Very fine, and warmer. Finished "Hedda", and began the other play. Wrote 4½pp.

Wed. Nov. 4. No sun; trying to rain. Wrote 4½pp. This morning wholly altered my plan for the upshot of the story. Hitherto I have meant Glazzard's plot to be carried out in its entirety. But what I have decided now is more probable, and less obvious.- Wrote to Alg and Roberts.

Thursd. Nov. 5. Not much sun. Banging of fireworks. Did 5pp., but shall have to rewrite the last two.

Frid. Nov. 6. No sun, cold. In morning came a note from A.H. Bullen, saying he would be in Exeter this evening, and inviting me to dine with him at the Clarence, Cathedral Close. Also letters from Roberts and from Alg, the latter much depressed. Wrote 3pp., and dined with Bullen, a much younger man than I expected, and rather less intellectual. How consistently I am disappointed when I meet men of whom I have heard! He is going round the country introducing self, as a new publisher, to the booksellers. Talked very hopefully of my work. Wants to print "The Radical Candidate" in America, if possible. Am to send him the MS at the end of next week. Home by 11.30.

Sat. Nov. 7. Sunless day. Letter from Nelly. Wrote to her and to Alg, urging latter to try to change his abode for a house near here.- Wrote 7pp., a tremendous day. Rapid and I think good.

Sund. Nov. 8. Sunless and cold. In morning rewrote 2pp. of Chap. II. Afternoon and evening Greek antiquities.

Mond. Nov. 9. Dull, with rain at night. Did nearly 7pp.- Letter from Bertz.

Tuesd. Nov. 10. Fine morning, then wind and rain. Did 5½pp. Smooth now to the end.

Wed. Nov. 11. In the morning a most violent storm. Afraid of the windows crashing in; could not work. Finally did 4pp.- Letter from Alg, who tells me that he has taken his Willersey cottage for 5 years.

Thursd. Nov. 12. Still wind and rain; storming at night. Did 4½pp., and finished "The Radical Candidate". Wrote to Roberts. Letter from Walt. Grahame.

Frid Nov. 13. Fine morning, then rain. Revising story.- Read some of the "Protagoras" [by Plato].

Sat. Nov. 14. Heavy rain. Reading Anakreon all day.- Sent "The Rad. Candidate" by registd parcel post to Bullen c/o Ja. Steuart, Dalkeith Park, Dalkeith, N. 13.-

Sund. Nov. 15. Morning pleasant; later, rain. Finished reading of Anakreon.

Mond. Nov. 16. Fine day once more. Wrote couple of pages of short story called "A Casual Acquaintance." Don't know whether I shall succeed in finishing it.

Tuesd. Nov. 17. Dull. Letter from A.J. Smith. In morning rewrote the work of yesterday. Afternoon, 2 more pp.

Wed. Nov. 18. Dull. Wrote 4pp.

Thursd. Nov. 19. Very beautiful warm day. In morning finished "Casual Acquaintance", and sent it to *Macmillan's Mag.* Recd from Roberts copies of his book "Land Travel and Sea-faring" and [of his brother] Cecil's "Adrift in America" [both published by Lawrence & Bullen].- In afternoon elaborated a story I have had in mind—"A Victim of Circumstances", and in evening began it.

Frid. Nov. 20. Again a fine day. Worked through morning without a fire, as yesterday.- Letter from Nelly.- Wrote 4pp. of story.- Forgot to note that last night came letter from Bullen, asking for a change of title for "The Rad[ical] Cand[idate]", because booksellers have assured him that women will be frightened. Confounded nuisance.- Reading "Adrift in America".- Took in a little stray cat.-

Sat. Nov. 21. Again fine day, with a few light showers. Reading [George Sand's] "Elle et Lui" once more.- Wrote 4pp.

Sund. Nov. 22. My birthday; thirty-four.- Beautiful morning, dull and cold after. Finished "Elle et Lui", and read 300 ll. of 18th Iliad.- No letters.

Mond. Nov. 23. Frost in the night; day dull and cold, ending in a thick fog. Wrote 3½pp.

Tuesd. Nov. 24. Hard frost all day, and at night again a thick fog.- Wrote only about 2pp.- Little cat reclaimed by people in the neighbourhood.- Wrote to Alg.- Telegram from Bullen, asking me to send copies of the American "Demos" and "Nether World". Did so.

Wed. Nov. 25. Thaw; miserable day. Finished story and sent it to Blackwood's—though I don't for a moment suppose it will be accepted.- Letter from Bullen, promising hundred guineas in a few days. But he adds that the story doesn't seem to him very strong. It will be called "Denzil Quarrier".

Thursd. Nov. 26. Rainy.- Frightful letter from Alg, saying that a week ago, when he had but two days more work at his novel, Katie fell ill and their servant went into hysterical mania! He is only just striving to finish the book.- Wrote to him and to Katie.—Bought a dinner and a tea service; 25/8 altogether. Hitherto we have made shift with kitchen utensils.- Read in [Balzac's] "Illusions perdues".

Frid. Nov. 27. Fine day.- Recd from Lawrence & Bullen cheque for £105, and agreement, which I signed and returned. Wrote to Exeter branch of Nat[ional] Prov[incial] Bank of England, asking if I can open account with this deposit.- Towards evening bad headache; went to bed at 8 o'clock.

Sat. Nov. 28. Ceaseless rain.- Bought Hardy's "A Laodicean". Wasted the day.

Sund. Nov. 29. Mist and at night thick fog. Read "Laodicean"—nothing else.

Mond. Nov. 30. Thick fog in morning, which cleared off; rest of day sunny. Deposited my £105 in the Natl Provl Bank of England—the first banking account I have ever had. Wrote to A.J. Smith, at Sheffield. Began the planning out of a new novel.

Tuesd. Dec. 1. Rain all day.- Recd from Mother £12.10, the last of my money in her hands. Bought odds and ends of furniture for the house.- Suddenly deserted by our servant, on plea of her mother's illness; we suspect her of fearing the extra work during Edith's confinement. Lest we should be alone all night, I rushed off to the nurse, Mrs Phillips, and got her to come and sleep here.- Of course a wasted day. Sent Alg £5 to aid in his calamities.

Wed. Dec. 2. Very beautiful, warm day. In the morning went to several registry offices, servant-hunting. From one of them got a good idea for the opening of a novel. Day otherwise wasted.

Thursd. Dec. 3. Duller in morning, but still warm and a good deal of sunshine. Servant-hunting. Ordered at Eland's two books—Daudet's "Sapho" and Dostoieffsky's "The Friend of the Family". Letters from Alg and Roberts. Wasted day.

Frid. Dec. 4. Beautiful day. Did nothing, and in misery about servants.

Sat. Dec. 5. Fine, warm. To another Registry Office, and thence to call at mean houses. Vain search. Wrote to three servants. Worn out.- Batch of proofs from L[awrence] & B[ullen].

Sund. Dec. 6. Fine, but duller. More proofs; corrected them. Nelly [the servant] came with unsatisfactory stories; promised to send girl to-morrow for a week or two.- Reading "Sapho"; otherwise, day wasted.

Mond. Dec. 7. Furious N.W. wind all day, with rain. Young girl came, heaven be thanked, and we received letter from another servant at Torrington to whom we had written. Wasted day.

Tuesd. Dec. 8. Dull, rain. Day utterly lost.- Read Dostoieffsky's "The Friend of the Family".—Letter from Alg.

Wed. Dec. 9. Rain and wind. E. beginning her troubles, we sent at 10 o'clock in the morning for Mrs Phillips, who after sleeping here, had gone away again. Vain endeavours to have a fire in the bedroom; the chimney smokes vilely—of course the only one in the house that does. Had to put it out at last. At 8 in the evening came Dr Henderson, and stayed for an hour. Fire in my study keeps going out, and each time takes me a quarter of an hour to relight. Our substitute servant—little girl of 14—comes back from a visit to her home in the evening weeping: her sister's "young man" has been killed to-day on railway. An accumulation of miseries.- Wrote engaging as servant one T. Easterbrook, of Torrington, asked her to come next Monday.- Expense for Bass's ale, and so on. A day of misery, unable to read or think.

Thursd. Dec. 10. 4.15am. Have been up all night. A furious gale blowing. E. in long miserable pain; the Doctor has just given her chloroform, and says that the blackguard business draws to an end.
    5.15. Went to the study door, and heard the cry of the child. Nurse, speedily coming down, tells me it is a boy. Wind howling savagely. So, the poor girl's misery is over, and she has what she earnestly desired.
    Sent notes to E.'s people in London, and one to Mother. Got through day without going to bed. Corrected some proofs. The wind, after lulling at mid-day, grew furious again towards night.
    The baby has a very ugly dark patch over right eye. Don't know the meaning of it.

Frid. Dec. 11. Wind still high until evening, then calm and fine. Doing nothing but correct proofs—though I try now and then to think of a new novel. Wrote to Alg. Then to A.P. Watt, telling him I am bound to sell "Godwin Peak" before end of year. In fact I wish it had never got into his hands.- All goes well in house. Mrs Phillips an excellent nurse, and our substitute servant does very well.

Sat. Dec. 12. Rain and stormy wind. Letters from Mother, Madge and Nell. Recd back from *Macmillan's Mag.* my story "A Casual

Acquaintance"—as I expected. "Fear I cannot make room for this", writes the editor [Mowbray Morris], "but I hope you will give me another chance some time." I am not likely to.- Racking my head to find subject for another long book.

Sund. Dec. 13. N.W. gale continued all night, and again all to-day. The perpetual roaring drives me crazy. No fire possible in the bedroom.- This morning reply from Watt, saying that the MS is now in Bentley's hands. Letter from Alg, who has given up idea of going to Jersey, and will go to Wakefield instead.- Wrote to Roberts. A day of absolute do-nothing; unspeakably weary.

Mond. Dec. 14. Gale all night; ceased by mid-day, then came steady downpour. Did nothing, except go and spend 18/- on a chest of drawers for the new servant, who came before dinner. E. suffering much in her breasts, and baby consequently fretful.

Tuesd. Dec. 15. Dull and rather windy.- Proofs.- Did nothing.- Note to Mother.

Wed. Dec. 16. Beautiful and mild day. E. and nurse on bad terms; had to take latter aside and talk for a quarter of an hour in the conciliatory vein. She feels herself too important, and of course we are greatly at her mercy. This situation suggested to me a book to be called "Jack in Office".- Letter from L[awrence] & B[ullen] saying: that Macmillan will pub[lish] American edition of "Denzil Quarrier", and allow them 10% on pubn price; that in Australia Messrs. Petherick will buy of them 1500 copies in sheets, paying 11¼d a copy; and that they hope to come to terms with Heinemann & Balestier for the Continent. I am to have half in each case.- Replied to them.- Got from lib. Quatrefages' "The Human Species"[10], and tried to read at it. But too tremulous and troubled, after scene with nurse.- Saw roses blooming to-day in a sheltered garden.

Thursd. Dec. 17. Beautiful morning, dull afternoon. Wrote to Bertz. Note from Alg. Proofs. Feeling severely the oppression of this lonely provincial life. Constant crying of the infant very hard to bear.

Frid. Dec. 18. Dull and colder. Read Quatrefages. Letter from Mother. Bought a sofa for E.—23/6.

Sat. Dec. 19. A brilliant day, but cold. Proofs to end of volume. Thinking over the "Jack in the Office" book—though that name won't do.- Wrote to Alg, asking him how to fill up cheques payable to self.

Sund. Dec. 20. Fine, frost.- Returned last proofs.

Mond. Dec. 21. Hard frost in night.—Had to draw £10 from bank. Note from Dr. Henderson, saying E. can go on alone now, and saying his fee is £3.3. Sent him a cheque.—Note from Alg saying Mother has slight bronchitis.

Tuesd. Dec. 22. It is remarkable that if I omit to chronicle a day, on the day after I can scarcely recall an item of it—so wearily and unprofitably do I spend my time. Hard frost—overflowing of a cistern—troublesome baby—general misery. Wrote to Mother.

Wed. Dec. 23. Bright weather again, but everything frozen. Reading from liby [E.B.] Tylor's "Anthropology", but with scant attention.- Trying to think out new story.- Bought Christmas cake and so on for the nurse and servant downstairs; E. and I shall have nothing of the kind.

Thursd. Dec. 24. Still hard frost. Much general discomfort; quarrelling with nurse etc. Of course nothing done. To my suprise, recd from Lawrence & Bullen, as a present, their 3-vol. edn of Herrick.

Frid. Dec. 25. Mist all day, and at night dense fog. Perhaps the most uncomfortable Christmas I have ever known. E. downstairs, but not able to walk. Much quarrelling with nurse, who is vulgar, meddlesome, and conceited. Wrote to L[awrence] & B[ullen] to thank them for Herrick; with difficulty composed even this short letter. Heard from Bertz. Yesterday and to-day made a poor pretence of reading "Measure for Measure".

Sat. Dec. 26. Rain all day. Read "The Faithful Shepherdess" [by John Fletcher, c.1610]. E. better. Paid my quarter's rent.

Sund. Dec. 27. A magnificent day, but rain at night. E. up all day, but towards night feeling ill. Baby quiet, seldom troublesome. Nurse ill-tempered. Read "The Knight of the Burning Pestle" [by Beaumont and Fletcher].

Mond. Dec. 28. Dull weather, mild. A day of misery; E. violently bilious, and unable either to be up or down. Idled miserably. Bought Whittaker.

Tuesd. Dec. 29. Windy, dull, warm. Letter from A.P. Watt, who at last has sold "Godwin Peak". A. & C. Black, of all people in the world, will give £150 for British rights, paying £75 now and rest on publication, which is not to be till next October. Replied to him. Wrote to Alg and Roberts.- E. still ill; house intolerable. Poor infant relegated to the kitchen, where he has to be hand-fed. I seldom hear his poor little voice. To-day went and registered his birth, giving his name as Walter Leonard.

Wed. Dec. 30. Windy, mild. Horrible day with E., who seems to have got the influenza. Henderson came. She in brutal temper, reviling everyone and everything. A day of misery, once more, and bitter repentance. Did nothing.

Thursd. Dec. 31. Bad day again with E., though she seems better.- Re-read Heine's "Die Götter im Exil" [*The Gods in Exile*].

1892

Frid. Jan. 1. Bright, but cold wind. E[dith] much better in mind and body.- Spent day at reading room over the new magazines. Making notes for new novel—perhaps "The Laughing Doctor".- Futile attempt in evening to read some Homer.

Sat. Jan. 2. Cold and bright. Day utterly wasted. E. still better, but has to keep in bed. Bought blind and carpet for back room upstairs, that she may go there when able to leave bedroom.- I see that in the literary review of 1891 in the *Athenaeum* to-day, no mention whatever is made of my name.- Spending a fearful lot of money in house expenses; £8 gone in less than a fortnight.

Sund. Jan. 3. Dull day.- E. out of bed in evening.- Did nothing, and had to nurse the yelling baby from time to time. Each night finds me wearied out with anxieties and sheer physical fatigue.

Mond. Jan. 4. Frost. E. in bed all day. Child so troublesome that we think of trying to send him out to nurse. Driven all but to desperation. To add to comforts, nurse told me as I was going to bed that our servant (whose name by the bye is Thyrza) had every symptom of influenza, and probably wouldn't be able to get up to-morrow.

Tuesd. Jan. 5. Rainy. E. better. Did nothing. Thyrza happily well again.

Wed. Jan. 6. Cold, dry. Recd from Watt a cheque for £67.10—the £75 due from A.C. Black with half his 10% commission deducted. Banked it.- Heard from Ottmann of Leipzig, who says the German "Demos" will soon be out, and asks me for my portrait for his catalogue. Sent it.- Reading Anstey's "The Giant's Robe"; very poor stuff.

Thursd. Jan. 7. Snow in morning; mild and beautiful afternoon. Did nothing. E. still unable to stand up. Letter from Nellie, who is spending a day or two with Alg at Ingleton.- Day after day worse than wasted.

Frid. Jan. 8. Snow and frost. Misery. Got from liby "Joseph's [Little] Coat" [by the author of *A Fellow of Trinity*]. Have heard of the book as good; of course find it very poor.- E. better.- Wrote to A. & C. Black, saying I must revise "Godwin Peak".

Sat. Jan. 9. Snow and frost.- Got in a ton of coals.- Paid bill at Eland's, the bookseller's.- From Roberts recd his "King Billy of Ballarat".-

Sund. Jan. 10. Snow and frost. Misery.

Mond. Jan. 11. Snow and frost. Wrote to Madge and Nell. Nurse at last left us, and little Margaret came back to help with child. Paid nurse £6-13-3, and gave half sov[ereign] gratuity for her extra trouble. Got "The Wages of Sin" [by Lucas Malet] from liby.

Tuesd. Jan. 12. Snow and frost. Last night terrible with the child; little sleep; constantly up mixing milk for bottle. This morning E. broken down again. Rushed to two newspaper offices, and inserted advts for someone to take child and keep him for a while. Wrote to nurse, asking if *she* could have him. In vain tried to read page or two. Dreadful worry and bodily ache.- Recd MS of "Godwin Peak" from A. & C. Black. Sent *Bookman* to Alg.- Wrote to Vicars of Brampford Speke and Stoke Canon, asking if they can recommend anyone to take the child.

Wed. Jan. 13. Frost still. Revd T. Blundun of Brampford sent over a Mrs Phillips, whom he recommends for the child in kind gentlemanly letter. Could not decide at once, as we had asked *our* Mrs Phillips if she could have the boy. Reply from her in negative came whilst other person was in the house, but we did not know it till too late. So I wrote off to Brampford (to Mrs. P. and the Revd) saying I should come over to-morrow morning. Payment asked only 6/- a week.

Thursd. Jan. 14. Slight fall of snow early, then a quick thaw with rain. By the 8.25 went to Brampford, and found Mrs Phillips at little farm-house called Mount Pleasant. Beautiful place, full of queer, ugly pictures and china of every description. Brought Mrs P[hillips] back by the 10.53, and immediately prepared child for removal by the 12.55. Cab kept to the last minute, because nurse-girl Margaret, who had been despatched to buy cap and veil was not returned. Drove off without these needments, but passed Marg. at short distance, pulled up, and finished Gubbins's equipment.

Frid. Jan. 15. Frost again. Finished "Wages of Sin"—a *wooden* book, without a living character or touching scene. The dialogue preposterous. So much for popular success.- Did nothing.

Sat. Jan. 16. Thaw, rain and wind. In afternoon went over to Brampford, and saw baby, who seems to be doing well on diet of pure milk straight from cow. Back from Stoke Canon Station—wet through.- Read nothing.

Sund. Jan. 17. Ceaseless rain. Day of utter idleness. Tried to read a little Horace, but in vain. Yesterday sent the doctor a cheque for £1-1, payment of a/c just received. He evidently cannot trust me for more than a fortnight.

Mond. Jan. 18. Dull, warmer. E. spent day downstairs once more.- Revised first 2 Chaps. of "Godwin Peak". Altered name Vinnicombe to Warricombe, and Peak to Peek. Trying to find another title for the book.

267

Tuesd. Jan. 19. No Sun. Still warmer. On with revising.

Wed. Jan. 20. No sun. Got from liby "The Gaverocks" [by Sabine Baring-Gould].- Our servant Thyrza, who has done precisely nothing since she came, gave notice, and will depart to-morrow. Little Margaret remains.- All shops closed to-day for funeral of P[rince] of Wales's son; tom-foolery.- Bad headache.

Thursd. Jan. 21. Weather dull. E. out for first time.

Frid. Jan. 22. Dull, windy. Letter from Bullen, hoping to have my next novel, and asking if they could get hold of my former work for cheap republication. Replied, mentioning "The Emancipated". They have sold Continental rights of "Denzil Quarrier" to Heinemann & Balestier for 25 gu[ine]as; half falls to me.- Think of calling "Godwin Peek"—"Born in Exile".- Wrote to Alg, and replied to Bullen.

Sat. Jan. 23. Dull, but a little sun in afternoon. Finished revision of MS., but find I must rewrite a good deal of it; the end especially is very feeble. Got a few ideas for improvement.

Sund. Jan. 24. Sunny. Out with E. in afternoon. Worked at "Born in Exile" morning and evening; rewriting several pages in vol. I.

Mond Jan. 25. Fine; cold wind. Worked morning and evening at revision. Letter from Alg, saying he will probably go by himself to Wooler, to work.

Tuesd. Jan. 26. East wind, sunny afternoon. E. went to Brampford and saw little Gubbins, who is getting very fat. Worked at novel.

Wed. Jan. 27. Sunny morning, rainy and windy afternoon. Finished revisal of vol. II.

Thursd. Jan. 28. Windy, rainy. E.'s birthday; gave her [J.G.] Wood's "Pop[ular] Nat[ural] History". Worked at vol. III—the very difficult love scene bet. Peek and Sidwell. Shall have to write it yet again to-morrow.

· *Frid. Jan. 29.* Windy, warm. Got on with vol. III. No reading nowadays.

Sat. Jan. 30. Windy, dull. Finished at last with the love chapters—always very difficult to me.

Sund. Jan. 31. Dull, close.- Did nothing, and thought of taking a holiday at Penzance when the book is out of hand.

Mond. Feb. 1. High wind, sunny. Letter from Nelly, saying that Alg went to Wooler last Monday.- Wrote 6pp.

Tuesd. Feb. 2. Gale and rain, with some sun.- Wrote 6pp.- Letter from one H. Vanwyke of Hampstead, asking me to let him send novelette for criticism.[1] Replied that he had better try the editors.- Wrote to Nelly.- First advt of "Denzil Quarrier", in *Daily News*. To be pubd on Feb. 5th.

Thursd. Feb. 4. Windy, rainy, warmer.- Wrote 4pp.- In afternoon to Brampford, and saw little Gubsey, who grows and thrives.

Frid. Feb. 5. Sunny, but cold wind. At last finished with "Born in Exile", so shall probably go to Penzance on Monday.

Sat. Feb. 6. Rain all day. Sent off "Born in Exile" to A. & C. Black.- Sent to Brampford a vaccination shield for Gubsey, and 24/- for the first 4 weeks of his nursing, due next Thursday.- Eland has got me a 2nd hand copy of Dostoieffsky's "Injury and Insult"—book out of print.- Got from liby Hardy's "Woodlanders".- Letter from Roberts, great gloom. Postcard to Mother.

Sund. Feb. 7. High wind.- Reading "The Woodlanders", and packing for to-morrow.

Mond. Feb. 8. High-wind, and occasional slight rain. Left by the 8.40 train, and got to Penzance at 2.45. Found lodgings at Miss Bolitho's, 7 Regent Terrace. No sea-view, but comfortable; 15/- a week. Magnificent night; a double halo round the moon.

Tuesd. Feb. 9. A magnificent day, hot as summer. In morning walked to Newlyn—couple of hours there and back at slow pace. A dirty, picturesque place, piled on the cliffs. Large village. Much washing hanging about. Nets drying everywhere. Old women carrying baskets by a band across their foreheads. Steep narrow alleys. Houses all of grey granite. Fine views across to Michael's Mount.- Afternoon along towards Marazion, turning off across cabbage fields to village of Gulval.- Letter from A. & C. Black, thanking for trouble I have taken, and saying they like the new title.- Both of us have slight cold.- Wrote to J. King Lewis, surgeon of Thorverton, asking him to vaccinate little Gubsey.

Wed. Feb. 10. Unbroken drizzle all day, and no sun. Walked about in a dreary way; and killed the time.- Yesterday all the crocuses in the garden were out; to-day they have kept shut up.

Thursd. Feb. 11. A grey day, with slight E. wind; sky formless and unchanging. We walked to St Just,- seven miles, through treeless country; fields tending to moorland. Beyond the top of the ridge where the descent to St Just begins, several mines. The tall grey chimney and shattered building by it which always indicates a mine. St Just stands on high ground; straggling grey little town grouped about the old church, with its three parallel roofs and square tower. Had dinner at the Commercial Hotel.

Close by it is the old amphitheatre, now level with the street, a great circle enclosed with grassy slope some six feet high; admission to it by iron gates. Seems to be used as a playground. A bit of sea just visible from the grassy mounds—above roofs of houses.- Returned by coach, leaving about 2 o'clock. The man with mobile face, parrot eyes and big mouth; had been to Kimberley, S. Africa; talked much of mining speculations, and used slang. Kimberley a "tough camp"; "I should have been euchred"—and so on. Painful contrast, this, to the old legendary atmosphere of St.Just.

High road bordered in some places by wall made of huge blocks of granite, set in earth. The few trees sea-blown. Far off swelling moorland away to Land's End, and eastward. View of Mount's Bay from top of ridge; then lost. Iron gates to fields.

Letters from Katie and Mother. Note from Lawrence & Bullen, telling me they have sent ten copies of "Denzil Quarrier". Acknowledged this.

Frid. Feb. 12. Again a grey, still day; no sun. Walk round the coast road to Newlyn and Mousehole, but did not see the cave.- Re-reading, these days, Dostoieffsky's "Injury and Insult".- Bought three photographs.- Miss Bolitho says that only old women now carry the *cowel*, so that in a few years it will be unknown. The people of Mousehole, on same authority, are much given to thoughts of "fashion"; fishermen's sons aspire above their birth, and so on. A woman there, who offered us a guide to the cave, said that her daughter was just "wiping her skin"—a remarkable expression for washing the face.

Sat. Feb. 13. Brilliant morning. Went by the 10 o'clock to St Ives (change at St Erth) and spent the day there; back by the 5.50. Afternoon clouded, and cold E. wind. Walked about a good deal. Delighted with the place—its old streets, rocky headlands, sandy bays.- Letter from Frau Adele Berger, Zelinkastrasse 10, Vienna, saying that she is translating "New Grub Street" for the *Pester Lloyd* [Supplement] (already publishing) and wishing for right to translate my next novel. Replied, asking her to send me a copy of the paper.[2]

Sund. Feb. 14. Dull, and rainy in afternoon. Edith bad toothache. In morning I walked to Marazion and back. Rest of day sat by a fire. Wrote to Mother, Katie and Roberts.

Mond. Feb. 15. Bright, clouding and rainy later. Returned to Exeter by the 11.10 express.

Tuesd. Feb. 16. Bitter east wind. (Snow in most other parts of England.) Wrote to Bertz and Alg. Letter from Bertz, saying that the German transl. of "Demos" is ludicrously bad. Sent copies of "Denzil Quarrier" to Wakefield, Roberts, A.J. Smith and Bertz.- Thinking over new book

Wed. Feb. 17. Hard frost, but sun in morning. Did nothing. E. went to Brampford. Gubsey was vaccinated yesterday; is very well. Short clothes in preparation for him.

Thursd. Feb. 18. Cold, but sunny. Got together my names, and leading ideas. Planned first chapter. Depressed letter from Alg; replied to him.

Frid. Feb. 19. Snow and whirlwind. Letters from Roberts and A.J. Smith. In evening made a beginning of my novel.

Sat. Feb. 20. Early this morning it thundered and lightened—though snow was still falling. Afternoon began a thaw. Laboured at my first pages, rewriting as usual.

Sund. Feb. 21. Sunny and warm all day. In afternoon walked with E. to Topsham and back. Reading "Wilhelm Meisters Wanderjahre" [by Goethe],- the first German for a long time. I have very little taste left for German literature, that's the truth.

Mond. Feb. 22. Heavy rain all day.- Threw aside the pages I have written, and took up another subject, that of the competition among shopkeepers. Thus it always is with me; I fall back on old subjects which have had time to ripen in my mind. Wrote 2½pp.; satisfactory, I think.- Got from lib. "The Monks of Thelma" [by Besant and Rice, 1878]. Read on at the "Wanderjahre".- Letter from Alg, who is shortly returning to Willersey.

Tuesd. Feb. 23. Dull morning, warm and fine afternoon. Letter from Bertz, with praise of "D.Q.".- Wrote and rewrote 2pp.

Wed. Feb. 24. Dull. Wrote nothing. Quite undecided. Recd from Bertz a copy of a play by one [Arthur] Zapp: "Ausserhalb der Gesellschaft" [*Outside Society*]—said to have great resemblance in plot to "Denzil Quarrier".

Thursd. Feb. 25. Sunny, with cloud. Did nothing, except look into Zapp's play.

Frid. Feb. 26. Sun and rain. Have abandoned my story, and am thinking of the old idea "For Art's Sake".- E. suffering for a week from toothache. Read "Vivian" [by Maria Edgeworth, 1809].

Sat. Feb. 27. Cold, gloomy. To my surprise, recd first proofs of "Born in Exile". See it is mentioned among A. & C. Black's forthcoming books in the *Athenaeum*. Suppose they will publish in the spring.- E.'s toothache worse; can do nothing on that account.

Sund. Feb. 28. Dull and cold. A frightful day; E.'s tooth so bad that in the evening we went searching for a dentist. On second trial, found a man (Mundall, Bedford Circus,) who would give the gas. He charged me 2 gu[ine]as—including attendance of a man whom he presented as Dr Brown, but who looked very much like a pretender. Had only 30/- in pocket, and must pay the rest to-morrow.- More proofs this morning. Managed to get all corrected.

271

Mond. Feb. 29. Went and paid the 12/-. Then, as it was a magnificent morning, took E. for a walk—she still suffering.- Made a beginning of "For Art's Sake",- the third attempt at a new novel. Think I have hit my subject this time.- Read a little more of the "Wanderjahre". But it is hard to get on with.

Tuesd. March 1. Cold, dull, but occasional sunshine. Worked morning and evening, doing some 4pp.- Letter from Roberts.

Wed. March 2. Bitterly cold, gloomy. More proofs. In morning corrected them, and in evening wrote 1p., finishing the 1st Chap.

Thursd. March 3. Still the E. wind that has blown for a week. Trying to snow.- Proofs. Recd from Vienna three of the feuilleton bits of the transln of "New Grub Street". She calls it "Ein Mann des Tages", but says in letter that she hopes to find a better name when it is pubd in volume.

Frid. March 4. Bitterly cold, gloom.- Proofs. No writing.- Postcard from Nelly, acknowledging "D[enzil] Q[uarrier]".

Sat. March 5. Brilliant, but still cold. See that a reviewer of novels [H.D. Traill] in *The New Review* [for March] says "D[enzil] Q[uarrier]" has "a certain force of outline", but is utterly unpleasant, and has a "crude violence of colour to set the teeth on edge". This is deliberate, purposeful lying—I have no doubt.- E. went to Brampford, and found Gubsey very well; vaccination had to be repeated, but finally took.- Sent a copy of "D[enzil] Q[uarrier]" to Adele Berger, and wrote to Lawrence & Bullen to tell them of her request.

Sund. March 6. Cold, dull.- Proofs.- Read some Boswell.

Mond. March 7. E. wind still, but bright.- Sent Alg copy of "D[enzil] Q[uarrier]". He is at Willersey once more. Wrote to Editor of *Blackwood*, asking about my short story.- Took up Goethe and Schiller Correspondence.

Tuesd. March 8. Very bright, but cold. This afternoon E. went to Brampford Speke, on Mrs Phillips's invitation, to stay till Saturday. I shall be alone in house. Our little servant is to come in for an hour each afternoon.- Read at the G[oethe] and S[chiller] Correspondence.- Letter this morning from Ella Gaussen. Replied and sent copy of "New Grub St.".

Wed. March 9. Sunshine, high wind, a little snow. Reply from Blackwood; my story is accepted—greatly to my astonishment.- Proofs.- Wrote to E.- Read [H.R.] Haweis's "My Musical Life".

Thursd. March 10. Day of wild storm, with much snow. E. wind still roaring.- Read some Goethe.- Have abandoned my novel again, and am trying to get new ideas.

Frid. March 11. Sun all day; snow melting. Letter from Bullen; says that "D[enzil] Q[uarrier]" is selling steadily.- Read some Goethe. Worked out a few ideas for possible book.- Proofs.

Sat. March 12. Bright, cold. At mid-day E. returned. She reports that little Gubsey never has a proper bath, but is merely wiped in a basin; also that his milk bottle is never cleaned. Strange that this rough and ready treatment seems to suit him so well.- Note from Ella Gaussen, acknowledging "N[ew] G[rub] S[treet]".—Good review of "D[enzil] Q[uarrier]" in the *Times* to-day.- Elaborated my story.

Sund. March 13. Sunny, cold.- Proofs.- Walk with E. in afternoon.- Read Goethe's "Epigramme". in which I have always delighted.

Mond. March 14. Bright, cold.- Letter from Nelly, expressing dislike of "D[enzil] Q[uarrier]". Of course. She mentions an astonishing thing. Someone has told her of a long report in *The Queen* [for March 5] of a lecture delivd by a lady to the London Ethical Society on "The Novels of George Gissing". I must inquire about this.- Replied to her.- Recd from Bertz a new issue of Ottmann's *Litterarisches Echo*, containing his "Victoria Schulze", and a short biography of him, in which it is said:"Schon im Beginn seines Aufenthalts in London, hatte er das Glück, den englischen Romanschriftsteller George Gissing kennen zu lernen, mit welchem ihn seitdem die herzlichste Freundschaft verbindet." [Right at the beginning of his stay in London, he had the luck to make the acquaintance of the English novelist George Gissing, with whom he has since been on most friendly terms].- Bertz's life reads strangely; sounds very varied and adventurous. How would *mine* read, if truly written?- Began a paper on "The Domestic Appeal for Reticence in Art".

Tuesd. March 15. Rain and gale, but warmer.- Once more began a novel. title uncertain; worked all day, and wrote and copied 1½p. (Yesterday's paper thrown away.)

Wed. March 16. Rain. A day of proof-reading. Bad headache, went to bed early. Heard from Roberts.

Thursd. March 17. Fine. Wrote to Bertz. Re-read [Ibsen's] "Hedda Gabler". Thought out details of story, but wrote nothing.

Frid. March 18. Magnificent, warm day, but windy.- Proofs.- Did little or nothing.

Sat. March 19. Again unbroken sunshine.- Have sore throat.- Read A. Hayward's life of Goethe—poor stuff. Recd copy of the *Queen* for March 5th, in which I find report of the lecture mentd by Nelly. It was delivered (date not given) by a Miss Clara E. Collet M.A. Very poor report; can't make out what the lecture really was—except that she maintained the "healthiness" of my mind.- "Born in Exile" announced in Black's list in *Athenaeum*; no date.

Sund. March 20. Again fine, though clouded in afternoon. Throat and chest very bad. Read Goethe's "Elegien," and about 900 ll. of Lucretius I.- Proofs.

Mond. March 21. Dull, rain in evening. Cold very bad; did not get up till dinner. Finished Book I of Lucretius and 200 ll. of II. Some De Quincey.

Tuesd. March 22. Dull and colder. Did not go out. Read De Quincey's "Protestantism" and finished Lucret. II.

Wed. March 23. Fine, but E. wind, as for many days. Did not go out. De Quincey, and 200 ll. Lucretius III.

Thursd. March 24. Fine, warmer. Went out, though cold still bad.- Read some 400 ll. Lucretius, and the life of Epimenides in Diog[enes] Laert[ius].

Frid. March 25. No sunshine, but no wind.- Proofs.- Got from lib. [Walter] Besant's "The Bell of S. Paul's".- Tried to read a play of Lessing's, but failed through blank lack of interest.

Sat. March 26. Dull, warm. Idled over Besant's absurd and empty book.- Proofs.- Letter from Bertz.

Sund March 27. Sunny, but dull. Did nothing.

Mond. March 28. Fine, but fierce E. wind.- Read De Quincey's transl. of Kant's "Idea of a Universal History on a Cosmopolitical plan".- Wrote to A.J. Smith.-

Tuesd. March 29. Brilliant day, but bitter E. wind as usual. On receiving final proofs of "Born in Exile", found that vol. III runs only to 249pp. This is too short. Resolved to insert a chapter before the last, and wrote to publishers saying this should be sent. Afternoon and evening did 3½pp. of said Chapter. Recd from Alg "A Masquerader" [his fifth novel].

Wed. March 30. Very fine, and warmer. E. spent day at Brampford. Working from 9 to 2, I finished my supplementary chapter, and sent it off.

Thursd. March 31. Brilliant day and warm. In afternoon to dig up primroses, which I set in the garden.- Finished Alg's book, and wrote to him. On the whole it is much the best he has yet done.- E. constantly suffering from neuralgia.

Frid. Ap. 1. A day of summer; cloudless, no wind.- Read Bret Harte's "Cressy" [a novel in 2 vols., 1889].- E.'s neuralgia giving great trouble.

274

Sat. Ap. 2. As fine as yesterday. Spent most of day reading the new magazines at Reading Room of Lit. Society. Finished Lib. III of Lucretius. Read one act of Jonson's "The Sad Shepherd".

Sund. Ap. 3. Again fine. Began Lucret. IV.- Read 1st and 2nd part of Shak.'s "Henry VI".- Letter from Alg.-

Mond. Ap. 4. Fine and warm. By the 10.30 E. went to London, to see her relatives and to consult a doctor. In evening I settled once more to a novel, and rough-wrote 1p. Letter from [Alfred] Hartley, acknowledging "D[enzil] Q[uarrier]".

Tuesd. Ap. 5. Still fine. Letters from Nell and Madge. Note from Roberts, saying he has written a sketch of me for the *Novel Review*.[3] Replied to him, and wrote to E.- Worked morning and evening, copying yesterday's page, and doing 4 more.

Wed. Ap. 6. Fine, hot. Marvellous days these; not a cloud from morning to night. All the apple-trees are suddenly bursting into bloom.- Wrote 1p., but half-heartedly. Read Lucas Malet's "A Counsel of Perfection". Not bad.

Thursd. Ap. 7. Weather unchanged.- Letter from E.; unsatisfactory. Wasted the day utterly.

Frid. Ap. 8. Same weather. Thought about my story, but did nothing. In evening E. returned from London.- Reading through [Lamb's] "Elia" in these days.

Sat. Ap. 9. Same weather—astonishing. Letter from Alg, saying he is invited to send his portrait to the *London Figaro* [See April 29]. Letter from Ella Gaussen, about "New Grub Street".

Sund. Ap. 10. Weather unchanged. Read 3 books of "The Task". Cowper rather a favourite of mine, oddly. In afternoon walk with E. to Ide. Read a little "Faerie Queen".

Mond. Ap. 11. Cloudless, as usual. Got from lib. Grant Allen's "Philistia". Paltry trash. Recd from Hartley, the Painter's Camp in the Highlands, and Guide to Guernsey, which I lent him two or three years ago.

Tuesd. Ap. 12. Still cloudless, but cooler. Wrote to Hartley and to Madge and Nell. Note from Roberts. Read three acts of "King John".

Wed. Ap. 13. Close of the fine weather. Clouded and cold. Of course the change comes on the very day when we expect the infant home from Brampford Speke. Mrs Phillips brought him in afternoon—one eye red and swollen. Of course an evening of disorder followed.- Alg sends a new photograph of self.

Thursd. Ap. 14. Cold, slight attempt at snow—which fell heavily in northern counties yesterday. Better in afternoon. Cannot attempt to read, much less think. Day entirely taken up with child. Perhaps one hour of sleep last night.

Frid. Ap. 15. Dull and cold. Letter from Roberts. No sleep last night.

Sat. Ap. 16. Brighter, but very cold. Hour or two of sleep last night. Child cried incessantly for a couple of hours this evening. Got from lib. Henry James's "The Tragic Muse", but of course can only pretend to read.

Sund. Ap. 17. Cold, sun and cloud. Day wasted.

Mond. Ap. 18. Bitterly cold. Sunny, with dark intervals, and rain. Day wasted.

Tuesd. Ap. 19. Beautiful day, but cold. Bought perambulator (with rug, 25/6) and Gubsey went out in it twice.- Did nothing.- Letter from Alg.

Wed. Ap. 20. Wind and rain.- Advertizing for a nurse.- Day wasted. Letter from Katie.

Thursd. Ap. 21. Sun and cloud, warm.- Letter from Alg. Wrote to Madge.- Day wasted.

Frid. Ap. 22. Fine. I have advertized for a nurse girl—as it will be impossible for me to do anything until we have one—and some dozen people have been in reply. E. of course unable to select. The child crying day and night.

Sat. Ap. 23. Magnificent day. Utterly lost, of course. From morning to night I have to make the child's food and to help in nursing. We are mixing with his milk some stuff called Mincasea—heaven knows if it is good for him.- Settled upon a nurse girl, but doubtful after all if she will do.- Letter from A. & C. Black, asking me to mark, in a huge list, the periodicals to which they are to send copies of "Born in Exile", and to name the private persons for like purpose. This courtesy has never before been paid to me.

Sund. Ap. 24. Fine. Read some of [J.A.] Froude's "Short Studies [on Great Subjects]" [1867-83].

Mond. Ap. 25. Fine, but cloudy, and colder. Did nothing. The bad nights are ruinous.

Tuesd. Ap. 26. Very fine. Rich sunset, as yesterday. Got from lib. "Reuben Sachs" [by Amy Levy, 1889]. Day wasted; headache and sore throat.

Wed. Ap. 27. Cold, rainy. Wasted.

Thursd. Ap. 28. Bright, but cold wind. In the afternoon came a nurse girl we have engaged. Not very promising, but the best that had presented herself. Margaret is to come henceforth every day from 7.30 to 11.

Frid. Ap. 29. Dull, bitter wind. Nurse girl already proved useless, or nearly so. Days utterly wasted.- On Wednesday appeared a portrait of Alg, with sketch of career, in the *London Figaro.*[4] Wood-cut of course ludicrous.

Sat. Ap. 30. Fine, warmer. Nurse giving much trouble. Cannot even read nowadays.

Sund. May 1. Bright, windy. Of course did nothing—except write to Alg and Bertz.

Mond. May 2. Dull, cold. Recd from Black one copy of "Born in Exile"— much to my surprise. As they have sent away three for me (Bertz, Alg, and Roberts) this makes only four that I shall receive. I had meant to send one to Bullen, but now cannot.

Tuesd. May 3. Rainy, cold. Recd from Watt cheque for £67-10—second half (minus his commission) of the £150 for "Born in Exile". As he says nothing, I suppose he has not been able to sell the foreign rights. I shall not mention the matter[5].- Feeling constantly sick these last few days.

Wed. May 4. Brighter, but cold. Feeling rather better. Postcard from Alg. No reading, no thought. Domestic arrangements a little calmer. Letter from Mother.

Thursd. May 5. Sunny, warmer. Did nothing. See by advt that Roberts' character sketch of me, with portrait, is in this month's *Novel Review.*

Frid. May 6. Sunny, cold. Letter from Roberts. Replied. Got from lib. Maspéro's "Ancient Egypt and Assyria", and tried to read a little of it.- Begin to fear I shall never get to work again until the child is out of his first year. E. constantly groaning with neuralgia, and discontent at our loneliness.

Sat. May 7. Fine, but still E. wind. Did nothing.

Sund. May 8. Magnificent day. Did not go out. Read Maspéro, with little profit. Asked Dr Henderson to come to-morrow, for child and E.

Wed. May 11. Glorious weather has set in. Of course quite unable to enjoy it. Daily domestic uproar. Dr Henderson coming for E. Letter from Bertz.- Measured for cheap summer suit—50/-.

Thursd. May 12. Hot splendid day. Read last 100 ll. of 4th Georgic. Wrote to Nelly. As Margaret cannot continue to come daily, advertized for girl to take her place.

Frid. May 13. Hot, clouded. Uproar in the house, owing to breakage of plates and dishes. Misery.

Sat. May 14. Fine.- Very severe review of "A Masquerader" in the *Saturday.*—Recd two copies of the Continental "Denzil Quarrier" from Heinemann & Balestier.- Reading the Bancrofts' Memoirs.[6]

Sund. May 15. Dull, rainy. Read the Bancrofts.

Mond. May 16. Dull, furious wind. Morning and evening sat thinking about new book, but wrote nothing. Letter from Adele Berger, asking price for translating "D[enzil] Q[uarrier]", and saying she has heard nothing about "Born in Exile". Replied, and sent her the proofs to see.

Tuesd. May 17. Fine. Sat all day at desk, and made a beginning.

Wed. May 18. Dull, windy. E. and Grobs spent day at Brampford Speke.- Letter from Nelly; replied.- I made a new beginning and wrote 1 page.

Thursd. May 19. Fine, but furious wind. Copied yesterday's page, and wrote 3½ more. Good start, I think.

Frid. May 20. Fine, furious gale. Letter from Bertz; replied. Wrote 3½pp.; good.

Sat. May 21. Fine, calm. Wrote 4pp., finishing Chap. II.

Sund. May 22. Fine, calm. Finished Stevenson's "Inland Voyage"—the first of his books I have read.

Mond. May 23. Fine, but dull. Morning and evening wrote 3pp. Read 100 11. of Lucretius.

Tuesd. May 24. Day of rain, much needed. Clear at evening. Wrote 3pp.

Wed. May 25. Fine, warm. Worked all day, but still have to rewrite the 2pp. done.

Thursd. May 26. Rainy. Rewrote 2pp. of yesterday, and one more.- Recd the 3 vo. of German "Demos" from Ottmann. Letter from Bertz.

Frid. May 27. Misty early; sun and rain. Wrote to Madge and Nell. Did 3pp.- Reading Baring Gould's "Richard Cable, [the Lightshipman]" [1888]—poor stuff.

Sat. May 28. Rain and sun. Recd from Roberts a copy of Thursday's *Daily Chronicle,* in which there is a column of praise of "Born in Exile", headed "Our One English Realist"[7].- Did my 3pp.

Sund. May 29. Fine. Did not go out. Read half Book XIII of the "Iliad".

Mond. May 30. Fine. A new girl began to come daily for kitchen work; pay 12/- a week.- Did 3pp.

Tuesd. May 31. Very fine. Letter from Madge, saying she hopes to come on June 13th.- Rewrote 2pp. of yesterday, and did two more.- Wrote to Roberts.

Wed. June 1. Fine, some rain. Wrote only 1 page. Domestic disturbance, because the oven is out of order. Read Homer.

Thursd. June 2. Fine. Morning and evening 4pp. Wrote to Madge. Homer, 100 ll.

Frid. June 3. Fine. Bad headache; did only 2pp.

Sat. June 4. Stormy. Not feeling very well. Rewrote 1p. of yesterday and did 1 more. Got from lib. Jefferies' "The Open Air".

*   *   *

Wed. June 8. Intervening days wasted. Domestic trouble. Magnificent weather all the time, and hot. To-day got to work again and did 4pp.

Thursd. June 9. Very hot. In morning wrote 2pp., but evening once more plunged me into doubts. Don't think I can go on with the story.- Received from Lawrence & Bullen a presentation copy of their Andrew Marvell, the Muses' Library. Wrote and thanked.

Frid. June 10. Very hot. Did nothing. Letter from Madge, saying she comes on Monday.- Read Kipling's "Plain Tales from the Hills".

Sat. June 11. Fine, but clouded and cooler. Did nothing.

*   *   *

Sund. June 19. Last Monday, Madge arrived at about 5.45. Since then, the weather has been unsettled and coldish, but we manage to get a daily walk. Yesterday went to Budleigh Salterton, where we found a great quantity of yellow iris, and some orchids. Madge's visit fairly successful, but of course no hope of genuine understanding bet. her and Edith. Little Grobs still has very bad cough; we keep him in the house. Sunny and hot yesterday, but to-day overclouded, with showers.

Have recd Ottmann's *Litterarisches Echo* for June, which contains my portrait and Bertz' article on me. Acknowledged this to-day; wrote also to Bertz and Alg.

*   *   *

Sat. June 25. After another week of fairly fine weather, Madge left at 10.35 this morning. She goes to Broadway for a week. Visit, as regards E., profoundly disagreeable, and rendering prospects of future intercourse with Wakefield very doubtful.- On Thursday we went to Teignmouth, and walked thence to Dawlish.- Ascended Cathedral Tower yesterday.

Sund. June 26. Fine, but did not go out. Read a chapter or two of Gibbon.

Mond. June 27. Brilliant and hot. Once more sat down to a novel, in the evening, and did about a page. Got from liby. [John Stuart] Mill's Autobiography.

Tuesd. June 28. Misty and very hot. Came down from the garret to my study on ground floor again. Did three pp.- See it mentioned in a paper to-day that Hardy writes in copying ink, and thus supplies himself with a duplicate. Think I must do the same, to avoid the fearful possibility of lost MS.- Letter from a madman who wrote to me some months ago, from Fulham; signed Ernest E. Fisher. One sentence is "I am a theosophist; you are Martin Luther".

Wed. June 29. Windy, but fine. Wrote 3½pp. Bought a copying press, for 10/6.

Thursd. June 30. Fine, cooler. Wrote 4pp.- In afternoon E. went to Brampford Speke.

Frid. July 1. Exquisite day. Wrote 4pp.- Good notice of "Born in Exile" in *The Times*[8].- On looking back I see that this novel I have now begun is the *seventh* attempt since my last was finished. Each time a new subject. Something wrong here.

Sat. July 2. Fine, warm. Did 4pp.- Paltry notice of "B[orn] in E[xile]" in *P*[*all*] *M*[*all*] *G*[*azette*] of yesterday. "The material is of the slightest, but it is cleverly worked up." Ye gods!- Wrote to Alg.- Bought a new kind of ink to experiment again with my press.

Sund. July 3. Fine, very warm. Worked in morning and did 2pp.—Read Bret Harte's "Gabriel Conroy" [1876].

Mond. July 4. Fine, cooler. The polling day in Exeter (general election). Sir Staffd Northcote[9], and a man called Dunn, ugly looking fellow. Blue and yellow rosettes; former vastly preponderant; seemingly worn by all but the lower sort of people.- Worked morning and evening; rather more than 4pp.

Tuesd. July 5. Day of rain.- I see [William] Summers was re-elected yesterday for Huddersfield.- Wrote 4pp., in good spirit.

Wed. July 6. Dull, but no rain. Bought new hat—10/-. Letter from Alg, saying he has sent his new MS [*Between Two Opinions*] to Lawrence & Bullen.- Worked well; 4pp.

Thursd. July 7. Dull. A day of illness; violent headache and diarrhoea. Of course did nothing. Letter from Madge to E.

Frid. July 8. Fine, warm. Well again, and did my 4pp.- Got from liby, "A girl in the Karpathians" [by Ménie Muriel Dowie, i.e. Mrs Henry Norman, 1891].

Sat. July 9. Cloudy, a little rain. All over with work. Decided to begin a new story.

Sund. July 10. Magnificent day. Positively began for the eighth time, and wrote a few paragraphs.

Mond. July 11. Fine and hot. Paid a doctor's bill, £1—very moderate. Worked well, doing 3pp.- Odd letter from one G. Gissing, of Maryville, Stanton Road, W. Croydon, who says that a Mr Steinitz has called there and left the German "Demos", with a letter for me. Adding that he is often congratulated on his work as a novelist—in mistake for me. But how the deuce did Steinitz get that address? Must write to him and to G. Gissing to-night.
   Alarmed by a slight effusion of blood from the baby's lips. Think it may be that he has scratched his gums. Noticed the same thing some three months ago. Poor little fellow!

Tuesd. July 12. Hard rain all last night. Fine, second half of to-day. Did 5pp., but must rewrite 2.

Wed. July 13. Heavy rain in morning, then fine. Wrote 4pp. Re-reading Dostoievsky's "The Gambler".

Thursd. July 14. Fine. Letter from Alg, asking to borrow £10. Sent it to him. Worked afternoon and evening. Rewrote 1p. of yesterday, and 3 more. Letter from Nelly, speaking of her new friends, the Lowther Clarkes.

Frid. July 15. Fine on whole, but a little rain. Rewrote whole of first chapter, 5pp.

Sat. July 16. Rainy. Rewrote 1p. and did 3 more.

Sund. July 17. Rainy. Postcard from Alg. Worked in morning, 3pp. Began to re-read Balzac's "Le Curé de Village".

Mond. July 18. Rainy, no sun. In morning rewrote 3pp. of yesterday, and did 1 more. Evening, 1½. E. bought a high chair for little Grobby. Only 3/11; we cannot afford a good one.

Tuesd. July 19. Rainy, east wind. Wrote 4pp. In afternoon went with E. to the Horse Show. Rather miserable, owing to weather. Wrote to Madge and Nell.

Wed. July 20. Very fine once more. Did only 2pp. Disturbance caused by departure of nurse, and arrival of new one from Ottery St. Mary. Clear at once that *she* will never do. A feeble and pretentious idiot, lamenting because she finds this is only a small house.

Thursd. July 21. Fine, hot. Did 3pp. Great trouble with new nurse.

Frid. July 22. Fine and very hot. Worked morning, evening, and after supper; 4pp. This morning our new nurse took her departure at moment's notice.

Sat. July 23. Fine, hot. In spite of disturbances, did 4pp. Skimming some stuff of [Walter] Besant's.

Sund. July 24. Dull, close. In morning wrote 2pp. Little Grobby very unwell.

Mond. July 25. Dull. Grobby a little better. Wrote 4pp.—In evening came new nurse, a sister of the girl who is doing housework for us.

Tuesd. July 26. Fine, warm. Did my 4pp. Getting on fairly well. Read a little Balzac.

Wed. July 27. Fine, very hot. In morning did 2pp. Evening, thought. Little Grobby giving great trouble; seems to be teething.

Thursd. July 28. Very hot. E. sufering from headache and fever; Grobby still troublesome. In spite of perpetual interruptions, did 4pp.- Don't know how.

Frid. July 29. Very hot. From 4 to 8 in the morning I had to amuse Grobby. E. suffering still. We think it may be caused by bad drains, as our servant Flossie is also ill. Bryan brought the sanitary inspector to give opinion; he thought the drains bad.- For all this, managed my 4pp.- Got from liby. H[enry] James's "Princess Casamassima".- No letter for a long time.

Sat. July 30. Hot. Day of headache and misery. *Decided to throw aside all I have written*!

Sund. July 31. Close, few drops of rain. Worked morning and evening at a new novel, in the first person, "No Character to Lose". Did 3½pp.

Mond. Aug. 1. Fine; high wind. Gave up the story I began yesterday, and decided merely to recast the vol. I have nearly finished.

Tuesd. Aug. 2. Fine, hot. Letter from Nelly, who is with mother at Broadway. Rewrote Chap. I.

* * *

Sat. Aug. 6. A wasted week. Yesterday, in despair, went by myself to Seaton, a very beautiful spot. There managed to think out an entirely new story. To-day got to work on it, and did 5pp., a rare day's work.- Letter from Alg, who has not yet heard from L[awrence] & B[ullen].

Sund. Aug. 7. Dull, close; few drops of rain. Wrote 5pp. Letter to Bertz.

Mond. Aug. 8. Dull, close. Wrote 5½pp., and went to bed with bad headache.

Tuesd. Aug. 9. Cloudy, cooler. Very little rain.- Letter from Madge.- Wrote 5½pp.

Wed. Aug. 10. Cloudy, but fine. Did 6pp.- Reading Stepniak's "Career of a Nihilist".

Thursd. Aug. 11. Magnificent day. Went with E. to Seaton. Walked to Beer.

* * *

Mond. Aug. 15. Again a waste of days. Once more to begin a new story. Very bad cold, caught at Seaton, I suppose. To-day wrote 3pp.- Letter from Bertz.

Tuesd. Aug. 16. Fine. Wrote 5pp. Cold still bad, and swollen eyelid.

Wed. Aug. 17. Magnificent day. Very hot. Wrote 4pp., working till 11 at night.

* * *

Frid. Sept. 2. Sick of chronicling endless beginnings, I left off writing in this book sixteen days ago. But on that same day I began once more a new story, and now I am able to note that I have *finished the first vol.*, and with some satisfaction.

For a week the weather has been very wild, and much cooler. Of course have done little but write, generally until 10.30 in evening. Have bought Karl Pearson's "Grammar of Science", and Mantegazza's "Physiognomy and Expression". Studying both when I can.

Sat. Sept. 3. Cloudy, cold, windy. Did 5pp.

Sund. Sept. 4. Wrote only ½page. In afternoon came Edith's sister and her husband [the Boshers or the Lloyds], by excursion from London, returning at six. Fine day.

Mond. Sept. 5. Fine, but cold. Had a fire for the first time. Wrote 5pp. Letter from Roberts.

Tuesd. Sept. 6. Dull and cold, but did without fire. Wrote 5pp. Replied to Roberts. Reading Pearson.

Wed. Sept. 7. Fine, but still cold. Wrote only 3pp. Letter from Mrs Bedells of Bristol, asking for advice in literary effort.[10] Replied as usual. Present of parkin from Wakefield. Wrote to Mother.

Thursd. Sept. 8. Fine, warmer. Long day's work, writing till 11.30. Did 6pp. Recd from Roberts his new book, "The Reputation of George Saxon and other Stories."

Frid. Sept. 9. Dull, warm. Headache. Wrote 4pp.

Sat. Sept. 10. Fine and warm. Good day's work; 5pp.

Sund. Sept. 11. Fine, warm. Wrote 4pp. Letter from Paris (Hotel Louis Le Grand) from a certain Jennie Bullard Waterbury, who writes in praise of "New Grub Street", and says she is a struggling author.[11]- Wrote to Roberts.

Mond. Sept. 12. Gloom, with a little rain. Wrote only 4pp. See that my letter in reply to the question "Why I don't write Plays?" appeared in the P[all] M[all] G[azette] on Saturday.[12] A little over a column.

Tuesd. Sept. 13. Dull, windy. Wrote 5pp.

Wed. Sept. 14. Fine. Did 5pp.

Thursd. Sept. 15. Fine. Poor work, only 3½pp. Disturbance with servants.

Frid. Sept. 16. Very fine. Wrote 5pp., *finishing the 2nd volume.*

Sat. Sept. 17. Very fine, cooler. Wrote 4pp. Letter from Nelly. Wrote to Alg.

Sund. Sept. 18. Brilliant weather.- Astonishing letter from one Bernard Traille, "Business Manager of the Opera House, Sydney", who writes from London to say he should like to see me about dramatizing "New Grub Street". Replied that I was very busy; but should like to hear from him again.- Wrote to Bullen, saying that my novel draws to an end, and asking if he will care to have it.- Wrote only 2pp., but planned all the knotty part of the story to come.

Mond. Sept. 19. Very fine. Wrote 5½pp.

Tuesd. Sept. 20. Fine morning, but close. Afternoon and evening some heavy rain. Wrote 5pp. Letter from Alg. Replied.

Wed. Sept. 21. Dull, close. Wrote 5pp. Reading Kipling's "Barrack-room Ballads".

Thursd. Sept. 22. No sun. In morning an attack of inexplicable nausea, which stopped my work. Did only 2pp.

Frid. Sept. 23. No sun. Far from well all day, but did 4pp.

Sat. Sept. 24. Dull. Wrote 3pp.

Sund. Sept. 25. Only a little sunshine; very warm. Worked hard and did 5pp.

Mond. Sept. 26. Fine. Wrote only 3½pp., struggling. Answer from a woman at Weymouth, to whom I had written (from an advt) asking about lodgings. We have made up our minds to go to Weymouth for a week in October. We are to meet Katie there on her return from a month in Jersey, and I shall go with her to Willersey, whilst Edith and Grobs go to London, where they will lodge for a time with Edith's sister, Mrs Bosher.- Sent postcard to Alg, to determine dates.- Recd from Roberts his new book, "The Mate of the Vancouver".

Tuesd. Sept. 27. Good deal of rain. Wrote 4pp.

Wed. Sept. 28. Sunny, with showers. E. went to Brampford Speke for the day with Grobby. Wrote only 1p. Note from Alg, agreeing to the Weymouth plan.

Thursd. Sept. 29. Great deal of rain. Wrote 4pp. Paid my rent.

Frid. Sept. 30. Moderately fine. Wrote 4pp.

Sat. Oct. 1. Cold and rainy. Wrote 4pp. Mentioned in gossip column of *The Bookman* [for October] that "Mr Hardy is known especially to admire the writings of George Gissing".- Reading some short stories of Henry James.

Sund. Oct. 2. Cold and much rain. Wrote 1p.

Mond. Oct. 3. Wind and rain. Wrote 5pp. Bought Landor's "Pericles and Aspasia".

Tuesd. Oct. 4. Fine, mild. Wrote 5pp., and then *finished the last chapter.* Shall call the book "The Odd Women". I have written it very quickly, but the writing has been as severe a struggle as ever I knew. Not a day without wrangling and uproar down in the kitchen; not an hour when I was really at peace in mind. A bitter struggle.-

Wed. Oct. 5. Copied Chap. I, with corrections, and sent off MS to Lawrence & Bullen, to whom I had promised the refusal of it.- News that Tennyson is on his death-bed.- Walk in afternoon onto the hills below Wonford. Mild air, windless. Sky thickly strewn with manifold cloud-shapes, some of rain; bright blue between. Golden sunlight on the trees, making their autumn foliage a rich brown. An exquisite afternoon. And later rose a full moon, one of the most brilliant I have ever seen.

Thursd. Oct. 6. Fine, but showery; warm. Went to reading-room for news of Tennyson. Morning papers only report that he was sinking. In afternoon noticed, in Eland's window, a card with "Works of late Lord Tennyson". After tea went to reading-room again for the London evening papers. He died at half-past one, in the night. A gloriously peaceful death, the room full of that moonlight which we had here. Not long before death, he asked for a Shakespeare and turned for a few minutes to "Cymbeline". Once or twice smiled at those about him.
 Wrote to Roberts.

Frid. Oct. 7. Cold and rainy. Bought Hardy's "Tess". Wrote to Alg.

Sat. Oct. 8. Cold and wet. Reading "Tess". Wrote to Weymouth lodgings, to make final arrangts for next Friday.

Sund Oct. 9. A wild day; furious wind and much rain; brief sunshine in afternoon. Read some Tennyson. Getting on with "Tess".- Letter from Alg. Blackett offers him the usual £50 for his new book.

Mond. Oct. 10. Fine, mild, nothing done.

Tuesd. Oct. 11. Fine, cold. Stray reading. Thinking about a new book.

Wed. Oct. 12. Fine, cold. Tennyson buried to-day.- Bought Björnson's "Heritage of the Kurts". Wrote to Madge and postcard to Roberts.

Thursd. Oct. 13. Gloomy and cold. Preparing for departure to-morrow. Finished Björnson's book.

Frid. Oct. 14. Sunny day. Left Exeter by the 10.45 and reached Weymouth at four o'clock. Address of lodgings: Mrs Craig, 8 Belgrave Terrace, Dorchester Road. Two comfortable rooms at 15/-.

*   *   *

286

Sat. Oct. 22. Have had a fairly enjoyable week, though little Grobsey makes it impossible to more than pace the sea-front, with hired perambulator. Weather very bright, but bitter winds. Heard yesterday from Katie that she cannot return from Jersey, as agreed; little Enid suddenly taken ill. So had to go on without her. Left Weymouth by the 10.20, in through carriage for Paddington, where Edith was to be met by her sister. At Swindon I quitted the train, and went on to Evesham. Grobsey very good on the journey, as he nearly always is, little chap. Got to Evesham at 4.12, and waited at Station till 5.28, because it was possible, owing to a mistake of mine, that Alg might come to meet train at this time. But he did not come, so I set off and walked to Willersey, via Broadway, in dusk and dark, a distance of some seven miles. Fine evening, and the walk enjoyable. Found Mother staying with Alg.

Whilst at Weymouth, heard from Bullen about "The Odd Women". He likes it much, save the first chapter, which I shall change. Offers royalty of 3/- on the 3-vol. edition, and of 6d on the subsequent 3/6 edition, and they will advance 100 gu[ine]as. Of course accepted. As he expresses a wish to publish "The Emancipated" in cheap edition, I wrote to Bentley about the book. They reply that it has cost them £444, and they have recd £392, and if I can relieve them from the loss they will be glad.[13] Sent letter on to Bullen.

*   *   *

Tuesd. Oct. 25. Fine mornings, but frosty. Paid Dr King Lewis, of Thorverton, 10/6 for vaccinating little Grobsey some months ago. Wrote to Katie and to Nelly.- Yesterday heard of Edith's safe arrival; wrote to her, and sent a box of flowers and coloured leaves.

Wed. Oct 26. Hard frost; beautiful misty morning. Walk on the Cotswolds. Letter from Bullen. He is frightened by Bentley's letter about "The Emancipated", and says we will postpone consideration of the 1-vol. issue.

*   *   *

Sund. Oct. 30. Exquisite day. Climbed the hill with Alg, and, amid clear sunshine, looked down on the plain covered with mist, Bredon, the Malvern summits, standing out precisely like islands from a sea. No wind, and warm. Colours of trees this autumn are very fine, owing to long, dry summer. The beeches a magnificent russet; the elms a rich yellow (beautiful with sun through them); hawthorns warm; wayfaring-tree frequent, with its noble leaves; maple bright yellow. At 9 in evening, when mist was thick, Alg and I again went up the hill to hear the owls crying. There were several of them, answering each other far and near;- "Tu-tu-whoo-oo!" is the general cry. Some voices deeper and more tremulous than others, as if with age.

Letter from Edith, saying, as I quite anticipated, that her sister is already tired of her, and has as good as expressed a hope that she will soon depart. No dealing with these low-class Londoners.

Mond. Oct. 31. Fine, warm, misty. In morning walked alone to Honeybourne and back. Wrote to E., saying that I shall take lodgings for us all at Birmingham.

*   *   *

Thursd. Nov. 3. Fine and warm, after a long fog. Left Willersey in morning, by cab to Evesham, and travelled with Mother as far as Birmingham, where we had dinner together at the Station. Mother then went on to Wakefield; and I, after a little searching, took two rooms at 129 Ladywood Road,- 11/6 a week. Sent off several postcards. Visited the Central Library. Alg goes to-night to Jersey, to join wife and Enid.

Frid. Nov. 4. Rain all day long, but warm. Spent most of my time at the Public Library. Inserted in [*Birmingham*] *Daily Post* an advt for three furnished rooms.- Dull and headachy; solitude weighing upon me as usual. How few men there must be who have spent as much time as I have in absolute loneliness.

Sat. Nov. 5. Fine, mild. Art Gallery and Library. In evening rode by steam tram to Aston Lower Grounds and walked back. Some good notes.- Note from Mother and Nelly.

Sund. Nov. 6. Foggy.- The Reference Library is happily open from 3 in afternoon on Sundays.- Reading [Meredith's] "One of Our Conquerors".

Mond. Nov. 7. Four answers to my advt. Went to look at two, but they discouraged me. Wrote to E. sending her £1.- At night a thick fog.

Tuesd. Nov. 8. Fine and warm. In morning long walk through Handsworth and Aston, getting ideas. Afternoon to Moseley, where I found two comfortable rooms, far better than those I am occupying, at 160 Brighton Road, just under the station. Only 10/6 a week, including fire and light. Took them from Thursday.- Note from Roberts, and letter from Alg.

Wed. Nov. 9. Fine. Letter from E. Replied to her, and sent off letters to Roberts, Bullen, Mary Bedford, and Bryan. Morning at library; afternoon at Aston Hall.- Wrote to Alg.-

Thursd. Nov. 10. Very fine day. Got to my new rooms about 10 in the morning, and had a walk out to King's Heath; country pleasant. In afternoon to Library; reading Arlidge's "Diseases of Occupations". My landlady, Miss Rowe, a curious old creature. Evening at home; comfortable.

Frid. Nov. 11. Again very fine. Spent the day at Dudley, and made some useful notes. Too tired to stay late, so must go again for the night effects. Bought some new pipes.

Sat. Nov. 12. Rainy and misty. Letter from one Walter Blackburn Harte, co-editor of the *New England Magazine,* Federal St., Boston Mass., who says he has just read "New Grub Street", and sends me a paper of his printed in the Mag., on the Philosophical Basis of Fiction. Poor stuff. Replied to him.-At Library.-

Sund. Nov. 13. Warm and rain all day. Walked a little; and in evening got some notes in town. Wrote to E.

Mond. Nov. 14. Bright and very warm. Windy towards night.- Library.- Letter from E.-

Tuesd. Nov. 15. Fine, dull. Sent E. the *Rev[iew] of Reviews.* Wrote to Mother, sending bit of little Grobsey's hair.

Wed. Nov. 16. Fog all day. Waiting in vain for the promised proofs from Bullen, and merely wasting time, for I have got all the material I can hope for out of Birmingham. Have read H[enry] Kingsley's "Geoffrey Hamlyn",- unliterary stuff. At the liby, read "L'Abbesse de Jouarre" [a play by Ernest Renan, 1886], with no great delectation. Wrote to E. Also to Mrs Frederic Harrison.

Thursd. Nov. 17. Dense fog all day, and cold. No proofs yet; feeling wretched. Letter from Alg. One from Bentleys, in which they offer to let me have copyright of "The Emancipated" for a "normal payment" of twenty guineas. Don't know how to get out of this.- Ashamed to draw back, but cannot possibly afford the sum. Wrote to *Blackwood's Mag.,* about my short story "A Victim of Circumstances", which they have had, accepted, for more than a year. Said I must either be paid for it, or have it back.- Basket of apples from Mrs Shailer.- At Liby looked through [J.A.] Symonds's Life of Michelangelo.- Wrote to Mrs Shailer.

Frid. Nov. 18. Still misty. Read at liby parts of [Sir Walter] Scott's Journal [published in 1890]. On coming home found a huge packet of slip-proofs of "The Odd Women". Fell to work.- Letter from E., anxious to get home.- Reply from Mrs [Frederic] Harrison, inviting me to stay at their house when I come to London.

Sat. Nov. 19. Mist and rain; a little warmer. Letter from Blackwood, enclosing £20 for my story—to my vast astonishment. Says it will appear in Jan. number. Worked at proofs all day. Sent B[lackwood]'s cheque to the bank at Exeter and a cheque of my own (£10) to be cashed and remitted here.

Sund. Nov. 20. Misty. Wrote to Blackwood and to E.- Read Scott's Journal at Library. Worked at correcting proofs.

Mond. Nov. 21. Colder; misty. Worked at proofs. Have to rewrite here and there.- Gave my landlady, Miss Rowe,- decent old body,- a copy of "The Nether World". 2/6 edition.

Tuesd. Nov. 22. Clear, cold. Returned batch of proofs to Bullen, minus Chaps. 1 and 2, which I must rewrite at Exeter; couldn't do such work in lodgings. Sent E. £2-10, having recd cash from bank. Wrote to Alg, and sent postcards to Wakefield and Bryan, about my journey on Thursday. Sent a note to Edmund Gosse, saying how delighted I am with his "Tennyson" paper in this month's *New Review*,- in which he scoffs at the universal assumption that Tennyson was appreciated by the populace. Couldn't resist the impulse to do this, though perhaps it is infra dig.—Went out in evening and had excellent tripe supper at Jackson's in High Street. Some good ideas for new book, in consequence.- Finished Disraeli's "Venetia".

Wed. Nov. 23. Clear, cold. In afternoon went to Dudley again, and made notes of night aspect. Letter from E.

Thursd. Nov. 24. Misty.Left Brighton Road by 8.24, and changed for the express at Barnt Green. Exeter by 1.48. On way home stopped at newspaper office to insert advt for servant. After the ceaseless rain and fog of last month, I find everything in the house very damp. Lit three fires, and got a sort of tea. Supper at the Coffee Tavern.

Frid. Nov. 25. Working to get the house in order. Dinner at Coffee Tavern.

Sat. Nov. 26. Working as yesterday. Read [Walter] Besant's "With Harp and Crown". Weather bad. Engaged a servant for next Wedy.

Sund Nov. 27. Weather improving. Sunshine, warm. Could not get to my proofs. Pleasant letter from Gosse, acknowledging that I wrote him fromBirm'ham.

Mond. Nov. 28. Bright and warm. E. and Grobsey came by the Flying Dutchman. I had everything ready for them. The little chap recognized me at once—at all events he laughed on seeing me, at the station.

Tuesd. Nov. 29. Dull again. No sleep last night, Grobsey so restless. Racking headache all to-day. Nothing but domestic labour possible till after tea. E. went to bed, worn out, about 7, and I, in spite of headache, worked at proofs till 9. Note from Bullen this morning, saying he will purchase "The Emancipated" for 20 gu[ine]as from Bentley, and give me half profits of cheap edn.

Wed. Nov. 30. Brilliant day. New servant came, from Budleigh Salterton, named Ellen. Bought little Grobsey a cot. After tea got to work, and wrote a little of the new first Chapter for "The Odd Women".- Wrote to Mother.

Thursd. Dec. 1. Rain all day. Morning wasted by the arrival and setting up of a gas cooking-stove. Worked afternoon and evening, and at night sent off the new first Chap. of my novel to Bullen.

Frid. Dec. 2. Dull. Wrote to Bertz and to Walter Grahame.

Sat. Dec. 3. Warmer; some sunshine, with showers. Got from lib. the life of Laurence Oliphant [*Laurence Oliphant and his Wife,* by M.O.W. Oliphant, 1891].

Sund. Dec. 4. Wild day. Bright sunshine broken by snow-storms.

Mond. Dec. 5. A little snow still; very cold. Paid my half-year's rates. Recd proof of "A Victim of Circumstances", with note from Blackwood inviting new contributions.- The expected uproar with new servant beginning. Had to go down into kitchen, and map out on paper a daily scheme of house-work. Bah!- Began to take the *Magazine of Art.*

Tuesd. Dec. 6. Sunny, cold. Returned proof. Reading my collection of dear old Will's letters.[14]

Wed. Dec. 7. Sunny and cold. Not much progress with plan of new novel. Letter from Mother; replied. House affairs in somewhat better order.

Thursd. Dec. 8. Frost. Bright. In morning a walk round by St Mary Clyst. Getting my new story into shape. Letter from Bertz. Sent a newspaper to Alg, with report of National Agricultural Conference at St James's Hall yesterday. Note from Roberts.

Frid. Dec. 9. Bright, cold. Did little or nothing, except settle a few names for the book. Wrote to Roberts, telling him, in reply to his proposal that he should come here for a day or two, that our domestic confusion makes it impossible to receive visitors. Another newspaper to Alg.

Sat. Dec. 10. Cold, rainy. *Little Grobby's birthday.* Present from Wakefield. He can just stand by himself, but not walk. Speaks no syllable, but understands a few words, such as "window", "fire". Only two teeth. On the whole in very good health, feeding exclusively on Allen & Hanbury's Malted Food. First thing in the morning, I crowned him with a wreath of ivy.

Sund. Dec. 11. Bright morning; rain later. Note from Bullen, asking me to send a corrected copy of "The Emancipated" for cheap edition. Went through the 3 vols., and made many corrections.

Mond. Dec. 12. Dull, mild. Found with astonishment that one of the primroses in our garden has come into flower.- Sent Bullen corrected "Emancipated", and the first six sheets, revised, of "Odd Women".

Tuesd. Dec. 13. Very fine day.- The man [Walter Blackburn] Harte, sub-editor of *The New England Magazine.* keeps sending me proofs of articles of his own writing—deuce take him! Very little in them.- Got to work this morning, and by 11 at night wrote the first chapter of a short story called "In the Cause of Humanity". Only thought of it yesterday.- Letter from Alg., who is working in Jersey.

Wed. Dec. 14. Dull, warm, Wrote a little more of my story, which interests me.

Thursd. Dec. 15. Dull, mild. Things going so badly in the house that I had to go and engage a sitting-room, at 7 Eaton Place, Heavitree Road, to use daily as a study. Cannot do anything at home. Rent to be 6/- with fire extra. Begin next Monday.- Corrected proofs. To bed in utter wretchedness.

Frid. Dec. 16. Dull, very warm. Walked in morning; evening wrote a page or two of story.

Sat. Dec. 17. Dull, mild. There is a second primrose out in the garden. These roots were dug up from a lane last spring.- Wrote out a list of 12 resolutions for the new year, and said to myself: Hic incipit vita nova. Now for work!- Got [F. Marion] Crawford's "Dr Claudius" [1883].

Sund. Dec. 18. Dull, mild. In morning went out with my bag, and brought home a lot of holly. The little boy, on being brought into the sitting-room after the holly had been stuck on the pictures, at once noticed the change, and afterwards kept pointing to the holly, with exclamations.- Letter from Roberts, telling of the death of Bertz's dog Don.

Mond. Dec. 19. Dull, warm. Went to my room at Mrs Couldridge's morning and evening; and thought about first chapter of novel.

Tuesd. Dec. 20. Very dull, warm, In morning wrote 1st page of novel. Read 50 ll. Homer. Evening to a performance of "Elijah" at Victoria Hall[15], with E.

Wed. Dec. 21. No sun for several days, but warm still, and dry. Bungled at 1st chap. all day, but at last hit the right beginning.- Letter from a man this morning, who proposes to dramatize "A Life's Morning". Impudently written: "I shall want your assistance in dialogue".- No reply, I think.- 50 *ll.* Homer, and 50 Æschylus.

Thursd. Dec. 22. No sun again, and very cold wind.- Present from Jersey to Grobs, a squeaking ball. Little chap afraid of the squeaking.- Worked well, and did 4pp.- Several Greek epigrams. Reading Pearson's "Grammar of Science" again.

Frid. Dec. 23. No sun; bitterly cold. Wrote 2½pp.- Some Greek.

Sat. Dec. 24. Gloomy, very cold; gleam of sun later. Wrote about 2pp.- Got from liby "Recreations of a Country Parson" [by A.K.H. Boyd].

Sund. Dec. 25. Very fine day; bright, sunny, cold. Goose for dinner; walk in afternoon. Read "Country Parson". Wrote to Alg. Proofs from Bullen.

Mond. Dec. 26. Bright day, but hard frost. Wrote about 1½p. Corrected proofs.

Tuesd. Dec. 27. Bright, but still hard frost. Foggy again at night. Wrote about 2pp.- Read 50 *ll.* Homer, and some Gibbon.

Wed. Dec. 28. Dull, foggy, bitterly cold. All water in house frozen since night before last.- Rewrote 1p.; a poor day. Bryan came to tea, and brought Grobsey a toy. Read some Homer. Recd *Blackwood's Mag.* for Jan[uary], with "A Victim of Circumstances" in it.

Thursd. Dec. 29. Brighter, and less cold. Wrote 2½ pp. Read the *Bookman,* and 40 *ll.* Homer. Pleasant letter from Blackwood, asking for further contributions. Replied to him.- Some Gibbon.

Frid. Dec. 30. Bright; cold wind. Wrote 2pp. Letter from Nelly; replied and sent her "Blackwood". Some Homer and Gibbon.

Sat. Dec. 31. A thaw, but with bitter s.e. wind and no sun. Bursting of pipes in the house; rushing for plumber. Proofs from Bullen. Corrected them, and wrote 3½pp. 50 *ll.* Homer, and Gibbon.
    The year 1892, on the whole profitless. Marked by domestic misery and discomfort. The one piece of work, "The Odd Women", scribbled in 6 weeks as the autumn drew to an end, and I have no high opinion of it. Have read next to nothing; classical studies utterly neglected. With my new plan of having a study away from the wretched home, may hope to achieve more in year to come.

1893

Sund. Jan. 1. Bright, but a deadly e. wind. Wrote to W. Blackburn Harte, of Boston, acknowledging a lot of his essays that he has sent me. Read poetry all day. Learnt a sonnet of Shakspere: "When to the sessions" [Sonnet XXX].

Mond. Jan. 2. Bright, terribly cold. Wrote only 1½p. Little Grobsey very bad cold. 50 *ll.* Homer and some Gibbon. Saw announced in the papers the death of William Summers, of smallpox, at Allahabad.

Tuesd. Jan. 3. Beautiful day, still frosty. Wrote 3pp. Another article from W.B. Harte. Got from lib. "Armorel of Lyonesse" [by Walter Besant, 1890]. 50 *ll.* Homer.- Learned from the newspaper that, four years ago. Alfred Summers was killed by a train, at a crossing, at Stalybridge.- Proofs recd and returned.

Wed. Jan 4. Still bright and cold. Wrote 3pp. 50 *ll.* Homer.

Thursd. Jan 5. Dull, cold as ever. Wrote 3½pp. Homer, Gibbon.

Frid. Jan. 6. Dull, warmer, in evening snow. Wrote 2pp. and corrected proofs. Homer.

Sat. Jan. 7. Thaw, raw, cloudy. Rewrote the 2pp. of yesterday, with much toil. Corrected proofs.

Sund. Jan. 8. Day of thaw and drizzle. Read the prophets Amos, Nahum and Habakkuk. Made notes for book. Wrote to Roberts.

Mond. Jan. 9. Rain all day, no sun. Wrote nothing; busy with development.

Tuesd. Jan. 10. Dry, colder again. In morning corrected proofs, and did some rewriting at beginning of new book. Evening wrote 2pp.- 50 *ll.* Homer. Vasari's life of Fra Angelico, and a Chap. of "Viaggio di due Asini". Must read a little Italian, or shall be forgetting it.

Wed. Jan. 11. Sunny, cold. Wrote 3pp. and corrected a lot of proofs.- Greek, Italian.

Thursd. Jan. 12. Dull, less cold. Wrote 3pp., and corrected proofs.- "Due Asini".

294

Frid. Jan. 13. A little sun, and some rain. Wrote 4pp.- Homer, Italian.

Sat. Jan. 14. Rainy, changing to a little snow in evening, then frost.- Wrote 4pp.- Italian.

Sund. Jan. 15. Hard frost. Corrected proofs. Wrote to Roberts.

Mond. Jan. 16. Thaw, then snow in night. Wrote 4pp.- *Review of Reviews.*

Tuesd. Jan. 17. Sunshine and rain. Corrected proofs. Wrote 2½pp.

Wed. Jan. 18. Dull, milder. Wrote 3½pp.- Finished Bk I of Augustine's "Confessions". Finished "Due Asini".

Thursd. Jan. 19. Dull, warm, rainy. Wrote 4pp.- Much trouble with servant, who is proving filthy and lazy, like all her predecessors. Filthy beyond description.

Frid. Jan. 20. Bright and warm. Large batch of proofs and revises. Wrote 2pp.

Sat. Jan. 21. Bright; cold wind. Wrote 2pp., finishing vol. I of novel.—To bed with severe headache. Letter from Bertz.

Sund. Jan. 22. Changeable, rainy, mild. Did nothing in particular, except read Tourguéneff's "Un Hamlet russe". Wrote to Roberts.

Mond. Jan. 23. Dull, warm. Wrote 3pp. of a short story ("A Shrewd Investment"). Proofs.- At night, read Bk II of Augustine.

Tuesd. Jan. 24. Dull, warm. Wrote 4pp. of story.- On way home, at night, an anguish of suffering in the thought that I can never hope to have an intellectual companion at home. Condemned for ever to associate with inferiors—and so crassly unintelligent. Never a word exchanged on anything but the paltry everyday life of the household. Never a word to me, from anyone, of understanding sympathy—or of encouragement. Few men, I am sure, have led so bitter a life.- Read half Bk III St Augustine, and some pages of [Cicero's] "De Oratore".

Wed. Jan. 25. Beautiful morning, then rainy.- Proofs, and wrote 5pp.- Bought "Rois en Exil" [by Alphonse Daudet].

Thursd. Jan. 26. Dull.- Got to the end of my short story, but must rewrite first half.- Last proofs of "The Odd Women". Sent note to Bullen.- "Rois en Exil".

Frid. Jan. 27. Thick mist first thing, then brilliant day. Rewrote first 7pp. of story, the name of which I have changed to "A Minstrel of the Byways". Think it rather good.- "Rois en Exil".

Sat. Jan. 28. High wind; fine and rain. Thought over beginning of my vol. II. Revises.

Sund. Jan. 29. Very fine and warm. Infinite misery with servant. Wrote to Alg; read "Rois en Exil".- Little Grobsey now tries at these words: Book, Brush and Crust,- which take form of Boo'—Bur'—Cur'. He delights in pulling books out of the lower shelves of my cases, and can always be pleased with an illustd volume.- To-night his mother got cross with him about some trifle, in the kitchen. I went and fetched him up, and when his mother came I saw him fix his little eyes on her for a long time with look of grave resentment, sad and impressive. Evidently he had felt the injustice.

Mond. Jan. 30. Warm, sunny. Began vol. II, and did 3pp.

Tuesd. Jan. 31. Warmer than ever; dull. Wrote 3pp. Sent off last revises of "The O[dd] W[omen]".-

Wed. Feb. 1. Bright, breezy day. Wrote 3pp. Began to read, for third time, "Anna Karenina".

Thursd. Feb. 2. Warm, sunny. Rewrote 2pp. of yesterday, and 2 more. Note from Roberts.

Frid. Feb. 3. Bright morning, dull afternoon. Wrote 2½pp.

Sat. Feb. 4. Fine, but colder. Wrote 3pp.

Sund. Feb. 5. Fine, cold. In morning walked to Stoke Canon and back. Afternoon, with E. to Countess Weir and back by Alphington.

Mond. Feb. 6. Dull, drizzly. Wrote 3½pp.

Tuesd. Feb. 7. Wonderfully fine day. Letter from Bullen, with cheque for £59-1-9, being second fifty guineas for "The Odd Women", and £7-11-9, my share of American sale of "Denzil Quarrier", up to end of June '92. Full accounts of "D[enzil] Q[uarrier]" enclosed; anything but a success. Still, it brings me money. Much more in Bullen's letter. Says they have sold "The O[dd] W[omen]" to Heinemann & Balestier, for Continental issue, at 35 guineas, and to same people, for Colonial Library, 1500 copies in sheets at 1/- each. Macmillan is to publish in America. He concludes with proposal to pub[lish] cheap edition of "The Unclassed" and "Isabel Clarendon", adding: "We count it a privilege to publish your books. If we lose money in issuing popular editions of your earlier novels it won't trouble us. The pleasure of seeing your books collected would atone for any loss; but we fancy they might ultimately be profitable."- Was every struggling author thus addressed?- Replied to the good fellow.

Wrote 3½ pp. to-day. Getting on splendidly.

Wed. Feb. 8. Change of fine and rainy, warm and cold. Bad night with little Grobsey, so did only 2pp.- Note from Nelly.

Thursd. Feb. 9. Rain all day, with wild wind at night. Wrote 4½pp.—Letter from Alg. Replied.

Frid. Feb. 10. Rainy. Wrote 3pp.- Reading a little book "Through the Ranks to a Commission" [anonymous, 1881].

Sat. Feb. 11. Rainy. Wrote only 1p.- Recd from Lawrence & Bullen a copy of their Waller, in the Muses' Library.- Blackwood returns my story: "A Minstrel of the Byways". A disappointment.

Sund. Feb. 12. Fine, but high wind. Read Waller. Wrote to Nelly.

Mond. Feb. 13. Rainy. Wrote 2½pp. Making notes of "Through the Ranks to a Commission".-

Tuesd. Feb. 14. Sunny, with a little rain. Wrote 3pp. Alg's new book, "Between two Opinions", announced [by Hurst & Blackett].

Wed. Feb. 15. Much rain. Wrote 3pp.

Thursd. Feb. 16. Rain and sunshine. Did 4pp. No reading at present.

Frid. Feb. 17. Drizzly rain all day, and colder. Wrote 3pp. Note from Alg, saying they return from Jersey to Willersey on Monday.

Sat. Feb. 18. Dull day. Wrote 4pp.- Got from lib. a trashy book of reminiscences by the son of Archbishop Whately [probably *Personal and Family Glimpses of Remarkable People,* by E.W. Whately, 1889].

Sund. Feb. 19. Very fine morning, rainy afternoon. Read "Two Gentlemen of Verona", and part of "Merry Wives [of Windsor]".—Cutting out pictures from numbers of *Review of Reviews.*

Mond. Feb. 20. Dull, rain at night. Wrote only 2pp. From liby. [Charles] Reade's "Peg Woffington".

Tuesd. Feb. 21. Dull, rainy, windy. Wrote 3pp.

Wed. Feb. 22. Wind and rain. Wrote 2½pp.

Thursd. Feb. 23. Colder, dull. Wrote 3pp. Letter from Nelly.

Frid. Feb. 24. Cold, dull. Wrote 2½pp.

Sat. Feb. 25. Fine, cold, rain at night. Wrote 3pp., finishing vol. II. See that A. & C. Black are bringing out a 6/- edn of "Born in Exile". Glad of this.

Sund. Feb. 26. Shine and shower. Did nothing.

Mond. Feb. 27. Rain all day. Rewrote the last p. of Vol. I and added half a p.- Recd from A. & C. Black a copy of the new edn of "Born in Exile".

Tuesd. Feb. 28. Not a cloud all day, but coldish. Wrote nothing. Depressed by letter from Alg, asking, poor fellow, for £10. Posted it to him. Wrote to Roberts. In evening attended the annual meeting of the Literary Society. Miserable speaking—vulgar, foolish.[1]

Wed. March 1. Roaring west wind. Magnificent full moon at night. Wrote 2½pp.

Thursd. March 2. Fine and warm; rain at night. Wrote 2½pp. Received from Alg his "Between two Opinious".
Frid. March 3. Warm; moist. Wrote 3½pp. Note from Roberts.

Sat. March 4. Very fine. Wrote 3pp.

Sund. March 5. Fine. Read some De Quincey, but wasted the day on the whole.

Mond. March 6. Dull, rain at night. Wrote 2½pp.

Tuesd. March 7. Fine. Wrote 3½pp. Got from lib. [F. Marion] Crawford's "Tale of a Lonely Parish" [1886].

Wed. March 8. Wonderful day; like summer. Wrote 3½pp.

Thursd. March 9. Very fine. Did 3pp. De Quincey.

Frid. March 10. Again a wonderful day. In morning wrote 1p. Afternoon went by train with E. to Brampford Speke, and walked back.

Sat. March 11. Mist and white frost in morning, then very fine. Wrote 3pp., but must cancel the last.

Sund. March 12. Fine, but cold east wind. Did nothing.

Mond. March 13. Dull. Rewrote 1½p. of Saturday, and 1 more.

Tuesd. March 14. Dull, ending in rain. Wrote 4pp., a good day.

Wed. March 15. Showery to fine. Note from Bullen, asking me to write him a paragraph on "The Odd Women" for mention in the *Athenaeum*. I suggested this: "It deals with the lot of women, who, for statistical or other reasons, have small chance of marriage.- Among the characters, militant or conventional, are some who succeed, and some who fail, in the effort to make their lives independent".²- Wrote 3pp.

Thursd. March 16. Shine and shower. Wrote 3½pp.

Frid. March 17. High wind; sun and shower. Note from Bullen, saying he has sent my par[agraph] to *Athenaeum*. Letter from Walter Grahame, who is going to Salisbury, and asks if he could see me here next week. Thought about this all morning and decided to ask him to come to lunch—a bold decision, alas. Wrote to him. In evening did 2pp.

Sat. March 18. Very fine. Letter from Edmund Gosse, saying he would like to print as appendix to a collection of some of his critical papers, a letter from me on the subject of poetry among the poor,- an enlargement of what I wrote to him last December. Accordingly spent the day in writing such a letter.- Bought for a shilling Holden's edition of Xenophon's "OEconomicus", and began to read it.- De Quincey.

Sund. March 19. Very fine. Spent whole of the day in rewriting my letter for Gosse.

Mond. March 20. Very fine. Note from Grahame, saying he will come to-morrow. Copied Gosse's letter and posted.- Xenophon's "OEconomicus".

Tuesd. March 21. Morning spent in buying things for lunch, and laying the table. Grahame arrived at 1.39. Gave him for lunch a couple of fowls (cooked last night), apple tart (cold from pastry-cook's) with cream, and a bottle of Burgundy. Afterwards walked about with him. Left him at 6, and at eight he came to sit for an hour, having dined—I hoped—at the Clarence, where he stays to-night.- A superb day, one of the finest I have ever known.

Wed. March 22. A day like midsummer, cloudless and hot, but with slight east wind. In morning walked with Grahame, on his way to Budleigh Salterton, as far as St George Clyst, and back to dinner at 1. Evening, to work again and wrote 1p.- Note from Gosse, acknowledging my letter, and promising a proof. Letter from Hudson, with a copy of his "Idle Days in Patagonia".

Thursd. March 23. Again a perfect, cloudless day. In morning wrote 1p.; evening nothing. Reading Hudson's book.

Frid. March 24. Magnificent day. Recd from Roberts a new photograph of himself. Wrote 2½pp.- Hudson.

Sat. March 25. Again cloudless. The nights are cold and misty.- Wrote 1½p. As usual, am lagging wretchedly over the end of the book. Gave up my room at Eaton Place, as I am going to London next week for Easter. Sent the quarter's rent to Bryan, and gave him notice of leaving at Michaelmas or sooner.- Xenophon.- Bullen's paragraph in *Athenaeum* to-day. Also a very abusive notice of Alg's book [*Between Two Opinions*], whereas the *Saturday* is very laudatory.

Sund. March 26. Fine, but rather cloudy. Letter from Grahame, who is back in London. Read several chapters of the "OEconomicus".

Mond. March 27. Fine, but with tendency to dullness. Wrote 2pp. Got from lib. Anstey's "A Fallen Idol".

Tuesd. March 28. Glorious day again. Wrote 2½pp. Letter from Alg, in which he speaks of trying to find some supplementary source of income.- L[awrence] & B[ullen] announce "The Odd Women" for publicn in a few days.

Wed. March 29. Very fine and warm. Full moon. Wrote 1½p. Letter from Hudson.

Thursd. March 30. Just the same weather. Letter from Editor of *Illustd Eng[lish] Mag[azine]* [Clement King Shorter] asking for a short story "like the Bank Holiday scene in 'Nether World' ". Replied that I would write something. Wrote to Grahame. At 1.5 left for London, with excursion ticket allowing me to return on Thursd., Frid. or Sat. of next week. Reached Waterloo at 6.30, and went into Kennington Rd to search for lodgings. Took a bedroom at 186 Kenn. Rd, at 4/- the week. Then wandered about streets till 10.30, feeling as if I had never left London at all.

Frid. March 31. Very fine, hot day. Spent the whole of it on foot. First went to explore Brixton. Walked up Brixton Hill to Streatham Hill, and by a long circuit through Clapham back to Kennington Park, making a lunch of oranges on the way. Then concert at St James's Hall, but was too late for the cheap tickets. Again walked miles and miles. Home at 10.30, and then kept awake all night by bugs, fleas and crowing of cocks.- Posted a line to E.

Sat. Ap. 1. Fine and hot. Spent a little time at the Tate Library, and the Brit. Museum. Explored the region of Brondesbury. Bestial row in the house till 1am.

Sund. Ap. 2. Fine, but turning cold. In morning to the Abbey, evening to St Paul's. Aching in every limb, owing to my much walking and bad nights.

Mond. Ap. 3. Glorious day. Morning to Brit. Museum, afternoon to Rosherville Gardens. Many notes, of course.- Letter from E.

Tuesd. Ap. 4. Fine, but cold wind. Wrote to Hudson and to E. In morning to Streatham, thence to Herne Hill, and walked home. Evening to the Pavilion, chiefly to hear Albert Chevalier in his coster songs. A note of comedy in him much superior to the run of hall people.

Wed. Ap. 5. Weather the same; cold wind. In afternoon (having bought a new hat at Heath's) went to call on Lawrence & Bullen, in Henrietta St. Recd very kindly, and had a long talk. No great promise for "The Odd Women", I fear. Heinemann trying to back out of his offer to buy it for Continental Liby. Much talk of Roberts, who has disappeared from all his friends.- Had to pawn my watch-chain for 5/-, as I came with too little money.

Thursd. Ap. 6. Dull, cold morning. Left London by the 9.5, and reached Exeter at 1.39. After leaving town, the weather cleared up to its usual warmth and splendour. Found little Grobsey much out of sorts,- sickness and headache. Letters from Bertz and Madge. Nelly is ill, and when she recovers will go to Bridlington with Madge. They propose that mother should then come here for a fortnight. Wrote to say we should be glad.

Frid. Ap. 7. Fine. Had to call Dr. Henderson to little boy, who is feverish. Wrote to Nelly and Mother.

Sat. Ap. 8. Fine. Grobsey a little better.

Sund. Ap. 9. Fine as ever. Little boy still aching. Bad throat, with cough.- Recd back from London my pawned watch-guard. Doing nothing all these days; most of the time, nursing Grobsey.- Few lines of the "OEconomicus".

Mond. Ap. 10. Fine, cold wind. "The Odd Women" published.

Tuesd. Ap. 11. Fine. Grobsey much better. Did nothing. Wrote to Alg.

Wed. Ap. 12. Fine. Letter from Bullen, saying that Mudie has taken 100 copies of "The Odd Women"; Smith, 25; Grosvenor, 13; Cawthorne & Hutt, 13; Day's, 13; and some smaller libraries 7 apiece. Wrote to ask him to let me have half a dozen.

Thursd. Ap. 13. Fine, but cloudy. Got to work at my short story for the *English Illustrated,* and wrote rather more than a page. Call it "Lou and Liz".

Frid. Ap. 14. Fine. Decided not to go on with story I began, but to find another. Recd from L[awrence] & B[ullen] 6 copies of "The Odd Women". Also Bullen's two vols. of Lyrics from the Elizabethans.

Sat. Ap. 15. Fine still. Sent copies of "The Odd Women" to Alg, Wakefield, Hudson, Hartley and Bertz. To Roberts, as he has mysteriously disappeared from all his friends, I cannot send one yet.- Nelly has been ill; on Monday she goes to Bridlington to stay with the Carters.- Impossible to get to work at short story.

Sund. Ap. 16. Dull, and in the afternoon just a few drops of rain, the first since March 18th, but it led to nothing.- Read at Bullen's two vols. of Lyrics. Wrote to Bertz.

Mond. Ap. 17. Fine. Wrote a couple of pages of short story. "Lou and Liz".

Tuesd. Ap. 18. Fine. Wrote 2½pp. Note from Alg, saying that Mother arrived there yesterday. Replied, asking if she can come here next Monday.

Wed. Ap. 19. Fine, hot. Finished "Liz and Lou" [sic] (5½pp. altogether) and posted it to *Eng. Illustd* (Arnold).

Thursd. Ap. 20. Fine, very hot. Reading Newman's "Letters and Correspondence". Sent advt for four unfurnished rooms, at Brixton, to *Dalton's Advertiser.* Driven to this by perpetual rows in the house. Letter from Alg, saying Mother would like to come to us here in about a fortnight.- Wrote to Mother.

Frid. Ap. 21. Very hot. Note from Ed. of *English Illustd,* thanking for story and promising proof. Letter from Hartley, who has moved to larger studio (17 Notting Hill Grove), thanking for "Odd Women".- Day of domestic misery. Read at Newman.- Wrote to Madge.

Sat. Ap. 22. In the afternoon a few drops of rain, but came to nothing. High wind.- Recd from Gosse a proof of my letter to be printed in his book. He has combined the note I sent him from Birmingham with the long letter I recently wrote at his request. This rather troubles me, for readers will think that I had the impudence to send a stranger that long rigmarole, uninvited. In reality, what I sent first of all was only the first two paragraphs.- Corrected and returned.
    The white and pink may is coming out, and the laburnums are a mass of bloom.- Had thoughts to-day for a new book, to be called "A Girl's Wild Oats". Though I have only 20pp. to write of "The Iron Gods" I doubt whether I shall ever finish it. Am much dissatisfied. Would prefer to rewrite and re-construct the whole thing.

Sund. Ap. 23. In the night a good fall of rain. To-day brilliant and very hot. The weather is like August. Did not go out. Racking brains for a new novel.- Letter from Alg; replied.

Mond. Ap. 24. Brilliant and unsufferably hot. Read [F. Marion] Crawford's "A Cigarette-maker's Romance" [1890]. In the evening began a short story: "How a Misfortune Made a Philosopher".- Wrote to Mrs Elston at Clevedon, asking if her rooms are vacant. If so, I shall ask Mother to meet us there; here it seems all but impossible.

Tuesd. Ap. 25. Just as hot as yesterday. Finished my short story, but shall not try to get rid of it just yet.

Wed. Ap. 26. Weather the same. Did nothing.

Thursd. Ap. 27. Rather cooler. Surprised to receive from Mrs Buckley a letter saying that she is going to print for private circulation some of her brother Will Summers's writings, and asking me if I will write a memoir for the book. She writes from Torquay, and proposes an interview in London next week. Replied to her, and said I would come to Torquay, if she liked.- Letter from Bertz.

Frid. Ap. 28. Reply from Mrs. Buckley, and went over to Torquay. Lunched with her and her two great boys at the Imperial Hotel. (When I last saw her, she was a young girl on the point of being married.) We talked of W[illiam] S[ummers], and made some arrangements about the Memoir. "Terms" were mentioned, but I begged that nothing of the kind might be proposed[3].- Leaving hotel at 3, hunted about Torquay for a lodging, as I have decided to take E. and Grobs, with the girl, to seaside for a week. Soon found that nothing moderate was to be had in Torquay, so walked over to Paignton, and there took three rooms from next Monday, at 25/-. Address 20 Gerston Road. The day overclouded and sultry. Lingered about till a late train for Exeter.

Sat. Ap. 29. Windy and cloudy; in evening heavy rain.- About half-past six astonished to receive a note from Roberts, from the New London Hotel, asking me to go and dine with him. Went, and heard that he has been rambling over the Continent, together with H[enry] H[yde] Champion, the labour-party politician. He now lives with Champion in a villa at St. John's Wood. Makes a mystery of his whereabouts, I know not why. Proposed to come down to Paignton with us on Monday.- Wrote to Mother.

Sund. Ap. 30. Windy, sunny; calm at evening. Morning walk with Roberts. He had tea with us. Doubtful whether he will go to Paignton to-morrow. Urging me to write short stories, and make more money.

Mond. May 1. Warm, but with signs of coming change. Went to Paignton by the 11.9, Roberts with us.

Tuesd. May 2. Cold n.w. wind, cloudy, not much sun, drops of rain. In morning an exquisite walk to Cockington. Afternoon, loafed about. Evening with Roberts at Gerston Hotel. He in the usual unsatisfactory mood.

Wed. May. 3. The old fine weather again. In morning by steam boat to Brixham, and saw the Prince of Orange stone.

Thursd. May 4. Glorious day. Roberts paid me the £3 that he has been owing for some years [see entry for April 9, 1889]. At 4.20 he started back to

London. In evening came proofs of "Lou and Liz" from Arnold. Corrected them rather freely.

Frid. May 5. Fine, hot. In morning with E. by steamer to Torquay; back to dinner. In evening I walked along to Goodrington, and then about the shore.- From Torquay sent ¾ pound of cream to Willersey.- Posted proofs.

Sat. May 6. Postcard from Alg.- Acknowledgment of Roberts's cheque from Bank at Exeter. High easterly wind, sea rather rough. In morning to Goodrington Beach.- Bought *National Observer*[4], which I very seldom see.- Postcard to Mother and Bryan.

Sund. May 7. Very bright, but still a cold wind. Morning to Goodrington; afternoon, loitered in fields.

Mond. May 8. Same weather; sea rough. Left Paignton by the 11.5, and so back home. Wrote to two men who have answered my advt for rooms.

Tuesd. May 9. Fine, hot. Can do nothing. Loiter all day at home or at the reading-room.

Wed. May 10. Fine, hot. Note from Miss Clara Collet (one of the Labour Correspondents of Board of Trade,- who lectured on my books at the Ethical Society some time ago,) saying she would like to meet me, and asking if I could call upon her. Replied, saying I was too far off.

Thursd. May 11. Fine, hot. Letter from [C.W.] Tinckam, Brixton, about his rooms. Says he has been employed 20 years at Sampson Low's [the publishers], and asks whether I am author of etc. Replied, asking more questions about rooms.- Time utterly wasted, in nervous idleness. Sold some old clothes for 9/-.

Frid. May 12. Weather unchanged. Fitted up a bedroom for mother, whom we expect from Broadway to-morrow. Ordered some stout for her. Bought a camp-stool. Nothing read, nothing thought.- Wrote to Katie.

Sat. May 13. Same weather. Mother arrived at 4.5. Looking rather weak. Parcel of publications from Miss Collet.

Sund. May 14. Hot, dull now and then. Decided it would be impossible to make mother comfortable for a fortnight here, in our piggish house, so proposed to go to Burnham for a week next Friday.- Read the good article on my books, by Miss Collet, in the *Charity Organization Review*, Oct. 1891.[5]

Mond. May 15. In the night, enough rain to lay the dust. To-day sultry again, with threatening clouds and a little thunder. Sent letters to four people who have advd unfurnished rooms to let in Brixton. In morning walk with Mother about the city. In evening recd letter from Tinckam, offering the whole of top of his house (five rooms) for 13/- a week. No other inhabit[ant]s but himself and his wife. He will fit up a kitchener for us. Replied accepting.

Tuesd. May 16. Dull morning, ending in sunshine. In afternoon I went with Mother to Dawlish. Arrived there, we found ourselves in a cold mist, drifting from S.W. Had to return sooner than we meant. Evening heavy rain.

Wed. May 17. In the night much rain, so that the long drought is fairly broken.

Thursd. May 18. Rainy. Did nothing.

Frid. May 19. Sun and cloud. In the morning we all of us went down to Burnham, Somerset, reaching there at half-past twelve. Whilst Mother, Edith and Gubsey waited at the station I rushed to find lodgings, and took three rooms on the sea-front, 2 Royal Parade. Here we abode for a week. The weather fair on the whole, and generally hot, but often furiously windy, and with a day or two of occasional rain. The pleasantest day was that on which mother and I went to Wells. On our way back, we forgot to get out of the train at Glastonbury, and sat talking until the train for Burnham had gone,- the porters of course taking no pains to see that passengers had changed. By this accident, Mother was enabled to see Glastonbury Abbey. I telegraphed from the P.O. to Edith, explaining delayed return. When we reached home at 8.30, I found this telegram had not reached Edith, and on inquiring of the servant there came a mooning reply—"Oh, yes, there is a telegram downstairs". A remarkable instance of West Country stupidity.- On the whole, our week at the sea was successful; all of us better for it. On Friday the 26th we left, Mother going straight to Wakefield. We reached Exeter at noon. Our servant had promised to be with us at 2, and of course did not come till 7,- again the nature of the beast.

Sat. May 27. Fine, hot. A good notice of "The Odd Women" in *Athenaeum,-* except that the fool charges me with writing "journalese"[6].- Yesterday I had another letter from Miss Collet, to which I replied. Whilst away, I finished agreement with Tinckam, taking his five rooms for 12/6 a week.- Sent Nelly, who is still convalescent in Bridlington, [Joseph] Knight's Life of Rossetti [1887].- Must now go through my papers, and destroy freely, in view of removal to London.

Sund. May 28. Fine. Spent day in reading my collections of old letters. Burnt a great many.

Mond. May 29. Fine. Note from Miss Collet, inviting E. and me to spend Sat. to Mond. with her at Richmond on our arrival in London. Replied that it was impossible.- Very good notice of "The Odd Women" in *P[all]* *M[all]* *G[azette]*.[7]

Tuesd. May 30. Fine, sultry. Doing nothing. Wrote to Mother.

Wed. May 31. Fine. A magnificent walk, in afternoon, to Brampford Speke and back, to ask Mrs Phillips if she could have E. and Grobsey whilst I am getting the house cleared of furniture.- Read a little "OEconomicus".

Thursd. June 1. Fine, occasionally dull. At reading-room, over the new magazines. A letter from the madman Fisher, who writes to me from time to time.- "OEconomicus".

Frid. June 2. Fine, hot. Letter from Miss Collet, sending her portrait. Read a little "OEconomicus". Wrote to Bertz, and sent Alg *The Bookman,* as usual.

Sat. June 3. A little rain and thunder. Got from lib. Grant Allen's "This Mortal Coil". The time I waste in reading trash such as this. But I can settle to nothing till I get to London.- "OEconomicus".

Sund. June 4. Very fine. Wrote to Miss Collet. Read two or three Chaps. of "OEconomicus".

Mond. June 5. Fine, hot. Nothing final yet from Tinckam. Got from lib [George] Borrow's "Bible in Spain" [1843]. Have as yet read nothing of his. Letter from Alg, saying that Katie and Enid go to stay with relatives of K.'s next Wednesday; he himself works on at Willersey for a fortnight.

Tuesd. June 6. Fine, hot. Reading Borrow. Waiting with extreme nervousness for news from Tinckam.

Wed. June 7. Fine, hot. Finished "Bible in Spain".- "OEconomicus".

Thursd. June 8. Fine, hot. Read on at "OEconomicus"". No letter from anyone just now. Frequent waking in the night with fears of the future.

Frid. June. 9. Fine, hot. Began to read [George Borrow's] "Lavengro" [1851].- "OEconomicus".- In evening received a card of invitation to dinner at the Mansion House, on July 1st, "to meet representatives of art and literature". Of course sent excuse.

Sat. June 10. Fine, hot. Grobsey is to-day a year and a half old.- "Lavengro".- Received from Gosse a copy of his "Questions at Issue", which has my Appendix.[8]

Sund. June 11. Dull, cooler. Finished "Lavengro".- Letter from one Miss Isabella Keer, governess in a family at Limerick, asking for sympathy. She is agnostic in orthodox household and has read "The Emancipated". Replied decently.

Mond. June 12. Colder wind. I see that Lawrence & Bullen have tacked on an advt of "Denzil Quarrier" to that of "The Odd Women", so presumably the latter is prospering. At all events the reviews are excellent.- Finished my reading of the "OEconomicus".- Wrote to Tinckam pressingly.

Tuesd. June 13. Sultry. Got from Lib. [George Borrow's] "The Romany Rye" [1857].- Letter, through L[awrence] & B[ullen], from Charles Stewart[9], of the Athenaeum Club, who addresses me on grounds of admiration, and invites me for Sat. to Monday at his country house near Tunbridge. Must of course refuse.- Letter from Alg and Mother. Replied to Alg.

Wed. June 14. Very hot. Letter from Tinckam, to say that rooms will be ready on the 26th. In evening call from Bryan, who, to my joy, told me that he has a tenant who will come into the house as soon as ever it is empty; so that, after all, I shall save the next quarter's rent.- Wrote to Alg.- Got papers from the Equitable Society about Life Insurance; must think of this when I get to London.

Thursd. June 15. Cloudless and very hot. Monsells agreed to do my removal for £15.

Frid. June 16. Cloudless, hot. Did nothing.

Sat. June 17. Cloudless, hot. Having finished "Romany Rye", I got from liby [Edward John Trelawny's] "The Adventures of a Younger Son".[10]- Recd from L[awrence] & B[ullen] an anonymous letter, (sent to them unstamped), virulently abusing "The Odd Women",—a curiously spiteful production.

Sund. June 18. Perhaps the hottest day yet. Reading Trelawny, and clearing up the house.- Sent cheque to pay Dr Henderson's account—10/6. Wrote to Mrs Phillips, to tell her that E. and Grobs will be with her at Brampford Speke next Thursday, to stay a week, whilst removal is completed.

Mond. June 19. Heat unbearable. We sleep at night on the outside of the bed, unable to bear even a sheet. Finished Trelawny's book, which pleases me very little.- Sold a lot of old furniture for 12/-.

Tuesd. June 20. Towards evening much cooler. Getting the house stript. Sent p. cards to Wakefield and Alg, and to Bertz. Wrote to Roberts, who is back from America.

Wed. June 21. Cooler, but fine. No thunderstorm here, though in many other parts.- Transferred my balance (£116-4-9) from Bank here to the branch of the Natl Provl Bank of England in Carey Street., Lincoln's Inn Fields. Out of this has to be paid cost of removal, and of new furntiture. A dreary outlook.- Packing etc.

Thursd. June. 22. Cooler, cloudy, but no rain. Packing books. At 3 in the afternoon, E. and Grobsey went to Brampford Speke. In evening Charles Bryan looked in, and I had a friendly talk with him.- Paid gas bill.- Worn out with work.

Frid. June 23. Fine. All the things away by 1.30. Ate a bit of bread and butter, and off to St David's. London by a quarter to eight, and put up at the Bedford Hotel, Museum St. Room for 3/- a night. Later went to Brixton, and had a look at the outside of Tinckam's house.

Sat. June 24. Fine. In afternoon to see Tinckam. The rooms still in disorder; workmen busy with gas, etc. Tinckam and his wife very ordinary people. With the whole of the upper part of the house to ourselves, there is some chance of comfort. Bought Zola's "Le Docteur Pascal", just out.

Sund. June 25. Cool, and occasional rain. Loitered in open streets all day, and read some Zola.

Mond. June 26. Fine, after rain in night. About 10 arrived the van, and a couple of hours sufficed to get furniture into the house. Made myself a bed amid the horrors. So henceforth my address is 76 Burton Road, Brixton, S.W. In afternoon to Oetzmann's; bought carpet, curtains and linoleum.- £5 odd.

Tuesd. June 27. Rainy. Toiling like a slave, with moments of wretched discouragement. Perspiration pours off me in streams. By night got something like order into dining-room and drawing-room,- i.e. the two rooms on the first floor, where also is a little kitchen.- Bought a geranium, fuchsia, and some leafy green plant.

Wed. June 28. Hot, windy, cloudy. Still toiling. Went to the Brixton Bon Marché, and spent some £6 or £7 in furniture for drawing-room. Took some engravings to be framed. Order ½ton of coals—and so on. Aching all over, and perpetually soaked in perspiration.- Letter from E.

Thursd. June 29. Close. Finished the furnishing of the drawing-room. Rash expenditure, about £12 in all. Got in some provisions, in prepn for E.'s arrival to-morrow.- Letter from Katie, saying she is going back home to-morrow from Norbiton.

*   *   *

Wed. July. 5. A terrible week, the last. Very hot weather, and ceaseless toil, bathed in perspiration. Little by little have got our rooms into some sort of order. On Monday a note from Bullen, saying that sale of "The Odd Women", up to end of June was 275, and they think it will continue. Of course unable to dream of work as yet; seeking in several directions for a servant—indispensable. Feel worn out and not very cheerful.

Thursd. July. 6. Terrifically hot. Still toiling at domestic work.

Frid. July 7. Perspiration and domestic dirt. Trying to get a servant.

Sat. July 8. Sweat and misery. But about four o'clock came a thunderstorm, and thereafter rain with a little coolness and wind. Engaged a temporary girl to come for first half of each day.- No reading, nothing.

Sund. July 9. Good deal of rain in night and morning; then clear cool afternoon. Had tea with the Tinckams. Feel a bit easier, owing to arrival of temporary servant.

Mond. July 10. Fine, but no longer excessively hot. Walking about Camberwell. Think of calling my book—"Miss Lord of Camberwell".

Tuesd. July 11. Rain in evening. Domestic miseries. Letter from the Scotch governess, Miss Keer, thanking for my reply.

Wed. July 12. Day of thunder and heavy rain. Letter from Mother.

Thursd. July 13. Dull and damp. Letter from Miss Black, from whom I have not heard for years. She speaks of a lady at Brussels who is translating "New Grub Street", and who wishes to write to me.- Decided, from tomorrow, to do my work (or try to do it) at the Brit[ish] Museum.

Frid. July 14. In the morning a grey fog. Went to Museum.

Sat. July 15. Fog again, but slighter. Again to Museum. Have decided to rewrite my Birmingham book, before setting to the Camberwell one. Took a bare attic, at 38 Cranmer Road, Kennington, for 3/- a week. The only furniture a table and chair; used as a lumber-room. Here I shall work quietly. Thought I might manage to write at Museum, but find it impossible.- Note from Roberts. Letter from Alg, enclosing some buffoonery about me, by [Israel] Zangwill, in the *Pall Mall Magazine*.[11] Recd my new suit of clothes from Crossley's.

Sund. July 16. Fog in morning, at evening sunny. Wrote to Miss Black, Miss Collet, Alg and Mother.

Mond. July 17. Began work at 10 o'clock, and wrote till 4.30.

Tuesd. July 18. Fine. Worked from 9.30 to 12.30, then ate some sandwiches brought from home, and went out for a glass of beer, walking about for half an hour. Back at a little after 1, and worked till 3.30, then home and had dinner at 4. To Waterloo to catch the 5.45 express to Richmond, where, by arrangement, I called on Miss Collet at 34 Hill St. We at once went out on to the river, and rowed to Kingston and back. Home by the 8.45 train. Miss Collet younger than I had expected. She wishes to come and call on E., but I fear.

Wed. July 19. Dull and close with some rain. Worked 9.30 to 1 and 2 to 3.30, with sandwiches and lemonade in interval. Had to begin book anew, and did 4pp.

Thursd. July 20. Rainy, fine at evening. Wrote 2pp., then into town, to buy some books for Alg. In evening wrote another page.- Letters this morning from Mother and Miss Black.- Reading "The Gadsbys" [by Rudyard Kipling, 1890].

Frid. July 21. Fine, close. Worked till 1.30, and did 3½pp. In afternoon to the Authors' Club, where I met Roberts by appointment. Had a chop with him at Monico's, and home by Victoria and Loughborough Junction.

Sat. July 22. Fine, warm. Wrote 2½pp.- Parcel from Roberts, with Maupassant's "Mlle Fifi" and "Notre Coeur", and Zola's "L'Argent",- also some of his own short stories.

Sund. July 23. Fine, heavy rain at night. Finished "Mlle Fifi", and began Oscar Wilde's "The Picture of Dorian Gray".- Mr and Mrs Tinckam to tea. Paid my first month's rent, £2-10. Wrote to Miss Collet.

Mond. July 24. Fine, very hot. Worked 9.30 to 3, and did 3pp., then into the City for an hour. Read Henry James's "The Real Thing". Recd Aug. number of *English Illustrated* with my story "Lou and Liz" in it.

Tuesd. July 25. Fine, but cloudy. Worked 9.30 to 1, then went to the Museum, where E. came to meet me. Took her over a part of it. Home by 5, and worked from 6.30 to 8.30. Wrote altogether 3pp. Letter from Miss Collet.

Wed. July 26. Fine. Wrote 3pp. Note from Editor of *Illustd Lond. News* [Clement King Shorter], asking for a story for the Christmas number.

Thursd. July 27. Fine. Got up at 3.30am., to explore the City; idea for a short story. Went to Waterloo to see the 5.50 newspaper train off. Home to breakfast at 8. Then to work as usual, and wrote 3pp. of "Hester the Fleet-footed". Recd from [W.H.] Hudson his "Birds in a Village".

Frid. July 28. Fine, but heavy. Recommenced short story, calling it "Fleet-foot Hester", and wrote 3½pp.- "L'Argent".- Wrote to Hudson and to Miss Collet to invite her to come here next Wednesday.- Recd from Ed.

Arnold cheque for 11 gu[ine]as, for story in *English Illustd.* Not quite enough, I think.

Sat. July 29. Rainy. In morning worked at home, and finished "Fleet-foot Hester"; posted it to Shorter. Then to lunch at the Café Royal with Roberts and John Davidson, whom I met for the first time. Letter from Hudson.

Sund. July 30. Doubtful at first, then fine. In afternoon went with E. and Grobs to Streatham Common. Carried old Grobs in my arms from Streatham Hill Station to the Common. Had tea there. Back and an hour at the reading-room. Finished "Notre Coeur". Wrote to Miss Keer, and sent receipt to Arnold.

Mond. July 31. Rainy. Wrote 9.30 to 3, then into the City. In evening got from Brixton Lib. [W.E.] Henley's "Views and Reviews".

Tuesd. Aug. 1. Fine, close. Grew sick of my Birmingham story. Doubt whether I shall go on with it.- "L'Argent".-

Wed. Aug. 2. Fine.- Began a short story called "His Brother's Keeper" [published in *Chapman's Magazine.* June 1895].- At 6 o'clock came Miss Collet, had tea with us, and stayed till 9. Invited E. to spend day with her at Richmond next Thursday.

Thursd. Aug. 3. Fine, windy. Finished short story.- "L'Argent".- Invited Mr and Mrs Hudson for next Wednesday.

Frid. Aug. 4. Furious storm, rain and thunder in middle of day,- then beautiful evening. Worked 9.30-3.30, and wrote a short story called "Under an Umbrella" [published in *To-day,* January 6, 1894].- Got from lib. [S.H.] Butcher's "[Some] Aspects of the Greek Genius" [1891].- Column notice of "The Odd Women" in *Illustd London News.*[12]

Sat. Aug. 5. Fine, except for shower in afternoon. Began short story called "The Pilgrim Pedagogues". In evening went with E. to the Gardening and Forestry Exhibn at Earl's Court—a squalid affair. Back by 10. Our servant had remained to put little Grobs to bed.- Letter from Bullen, saying that in July they sold 57 of "The Odd Women".

Sund. Aug. 6. Fine. In afternoon took E. and Grobs by train to Westminster Bridge, and walked as far as Temple. Back by steamboat, and home. In evening to news-room.

Mond. Aug. 7. Bank-holiday. A brilliant, hot day. Worked 9.30 to 3, and wrote 3pp. of a short story, "A Capitalist" [published in the *National Review,* April 1894].- "L'Argent". Finished Butcher's "Aspects of Greek Genius".

Tuesd. Aug. 8. Brilliant, hot. Finished short story. Got from lib. [A.J.C.] Hare's "Walks in London" [1878].- "L'Argent".-

Wed. Aug. 9. Extremely hot. Spent morning in London Bridge district, and got ideas for a story. Wrote nothing. Home at 3.30, and at 5 came Hudson and his wife, who stayed till 9.- Wrote to Alg.-

Thursd. Aug. 10. Very hot. E. went to spend the day with Miss Collet at Richmond. They boated up to Kingston. I looked after Grobsey at home. Reading Asia Minor [perhaps H. Barkley's *Ride through Asia Minor and Armenia,* 1891].

Frid. Aug. 11. Hot as ever. Worked 9.30 to 4, writing 3pp. of short story called "A Lodger in Maze Pond" [published in the *National Review,* February 1895].- Reading, at intervals, Hare's "Walks in London". Wrote to Shorter, asking if he recd my "Fleet-Foot Hester". also to Miss Collet. Letter from Nelly.

Sat. Aug. 12. Hot. Wrote 3 more pp. of story. Recd from Shorter the proofs of "Fleet-foot Hester". He says: "I am presuming that you will accept 12 gu[ine]as for the story",- suppose I must. Letter from Alg, and one from Mme Rottimaler, of Brussels, the person spoken of by Miss Black recently. She wants to translate "New Grub Street" in an abridged form.

Sund. Aug. 13. Heat very oppressive. Corrected proofs for Shorter. Unable to do much else.

Mond. Aug. 14. Hot and fine. Finished story "A Lodger in Maze Pond".- "L'Argent".

Tuesd. Aug. 15. Hot, fine. In morning stayed at home, and made some rearrangement of furniture. Afternoon went to Lawrence & Bullen's. Both of them away. Brought back some proofs of the cheap edn of "The Emancipated".

Wed. Aug. 16. A day of terrible heat. Corrected proofs of "The Emancipated", but was at length driven out of my baking garret. E. not well.- Invitation from a Mrs. Waller Ward, of 39 Ladbroke Grove. Of course refused.

Thursd. Aug. 17. The ninth day on which thermom[eter] has been above 80 in the shade. Heat really maddening. From morning to night a bath of perspiration. For a fortnight we have slept on outside of bed, all through the night. Men have begun to wear cummerbunds.- Did nothing, of course.

Frid. Aug. 18. Hotter than ever. People dying of sunstroke etc; bus-horses falling dead. Having recd letter from Miss Collet, asking me to send her some French books[13], I went into town. Spent few hours at Museum. Letter from a man [Philip Bergson] who wants an explanation of the last words of "Thyrza".- At evening, sky clouded over; a little cooler.

Sat. Aug. 19. Decidedly cooler, but still warm enough. Wind from west, making the sky an exquisitely limpid blue. Replied to the man about "Thyrza", and wrote to Miss Collet, who is staying with the Chas. Booths at Leicester[14]. Posted her French books.- Worked 9.30 to 3, writing 2pp. of short story called "The Day of Silence" [published in the *National Review*, December 1893].

Sund. Aug. 20. Much cooler; windy, sky clouding; in afternoon a little rain. Went with E. and boy to Clapham Common. In evening finished 2nd vol. of [A.J.C.] Hare's "[Walks in] London".

Mond. Aug. 21. Morning cloudy, windy, and a little rain; then finer. Wrote 2pp. of story.- Finished "L'Argent".- Letter from Miss Collet, and one of acknowledgment from P. Bergson who says that he takes my books with him everywhere, and that they continue the qualities of Shakespeare, Marlow and Euripides!- Rent paid.

Tuesd. Aug. 22. Changeable. The hot weather seems to have gone for good. Finished "The Day of Silence". Reading [E.] Chesneau's "Education of the Artist" [translated by Clara Bell, 1886].- Wrote to Hicks & Nash, of Pickle Herring Warf, asking if they will let me see working of such a place.

Wed. Aug. 23. Rainy. Did nothing. In afternoon to Museum. Letter from Shorter, asking for a story for the ordinary issue of the *Ill[ustrated] Lond[on] News,* and for my portrait to be used in the *Sketch.*

Thursd. Aug. 24. Fine. Thought out a short story, then to Museum, to read books about advertising.- Wrote to Bertz.

Frid. Aug. 25. Fine. Began short story, "A Midsummer Madness". Got from lib. [Robert] Browning's "Inn Album" [1875] etc.- The wharf people don't reply to me.

Sat. Aug. 26. Fine. Bungling in uncertainty about the short story.- Got Stevenson's "Travels with a Donkey [in the Cévennes]" [1879].

Sund. Aug. 27. In afternoon rainy. Finished "The Inn Album". Wrote to Madge, Miss Collet and A.J. Smith.

Mond. Aug. 28. Fine, cool. Leaving "A Midsummer Madness", began a story called "Our Mr Jupp". In afternoon with E. to the Tower.- Read hist. of the Tower in "Old and New London" [by G.W. Thornbury], and finished Stevenson's "Cévennes". Corrected proofs.

Tuesd. Aug. 29. Fine. Finished "Our Mr Jupp" [published in the *English Illustrated Magazine,* March 1894]. Got from lib. [Reinhold] Pauli's "Pictures of old England" [translated by E.C. Otté, 1861].

Wed. Aug. 30. Misty, fine in middle of day. Sent MS to *Ill[ustrated] Lond[on] News.* All day walked about in search of my Camberwell book. Finished [Robert Browning's] "Red Cotton Night-Cap Country" [1873].

Thursd. Aug. 31. Fine. Did nothing in particular.

Frid. Sept. 1. Fine, but threatening. Worked out scheme for beginning of "Miss Lord of Camberwell".

Sat Sept. 2. Fine. In morning to Alfred Ellis, Upper Baker St., to be photographed.[15] Ordered 6 Cabinets, sat four times. Heavy expense: £1. Afternoon with E. to National Gallery.- Morning looked in to see old Lane, the agent for Cornwall Mansions, and learnt from him that my successor in 7K committed suicide—not at home, but in the City. The atmosphere I left behind me, some would say, overcame the poor man.- Read Grammont.[16]

Sund. Sept. 3. Fine, but rather dull. Bilious headache all day. Reading Jusserand's "[Englich] Wayfaring [Life in the Middle Ages", 1889].[17] Wrote to Roberts, and sent cheque for £1 to Alfred Ellis.

Mond. Sept. 4. Fine. Much out of sorts. For one thing, getting heartily sick of my garret in Cranmer Road, and determined to make other arrangements.

Tuesd. Sept. 5. Fine and warm. E. found for me an empty room at 32 Crawford Street., Camberwell, not far from the Station. I took it for 2/6 a week, and shall put in table and chair.- In Westminster, met Miss Collet. Did nothing all day; have given up "Miss Lord".- Finished Grammont and began to read the Boscobel Tracts [relating to the escape of Charles the Second after the battle of Worcester, and his subsequent adventures, 1830].- My letter to A.J. Smith returned from dead-letter office.

Wed. Sept. 6. Hot. Did nothing. Finished "Wayfaring Life". Did not go to Cranmer Rd.

Thursd. Sept. 7. Fine. Did nothing. Letter from Madge, at Edinburgh.

Frid. Sept. 8. Went for first time to my new room, and there meditated a while.- Reading *The Times* at news-room, yesterday, came across a review of a book called "The Social Problem", by one Revd Osborne Jay, of Shoreditch. In a passage quoted from him I recognized whole sentences taken bodily from "The Nether World". Wrote letter to *The Times.*

Sat. Sept. 9. Fine, but much cooler. My letter in the *Times,* headed, unfortunately, "Borrowed Feathers". Commented on in *Star,* to which I cannot write to explain that the phrase "borrowed feathers" was not of my choosing.- Reading [Thomas] Hughes' "Alfred the Great", and once more thinking over my Camberwell book. Sent Alg a copy of *The Times*.

Sund. Sept. 10. Fine. In afternoon came Miss Collet, and stayed till 9.30. She invited E. to go with her to theatre next Saturday.

Mond. Sept. 11. Fine. I see that the *Westminster Gazette* of Sat. had a paragraph on the Osborne Jay affair. To-day the Revd O.J. writes in the *Times* that I am hard upon him, that he of course meant to quote me, that by some mistake he did not see the proofs of his book, etc. The lamest excuse.- Sent one of my new portraits to Shorter.- Sat all day in my room, vainly struggling to get new ideas.

Tuesd. Sept. 12. Fine.- The *Westminster Gazette* and the *Globe* of yesterday had ironical paragraphs concerning Revd O[sborne] J[ay], declining to believe his excuse.- At last got to work on Camberwell book, and wrote a page.- By the bye, little Grobs has just uttered, for the first time, some connected words, viz. "park and trees". Very comical effect.

Wed. Sept. 13. Fine.- One W.C. Hunt writes to the *Times* to say that the Revd O. Jay entrusted to him the correction of his proofs, and *he* is responsible for the omission of inverted commas and of "some names". Referring to this the *Westminster Gazette* heads its par[agraph] "A Printer's Marvellous Confession". Indeed, it is remarkable enough.- Worked all day, and wrote 3pp.- Letter from Shorter, asking for 3 more stories, to be pubd in *English Illustrated*, and offering 12 gu[ine]as each for "all world serial rights". But I think this won't do.- Note from Miss Collet, with some MSS of hers. Letter from Nelly, from Bridlington.

Thursd. Sept. 14. Beautiful autumnal day. Worked well, and did 3pp. See that the *Globe* last night had another par[agraph] concerning Revd O. J[ay].- Wrote to Miss Collet.- Reading [Augustus] Jessopp's "Coming of the Friars [: Historical Essays]". Some short stories of Aldrich.[18]

Frid. Sept. 15. Fine and warm. Wrote 2½pp. Par[agraph] about Osborne Jay in the new *Black and White* [of September 16]. Wrote to Alg. Replied to Shorter, saying that for all-world serial rights I must have 18 gu[ine]as a story.

Sat. Sept. 16. Fine, warm. Thought, but wrote nothing. In afternoon, E. went with Miss Collet to the Globe Theatre. During her absence came a letter from Miss Collet, asking me to promise that, if I should break down any day, I will allow her to be responsible for all the costs of little Walter's bringing-up. A wonderful piece of kindness.

Sund. Sept. 17. Dull. Finished Jessopp's book. Replied to Miss Collet. In morning walked about Camberwell, and got some good ideas.

Mond. Sept. 18. Dull. Spent morning in town, where I bought MS paper and a pair of boots. At Museum met by chance with John Davidson. In evening worked 5 to 8. Made new beginning of "Miss Lord", and did 1½p.- Paid rent. Sent one of my portraits to Roberts.

Tuesd. Sept. 19. Windy, fine. Worked 9 to 1 and 5 to 8, doing 4pp.- The *Echo* of this evening gives, as its daily quotation from literary [work], a passage from "Thyrza"[19].- Note from Miss Collet. Made up my mind at last to write to Colles, of the Authors' Syndicate and ask him if he will sell short stories for me. Seems the best way of discovering my price in the market. Scoundrel Shorter has not replied to my last letter yet.

Wed. Sept. 20. Some rain; getting much cooler. Worked usual hours and did 3½pp.

Thursd. Sept. 21. Dull and cold. Feeling unwell, but did 4½pp. Got from lib. [E. de] Pressensé's "The Ancient World and Christianity" [1888].- Cordial reply from Colles, asking me to see him to-morrow at 12. He says: "Will you let me express my admiration of your work. It has for years been to me a revelation".

Frid. Sept. 22. Beautiful day. Went to see Colles, and on way looked in on Bullen, who gave me cheque for £18-7-6, half Continental money for "The Odd Women". Colles cordial; a fat, red-faced, vivacious man, and great talker. He tells me that in selling short stories, I ought to get 3 gu[ine]as a thousand words, for the English serial rights. Left with him five short stories to dispose of. Home at 2.30, and worked from 5 to 8, doing 2pp. In evening letter from Shorter. Says that he will take *one* story, for Christmas no. of *English Illustrated,* for 12 gu[ine]as. Will arrange for others later.

Sat. Sept. 23. Very cold. Made an arrangement with landlady at Crawford St. about a fire. Began to write story for Shorter, but had to go home early with bilious headache. Note from Alg, saying that Blackett, after agreeing 'for a 2-vol. edn of his new book [*At Society's Expense*], is going to issue it in three.

Sund. Sept. 24. Cold, bright. Our first fire at home. Coals at terrible price, 30/- or more a ton. Read a book on the Bahamas—"The Land of the Pink Pearl" [by Louis D. Powles, 1888]. Decided to call my story for Shorter "The Muse of the Halls".

Mond. Sept. 25. Bright. Recommenced short story, and wrote 4½pp. Got from lib. the life of Raja of Sarawak [Sir James Brooke] and [Thomas] Wright's "Celt, Roman and Saxon" [1852].

Tuesd. Sept. 26. Fine, warmer. In morning finished "The Muse of the Halls" [published in the *English Illustrated Magazine,* Christmas 1893].

Afternoon left it at the London News Office. Went to Museum, and there read [John] Davidson's "Fleet Street Eclogues", and "In a Music Hall".

Wed. Sept. 27. Warm again; fires unnecessary. Went to my room, but did nothing.- Letter from Mother. I must note the progress of little Grobsey. He says no distinct words yet—except perhaps "chair"—but is beginning to chatter strange sounds with a fluency that shows his tongue all but ready for language. The syllable most commonly on his lips is "na", which means "man".- "Ka" signifies dirt of any kind, and ugliness. He understands very well most things we say to him, and will even go on simple errands, - to fetch a hammer, for instance. Pictures of people and animals delight him. All female figures he calls "gur" i.e. "girl". Pictures of snakes he dislikes extremely, saying "Ka! Ka!". As if to signify that his infancy draws to an end, he yesterday let his teat-bottle fall, and it broke. He is still in the habit of using it for milk at meals, but can drink pretty well out of a cup. Every morning, when he is dressed, he comes from the bedroom to the top of the stairs and calls out "Da ! Da !" and I go and bring him down, and give him breakfast. Whilst having his bread and milk sop, he insists on spoonfuls being offered to his favourite pictures, which happen to be lying by; or even to those on the walls. His ordinary game is to "build a sha" i.e. a house, with bricks.

Thursd. Sept. 28. Inclined to rain. In morning walked through Camberwell to New Cross, and thence all along Old Kent Road.- Evening thought over book.- Wrote to John Davidson, in praise of his "Eclogues". Note from Roberts.

Frid. Sept. 29. Rainy. Morning walked about Camberwell. Afternoon to meet Roberts at Authors' Club. Last night they gave a dinner to Zola at the Metropole, but Roberts was not present.- Finished Raja of Sarawak.

Sat. Sept. 30. Fine. Morning wasted. Evening went by train to Dulwich, and there wandered for an hour or two.- "Celt, Roman and Saxon".

Sund. Oct. 1. Rain at mid-day, then fine. In afternoon with E. and Grobsey, by car, to Norwood and back.

Mond. Oct. 2. Fine. Have a sore throat and the old rheumatism across shoulders. Did nothing.

Tuesd. Oct. 3. Fine. Sore throat better. In morning recd from Shorter proof of "The Muse of the Halls", and returned it. In evening began—for the how-manyeth time? - "Miss Lord of Camberwell", and wrote 2pp.- Got from lib. [Sir Austen Henry] Layard's "Early Adventures [in Persia, Susiana, and Babylonia]" [1887], and Van Lennep's "Travels in Asia Minor".- Invitation from Miss Collet to go with her and her sister next saturday week to Gilbert and Sullivan's new opera at the Savoy [*Utopia, Limited*].

317

Wed. Oct. 4. Fine. Did 2 more pp., but foresee that I shall have to begin again once more.- Reading Layard.- In *Echo* of Monday was an article on [Walter] Besant, wherein I am lauded at his expense.[20] Sent it to Mother.

Thursd. Oct. 5. Fine. Once more began novel, and wrote 3pp. Am able to sit without a fire. A good thing, as the price of coals is terrific, owing to long miners' strike.[21]

Frid. Oct. 6. Beautiful day. Did 4½pp.- Lennep's "Travels in Asia Minor" good example of subject spoilt by a writer who has nothing in him. Can't read it.- Recd from Mother 3 pairs of socks knitted by her for Grobsey.

Sat. Oct. 7. Rainy and fine. Did 2½pp.- Began to re-read Carlyle's Life [by J.A. Froude].- Lawrence & Bullen announce 6/- edn of "The Emancipated" in *Athenaeum* to-day.

Sund. Oct. 8. Fine, warm. In morning walked to Goose Green. Hard thinking all day. Layard.

Mond. Oct. 9. Fine, ending in heavy rain, which lasted all night. Wrote 3pp.- Layard.

Tuesd. Oct. 10. Dull, ending in rain. Wrote about 3pp. Letter from Bertz.- Finished Layard's "Early Adventures", which is to me one of the most interesting of books. Shall read it again some day. Enough adventure to stock several Rider Haggards.

Wed. Oct. 11. Miserable day, much rain. In spite of bad cold and racking headache, did 3pp. Letter from Bertz.

Thursd. Oct. 12. At home all day; wretched.

Frid.·Oct. 13. Weather dull and rainy. Went to room in morning, but did nothing.- Got from lib. [E.L.] Mitford "Land March from England to Ceylon [Forty Years Ago]" [published in 1884].- Cold getting onto the chest as usual.

Sat. Oct. 14. Dull and rainy, warm. Did nothing. In afternoon to Savoy Theatre ("Utopia") with Miss Collet, who had invited us. Tea afterwards in the Strand. Had to take a cab home from Waterloo, for fear little Grobsey would be left too long alone with the girl.

Sund. Oct. 15. Dull, warm. Cold still bad. Reading Mitford's "Land March". Shall know something about Asia Minor presently.

Mond. Oct. 16. Bright and very warm. Yet once more re-began "Miss Lord", and did 3½pp. Did ever man work on such a method as this? Paid my rent, and went to the bank for money; supply there dwindling. Letters from Hudson, A.J. Smith and Nelly.

Tuesd. Oct. 17. Day of rain and gloom—indeed the first fog. Worked usual hours, and did nearly 4pp. In the *Echo* of yesterday, I figure under the head of "Novels and Novelists"—column or so.[22] Sent copies to Wakefield and to Bertz.

Wed. Oct. 18. Very fine once more. Wrote 4pp. Cold nearly gone.

Thursd. Oct. 19. Fine, colder. In morning wrote 1½p. In afternoon to Hudson. Home by nine.

Frid. Oct. 20. Fine. In morning very unwell, but wrote 1p., and in evening 2. Think I am fairly launched upon the new book—at last. Look forward with pleasure and some energy.

Sat. Oct. 21. Fine and warm. Feeling better, and did 4pp. Letter from Bertz, and note from Roberts. Got from liby. Carlyle's Life in London [by J.A. Froude].- So this week I have done 20pp., and think I shall not again turn back.- John Davidson never made any reply to the letter I sent him; why not? And no news yet from Colles about my short stories.

Sund. Oct. 22. Day of miserable fog and rain. Did not go out; read Froude. Wrote to Alg and Nelly.

Mond. Oct. 23. Dull. In morning wrote 2pp., but shall have to rewrite them. In afternoon came telegram from Roberts, saying he would come at 7, so lost the evening. R. *boasts* that he has spent weeks in Paris without so much as entering the Louvre!

Tuesd. Oct. 24. Dull. Rewrote the last 3pp. Letter from Miss Collet at Paris. Also from Alg, who is to get more money from Blackett, because his novel is being printed in 3 vo[lumes] instead of 2.

Wed. Oct. 25. Dull day. Very bad with cold and headache, yet did 3pp. Home to bed, supperless and with medicine, at 8.30.

Thursd. Oct. 26. Fine. Feeling better, but nothing to boast of. Did 3pp. Last 2 however must be rewritten.- Letter from Colles, to say that Jerome K. Jerome (eheu!) wants me to do for him some "London types" about 500 words each. Replied that I would think of it, but was too busy, just now.

Frid. Oct. 27. Fine. Again much out of sorts, and did not work. After hopeless struggle, decided to take a week's holiday, and to go down to-morrow to Willersey. Also, I shall give up my room in Crawford St., it is too squalid. Whilst I am away, E. will move the furniture. On returning, shall try to work at home, though heaven knows if it will be possible. Got from lib. [W.E.] Henley's "Book of Verses".

Sat. Oct. 28. Left by the 10.5, and got to Honeybourne at 1.36, where Alg and little Enid were awaiting me. Walked to Willersey.

Sund. Oct. 29. Bright and cold; cheerful idling.

Mond. Oct. 30. Sunny, cold day. With Alg to Stratford. We walked to Shottery, and went over the cottage.

Tuesd. Oct. 31. Letter from Colles, saying he has sold my "Under an Umbrella" to Jerome, for 3 gu[ine]as a thousand words. I think it is about 3000.- Read [William Dean] Howells's "The Shadow of a Dream" [1890].

Wed. Nov. 1. Sharp frost. My cold rather bad still. Spent the day alone at Evesham.

Thursd. Nov. 2. Dull weather. At home all day. Read Howells's "A Fearful Responsibility" [1881]. Inane triviality.

Frid. Nov. 3. Pleasant day. Had dinner with Mrs. Shailer and Mary at Broadway.

Sat. Nov. 4. Wretched drizzly morning. Could not walk to Honeybourne, so went to Evesham by the mail, and caught the 11.56 for London. Home about 5. All well.

Sund. Nov. 5. Gloomy, but not cold. Reading a book of travels in Morocco.

Mond. Nov. 6. Suffering much from coldness of this front room, which faces North. But managed to do 3¼pp. In afternoon a sharp walk to Streatham, which I mean to take daily. Sent [W.H.] Hudson's "Birds in a Village" to Alg, and the Catalogue of the Brixton library; am going to let him have the use of my ticket, books to go backwards and forwards.

Tuesd. Nov. 7. Struggling with cold. Did only 1¾p. In the evening came Miss Collet, and stayed till 10.- Letter from Colles, to say that he has sold "The Day of Silence" to the *National Review* at 30/- a page of 460 words. He calls it "an inimitable piece of work"—pooh! But good news.

Wed. Nov. 8. Bright and cold. Worked morning and evening, and did 3pp., ending up with bad headache,- now such a common experience. Unexpected present of parkin from Wakefield, In afternoon walked to Westminster and back, and left borrowed French books for Roberts at the Authors' Club. Postcard to Alg, letter to Colles.

Thursd. Nov. 9. At sea again about my novel. Got from lib. [H.F.] Tozer's "AEgean Islands" [1890].

Frid. Nov. 10. Did nothing. Wrote letter to Enid, for her birthday to-morrow.

Sat. Nov. 11. No work. In afternoon to the concert at St James's Hall, with E.- Proof of "The Day of Silence", and encouraging note from Colles.- At the concert got some ideas for reconstruction of first chapters of my book.

Sund. Nov. 12. Bright, beautiful day.

Mond. Nov. 13. Bright, cold. Yet once more turned back to the beginning of my novel, and wrote 2½pp.

Tuesd. Nov. 14. The first fog. Hung thick all day (though not black) and in the evening turned to heavy rain. Rewrote my work of yesterday. In afternoon came Miss Collet, and stayed till 6.

Wed. Nov. 15. Wretched weather again. Did 4pp. Reading G.B. Shaw's "Quintessence of Ibsenism".

Thursd. Nov. 16. Weather improved. Did 3pp., in better hope. Poor little boy has a most severe cold; croup-like cold. Got from lib. Mrs Scott-Stevenson's "[Our] Ride through Asia Minor" [1881].

Frid. Nov. 17. Fine, to rain in evening. Doctor came to see little boy, and declared him suffering from bronchial catarrh. Had to light bedroom fire, use a bronchitis kettle, and sew the little body into cotton wool. Of course could do no work. No sleep after 3 this morning.

Sat. Nov. 18. No sleep last night. Keeping fire up, etc. To-day little boy much better; we have caught it in time. Fog, rain, and in the evening a furious gale. It shows how much I have benefited by recent holiday, and the cod liver oil, that in spite of two sleepless nights, I got to work this evening, and from 5 to 7.30 did 2pp. No headache.- Yesterday a Conference put an end to the great coal-strike of 16 weeks. Miners go to work on Monday. To-day coals have fallen to 1/10 a cwt.

Sund. Nov. 19. Wind still furious; gloom and cold. Finished Mrs Scott-Stevenson's book. Wrote to Nelly, Miss Collet and Bertz.

Mond. Nov. 20. Wind still high. Did 4pp., but—shall have to begin yet once more. Got from lib. [Henry Baker] Tristram's "The Land of Moab [; travels and discoveries on the east side of the dead sea and the Jordan]" [1873].

Tuesd. Nov. 21. Finer. Little boy still in bed, but decidedly better. Keeps up his spirits wonderfully. Recommenced "Miss Lord", and did 3pp. Read some Tristram.

Wed. Nov. 22. Kept in by a cold on the chest. No work. In evening came Miss Collet, with a present of bricks for Grobsey. Letter from Alg, saying he can come here on Dec. 4th. Letters from Mother and Nelly. My birthday; age, 36.

Thursd. Nov. 23. Dull, cold, windy. Still unable to go out and to work. Finished "The Land of Moab", and began the history of Saracens in Gibbon. Wrote to Alg.

Frid. Nov. 24. Dull, warmer. Finished vol. VI of Gibbon. No writing. Recd proof of "Under an Umbrella".

Sat. Nov. 25. Dull, rain towards evening. Little boy got up yesterday, but is still kept to the bedroom. My cough bad. Worked morning and evening, and did 4pp. Got from lib. [James] Bryce's "Transcaucasia and Ararat [Notes of a Vacation Tour in Autumn of 1876]".

Sund. Nov. 26. Hard rain. E. went off to see her people; back at 5. Finished Bryce's book.

Mond. Nov. 27. A little sun. Wrote morning and evening, and did 4pp. Colles sends cheque for £13-10, for "A Day of Silence" (£15-0-0 minus his commission). Very glad of this.

Tuesd. Nov. 28. Dull and warm. Wrote 3½pp. Got from lib. [W.F.] Ainsworth's "[Narrative of the] Euphrates Expedition" [1888].

Wed. Nov. 29. Weather unchanged. In morning (10 to 1 are about my hours now) did 1½p. In afternoon to town; bought copies of the *Illustd London News* and the *English Illustrated*,- as the blackguards haven't sent them to me. Evening worked 6-8, doing 2pp.- Wrote to Miss Collet.

Thursd. Nov. 30. Fine and warm. In morning wrote 2pp. In afternoon, telegram from Roberts, asking me to dine at the Club. Went, and found several men. McCormick, who recently went with exploring party to the Himalayas. H.H. Champion, who surprised me favourably. A man called Best—Greek scholar and medical student. Francis Gribble. And one Mackenzie, young man from Aberdeen, writing for "Funny Folks"[23]. McC[ormick] told me he had come across my books in India. Home at 12 o'clock.

Frid. Dec. 1. Cloudy; north wind. I have not yet received cheques from Shorter nor copy of the *English Illustd.* I suppose this is a new meanness. Worked morning and evening and did 3pp.

Sat. Dec. 2. Hard frost. Did nothing. In afternoon came Miss Collet, and stayed till 9.30.

Sund. Dec. 3. Bitterly cold, and foggy. Nothing done; nothing read.

Mond. Dec. 4. Dull, warmer. In the afternoon went to see Shorter, and had rather a brusque conversation with him. However, he asked me to undertake a serial for the *Illustd London News,* to commence in a year's time or so. Got from him no cheques, but forms of account to fill up and send. In the office met L.F. Austin, who has occasionally reviewed my books,- a pallid young fellow. Thence went to see Bullen. They have sold some 250 of the new edn of "The Emancipated". [H.W.] Lawrence came in, and showed us a little copy of "The Dance of Death" [by Holbein, with introduction by Austin Dobson, 1893], which he has just had bound in human skin—silly fellow. Presents of last two numbers of Muses Library, and two other books, to be sent to me; also 10 copies of "The Emancipated". Bought copies of *National Review* (my story "The Day of Silence") and some other things to send to Wakefield and to Bertz.

Thinking I had anything but pleased Shorter, I was astonished to receive by last post a note from him, which must have been written immediately after my departure. He will be "exceedingly glad" to have 6 stories from me for the *Eng. Illustrated,* at 12 guineas each, I to keep the American rights. Moreover, he hopes I shall be able to dine with him shortly, and would like to "see more of" me. Evidently he thinks me of some commercial value. I replied, saying I would do the stories, and that he should have all the serial rights, as I can't sell the American myself.

Tuesd. Dec. 5. Dull, warm. Note from Alg, saying he will come on Thursday. Sat to work at a short story I have long had in mind—"The Poet's Portmanteau", and wrote 3pp.

Wed. Dec. 6. Fine day, warm. Wrote another p. of the story, but shall put it aside till I have written a better one I have in mind. No cheques yet from Shorter, and no books from Bullen. Confound these delays! Went to bed with headache.

Thursd. Dec. 7. Very fine. In morning did 1p. of "The Pessimist of Plato Road". At 4 o'clock met Alg at Westminster. He is going to stay with us for a time.

Frid. Dec. 8. S.W. wind, and occasional rain. Finished "The Pessimist" [published in the *English Illustrated Magazine,* November 1894]. So there is one of Shorter's 6 stories. Alg all day at the Museum.

Sat. Dec. 9. Fine. Got to work again at "The Poet's Portmanteau". Mother sends 2/6 to buy toy for Grobsey.

Sund. Dec. 10. Rainy. In morning wrote 3pp. Afternoon with Alg to Brixton reading-room. Wrote to Miss Collet, to ask her to come next Saturday.- Little boy's birthday. In good health and spirits. Calls Alg the "na" = man.

Mond. Dec. 11. Fine. Wrote 3pp. and finished the "Portmanteau" [published in the *English Illustrated Magazine,* February 1895]. Evening wrote two pages of next story, "A Midsummer Madness". In afternoon walked with Alg to Westminster.

Tuesd. Dec. 12. Furious gale, with rain; but warm. Did no work. Bullen has sent my copies of "The Emancipated", but not the other books he promised. In afternoon Alg and I went to see Alfred Hartley, at his large studio, 14 Aubrey Walk, Campden Hill.

Wed. Dec. 13. Still high wind, but fine. Letter from Nelly. Worked morning and evening, and finished "A Midsummer Madness" [published in the *English Illustrated Magazine,* December 1894]. In afternoon walked with Alg to Clapham.

Thursd. Dec. 14. Began "A Honeymoon", and wrote 2pp. Recd from Bullen new vols. of "Muses' Library".

Frid. Dec. 15. Fine. Wrote 1½p. In evening came Miss Collet. Little boy spoke his first perfect words, viz. "Good day!" which he seems to have learnt from the girl Lizzie. Letter from Mother, acknowledging my Xmas present of wine.

Sat. Dec. 16. Beautiful day. Received 12/12/- from *English Illustrated,* for "The Muse of the Halls". The scoundrels only pay in the middle of the month after publication. An astonishing letter from Roberts, from Genoa, telling me that he has run away with Mrs Hamlyn,- a thing that might have happened any time these three years. I met Mrs Hamlyn once at the Fennessys', and then suspected what was going on. Now, I suppose, there'll be the devil to pay. He enclosed a note for me to post to her sister, Mrs Fennessy. The sister and the mother, he says, both approve of what is done.- Worked all day, and finished "A Honeymoon" [published in the *English Illustrated Magazine,* June 1894].

Sund. Dec. 17. Fine. Alg went till to-morrow to visit one of Katie's sisters at Norbiton. Reading "Alone through Syria", by Miss [Ellen E.] Miller [1881]. Wrote to Hudson.

Mond. Dec. 18. Fine. No work. Sent to Bertz and Miss Collet copies of "The Emancipated".

Tuesd. Dec. 19. No work in morning. Fine. At 1.30 went with Alg to Gatti's, where Hudson came to lunch with us. Cost me about fifteen shillings; very enjoyable. Home at 4, and in evening began new story; 2pp.

Wed. Dec. 20. Stormy, much rain. Story of yesterday won't do. Began another, "Comrades in Arms", and did 2pp. Shorter sends a letter from one Albert Bachelor, of the Outer Temple, who writes complaining that I have used his name in the *Ill[ustrated] Lond[on] News.* Wrote a line to the man.-

Last night had a note from Roberts, from Livorno, with enclosed letter to post on to Mrs Fennessy.

Thursd. Dec. 21. Wonderfully fine. Wrote 4pp., and finished "Comrades in Arms" [published in the *English Illustrated Magazine,* September 1894]. See that the *Star* of yesterday had a whole column review of "The Emancipated", which it supposes to be a new book.-

Little boy amusing us much by having learnt to call the portrait of Shakspeare "Shik-pear". Tennyson he calls "Good Na", with a funny pipe on the "good".

Frid. Dec. 22. Wet. Began my sixth story "In Honour Bound", and wrote 2pp.

Sat. Dec. 23. Very fine. Rewrote the 2pp. of yesterday, and 3 more. Note from A.J. Smith, saying he is coming to London. Wrote to invite him. Box of flowers from Miss Collet.

Sund. Dec. 24. Fine. In morning finished "In Honour Bound" [published in the *English Illustrated Magazine,* April 1895], which is the last of my six stories for Shorter. Afternoon walked with Alg up to Streatham Hill.

Mond. Dec. 25. Cloudless from dawn to sunset, and very warm; afterwards some rain. In morning Alg and I walked over to Dulwich, and back by Lordship Lane.- Reading [William Gifford] Palgrave's "[Narrative of a Year's Journey through] Central and Eastern Arabia [1862-63]".

Tuesd. Dec. 26. Misty but fine, and warm. In evening came A.J. Smith, and stayed till 10. Did nothing.

Wed. Dec. 27. Mist hanging about, and thickening at times. Did nothing.

Thursd. Dec. 28. A dense fog. E. went to Olympia for the day. In the afternoon I went by invitation to see A.J. Smith at his brother Watson's house, 34 Upper Park Road, Haverstock Hill. Watson's wife originally a Swiss peasant girl; now a strong, amiable, energetic woman, with seven children.- Letter from *Pearson's Weekly,* asking me to state, for publication, some facts about my work and tastes in literature. Regard it as an advertisement, and shall reply [see entry for June 23, 1894].

Frid. Dec. 29. Still foggy. In afternoon with Alg to Brockwell Park. Then telegram from [H.H.] Champion, to come to New Travellers' Club, Piccadilly, and there met Roberts back from Italy.

Sat. Dec. 30. Very fine. Spent day with Alg at Bethnal Green Museum.

Sund. Dec. 31. A cold and wretched day. Afternoon, as usual, to reading-room. Wrote to Nell.

1894

Mond. Jan. 1. Yet once again recommenced "Miss Lord". Worked morning and evening, and did 4pp.

Tuesd. Jan. 2. Bitterly cold. A little snow. Did 4pp. Wrote to Miss Collet. Finished Palgrave's delightful travels in Arabia.

Wed. Jan. 3. Snow, and terribly cold. With difficulty did 3pp. Hands frozen.

Thursd. Jan. 4. More snow, and still colder. No work. Idiotic domestic troubles. Letter from Miss Collet.

Frid. Jan. 5. Deep snow, no wind, and many degrees of frost. In spite of great difficulty from the cold, wrote 5pp.- Had to go back to Chap II. Postcard to Nelly.

Sat. Jan. 6. Weather unchanged. Fog gathering. Wrote 3½pp.

Sund. Jan. 7. Terrible day. Thick fog, never moving. Wrote 3pp. Afternoon to reading-room.

Mond. Jan. 8. In the morning no change except that fog had gone. In afternoon a slight thaw began. Wrote 4pp.- Little boy has learnt to call "Shakspeare's House" when he sees the little photograph, now on mantelpiece, which I brought from Stratford. In his language it is "Shikbeard's shah". "Shah" has always been his pronunciation of house. We say to him, when we get out his toy-bricks: "Let's build a shah!"

Tuesd. Jan. 9. Thorough thaw, with rain. Worked as usual (morning 9.30 to 1; evening 5 to 8, and 9.30 to 11) doing 4pp. Reading [Alfred] Austin's "Fortunatus the Pessimist [: a Dramatic Poem]", [1892].

Wed. Jan. 10. Yesterday and to-day water pouring through the kitchen ceiling. Moderately fine day. In morning could not work, evening did 2½pp., and should have written more, but that Tinckam came up.

Thursd. Jan. 11. Very fine and warm. Wrote 2½pp.

Frid. Jan. 12. Wonderful day; like summer. Wrote only 1p. In evening came Miss Collet, who told me that my "Under an Umbrella" appeared in last week's *To-Day* [on January 6]. Letter from a Mr. Hamilton of Paisley, informing me that "Demos" is to be discussed at a meeting of the Paisley Philomathic Society, on Feb. 23rd, and asking for biographic details. By the card he sends, I see that the book chosen for the preceding meeting is the Canterbury Tales!

Sat. Jan. 13. Fine. Alg left for Evesham by the 10.5. I went to Paddington with him, and thence to Brit[ish] Museum, where I looked up some things in newspapers. Home to work, and did 2pp., but must rewrite them.

Sund. Jan. 14. Day of rain and fog, but warm. Worked 9 to 1, 4.30 to 8, and 9.30 to 11.30, rewriting the last 4pp. and doing 1 more.- Reading Isaac Taylor's "History of the Transmission of Ancient Books [to Modern Times]" [1827].

Mond. Jan. 15. Fine. Wrote 4pp. Afternoon to see Shorter to whom I gave the 6 stories I have written for him. He promises they shall all be paid for at once, in a few days. Agreed with him to write a serial story for *Illustd London News,* probably to be pubd early next year. Consist of 60,000 words, to run 13 weeks; payment £150.- Sent in an application for membership of the Society of Authors. Don't like to make use of Colles without doing this.

Tuesd. Jan. 16. Very fine, and warm as summer. Worked same hours as yesterday, and did 5pp. Note from Bertz. Letter from the Paisley man, thanking me for information.

Wed. Jan. 17. Much rain all day. In morning had to think. Afternoon and evening did 3pp. Wrote to Katie.

Thursd. Jan. 18. Rainy. Wrote 3pp. and went to bed early with one of my bad headaches.- Became a member of the Society of Authors.

Frid. Jan. 19. Fine; clouded in afternoon. No work in morning. After early dinner, went by train with E. to Sydenham Hill, and walked home. Evening rewrote 2pp. of last chapter and did a 3rd.- Wrote to Bertz.

Sat. Jan. 20. Fine, with showers. Wrote only 3p.- Yesterday recd a wedding card, announcing, to my surprise, the marriage of Annie Black with a Mr. M.H. Larmath of Manchester. Acknowledged it to-day.

Sund. Jan. 21. Dull, rainy. Reading [Dostoievsky's] "Le Crime et le Châtiment". Wrote to *National Observer;* letter suggested by correspondence on "Speech of Characters in Fiction".[1]

Mond. Jan. 22. Rain all day. Worked 9.30 to 1, 5 to 8.30, and 9.30 to 10, doing 5pp.

Tuesd. Jan. 23. Very fine. Little boy in bed with a cold.- Letter from Bullen, sending account up to June 93 of American sale (Macmillan) of "The Odd Women", and "Denzil Quarrier". Of the former, 915 were printed; 221 presented (good heavens!); 349 sold at royalty to Bullen of 10%; which brought £7-3-11. Of "Denzil Quarrier", only 35 copies sold since June 92; which brought 14/5. Bullen is debited with £61-11-3 for half cost of printing[2]; so that he owes Macmillan £53-12-11. Hugely unsatisfactory. However he says he will soon make acct of English sale last year, and sends me a cheque for 25 gu[ine]as on account. This seems absurd. Nothing can possibly be owing to me, and I can't take the money.- At night a letter from Shorter, recounting our agreement for a serial for the [*Illustrated London*] *News.* Says he thinks it will be pubd in last quarter of this year, and that he should like to have the copy by June or July.- Wrote 3pp.

Wed. Jan. 24. Beautiful day. Little boy better, but still in bed.- Did 5pp. Wrote to Bullen and to Shorter.

Thursd. Jan. 25. Rainy. Little boy up.- Wrote only 3pp. Reading [Sir J.F.] Stephen's "Horae Sabbaticae" [articles from the *Saturday Review*]. Every morning, when he wakes, little Grobs asks for the story of the Three Bears, and generally has it repeated two or three times.

Frid. Jan. 26. Sunny, but cold wind. Wrote 4pp., finishing vol. I, heaven be thanked.

Sat. Jan. 27. Dull, with s.w. gale. Grobsey bad again—had to send for doctor.- My letter appears in *National Observer.*- Did no writing. In evening came Miss Collet.

Sund. Jan. 28. Brilliant day. In spite of no sleep last night—through having to keep up bedroom fire—wrote 4pp. Wrote to Alg.

Mond. Jan. 29. Fine. The doctor says it would be well to take boy away for rest of winter. So I at once sent off an advt for rooms to a Hastings newspaper. Shall probably go for 3 months, then back here for summer.- Did 4pp.

Tuesd. Jan. 30. Brilliant day. Wrote 4pp.- In afternoon to Bank, and went over some chambers in Staple Inn, for my novel.

Wed. Jan. 31. Rain and gloom all day. Letters from Alg and Miss Collet. In morning wrote 2pp., but had to destroy them. In evening wrote 3. Sent note to Shorter, reminding him that I have not yet had promised cheque.

Thursd. Feb. 1. Fine morning, rain later. Wrote 5pp. Note from Colles, saying he has sold "A Capitalist", and "A Lodger in Maze Pond", for £30 to the *National Review.*- Wrote to Alg, Madge and Colles.

Frid. Feb. 2. Dull, a little rain. Wrote 2pp. in morning, but had to destroy them. At night, 3pp.

Sat. Feb. 3. Very fine. Little chap went out for first time. Wrote 4pp. Recd from Colles typescripts of the two stories to revise.

Sund Feb. 4. Very fine and warm. Wrote 4pp. Letter to Miss Collet and to Colles.

Mond. Feb. 5. After receiving about 30 replies to my advt for lodgings, went down to Hastings. Of course a day of ceaseless rain, miserable; got wet through. No one of my replies any use. Took rooms at house recommended by Miss Collet; 23 East Ascent, St Leonards. Sea-view happily. For my study, shall have to use a back bedroom. Home at 10 o'clock, worn out.

Tuesd. Feb. 6. Gloomy, windy. In aft. went to see Bullen. Evening came Miss Collet.

Wed. Feb. 7. A little sun in morning; gloomy later. Drove by cab to Charing Cross, and left by the 11.15, reaching St Leonards at 1.18. Dinner ready for us.- A comical mistake on arrival. The landlady, Mrs Gardner, met me with a grave face, and said she couldn't take in a *cat.* "Cat ? who talked about a cat?" And then it struck me. Yesterday I sent her a postcard, saying that "the cot" had been dispatched, and might arrive before we did! Oh, the asininity of people!

Thursd. Feb. 8. Glorious day, sunny and warm. In morning, with fearful efforts, got to work, and did 1p. Of course had to destroy it in evening, but did 3 more. Proof from Shorter of "Comrades in Arms", and note promising cheque next week. Managed to sit in my top room without a fire. We are remarkably comfortable in these lodgings. The landlady's husband, a former butler, waits upon us at table.- Before going to bed, corrected the proof.

Frid. Feb. 9. Wild s.w. wind again, and high sea. Wrote 1p. in morning, but had to destroy it. Evening wrote 2. Returned proof to Shorter. Postcard to mother.

Sat. Feb. 10. Strong wind, high sea; fine. Wrote in better spirits; 4pp. Letter to Colles, assuring him, as he desires to know it, that L[awrence] & B[ullen] do not swindle me. See in *Athenaeum* to-day a notice of a "cheap edition" of "Born in Exile", at 3/6. Must inquire about this.

Sund. Feb.11. Still the s.w. gale; sea very high. In morning had a walk alone. Evening did 2pp., and wrote to Miss Collet.

Mond. Feb. 12. The gale falling, very fine. Wrote 4pp.

Tuesd. Feb. 13. Very fine; wind fallen. Wrote 4pp.- Still reading "The Cloister and the Hearth" [by Charles Reade]. Buy the *P[all] M[all] G[azette]*, each day. Little boy enjoying himself much by the seaside.

Wed. Feb. 14. Fine. Did only 1½p. In no mood for writing.

Thursd. Feb. 15. Dull and rainy. Wrote 4½pp. Letter from Roberts.

Frid. Feb. 16. Cloudy but fine; no wind. In afternoon, E. being gone to purchase in Hastings, I walked alone with little boy. Wrote 3pp.

Sat. Feb. 17. East wind, and rain. Boy got a cold again. Did 4pp. Note from Miss Collet, to say she is coming down for next week.- At 10.30, just after I had got into bed, was terrified by a deep barking cough from little boy. Dressed at once, and rushed out to fetch Dr Batterham, who came with me. Then bought medicines and linseed meal. Of course no sleep.

Sund. Feb. 18. Same wind, but brilliant sunshine. Boy has bronchitis again. Of course nothing done but nursing.

Mond. Feb. 19. Same weather; glorious sky all day. Boy seems a little better. In afternoon Miss Collet came for an hour or two. Afterwards, though sick and headachy, wrote about half a page.- Letter from Tinckam, and note from a Caernarvon man, asking for autograph,- replied to him.

Tuesd. Feb. 20. Same weather; still the accursed east wind. Boy rather better. In the morning struggled vainly to work; evening did 2pp. Afternoon, a walk with Miss Collet.

Wed. Feb. 21. Same weather. Boy still better. No work. Miss Collet to supper.

Thursd. Feb. 22. Same weather. Boy for few hours in the front room, but not dressed. Wrote 3½pp., finishing vol. II.

Frid. Feb. 23. Change of wind to s.w., but still very fine. First thing in morning sent vols 1 and 2 of "Miss Lord" to Bullen. Wrote 1p. Miss Collet to supper.

Sat. Feb. 24. Glorious weather. Boy able to be dressed. Wrote 2pp. In afternoon walk with Miss Collet. Received, at last, cheque for £88-4 from *English Illustd Magazine,* for my seven stories. Heard from Bullen of receipt of parcel.

Sund. Feb. 25. Rain, mist, s.w. gale. Wrote to Bullen and Tinckam. Finished "The Cloister and the Hearth". Miss Collet spent evening here.

Mond. Feb 26. Continuation of yesterday's weather. Morning did nothing; evening wrote 1½p.- Little boy has badly swollen tonsils. The doctor thinks they have been so for a long time, and have caused his snoring at night. We have to apply alum to them, a difficult thing. In afternoon Miss Collet returned to London.

Tuesd. Feb. 27. Dull and misty morning; later fine and warm. Wrote 3½pp. Struggling with fearful difficulty against the oppression caused by little Grobsey's illness. Sent for Reigate newspapers. Thinking of going to lodgings there when we leave St Leonards. But the outlook is full of difficulties. Letters from Alg and from A.J. Smith.- The new *English Illustrated* contains "Our Mr Jupp",- of which, by the bye, I have never had a proof.

Wed. Feb. 28. Dull, rainy morning. Afternoon very fine. Began to give little boy cod liver oil. He takes all medicines without the least objection.- Wrote 4pp.

Thursd. March 1. High gale, cloudy. Wrote only 3pp.- Letters to Alg and to A.J. Smith.

Frid. March 2. Very fine. Boy went out for the first time.- Have broken down; could do no work. Bought Hardy's new book—"Life's Little Ironies",- and read most of it.

Sat. March 3. A marvellous day. Windless, hot, glorious sky. Boy out for three or four hours. At night did 1p. It took me four hours. It is long since I found work so difficult.

Sund. March 4. Fine still, but cloudy and cooler. Managed to write 2pp.

Mond. March 5. Bright morning, dull afternoon, windy. Wrote 3pp. Sent cheque to Tinckam.

Tuesd. March 6. Fine. Did nothing. All but gave up hope of finishing "Miss Lord" here. Note from Colles, asking if I am still here, as he wants to send cheque.

Wed. March 7. Fine. Reading [Mrs Gaskell's] "Wives and Daughters" left here by Miss Collet. In evening got to my work again, though it was a fearful struggle. Rewrote the last 2pp. Letter from Tinckam, and from Miss Collet.

Thursd. March 8. Rainy. Did nothing. Recd from Colles £25-8 for the two stories sold to *National Review* ["A Capitalist" and "A Lodger in Maze Pond"].

Frid. March 9. As morning promised sunshine, I went to Reigate, but had a cold day, with a little rain, and back by 2.30. No good, either for lodgings or

331

a house. Pretty place, but spoilt by the builders. We shall have to find new lodgings here, after 20th March, as these rooms are let from the 21st.

Sat. March 10. Very fine. In evening wrote nearly 2pp.- Note from Colles, saying that Jerome has not yet paid for the story he published in *To-Day* ["Under an Umbrella"].

Sund. March 11. Dull, very high wind. Worked morning and evening, and did 4pp. Letter from Roberts. Replied to him.

Mond. March 12. Rainy and stormy. Worked morning and evening, and did 4pp.

Tuesd. March 13. Very high sea. Brilliant sunshine. Wrote 5pp. Postcard from Bertz, who is removing from Frankfurt to Berlin.- The boy much better in general health. Talks a great deal, and very accurately. "That's the proper way-" "This is the way that da does it"—"Just a little jam please— not much"—and so on. He is taking cod liver oil, and drinks it out of a spoon, without showing any distaste.

Wed. March 14. Fine, but cold. Suffering from sore throat. Did 4pp.

Thursd. March 15. Dull, a little rain. Wrote 4pp. Throat better. Thank heaven the end of book is in view. Think it won't be bad, on the whole, and it has been written under fearsome circumstances.

Frid. March 16. Very fine, but I had to stay at home, because of my bad cold. Wrote 5pp.

Sat. March 17. Fine. Cold so bad that I didn't work in morning. Evening did 2pp.

Sund. March 18. Fine, but east wind. Cold still bad; didn't go out. Wrote 4pp.

Mond. March 19. Glorious day. Went over to Eastbourne, and took 2 rooms at 6 Grove Road, opposite the Station,- 25/- a week (Mrs Brewer). Back at 4 o'clock. But did no work.

Tuesd. March 20. Dull, very warm, though east wind. Wrote 4pp. Sent off postcards about change of address. Paid Batterham's medical bill.- £4, confound him! Decidedly too much.- Card of invitation from Alfred Hartley, for exhibn of pictures on Ap. 1st.

Wed. March 21. Fine. Left St Leonards by the 10.49 for Eastbourne. All well.

Thursd. March 22. Fine, but easterly wind still. As I have only two rooms here, I cannot write till the boy has gone to bed. Worked till midnight, and did 3pp. Proof of "A Capitalist". Bought Balzac's "Physiologie du Mariage".

Frid. March 23. Very fine; still east wind. Have given up my work; can do nothing here; must finish the last chapter when I get home. Walked to Willingdon.

Sat. March 24. Very fine; wind still east. In morning walked to Jevington and back.

Sund. March 25. Fine; wind the same. Boy seeming to get much better. Tonsils decidedly getting normal.

Mond. March 26. Cloudless day; still east wind. Took boy up onto the Downs.

Tuesd. March 27. A golden day; cloudless, warm, and with very little wind. Went by train to Polegate, and walked from there, through Wannock, to Wilmington, then on to Alfriston, where I had dinner at the Star, a fine old inn; but spoilt, as such places seem always to be in the south of England, by churlish people. Then by another road back to Wilmington, where I smoked at the Black Horse. On to Polegate, and home thence by train, at 6 o'clock. A day of exquisite spring. Primroses abundant. Ceaseless songs of larks, the bleating of lambs. Gathered a twig of blackthorn, all but out.- I saw workmen engaged in re-roofing the tiny old church at Litlington, which, when I was last there, I sketched in my Black's [Guide Book to] Sussex.- The "long man" at Wilmington gleaming like silver in the morning sunlight; in afternoon scarcely to be distinguished. On inquiry I learnt that a Mrs Carpenter used to let lodgings in the village, and might be induced to do so again.
   Posted letters to Alg and Bertz.

Wed. March 28. Again cloudless. Hired a mail-cart for the boy, and in the morning started over the downs to Jevington, which was reached about 1 o'clock,- a hard tug in some places. Had dinner at a cottage where meals are supplied; rested for an hour; then on again, thinking to come home by road through Willingdon. Found it would be too much, so took the 4.18 train from Polegate. A magnificent day, and did the boy much good.- Sent an advt for servant to the *South London Mail.*

Thursd. March 29. Foggy in the early morning, but the day again cloudless; very warm, light breeze still from the east. In the afternoon I walked alone to Pevensey, had a couple of hours there, and back by the 7.5.- Boy spent the afternoon down on the shore. His breathing is much improved; scarcely snores at all in the night.- Thinking of my story for the *Illustd London News,* and got some ideas.

Frid. March 30. Weather unchanged. In morning I walked up to Beachy Head and lay there for half an hour, thinking out story. Letter from Miss

Collet. One from Alg, saying he has been away for a fortnight, at Wakefield and Wooler. On returning he found Katie ill.- Bought "The Egoist" [by George Meredith].

Sat. March 31. Change of wind to west. A very warm and brilliant day. A cool letter from a German governess at Chiswick, beginning "Dear Mr Gissing", and asking me to send her, as a present, two or three of my books.- Idled about the shore. I see that "A Capitalist" is in the April number of the *National Review*.

*   *   *

Mond. Ap. 2.

Wed. Ap. 4. Left Eastbourne by the 9.55, and got home at 1 o'clock. The last days have been magnificent, as hot and bright as midsummer. Found letter from Nelly; answered.

Thursd. Ap. 5. Fine, but cold wind. Of course can do nothing until we get a servant.

Frid. Ap. 6. Went into town; and put advt for servant in the *Daily Chronicle*. Fine, but dull and coldish wind. Reading the first number of the *Revue de Paris*.- Invitation from Society of Authors to be on the list of stewards at their annual dinner.- The boy is beginning to learn the names of portraits and pictures hanging round the room: Michael Angelo, Shakspere, Schopenhauer, Kant, Turner, Daudet, George Sand etc.

Sat. Ap. 7. Fine, warm. Got from liby. [Henry] Sidgwick's "[Outlines of the] History of Ethics" [1886].

Sund. Ap. 8. Spent the morning at Streatham, where I am thinking of taking a house. Walked many miles. Fine, and very warm.

Mond. Ap. 9. Fine, hot. After much trouble with dirty applicants, engaged as servant, to live in the house, a young girl (said to be slow and stupid) who has been working at Stockwell Orphanage. She comes to-morrow. Letter from John Davidson, asking me to see him shortly. Made engagement for next Thursday.- Of course do nothing.

Tuesd. Ap. 10. Fine, hot. Got from liby "Charicles" which I have often wished to read, but never yet saw.[3] Visited Colles, and listened to his suggestions that I should seek other publishers than L[awrence] & B[ullen]. It seems Methuen wants me. Then looked in on Bullen. They have sold about 400 of the new edn of "The Odd Women".

Wed. Ap. 11. Fine, hot. In afternoon to Streatham; saw houses and talked with agent.- Davidson writes to put off our meeting till next week.

Thursd. Ap. 12. Fine, cooler. The new servant does fairly well. To-day I sat down to the final chapter of "Miss Lord", and wrote 2½pp. with indescribable struggle. I am utterly tired of the thing, and within a page of the end cannot realize that it will ever be finished.

Frid. Ap. 13. Fine. In the evening *finished my interminable novel.* Very slovenly the last pages. Gave up my idea of taking a house at Streatham. We shall probably go into Yorkshire at midsummer.- Letter from Katie, with portrait of Enid.

Sat. Ap. 14. At length some rain; heavy in the evening. Took my 3d vol. and left [it] at Bullen's. Then to Museum, where I spent an hour or two. Then to Gough Square, to see Johnson's house—the last remaining of those he inhabited—which is shortly to be pulled down. It has a tablet on the front. Occupied at present by stationers and printers, and some sort of club. I walked part of the way up the old stairs, which are wainscotted. A large house, twelve rooms, I should think. Rent must have been low in Sam's day.- Note from Bullen acknowledging receipt of MS.

Sund. Ap. 15. Rainy. Did nothing.

Wed. Ap. 16. Rainy. Planning out my new story. Note from Colles, saying that Messrs. Methuen wish to offer for it in vol. form. Letter from Nelly, to say she will be at Kingston on the 24th.

Tuesd. Ap. 17. Rainy to fine. Worked out list of names for my book. Wrote to Nelly and to Colles, telling latter I cannot decide until autumn.

Wed. Ap. 18. Fine. Made a beginning, and wrote rather more than a page.

Thursd. Ap. 19. Sunless and cold. In morning wrote a page, but in evening went back to beginning and rewrote 1½p. I am using as much as possible of my old Birmingham story.

Frid. Ap. 20. Weather unchanged. In afternoon met [John] Davidson at Grosvenor Club, and we remained together till 8 o'clock. No writing.

Sat. Ap. 21. Sky clearer. No work. Got from lib. Joseph Thomson's "Travels in [the Atlas and Southern] Morocco" [1889].

Sund. Ap. 22. Went nowhere, did nothing. Gloomy.

Mond. Ap. 23. Windy and rainy. Did nothing. Sent my guinea to the Authors' Society for the Annual Dinner, saying I should be able to be present.

Tuesd. Ap. 24. Heavy rain. At 1.55 met Nelly at Kings Cross, had dinner with her at restaurant, and came on to Brixton. As we have no spare bedroom, I have had to get one for her at 35 Burton Road.

Wed. Ap. 25. Began with rain, but at ten o'clock cleared, and became beautiful day. Went with Nelly to the Tower. In afternoon, E. met us, and we went to a so-called matinée of "Twelfth Night" at Daly's Theatre. Ada Rehan as Viola.[4] The most offensive performance I ever sat through. Only 3 acts were given, and then, to fill up the time, a concert followed! The Viola very absurd in slow tragic utterance. The Maria an impudent barmaid. Sir Andrew a circus clown, and so on. Grieve over the guinea I had to pay for our three places.

Thursd. Ap. 26. Fine morning, afternoon showery. With Nelly to service at St Paul's. Thence westwards. Looked in at St. Clement's, and saw Johnson's pew. Also his house in Gough Square. Then to Westminster Abbey. Home to dinner at 2.30. At 4 o'clock Nelly went from Loughborough Junction to Norbiton, where she is to stay for ten days with Vic.- Note from Miss Collet, asking what has become of me.

Frid. Ap. 27. Fine. Made an attempt to work, but have no grip of the story. Thought of a new one.- Note from Nelly.

Sat. Ap. 28. Showery to fine. Got from lib. Lady Anne Blunt's "Pilgrimage to Nejd" [1881]. No work.

Sund. Ap. 29. Fine. Spent morning in a walk to Chelsea.- Looked at Carlyle's house, which now has a marble tablet with Thomas's head. Wrote to Nelly and Miss Collet.

Mond. Ap. 30. Wretched day; cloud, fog and rain. Within, utter misery.

Tuesd. May 1. Left by an early train, and went by the Baker Street line to Aylesbury. Back to Wendover, a beautiful place, where I had dinner. Home by 5 o'clock. Day of cloud, with a little sunshine. Letters from Alg, and Miss Collet.

Wed. May 2. Dull. Thinking out my story. Made inquiries about warehousing the furniture, and find it will only cost 4/- a month. Wrote to Miss Collet.

Thursd. May 3. Dull, some sunshine. Made yet another beginning, but in vain. Think I can begin once more to-morrow. Letter from Miss Collet. Wrote to Alg, and sent him a lib. book.

Frid. May 4. Windy, cold, cloudy. Made a new beginning, and did 4½pp.

Sat. May 5. Finer and warmer. Did 5½pp. Getting on at last.

Sund. May 6. Fine. Wrote 2pp.

Mond. May 7. Fine. Wrote 2½pp. Got from lib. Mrs. Oliphant's "Makers of Venice".

Tuesd. May 8. Fine. Nelly and Ethel Hick came at dinner-time. Spent the night where Nelly stayed before.

Wed. May 9. Rainy in afternoon. Visitors took leave of us at 9.30 in the morning. They go home—to Wakefield—to-morrow.- In evening made yet another beginning of my story. Wrote 1½p.- Recd a copy of Roberts's new vol. "The Purification of Dolores Silva".

Thursd. May 10. Rainy. Wrote 1½p. In evening came Miss Collet.

Frid. May 11. Rainy. Wrote 3½pp. Recd from [W.H.] Hudson his pamphlet "Lost British Birds".

Sat. May 12. In morning gloom and high north wind. A very little better afterwards.- Unable to satisfy myself with the first part of my story. I left it aside, and began at a later point. Did 3pp., writing from 9-1, 4-8, and 9.30 to 12.

Sund. May 13. Once more, fine weather. Wrote 3pp. Hours 9-1, 4.30-8, and 9.15-10. Letter to Hudson.

Mond. May 14. Whit Monday. Very fine and warm. Wrote 9 to 11; 5 to 8; 9.30 to 11.30, and did 3pp.

Tuesd. May 15. Fine. Wrote 9 to 1, and 5 to 8.30. Did 3½pp. Letter from Alg.

Wed. May 16. Wretched day, close and foggy, with spots of rain. E. went to Miss Collet at Richmond. I, with little boy, of course did nothing.

Thursd. May 17. Fine. Once more the poor boy has a bad cold; kept him in bed.- Wrote 4pp.- At night told Tinckam that I shall give up these rooms at midsummer.

Frid. May 18. Fine. Boy rather hoarse in morning, but better during day. Poultices etc.- Yet again, began a new story, to be called, perhaps, "The Woman-Queller". Wrote to Shorter, asking if he cared for this title.

*   *   *

Sat. May 26. In utter misery, left off chronicling the useless days. Gave up "The Woman-Queller" within a few hours, and wrote again to Shorter, saying I had altered my mind. The blackguard has answered neither letter. Weather wild, rainy, cold. Boy has got better, but not able to leave the house yet. I have not touched work, and shall not whilst I stay in London.

This morning left home at 3.30, walked to L'pool Street, breakfasted at Coffee stall, and took 5.10 train for Southwold—to see if the place would do. Found it quaint and pretty, but a miserable beach of shingle; no use.

Weather too, was discouraging; bitterly cold, with frequent showers and some hail.- However I spent three or four hours at Halesworth. Found the sexton (Jarmey, by name) and got him to show me the birth register in church. There I discovered "June 27, 1830. Thomas Waller Gissing, son of Robert Foulsham Gissing and Jane Hall". I think the baptism must have been two years after birth. Jarmey said that his old father (now breaking up) "went to school with a Tom Gissing"—no doubt Father. Altogether this visit to Halesworth pleased me much. I had dinner at the Swan, with a beautiful view of the church from the window. Old, quiet town. Boys and men on the roads still touch their hats to a stranger.- At the railway station I bought the June *English Illustrated* where Shorter has printed one of my stories ["The Honeymoon"] (without having sent me a proof). How proud he would have been, the dear, kind Father! How little could he dream, when a lad running about lanes and fields, that, more than half a century hence, his son's literary work would be sold, to that son himself, at Halesworth!

Sund. May 27. Furious n.e. gale all day, with heavy rain and hail. Towards night came calm.- Decided that we shall go to Clevedon. Wrote to Alg and to Miss Collet. We shall leave next Saturday.

Mond. May 28. Sunny, but very cold. Paid Tinckam rent up to midsummer. I suppose few men have spent more superfluous rent, wages etc. than I.- Bought Holden's edn of Plutarch's "Gracchi".

Tuesd. May 29. Rainy. In afternoon came Miss Collet.

Wed. May 30. Great deal of rain; little sunshine. Heard from Alg. Busy packing.

Thursd. May 31. Rain, hail, thunder and last a brilliant evening. Packed all the books. Took a bedroom for to-morrow night, at the house where Nelly slept.

Frid. June 1. Removing people came at 8.30, and had done by 12 o'clock. Goods taken to be stored at Dougharty's, Barrington Road. Hope I have not seen the last of them. Dull day, but happily did not rain. In evening came Bullen's agreement for publn of "Nancy Lord", with his cheque for fifty guineas.

Sat. June 2. Dull, close. Went by cab to Westminster Bridge, thence by train to Praed St., and left by the 10.15 for Clevedon. Arrived at 2.23. Whilst E. and little boy waited at station I went to Mrs Elston's, and succeeded in getting our old rooms, together with a third, which I shall use as study. (Address 84 Old Church Road). Rent 20/- a week, with a few extras.- Utterly worn out.

Sund. June 3. Rainy, close, little sun towards evening. Wrote several letters.

Mond. June 4. Cloudy morning with rain. Hot sun in afternoon, then clouds again. Sat down to my work, and did 2pp. A horrible struggle—sinking misery. At night read a chapter of Plutarch's "Gracchi".

*Tuesd. June 5.*Morning of thick cloud and rain. Fine afternoon, then cloudy evening. Wrote 3pp. To bed early, feeling ill.

Wed. June 6. No sun all day; and cold. Did 3½pp. Letters from Tinckam and Nelly.

Thursd. June 7. Vast improvement in weather. Bright sun nearly all day. Did 4½pp. Letter from Alg.

Frid. June 8. Fine morning. Rain late in afternoon. Did 4pp.

Sat. June 9. Fine. Did 2pp. Reading Anstey's "The Pariah".

Sund. June 10. Fine, with a shower or two. Did nothing. Postcard to Bertz, and notice of change of address to London P.O. My letters to be sent to Bullen.

Mond. June 11. High wind, showers. Wrote 4pp. "The Gaverocks" [by Sabine Baring-Gould] from the liby. Letter from Bertz, and one from Madge, who is at Criccieth, in N. Wales.

Tuesd. June 12. Cloudy, but fine and warm. Wrote 4pp. Letter to Madge, and postcard to Tinckam.

Wed. June 13. Fine, but cloudy as usual. Wrote 4pp.

Thursd. June 14. Weather improving; sunshine all day. Did 4pp.

Frid. June 15. No sun, and rain at evening. Letter from Bullen, saying that postman brought a letter to Henrietta St., redirected for me from Burton Road, but refused to leave it, on the ground that I, not having been householder at Brixton, had no claim to have my letters readdressed gratis.- I wrote to the General P.O. about this.- It spoilt my morning, and all day I only wrote 2pp.

Sat. June 16. A beautiful day, but no work. We are tortured here with fleas, rest broken, and the poor boy a mass of bites. Moreover, cannot get wholemeal bread, necessary for E. In the morning I walked over to Yatton, to try the whole-meal of a baker there. Evening read a little Plutarch.

Sund. June 17. Morning rain. Evening very beautiful. After tea a walk half way to Kingston Seymour, boy in his cart. Wrote to Miss Collet and Alg.- Am thinking of trying to get a house at Hitchin.

Mond. June 18. High wind and much rain. Did 3pp. Got from liby. Kipling's "Many Inventions".

Tuesd. June 19. Fine, but cloudy. Last night ruined by fleas, which torment us sorely. To-day did only 1p. Letter from [William Thomas] Stead of *Review of Reviews,* asking me, as one of the foremost of the novelists of Great Britain, for my signature to a Memorial in the International Peace cause. Of course gave it.

Wed. June 20. Cold and rainy. Did 3½pp.- Letter from Ella Gaussen, who says she is going to marry an officer.

Thursd. June 21. Fine, hot day. Did 3½pp. Bought "The Trumpet Major" [by Thomas Hardy].

Frid. June 22. Cloudy but fine. Did 3pp. Feeling better about my work. It may not be utter trash, after all.

Sat. June 23. Weather still doubtful. Did 3pp. Intimation from *Pearson's Weekly* that my letter, which they asked for six months ago, has just appeared.[5]

Sund. June 24. Cloudy, but no rain. In morning wrote to Bertz and Ella Gaussen. Afternoon we all went to Kingston Seymour, and had milk there fresh from the cow. Read some Plutarch, and some Shakspere.

Mond. June 25. Cloudy; very little sun. Did 3½pp. Got from lib. "A Window in Thrums" [by James Barrie]. Am having a summer suit made here, 50/-.

Tuesd. June 26. Sultry and sunless. Did 3pp.

Wed. June 27. Brilliant day. Had to rewrite the 3pp. of yesterday, and did 1 more. Wrote to Shorter, saying that I had finished the story, and asking if I shall send the MS at once.

Thursd. June. 28. Cloudless, very hot. Did only 1p. My usual difficulty in finishing.

Frid. June 29. Weather the same. Reply from Shorter, saying he will be glad to have the MS at once, to give the artist as much time as possible. Heaven be thanked, finished the thing, and decided to call it "Eve's Ransom". A poor title, but my head whirls.

Sat. June 30. Weather the same, very hot. Sent off MS to Shorter. In afternoon took the boy on a steamer round the light-ship. Weighed him on automatic machine which registered 2 stone 4 lb. A fair weight, I suppose. Bought "Desperate Remedies" [by Thomas Hardy].

Sund. July 1. Very hot. Wrote to Alg, saying that I shall be at Willersey next Wednesday. Read "The Tempest".

Mond. July 2. Misty and rainy morning. Fine afterwards. Reading "Desp[erate] Remedies".

Tuesd. July 3. Dull morning; afterwards fine, windy. Recd from bank £15. Shorter acknowledges MS. Letter from Nelly.- Announcement that Mudie's and Smith's will give the publishers only 4/-a vol. for 3-vol. novels after end of this year. Grievous outlook for some unfortunate writers.- Am thinking of making my next book a vol. of essays.[6]

*   *   *

Frid. July 13. On Wed. 3rd [*sic*] I set off for Willersey, and stayed with Alg until the morning of the following Tuesday. The first day or two hot bright weather, so that we had an occasional meal out in the orchard. After that, the sky began to be swept by masses of cloud, which rarely broke in rain. From Willersey I went on to Hitchin, where I stayed only an hour, finding it at once utterly unsuitable for a place of abode. Went on to Bury St Edmunds, and put up there at the Temperance Hotel, where I stayed two nights. Very pleasant old town, but weather cloudy and rainy. Doubt whether I should care to settle there. Back to Clevedon on Thursday (yesterday). To my suprise, found proofs of the first two chaps. of "Eve's Ransom" awaiting me.

To-day corrected the proofs and returned them. Still cloudy, with light showers, and cool.

Sat. July 14. Fine on the whole, but clouds still about. Another batch of proofs; corrected and posted. Read some Plutarch. Wrote to Alg.

Sund. July 15. Cloudy. Finished life of Tib[erius] Gracchus, and read 150 *ll.* of 13th "Odyssey".

Mond. July 16. Mist and rain. Began revision of "Nancy Lord", and worked all day. Got from lib. [Andrew] Carnegie's "Triumphant Democracy" [1886].

Tuesd. July 17. Cloud and wind. Recd Alg's new book, "A Vagabond in Arts". Worked at my revision.

Wed. July 18. Cloud and wind, with light showers. Worked, doing a page of rewriting—cursed toil. Read to end of 13th "Odyssey". Recd proof of "In Honour Bound", for *Eng. Illustrated.* Letter from Miss Collet.

Thursd. July 19. In afternoon we all went to Weston, chiefly to buy some clothing for boy. Found it was the day of a horse-fair and that shops had closed at 2. Moreover, a demonstration of the Salvation Army in full blast.

With difficulty found one shop still open and made purchase. Very high wind and showery clouds. Home by 7 o'clock, having had merely a glimpse of the sea-front. Read 150 *ll.* of 14th "Od[yssey]".

Frid. July 20. Cloudy and threat of rain all day. The boy got a cold, from yesterday. [Edward] Clodd's "Story of Creation" from liby. Some "Odyssey".

Sat. July 21. Fine and hot. Boy's cold very bad, but only in the head. We have let him run about all day, to see the result. Finished my revisal of "Nancy Lord". Colles writes that he has sold "His Brother's Keeper" to a new mag[azine] which is to start early next year [*Chapman's Magazine*]. In evening I walked to Walton. Wrote to Alg about his book.

Sund. July 22. A day of thin, steady rain. Read at Clodd. Some Shakespeare. Wrote to Nelly and to Colles.

Mond. July 23. Sunless, and occasional light rain. Read several chaps. of Caius Gracchus, and some "Odyssey". Letter from Roberts, who is back from Australia, saying that he saw it mentioned in *Echo* of last Saturday that I was in Somerset.[7]

Tuesd. July 24. From 11.30 in the morning to 10 at night, ceaseless heavy rain. Wrote to Roberts. Finished "Caius Gracchus".

Wed. July 25. Changeable; very fine morning. Wrote to Hudson.

Thursd. July 26. Fine, hot. A little Plutarch. Barrie's "The Little Minister".

Frid. July 27. Fine, but heavily clouded at times. A clear sky is unknown this summer. Did nothing. Letters from Bullen and Hudson.

Sat. July 28. Fine. Did nothing. Took boy to be photographed for the first time.

Sund. July 29. Rain.

Mond. July 30. Hot and fine. The boy paddled in sea. Reading "Katherine Lauderdale" [by F. Marion Crawford, 1894]. Letter from McCormick, asking me to get him the illustration of "Eve's Ransom". Decided at last to call my novel "In the Year of Jubilee", and wrote to Bullen about it.

Tuesd. July 31. Fine, rain at evening. Doing nothing.

Wed. Aug. 1. Doubtful all day, and rain at evening. In afternoon walked to Portishead and back.- [William] Black's "Judith Shakespeare" [1884].

Thursd. Aug. 2. Rainy.

Frid. Aug. 3. Clouded and windy, but on the whole a fine day. I walked from Cheddar to Wells, and enjoyed myself—excogitating three short stories. Liked Wells better than ever. Back by train at night. Letter from Alg.

Sat. Aug. 4. Dull, rainy. Shorter sends a letter addressed to him by Fred Barnard, who is illustrating "Eve's Ransom", and who wishes to know whether I like the sketches of heads which he encloses. Dengate and Hilliard won't do; wrote to Barnard with suggestions. His address 3 Park Road, Stevenage. Replied to Shorter. Wrote to Alg.- Reading some of Tolstoi's short stories.- In *Athenaeum* to-day a paragraph announcing death of Cecil Roberts, and saying that M[orley] R[oberts] thinks of writing his life.[8]

Sund. Aug. 5. Fine morning, then dull. Read [Anstey's] "Vice Versa". Wrote to Roberts.

Mond. Aug. 6. Dull morning, fine later. Thinking over a short story. Began re-reading of the "Gracchi".

Tuesd. Aug. 7. Fine during day, but ending in rain; as usual. Took the boy to Walton. As we were going through a shady lane, he said "Let us get into a *light* place". Has made this remark before. He likes the tops of hills.

Wed. Aug. 8. Fine till evening, then rain. In afternoon took boy up to Dial Hill and Walton Castle. He enjoyed the castle much, and asked many questions.- Reading Memorials of Lady Canning and Lady Waterford (Hare)[9].- Note from Fred Barnard, thanking for my letter.

Thursd. Aug. 9. Fine morning, dull afternoon, rainy evening. Read Hall Caine's "The Manxman", which has just appeared in 1 vol., instead of 3,- a result of the recent Mudie revolution. (How, by the bye, will it affect poor Alg?) Mudie and Smith have sent a circular to the publishers, saying that after end of this year they will pay only 12/- for 3-v[olume] novel. The publishers seem disposed to give up the 3-vol. publication altogether, and the Authors' Society has passed a resolution to the same effect. My own interests in the matter are entirely dubious.- Caine's book very poor.

Frid. Aug. 10. Fine, cool. Recd and corrected some proofs of "Eve's Ransom".

Sat. Aug. 11. Fine, though cloudy, day; rain at evening. Corrected proofs of "The Pessimist of Plato Road". Got from lib. "Life of Dean Stanley" [*The Life and Correspondence of A.P. Stanley,* Dean of Westminster, by R.E. Prothero, 1893].

Sund. Aug. 12. No sun, and after noon heavy rain. Reading Stanley. Wrote to Alg.

Mond. Aug. 13. Windy, but fine afternoon. Walked with E. and boy to Yatton and back by train. Wrote to John Davidson.

Tuesd. Aug. 14. In spite of cloudy, windy and altogether threatening morning, we started by the 11.20 to go to Wells, taking the boy for once without his cart. It turned out a beautiful day on the other side of the Mendips, though Clevedon had storms. We had dinner and tea at the Temp[erance] Hotel in Market Place. Heard afternoon service in Cathedral, the boy sitting very quietly, much impressed by organ. Showed him the iron men striking the quarters on the old clock. Went up Tor Hill. Rambled about the moat.- Boy chiefly anxious to throw stones into the water. Back by the 5.40 train.- The first proofs of "In The Year of Jubilee"—as we have now decided to call "Miss Lord of Camberwell".

Wed. Aug. 15. An astonishing day for this time of year; but for the warmth like a wild day of March. Furious wind, with frequent sharp showers. Reading all day at the 3d vol. of Lady Canning and Lady Waterford.

Thursd. Aug. 16. Wind has fallen. No sun till afternoon; fine evening. Read [E.F. Benson's] "Dodo"—the astounding success of 1893. More proofs. Temperature rarely above 60 nowadays.

Frid. Aug. 17. Heavy clouds but no rain. In afternoon I took train to Yatton, and walked to Wrington. Back to Yatton by way of Congresbury, where I had tea at the Ship and Castle Inn. Interesting monument in Congresbury churchyard, to a man named Hardwick, who died in 1849; the granite cross raised to his memory by friends in 1871. "So fearless was he, that having been attacked by a highwayman (Oct. 1830) on the heath in the parish, and fearfully wounded by him, he pursued his assailant as far as the middle of this village, where he seized him and handed him over to justice."- Letter from Roberts.

Sat. Aug. 18. Heavy clouds; rare glint of sun. Reading [J.T.] Coleridge's Memoir of Keble [1869]. More proofs.

Sund. Aug. 19. No sunshine; heavy clouds, windy and cold. Finished Keble. Wrote to Mother and Madge.

Mond. Aug. 20. Cold, gloomy. Read Laurence Oliphant's "Haifa [; or Life in Modern Palestine]" [1887].

Tuesd. Aug. 21. Cloudy, warmer. Read "The Lancashire Life of Bishop Fraser" by [John William] Diggle [1889].- Proofs.

Wed. Aug. 22. Cloudy, warm. Read Mary Somerville's Memoirs.[10] The boy has a bad cold again.- His photographs not being good, he has sat a second time, with better result.

Thursd. Aug. 23. Sunless, rainy, steamy. Boy's cold has got onto his chest. (N.B. Last Tuesday, when already it was very bad, E. let him paddle in the sea!)- Letter from Mother. Proofs.

Frid. Aug. 24. Sunless day, faintly brightening, with rain, at evening. Boy in bed. Letter from Nelly.

Sat. Aug. 25. Hard rain till afternoon; then sunless gloom till late evening; then through the night, a violent thunderstorm, with furious rain. Letter from Miss Collet, objecting to title "In the Year of Jubilee". Answd her[11], and wrote to Nelly.- Boy in bed.

Sund. Aug. 26. Brilliant and hot all day. Packing for my departure to-morrow. Boy up, but has bad cough.

Mond. Aug. 27. Cloudy again till evening.- Left Clevedon by the 8.30, got to London 12.25, left some heavy luggage at the station, and went on to Berkhamsted in search of an abode for us all. Put up at the Goat Inn. Same evening found that this district would not serve my purpose. To bed worn out. Sent note to E.

Tuesd. Aug. 28. Bright and hot day. Walked to Boxmoor, only to be disgusted. Thence by train to St Albans, a picturesque spot but as unsuitable as the others. Back in evening to Berkhamsted so exhausted that I had to lie on the bed for an hour before I could eat.- Note from E. Much troubled all last night with anxious thoughts about little boy.- Shall have to give up Herts. To-morrow go into Surrey.- Wrote to Tinckam, to thank him for gift of "Perlycross" [by R.D. Blackmore, 1894].- Objects. to Herts are a certain squalor of the towns and villages, due, doubtless, to influence of London. Country seems, too, to be damp. At all events, I can't get to like it.

Wed. Aug. 29. Fine and hot. Travelled to Leatherhead; low-lying, squalid rather, and looking damp. Thence walked to Ashtead, where I engaged two rooms over a corn-dealer's shop. But scarcely had I got away than I repented. Resolved at length to write and excuse myself—sacrificing the 10/- deposit I had paid. Alas for my instability and impractical folly! Back by train to Leatherhead, to fetch the handbag I had left there at station; then, in sheer distraction of mind, took train for Wimbledon, where I haunted the ways uselessly, for all the houses are big, and utterly beyond my means—even if the place were not detestable. Spent a terrible night at the "Dog and Fox", having telegraphed to E. asking her to write at once to Wimbledon P.O., to say how boy was.- Heavens, what a day of misery!

Thursd. Aug. 30. White mist early; it cleared, and there followed a blazing day, throughout which I travelled and tramped many a weary mile. Having recd E.'s letter, saying boy is better, I went by train to Dorking and looked for rooms. Saw some at 3 Clifton Terrace, s. end of town, which looked possible. Felt I *must* come to a stop somewhere. Yet, remembering Ashtead, I resolved first of all to see Sutton. Thither by train, and talked with a house-agent. No house in the high ground under £40. Took train to Banstead station, and walked a useless two miles, under broiling sun, to the wretched little village. Returned to Sutton, and thence back to Dorking, where at length I took two rooms at 3 Clifton Terrace, for a fortnight from Saturday. Terms 25/- and small extras. Dry, sandy soil, beautiful view, and nice little garden behind. Paid 5/- deposit. Wrote at once to E., and sent new address to Bullen. Put up for the dreary night at the Temperance Hotel in West St.- Another week such as this would kill or madden me.

Frid. Aug. 31. Brilliant, and still hotter. Till evening felt very miserable; then was vastly cheered by learning from a review that Hare, in his handbook to Sussex, quotes my description of West Dean, from "Thyrza"[12].- Sent off three postcards to house agents in Kent. Spent evening up in Glory Woods, where I was astonished and delighted to hear owls hooting.- Got from lib. "A Group of Noble Dames" [by Thomas Hardy].

Sat. Sept. 1. Took my bag to 3 Clifton Terrace, and started for London, allowing myself an hour to get from Victoria to Paddington. But train was of course half an hour late, so I had to take a cab. Met E. and boy at 12.25, grappled with their luggage, together with my own, which I took out of the cloak-room, and cabbed to Victoria, where we had dinner. On by 2.14, via Croydon, to Dorking. No carriage there procurable; so we put boy in the mail-cart, and walked all the way to our lodgings. E. brings batches of proofs.

Sund. Sept. 2. Fine and very hot. In morning we walked to the woods. Boy is better, but a little cold still clinging to his chest. He said to me to-day, holding up a little apple which had fallen off the tree: "Da, put this on the tree again till it has grown bigger." Corrected some proofs.

Mond. Sept. 3. Rain once more; all day. Walked about, looking vainly for suitable house. Only two or three houses to let in Dorking, and expensive. Boy's cold better.

Tuesd. Sept. 4. Fine. Went to Epsom, and there at length found a house that pleases me—Eversley, Worple Road. Soil, chalk and gravel. Rent £40. It has a bathroom, of which I had begun to despair. Decided to take the house, on yearly tenancy. Wrote to ask the furniture people what cost would be of removing my things to Epsom.

Wed. Sept. 5. Fine. Recd proofs and corrected. Letter from Alg, mentioning that Enid seems likely to have whooping-cough.

Thursd. Sept. 6. North wind and much rain, with thunder. No reply yet from the furniture warehouse at Brixton. Begin to feel anxious about it.

346

Frid. Sept. 7. Fine on the whole. Boy much better since he came here. Nothing yet from Brixton; sent postcard to the people. Walks in this neighbourhood. Delightful scenery, and comfort from the fine sandy soil. I wish we had been here all the summer—though of course only for the boy's sake.- Proofs.

Sat. Sept. 8. Doubtful. High north wind. We went up onto Holmwood Common. Letter from Bullen, saying they have sold to Bell & Co., for a new Colonial Liby, 1200 copies of "Denzil Quarrier" and 750 of "The Emancipated", in quires, at 10d½ a copy. Bell will also take 1500 of "In the Year of Jubilee" at 1/- a copy, in quires. Also letter from Lawrence saying that Houghton & Mifflin of Boston will possibly pub[lish] "Jubilee".- Proofs.

Sund. Sept. 9. Early part of day wind and rain; later fine. Wrote to Bullen and to Lawrence.

Mond. Sept. 10. Fine. Went over to Epsom and saw agents. Agreement not ready yet, but promised for to-morrow at latest. Walked back to Ashtead and thence by rail. More *Illustd L[ondon] N[ews]* proofs.

Tuesd. Sept. 11. Magnificent day. Cloudless. Blackguard agents have of course broken their promise; no news.

Wed. Sept. 12. Fine. Went over to Epsom, and signed agreement for the house. Yearly tenancy at £40.

Thursd. Sept. 13. Day of rest before the horrors that begin to-morrow. Sent off great batch of letters, announcing new address.

Frid. Sept. 14. Weather still fine, but cloudy. Leaving E. and boy to follow to-morrow, I started for Epsom in the morning. Found charwoman, whom I engaged on Wednesday, at work in house. Furniture promised for 3-4 o'clock; of course came at 6. By 7 was able to send off note to E. that all was safely in. Tired to illness, went for the night to the Spread Eagle.

Sat. Sept. 15. Fine. At the hotel they charged me 7/- for simple tea, bed and breakfast; too much. Worked with charwoman and got house in some sort of order. At half past two came E. and boy. Through registry office, E. engaged a servant to come in on Monday night. £14 a year. Batches of proofs. "Jubilee", "Eve's Ransom", and "A Lodger in Maze Pond" for the *National Review*. Got my books out of the 11 packing-cases, which have to be returned at my expense to London.

Sund. Sept. 16. Fine, but dull. Put up curtains etc., and did a little gardening. Proofs. Enjoyed my new bath.

Mond. Sept. 17. Dull, and spots of rain. Ordered notepaper printed with new address. Went early to London, and spent £20 at Oetzmanns—

bedroom furniture, fenders, lamp, curtains etc. Then to see Bullen and Lawrence. Thence to Shorter, who told me that, owing to Fred Barnard's breakdown, the publication of my novel is unavoidably postponed to Jan[uary]. As yet he has actually advertized it for Oct. in the new *English Illustrated*. He asked me for some more short stories, and promised cheque for "Eve's Ransom" at once. Accepted his invitation to dine with him and meet Dr. Robertson Nicoll, at Devonshire Club, St. James's St., at 7.30 on Wed. week. Also promised Lawrence to dine with him and Bullen to meet Miss Orme shortly.

Tuesd. Sept. 18. Dull. Grappling with disorder of the house. Servant promises to be far better than any we have had yet. A couple of pounds spent in casual small purchases.- Recd £150 from *Illustd London News.*

Wed. Sept. 19. Very fine day. Toil in the house. Letter from Nelly.

Thursd. Sept. 20. Heavily clouded, but dry. Oetzmann's furniture arrived; tremendous unpacking.- Proofs.- Letter from Colles asking for Xmas story. Line from Lawrence.

Frid. Sept. 21. Sunless, foggy day. Find that the looking-glass won't fit into the new dressing table. Wrote to Oetzmanns about it. Letter from Roberts.

Sat. Sept. 22. Sunless. In afternoon came Miss Collet and stayed till after supper. *Athenaeum* states that my story in the *Illustd L[ondon] News,* which it miscalls "Eve's Pardon", won't appear in Oct. as advertised because the illustrations are not ready.

Sund. Sept. 23. Rainy to fine; heavy clouds. Letter from Bertz. In afternoon walked on Epsom Common.

Mond. Sept. 24. Dull, close. Unable to get to my work yet. Wrote again to Oetzmanns, who have paid no attention to my letter.

Tuesd. Sept. 25. Mist and fine rain; warm. In morning came Roberts, and stayed till supper. Miss Collet sends the boy "Struwwelpeter" [*Shock-headed Peter,* by Heinrich Hoffmann].- Lent Roberts £5.- After all, find the looking-glass can be made to fit the dressing-table.

Wed. Sept. 26. Dull, rainy at first, clear towards evening. Went to London at mid-day, to do several things and to dine with Shorter. Dinner was to be at the Devonshire Club, which just now is housed at the Reform; so I went to the Reform, and for a time waited vainly for Shorter. Then came a telephone, asking me to go to the National Liberal. Of course I had to cab it. Seems that Shorter had telegraphed the change to Epsom after I had started. The party consisted of Robertson Nicoll (of the *Bookman* and *British Weekly*), Massingham (political editor of [*Daily*] *Chronicle*), a lawyer whose name I didn't catch [George Whale], and an American,

Gilder, connected with New York *Critic.* Very pleasant evening. Liked both Nicoll and Massingham better than I had expected. Caught last train at Waterloo, and home at 12.30.- Proofs.

Thursd. Sept. 27. Fine, but getting coolish. Took a quarter's subscription at Andrews's library, connected with Mudie's. Letter from Nelly.

Frid. Sept. 28. Fine, coldish. Note from Colles, asking for 2 stories. Replied, promising them in a fortnight.- Proofs.- Afternoon, walked up to the Downs. Trying vainly to think of the stories.

Sat. Sept. 29. Fine, cold. In afternoon, walked to Wimbledon, by devious way, which made it 10 miles. Saw some papers at the free library—the nearest to here, I think. Back by 7.30.- Proofs.- Wrote to Nelly.

Sund. Sept. 30. From sunshine to gloom; less cold. In afternoon walked over Epsom Common into the Forest.- Evening began a short story: "Simple Simon". Wrote only three lines, and preparation for to-morrow.- Proofs.

Mond. Oct. 1. Cloudy, but fine on the whole; warmer. Worked morning and evening and finished "Simple Simon"; posted to Colles.- Proofs.

Tuesd. Oct. 2. Beautiful day.- Trying to think out another story. Wrote to Bertz.- Proofs.

Wed. Oct. 3. Fine. Got idea of story, but wrote nothing. Note from Colles, about "Simple Simon" [published in the *Idler*, May 1896]; says it is just what he wants, and asks for as much more of that sort as I can send him. Wrote to Alg.- Proofs.

Thursd. Oct. 4. Began and finished "Their Pretty Way"[13]. Got from lib. Eng[lish] tr[anslation] of M[axime] du Camp's Memoirs [*Literary Recollections*, 2 vols., 1893]. and Hare's Sussex. Found in latter's quotation from "Thyrza" a misprint about which I must write to him.- Day of rain.

Frid. Oct. 5. Gloom and rain. Reading Du Camp all day.

Sat. Oct. 6. Gloomy and rainy. Wrote at a short story, but gave it up at night. Letter to Alg.- More "Eve Ransom" proofs. Last proofs of "Jubilee".

Sund. Oct. 7. A little better weather. Finished Du Camp.

Mond. Oct. 8. Mist all day. E. went to London to buy a jacket, and so I spent the day with little boy. In the morning we ran about the garden for an hour; then he had his midday sleep (generally from 12 to 2). It took him some time to get to sleep, and he told me that the cause was his trouble about "the crumpled horn". We had just been looking at a picture of "the cow with the crumpled horn", which caused him much concern. "How did the horn get crumpled?" he asked, with distress. (In the same way, he used to be much troubled about "the bent tree" at Clevedon—a tree grown bent under the sea-wind.) In the afternoon we walked about Ashley Road, much engaged in looking at a steam-roller at work. At 6.45, I put the dear little chap to bed.- He seems to have a wonderful memory. Already he knows by heart the whole of his "Struwwelpeter", which Miss Collet gave him a fortnight ago. Incidents long past—our seaside visits chiefly—are very firm in his mind. Health much better; breathing in day time all but normal, not very bad at night. He is now taking Squire's Chemical Food and Cod Liver Oil.

Got from lib. the Life of Coleridge by J.D. Campbell [1894], and "A Lotos-Eater in Capri" [by Alan Walters, 1893]. Letter from Alg, very dark about his prospects.

Sund. Oct. 9. Still misty and some rain. Read Campbell's Coleridge. Trying hard to think of new stories.

Mond. Oct. 10. Rain all day; boy's breathing a little worse again. Began a story, but gave it up—in the old way.

As examples of the kind of torment I am silently bearing all these days and years, I will set down two stories, of recent date.

(1) In coming to live in the house, which I have furnished with special view to E.'s wishes and vanities, I made it my one request that she would keep out of the kitchen, and not quarrel with the servant. After the servant's arrival (and she is very hard-working) I hear tumult from the kitchen. There stands E. cleaning a pair of boots, and railing at the servant in her wonted way.- I had to put a stop to that by an outbreak of fury; nothing else would have availed; and this will only be effectual for a week.

(2) To-day, the little boy has not been very well, owing to wet weather. At eight o'clock to-night, as E. did not come down to supper, I went quietly to the bedroom door, to listen, as I often do, whether the boy was asleep. To my amazement I heard E. call out "Stop your noise, you little beast!" This to the poor little chap, because he could not get to sleep. And why not? Because the flaring light of a lamp was in the room. I have begged— begged—again and again that she will *never* take a lamp into the bedroom, but she is too lazy to light a candle, and then uses such language as I have written.

But for my poor little boy, I would not, and could not, live with her for another day. I have no words for the misery I daily endure from her selfish and coarse nature.

Thursd. Oct. 11. Heavy sky and close air. Began a story "The Vision of Humphrey Snell". Letter from Alg.

Frid. Oct 12. Fine once more.- Put aside yesterday's work, and began a new story.- Paid rates £2-16-10. Got from lib. Miss [Agnes] Repplier's "Essays in Idleness" and "A Book of Strange Sins" by [Coulson] Kernahan [both published in 1893]. Latter rubbish. Sent to Alg, "The Heritage of the Kurts" [by B. Björnson, 1892]. Dismissed last revise of "Jubilee".

Sat. Oct. 13. Very fine. Finished "The Tyrant's Apology", 5½pp. [published in the *English Illustrated Magazine,* July 1895]. "In the Year of Jubilee" announced by L[awrence] & B[ullen] in *Athenaeum.*

Sund. Oct. 14. Fine, cold. Afternoon walked to Ashley Park. Read several books of [William] Whiston's [translation of the works of] Josephus.

Mond. Oct. 15. Dull, cold. Frost last night. Wrote 2pp. of "The Fate of Humphrey Snell".

Tuesd. Oct. 16. Dull, cold. I and the little lad went for a walk in afternoon, as we have several times done lately. Wrote 2pp. Letter from John Davidson.

Wed. Oct. 17. Fine. Wrote 1½p. Letter from Tinckam. More proofs of "Eve's Ransom".

Thursd. Oct. 18. Fine morning, then gloomy. In afternoon walked with boy to Woodcote. Finished "Humphrey Snell' [published in the *English Illustrated Magazine,* October 1895]. Letter from Innes & Co., who ask me to write story for the first number of a new magazine "on Church lines" to be edited by one of the Chaplains of the Archb[isho]p of Canterbury [*The Minster*]. I replied asking for further information. Reading the 7th vol. of Goncourts Journal.

Frid. Oct. 19. A little rain. In afternoon walked to Burgh Heath. Wrote 1½p. of "A Freak of Nature".

Sat. Oct. 20. Mist and gloom. Gave up the story. Reading Léon Daudet's "Les Morticoles". Letter from Innes, agreeing to my proposal about the story (12 gu[ine]as, and free to choose my subject) and asking for a novel next year.

Sund Oct. 21. Gloomy, cold. Did nothing.

Mond Oct. 22. Tolerably fine, cold wind. Began "The Flowing Tide". Reading "Gli Amanti" of Matilde Serao.

Tuesd. Oct. 23. Gloomy, no rain. wrote 1½p. Postcard from Nelly.

Wed. Oct. 24. High gale and rain. In afternoon E. went to London; and back at 10.30. Altered my story, and called it "The Salt of the Earth".

Thursd. Oct. 25. Gale and rain. Worked morning, and till 12 at night, and finished story, 5pp. [published in *The Minster,* January 1895]. A maddening drum and fife band, planting itself before the house at 8 o'clock compelled me out in a rage, and I sent them packing. Invitation from Lawrence to dine with him and Bullen and meet Miss Orme. Answered that it must be week after next.

Frid. Oct. 26. Gale and furious rain. all but helpless with lumbago; crawled painfully to liby, and got Rovetta's "Il primo Amante" [1892] and Le Gallienne's "Prose Fancies" [First Series 1894]. Invitation from Colles to dine with him at house dinner at the Authors' Club on November 19. Accepted, and so shall be drawn at last to get a dress suit,- even if I hadn't needed it for Lawrence's dinner.- Began "A Merry Wooing".

Sat. Oct 27. Wind and rain; terrible weather. Lumbago still very bad. Wrote 2pp.

Sund. Oct. 28. End of gale. Fine day. Reading Italian novels.

Mond. Oct. 29. Fine, then furious rain, then fine afternoon. Finished "Merry Wooing" [no record of publication]. In afternoon went to London, and ordered dress suit and Inverness cape (together 9 gu[ine]as)[14]. Bought some things for E. See that "The Pessimist of Plato Road" is in the new *English Illustrated.* Letter from Alg, who proposes to come here for a week or two. Sent him £10.

Tuesd. Oct. 30. Ceaseless rain from dawn to midnight. Began a story, but gave it up. Wrote to A.J. Smith and John Davidson. Lawrence's dinner appointed for to-morrow week.

Wed. Oct. 31. Fine, but inclined to rain in afternoon. Letter from Fred Barnard, saying he is at work again on the illustrations. Replied to him. Read Mme Octave Feuillet's Memoirs; poor, and reveal a poor character.

Thursd. Nov. 1. Very fine. In morning began "An Inspiration", and wrote 1½pp. Afternoon to London, to tailor's. Letter from Innes, saying they think they could sell the American rights of the story I am doing for them, and asking my price. Replied that I don't know what to ask.- P.C. to Alg.

Frid. Nov. 2. Dull and a little rain; warm. Wrote 2½pp.- Reading "Cuore Infermo" of Matilde Serao [1881].

Sat. Nov. 3. Fine morning, rainy afternoon. Warm. Finished "An Inspiration" [published in the *English Illustrated Magazine,* December 1895]. Wrote to Alg, who has altered his mind about coming here for a week or two.

Sund. Nov. 4. Very fine. Spent day reading Josephus ['s works translated by William Whiston].

352

Mond. Nov. 5. Rainy. In afternoon to London. Called on Shorter, and gave him the three stories I have written. Sent story to Innes.

Tuesd. Nov. 6. Very fine day. Finished "Cuore Infermo". In afternoon, I and boy walked up to the Downs.

Wed. Nov. 7. Reading "La Tourmente" (Paul Margueritte[15]). Letter from Henry & Co., asking for a novel. Shall decline. In evening went up to town, to dine with Lawrence & Bullen and Miss Orme. Put on my new dress clothes, which I found was needless. We dined at the Adelphi Restaurant, and then went back to Henrietta St. and smoked, Miss Orme taking a cigar as a matter of course. [Half a line crossed out and illegible] Bullen gave me his "Anacreon". Pouring rain all the evening.

Thursd. Nov. 8. Cloudy and some rain. Bad headache; did nothing. Sent as present to Bullen my old copy of Randolph.[16]

Frid. Nov. 9. Rain all day. Read "The God in the Car" (A[nthony] Hope). Of course vastly inferior to what I had supposed from the reviews. Letter from Nelly.

Sat. Nov. 10. Lovely morning. Walked Burgh Heath way. Then heavy rain. Got [C.R.B.] Barrett's "Somerset[shire Highways, Byways, and Waterways]", [1894]. Thinking over a new novel.

Sund. Nov. 11. Fine all day, rain at night.- Thinking.

Mond. Nov. 12. Rain all day, and at night great storm, with thunder and lightning. Sent off as wedding present to Mary Bedford (who will be married on 28th to Austin Williams, after many years engagement) copies of "Thyrza" and "New Grub Street", and a little wall-frame for photographs.- Wrote to A.J. Smith, asking him how to make our hard water soft.

Tuesd. Nov. 13. Very fine. In morning walked on Burgh Heath road, and thought out a book called "Among the Heathen". Note from Colles, asking if I will read a story at the Authors' Club dinner on Monday. Heaven forbid!- Evening worked at plan of my book.

Wed. Nov. 14. Rain and gale all day. Newspapers full of floods and wrecks.- Thinking over book.- Josephus, and Lamartine's "Girondists".

Thursd. Nov. 15. Rain all night and till mid-day. Katie and Enid were to have come over from Kingston, but weather prevented. Reading Emile Bergerat's "La Vierge"[17].- Letter from Mary Bedford, acknowledging presents.

Frid. Nov. 16. Rain first of all, then very fine day. At 12 came Katie and Enid, and left us at 4.

Sat. Nov. 17. Fine. Sent Enid the "Arabian Nights", for birthday.

Sund. Nov. 18. Very fine, all day.

Mond. Nov. 19. Fine, cooler.- Dinner at the Authors' Club, the honoured guest Anthony Hope (real name, Hawkins; a relative, I find, of Walter Grahame). About 40 present, and as dull an evening as ever I spent. A mere gathering of tradesmen, and very commonplace tradesmen to boot. Oswald Crawfurd in the chair; his speech ludicrously feeble. In the middle of Hope's reply, the electric light went out, and we all had to strike matches to keep him going. I sat near to [Walter] Besant, and talked with him. His face precisely that of an owl—a resemblance strengthened by his gold-rimmed *pince-nez.* Commonplace to the last degree; a respectable draper. Talked a little with Hope, of whom little is to be expected. Crawfurd told me that he is going to edit a new periodical for Chapman & Hall [*Chapman's Magazine of Fiction*], and asked me to write. On going away, I was stopped by some fellow (don't know who) demanding my address. Said he wanted it for Mrs. George Edwardes, wife of the manager of the Empire; and this Mrs G.E. turns out to be Julia Gwynne, who has kept me in remembrance.[18] In the doorway, met R.H. Sherard, and was introduced to him. A walking skeleton, tall, upright, ghastly, with warts on face and neck.[19]

Tuesd. Nov. 20. Fine till night, then rain. Read Matilde Serao's "Gli Amanti".

Wed. Nov. 21. Very fine. Note from Henry & Co., saying they would be willing to agree for a novel for 1896.- Miss Collet sends me the life of W.H. Widgery [*William Henry Widgery, Schoolmaster.* by William Kirkpatrick Hill, 1894], and a volume of Maria Edgeworth.- Still pestered by the blackguard drum and fife band. They play to-night *in the garden* of the house opposite, and defy me from private ground, the people of the house encouraging them. I went again to the police station, but found there is no help.

Thursd. Nov. 22. My birthday; 37. Letters from Mother and Alg. Went early to London, and did a lot of things. Bought some crocus and hyacinth bulbs. Went to see Tinckam at Sampson Low's. Looked up some things at Museum. In afternoon to see Fred Barnard, at 105 Gloucester Road, Regent's Park. Wretched lodgings; his wife and two daughters in the country, and, I surmise, living at someone else's expense. The poor man very drunk, in a torpor, and only just able to talk connectedly. Has done only one drawing for my story, and the *News* people are getting very impatient with him. I think it very unlikely that he will finish the job. Looks very young for his age, but has grizzled hair. Subject, I think, to delusions; says a man is going about offering forged work in his name. Told me he had got up at 5 that morning (as often) to wander about the streets, but I don't believe it. He probably used to do so in better days. Talked in melancholy strain of his son (animal painter) who died at 21. When I left he came out with me, and insisted on drinking brandy at the nearest public-house.- Home at 7 o'clock.

Frid. Nov. 23. Misty, fine, cold. Put crocuses into the garden. Got from lib. Baring-Gould's "The Tragedy of the Ceasars [: Julian and Claudian]", [1892] and Rovetta's "La Baraonda" [1894]. Wrote to Mother and Nelly and Miss Collet.

Sat. Nov. 24. Misty, cold. Reading the Ceasars. Wrote to Bertz and Alg.

Sund. Nov. 25. Sunny, cloudless sky; cold.

Mond. Nov. 26. Grey and cold; no sun. Troubled by the necessity of having fires in so many rooms. Spending the days, at present, down in dining-room, to save fire in study. Still at the Caesars.

Tuesd. Nov. 27. Sunless, cold. Reading "La Baraonda". Letter forwarded by Bullen from Blaze de Bury (I know not whether male or female) of Paris, asking for permission to translate "The Odd Women". Writer says that he (or she) has heard much of me from Mrs Cornish of Eton. Who the deuce is Mrs Cornish?[20] Wrote to Bullen for advice.- Proof from Innes of "The Salt of the Earth", the worst proof I ever had in my life. Asked for revise.

Wed. Nov. 28. Sunless, a little warmer. "La Baraonda", which I like. Invitation from Douglas Sladen to the *Idler* office, which I decline. Note from Roberts.

Thursd. Nov. 29. Sunless, grey. Letter from Bullen, advising me to ask a fee of 20 gu[ine]as for right of translating "The Odd Women". He tells me that Bells have taken 500 more of "The Emancipated" for their Colonial Library. The subscription for "In the Year of Jubilee" is about the same as the last. He wants to republish "The Unclassed" next year.

Frid. Nov. 30. Fine day. Walk with little man in afternoon. Bullen sends 6 copies of "In the Year of Jubilee". Finished "La Baraonda". Not an original book; recalls too strongly French and Russian novels.

Sat. Dec. 1. Went to London in afternoon, merely to decide who "Blaze de Bury" is. At Wimbledon began fog, and in town it was horrible. I felt asthmatic pains; could not live in that atmosphere now. Went to Museum, and from the Catalogue learnt that my Paris correspondent is Mlle (Yetta) Blaze de Bury, evidently daughter of the Baroness of that name. On returning found cheque from *English Illustrated* for my three new stories (£37-16). Also revise of the horribly printed story for Innes.

Sund. Dec. 2. Misty, cold. Wrote to Mlle Bl. de Bury. P.C. to Bertz.

Mond. Dec. 3. Very fine and clear. Letter from Miss Collet, saying she likes "Jubilee". Wrote to Alg and Nelly. Got from lib. "Castigo" by M. Serao.

Tuesd. Dec. 4. Foggy.

Wed. Dec. 5. Foggy. Wrote to John Davidson, asking if he will dine with me at end of next week.

Thursd. Dec. 6. Clear, but grey; no sun. In afternoon walked with boy to "the dark tree". He saw a child going to school, and said: "When I go to school, I will work hard"-with a pathetic little earnestness.- Telegram from John Davidson, appointing Café Royal at 6.30 on Saturday.- Letter from Roberts, from 20 Rampa Brancaccio, Naples. Replied to him.

Frid. Dec. 7. Very fine and mild morning, later rain. I had a walk in the Oxshott direction. Got from lib. Swinburne's "Studies in Prose and Verse" [1894], and [George Moore's] "Esther Waters" [1894].

Sat. Dec. 8. Moderately fine. Spent the day in town, chiefly buying things for house, and in evening dined with Davidson at Cranford's, Sackville St.- an astonishing 2/6 dinner. John Lane, the publisher, came in, and we went with him to his rooms in the Albany, which were Macaulay's rooms. But he had to go off to Bath, and left us to stay alone as long as we liked, which was till 11, smoking his cigars and drinking his whiskey. Davidson gave me a copy of his "Ballads" and said: "The first edn of 5000 copies is sold out".

Sund. Dec. 9. Gloomy day. Read "Esther Waters". Some pathos and power in latter part, but miserable writing. The dialogue often grotesquely phrased.

Mond. Dec. 10. Gloomy. The boy's birthday: gave him [Edward] Lear's "Owl and Pussy-cat". Wrote to Nelly and Miss Collet. Read Davidson's book, which gives me thoughts.

*   *   *

Tuesd. Dec. 18. Nothing to note of late. Weather still very mild.- This afternoon, our servant took herself off, having secretly had her box removed beforehand. Good riddance. E. got a young girl to come in daily. To-day appears *The Minster,* with my story "The Salt of the Earth". A poor get-up, and badly illustrated. Jerome writes asking for my portrait to use in review of "Jubilee" in *To-day* [published on January 12, 1895]. Sent it.- Have read Maria Edgeworth's Letters, and A[rthur] Morrison's "Tales of Mean Streets" [1894]. Last Saturday came Miss Collet. She sends me [Robert] Buchanan's "Book of Orin" [1868].

Wed. Dec. 19. Fine. In afternoon to town, on appointment with Jerome at 3. Having seen from an advt that "Eve's Ransom" is after all to be illustrated by some man [Wal Paget] whose name is new to me, I called at the *Illustd Lond[on] News*. Shorter out at lunch. In Arundel St. I met him, with Bowden (of Ward, Lock) to whom he introduced me. Barnard, as I anticipated, has hopelessly broken down. On to the office of *To-Day*. Jerome wants a series of articles on every-day lower-middle-class London folk. Promised to try my hand. Home by 7.30.

Sent Alg 30/-, for his immediate needs. Wrote to Fennel of Wakefield, ordering 3 bottles of sherry for mother. Little boy has a glandular swelling in neck, confound it. Painting with iodine.

Thursd. Dec. 20. Fine. Reading [R.H.] Sherard's Daudet, and trying to think out work for Jerome. Posted presents to M[argaret] and E[llen]— two silk handk[erchie]fs. Bought Christmas Tree.

Frid. Dec. 21. Rain all day. Reading [Henry Kingsley's] "Ravenshoe". Astonished by letter from Revd Osborne Jay, of Holy Trinity, Shoreditch (the man whose plagiarism I had to write to the *Times* about, last year) inviting me to visit him. Replied genially, of course, and promised to go some day.

Sat. Dec. 22. Furious gale. In the afternoon I took the boy out, and he came back complaining of aches and pains. Seems to have a cold. Letters from Mother, M[argaret] and E[llen].

Sund. Dec. 23. Very fine, but could not leave house. Boy has cold on chest. Dreary times, these.

Mond. Dec. 24. Gloom and drizzle; very warm. From Miss Collet, for "George and Walter Gissing" a beautiful little "Alpine Flora" bought at Zürich. For E[dith], two silk handk[erchie]fs. Letter from Alg, saying he thinks of changing abode in Edinbro'.

Tuesd. Dec. 25. Gloom and drizzle. Boy's cold better; he has not been kept in bed this time. Present for him from Willersey. Still amused himself with the Christmas Tree,- crackers etc. We lighted the plum-pudding for him.- E., her cold severe, went to bed at 6, and I sat alone through the evening; mind untuned for thought.

Wed. Dec. 26. Gloom, but no rain. All our colds bad. Of course doing nothing at all.

Thursd. Dec. 27. Very bright. Could not go out. Sent my rent to the agents.

Frid. Dec. 28. Gloom again. All have bad colds; no one leaves the house.

Sat. Dec. 29. Bright, cold. Sent a little present to Willersey. Read Mary Deland's "Philip and his Wife" [1894].

Sund. Dec. 30. Bright and cold. Edith kept in by throat. Boy struggles well against his catarrh. Wrote to Bertz.

Mond. Dec. 31. Hard frost, clear. Sent off another servant advt.- Find that I earned by literature in 1894 no less a sum than £453-12-5. Bravo! I see that my total expenses were £239-6-9.

1895

Tuesd. Jan. 1. Clear, freezing. Reading "Fantasia" [by Matilde Serao, 1883]. In the new number of *The Author* [Walter] Besant has a well-meaning par[agraph] on the "comparative silence" with which my "fine works" are received. He begins, however, with the amazing statement that my story in *The Minster* is the first piece of writing that to his knowledge, I have ever pubd serially!- I am amazed at the ignorance of these men in current literary news.

Wed. Jan. 2. A little snow; clear sky. Boy still in house. Letter from Nelly, who is going for fortnight to Bridlington. She sends me a cutting from last Thursday's *Times*, an astonishing item of news by the Paris correspondent. It seems that Mlle Blaze de Bury has just been lecturing on me in Paris, with huge eulogium[1].- Sent the cutting off to Bullen.

Thursd. Jan. 3. Cold, more snow, but sunny. Walked in afternoon to Banstead. Reading "New Arabian Nights [: Tales not included by Galland or Lane]".

Frid. Jan. 4. Cold, dull. Can do nothing at all. Advertising for servant is quite useless.

Sat. Jan. 5. Very cold. Snow still lying. I see that Bullen advertises "Jubilee" largely. Wrote to Miss Collet. Reading "Where Three Empires Meet" (travels in Kashmir etc.) by E.F. Knight [1893]. First part of "Eve's Ransom" appears in *Ill[ustrate]d Lond[on] News* [weekly instalments, January 5-March 30].

Sund. Jan. 6. Freezing hard, gloomy.

Mond. Jan. 7. Bright, hard frost. Boy went out again for first time, and was greatly astonished at seeing a frozen pond. He is taking Scott's Emulsion now, and it evidently does him much good. Letters from Miss Collet and Bertz. Getting a new book clear in my head. Think of calling [sic].

Tuesd. Jan. 8. Frosty, fine. Boy out again.

Wed. Jan. 9. Hideous day; thick fog and frost still. Shorter sends me *The Sketch*, with my portrait and article on "Jubilee"[2]. He writes asking me to go and sit to Russell for a large portrait, to be included in series of sixteen leading novelists.- Most serious letter from Alg. Blackett says he sold, of the last novel, 100 fewer than of any before, and declines to take the new book. I wrote advising A[lgernon] to correspond with [A.P.] Watt, the agent.- Sent *The Sketch* to Wakefield, and another copy to Bertz.

Thursd. Jan. 10. Continuation of hard frost. Reading [Lionel] Johnson's book on Hardy [*The Art of Thomas Hardy,* 1894].

Frid. Jan. 11. Weather the same; thick mist. Sat down at last to write something for Jerome. Finished a sketch "A Drug in the Market" [published in *To-Day,* May 11, 1895]. Wrote to Alg, promising money in a day or two. The editor of a forthcoming weekly, *The Hour,* sends for a portrait. Sent him one.³

Sat. Jan. 12. Clear sky, but still freezing. Letter from Roberts, praising "Jubilee". Cheque for *Minster* story, from Innes. In afternoon, to my astonishment, formal letter from Smith, Elder, asking for a novel for a 1-vol. series. I never conceived it possible that they would come to me. Times are altered.- Great advt of my books, by Bullen, in the *Spectator,* and excellent notice of "Jubilee" in *Athenaeum.*- In evening wrote a second sketch "The Friend in Need" [published in *To-Day,* May 4, 1895].- Reading George Egerton's "Discords" [1894].

Sund. Jan. 13. A thaw, with rain. Sent sketches to Jerome. Replied to Smith, Elder, saying I will some day write a book for them if I have time. Wrote again to [Fisher] Unwin (second letter from him this morning) explaining what I could do for the Autonym series.

Mond. Jan. 14. Thaw, fine. Took boy out in afternoon. Reading my old diary to get material for new story for Unwin. Note from the *Idler,* asking for 200 words on question of who is to be next laureate. Did it after supper [published in April number].

Tuesd. Jan. 15. Rain all day. Began writing my new story, to be called, I think "Sleeping Fires". Did 1½p.- Proof from Shorter for "The Fate of Humphrey Snell".

Wed. Jan. 16. Rainy. Went to town by the 11.9, and straight to Russell's, where I sat five times for head and shoulders and once for three quarter length⁴. Thence to Unwin's. Could not see Unwin, who was detained somewhere, but had a talk with his manager.- At St Martin's Lane reading-room which I frequent for want of better, saw a paragraph in the *Literary World* [of January 11], to effect that my "boom", set going by W[alter] Besant, must have startled its originator. (Didn't know of the "boom".) Also that I spend most of my time in Italy, but am at present in England.- The boy, who likes to tear open my letters in the morning, says that he knows who "Fisher Unwin" is—"the man who sends our fish".- Sent £10 to Alg.

Thursd. Jan. 17. Fine. Telegram from Colles, asking if he may quote terms to Methuen for "Eve's Ransom". Said no, but that I would write them another book, if they liked.- Jerome writes, asking terms for my sketches; referred him to Colles.- Wrote to Unwin from whom a letter this morning, asking his terms for copyright of an Autonym book.- Wrote to Miss Collet.- Did ½p. of the book.- Copy of *Wakefield Free Press* [of January 12], with paragraphs about me.

Frid. Jan. 18. Fine. Wrote to Besant as follows: "Dear Mr. Besant, it would be a proof, I think, of insensibility if I refrained from speaking of that paragraph in the current number of *The Author* which has undoubtedly done me so important a service. For the kindness which prompted you to write those lines, permit me to express with all simplicity my sense of grateful indebtedness.- I am, dear Mr. Besant, very sincerely yours, G.G."- No writing.

Sat. Jan. 19. Rainy. *Sat[urday] Review* has article on "Mr Gissing's new book".- Unwin writes offering £150 for all rights of story of 30,000 words, to be ready by 31 March. As I know not a soul here, I have to post the Agreement to Miss Collet, to sign as witness.- Letter from Colles, in which he says Jerome offers £3 for my sketches.- No work.

Sund. Jan. 20. Fine. Read [A.H.] Japp's "De Quincey Memorials" [1891]. Wrote to Colles again.

Mond. Jan. 21. Gloomy, high wind. Returned agreement to Fisher Unwin. Letter from Roberts. One from Nelly, telling me that Alg is at Wakefield.- In evening made new beginning of "Sleeping Fires". Did 2pp.

Tuesd. Jan. 22. Heavy fall of snow. Worked amid much discomfort and did 3pp. Letter from Colles, saying he had heard Ward Lock were to issue "Eve's Ransom". Wrote to him to make appointment for Thursday; also to Roberts.- In reply to a remonstrance of mine, Mudie writes that their new Catalogue gives my books under my name. It was intended to be done for the '94 Cat., but "unfortunately overlooked".- From a letter from Miss Collet I learn that Jerome and Shorter both wrote to the [*Daily*] *Chronicle* apropos of their quotation of Besant's paragraph. Must see these letters.[5]

Wed. Jan. 23. Day of violent winds and storms; a little snow, then thaw again.- Presentation copy of Mudie's Catalogue.- Wrote 3pp.

Thursd. Jan. 24. Letter from Alg from Wakefield.- Went up to town by the 10.10. Day of extraordinary variations of weather: snow, fog, sunshine, hail, rain. An hour's talk with Colles at office. Story to be done for Xmas Annual edited by Anthony Hope, and several other things suggested. With Colles to lunch at Authors' Club. There found Roberts. With him sauntered about, and dropped in for a moment at Bullen's.- "A Poet's

Portmanteau" put first in the Feb. *English Illustrated.*- Bought a shawl as present for E. on birthday. Gloves for myself. Home by 7.30, worn out with excitement.- Before going to bed wrote letters to three servants.

Frid. Jan. 25. Snowy and sloppy. Did 3pp. Letter from Bullen, inviting me to dine some day next week.- James Payn, in his *Illustd Lond[on] News* page to-day, has a paragraph about me.[6] Meant as laudatory, but showing little understanding of my work.

Sat. Jan. 26. Hard frost, fine. In *Athenaeum* to-day a column advertisement of my books. Letter from Alg's sister-in-law at Kingston Hill, asking me to lend her "Jubilee". Sent it.- No writing. Read Huxley's "Evolution and Ethics".

Sund. Jan. 27. Hard frost, beautiful day. Wrote 1½p.- Recd two proofs of photographs from Russells. Don't much like either, and wrote asking if they are the last.

Mond. Jan. 28. Still terribly cold. Wrote 3pp.

Tuesd. Jan. 29. Fine. E. went to London. Wrote only ½ page. Reading [R.L.] Stevenson's "[Familiar Studies of] Men and Books" [1882].- Ward & Lock write to ask if they can have "Eve's Ransom".

Wed. Jan. 30. Terribly cold, with light snow. Struggled to write with frozen hand morning and afternoon, doing 1p.- In evening went up to town, and dined with Bullen. He gave me detailed accounts of my books up to end of last year. They all show deficits, unfortunately, but he generously proposes to "write off" everything, and begin anew, paying me a royalty of 1/- on each copy from Jan. 1 '95. He will bring out "Eve's Ransom" soon. I offered to forego advance on royalties, but he insists on paying 50 gu[ine]as. We had a long evening, ending up in the cosy bar-parlour of Stone's in Panton St.- On getting home, I found that the "Autolycus" article in to-day's *P[all] M[all] G[azette]* is devoted to me [a review of *In the Year of Jubilee*].

Thursd. Jan. 31. Too cold to do anything. Reading Life of Symonds [H.F. Brown, *John Addington Symonds: a biography,* 2 vols. 1894].

Frid. Feb. 1. Snow. Cisterns frozen. Bad headache.- Bullen sends as present their edn of Catullus, and a little book "Tales of the Masque" [by J.H. Pearce, published by Lawrence & Bullen in November 1894].

Sat. Feb. 2. Sunless; ice and snow. In afternoon came Miss Collet.- No work.

Sund. Feb. 3. Weather unchanged. Read a little Catullus. No work.

Mond. Feb. 4. Ice and snow. Letter from Alg, saying he will be in London shortly.- Miss Ella Hepworth Dixon, as editor of a new paper *The English*

Woman, writes to ask for story, but can only give £2 a thousand. Must refuse.- Thinking all day of my story, shall have to recast it.- Wrote to Madge, asking her to lend me Crabbe, for there is a possibility that I may edit [George] Crabbe in the Muses' Library. Bullen suggested it.[7]

Tuesd. Feb. 5. Sunshine, but cold as ever. Letter from Colles, saying that Methuen have abandoned their Annual.- In evening arrived our new servant, Annie Medhurst (£16) got through Hetherington's.- Wrote to Alg.

Wed. Feb. 6. Colder yet. Letter from Bullen, saying that Mudie has had 25 copies more of "Jubilee". Sends Agreement for "Eve's Ransom". It is to be published in April, and, to secure American copyright, will have to be printed (alas) from American plates. Replied to him. Wrote to Colles.- In evening, despite numbness, made a new beginning of my story and did 1¼p.

Thursd. Feb. 7. Terrible weather. Reports of 35° of frost from the Midlands. Worked well, though against terrible odds—hands frozen and feet like stones. Did 4pp.- Got from lib. "Children of the Ghetto" [by Israel Zangwill]. Received Crabbe. Present of parkin from Mother.- New servant seems satisfactory.

Frid. Feb. 8. Same weather. Reports from Midlands and Yorkshire of 35° and 37° of frost!- Wrote 2½pp.

Sat. Feb. 9. Frost harder than ever. Wrote only ½p.- Article of 2 cols. in *Spectator* to-day, an attack on me for my "perverse idealism".- Roberts writes to ask if he may write a critical article on me for the *Fortnightly.*

Sund. Feb. 10. Cold terrible. Wrote to Mother, and to Roberts replied a long letter, with suggestions of defence agst *Spectator* misrepresentations.[8] - Reading Crabbe's Life.

Mond. Feb. 11. Bitter wind, but slight beginnings of thaw. Wrote 3pp.

Tuesd. Feb. 12. Not quite so cold. Did 2½pp.

Wed. Feb. 13. Terrible frost again. Wrote 3pp.- In the afternoon, as I walked towards Ashtead Park, I found a little greenfinch fluttering helplessly at the roadside. He seemed to have injured a wing, but perhaps was only starved and frozen. I brought it home; we put it in an extemporized cage, and gave it food, which it soon ate heartily. Must keep it to see if it recovers power of flight.- Letter from Roberts, asking for £5. Alas, must send it; though I can ill afford.

Thursd. Feb. 14. Hard frost, and bitter wind. Did 3pp. Sent Roberts his cheque.

Frid. Feb. 15. Same weather. Bad headache, did only 1½p. Letter from Bertz. Colles writes, saying he has application for "A Lodger in Maze

Pond" to be translated for the *Revue Bleue* [published on March 16, 1895].
Replied.

Sat. Feb. 16. Furious east wind. In afternoon, much warmer. Did 2½pp.-
Letter from Roberts.

Sund. Feb. 17. Dark, cold. The poor little bird that I brought home died,
whilst we sat at dinner.- Finished "Children of the Ghetto", a powerful
book.

Mond. Feb. 18. A slight thaw. Wrote 2pp.

Tuesd. Feb. 19. A thaw. Wrote 1½p.

Wed. Feb. 20. Thaw slight still. Cannot work; reading [A.P.] Stanley's
"Sinai and Palestine" [1856]. Recd some more proofs of photographs
from Russells, and sent an order for some.

Thursd. Feb. 21. Thawing slowly. Still unable to work. Astonished to
receive a letter from Martha Barnes, of Waltham, Mass., one of my old
High School pupils. It seems she has read some of my books; writes very
nicely, and like an intelligent woman. Replied to her. Strange, strange!-
Note from Appletons' English agent, asking for photograph to send to New
York. Sent it.

Frid. Feb. 22. No sun; thaw very slow. Did nothing. Note from Lawrence,
telling me that Appletons are to publish "Eve's Ransom" in America.-
Wrote to M[artha] B[arnes]. Letter from Katie, at Wakefield, saying Alg is
looking for rooms at Newcastle. Replied, and wrote to Nelly.

Sat. Feb. 23. Warm and in afternoon bright. Read [J.R.] Seeley's "Goethe
[Reviewed] after Sixty Years" [1893]. Letter from Mrs Henry Norman
(M[énie] M[uriel] Dowie, the girl in the Carpathians) asking me to go and
see her. She says that on the occasion of the publication of her novel
"Gallia", she has purchased *all* my books in the 3-vol. form, and that she
ranks me as one of the *three* first novelists.- Replied that I don't feel well
enough to go at once, but that I will write again.- Letter from Miss Collet.

Sund. Feb. 24. Thaw going on. Reading [Sir Richard] Burton's
"Pilgrimage [to El-Medinah and Meccah]", [3 vols., 1855-56]. Wrote to
Bertz and to Miss Collet.

Mond. Feb. 25. Woke up to find snow again, but it soon melted.- Wrote
3pp.- My portrait in *The Album* to-day.[9]

Tuesd. Feb. 26. Frost again last night, but day pleasant. Wrote 2½p.
rewritten from yesterday. Recd from America a copy of "Meditations in
Motley", by W[alter] B[lackburn] Harte.

Wed. Feb. 27. Frost in night, thaw in day. Did 1½p.- Letter from Alg, who has given up his northern projects, and is again at Willersey.

Thursd. Feb. 28. Very fine and springlike. But no thawing of waterpipes yet. In afternoon, Miss Collet. Letter from George Whale, whom I met at Shorter's dinner, asking me to dine with him at the Devonshire Club on March 17th. Accepted. Wrote 1p.

Frid. March 1. Fine, with the first shower for many weeks. Letter from Nelly.- Wrote 2pp., and finished "Sleeping Fires".

Sat. March 2. Frost in night, and a little snow this morning. Reading [J.R.] Seeley's "Expansion of England [: Two Courses of Lectures]", [1883]. Letter from Bertz.

Sund. March 3. Cold, still snowing a little. Reading [J.A.] Froude's "[The Life and Letters of] Erasmus" [1894].

Mond. March 4. Snow and wind. Went to town in morning, and took my MS to Miss Gill to be type-written. My writing has got so minute that I am ashamed to send the MS to Fisher Unwin. Note from Roberts.

Tuesd. March 5. Fine. At last we have our water supply in the house. Wrote to W.B. Harte of Boston, about his book.

Wed. March 6. Fine. Absurd letter from Colles, saying that Methuens have told him that Hurst & Blackett are going to publish "Eve's Ransom". Replied bluntly.- Began short story called "The Gentle Bagman", and did 3pp. Finished "Erasmus".

Thursd. March 7. Fine. After working all the morning at story, threw it away as useless. In evening wrote 3pp. of another—"A Freak of Nature". Reading [G.S.] Street's "Episodes" [1895].

Frid. March 8. Fine. A little rain at evening. Letter from Alg. One from Colles.- Finished story and sent it off [published in *London Magazine* in April 1895]. Reading [Max] Nordau's "Degeneration" [1894].

Sat. March 9. Rain. Finished Nordau.

Sund. March 10. Very fine. Reading [T.E.] Kebbel's little book on Crabbe [in Great Writers series, 1888].

Mond. March 11. Glorious day, very warm. Reading Crabbe, and noting.- Another letter from Mrs. Henry Norman. Wrote and offered to come towards end of week.- Got up at 2 in the morning, to see eclipse of the moon, which began at 1.52, and was over in about two hours. Splendid full moon, and at 2 o'clock the curved shadow already creeping upon it. Sorry I could stay only for a quarter of an hour or so.

Tuesd. March 12. Fine. Recd type-written copy of "Sleeping Fires", and worked in some additions. Man at Birkenhead sends for autograph. Mrs. Norman writes appointing Thursday.

Wed. March 13. Fine. Spent the morning over my story, and then sent it off to Unwin. Recd bill for the type-writing. It is 33,000 words (£1-13). As I cannot get [Mrs Norman's novel] "Gallia" [just published] through the library, had to buy it, and spent afternoon reading it. Not at all a bad book.

Thursd. March 14. Fine. Went early to town. Jerome has written for some more "Nobody" papers, and I have to think them out.[10] In afternoon to Mrs Henry Norman, 27 Grosvenor Rd. Spent, alone with her, a pleasant two hours.

*   *   *

[Notes concluding the second copy-book]

The Emancipated. Agbrigg. June 3-Aug. 13. 1889 (10 weeks)
New Grub Street. Cornwall Mansions. Oct. 6-Dec. 6. 1890 (9 weeks)
Born in Exile. Exeter. Clevedon. March 10-July 17. 1891 (18 weeks)
Denzil Quarrier. Exeter. Oct. 7-Nov. 12. 1891 (5 weeks)
The Odd Women. Exeter. Aug. 18-Oct. 14. 1892 (7 weeks)
In the Year of Jubilee. Brixton. Jan. 1-Ap. 13. 1894 (15 weeks)
Eve's Ransom. Written at Clevedon. June 4th-29th 1894 (25 days)

*   *   *

	Eve's Ransom	*Sleeping Fires*	*The Emancipated*
Illustd London News			
Sept. '94	£150		
Unwin			
March 25 '95		£150-0-0	
Lawrence & Bullen			
Ap. 15. 95	£52-10		
June 30. 95	£23-2-1		
L & B a/c June '95			£5-3

Wed. March 27. A gap in my diary of more than a week—unusual thing. On Mond. March 18th, we all went to Eastbourne, to Mrs Brewer's (6 Grove Road) and had a very poor week. Lodgings bad, and weather worse. Thursday the only fine day, and that we spent at Pevensey. I had a bad cold, due to damp sheets, and the boy caught it from me. We returned on Mond. the 25th, a tedious journey: changing at East Croydon, Norwood and Sutton, and wait of half an hour at each place. Recompense on reaching home to find that Annie had given the house a genuine spring cleaning from top to bottom. At Eastbourne I wrote two sketches for Jerome.-

To-day received £150 from Fisher Unwin for "Sleeping Fires". Wrote to Mother, asking if I could come to Wakefield next monday.- Weather rainy.- Read "The Prisoner of Zenda" [by Anthony Hope, 1894].

Thursd. March 28. Gale, with rain. Headachey. Struggled desperately, and wrote most of another paper for Jerome. Poor rubbish. Reading [R.L. Stevenson's] "The Master of Ballantrae" [1889]. Apologetic letter from Max Pemberton, offering £50 for a 25,000 word story for Cassell's Pocket Library. Shall think about it.

Frid. March 29. Wind and rain, fine after dark. Struggled desperately, and wrote the last of the 6 sketches for Jerome. Replied to Pemberton, promising story for autumn. Finished "Master of Ballantrae". Note from Wakefield, saying I can come on Monday.

Sat. March 30. Rainy and fine. In afternoon, Miss Collet.- Letter from a Miss Rosalind Travers, of Dorney House, Weybridge, asking me, in name of her father and mother, to make their acquaintance. Very troublesome, all this.- Letter from W.B. Harte.

Sund. March 31. Fine. In morning to [Alfred] Hartley's, Campden Hill, to see his new pictures. Afternoon to Shoreditch, where I stayed till 6 o'clock with Father [Osborne] Jay, as he is called. Think I see my way to a big book.

Mond. Ap. 1. Very fine morning. Left home at 9.5 and spent the morning in London. Then, by the 1.30, went to Wakefield. Took a brace of ptarmigan. Cold rain began in the Midlands.

Tuesd. Ap. 2. Fine, but cold and windy. In morning tried to find Mr. Hick, but failed and walked on to top of Lawe Hill. Thence to Back Lane School, where, in prowling about, I was addressed by a man who proved to be Andrew Chalmers, minister of the Unitarian Chapel. When I mentioned my name, he became very genial, and took me to his house at St John's. Invited me to dine this evening, and again on Thursday. Dined accordingly, meeting a young man called Latham, and Frank Wood, the doctor. Home at 1am.

Wed. Ap. 3. Gloomy, very cold, ending in a little snow. Spent afternoon with Mr. Hick. Called on the Bruces. Letter from Miss Blanche Wilmot, of

	Denzil Quarrier	The Odd Women	Short Stories	In the Year of Jubilee
From Hein[emann] & Bal[estier] (Continental)	£13– 2–6	£18–7–6		
Macmillan (N.Y.) to June 30th '92	£6–11–9			
Lawrence & Bullen (acct of royalties) June 95	£105– 0–0 13/-	£105–0–0		
L[awrence] & B[ullen] on acct of royalties Jan 94		£26–5–0		
Blackwood Jan 93			£20– 0–0	
Eng. Ilustd Mag. Aug 93			£11–11–0	
” Dec 93			£12–12–0	
Illust. L. News Xmas 93			£12–12–0	
National Review Dec 93			£13–10–0	
Eng. Illustd Mag. Feb 94			£88– 4–0	
National Review March 94			£25– 8–0	
To-Day Jan 94			£5–13–5	
"His Brother's Keeper" June 95			£15– 6–0	
Lawrence & Bullen July 94				£52–10–0
” Dec 94				£52–10–0
English Illustrated Dec 94			£37–16–0	
The Minster Jan 95			£12–12–0 (An Inspiration)*	
For transl. of "A Lodger in Maze Pond" in Revue Bleue March '95				
The Idler March 95			£1– 0–0	
The Humanitarian July 95			£1– 1–0	
The Minster June'95			£1–11–6	
a/c June 95		£1–16–0	£12–12–0	

*[The Minster for January 1895 contains "The Salt of the Earth", not "An Inspiration", which appeared in The English Illustrated Magazine, December 1895]

Temple Bar pubd in Aug 1891 "Letty Coe"—written 1884

[There follow notes in pencil, first illegible quotations in Greek, then]

Gibbon begun Dec 17 1892
Grahame's visit at Exeter March 21, 1893
May 10, 1893   1st letter from Miss Collet

[Finally, there are two references to Bertz, on p. 30 and 31 of the original of the Diary, to Newman's *Phases of Faith*, to the entry for Dec. 5, 1890, to the life of Bertz on p. 83, March 14, 1892].

St James's Theatre, asking for autograph. Wrote to E., to Lawrence, and to Miss Travers, of Weybridge, saying I wasn't able to go to see them.- Lawrence writes that "Eve's Ransom" was pubd yesterday; that more than 800 copies have been subscribed in London, and they hope to get rid of 1000 this week.

Thursd. Ap. 4. Cold and cheerless. Called on Mrs Binks. Dined again with Mr. Chalmers. Excellent dinner; home at 1.15. A family named Booth, intelligent women, called in the evening. Chalmers gave me a copy of his "Red Cross Romance" [1893].

Frid. Ap. 5. Cold, but dry. Called on Benington [a relative of James Wood, Gissing's former schoolmaster], and sat for an hour. Dined with Frank Wood. Present C. Atkinson, Leeds magistrate, and Dr Statter. Chalmers came in afterwards, and, as we walked homeward, at 12.30, he urged me to go with him to have an oyster supper! With difficulty resisted.

Sat. Ap. 6. Gloomy, but no rain. Left in afternoon for Manchester, by the 3.22. Express, with no stop, and journey done in less than an hour. Walked about Manchester, and ate. Then on to Alderley Edge, where I put up for the night at the Queen's Hotel.

Sund. Ap. 7. Fine but misty. In morning walked to Wilmslow, and saw Willie's grave in the churchyard. It is in fairly good order. Tis my first visit to Wilmslow since I left Wood's school in 1876. Willie died in 1880, poor boy. Came back to Alderley, and climbed to top of the Edge. Too misty to see horizon. But little changed in the past twenty years.- My bill at hotel 9/-.- Left at 4.55, and reached Birmingham 7.30. Put up at Victoria Temperance Hotel, Corporation Street.

Mond. Ap. 8. Sunny but cold. Went to Willersey. Found letter, an angry letter, from Shorter, complaining that we have pubd "Eve's Ransom" so soon after it came to end in *Illustd London News.* Replied civilly but firmly, saying I couldn't see how we had infringed his rights.- Invitation to be Steward at dinner of Royal Literary Fund. As it involves payment of £5-5, must refuse.- Innes writes for another story for *Minster.*

Tuesd. Ap. 9. Gloomy. Walking about the fields.

Wed. Ap. 10. Windy, but fine. Left Honeybourne by the 10.37, and got to Epsom at 5 o'clock. Find apologetic letter from Shorter, ending with request for new stories. Evidently I hit on the right tone to use with him. Boy very well.

Thursd. Ap. 11. Fine and hot. Recd from Lawrence cheque for fifty guineas. Got from lib. the English translation of Alex[andre] Dumas's Memoirs. Sent off eight presentation copies of "Eve's Ransom".

Frid. Ap. 12. Fine. East wind. Idling. Must try to have a 2 hrs walk each afternoon.

Sat. Ap. 13. Fine. East wind. Reading Mahaffy's Hist[ory] of Greek Lit[erature].

Sund. Ap. 14. Fine. East wind. Did nothing.

Mond. Ap. 15. Weather same. Wrote ½p. of my story for *The Minster*: "Merely Temporary".

Tuesd. Ap. 16. Same weather. Gave up yesterday's story, and thought all day of another. These short stories are becoming a great trial. Letters from Frank Wood, Mr Hick and Alg.

Wed. Ap. 17. Close and cloudy. In morning wrote 1p. of new story "A Calamity at Tooting". Afternoon walked to the woods, and heard the first cuckoo. Caught without umbrella in a thunder-storm.- Sent copy of "The Emancipated" to Chalmers.- Cheque for £15 from *The London Mag.*, for "A Freak of Nature"; but as they have sent a form of receipt for the "entire copyright" I had to refer it to Colles.- Impertinent letter from a vulgar admirer called Sheffield.

Thursd. Ap. 18. Fine and warm. Finished the story [published in the *Minster*, June 1895].

Frid. Ap. 19. Very fine. Letter from Colles, saying that of course he only sold serial rights to the *Lond. Mag.*- Letter from Miss Collet. One from Lawrence, saying that his friend young MacWhirter, son of the R.A., wants my address to write to me.- Proof of one of my sketches from *To-Day.*- Read a little Diogenes Laertius.- Called on Dr Alexander, to ask him to come and see the boy, for advice about tonsils and swollen glands.

Sat. Ap. 20. Wonderful day. In afternoon took boy to Ashtead Park.- Dr. Alexander came to give opinion about boy's tonsils. Said nothing need be done at present.- Letter from Bertz. Ed[ward] Clodd writes, inviting me to Aldeburgh for May 31st to June 5th.- Letter from Editor of the *London Magazine,* saying he wants as much of my work as possible.- Returned proof to *To-Day.* and sent my story to *The Minster.*

Sund. Ap. 21. Dull. Wrote to Miss Collet, who has invited E. to stay with her at Richmond, explaining frankly that E. cannot make friends with people, and is merely uncomfortable away from home.- Replied to Clodd, accepting invitation. Wrote also to Colles, and editor of the *London Magazine.*- Reading [S.R.] Crockett's "Raiders [: Passages in the Life of John Faa]," [1894]. Find it wearisome.

Mond. Ap. 22. Dull, trying to rain.- Thinking out "The Spendthrift".- Paid property tax and house duty (14/6).- Reading Crabbe again.

Tuesd. Ap. 23. Fine. Thinking away, all day and half the night.

Wed. Ap. 24. Fine, changing to rain. Drew up my list of names.- Recd batch of proofs of "Sleeping Fires" from Fisher Unwin. Advt of "Eve's Ransom" says "Second Edition ready shortly".

Thursd. Ap. 25. Rainy morning, then fine but cooler. Got from lib. "Fleur d'Abîme", by Jean Aicard.

Frid. Ap. 26. Rainy. Can't get my story into working shape.

Sat. Ap. 27. Rainy. Bought the little boy his first suit of knickerbockers— looks well in them. In afternoon came Miss Collet. Letter from Mr. Bruce, and one from Roberts. From Cassells, the agreement for my story for the Pocket Library.

Sund. Ap. 28. Dull.- Henry Hick, who is staying with relatives at Putney, came over and spent the day. A most genial, gentle fellow.

Mond. Ap. 29. Very fine. Spent day in town. Called on Lawrence, and on Unwin. Bought Nelly two French books, for her teaching. Find my balance at bank is £436.- Letter from Alfred Ellis, saying he has had applications for my photograph, and will be glad to send gratis copies if I permit him to supply. Of course agreed.- Rather more than 1000 copies sold of "Eve's Ransom".

Tuesd. Ap. 30. Fine. Working out details of story. Recd from Miss Collet "Mademoiselle Mori [: a Tale of Modern Rome]", [anonymous, new ed. 1886], and began to read it. Got from lib. [H.F.] Tozer's "[Researches in the] Highlands of Turkey" [1869].

Wed. May 1. Windy, fine. Wrote to Nelly and Alg. Hoed the potatoes in garden.- In evening actual beginning of "The Spendthrift", and wrote 1p.

Thursd. May. 2. Beautiful day. Wrote 2pp.- Received from Miss Travers, of Weybridge, a present of asparagus. Wrote to thank her.- Corrected proof of "A Calamity at Tooting".- Recd copy of *Woman* [of May 1] with my portrait [and a review of *Eve's Ransom*]. Also letter from one John Northern Hilliard, of Rochester, N.Y., with a long review of "Eve's Ransom" which he has pubd in some American paper.[11]

Frid. May 3. Fine, but very windy. Wrote 1p.- Invitation from Mrs Norman to lunch next Tuesday. Request from Elliott & Fry that I will sit to them.- Letter from Alg.- Wrote to Hilliard.

Sat. May. 4. Very fine. Wrote 1p., but fear this will be the last. The old indecision. Don't like my story.

Sund. May 5. Gloomy. Clodd sends copy of his presidential address of Folk-Lore Society. Wrote to him. Note from Miss Collet.- Reading [E.A.] Freeman's Hist[ory] of Exeter.

Mond. May 6. Glorious day. Seem to see my way to reconstruction of story.

Tuesd. May 7. Same weather. At 11 went and sat to Elliott & Fry[12]. Then to lunch with Henry Norman and his wife. Then to have tea, at my invitation, with Tinckam. Bought Church and Brodribb's selections from Pliny's Letters.

Wed. May 8. Very warm. Can do nothing nowadays but think fruitlessly of a story.- Cannot even read.

Thursd. May 9. Weather unchanged. Did nothing.- Astonished to receive from Bertz the sum of £27—a debt due to me for more than ten years. Wrote to him.

Frid. May 10. Very hot. Reading Daudet's "La Petite Paroisse". By the by, Daudet is just now in London for a fortnight. No chance of seeing him.

Sat. May 11. Wonderful day. In afternoon walked to Chessington.- Letter from Miss Barnes.- Have got my story into better shape.

Sund. May 12. Read "La Petite Paroisse", a sad falling from the old Daudet. No character that is a creation.- Read also several letters of Pliny.

Mond. May 13. Oppressively hot. In morning another false start at my story; wrote 1p., only to tear it up again. Letter from Nelly.

Tuesd. May 14. Just as hot. Another false start; 2pp. written to be torn up.- The P[all] M[all] G[azette] reviews "Eve's Ransom", and warns me agst "beating out too thin" for serial purposes. Troubled rather by this.

Wed. May 15. High wind, and much cooler. Reading [Arsène] Houssaye's "Mlle Cléopâtre"[13]. Letter from Alg. Announces that a son [Roland] was born to him at 6.30 yesterday morning, and all well.

Thursd. May 16. High wind, and coldish. Beginning of a new novel, and more hopeful. Wrote 2¼ pages. Recd a dozen of my portraits from Ellis.

Frid. May 17. Cold. News of snow and frost. Wrote 1p.

Sat. May 18. Cold, cheerless. Wrote 2pp. Reading "Solomon Marmon".

Sund. May 19. No sun. Last night recd request from editor of *The Humanitarian* [W.W. Wilkins] for contribution to a symposium on "Realism". Wrote it to-day, 1000 words [published in July 1895].

Mond. May 20. Cold and gloomy; spent day in town. Bought (at last) a writing-table; second hand, £6-10, in Tott[enham] C[our]t Road. Also a reading-lamp.

Tuesd. May 21. Finer and warmer. Letter from Bertz. Wrote 1p. Reading "Kidnapped" [by R.L. Stevenson, 1886].

Wed. May 22. Fine. Letter from Colles, asking for first chapters of story;- there is an opening in *Good Words.* Replied promising to send some pages to-morrow. At mid-day telegram from him, inviting me to dine at Authors' Club to-morrow. Declined.- After applying for it, at last got my guinea from the *Idler,* due from April number.- Wrote 3pp.

Thursd. May 23. Fine.- Letter from a Miss Hamel, who asks me to find her a secretaryship on the strength of her having typed a story of mine. Replied.-. Wrote 4pp., finishing 3rd Chap., and sent off MS to Colles.

Frid. May 24. Fine and warm. Wrote 2½pp.

Sat. May 25. Fine, hot. Wrote ½p. Miss Collet came. Proofs of photographs from Elliott & Fry.

Sund. May 26. Same weather. Finished "Kidnapped", and read—first time for long—some Schopenhauer. Recd June number of *Minster,* with "A Calamity at Tooting" in it.

Mond. May 27. Rather close. Wrote 2pp. Reading a book of [John?] Runciman's.

Tuesd. May 28. Very hot. Did nothing, oppressed by atmosphere of the races.

Wed. May 29. Very fine, with breeze. As blackguardism reached its height to-day, I went off by train to Bookham, walked thence to Box Hill, and back through Norbury Park to Leatherhead. Grand walk.

Thursd. May 30. Terribly hot for time of year. Thermom. 70° at 10 o'clock, and much higher, I should think, afterwards. Did nothing. Preparing for departure to-morrow.

*   *   *

Thursd. June 6. On Friday last I left L'pool Street by the 3.20 for Aldeburgh. Great crowd, and recognized nobody. At Saxmundham encountered L.F. Austin and Grant Allen. Reached Clodd's house just in time for dinner. There were five guests beside myself. Sir Benj[amin] Ward Richardson, Shorter, George Whale the Solicitor, L.F. Austin and Grant Allen. These men's parties at Whitsuntide have been an institution with

Clodd for many years; he has had numbers of well-known men down at his house. Everything simple, but great geniality and heartiness.

On Saturday we sailed in Clodd's boat, the "Lotus", to Orford, and had our lunch in the banquetting room of the Castle. Splendid view from the top; Sunday we boated to Iken, up the river, and ate there on the cliff; perfect weather. On Monday morning we sailed up and down for a couple of hours, returning for lunch. This being our last day, I was asked to write some verses to celebrate the holiday. They were copied seven times, and each copy signed by all of us[14].

Grant Allen I liked much better than I had expected. He is white-haired; and all but white-bearded (a little sandy remaining) though only 47. Very talkative, and, with me, confidential about his private life. Says his wife suits him admirably, and shares all his views of sexual matters. Showed me a letter just received from her, beginning "My darling Daddy". Has a wonderful memory; mentioned that he could name 40,000 plants. His special study is anthropology. Thinks there never was a man Jesus: his whole story a slowly perfected mythus. Has rather high-pitched and sing-song voice, to me pleasant.

Sir Benj. Richardson a wonderful old man. Endless stories, which he tells admirably; never at a loss for a name or date.

On Sunday evening there dined with us Sir H[enry] Trueman Wood, Sec. of Society of Arts, and late British Commissioner at the Chicago Exhibition. Man of no account.

I note some of the stories told.- A doctor, accustomed to attend to Lady Huntingtower at Bosworth Park (don't remember the date) was one day called in to see a young woman of sprightly kind somewhere in the neighbourhood. She talked much of "Huntingtower", and seemed to make out that he was her husband. At length, as they lunched together the doctor told her plainly that she could not be lady H., as he knew that lady. "Oh", said she, "that is the brazen hussey that goes about in public. I am his private wife."-

Edward Clodd once recd abusive letters from Ruskin, apropos of his treatment of Christianity. In one of them Ruskin wrote: "If you came into my study and made water on the hearth-rug, your behaviour would not be more offensive to me than this book of yours is." When Clodd read this letter to Cotter Morison, the latter exclaimed "Insolent capon!"

By the bye, Holman Hunt's account of Ruskin's divorce is this. Ruskin married merely to please other people, and after the wedding told his bride they were merely to be brother and sister. Impotency may or may not have had anything to do with it. Wife sued for nullity.

Macmillans and Longmans both refused [Cotter] Morison's "Service of Man", which was pubd at length by Kegan Paul. Morison much disturbed by these refusals.

Grant Allen told me he is drawing £25 a week from "The Woman Who Did", and will soon have had £1000. But, owing to the reaction consequent on the Wilde case, two publishers have just refused another book of his, greatly to his astonishment.

John Morley promised to write a memoir of Cotter Morison, to be prefixed to a collection of papers. But he has backed out of it.

Bernard Harrison, my old pupil, now an art student at Paris, has been converted to Roman Catholicism.

[L.F.] Austin told of Will Watson's madness. Once, in a hotel, in presence of a stranger, Watson told Austin that the Almighty had declared to him he was to be Laureate. Shortly after, he sent Austin long incoherent telegrams, abusing his publishers—Macmillans; these Austin sent on to [R.H.] Hutton [editor] of the *Spectator*. It appears that Watson will never talk about anything but his own poetry.

[here Gissing left half a page blank]

On Tuesday morning we all left Aldeburgh together (Clodd excepted) by the 8.55. At Saxmundham I parted from the others, and went to Yarmouth, where I put up at the Cromwell Temperance Hotel,- very cheap and very good. Went to Gorleston to look for lodgings for our summer holidays, and noted an address.

On Wednesday I left early, for Southwold. Walked from Southwold to Wenhaston, up Blythe valley. Splendid day. Then home by express from Halesworth, and found all well.

Letters. From Alg, to say that Katie is down again, and child (Roland his name) hearty.- From Henry Gibson Smith, telling me that A.J. died suddenly last Friday, of colic. (Is it possible that this veils a suicide? I should not be at all surprised, for one of the brothers did poison himself years ago, and H.G.S. made an attempt to cut his throat at Oxford.) My poor old friend, A.J.!- Letter from Henry Hick, inviting us all for next week to Romney. Of course can't go.- A line from Miss Collet.

At Aldeburgh, I agreed with Shorter to write 6 stories for the *English Illustrated*, at 12 gu[ine]as apiece, and 20 sketches for *The Sketch*, like those now running in *To-Day*, at 3 gu[ine]as each.

Frid. June 7. Fine, windy. Tried to make a beginning with the stories for Shorter—having put aside "The Enchantress" till I hear from Colles. No success. Recd from Elliott & Fry ½ doz. of my photographs.

Sat. June 8. Very hot. Decided to call my stories "Great Men in Little Worlds". Wrote 2½pp. of the first: "Our Learned Fellow-townsman". Letter from Shorter confirming our agreement.- Got from lib. 2 vo[lumes] of Montalembert's "Monks of the West" [1860-77].

Sund. June 9. Hot. Wrote to Hudson, Alg, Shorter and Nelly. In evening did 1p. of work—good for Sunday.

Mond. June 10. Hot. Finished first story [published in the *English Illustrated Magazine*, May 1896], and began the second. Letter from mother.

Tuesd. June 11. Fine, cooler. On with second story, "The Patron of the Drum and Fife", and wrote 2½pp.- Reading Montalembert.

Wed. June 12. Fine. A wasted day. Wrote and destroyed.

Thursd. June 13. Fine. Began new story, "A Despot on Tour", and did 3pp.

Frid. June 14. Fine. Finished the story [published in the *Strand Magazine*, January 1898].

Sat. June 15. Fine. Idled. Reading Montalembert.

Sund. June 16. Fine. Finished vol. II of M[ontalembert]. Wrote to H. Hick, sending a photograph; the same to Mary [Bedford Williams] of Broadway.

Mond. June 17. Fine. Went with E. to Kingston, where Miss Collet met us. In her boat a mile or two up the river, where we picknicked. Returning, at Molesey Lock met by appointment a friend of Miss Collet, one Mr. Barnes, teacher. With him we had tea. At Kingston Station, on way home, was astonished to meet May Baseley and her sister Mrs. Vandermirden [sisters-in-law of Algernon Gissing]. They had been on the river and were returning by train to Norbiton.
Letter from Mrs. Norman. Invites me to At Home for the 28th.

Tuesd. June 18. Hot. A few drops of rain at mid-day. Box of magnificent roses from Miss Travers. In replying to her asked if I could go and see them at Weybridge the first week of July. Wrote to Miss Collet, and to Roberts.- In evening got to work again, and did 1p. of "The Justice and the Vagabond".

Wed. June 19. Close. Much rain last night. Wrote 2¼pp. Letter from Nelly.

Thursd. June 20. Fine. Finished "Justice and Vagabond" [published in *English Illustrated Magazine*, June 1896], and began next story "The Firebrand". Postcard from Bertz.- The July *Eng. Illustd* has my story "The Tyrant's Apology".- Letter from Mrs Travers, asking me to go to Weybridge on 3rd, 4th or 5th of July.- Reading the Arian question in Gibbon.

Frid. June 21. Fine. Wrote 1p. in morning, and afternoon went to town— bank and elsewhere. I see that Shorter mentions in *Illustd Lond[on] News* of this week [June 21] that I am writing a series of stories for *Eng[lish] Illustd.* Bought [J.H.] Slater's little book on "Book-Collecting" [*Round and About Bookstalls : Guide to Book-Hunters,* 1891]. Letter from the curious Irishwoman Isabel Keer.

Sat. June 22. Fine and hot. Wrote 2½pp., and finished "The Firebrand" [published in the *English Illustrated Magazine*, July 1896]. Letters from Mary [Bedford Williams] of Broadway, and Harry Hick. Invitation to annual *Illustd Lond[on] News* dinner at Star and Garter, on July 20th, at the odd hour of 4 o'clock. Shall be at Yarmouth then.

Sund. June 23. Fine, very hot. Read some Gibbon, and [E.H.] Palmer's "Desert of the Exodus"[15]. Wrote to Bertz, Miss Keer and Mrs Travers.

Mond. June 24. Very hot. A little rain. Thinking out story for Cassells. Paid rent. Sent some of my photographs to Mother, and to Nelly. "Lebenslänglich-verurtheilt" [by Jonas Lee].

Tuesd. June 25. Fine, hot. Thinking hard and suffering as usual. Glance through [Sir Richard] Burton's "Unexplored Syria" [1872].

Wed.June 26. Weather the same. Thinking still. Read chapter or two of [Charles] Merivale [author of *The Romans Under the Empire,* in 8 vols., 1850-64].

Thursd. June 27. Somewhat cooler. Began story for Cassells, and wrote 3pp. Note from Alg.

Frid. June 28. Not so hot. A few drops of rain.- Wrote 3pp. Reading 1st vol. of Hodgkin's "Italy and her Invaders". Letter from Roberts, from Howtown, Ullswater.

Sat. June 29. Fine. Wrote 2½pp.

Sund. June 30. Fine. Finished Hodgkin's first vol. Letter from Miss Keer, asking advice about a proposal of marriage. The man is "nice" and rich, but has "no more brains than an ape".- Replied, rather persuading her to the marriage!

Mond. July 1. Much rain. Broke down again in my work. Recd from *Humanitarian* £1-11-6.

Tuesd. July 2. Heavy rain and high wind. Made a new and vigorous start; story to be called "The Paying Guest". Wrote 4pp. Reading 3rd vol. of Montalembert. Invitation from Shorter to be his guest at the dinner of the Omar Khayyám Club[16], at Burford Bridge Hotel, on Sat. of next week; George Meredith to be there. Accepted.

Wed. July 3. Weather improved. Wrote 3pp. Recd from Miss Collet a Board of Trade Report by her.

Thursd. July 4. In morning went to Weybridge. As it looked rainy, drove from the station to Dorney House. Found the Travers's excellent people. After lunch we went on the river and in pouring rain visited Matthew Arnold's grave at Laleham. Dined, and home by 10.30. These people are well acquainted with my books—not a mere pretence of knowing them.

Frid. July 5. Dull and close, no rain. Wrote 2½pp. Invitation from Osborne Jay to the laying of foundation stone of his new church; can't go. Sent note of thanks to Mrs Travers.

Sat. July 6. Fine. Wrote 3½pp.

Sund. July 7. Fine and hot. Reading all day at Hodgkin, except for an hour or two, given to Milton.

Mond. July 8. Same weather. Wrote 3pp. Finished vol. II of Hodgkin.

Tuesd. July 9. Same weather. Wrote 3pp.

Wed. July 10. Weather same. Wrote 3pp. Making notes of Hodgkin.- Interested in a great Evening Primrose which has come up in our garden. Went down at 7.30 this evening, and watched four buds open.

Thursd. July 11. High wind, with sun. Wrote 3pp.- Reading [Israel] Zangwill's "The Master" [1895].

Frid. July 12. Wind still. Wrote 1½p. Recd from *The Minster* 12/12/- for story in June number. Wrote to Alg and Miss Collet.

Sat. July 13. Fine. Early in afternoon went to Box Hill and had enjoyable time. The Omar Khayyám Club seems a queer mixture of people—some of them by no means intellectual. Before dinner a few of us walked up the hill. Present at the dinner were Clodd (President), Hardy, Henry Norman, [Harry] Cook (ed[itor] of *Westminster Gazette*), [Henry] Cust (ed[itor] of *P[all] M[all] G[azette]*), Robertson Nicoll, Shorter, Max Pemberton, L.F. Austin, George Whale, Forestier the artist, Edmund Gosse, Theodore Watts, William Sharp, and many others whom I knew not. As soon as dinner was over, Meredith entered; we all stood up and received him with applause. Clodd began the speeches by a toast to Meredith, who briefly replied. He said it was the first time in his life he had spoken publicly— strange fact. Then Austin gave "The Guests" in a capital speech. Hardy replied, very shortly, just mentioning that 26 y[ea]rs had passed since he first met Meredith, which was in a back room of Chapman & Halls. Then my name was shouted, and there was nothing for it. I told the story of Meredith's accepting "The Unclassed" for Chapman, and my interview with him, when I didn't know who he was. Got through the speech somehow. Cust then spoke and Cook.

Meredith grievously aged; very deaf, and shaky, but mind clear as ever. As he came round the tables on entering, someone mentioned my name to him, and he said "Mr Gissing! Ah, where is Mr Gissing?" And we shook hands. Then he sat at the top of the table, talking with Clodd and Watts. On going, I went to shake hands with him, and he asked me to go to his house some day.

With Hardy I talked a little, and he asked me to write to him. Seems to wish to leave Dorchester, and settle in or near London. In his talk to-day I caught a few notes of the thick western utterance.

Sund. July 14. Fine. Tormented to death with thinking of my speech last night. This retrospective shyness a dreadful thing. In vain tried to read a little.

Mond. July 15. Fine. Wrote 1½p.- Long account of Saturday's dinner in the *Chronicle,* which speaks of Meredith, Hardy and me as the three foremost novelists. I much fear that this boldness of [Henry] Norman's does me no good in the end. Sent a copy of paper to Mother, and one to Bertz.

Tuesd. July 16. Fine. Wrote 1½p. and finished "The Paying Guest". It is not due till end of October. In evening came Miss Collet.

Wed. July 17. Close. Few spots of rain. Reading "Wild Life in England of To-Day" by [C.J.] Cornish [1895].

Thursd. July 18. Preparing for departure to-morrow. At sunset began a steady rain, which is grievously wanted.

Frid. July 19. Of course a rainy morning. Left home at 8, and caught the 10.15 to Yarmouth at L'pool St. Reached Gorleston at 2.30 (1 Sunrise Terrace, Mrs. Bunn; two rooms 30/-). Sunny evening, but high wind.

Sat. July 20. Day of wild wind and rain. Of course the first bad day for many weeks. A little better in afternoon. Boy dug on the sands a little.- Reading [Hermann] Sudermann's "Es War" [*The Undying Past,* 1894].

Sund. July 21. Weather as bad as yesterday. Gloom, wind, and deluges of rain. Now and then, a brief, pale sunshine.

Mond. July 22. Weather a little better. Before breakfast went down the shore and bathed; the boy and E. had a machine. Letters from Mother and Nelly.

Tuesd. July 23. The first fine day. But the sky hung with clouds, and thunder-shower at dinner-time. In the afternoon I walked alone to Burgh Castle, about four miles. The ruins stand amid corn-fields; wheat is growing in the space they enclose; and only by a narrow path on either side can they be walked round. At the S.W. corner a huge mass has broken away, and leans threateningly. They are on high ground, overlooking the Yare at its junction with Breydon Water; view over wide plain, with windmills and sails of boats. Very lonely and quiet.- The church of Burgh (pronounce Borough) has a *round* tower, of flints—perhaps taken from the Roman walls.- Home to tea, rather tired.

Wed. July 24. In night very heavy rain, and to-day scarcely any sunshine. Answered some Latin questions sent by Nelly. The boy digging bravely on the sands.- Wrote last night to Bullen, merely telling him of my engagements.

Thursd. July 25. Tolerably fine. E. sulking all day in bedroom, with no meals. Letter from Alg, asking for £2.

Frid. July 26. Morning dull, afterwards very fine. In afternoon all went to Yarmouth, and boy came back with bad headache. Sent £2 to Alg.

Sat. July 27. Boy feverish all night. In morning called in Dr Bately, of High St., who made light of the case. Weather terribly hot. Kept boy in bed all day. Great discomfort here in lodgings; wretched cooking. Arranged to leave at end of second week.

Sund. July 28. Heavy rain all night, and lighter downfall all to-day. Boy better, but with slight sore throat. Letter from our servant, Annie, saying she won't be able to return to us. Sent to Hetherington's, to find another.

Mond. July 29. A few bright intervals, but on the whole clouded and gloomy. Letter from Alg, in which he speaks persistently of his hope to earn £150 a year by literature, poor lad! - Sent three stories to Shorter.- E. spent some hours in Yarmouth trying to find lodgings, as this place is intolerable. She got two rooms at last, near the pier, for 27/-: an attic and a basement sitting-room. A terrible holiday, this! The woman Mrs. Bunn outrageously coarse and brutal.

Tuesd. July 30. Weather fine, but a day of horrors. Arranged to leave the house after dinner. Paid the bill (rent up to next Friday, according to agreement with Mrs Bunn,) and E. and the boy left, whilst I waited for arrival of parcels delivery cart to take the luggage. Presently Mrs Bunn enters room, and begins to be abusive. I walked out; whereupon she locked the door, and refused to allow luggage to leave until I had paid whole of rent for three weeks. I sought a policeman, who could only advise me to see the inspector. Meanwhile E. and the boy returned to see the cause of my delay. Wrangling between E. and Mrs Bunn, who at length refused us admission to the rooms, which we had paid for till next Friday! I then discovered that, on the plea of not being able to write (a lie) she had given E. no receipted bill.

We had to walk about from 3 to 5.45, till we could see the inspector at the police-station. A horrible time; spent part of it in the public reading-room, next door to Police. Poor little chap ate buns there. At 6.45 [sic] found Mr and Mrs Bunn with the inspector, and a tragi-ludicrous scene ensued. The Bunns violently insulting, of course damaging their case. Bunn, whom I had so innocently taken for a plain, honest seaman, turned out rampant rogue and blackguard. Asked me why I had spied after him this morning to see that he was going to be away from home. On my answering that I didn't know but what he was at home all day, he roared "You're a liar!" - In the end, the inspector gave the case against the Bunns, and advised them to surrender luggage at once. I thereupon demanded safe-conduct of policemen, in whose company I got a fly, and drove up to the house with constable on the box.- E. and the boy walking slowly the while towards Yarmouth, to be picked up afterwards.

At the house an exhibition of ruffiandom. As we drove up to the front door, Bunn comes out shouting: "Go to the back! We don't want *tramps* here".- (It has since occurred to me that he alluded to my *walk* to Burgh Castle. The fellow thought I *walked* to save money!) Amid jeers and brutal insults, we got luggage onto the cab, and so off, heaven be thanked. Of course I spoke not a syllable. In my flurry, I even forgot to demand the receipt of payments, but I dare say that doesn't matter.

The constable tells me that these Bunns are Salvation Army people, and *therefore* worthless.

I picked up E. and the poor boy, and we reached our Yarmouth lodging about 6.30. A great contrast; decent woman, and nice house, though no view, and might be in Brixton. Address: 15 Paget Road, near the Pier. The landlady, Mrs Squire, has made arrangement by which we have a ground-floor bedroom, and, until Saturday, a ground-floor front sitting-room, generally occupied by a curate—one Frank Eardley, I find.

Wed. July 31. Bad night in consequence of fleas, but this we felt to be a trifle after recent troubles. Very fine day. All went by the "Yarmouth Belle" up the river to Norwich, starting at 9.30, and getting to Foundry Bridge about 1.30. For last half hour, boy slept on my lap. Had dinner at restaurant in London Street, then to the Cathedral. Unfortunately, no service till 5, which was too late. Walked to the top of the Castle Hill, and just entered the Museum, where boy was much interested in a stuffed group of a great snake crushing a tiger. Back by train to tea.- Have sent advt for new servant to Hetheringtons.

Thursd. Aug. 1. Very fine day, but of course gloomy at sunset. Wrote to Miss Collet. A fine bathe up to the north at low tide—hard sand.

Frid. Aug. 2. Showery; no bathe. The boy getting into fine health and appetite. The landlady's cooking is excellent.

Sat. Aug. 3. Uncertain weather, but in morning had good bathe. By the 2 train went to London, and got to Epsom by 7. Found that storms had pulled down the creeper in front of the house so that it hung all over the front door, and had laid flat the beautiful sunflowers. A heap of letters and papers waiting: from Miss Collet, Mrs Norman, Shorter, Colles etc.- In heavy rain went to get food; bought a small currant-cake, a penny loaf, and some fried fish; this will last me over dinner-time to-morrow. Went to the gardener, about creeper.

Sund. Aug. 4. Bright early day; then heavy rain. Wrote to Mrs Norman (at Shaftesbury, Dorset), to Bullen, and to Colles. Washed up a lot of dirty things we had left on the table, and so put the house in order. Left Epsom by the 2 o'clock, and got to Yarmouth again, very late, at 9 o'clock.

Mond. Aug. 5. A few gleams of sunshine; the rest gloom and rain. Replied to a letter from Arrowsmith of Bristol, who asks me for a novel for '96; say I can't.- Writing to some addresses of servants.

382

Tuesd. Aug. 6. All morning heavy rain. Afternoon clouded, but dry. Came across a paragraph describing myself in the *Norfolk News* of Aug. 3rd, and bought a copy. Wrote to Alg.-

Wed. Aug. 7. The sky still burdened with great gloomy clouds, frequently breaking into showers; cold and windy. Afternoon warmer and brighter. Went by the 2.40 to Ormesby, walked back to Caister, and thence home again by train. Caister a rather squalid village, but pleasant shore.

Thursd. Aug. 8. The first very fine day since we left home. I went alone to Cromer, and spent a few hours there. Quick building going on, and the place crammed with people. Can see how beautiful it must once have been. Letter from Miss Collet and Alg.-

Frid. Aug. 9. Very fine. Morning on pier, afternoon to Caister. Fine sands here, and I decided it shall be our place for a holiday next year.

Sat. Aug. 11. Fine. Loitering about. Wrote 6 letters to servants.

Sund. Aug. 11. Great storm last night; to-day high wind but fine. Finished "Es War". It is the work of a playwright, and, as such, strong. But the character-drawing seems to me superficial. Best is the Pfarrer Brenckenberg. The long conversation between him and Leo, in middle of the book, very fine indeed.- *Athenaeum* of yesterday says "That remarkable novel of Mr Gissing's "In the Year of Jubilee", has just been issued by Messrs L[awrence] & B[ullen] in one handsome volume."-

Mond. Aug. 12. Fine, but high wind, and thunder in distance. All spent the day at Reedham, a very delightful place. Had dinner (bacon and eggs) at the Station Hotel. Long talk with decent old man who owns a cottage and ground on the shore of the river; he lets lodgings and had, he told us, an artist family named Luker from Notting Hill[17]. A pleasant house to live in, if cooking were decent. The boy enjoyed himself, but on return was rather overtired.

Tuesd. Aug. 13. Left Yarmouth by the 8am., and reached L'pool St. at 11.30. Pouring rain. Had dinner at station, and on to Epsom. Fine evening. Found letter from John Lane, asking for story for *Yellow Book* for October. But how am I to write, in our life here without a servant? Everything will be very hard for some weeks, I expect.

Wed Aug. 14. Fine. Fear I shall do nothing till we can get a servant.- Had a first dish of potatoes from our garden; very large, and fine flavour. Sent advt for servant to the *Guardian*.

Thursd. Aug. 15. Very sunny and warm. Read Loti's "Madame Chrysanthème", and did not think much of it. Sent copies of "Jubilee" to Edward Clodd and Grant Allen. Wrote a short letter of approval to author of article "Londoners at Home" in the current *Quarterly*.[18]

Frid. Aug. 16. Fine. Did nothing.

Sat. Aug. 17. Very fine and hot. Letter from Clodd. In afternoon came Miss Collet. Making inquiries with a view to sending boy to a day-school.

Sund. Aug. 18. Very fine. Reading a little Gibbon.

Mond. Aug. 19. Glorious day. A little box of Alpine flowers from Miss Travers, in Switzerland. The boy, who knew many of them from his Alpen-Flora, delighted with the gentians.

In afternoon unexpectedly came Roberts. An evening of exquisite beauty; Roberts and I walking the railway platform just at sunset.

Tuesd. Aug. 20. Very hot. In afternoon boy and I made our first expedition alone together. We went up to town, and to the National Gallery. Boy recognised the portrait of Turner, "The Death of the Stag", and other pictures which he knows from our book of photographs. We had tea in the Strand, and got back by 7.30.

A time of great domestic misery. No servant heard of yet, and of course no work possible.

Wed. Aug. 21. Oppressively hot. Read a new novel called "Into the Highways and Hedges" [by F.F. Montrésor, 1895]; poor. Got 1st vol. of Coleridge's Letters, just pubd by Ernest Hartley Coleridge. Endless correspondence going on about servants.

Thursd. Aug. 22. Sultry day, ending in great thunder-storm, with brilliant lightning scarcely stopping for an hour. By the bye, I recd the other day a line from Prothero, ed[ito]r of *Quarterly,* saying he had sent on my letter to the author of "Londoners at Home". Yesterday came a note from this latter person, signed merely "The Writer of the Article" and with postmark Kentish Town. To my astonishment it is an almost illiterate scrawl, with a mis-spelling "encouragment". What the deuce can this mean?- Poor Madge has just undergone a surgical operation. I know not for what disease [several words crossed out]. For some reason a mystery is made of it. Nelly says she bore the trial well, and is progressing to recovery.

Frid. Aug. 23. Fine day and cooler. Several answers to my *Guardian* advt, but not one that seems really satisfactory. Read "Misunderstood" by Fl[orence] Montgomery [1869].

Sat. Aug. 24. Fine. Read "Vanitas [: Polite Stories]", [1892], by Vernon Lee. Engaged on trial a young Epsom girl, all efforts to get mature woman having failed.

Sund. Aug. 25. Fine. In afternoon went with E. and boy to Box Hill and walked into Norbury Park.

Mond. Aug. 26. Rainy, then dull. Our new servant came.- Read [Sir Thomas Browne's] "Religio Medici" again.

Tuesd. Aug. 27. Rainy morning, then fine with high wind. Began the series of sketches for *The Sketch*, and did one: "The Medicine Man" [published October 9, 1895].- Read some Pliny. Wrote to Katie and to Bertz.

Wed. Aug. 28. Fine and hot. Wrote another sketch: "Raw Material" [published October 16, 1895].- We are getting excellent potatoes out of our garden now, and a lot of scarlet runners.

Thursd. Aug. 29. Very fine. Wrote two sketches: "At Eventide" [apparently unpublished], and "An Old Maid's Triumph" [published October 30, 1895]. Reading Lombroso, "The Female Offender" [1891].-

Frid. Aug. 30. Weather the same. Wrote one sketch "The Invincible Curate" [published November 6, 1895]. Reading Turgueneff's "Rudin".

Sat. Aug. 31. Beautiful day. Wrote "The Tout of Yarmouth Bridge" [published November 13, 1895]. Whilst I was working at it, in rushed E., in a fury, bringing a *pudding*,- just to show me the bad cookery of new servant. One of a hundred such things, which I never trouble to note.- Letter from Bertz with portraits.

Sund. Sept. 1. Very fine. Read the 3rd vol. of the Verney Memoirs [during the Civil War]. Wrote to Miss Collet.

Mond. Sept. 2. Very hot. Wrote 2 sketches: "A Well-Meaning Man" and "A Song of Sixpence" [published November 20 and 27, 1895].- Letter from Miss Collet. Sent Alg copy of my "Jubilee".

Tuesd. Sept. 3. Hot, hot. In morning wrote "A Profitable Weakness" [published December 4, 1895]. In afternoon went over to Box Hill, and called on Meredith. Found him sitting in little drawing-room, unoccupied, smoking cigarette; very old house-coat over waistcoat of different colour; trousers of yet another cloth. Very soon came in his daughter and her husband, who were driving past; they invited me to call (house near Leatherhead) any Sunday. When they went, Meredith led me out into the garden, which lies beautifully on the slope of the hill, and high above, his chalet. In the chalet only two rooms, - splendid view southward. The writing room has book-cases all round the walls.- His talk of simple enough matters; strong interest in women often appearing. Pleaded for imagination in the novel- "must be fruit for the reader to take away". After an hour or so, Lady Lawrence[19] called, and I took my leave,- with invitation to dine next week. M.'s manner to Lady L. extremely deferential; "yes, my lady", and so on. This jarred upon me. But I am pleased and proud to be thus received by the old man. He walks with sign of severe lameness in left leg,- ataxy. Mentioned the journalism for *Saturday Review* in old days;

hated it for the trouble it gave him. Said he had a miserably hard time in his youth. Thinks he will now rest—write no more.- Wrote at night to Thomas Hardy.

Wed. Sept. 4. Fine again. Wrote "The Beggar's Nurse" [published December 11, 1895].- Infinite domestic misery going on from day to day. I keep as silent as possible.

Thursd. Sept. 5. Fine; hot. Wrote "Two Collectors" [published October 23, 1895], to take the place of "At Eventide", which won't do. This completes ten sketches, and I sent them off to Shorter.- Read "As Others Saw him [: a Retrospect, A.D. 54]" [anonymous, 1895], attempt to write story of Jesus on lips of a contemporary; neither very bad nor very good.

Frid. Sept. 6. Fine. Spent day in town. Saw Bullen, who returns to subject of "The Unclassed". Suppose he had better publish it and have done. Bought F. St John Thackeray's Anthologia Latina, and read in it.- Reading Serjeant Ballantyne's Memoirs [*Experiences of a Barrister's Life,* 1882].

Sat. Sept. 7. Fine, very hot. Note from Hardy, inviting me to stay with him from Sat. to Monday next. Accepted, and decided to take E. and boy to Weymouth for a week, at same time.- In afternoon took boy to see his schoolmistress, Miss Taylor, in Ashley Road. Unfortunately she is rather deaf, but seems a nice woman. She gave the boy two apples.- Read [F.A.] Gasquet's Hist. of Black Death [*Great Pestilence (A.D. 1348-9): the Black Death,* 1893].

Sund. Sept. 8. Fine, cooler. Read a little Martial. With agonies untellable, went through 1st vol. of "The Unclassed", and cut out nearly half.- Wrote to Alg. Also to Meredith, asking whether next Thursday will do for me to dine with him.

Mond. Sept. 9. Fine, hot. Little boy's first day at school. Went off like a Trojan, and was perfectly good. Rather awed by the fact that a little girl had her hands caned.- Reading in the Anthologia Latina.

Tuesd. Sept. 10. Dull, with spots of rain in afternoon. E. called to London by sister's illness.- Recd from Bullen account up to end of June. My balance £30-14-1 - wonderful!-Anthologia.- To-night I have put little boy to bed, in E.'s absence, and I sit in my study whilst he gets to sleep in the next room. He is singing "When cats come home". Having changed the tune, he cries out: "This is a different song".- "No", I say, "it is the same." "No, it is a different song", he rejoins, "but the same language as the other". Very odd sound on the little lips, this unexpected phrase.- Note from Meredith, saying Thursday will do, and begging me to come early.

Wed. Sept. 11. A little rain, high wind. Proof of my first story for *The Sketch.* Astonishing letter from poor Alg, asking me to lend him £25 to pay debts at Willersey, and get away to the North for a change. Replied that I could let him have £10.- Toiled all day at "The Unclassed", a terrible job.

Thursd. Sept. 12. Fine again. At 4 o'clock went over to Box Hill, and stayed to dine with Meredith; he, very cordial. His son William, with wife and baby boy, arrived on a visit just before dinner. William, a smooth-shaven young man, seemingly of no particular ability (partner in firm of electrical engineers), and his wife a pleasant, unimportant woman. Meredith banters his son for Toryism, for lack of humour, etc. Imagine they feel little in common.- Among the books lying about, I noted Kennedy's "Agamemnon" (present from Cotter Morison); Mommsen (in original); the Memoirs of Barras, Léon Daudet's latest novel ("hommage d'admiration et d'affection"), William Watson's last volume (from author).- Dinner poor; servants seem awkward and careless.- M[eredith] mentioned that his daughter had carried off the piano, so that he could never have any music.- His son by first marriage is dead.- He has never been to Rome, though so familiar with North Italy.- Only slight acquaintance with Hardy.- Spoke of Charles Dilke, and too sorely tempted he had often been to use the story. Says that Mrs Mark Pattison, being in India at time of Dilke scandal, telegraphed to all the London papers that she was coming back to marry Dilke. Dilke heard of this, almost at once, in telegram from Grant Duff, and was too late to stop appearance of paragraphs; then yielded to what seemed inevitable; had never thought of marrying the woman.- M[eredith] says he knew Sir Willoughby Patterne in the flesh.

Frid. Sept. 13. Fine. Sent Alg £10. Reading [E.A.] Freeman's "English Towns and Districts [: Addresses and Sketches]" [1883].- Finished revisal of "The Unclassed", and sent it off.

Sat. Sept. 14. Fine. Went up to Waterloo, and by the 2.25 to Dorchester, arriving ¾ hour late. Hardy to meet me at the station. Found he had his publisher, McIlvaine staying with him—a very young man, and seemingly rather dull-witted. Pleasant house, in garden which has not yet had time to mature. Signs of easy circumstances, but cooking of course bad. Mrs Hardy a foolish, unrestful person, and disagreeable in face. Slept well.

Sund. Sept. 15. Clouded over, hot. After breakfast, Hardy walked through the town with us; and as far as the amphitheatre; then showed us the way to Maiden Castle, the old Roman camp, which McI[lvaine] and I climbed alone. In afternoon a walk all together to the edge of "Egdon Heath". Hardy talking a little about his new book, which is to be called "Jude the Obscure". (At its beginning in *Harper's*, it was named "The Simpletons", and then the title was changed to "Hearts Insurgent"; now a third change.) He spoke of the difficulty he had in describing in decent language an odd scene—that in which, at a pig-killing, a girl throws the pig's *pizzle* at a man and hits him. Thomas is of course vastly the intellectual inferior of Meredith. I perceive that he has a good deal of coarseness in his nature— the coarseness explained by humble origin. He did an odd thing at breakfast—jumped up and killed a wasp with the flat of a table-knife! He seems to me to be a trifle spoilt by success; he runs far too much after titled people, and, in general, the kind of society in which he is least qualified to shine. He read aloud a poem of [William] Barnes, but by no means rendered the dialect well. It surprised me that he does not know the names of wayside flowers—comfrey, for instance; surely an indication of something wrong. Cannot let himself go in conversation; is uneasy and preoccupied.

He tells me Mrs Procter (Barry Cornwall's widow) once took him to see Tennyson. The first thing Tennyson said, was: "Who is the first man mentioned in the Bible?"- Answer "Chap First". And, throughout, Tennyson spoke only of the most trivial things.

Mond. Sept. 16. Very fine and hot. In morning we went to see [William] Barnes's grave and parsonage. Home to early lunch. In a short private talk with Mrs Hardy, she showed me her discontented spirit. Talked fretfully of being obliged to see more society than she liked in London, and even said that it was hard to live with people of humble origin—meaning Thomas, of course. She then scolded her servants noisily for being late with lunch—oh, a painful woman!

As McIlvaine was going back to London to-day, I travelled with him, which meant (to my surprise) that I had to get a first-class ticket - 28/- instead of 12/-. Home by 6.30.

A good story of Meredith, who, when Sturgis[20] was constantly coming, to pay court to Miss Meredith, did not suspect the real reason, and thought the man came out of respect for *him*! Amazed when the truth was revealed.

On the whole, very little pleasure from this visit. It is disagreeable to see a man like Hardy so unsettled in his life. Talks of leaving Max Gate, and getting a house near London. Of course all this is the outcome of misery in his marriage. I suppose he has done his best work; the atmosphere of success does not suit him. Vastly better, no doubt, if he had married an honest homely woman who would have been impossible in fashionable society.

Tuesd. Sept. 17. Fine. Wrote to Mrs. Hardy and to Miss Collet. Set to work at the second ten of my papers for the *Sketch*, and nearly finished "Transplanted" [published December 25, 1895]. The boy went to school yesterday, but to-day is at home again with his cold.

Wed. Sept. 18. Fine. Finished "Transplanted", and wrote "A Parent's Feelings" [published January 1, 1896]. Letter to Miss Collet.

Thursd. Sept. 19. Heavy fog. Wrote "Lord Dunfield" [published January 15, 1896]. Letter from Madge, who is at Flamboro', much better after her illness. Wrote to her. McIlvaine sends me 3 vols. of the new edition of Hardy.- Reading the first 2 vo[lumes] of the Verney Memoirs.

Frid. Sept. 20. Beautiful day. Wrote "The Little Woman from Lancashire" [published January 29, 1896].- In evening made a conspectus of my earnings by literature from the beginning in 1880. Find that I shall have made more than £500 this year.[21]

Sat. Sept. 21. Fine but cold. Wrote "In No-Man's Land" [published February 12, 1896]. Reading [E.A.] Freeman's Historical Essays [Four Series 1871-92].

Sund. Sept. 22. Fine. Busy all day with Spruner's Atlas, and Freeman's Little European History [Oxford Lectures, 1886]. Wrote to Alg and to Bertz.

Mond. Sept. 23. Warmer again. A wasted day. Boy went to school again, after his cold. Invitation from Mrs. Travers.

Tuesd. Sept. 24. Fine and very hot. Wrote "At High Pressure" [published February 19, 1896]. Invitation from Harry Hick down to Romney, which I think I shall accept for next Saturday. Wrote to Mrs Travers, appointing Oct. 13.

Wed. Sept. 25. Fine, hot. Letter from [Max] Pemberton, offering to negotiate (I don't know why) with Dodds, Mead & Co., the Americans, for my story in Cassell's Pocket Library Series. Replied, thanking. Letter from Alg. From Colles, account up to 24th, with cheque for £23 odd. He says M. [Georges] Art, of Paris, wants to translate "Eve's Ransom". In replying, sent him a rubbishy little story, "A Despot on Tour", to try and get rid of.- Wrote "A Conversion", which I don't think will stand [published February 26, 1896]. Received more proofs of "The Unclassed", and read them.

Thursd. Sept. 26. Terribly hot. Reading 3rd vol. of Hodgkin's "Italy and her Invaders".- Wrote "A Free Woman" [published March 4, 1896].- Late at night made out in rough the draft of my *will*.- Astonished by a letter from Dr Zakrzewska, my old Boston acquaintance. She encloses a letter to her from Frank Garrison, who tells her I have become an author "of reputation and some popularity". Wrote to her, and sent my photograph.

Frid. Sept. 27. Heat unbearable. But wrote two sketches, "A Son of the Soil", and "Out of Fashion" [published March 11 and 18, 1896], thus finishing my twenty. See that "The Fate of Humphrey Snell" is in the October *Eng. Illustrated*, with an excellent frontispiece by Fred Barnard. Wrote a line to him.

Sat. Sept. 28. N.E. wind, but hot as ever. Barnard's illustration to "Humphrey Snell" is reproduced in *Illustd London News*. In afternoon came Miss Collet.- New servant has of course given notice. Sent advt to the *Church Times,* and paid fee at the Norfolk Registry Office.- Proofs of "The Unclassed" are arriving.- Spoke with Miss Collet of my will; she consented to act as guardian with Alg, provided that my wife was made guardian with coordinate powers.

Sund. Sept. 29. Hot. Finished drafting of my will, and copied it. Read a little of [Ernst] Kroker's "Archaeologie".

Mond. Sept. 30. Fine. Went to Romney, to stay with Henry Hick.- Letter from Miss Orme, enclosing one from the widow of P. Taylor, erewhile radical member for Leicester[22]—an old woman of 84; she has been reading "The Odd Women", and wants more of G.G.

Tuesd. Oct. 1. Fine, but high wind. Down to seashore; view of Dover cliffs. Then driving with Harry on his medical rounds to Bilsington. Horse very skittish, and I thought we should end in the ditch. Call in evening from a Mrs Sampson, of the town; unusually intelligent woman.- Got the Hicks to sign my will.

Wed. Oct. 2. Heavy rain in night. To-day fine, but cool and windy. Reached London about 12, and made some purchases. Left my second ten sketches for the *Sketch* with Shorter's substitute.- Shorter away in Italy. Home at 5 o'clock.- Letter from Barnard promising to give me the orig[inal] drawing of the illust[ratio]n to "Humphrey Snell".- Wind, as usual, has given me a sty in the eye—making evening miserable.

Thursd. Oct. 3. Rainy and windy; cooler. Sent "The Paying Guest" to be typed, for America. Wrote a preface for "The Unclassed", and sent it to Bullen. Wrote to Miss Orme, and to Miss Collet.

Frid. Oct. 4. Wind, rain and cold. Letter from Miss Collet. Reading vol. 3 of Hodgkin.

Sat. Oct. 5. Weather bad. Attacked by inflammation of the testicles, and groaned all day.

Sund. Oct. 6. No sun, and much rain. In bed all day, groaning. Read at Hodgkin.

Mond. Oct. 7. A very bad night and much suffering. To-day sent for Dr Beaumont, who came and prescribed. Weather bright and cheerful. Wrote some letters, and read at Hodgkin.

Tuesd. Oct. 8. Dull weather. My ailment improved. Find that Dr Beaumont a decent fellow. Knows my books.

Wed. Oct. 9. Dull but no rain. First of my "Human Odds and Ends" appeared in the *Sketch*.

Thursd. Oct. 10. Fine. E. went to town yesterday and made a lot of purchases at Shoolbred's. Things arrived to-day. Read the *Quarterly Review*.

Frid. Oct. 11. Fine. Letter from Alg; Heinemann refuses his novel. The state of things there keeps me constantly uneasy. To-day I have a very bad cold. Can do nothing. Reading "Herr Paulus" [by Walter Besant, 1888].

Sat. Oct. 12. Dull. Cold very bad. Did nothing.

Sund. Oct. 13. Sunless. Cold getting better. Reading some chapters of [Sir G.W.] Cox's Greek History, and some pp. of the Latin Anthology.

Mond. Oct. 14. Most beautiful day. Hear from Hudson that he is going to Willersey to-morrow. Lane writes to ask for a story for the Jan[uary] *Yellow Book*. Promised it if he could give me a month. Racking my brain for a subject.

Tuesd. Oct. 15. Fine morning; rainy afternoon. Worked out a story: "The Magnanimous Debtor".- Colles writes that a transln of my "The Day of Silence" has appeared in the *Revue Bleue* [on October 5, translated by Georges Art], and £1 paid for right.

Wed. Oct. 16. Cloudy and n. wind. Thinking. Began [J.R.] Green's "Making of England" [1881]. Reply from Lane.

Thursd. Oct. 17. Beautiful day. Went early to town, and in Fleet St. met Shorter, just back from Italy. He asked me to write 9 stories, instead of the 6, for the *Eng. Illustd.* To Albemarle St., where I found McIlvaine and Roberts. Took them to lunch in the East Room at the Criterion: a jovial occasion. Then tried to see Bullen, but he was out. Passing the Record Office, it occurred to me to go in and see [John George] Black. The man has not changed at all. Has had seven children, six of them living.- Bought the "Arabian Nights", also second-hand copies of Bacon's "Advancement [of Learning]" and [E.A.] Freeman's "Old Engl[ish] History [for Children]" [1869].- Back home by 8.30.

Frid. Oct. 18. Fine. Reading Green's "Making of England".- In evening began my story, "The Foolish Virgin", and wrote ½p. Letters in reply to my advt for servant in *Daily News*.

Sat. Oct. 19. Dull, wild. Wrote 2½pp., but shall not go on with this story. Note from Burgin, asking me for information about my modes of work, to be used in *To-Day*23. Suppose I must send it. Wrote to Miss Collet. Letter from Alg, saying that Hudson stays at Willersey till this morning, and is enjoying himself.

Sund. Oct. 20. No sun, misty. Reading Freeman's "Old Eng[lish] History". Replied to Burgin, and wrote letters to servants.

Mond. Oct. 21. No sun. Letter from Mrs Norman, from Pera Palace, Constantinople. (Norman in Montenegro, writing good letters for

Chronicle.) She says she dare not go out alone; streets unsafe just now for Englishwomen.- Pemberton writes with satisfaction about "The Paying Guest", and says Dodd Mead & Co. have bought American right for £25 down and 10% royalty.- Replied to him.- Reading [James] Bryce.- Thought out a new story for *Yellow Book.*

Tuesd. Oct. 22. Hideous day; rain, fog and wind from morning to night. Began "The Ewe Lamb", and wrote 1p.

Wed. Oct. 23. Dull and cold. There came, for an interview, a young woman called Janet Sparkes, who has replied to the advt for servant. Think she may do.- Reading Bryce.

Thursd. Oct. 24. This morning everything white with frost, and chestnut leaves tumbling thick. The sun shining once more. Wrote to engage Janet Sparkes, for £25. Got from lib. the Life of Freeman [*Life and Letters of Edward Freeman,* by W.R.W. Stephens, 2 vol., 1895], and read first vol. The *Daily News,* in a literary paragraph, says that Cherbuliez is at present reading "the works of George Gissing".

Frid. Oct. 25. Frost again, but bright and sunny. In afternoon I had a walk with boy to the birch-wood over the downs.- Finished Freeman's Life. On p. 450 of vol. II, I find, in a letter replying to one from Edith Thomson, the foll.:"I read a bit of 'Blanche Lady Falaise', as she lay on the table, but I could make nothing of it. How could anybody be 'Lady Falaise'? And of George Gissing and *New Grub Street* I knew nought."- The editor appends a note: "A novel in three vols., by G. Gissing" - worthy man.- Reading also at Bryce.- Wrote to engage Janet Sparkes for next week.

Sat. Oct. 26. Fine. In afternoon came Miss Collet.

Sund. Oct. 27. Fine morning, then gloomy. Still frost at night. Finished Bryce, and made notes from him. Read some Gibbon.

Mond. Oct. 28. Splendid day, but very cold. Settled on a story, "The Light on the Tower", and in evening wrote 2pp. Card from Alg saying that Blackett has taken his novel. Tinckam writes that his wife died on Saturday.

Tuesd. Oct. 29. Rain in night; to-day dull and cold. Wrote nothing; threw aside yesterday's work. Letter from Sec[retar]y of Omar Khayyám Club, telling me I have been elected Member on motion of Clement Shorter.

Wed. Oct. 30. Very fine. Reverted to my former story, "The Foolish Virgin", and wrote 2¼pp. Recd Roberts's new book "A Question of Instinct". Reading [André] Vieusseux' Hist[ory] of Switzerland [1840].

Thursd. Oct. 31. Rain in the night, and again to-day. Wrote 3pp. Vieusseux.

Frid. Nov. 1. Fine, misty at night. Wrote 2½pp.- Alg writes that Blackett has given him £25 for novel in 2 vols.- Cassells write asking me to sit for portrait for their Catalogue. Reading Bourget's "Sensations d'Italie" [1891].-

Sat. Nov. 2. Fine. Recd from McIlvaine copy of Hardy's new novel "Jude the Obscure".- Wrote 1p.- Our new servant arrived. Much superior socially to any we have had. Perhaps too good for the place.

Sund. Nov. 3. Fine morning, then rain. Servant doubtful. Wrote to Roberts and McIlvaine.

Mond. Nov. 4. Rain all night and all day. Servant doing better. Finished "A Foolish Virgin" [published in the *Yellow Book,* January 1896].

Tuesd. Nov. 5. First rainy, middle day fine, then rain and gale. At 12 went to London, and sat to Mendelssohn, at Notting Hill, for Cassells[24].- Received the pictures I sent to be framed.- Of course the new servant says she cannot stay beyond the month; pretends she is wanted at home. Wrote letters to three more.- Bought in London a clock for dining-room, and some chairs for drawing-room.

Wed. Nov. 6. Horrible day of gloom and rain. Boy in bed; feverish. In evening I went to see Dr Beaumont, and asked him to come to-morrow. Reading Bourget's "Cosmopolis" [1893]. Wrote a letter to Frederic Harrison, to whom I have not written for many years.

Thursd. Nov. 7. Worse than yesterday: muggy, reeking, sunless. Doctor says that boy's disorder is either scarlet fever or roseola—will decide to-morrow. Poor little chap suffering much from fever. In afternoon an eruption began to show on his arms—mass of uncoloured pimples.- Mrs Travers sends some fine chrysanthemums.- Bad headache all day.

Frid. Nov. 8. Boy's fever bad, but still undetermined.- Sent birthday present for Enid.

Sat. Nov. 9. Boy a little better; doctor still unable to decide. Recd proofs of "The Paying Guest".

Sund. Nov. 10. Boy greatly better, and doctor thinks it is *not* scarlatina. Corrected proofs.- As my study will in future be needed as a bedroom, I began to make changes. Moved all books and cases down into the front room—miserable toil.

Mond. Nov. 11. Fine, and all night rain with squalls. Boy still improving. Reading "The Wrecker" [by Stevenson and Osbourne, 1892]. Long letter from Frederic Harrison.

Tuesd. Nov. 12. Beautiful day, calm and golden. Recd copies of "The Unclassed". Sent one to Bertz. Letter from Alg.

Wed. Nov. 13. Beautiful day. Boy able to get up. Mrs Travers sends ham, grapes and a fowl.- Mysterious arrival of great barrel of apples from unknown sender.- Read Book I of [Bacon's] "Advancement of Learning".

Thursd. Nov. 14. Very fine. A parson in N. Wales writes for my autograph. Tried to make a beginning of short story, but fizzled.- Reading Robert Bridges' "Shorter Poems" [five vols., 1873-93].

Frid. Nov. 15. Day of rain and wind. Began story "The Prize Lodger", and wrote 1p. Letter from *Sheffield Independent,* asking who has copyright of "Demos", as they wish to publish it serially.[25] Wrote to Madge and Nell, to Miss Collet.

Sat. Nov. 16. Fine morning; boy went out. Evening wild. Wrote 2pp. Reading "Catriona" [by R.L. Stevenson, 1893]. Letter from a Miss Groening, of Oldenburg, asking leave to translate "Jubilee". Bullen sends 50 gu[ine]as, on a/c of "Unclassed".- Editor of *Cassell's Magazine* writes for short story; can't do it.

Sund. Nov. 17. Fine. Read part of 2nd Book of "Advancement of Learning". Bridges' "Shorter Poems". Wrote to Bullen.

Mond. Nov. 18. Fine, cold. Towards evening, bad sore throat. Wrote 2½pp. and finished "Prize Lodger" [published in the *English Illustrated Magazine,* August 1896]. Reading Huysmans' "En Route" [1895].- Request for autograph from a Miss Ison, Ashby de la Zouch. Sent it.

Tuesd. Nov. 19. Gloomy. Suffering extremely from throat; returned to bed early in afternoon.- Recd announcement of Omar Khayyám dinner, at Frascati's, on Dec. 6th, and wrote asking Bullen to be my guest.

Wed. Nov. 20. Dull. Towards evening feeling a little better. Visit from the sanitary inspector, who looked about the house, and could see no sign of defective drainage. Letter from [John George] Black, asking for a meeting. Bullen accepts invitation. Wrote to Cassells, asking for cheque of "Paying Guest".

Thursd. Nov. 21. Still suffering greatly from throat. Reading Chronicles of the Crusades, in Bohn. Wrote to Black.

Frid. Nov. 22. Misty, but fine. Throat as bad as ever. A present for the boy from Mrs. Travers—Caldecott's story-books. Recd Cassell's £50.

Sat. Nov. 23. Dull, cold, windy. Throat very bad.

Sund. Nov. 24. Terrible n.e. wind. Throat a very little better. Wrote to Mendelssohn, ordering 1 doz. photos, which he is to let me have for 6 gu[ine]as instead of 8. A great outlay, but I can use some as Xmas presents. Wrote to Madge and to Alg, for his birthday to-morrow.

Mond. Nov. 25. Sunless, cold wind. In evening resumed work, and wrote 1½p. of "The Philanthropist". Reading Life of Adam Smith [by John Rae, 1895]. Letter from Mrs Norman.

Tuesd. Nov. 26. Fine. To town in afternoon. Called on Mrs Norman at 4.30, dined with her, and left at 10. Story given up.

Wed. Nov. 27. Gloomy. Read "The Ebb-Tide" [by Stevenson and Osbourne, 1894].

Thursd. Nov. 28. Day of mist and rain. Read Tolstoi's "Master and Man", and [Ian] Maclaren's "Beside the Bonnie Brier Bush" [1895].- Evening, some Ovid.

Frid. Nov. 29. Day of steady rain. Read some Ovid and Persius.

Sat. Nov. 30. Gloom, but only a little rain. Went to Weybridge, home at 8.30. Alg's new book announced by Blackett - "The Sport of Stars".-

Sund. Dec. 1. Fine. Out in morning and afternoon with boy. Read some Catullus.

Mond. Dec. 2. Beautiful day. The useless idiot woman named Sparkes happily left, and in her place came Mrs Mantle from a farm at Leatherhead. Age 45, seems decent.- Reading "Apocrypha" [1611 version, revised 1894].- Letter from the *Northern Figaro* (Aberdeen) asking for a copy of "The Unclassed", and a portrait. Notice of "The Unclassed" in [*Daily*] *Chronicle*[26].

Tuesd. Dec. 3. Fine. Spent the day in sluggish misery.

Wed. Dec. 4. Dull. Again did absolutely nothing.

Thursd. Dec. 5. Dull. Idleness and misery.

Frid. Dec. 6. Change to bright weather, and for relief a busy day. Went up to town, and had lunch with [John George] Black. Then on to see Dr Zakrzewska and Miss Sprague, my old American friends, who have just come over from Boston. Spent a couple of hours with them. Later to the Omar Khayyám dinner at Frascati's, where Bullen was my guest. A number of new acquaintances: Pinero the dramatist, Walkley the dramatic critic, Sir Herbert Mather, Moncure Conway, W.L. Courtney. Gosse proposed the new members, and named me first; of course I had to reply. Invitations from Massingham, George Whale, and others: everybody very cordial. William Watson was to have come, but did not.

Sat. Dec. 7. A little snow in the night; to-day bright and cold. Recd copies of "Sleeping Fires"; sent to Mrs Travers, Mrs Norman, Harry Hick, Miss Barnes, Bertz.

Sund. Dec. 8. Bright, frosty. Great domestic misery. Spent whole day with the boy,- whom I dressed and put to bed. Wrote to Miss Barnes and Miss Collet.

Mond. Dec. 9. Dull, warmer. The new servant, Mrs Mantle, better than any yet. Meals are well cooked and tasty; everything kept clean.- Recd from Mendelssohn my big photographs. Sent one to Mother.- Had some more shelves for books put up in dining-room.- Nothing done; nothing thought.

Tuesd. Dec. 10. Very beautiful day, soft air and sky. Did nothing.

Wed. Dec. 11. Went to town by the 9.5 to keep appointment with Dr Z[akrzewska] and Miss Sprague. Fearful fog; 1½ [hours] late. Had lunch (very bad) at the boarding-house, and in afternoon we all went to Carlyle's house, just opened as public exhibition. The affair cost me nearly 10/-, but the good old people seemed to enjoy themselves. Home at 8 o'clock.

Thursd. Dec. 12. Fine morning, wild and rainy afterwards. Read Fitzgerald's Letters to Fanny Kemble [1871-83, by W.A. Wright, 1895]. Sent some of my books to Dr Zakrzewska.

Frid. Dec. 13. Fine, cold. Read Spencer's "Education".- At tea, the boy was told he must not eat a *whole* cake. After eating a half, he asked for a second half. "But I told you you mustn't have a whole cake".- He was astonished, and only after careful explanation saw that the two halves made a whole. Then it delighted him.- Trouble again with servant. She declares herself generally dissatisfied, and says she can't stay long. This thing is become tragic.- Alg writes to say that Shorter has accepted a sketch of his for the *Eng. Illustrated,* £6-6 [probably "Between Night and Day", September 1896].

Sat. Dec. 14. Fine. Miss Collet came. Begun to take *The Portfolio,* to have good pictures for the training of the boy's taste.

Sund. Dec. 15. Fine. Did nothing.

Mond. Dec. 16. Much rain. At length got to work again, and did 2¼pp. of story for Shorter: "The Schoolmaster's Vision".

Tuesd. Dec. 17. Fine, but E. wind. Finished story [published in the *English Illustrated Magazine,* September 1896].

Wed. Dec. 18. Fine. Wrote 1 page of another story, "The Light on the Tower".- Proofs of "The Foolish Virgin".- Sad letter from Bertz; he has got scurvy, result of poor living. Replied to him.- Wrote to Fennell, of Wakefield, ordering a dozen of sherry for Mother.

Thursd. Dec. 19. No sun; foggy. Wrote 2pp.- Reading [Meredith's] "The Amazing Marriage".

Frid. Dec. 20. Gloom, fog, and wind. Finished story [published in the *English Illustrated Magazine,* January 1897], and sent 3 to Shorter.- Sent to L[awrence] & B[ullen], and to Miss Collet, presents of my big photograph by Mendelssohn.

Sat. Dec. 21. Day of hideous fog. Went to London. Bought some Christmas presents. Sent Alg a vol. by "A Son of the Marshes" [ed. J.A. Owen], and Katie two little manuals of science. Sent Madge and Nell each a vol. of the Golden Treasury Series. Bought "The Children's Garland [from the Poets", by Coventry Patmore], and a game of draughts for the boy. Some scent for E. Back at tea-time.

Sund. Dec. 22. Half inch of frost in night. Very fine morning; walked with boy to Ashtead Park.- Invitation from Clodd to dine with him at Savile Club on Jan. 11 to meet C.F. Keary. Accepted.- Recd from Sec[retary] of Omar Khayyám Club account of my share for last dinner—£1-3. Sent cheque.- Reading Grant Allen's little book, "The Story of the Plants".

Mond. Dec. 23. Fine, sunny. Last night had several strange dreams. I met deal old Willie [his brother who died in 1880]somewhere, and he told me had just come from Continental travels, and he had been in Rome. He looked well and cheery. Oddest of all, we conversed in German, and I remember correcting myself in a false past participle.- Then I dreamt that I had cancer, though unaware of its situation. Friends gravely assured me of it, and recommended operations, and I was much perturbed.- Then I was saying to someone that there was only one bit of Byron I could repeat with strong feeling, and it was the stanza beginning: "O Rome my country, city of the soul!" I repeated the following line, which I now forget. Queer thing is that I don't remember ever to have thought of this passage in verse.-
   Letter from [John] Davidson saying he sends me his new vol., and asking me to lunch next Saturday.- Lawrence thanks for my portrait, and says he is sending their new edition of Donne.- Present of sweetmeats from Willersey for the boy.- Sent my portrait to Mrs Travers.

Tuesd. Dec. 24. No sun, cold, damp. Wasted day.

Wed. Dec. 25. As bad as yesterday. Didn't leave the house. Our Christmas dinner a small joint of wretched beef, with a plum pudding like lead and a leathery mince tart.- Reading Huxley's little Physiology.- The poor boy managed somehow to enjoy himself, playing with a few new toys. Eheu!

Thursd. Dec. 26. Weather still gloomy, but less rain. A day of thinking over a new book—at last!

Frid. Dec. 27. Leaden sky; ceaseless east wind, and much rain. Making notes.

Sat. Dec. 28. Gloom and rain. Read Mrs Ritchie's "[Chapters from Some] Memoirs" [1894]. Also George Moore's "Vain Fortune" - a paltry book.

Sund. Dec. 29. Less gloomy. Read a paltry book of reminiscences by the journalist [T.H.S.] Escott [*Platform, Press, Politics and Play,* 1895]. In evening, read through "Childe Harold". Note from Clodd.

Mond. Dec. 30. Warm, moist, moderately fine. Spent day in getting my names for the new book. Book itself may possibly be called "The Common Lot". Wrote to Alg and to Nelly. No reading.

Tuesd. Dec. 31. Most beautiful day, mild, blue, sunny. In afternoon had a walk to Ashtead. From Mrs Travers comes a framed water-colour of her doing, bit of heath at Walberswick [in Suffolk]. Mrs Norman asks me to tea next Saturday. Read a little book "The Invisible Playmate" [by William Canton, 1894]. Some Huxley's Physiology. Saw the new year in.

1896

Wed. Jan. 1. Gloomy, warm. Reading "Herbert Vanlennert" [by C.F. Keary, 1895], and Stevenson's "Vailima Letters". Some more notes for "The Common Lot"—so I think of calling new novel.

Thursd. Jan. 2. Rain at first; dull, warm. Finished "Vanlennert", a long, conscientious, uninspired book. Some more notes for my book.- Huxley.- Appointment with Roberts for Saturday.

Frid. Jan. 3. No sun, misty, warm.- More notes.- Huxley.- Letter from Madge.-

Sat. Jan. 4. Gloom. To town, and got my pass-book at Bank. Find balance to be £560 and more; good. Lunch with Roberts, and afternoon of talk. Then to Mrs. Norman's, where I met a relative of hers—Allan Monkhouse, writer on the *Manchester Guardian,*- and Sidney Low, editor of *St James's Gazette.* Home by 8.30.

Sund. Jan. 5. Gloom. Day wasted.

Mond. Jan. 6. Gloom. More notes for book. Recd Alg's "The Sport of Stars", and read one vol.

Tuesd. Jan. 7. Gloom. Invitation from George Whale, to dine at the Bath Club, Dover St., on 24th inst.- Accepted. Read Alg's new book.- Letter from H.H. Champion (now editing newspaper at Melbourne) enclosing long laudatory epistle from one Joseph Woolf, solicitor of Melbourne.- Miss Collet writes offering to find us a servant.

Wed. Jan. 8. Gloom. Recd 6 copies of "Paying Guest" from Cassell. Sent to Wakefield, Alg, Bertz, Miss Collet and Mrs Norman. Replied to Woolf, and sent him copy of "Sleeping Fires".

Thursd. Jan. 9. A finer day. Did an hour's digging in garden. Reading "Novelle" of Giovanni Verga.[1]

Frid. Jan. 10. Dull, but fine afternoon. Dug in garden.

Sat. Jan. 11. Gloom and drizzle. Lunched with John Davidson at the Grosvenor. He in good health and spirits. His two boys have been sent to live at a farm in Sussex, and the experiment is a great success. Is having trouble with editors etc. because of his employing Watt as his agent. Asks £25 for any poem but the very shortest. Speaks with disgust of appointment of Alfred Austin to be Laureate.- We sat together till 6.30, when I went on to the Savile Club in Piccadilly, to dine with Clodd. Other fellows—C.F. Keary, Shorter and the artist John Collier (who has a bad stammer, but only now and then troubling him.) Keary a pleasant man, without much appearance of force. Shorter told of the process by which he has got into his hands all the remnant MSS of Charlotte Brontë. Last summer he went to the village in the middle of Ireland where, for many years, Nicholls, Charlotte's husband, has lived. Got round the aged man, and bought all MSS for some £500 (I suspect for less). Nicholls has hitherto refused all approaches.- Casual information. The man T.J. Wise, a great collector of literary curiosities, has income of some £800. He lives with his wife in very bourgeois way, in N. London, on about £250 a year, and spends all the rest on his hobby. Has things of immense value.- John Morley still reads for Macmillans, and gets for it £1000 a year. Meredith, as reader to Chapman & Hall, received £150 a year.- Universal contempt thrown on Alfred Austin, of course.

Recd my £25 for "The Paying Guest" from Dodd Mead & Co., of New York.

Sund. Jan. 12. Dull. Reading [J.W.] Oliver's "Elementary Botany" [1891].

Mond. Jan. 13. Beautiful day. Long walk with boy in morning. Oliver.- Wrote to Nelly and to Miss Collet. Letter from Harry Hick, with doleful account of his affairs.

Tuesd. Jan. 14. Gloom and rain. Letters from Mrs Norman and Bertz.- Oliver.- Wrote to Mrs Norman.

Wed. Jan. 15. High wind and rain. In morning a walk with the boy. Letter from Keary inviting me to Paris. Also from Hudson and Roberts.- Botany.

Thursd. Jan. 16. Beautiful day.- Botany.- Present from Dr Zakrzewska of Heinzen's "Rights of Women" [Boston, 1891].-

Frid. Jan. 17. Fine. Digging in garden. Our servant, the woman of forty, who has grumbled through a month or so left to-day. The old Annie (Tunbridge Wells) comes to-morrow. Edith's state required attendance of doctor and nurse. Misery, but a false alarm.- Wrote to Miss Collet about Dr Zak[rzewska] and Miss Sprague.

Sat. Jan. 18. Dull, but dry. Got up early, lit fires, got breakfast, peeled potatoes etc. In afternoon came the servant who, though coarse, is a willing creature. Of course, can do nothing at all, not even read, at present juncture.

Sund. Jan. 19. Dull. Things upset.

Mond. Jan. 20. White frost, and bright sunshine. In afternoon had to summon the nurse—one Mrs Barcock, of Woodcote Rise—and about 7 came Dr Beaumont. At 10.30 was born a boy. Wrote to Mother, Alg and Miss Collet. Walter and I (I must henceforth give him his own name) make our bedroom in my study, which must now be permanently turned into nursery. E. doing well—an easy time—no chloroform.

Tuesd. Jan. 21. Frost gone, fog. All well. A long day with Walter. Bought the Jubilee number of the *Daily News,* with facsimile of the first issue of the paper. A notice of "The Paying Guest" in [*Daily*] *Chronicle.*

Wed. Jan. 22. Most beautiful day. Spent time with boy.- E. going on well, but child constantly crying—unable to get milk from breast, and of course, half-starved. The nurse an old idiot.

Thursd. Jan. 23. Dull, foggy. E., struggling with breast difficulties, in her familiar mood of surly revolt and anger against everyone.- Busy with boy all day. Bought him Andersen's "Tales", and at night read him some, with curious results. First came "The Tin Soldier". This amused him, but, at the close left him grave and troubled. Then "The Ugly Duckling". Here I noticed reddening eyes, and a distress hardly relieved by the close. Lastly "The Whipping-top and the Ball". When it came to the ball being left forsaken in the dust-bin, the poor little chap burst into bitter tears, and was with difficulty consoled.- Wrote to Miss Collet and Alg. Letter from Mother.- Reading [C.H.] Pearson's "National Life and Character [: a Forecast]" [1893]. Of course I can only open a book after the boy is in bed.- Suffer much from cold and discomfort on my sofa bed at night.

Frid. Jan. 24. Beautiful day. In morning with boy to Ashtead Park, to see the deer. Taught him the relation between branches and roots of trees. E. succeeding in giving child the breast.

Sat. Jan. 25. Rain and fog all day. Didn't leave house. Reading Keary's "A Mariage de Convenance" [1890].

Sund. Jan. 26. Fog all day. Out for half an hour with boy in afternoon. Wrote to James Wood, Colwyn Bay, who has sent me a report of his school. Also to Dr Zakrzewska, and in reply to a man who asks me to sit on a Committee for "reforming" the Authors' Society.

Mond. Jan. 27. Fog and rain. Did nothing.

Tuesd. Jan. 28. Magnificent day. In morning with boy to top of downs.- Letter from Dr Zakrzewska.

Wed. Jan. 29. Fine. With boy to Ashtead Park. Reading Keary's "The Two Lancrofts" [1893].

401

Thursd. Jan. 30. Glorious day, after misty morning. Saw the crimson tufts out on hazels.

Frid. Jan. 31. Fog, no sun. As usual, occupied all day with boy.

Sat. Feb. 1. Gloom. Read Keary's "Norway and the Norwegians" [1892]. Wrote to Miss Collet.

Sund. Feb. 2. Mist, gloom. Reading Mrs [Frances] Elliott's "Roman Gossip" [new edition 1896].

Mond. Feb. 3. Fine. Usual day with boy. Odd thing that the postman brings no letters nowadays.

Tuesd. Feb. 4. Fine. Reading vol. I of Michelet's "Hist[oire] de France".

Wed. Feb. 5. Gloom. Read a vol. of stories by H.G. Wells. Michelet. Of course I can only read after Walter is in bed. He goes about six.

Thursd. Feb. 6. Gloom.- Michelet.

Frid. Feb. 7. Gloom. Unwin sends batch of notices of "Sleeping Fires".- Michelet.

Sat. Feb. 8. Very fine. Recd Bullen's Accounts for July-Dec. 95. Balance due to me £29.

Sund. Feb. 9. Dull. Much quarrelling between E. and the nurse.

Mond. Feb. 10. Fine morning. The boy begins to read simple sentences.

Tuesd. Feb. 11. Cloudy morning, and brilliant afterwards—hot as ordinary June.

Wed. Feb. 12. Brilliant and warm. Went to town in morning, and lunched with Dr. Zakrzewska and Miss Sprague, who are soon leaving for America. At Mudie's bought copy of "Isabel Clarendon", with view to new edition. Man at counter, of course not knowing me, remarked genially that George Gissing was a very popular man—thought by many one of our cleverest writers.- Bought for boy [Charles] Kingsley's "[The] Heroes [: Greek Fairy Tales for my Children]". For myself, an 8 vol.old edition of Swift; Lockhart's Life of Burns; [Sir J.D.] Hooker's "Himalayan Journals" [1891]; [J.H.]Ingram's Life of Poe [1891]; "Moll Flanders".- In evening, on looking over "Isabel Clarendon"—on which I wasted 3/6—found it impossible, and wrote to tell Bullen so.[2] Also wrote to Miss Collet.

Thursd. Feb. 13. Dull.. Reading "Moll Flanders". Endless misery in the house.

Frid. Feb. 14. Dull. Finished "Moll Flanders". Child very troublesome—of course poisoned by his milk, E. being constantly in sullen rage, at nothing at all.

Sat. Feb. 15. Dull. Nurse-maid (£8) came, and monthly nurse departed. The flaring up (all but explosion) of hall lamp last night decided me to have gas in the house.

Sund. Feb. 16. Gloom. Within, misery and uproar. Trying to read, in intervals of rage, [Zola's] "La Débâcle".- Wrote to Dr Zakrzewska and Miss Sprague, farewell letters. Sending them, as presents, two vol. of Golden Treasury Series. Also two of my books for William Smith, of Waltham, and Mr Elson of Boston—old acquaintances of mine.

Mond. Feb. 17. Dull and misty. Reading "La Débâcle".

Tuesd. Feb. 18. Dull. Went up to town, and bought cheap gas-fittings for the house. Picked up a Baedeker (E. Alps) for 6d. Dined with Bullen at Comedy Restaurant, and finished evening with him at Stone's.

Wed. Feb. 19. Dull. Get no walks, since the nurse-girl takes the boy out.

Thursd. Feb. 20. Fine. No event.

Frid. Feb. 21. Gloom, fog, rain. Registered child's birth, name Alfred Charles. Read Francis Peek's "Social Wreckage [: Laws of England as they affect the poor", 1883].

Sat. Feb. 22. Very fine. In a walk with the boy, saw the first celandine.- Invitation to be a steward at dinner of Literary Fund; declined. Letter from Nelly, saying that she and M[argaret] think of starting a preparatory school.

Sund. Feb. 23. Frost, dull. Reading Omar Khayyám, in copy given me by Bullen.

Mond. Feb. 24. Frost, sunshine. Young Alfred out for first time. Wrote to Nelly, and sent her £5 towards expenses of starting school. Reading Ingram's "Poe". Having gas put into the house.

Tuesd. Feb. 25. Frost and sun. Gasfitters still in house.

Wed. Feb. 26. Hard frost, dull. Can't get gas yet, because it has somehow been cut off, and nobody knows where or how.- Reading Herbert Spencer's "Man v. the State" [1884][3].

Thursd. Feb. 27. Frost over; bright and mild. Reading Mrs Jameson's "[Legends of the] Monastic Orders" [1890].

Frid. Feb. 28. Rainy. Great success at Lyceum last night of John Davidson's "For the Crown"—translation from [François] Coppée. Wrote to congratulate him.- Alg writes for loan of £5. Sent it. Letter from Bertz, and one from Stanley Wood, about "The Odd Women".

Sat. Feb. 29. Rainy. In afternoon came Miss Collet. Gas-pipe laid down to the main.

Sund. March 1. Fine.

Mond. March 2. A black day in memory, though weather fine. Went to town, to get measured for clothes etc. Bought some seeds for garden. Had dinner with Tinckam. Got home by 11 o'clock, and to my horror found all the front windows of house standing open. During my absence, man was to test the gas pipes; this he had done with a candle, and there resulted a bad explosion. Ceiling of drawing-room completely blown down, and a patch in the dining-room. In front bedroom a chair burnt up, bed-clothes damaged by fire, carpet drenched with water. All this happened at 3 in afternoon and on my return, E. with Walter and baby and two servants were sitting all together in the kitchen. Drawing-room a hideous wilderness of plaster. With difficulty made ourselves beds for the night.

Tuesd. March 3. Fine, but in afternoon a hailstorm, with thunder and lightning. Went to see landlord about explosion. Of course, I am not insured. Terrible labour to clear the drawing-room. More and more wonderful that the house was not burnt down. Someone might easily, but for accident of position, have been killed. Little boy was actually watching the workman, and had his hair singed at the back. Workman badly burnt on face and arm. All due to the blackguard incapacity of the man I employed to have the fittings put up.- Yesterday received Bertz's new novel—"Das Sabinergut"[4].

Wed. March 4. Morning showery, afternoon rain. Went to Dorking; and took rooms for E. and children; nurse-girl will go with them. They must be out of the house whilst repairs are done.

Thursd. March 5. Fine, windy. Reading Bertz's book. Arrangements with landlord for repairs.- Letter from Alg.

Frid. March 6. Gale, rainy. Letter from a man called [Herbert] Sturmer, about a story of mine in the *Sketch*. Announcement of next Omar dinner, which, for economy's sake, I shall not attend.

Sat. March 7. Steady rain all day. Finished Bertz's book. Read [Alphonse Daudet's] "Tartarin de Tarascon"—for first time, and began "Au Bonheur des Dames" [by Zola].

Sund. March 8. Rainy. Wrote to Bertz about his novel.

Mond. March 9. Bright morning, then rain. Edith, with children and nurse, went to the lodgings at Dorking. In evening got fiercely to work, and wrote 2000 word story for Colles—promised long ago, name "Joseph". Miserable trash, but had to be done [published in *Lloyd's Weekly Newspaper,* May 17, 1896].

Tuesd. March 10. Very fine. Had gas seen to, and found that the other man had absolutely neglected to stop an open pipe-end under bedroom floor—hence explosion. All is right now.- Wrote at night, but destroyed what I did.

Wed. March 11. Dull, but no rain. Plasterers got to work. Gardener dug and manured kitchen garden. At night wrote 2pp. of story "Spellbound".

Thursd. March 12. Fine. Went to London, to have new clothes fitted. In evening 1½pp.

Frid. March 13. Dull, cold. Finished "Spellbound" [published in the *English Illustrated Magazine,* October 1897]. Gardened: put in Jer[usalem] Artichokes.

Sat. March 14. Fine, and showery. Wrote 2pp. of "One of the Luckless". Gardened a good deal. Put in peas, cress, cabbages, radish and spinach. Read Taine's "Notes on England".

Sund. March 15. Dull, windy. Wrote morning and evening, 2pp. Reading Zola's "Une Page d'Amour".

Mond. March 16. Fine. E. and children returned from Dorking. We have to take meals in kitchen, and live up in bedrooms.

Tuesd. March 17. Fine. George Whale invites me to his house, after the Omar dinner on 27th. Refused. Roberts invites [me] to dine at Authors' Club. Refused.- Can do nothing again.

Wed. March 18. Rain and fog all day. Did absolutely nothing.

Thursd. March 19. Brilliant day. In midst of terrific difficulties wrote 1p. of "One Way of Happiness".

Frid. March 20. Rain all day. Wrote 1p., at night, by the boy's bedside. Plasterers at work again. Young Alfred vaccinated to-day. Read "When Valmond came to Pontiac" [by Gilbert Parker, 1895].

Sat. March 21. Rain mostly. Wrote 1p. Reading Taine's "Ancien Régime".

Sund. March 22. Most glorious day—if only one could enjoy it. Reading Taine. Wrote to Miss Collet.

Mond. March 23. Fine. Wrote 1p.- Letter from Alg, who, broken down in health, has fled to his old retreat in Northumberland—Harbottle.- Cleaned all my books and shelves.

Tuesd. March 24. Magnificent day, summer heat. Wrote 1p., and finished "One Way of Happiness" [published in *English Illustrated Magazine,* June 1898]. Alg writes for £15. Sent it.

Wed. March 25. Rainy. Reading Mrs [Isabella Lucy] Bishop's "Journeys in Persia [and Kurdistan]" [2 vols., 1892]. Gardener sowed peck of potatoes.

Thursd. March 26. Windy and colder. Whitewashers came, and finished ceilings. Note from Miss Collet.

Frid. March 27. Fine, but windy. Got dining-room habitable once more. Correspondence with poor Alg, who writes asking for £20 more. Sent him £5, and promised the rest on Monday.

Sat. March 28. Gale and rain. Bought Black's Guide to Wales. See that Shorter has sold some of my new *Eng. Illustd* stories for publication in the *New York Times*[5].- Tinckam sends me a copy with announcement.

Sund. March 29. Cold rain all day.

Mond. March 30. Dull morning, fine later. Utter misery in the house. Servant didn't come home last night, sending message (lie no doubt) that she was ill at a friend's house. Has not returned to-day. I went to town, to get money from bank; drew £35.

Tuesd. March 31. Cold, but dry. Servant still keeps away; wrote violent letter. In evening began "The Hapless Boaster", and did 1p.- Misery.

Wed. Ap. 1. Gloomy and cold. No writing. Read Dr [G.S.] Keith's "Plea for a Simpler Life" [1895], seemingly a very sensible book on diet and medicinal treatment.

Thursd. Ap. 2. Bright morning, then dull; still north wind. Wrote 1p. New girl engaged for the baby, to come next Monday.

Frid. Ap. 3. Dull. Wrote 1p.- Read Book of Tobit.

Sat. Ap. 4. Dull, a little rain. Wrote 1½p. and finished "The Hapless Boaster" [published in the *Illustrated London News*, September 11, 1897].

Sund. Ap. 5. Fog and a little rain. Read "The Tale of a Tub" [by Swift], for the first time. Letter from Mrs Travers, with present of book for Walter.- Great misery in the house.

Mond. Ap. 6. A little sun, then dull, but warm. Read part of "Gulliver".

Tuesd. Ap. 7. Brilliant day. Planted some peas.

Wed. Ap. 8. Fine and warm. Left Epsom at 8 o'clock and got to Wakefield by 1.30. The boy not much tired, and soon makes himself at home. Wrote to Mrs Travers.

Thursd. Ap. 9. Fine; but gloomy sky. In morning walk with Madge and boy. Wrote to Dr Zakrzewska.

Frid. Ap. 10. Very fine, but high wind. At night tremendous scene with the boy, over his bath. Madge bathing him, and of course he refused to come out. He fought and shrieked—a worse outbreak than I ever knew. I had to seize him and carry him to bed. When I reproached him with having hurt his aunt, he (sobbing in penitence) could only think of the fact that he had scratched *me*. "Oh, never mind me".- "But I think more of *you* than of aunt", wept the poor little chap. A doleful business altogether, and showing that it would be criminal to take him back to the old life in our home which is no home. He must stay here, evidently, and be tamed.

Sat. Ap. 11. Gale and showers.

Sund. Ap. 12. Gale and furious rain.

Mond. Ap. 13. Left Wakefield (boy staying behind) at 9 o'clock, and journeyed to Colwyn Bay. Had two hours in Chester. Found James Wood less antiquated than I had expected. Dinglewood a really beautiful spot. Stanley Wood seems to have talent for painting, but he does not impress one. Learn that my old schoolfellow [at Lindow Grove School, Alderley Edge], George Brook, died not long ago at a moment's notice.- Weather to-day very fine. View from Chester to Colwyn seen at its best.

Tuesd. Ap. 14. Dull, and a little rain. Sent p[post]c[ards]to Wakefield and London. Walked a little in the woods. Of course cannot collect my thoughts in this scene.

Wed. Ap. 15. Beautiful day. In morning, Wood's son Stanley started for the Italian lakes. I, at 1.26, left for my exploration of Caernarvon. Got to Pwllheli at half-past four, and, after half an hour's delay, went by old ramshackle coach to Nevin (7 miles, fare 1/-). Put up at the Nanhoran Arms. Two or three commercial travellers, one a young fellow named Currie, Liverpool representative of John Heywood's. Amusing talk till midnight.

Thursd. Ap. 16. A day of much pleasure. As I got up, I saw clouds on the hills, and there was rain. But it stopped after breakfast, and I started on a walk. Climbed the mountain which is being quarried (Gwylwyn); boggy and rough. When near top, overpowered with furious wind, and had to come down again. Back home by the shore. Began to rain hard and I got wet. But after dinner the sky cleared, and there came a glorious afternoon. I walked by the cliffs all round both bays (Nevin and Portcullaen). Splendid view of the Eifel, with its three peaks. Sea very blue and calm. Home by the sands and by Morfa Nevin.- Wrote to Walter, sending some flowers and ferns. Sent post-card of greeting to Lawrence & Bullen. To-night I am alone in the hotel.

Frid. Ap. 17. Unbroken sunshine, till half-past four, then cloudy. In morning climbed Carn Bodvean and lay on the top in the glorious air for two hours. Too misty to see the Snowdon mountains. Made some notes for my book. In afternoon gathered shells in the bay; then bought some photographs of W. Jones, Old Post Office—who promises to send me addresses of lodgings when I want them.- Sent letter to Bertz, and postcards to Colwyn and Wakefield.- On the whole, one of the days of my life to be looked back upon with joy.

Sat. Ap. 18. Dull morning; clouds thick on the hills. Left Nafyn (this is the proper way to spell it) by the coach at 9 o'clock. Bill at hotel rather excessive (£1-1-3). By when I reached Caernarvon, the weather beautiful. Dined there at the Castle Hotel (good) and spent two hours wandering about. Climbed Twt Hill; a splendid view. Got back to Colwyn at 6 o'clock, and found that a letter for me had been absurdly sent to Nafyn Post Office. Telegraphed to the post-master.

Sund. Ap. 19. Fine, then dull. In evening walked with Wood up to top of hill; fine view down on Conway. Letter from Madge enclosing few words from little lad.

Mond. Ap. 20. Left Colwyn by 8.18 express, and got to Wakefield at 1 o'clock. Boy well and delighted to see me. Fine day. Evening with Frank Wood.

Tuesd. Ap. 21. Fine and hot. In afternoon called on Chalmers, and stayed an hour. Spent evening with the Bruces; genial. (In morning went to Leeds, to buy some schoolbooks for girls.)

Wed. Ap. 22. Alg writes that I cannot go to Willersey; servant troubles etc. Wrote to him, and to Edith, telling the latter that I have decided to leave Walter here. (I shall pay £10 a quarter, and of course cost of clothing.) In morning walk with boy to top of Lawe Hill. Showed him Back Lane School, and our old house. In afternoon to Cemetery, where I cleared a few weeds from Father's grave. Evening spent at home.

Thursd. Ap. 23. Reached London at 1 o'clock, and went to bank. Epsom at 3.30. Of course a terrible scene with E.; won't bear speaking of. A heap of letters awaiting me. Wrote to Miss Collet, about what I have done.

Frid. Ap. 24. Very fine all day. Sent off a portmanteau to Wakefield, with boy's books and clothing. Tried to settle to work. Things quieter once more.

Sat. Ap. 25. Fine. Began to work steadily at construction of my book. Got several names settled, and lines of action.

Sund. Ap. 26. Fine. Read [D.G.] Hogarth's "A Wandering Scholar in the Levant" [1896].

Mond. Ap. 27. Fine and hot. Worked morning and evening. Gardened in afternoon. Miss the little lad grievously.

Tuesd. Ap. 28. Still fine and warm. Worked morning and evening, and wrote about a page. Thus the novel is actually begun. Letter from Madge, saying that boy's things have reached him. He is very good, and gives little trouble. Ah, but how I miss my dear little son!

Wed. Ap. 29. Fine with a few showers. Wrote 1½p.

Thursd. Ap. 30. Fine, with clouds.- As usual, have made a false start, must re-cast story.- Mrs Travers sends asparagus.-

Frid. May 1. Much colder, and rather cloudy, but no rain. Went to town, and lunched at Café Royal with an American, Joseph Anderson (brother of Mary Anderson the actress) who had written asking for an interview, to be used in the *Boston Transcript*. Very decent young fellow.- Bought at Philip's a geological Map of Brit. Isles.- Wrote to my boy.

Sat. May 2. Fine, but cold. Worked at re-casting my story. Think I have got all the names at last. Might call the book "Benedict's Household".- Letter from Roberts.

Sund. May 3. Fine, cold. Wrote to Roberts, and to [John Northern] Hilliard (Rochester, USA). Read [J.A. and Margaret] Symonds' "Our Life in the Swiss Highlands" [1892]. Also, with scant satisfaction, the notorious "Trilby" [by George Du Maurier, 1894].

Mond. May 4. Fine, cold. Letter from Nelly, with good account of Walter. Began writing again, and did 1½p.

Tuesd. May 5. Fine and warmer. Wrote 2½p. Wrote to Alg.

Wed. May 6. Fine. Wrote 2pp. Walked in afternoon to Ashtead Park.

Thursd. May 7. Fine. Wrote 2pp. Letter from Walter, and one from Nelly, giving good account of him.

Frid. May 8. Fine. Wrote 2½pp. Letter from Alg. Read "Clara Hopgood", by Mark Rutherford [1896].

Sat. May 9. Fine, but same n.e. wind that has blown for several days. Wrote 2½pp. and finished Chap. III.

Sund. May. 10. Weather unchanged; cloudless sky and hot. Wrote to Bertz and to Miss Sprague.

Mond. May 11. Very hot and cloudless; wind the same. Wrote 2½pp. Getting well on with the story.- Astonishing paragraph in paper to-day, that Rudyard Kipling has summoned his brother-in-law (Balestier) for attempt to kill him. Trial to be at Brattleborough (Vermont) to-morrow.

Tuesd. May 12. Weather unchanged. In morning wrote 1½p. In afternoon went to Box Hill, to see Meredith. Found the Meynells and their children staying there. Had tea and came home. Meredith bright and good. He is revising his works for the Library edition, and says he is "slashing" at them—probably a great mistake.

Wed. May 13. Fine, but hazy. Wrote 2½pp. Letter from Nelly, with good report of dear boy. Replied to her.

Thursd. May 14. Fine, very hot. Wrote 2½pp. Miss Sprague sends review of "Sleeping Fires" from a Boston paper.

Frid. May 15. Cloudy, but fine. Wrote 1½p. Mrs Travers sends more asparagus.

Sat. May 16. Fine, cooler. Wrote 2½pp. Letter to my boy. Reading Harold Frederic's "Illumination" [1896].

Sund. May 17. Fine, cloudy. Read "Two Summers in Guyenne" [by Edward Harrison Barker, 1894].

Mond. May 18. Fine, close. Wrote 2pp. Note from Mrs Norman. Reading "[In] The Land of the Tui" [by Mrs Robert Wilson, 1894].

Tuesd. May 19. Fine. Went to town early, and got some information of Museum. In looking over the *Journal of Botany* for [January] 1889, delighted to find Father's name, with biographical details in an "Index of British Botanists".- Was to have met Roberts, but he failed me.- Went over the National Portrait Gallery.

Wed. May 20. Rain at last, with high wind. Wrote 2pp. Wrote to Bertz and to Alg for information.- Roberts ill with his malaria.

Thursd. May 21. Windy, fine. Wrote 2pp. Recd from Joseph Anderson his article about me for *Boston Transcript*. Revised it and returned. Letter from Mother, Nelly and my boy. They have just taken a new house, in Wentworth Terrace [No. 9], better situation for the school.

Frid. May 22. Rainy all day. Wrote only 1½p.; very hard work; description of Carn Bodvean.- Got from lib. Zola's "Rome".

Sat. May. 23. Fine. Wrote 2pp. Headache.

Sund. May 24. Fine. Reading [Samuel] Smiles's "John Murray" [published as *A Publisher and his Friends*, 1891].

Mond. May 25. Fine. Rewrote a page of Sat[urday], and did 1 more. Letter from Alg.

Tuesd. May 26. Fine and windy. Rewrote a page of yesterday, and did 1 more. Have got over a knotty point, the story of Benedict's early life. Very difficult to tell this briefly. Wrote to Mother and Nelly, and sent the boy some flowers I gathered this afternoon—iris, horsetail and white bryony.

Wed. May 27. Fine, warmer. Wrote 2pp.

Thursd. May 28. Fine. A good day's work, 3¼pp. Letter from Bertz, and replied to him. Still reading Zola's "Rome".

Frid. May 29. Fine and hot. Wrote 2¾pp. Colles writes that [Georges] Art, of Paris, will give 250 francs for right to translate "Eve's Ransom". Ordered a copy to be sent to him.- Editor of *Cosmopolis* writes for a story. Wondering whether I dare do it. Late at night, wrote that I would do 6000 words for £20.

Sat. May 30. Fine. Wrote 1p. Letter from boy, who says he has been to Ryhill. In afternoon came Miss Collet.

Sund. May 31. Fine and hot. In morning a long walk, worrying over ideas for a short story—confounded interruption of my smooth work. Wrote to George Whale for legal information.

Mond. June 1. E. wind still, but a very bright, hot day. Wrote 2½pp. Mrs Travers invites me to Weybridge.

Tuesd. June 2. Same weather. *Cosmopolis* writes to accept my terms, and wants story by July 1st.- Lawrence writes asking me to write my name in three books of mine, for a charitable bazaar. He tells me, too, that they have just bought "Born in Exile" from A. & C. Black, and will soon bring it out uniform with my other books.[6] They will give me a royalty on it.- Joseph Anderson writes to thank me for revising his article.-
Did 2½pp. Still reading Zola's "Rome", an immense book.

411

Wed. June 3. A few light showers. In morning, wrote 1p.; evening thought over story for *Cosmopolis.*- The editor, Ortmans, sends formal invitation to dinner at Savoy Hotel on June 25. Accepted. Lawrence writes that they have sold plates of "The Unclassed" to a New York house [R.F. Fenno and Co.].

Thursd. June 4. Very hot, and rain with thunder late in evening. George Whale sends me legal information for my book. Received and returned the books sent by Lawrence for my autograph. I see that L[awrence] & B[ullen] have become a Limited Liability Co., but they have told me nothing about it.- Wrote 1½p. of short story, but it won't do; have a better idea to go at to-morrow.

Frid. June 5. Very fine. Worked hard all morning, but after it all again found the thing futile. In evening began a third attempt, "Twin Souls", and wrote 1p. This, I think, will do.

Sat. June 6. Fine and cooler. Wrote to my dear boy. Did 3pp. This story, after all, won't do for *Cosmopolis,* but I shall finish it, and lay it aside for future use.

Sund. June 7. Rainy. Finished Zola's "Rome".

Mond. June 8. Fine, no rain. Began "A Yorkshire Lass", and did nearly 3pp. Letter from Bertz.

Tuesd. June 9. Rainy. Wrote 3⅓pp.

Wed. June 10. Day of ceaseless rain. Wrote 1p. and finished my short story [published in *Cosmopolis,* August 1896]. Gladly turning again to the book.- Note from Roberts, from Montreux, saying he is married.- Letter from my boy, and one from Nelly.

Thursd. June 11. Fine and hot. Went to town, and read *Musical Times* at the Museum.

Frid. June 12. Same weather. Wrote 2pp. of my novel; glad to be at it again. Harry Hick sends me Banks's "Glossary of Wakefield Dialect"; very useful [William Stott Banks, *A List of Provincial Words in use at Wakefield in Yorkshire,* 1865].

Sat. June 13. Very hot. Wrote 2pp. Note from Bullen, explaining that they have merely issued preference shares, no debentures. Wrote to my boy.

Sund. June 14. Very hot. Read "The Revolution in Tanner's Lane" [by Mark Rutherford, 1887]. Wrote to Nelly about holidays, and replied to Harry Hick.

412

Mond. June 15. Terribly hot. Wrote 2pp. Again bother with servants; both wanting to leave at week's notice.

Tuesd. June 16. Same weather. A day of frantic uproar; servants demanding to go without notice, their mother sent for. I rushing into the kitchen, to stop clamour, and paying wages in wrath, etc. Of course no work done. In evening E. went and engaged charwoman, to come day by day.- Letter from Nelly, saying she had rather the boy went with her to Broadway than with us to the seaside. I daresay it would be better, but I daren't make such a suggestion.

Wed. June 17. Rainy. Wrote 2pp. Replied to Nelly. A man named Ainscough, who writes as "Rivington Pyke" sends me a story called "The Man Who Disappeared [: a Lancashire Story]" [1896][7]. Poor twaddle, but must write something to him.

Thursd. June 18. Fine, cooler. Wrote 2½pp. Reading again [Edward] Fitzgerald's Letters.

Frid. June 19. Fine. Wasted day, owing chiefly to worry about our summer holiday. Cannot fix upon the place,- Read a vol. of Fitzgerald's Letters. Reading Gaston Boissier's "The Country of Horace and of Virgil", a very bad translation, abounding in misprints and ignorant errors.- Miss Travers sends a lot of roses; sent some on to the boy at Wakefield. Invitation to At Home from Mrs J.M. Biddulph[8]; refused it. Wrote to Alg and Nelly. Sent Miss Barnes a copy of "The Paying Guest".- Wrote to my boy and to Alg.

Sat. June 20. Fine, but cloudy. Went by the 2.25 to Marlow, for the Omar Khayyám dinner, at the Crown Inn. New acquaintances J.M. Barrie, Maarten Maartens, Dr Walter Leaf, Harold Frederic. Again strange disappointment of expectation as to men. I had imagined Barrie rather tall, rather elegant; I found a small, slouching, boyish fellow, carelessly dressed. Frederic I had classed with Henry James; I found a burly man with hands like a blacksmith's, talking roughly and with American accent.

Barrie and I next to each other at dinner. He told me that, after leaving school (a college) he aimed at getting journalistic work in England, and sat at home answering Advts. At length heard from the proprietors of a Nottingham paper, who absolutely took him as Editor at £3 a week—he having had no sort of experience. The proprietors were brothers touched with lunacy. Barrie wrote as he chose at the moment, having no political principles.

Frederic was married at 20, afterwards parted with his wife (in America I suppose) and is now living with another woman by whom he has children [See entries from December 20, 1898 to January 7 1899, *passim*]. To support both women, has to earn £1400 a year.

Our joke late at night. We bought pots and pans from a cheap jack in the market-place, and presented them to Shorter—who is to be married in a few weeks.

No room for me at hotel; had to sleep over a furniture shop next door. George Whale took me to see the cottage where Shelley lived; an inscription is over it.

Dr. Leaf told me that F. Myers admires my books.

Sund. June 21. Very fine. Up at 7, and had breakfast at 7.30; Frederic and Whale coming down to keep me company, and going to station with me[9]. Got to London about 10 o'clock; and as there was no train to Epsom till 1.20, went to see [W.H.] Hudson, and spent time pleasantly.

Mond. June 22. Fine; with dull afternoon. Miserably unable to settle to work. Reading [George] Borrow's "Wild Wales" [1862].

Tuesd. June 23. Fine. Wasted. Bad news from Alg, that Blackett refuses his book.

Wed. June 24. Heavy rain. Read [R.L. Stevenson's] "Weir of Hermiston" [1896]. Gosse asks me to lunch on July 3rd. Wrote to Miss Collet. No work.

Thursd. June 25. Rainy morning, later fine. Went up to the *Cosmopolis* dinner at the Savoy, a great assembly. New acquaintances: Bryce, Justin McCarthy, Nisbet Bain (who sat next to me), [Israel] Zangwill. Saw Andrew Lang for the first time, but no speech with him. Met Frederic Harrison after a lapse of 6 or 7 years. He made a speech, and a sadly dull one—ponderous, slow. Zangwill decidedly a good fellow, as I have always felt from his books. Home by last train.

Frid. June. 26. Fine. Bad headache. Did nothing.

Sat. June 27. Fine. Went to Weybridge, to the Travers'. There met Mrs Travers's mother, Mrs Ellicott, wife of the Bishop of Gloucester—a fact I was heretofore unaware of. Also an unmarried daughter of the Bishop [Rosalind], meagre and musical[10]. The old lady decidedly vulgar. We spent the afternoon on river in an electric launch. At dinner came a man named Hadow, a young·Oxford don; pleasant fellow, and well read; something of a musician, too.[11]

Sund. June 28. Stayed over night, and returned to Epsom by early train. Utterly wasting my time now, and fear shall not do anything till after the seaside holiday.

Mond. June 29. Fine. In morning, lengthened my *Cosmopolis* story by ¾p., and sent it off. A poor thing, I fear. In evening got once more to my book, and wrote 1½p.- Sent plant-book to my boy. Read a little Ovid and Horace. Ah, if I had but the energy to give but half an hour daily to Greek or Latin!

Tuesd. June 30. Windy, but fine. Wrote 1p. In evening read again at my Latin Anthology.- Letter from Nelly, with good account of boy. He passed day and night during family's removal to Wentworth Terrace with the Bruces, and Mr Bruce went to talk with him when he was in bed.- Barrie sends me a vol. of Scotch stories, by one Malcolm McLennan, called "Muckle Jock" [1892]. Wrote to thank him.- Mother and the girls are now in a larger house, much better situated for the purpose of a school. Rent of course higher. We shall see if the school pays it.

Wed. July 1. Rainy and cool. No writing. Reading 2nd vol. of Fitzgerald's Letters.- Letter from Miss Sprague, enclosing Joseph Anderson's article on me, from *Boston Transcript* of June 13.

Thursd. July 2. Fine. In afternoon to Morris Colles'; long tedious journey to West Hampstead. Rather out of my element, among high hats, frock coats and furbelows[12]. Talk with Mrs Hodgson Burnett. Also with a French lady, Mme Thierry—I understood the name. Met old F. W. Robinson, who said to me, "Ah, we are both South London men". Of course a commonplace old fellow. Left with [Israel] Zangwill, and went for half an hour to his house hard by.

Frid. July 3. Fine, turning to rain at eve. To town, to lunch with [Edmund] Gosse at the National Club, Whitehall Gardens. Present: Austin Dobson, Andrew Lang, young Edward A. Fitzgerald (who has just published his feats on the New Zealand mountains), a Mr Bateman, head of commercial department of the Board of Trade (who says he reads Zola and me), an American named Armour, and Hamo Thornycroft the sculptor—rugged old fellow, whose look pleased me. Lang justified his reputation of being crusty to new acquaintances. Not an agreeable type: lolling and languid.

Sat. July 4. Fine, hot. Left King's Cross by the 12.30 for Sutton-on-Sea, to find lodgings for our holiday. Cheap week-end ticket, 8/6—less than the ordinary single fare. Got to Sutton about 5, and put up at the Bacchus. Much pleased with the place. Walk after tea, and got drenched with a sudden windy shower.

Sund. July 5. Fine. Could do nothing but lounge about. One attempt at inquiring about rooms led to a severe rebuke- "We never do business on Sunday".

Mond. July 6. Very hot; cloudless sky. First thing after breakfast began search in earnest. House after house had let all the rooms for August. Rents very high. About 11 o'clock walked to Mablethorpe, and here again had a hard search. Found at length good rooms (three) in Bank House, Mrs Dabb, situated on the back of the sandhills towards Trusthorpe. Engaged them for a month from July 22nd, at £2-5 a week for first fortnight, and £2-10 for the second—a queer inversion of ordinary agreements. Then at length breathed freely. Had some dinner, and left by the 3.20. But, owing to my sleepy inattention, I sat in the train at Willoughby till the Peterborough train had left. Had to wait two hours, and spent them with the stationmaster, who took me to his house for a cup of tea.- Reached Epsom at midnight.

At Sutton, the landlord said that Tennyson, in boyhood, used to stay at that inn, formerly called The Jolly Bacchus—they have dropped the "Jolly".

Tuesd. July 7. Hot. Wrote some letters—nothing else. Sent Alg £5.

Wed. July 8. Hot. reading "The World and A Man" [1896] by Zangwill's brother [Louis]—"Z.Z." Somebody at Rhode Island U.S.A. writes for my autograph, oddly enough mentioning "Workers in the Dawn". Has some pirate reprinted the book? [No record of pirated edition.]

Thursd. July 9. Hot, fine. Read "A Drama in Dutch" by "Z.Z." [1894].

Frid. July 10. Hot. Miss Collet writes from Scotland. Thinking over my book again.

Sat. July 11. Hot. Read Vol. I of Lady Eastlake's Memoirs [*Journals and Correspondence of Lady Eastlake,* ed. Charles Eastlake Smith, 2 vols., 1895]. Wrote to my boy.

Sund. July 12. Hotter than ever. Did nothing.

*　　*　　*

Thursd. July 16. Useless to chronicle the wasted days. To-day ceaseless rain, the first for a long time. Read Cunningham's "Travels in the Caucasus", and began [Lina] Eckenstein's "Woman under Monasticism" [1896]. A letter from my boy.- Paid Dr Beaumont's bill, £6-10.

Frid. July 17. Cloudy, but no more rain. Day wasted, as usual.

Sat. July 18. Fine again. Read [E.A.] Freeman's Hist. of Wells Cathedral [1870].

Sund. July 19. Fine, hot. Reading idly.

Mond. July 20. Terribly hot. Went to London, and bought a trunk for E. Also, at Piggott's, Bishopsgate, a tent for the sands, price £5-10.- Annoying telegram from Mablethorpe, asking if I could put off arrival till Friday; replied, impossible.- Wrote to Alg.- Made a few alterations in my will, which I must take to Wakefield, and get the girls to sign.

Tuesd. July 21. Very hot, but cloudy at evening. Busy preparing for departure to-morrow.

Wed. July 22. Fine, but cloudy, and much cooler. Left home at 10, crossed London by the G.N. Omnibus, and left King's Cross by the 12.30, reaching

Mablethorpe at 5 o'clock. Baby rather troublesome on journey. The nurse-girl with us.

Thursd. July 23. Fine. In morning I bathed. Tent arrived from London, and with Dabb's help I got it set up on the sands.

Frid. July 24. Fine. Left Mablethorpe early, and reached Wakefield at 1.30, having stopped to eat at Doncaster. Found boy well and excited about his coming holiday. The new house in Wentworth Terrace everything that could be wished.

Sat. July 25. Rain all night. At 7.42 boy and I started from Wakefield. It rained till we got to Lincoln, then cleared. Reached Mablethorpe in time for 1 o'clock dinner.

Sund. July 26.. Windy, cloudy, fitful sunshine; towards evening steady rain. In morning went with boy to Trusthorpe Church.

Mond. July 27. N.w. wind, with very high morning tide; it just entered our tent, but happily came no further. In afternoon I went plant-hunting, and found the splendid Flowering Rush, growing in a dyke. Also the Great Bur-reed.- Letter from Miss Collet, from Scotland.

Tuesd. July 28. Fine, turning to cloud and wind. In morning Walter bathed, with the result that he had a little sore throat at evening. His tonsils are very bad again, greatly to my distress, as he had come to breathe quite normally whilst at Epsom. Uncertain whether this is due to Wakefield air, or to a cold caught in coming here. His snoring and gasping all night break his own rest and mine—for he sleeps with me.

Wed. July 29. Sunny, but a fierce s.e. wind. Sauntered about all day. Tides getting lower.

Thursd. July 30. Cloudy, showery. In morning I bathed. Boy still has a little cold, but seems on [the] whole to be benefiting.

Frid. July 31. High wind, bright sunshine. Boy better. Letter from Madge, and replied to her.

Sat. Aug. 1. Morning rainy; later a little sun; dull and cold evening. Weather day after day like late autumn. Letter from Joseph Anderson, with his article on me from *Boston Transcript*[of June 13]. Found a few new plants.

Sund. Aug. 2. Sunny, but cold n.e. wind still. Wrote to Miss Collet and to Joseph Anderson. Walk with boy on sand-hills in afternoon. He still shows very great interest in every mechanical contrivances, is never tired of examining sluices, etc, or agricultural instruments. Perhaps has less of the aesthetic tendency than I hoped—yet it is very early to decide.- In morning all went to Mablethorpe Church.

Mond. Aug. 3. The hateful Bank Holiday. Day fine and warm, until 4 o'clock, then gloom and rain. I went to the railway station, to see the throng of people. These Midland trippers compare very favourably indeed with those of London. Great numbers of them, but no crushing, no yelling, no horseplay, a decency even in drunkenness. The women vastly better—even more tastefully dressed—than the harridans and trollopes of London.

Tuesd. Aug. 4. Black clouds, pelting rain, and severe N.E. wind. Kept awake at night by a bad cough.- Wrote to Bertz.

Wed. Aug. 5. Day of great rolling clouds, occasional rain, and violent N. wind. I see from the paper that yesterday was the coldest 4th August since 1890. Hardly possible to sit out of doors. The tent very useful, but constant fear lest it should be beaten down by wind, or swept away by a high tide. Wrote to Bertz.

Thursd. Aug. 6. Cloud and sun, wind falling, calm at evening. Cough very bad.

Frid. Aug. 7. A still day, with little sunshine, threatening rain at night. Warmer. Wasting my time. Utter foolishness to call this idle loafing holiday, but of course I am bound to be here. And the boy is benefiting.

Sat. Aug. 8. Sun and cloud. N.E. wind rising again, and at night blowing high. My cough still very bad. In the afternoon I got permission from the miller of Trusthorpe to go over his wind-mill. The boy enjoyed it very much. I learned that these mills still grind between stones, in the old old way.

Sund. Aug. 9. Nothing could be more difficult than my position as regards the boy Walter. All but every statement made to him he answers with a blunt contradiction; to all but every bidding he replies "I shan't". As I sit in the room, where the nurse-girl is present, he calls me all manner of abusive names. I said to him this afternoon, that, as it was too windy to go out, he had better rest an hour. "Not in *your* bedroom", was his harsh reply. "I'll rest in mother's room, but not in yours." And to-morrow, on some trifling provocation, he would make precisely the opposite reply. He knows there is no harmony between his mother and me, and he begins to play upon the situation—carrying tales from one to the other, etc. The poor child is ill-tempered, untruthful, precociously insolent, surprisingly selfish. I can see that Wakefield *may* have a good influence, but only the merest beginnings show as yet.- I should like to know how the really wise and strong father would act in this position. But no wise and strong man could have got into it. Talk of morals! What a terrible lesson is the existence of this child, born of a loveless and utterly unsuitable marriage.

A wretched day. Grey—gloomy, with savage N.E. wind. None of us left the house.

Mond. Aug. 10. Weather slowly clearing. N.E. wind all day, only falling at dark. Letter from Nelly. My cold passing away.

Tuesd. Aug. 11. Fitful sunshine to begin with, then a day of muggy gloom, with warm N.W. wind, dripping rain. In morning I tried to go for walk with boy, but we were driven back. Baby woke up in night with severe cough, seeming to threaten bronchitis; bad all day.- Letter from Roberts, who is back in London with his wife. Replied to Nelly.- Lady Tennyson died yesterday

Wed. Aug. 12. Hot day, much sunshine, but air heavy with moisture. Long walk in morning with boy.- Last night no sleep; poor little Alfred choking with bronchitis, or something like it. To-day he seems a trifle better. Of course usual lodging-house difficulties under such circumstances. The house is now packed—one family of 8 children only a fraction of the contents.

Thursd. Aug. 13. High N.W. wind, cloudy, but only few spots of rain; fine at evening. Letter from a Miss Lea of Cheshire, asking where she can find a story by me called "The Foolish Virgin". Replied. Letter from Toynbee Hall,[13] asking me to give a lecture in October to the "Society of Library Readers". Replied with refusal, on score of work.- Baby a little better.

Luckily, I went out after supper. A calm night, very starry, only a little cloud above sea horizon. Long sluggish rollers, at full tide, were breaking in brilliant phosphorence—a sight I never saw before.

Frid. Aug. 14. Day began cloudy and showery, but turned out fine. Letter from Mrs Frederic Harrison, inviting me for two days to Blackdown Cottage, Haslemere. Accepted for the 24th.

Sat. Aug. 15. Day of brilliant sunshine, but with the old fierce N.E. wind, furious at night. Letter from Miss Collet. Wrote to Madge, announcing our return to Wak[efiel]d for next Wednesday.

Sund. Aug. 16. A few gleams of sun at first, then a cloudy, sunless day, lightening at dusk. Wind N.E. changing to N.W. In morning we all went to Trusthorpe Church. Alfred's cold still bad, poor little chap.

Mond. Aug. 17. Very fine bright day, but wind rising in S.E., with cloud at night. The boy bathed in the morning.

Tuesd. Aug. 18. Fine, but clouded.

Wed. Aug. 19. Brilliant morning. We left Mablethorpe at 9.12, just caught London express at Louth, by which E. and Alfred and girl went off. Boy and I in more leisurely fashion on to Wakefield, where we reached house in violent storm of rain. Boy has a bad cold.

Thursd. Aug. 20. Cloudy but fine. In morning a walk with Mother, Nelly and the boy; gathered some flowers. Wrote to Miss Collet. Paid the girls Walter's next quarter in advance.

Frid. Aug. 21. Rainy.

Sat. Aug. 22. Fine, though heavily clouded. In morning a walk towards Stanley with Mother and boy. We were to have met the girls, but failed to do so. Boy's cold not well yet. Said good-bye to little chap, who is very cheerful, and left Wakefield by the 3.15; reached Epsom at 8.30. Letter from Martha Barnes, and one from Mrs Norman.

Sund. Aug. 23. Rainy.

Mond. Aug. 24. Went in morning to visit the Frederic Harrisons, at Blackdown Cottage. Austin Harrison met me at Haslemere Station; he knew me, but I could not recognize him, for it is nearly ten years since I last saw him. We drove the five miles to Blackdown. Bernard I found less changed than Austin. He has been for five years studying art in Paris, and has just sold his first picture, to his friend Lord Davey. Not very striking. Austin, preparing for Foreign Office, lives much on the Continent. Both are interested in literature, but neither strikes me as particularly intelligent. Bernard very nervous and sensitive; think I can understand his having gone over to Rome.

In afternoon Mrs Harrison drove Austin and me to Lord Davey's, a few miles away. Was to have been a tennis party, but rain stopped it. Gathering of very dull local people.

Tuesd. Aug. 25. Showery. In morning, Austin took me over Blackdown to look at Tennyson's house. He amazed me by telling me that young [Hubert] Crackanthorpe ("Wreckage" etc.) apprenticed himself for a year to *George Moore*—to learn English style! His father paid £200 for the privilege!

After lunch, I said farewell, and Bernard drove me to Haslemere Station. Home by 6.30.

At Haslemere Station there entered, and sat opposite to me, a lady whom I thought I knew. After travelling some miles, she said to me, "I think you must be Mr Gissing". And behold it was Mrs Maxse, formerly Kitty Lushington, my pupil. We talked, and she left the train at Guildford. I had not seen her for twelve years.

Wed. Aug. 26. Cold and rainy. In evening sat down and made a new beginning of my novel; wrote ½p.- Received £20 from *Cosmopolis*.- Wrote to [Israel] Zangwill and Burgin; also to Alg.

Thursd. Aug. 27. Cold, showery. Wrote 1½p. In afternoon gardened.

Frid. Aug. 28. Bright and warmer. Wrote 3pp. Good day's work.

Sat. Aug. 29. Fine. In morning worked hard, and did 2pp. In afternoon came Miss Collet. Wrote to my boy.

Sund. Aug. 30. Fine.

Mond. Aug. 31. Dull, close. Wrote 3pp. Reading Armstrong's Life of Velasquez. (Portfolio) [W. Armstrong, *Velasquez: a Study of his Life and Art,* 1896].

Tuesd. Sept. 1. Heavy rain in night, and a great deal to-day. Wrote 3pp. A letter from my dear little boy, whose cold is nearly gone. Reading Miss [Isabella L.] Bird's "[Six Months in the] Sandwich Islands" [1873].

Wed. Sept. 2. Heavy rain, night and day. See that Alg has a short story in the new *English Illustrated* ["Between Night and Day"]; better than most they print.- Did 3pp. Getting on well.

Thursd. Sept. 3. A fine day. Did 3pp.

Frid. Sept. 4. No sunshine and no rain. Did 3pp.

Sat. Sept. 5. Fine and warm. Did 3pp. Wrote to my boy.

Sund. Sept. 6. Heavy sky, no sun. Read [J.W.] Mackail's excellent little history of Latin Literature [1895].

Mond. Sept. 7. Dull, but no rain. In afternoon, dug a lot of potatoes, for storing. Wrote 3pp.

Tuesd. Sept. 8. Fine, sunny. Did nearly 3pp. Dug more potatoes. Reading [E.A.] Freeman's small history of Sicily [*Sicily, Phoenician, Greek and Roman,* 1892]. Note from Roberts. Wants to see me, but no getting to London just yet.

> Pegging away,
> Three pages a day,
> Groaning and moaning - the devil to pay.

Wed. Sept. 9. Great thunderstorm in the night; to-day sunny and showery. Hard work and did only 2¼pp.

Thursd. Sept. 10. Rain all day. Wrote 2¾pp.- A little Emerson.

Frid. Sept. 11. Rain all day. Wrote 3pp.- Emerson. Form to fill up of biographical detail for "Who's Who".[14]

Sat. Sept. 12. Rain all day. Wrote 3pp. Reading [Sir Francis] Galton's "English Men of Science [: their Nature and Nurture]" [1874]. Wrote to my boy.

Sund. Sept. 13. Rain all day. Finished Galton, and began Miss [Isabella L.] Bird's "Golden Chersonese" [1883]. Wrote to Alg and to Madge.

Mond. Sept. 14. Sunny morning, a little rain afterwards. Wrote 3pp.

Tuesd. Sept. 15. Fine. Wrote 3pp. Letter from Harry Hick, who is coming to London to send his eldest girl into Yorkshire. Invited him to come here for next Saturday and Sunday.

Wed. Sept. 16. Fine morning, then rain. Did 3pp.- A chapter of Plutarch's "Pericles". Long since I read any Greek.

Thursd. Sept. 17. Showery. Wrote 3pp. A little "Pericles".

Frid. Sept. 18. Very dull, a little rain. Heavy rain last night. Letter from boy, and from Madge, Nell and Mother. Wrote 2pp.

Sat. Sept. 19. Fine. In morning wrote 1p. In afternoon had telegram from Henry Hick that he was walking here from Guildford. Set out on high road, and met him at Leatherhead. As we have no spare bedroom, I put him up at the Fox Inn for two nights.- Wrote to my boy.

Sund. Sept 20. Very fine. Walked about with H[enry] H[ick]. At night took leave of him, as he goes back to Romney early to-morrow.

Mond. Sept. 21. Fine morning, then heavy rain till night. At 11, Edith went with baby to her relatives in London. Telegram at 8, to say she could not come back to-night because of the rain. Wrote 3pp. Letter from Alg.

Tuesd. Sept. 22. Rainy morning, fine afternoon, high wind. Wrote ½p., but no use. E. came back in afternoon.

Wed. Sept. 23. Sun and rain, high wind. Had to go back and rewrite the last chapter; did 3pp. Sent 1st vol. of [George Sand's] "Consuelo" to Nelly.- Plutarch.

Thursd. Sept. 24. Fine. Headache. Rewrote 2pp.

Frid. Sept. 25. Furious gale, with rain. Wrote only 2pp., very hard work. Finished [Sir James George Frazer's] "The Golden Bough" [12 vols., 1890-1915].

Sat. Sept. 26. Wind fallen. Showery. Wrote 3pp. Gale has blown down some of the tall Jerusalem Artichokes; dug a root, the first. Sent letter to my boy.

Sund. Sept. 27. Unutterable gloom all day. Reading Mrs Oliphant's "Miss Marjoribanks" [1866] and [F. Marion] Crawford's "Adam Johnstone's Son" [1896]. The former excellent, the latter rubbish. Wrote to Bertz.

Mond. Sept. 28. For a wonder, fine nearly all day. Wrote 3pp. A man [Herbert] Sturmer writes promising a book of his. Miss Collet writes. Replied to both. A chapter of "Pericles".

Tuesd. Sept. 29. Dull and cold morning, sunny afternoon. Wrote 3pp. Paid my rent.- "Pericles".

Wed. Sept. 30. The first mist. Sun broke through. Did 3pp. Letter from Nelly and little man.- "Pericles". Reading [Balzac's] "César Birotteau" again.

Thursd. Oct. 1. Misty, cold. Did 2pp. Sturmer sends his genealogical account of two English Huguenot families [*Some Poitevin Protestants in London*]. Read it.- "Pericles".

Frid. Oct. 2. Dull, no rain. Did 2½pp.- "Pericles".

Sat. Oct. 3. Moderately fine. Did only ½p. In afternoon Miss Collet. Wrote to boy and mother. Bullen sends cheque for £14-16—accounts from Jan. to June of this year.- William Morris[15] died to-day.

Sund. Oct. 4. Gloom and rain. Read Kuhe's "[My] Musical Recollections" [1896]. Wrote to Editor of *Blackwood's*, recommending Bertz's book [*Das Sabinergut*] for notice.

Mond. Oct. 5. Fine. In afternoon saw a grand thunder cloud, with lightning, pass towards London—all the rest of the sky brilliant. Wrote 3pp. Roberts invites me to dine at Authors' Club; refused, as I cannot spare the time.

Tuesd. Oct. 6. Gloom and rain, windy. Wrote 3pp.- "Pericles".

Wed. Oct. 7. Fine morning, then gale with rain. Wrote 3pp.- "Pericles".- Young Alfred is just able to stand, supporting himself by things. No tooth yet. On the whole, a good child, very easy to manage. Stronger, I think, than Walter, and nothing like so nervous. He is a dear little chap, but I think longingly of my own boy at Wakefield.

Thursd. Oct. 8. Fine, cloudy. Wrote 3pp.- Paddington Public Library begs for some of my books. Must send two or three, of which I have duplicates. Can't afford to buy.- "Pericles".

Frid. Oct. 9. Lovely day, after the gale. Bad for writing. In morning 1p., which I had to rewrite at evening, and did only ¼p. after all.- Colles sends cheque for £19. He has got £10 from M. Art for translation of "Eve's Ransom", which I am delighted to hear is to come out in the *Revue de Paris*.- Letter from William Blackwood, promising to review Bertz's book if possible.

Sat. Oct. 10. Fine. But could do no work. Hardly any sleep last night. Sat all day thinking over second half of book. Wrote to my boy, and to Madge and Nell. Read Harold Frederic's "Mrs Albert Grundy [: Observations in Philistia]" [1896].

Sund. Oct. 11. Gloomy and cold. Read Ben Jonson's "Bartholomew Fair". Wrote to Colles, telling him that I won't go into the serial market with my new novel, but will let any editor of a first rate periodical who really wishes for a novel by me, to see it when it is finished.

Mond. Oct. 12. Last night did not sleep at all; feverish and miserable. To-day still unable to work. Wretched weather, rain and n. wind.

Tuesd. Oct. 13. Bright morning, then rain and wind. Went up to town to see Colles about serialization of the novel; don't think it will be possible, on account of its length. Colles lunched with me at the Gaiety. Bought some note-paper, and a fur tie for E. (28/-). Looked in to see Bullen. Home again in terrible weather at 6.32.- Noticed in the *Bookman* an announcement that a novel by Alg - "The Scholar of Bygate" - is to be pubd by Hutchinson. Have heard nothing of this from Alg.

Wed. Oct. 14. Have got my sleep back again. Fine morning, wretched afterwards. Wrote 2pp. Have tried to begin fires.- I note here that young Alfred can already stand, holding by things, and even totters a few steps from one hold to another. His hair is coming, but no tooth through yet. A good little chap; scarcely any trouble.

Thursd. Oct. 15. Dull, but warmer. Wrote 2pp. Broken off at evening by E.'s neuralgia. Letter from Alg, who has £30 on account from Hutchinson for his novel.

Frid. Oct. 16. Heavy rain and gloom. Did 2pp. Letter from my boy, and from Madge. He is in excellent health, and very contented.- Reading the life of J. Gladwyn Jebb [*A Strange Career*, by his widow, Mrs Bertha Jebb, 1894].

Sat. Oct. 17. Sunshine again. Headache, could do nothing. E.'s neuralgia. Wrote to my boy. Reading a stupid book, "Romantic Love and Personal Beauty" by one [H.T.] Finck [2 vols., 1887].

Sund. Oct. 18. Sunny. In morning walked to Leatherhead. A little reading in "Ecclesiasticus".

Mond. Oct. 19. Fine, till late afternoon, then rain. Letter from Osborne Jay, saying his friend Lady Dorothy Nevill wants me to lunch in Berkeley Square next Saturday. Refused. Wrote 2pp.

Tuesd. Oct. 20. Gloomy, a little rain. Did 2½pp.

Wed. Oct. 21. Foggy. Did 2½pp.

Thursd. Oct. 22. Fine autumnal day, mellow sunshine. Wrote 2½pp.

Frid. Oct. 23. Fine. Wrote 2pp. Letter from my boy, and one from Nellie. Miss Collet writes that she hopes to be in Wakefield next week, and will call to see the boy. Replied to her and to Nellie.- Alfred has cut his first tooth.

Sat. Oct. 24. Gloomy. Did 1½p. Wrote to my boy.

Sund. Oct. 25. Sun, rain and wind. Old Tinckam came to spend the day; left at 9 o'clock.

Mond. Oct. 26. Very fine. Did 2½pp. Reading Grant Allen's "Anglo-Saxon England" [*Early Britain - Anglo-Saxon Britain,* 1881].- Nellie writes that they can offer Miss Collet a bed at Wakefield.

Tuesd. Oct. 27. Beautiful day. Wrote 2pp.

Wed. Oct. 28. Beautiful day again. The first hoar frost. Wrote 2pp. Invitation to dine from Keary. Accepted.

Thursd. Oct. 29. Thick mist all day. Did 2pp. Miss Collet writes that she will spend Friday night at Wakefield.

Frid. Oct. 30. Mist at first, then fine, then rainy. Did 2½pp. Reading [W.W.] Skeat's "A Student's Pastime [: Articles reprinted from *Notes and Queries*]" [1896].

Sat. Oct. 31. Fine. Wrote 1p. Reading "Samuel Brohl et Cie" [by Victor Cherbuliez, 1877].

Sund. Nov. 1. Dull and cold. Day of idleness.

Mond. Nov. 2. By first post recd letter from Miss Collet, asking if she could come to-day, to report as to her Wakefield visit. This created an uproar in the house—rage and fury. I was driven out, walked through rain to Ewell, (rather than wait at Epsom for a train,) and then sent telegram to Miss Collet that I would be with her at 1 o'clock. Idled miserably in town till that hour, then lunched with Miss Collet at a restaurant. Very good accounts of the dear boy, and all else.

Pottered about in wretchedness till seven o'clock, then home. A wasted day.

Tuesd. Nov. 3. Fine. Did 2pp. Clodd invites me for next Sunday to his house, Tufnell Park, to meet Louis Becke. Promised to go; though I shall have to stay overnight, and I suppose this will upset the house again.- Received from John Davidson his "New Ballads".

Wed. Nov. 4. Misty but fine. Chiefly owing to domestic miseries, have broken down; tried to write, and could do nothing. Went and dined with C.F. Keary, Gordon Place, Campden Hill, and had pleasant talk. But he is not a man of much account.

Thursd. Nov. 5. East wind and bright sun. In morning walked to Burgh Heath, thence to Cheam, and through Nonsuch Park to Ewell. First time I have seen Nonsuch. Home with appetite for dinner.- Reading "Life [and Letters] of G[eorge] J[ohn] Romanes" [written and edited by his wife, 1896].- The good Wakefield people have sent me, as usual, some November parkin, my great delight.

Frid. Nov. 6. Hard frost in the night—the first. Reading Von Thielmann's "Journey in the Caucasus etc" [translated 1875].

Sat. Nov. 7. Again a frost, but thawing soon, and at night rain. Reading [Kington] Oliphant's "[The Sources of] Standard English" [1878].

Sund. Nov. 8. Fine, and not so cold. In evening went to Clodd's house (19 Carleton Road, Tufnell Park) and had dinner, or as he calls it, supper. Louis Becke, the author of Polynesian stories was there—his first visit to England, an uncouth fellow with a slight stammer. Clodd's wife a nonentity; sits mute and grim; even less intellect, I suppose, than Mrs Hardy, but the sense to hold her tongue; and no one heeds her. A daughter of about seventeen present [Edith], and two sons. Eldest daughter [Amy] is married, and one son abroad. The inevitable Shorter, talking about his "Charlotte Brontë" and a "Byron" he is going to undertake.Says the "Brontë" will bring him some £800. The excellent Clodd genial as ever. As there is no late train for me on Sunday, I stopped over night.

Mond. Nov. 9. Bright and cold. Walked from Clodd's all the way to Victoria, and home to dinner. High time I got to work again. Must try to-morrow morning.- By the bye, Clodd told me about his beginnings. He lived at Lowestoft as a boy, his father having been a ship's captain. At 15, he came to London on a visit to an uncle, and being overcome by desire to stay in the town, applied on his own responsibility in answer to advt by an accountant, and got the place—£10 a year. Parents' protests no use; he lived with uncle and aunt and went steadily on to the Secretaryship of the Joint Stock Bank, which he still holds. He married at 22 on £120 a year.

Tuesd. Nov. 10. Sunny. Made a wretched effort to get to work again, and did 2pp.

Wed. Nov. 11. Fine. Editor of *Sun* writes for a short story for Xmas. Refused. Wrote 1p., finishing Part II. Made a beginning of Part III, but futile.- Read Kipling's "The Seven Seas" [1896].

Thursd. Nov. 12. Fine, and warmer. Did 1½p. Reading [Barrie's] "Sentimental Tommy" [1896], which I thoroughly dislike.

Frid. Nov. 13. Fine. Wrote 2pp. Letter from my boy, and from Nellie.

Sat. Nov. 14. Dull, ending in rain. Wrote 1½p.

Sund. Nov. 15. Fine. Baby has a cold again. Reading Lockhart's "Burns".

Mond. Nov. 16. Fine. Did 2pp.

Tuesd. Nov. 17. Gloomy. Did 2pp.

Wed. Nov. 18. Gloomy, with rain. Did 2½pp. Reading Swinburne's "Study of Ben Jonson" [1889].- Letter from Henry Hick; replied. Mrs Travers sends chrysanthemums; acknowledged.

Thursd. Nov. 19. Beautiful day, calm and bright. Did 2½pp.

Frid. Nov. 20. Very fine. Left for London 12.49, and spent afternoon in shopping. Bought a box of little wooden models for my boy on his birthday next month. Went to Aitchison's, the optician, and ordered a pair of spectacles—25/-. The man tells me my eyes are greatly astigmatic. Bought boots, ties etc.—the annual purchase of small articles of clothing.- Great difficulty in getting a red rose, for the Omar dinner, held at Frascati's, Oxford Street. There my guest, John Davidson, met me at 7 o'clock. Sixty-two diners all together. New acquaintances made: W.E. Norris, [J.W.] Mackail (author of "History of Latin Literature"), H.G. Wells and Conan Doyle. Guests of the club were Frederic Harrison and Sidney Colvin. Pleased to meet Hamo Thornycroft again. Wells amused me by rushing up, after dinner, introducing himself hurriedly, (only a minute, as he must go,) and telling me that, when he first read "New Grub Street", he himself was living in Mornington Road, poor and ill, and with a wife named Amy! Queer coincidence. As he told his story, Mackail, who had been talking with me, stood by and smiled. I rather liked Wells's wild face and naive manner. As usual, not at all the man I had expected.

Left with George Whale, and went home with him to Blackheath. Kept awake most of the night by whistles and sirens on the river, as the night was foggy.

Sat. Nov. 21. Fine morning, turning to fog. Long walk with Whale, through Greenwich Park and round Charlton Village. Afterwards pleasant talk in Whale's library. To lunch came Miss Adeline Sergeant, the novelist, a very plump, rosy and merry woman, with a touch of the old maid in her way of talking. After lunch I made my way homewards.

Sund. Nov. 22. Woke with a slight cold on the chest—the first for a long time. Gloomy day. Reading "Marcella" [by Mrs Humphry Ward, 1894]. Letter from a Miss Mary Krout, London Correspondent of a Chicago paper, from which she sends a long cutting about "The Odd Women".[16] Replied to her.

To-day, am 39 years old.

Mond. Nov. 23. Gloom. Cold bad. Day wasted. Letter from Barrie, inviting me to call and see him.

Tuesd. Nov. 24. Gloom. Day again wasted. My new spectacles came but are useless. Wrote to Alg for his birthday.

Wed. Nov. 25. Gloom. Cold better. Got to work again and did 1½p., but the ½ must be rewritten.

Thursd. Nov. 26. Gloom. Wrote 1½p.- An odd letter from H.G. Wells, asking me to go and see him at Worcester Park. He seems the right kind of man. Replied that I would go presently.

Frid. Nov. 27. First sunshine, but still deadly N.E. wind. Managed to leave the house, but cough very bad. Wrote 1½p. Reading [A.J.C.] Hare's "Story of My Life" [3 vols., 1896]. Letter from Alg, who is at Richmond, Yorks.

Sat. Nov. 28. Gloom and fierce wind. Wrote to my boy. Did 2pp.

Sund. Nov. 29. Sunny, but very cold. Short walk.

Mond. Nov. 30. Hard frost. Beautiful day. Did only ½p. I work with extraordinary difficulty and slowness nowadays. Shall I ever get done. More than 30pp. still.- Note from Wells. Alg calls at Wakefield to-day.

Tuesd. Dec. 1. Gloom and frost. Hard work to dig up some artichokes. Did 2½pp., better than of late.

Wed. Dec. 2. Gloom and rain. Did 1½p.

Thursd. Dec. 3. Sunny. Did 1p.

Frid. Dec. 4. Pouring rain, except an hour in afternoon. Did 2½pp. Reading Wells's "The Wheels of Chance" [1896], in which I find my name is mentioned.

Sat. Dec. 5. Fine. Did 1p. Letter from Miss Collet.- Wrote to my boy.

Sund. Dec. 6. Fine. Read G. Leslie's "Riverside Letters" [1896]. Also Frank Barrett's "A Set of Rogues" [1895].- At night some Tennyson. Wrote to Bertz and Miss Collet. Postcard to Wells, asking if I can come to see him on Wednesday.

Mond. Dec. 7. Gloom. Did 2pp.

Tuesd. Dec. 8. Gloom. Did 1p. A letter from Prof. Wilhelm Victor, of Marburg University, who says he is going to give five lectures on English Novelists of To-Day for the Freie Deutsche Hochstift in Goethes Vaterhaus, Frankfurt, and asks me for any notes I like to send. Wrote to him at some length.- Can't go to Wells's to-morrow, as he has an evening engagement.- Wrote to Madge, sending the quarter's money for Walter. Sent off a present for little boy's birthday, on Thursday—a box of model tables, chairs etc, to be built together.

Wed. Dec. 9. Gloom. Did 3pp; unusually good day. Sent birthday letter for boy.

Thursd. Dec. 10. Gloom and rain; warm. Did 2½pp. My boy Walter is 5 years old to-day. Madge writes that he is going to have tea with his grandmother at Mrs Bruce's.- Read some of Johnson's Poets.

Frid. Dec. 11. A little finer. Did 2¾pp. Reading "Margaret Ogilvy" [by James Barrie, 1896].

Sat. Dec. 12. Gloom and rain. Did 3pp.- In a letter to me a little while ago, Barrie recommended me to read "Nancy Noon", a novel by a Scotchman who calls himself Benjamin Swift. I have tried, but *cannot*; a duller book I never opened. Yet I see that the publishers advertise Barrie's opinion that the author will be a great novelist. We shall see.

Sund. Dec. 13. Pretty fine. For a wonder, wrote 1p. Read "The Task" [by William Cowper, 1784].

Mond. Dec. 14. Gloom and rain. Did 3pp. Letter from little boy. Mrs Bruce gave him, on his birthday, a cake marked "Walter", and a train.

Tuesd. Dec. 15. Black at first, changing to fine. Did 2½pp.

Wed. Dec. 16. Thick fog. Wrote 1½p. In afternoon went to see H.G. Wells at his house at Worcester Park, and stayed till 11 at night. He and his wife and her mother. Liked the fellow much. He tells me he began life by two years' apprenticeship to drapering. Astonishing, his self-education. Great talent. His wife a nice woman, formerly his pupil in biology, when, after taking the London B. Sc., he coached science.- Note from Mrs Norman.

Thursd. Dec. 17. Clearer; white frost. Wrote 1p.

Frid. Dec. 18. Gloom. Yesterday morning (as I learn from newspaper to-day) there was a shock of earthquake, all across England, at about 5.30. E. heard it shake the things in the bedroom. Worst at Hereford, where church pinnacles fell.- Wrote 1p. and *finished "The Whirlpool"*. The hardest bit of work I have done yet.

Sat. Dec. 19. Gloom. Made a few corrections in early chapters of the book.

Sund. Dec. 20. Gloom, fog. Re-reading [Meredith's] "Beauchamp's Career" [1875].

Mond. Dec. 21. Dull, a little snow. Spent day in town. Took my MS to Bullen, who offered 150 gu[ine]as on a/c, instead of the old 100. Paid half of it at once. Bought some books for Christmas presents.

Tuesd. Dec. 22. Very fine sunny day, mild. In afternoon went up to the heights with E., and cut a lot of holly for the house.

Wed. Dec. 23. Dull. Sent A. a present of "Lavengro" [by George Borrow, 1851].

Thursd. Dec. 24. Fine and mild. Read Wells's "The Wonderful Visit" [1895]. Walter sends Xmas cards.

Frid. Dec. 25. Beautiful day, cloudless and mild. In morning walk to Cheam and back. Present of a "pussy-cat" for young Alfred from children at Willersey. Read [Arthur] Morrison's "A Child of the Jago" [1896]. Poor stuff.

Sat. Dec. 26. Rainy. Reading "The Heart of a Continent [: a Narrative of Travels in Manchuria, Across the Gobi Desert etc., 1884-94"] ([F.E.] Younghusband).

Sund. Dec. 27. Cloudless and warm; wonderful day. A letter from J.H. Rose (my old acquaintance at Owens) who asks me to write a monograph on Dickens for a series to be pubd by Neville Bieman. Replied consenting, but asked for more detailed terms. *Shall be glad to have this change from fiction-grinding.-* Wrote to Miss Collet, asking her to come next Saturday, and to Roberts and Hudson, asking them to lunch in town on Thursday.

Mond. Dec. 28. Rain and dull. Trying to think out a story that would serialize.

Tuesd. Dec. 29. Brilliant and warm again, wonderful springlike day. In morning went to see Dr. Beaumont about my cough. He made an examination, and says that there is a weak point in right lung. This may be a grave matter, and may not. But I am to paint with iodine and take syrup of hypophosphites.

Wed. Dec. 30. Rain and dull.

Thursd. Dec. 31. Bright day and warm. Went to town, where Hudson and Roberts lunched with me. By a remarkable coincidence, Roberts has just proposed to his publishers, as title of his new book, "The Whirlpool".

Happily, I have priority, but thing is a nuisance.- Called at Mrs. Norman's, but no one at home.- First proofs of "Whirlpool" arrived. Letter from Alg.

1897

Frid. Jan. 1. Beautiful day. Having seen in paper that Meredith had just undergone an operation of some kind, I walked over to Box Hill in the afternoon to make inquiry. Found he was at his son's house in London. The servant said the operation was for his deafness.- Letter from Walter.

Sat. Jan. 2. Mist turning to thick fog. Miss Collet came.- Reading Rochefort's Memoirs.

Sund. Jan. 3. Cloudy, but fine. Correcting proofs all day.

Mond. Jan. 4. Fine, cold. In afternoon went to call on Barrie at his house, 133 Gloucester Road. House beautifully furnished. Mrs Barrie (formerly an actress) came in when we had been sitting for an hour in the study, and made herself agreeable; handsome, robust, and amiable—I should think. They have a magnificent St Bernard dog, a huge fellow. Invited to stay dinner, but thought it better to decline.

Tuesd. Jan. 5. Rainy, dull. Letter from Shorter, asking for "bright little love story" for the *Illustd London News*. Told him I couldn't do it.- Letter from Rose and note from Mrs Norman.- Proofs.-

*　　*　　*

Sat. Jan. 9. Days too miserable to chronicle; ceaseless quarrel and wretchedness. Weather foggy and rainy. To-day went to Brit. Museum, and there chanced to meet Joseph Anderson, who tells me he spends his days in Reading-room to save a fire at his lodgings. On way back home, looked in at Wells's, Worcester Park, and stayed till midnight. I like the people. Wells's wife a delightful little creature, a real companion for him, I should think.- "The Whirlpool" mentioned in *Athenaeum* gossip to-day.

Sund. Jan. 10. Dull, turning to rain.

Mond. Jan. 11. Thick fog all day. Didn't leave the house. A good idea for a short novel; thinking all day. Clodd invites me for the 24th. Wrote to Alg.

Tuesd. Jan. 12. Fog all day. Went to see Beaumont again. Nothing new.- Proofs.- Letter from Alfred Hartley, who tells me he has just been married [to Leonora Locking]. Invitation from Mrs Travers; declined. Wrote to Hartley and to Joseph Anderson.

432

Wed. Jan. 13. Gloom. Wrote to Nelly. Letter from little boy, beautifully written. Reading Shorter's "Charlotte Brontë" [1896].

Thursd. Jan. 14. Clear and dry, cold. Spent some hours at the Museum. Then to call on Mrs Norman. Home at 8.30.

Frid. Jan. 15. Dull, cold. Clodd sends me his "Pioneers of Evolution".

Sat. Jan. 16. Cold; at evening, heavy snow. Last of the proofs. Re-reading Dostoievsky's "Idiot". Wrote to my boy.

Sund. Jan. 17. Snow lying thick.

Mond. Jan. 18. Snow still on ground; bright day.

Tuesd. Jan. 19. Gloom; slow thaw. Received from Miss Sprague a picture calendar of Californian wild flowers. Invitation from the Royal Societies Club for evening of Feb. 5th, to meet Dr Nansen. Shall go. No idea how the invitation happens to be sent to me.- Editor of *Westminster Gazette* asks my contribution to a discussion on Reviewing. Sent a short letter[1].- Anonymous letter from some enthusiast who says that a friend of hers has established a "Gissing library" and lends my books to all his friends.

Wed. Jan. 20. Terrible wind. Didn't leave the house. Amazing note from Bullen, who wants to make suggestions of change in "The Whirlpool".

Thursd. Jan. 21. Gloomy and cold. Reading [P.G.] Hamerton's life [*An Autobiography 1834-58, Memoir by his wife 1858-94*, published in 1896].

Frid. Jan. 22. Heavy snow-storm. Had agreed to dine at Roberts's house, but had to telegraph excuse.- Reading Rosny's "L'Indomptée" [1894].

Sat. Jan. 23. Thick snow and gloom. Wrote to my boy; also to Alg, Nelly and Miss Collet. Finished "L'Indomptée".

Sund. Jan. 24. Bright, cold. In afternoon went to Clodd's, and stayed the night. People there: Selwyn Image, Grant Richards (who has just started publishing), and Grant Allen's son. Also Mme Blouet (wife of Max O'Rell), and a Mrs Lowndes (Marie Belloc)—nasty woman.

Mond. Jan. 25. Bad headache. Weather still severe.

Tuesd. Jan. 26. Fine, hard frost. Thinking about new story.

Wed. Jan. 27. Cold. Reading Sienkiewicz's "Quo Vadis?" [1894].

Thursd. Jan. 28. More snow. Made notes for "Polly Brill".

Frid. Jan. 29. Bright and frosty. Colles sends request from M. [Georges] Art for biog[raphical] details, and copies of my old books. Sent two.

Sat. Jan. 30. Dull and thaw. Miss Collet came. Wrote to my boy.

Sund. Jan. 31. Fog, thaw. Thinking hard over "Polly Brill". Getting names etc.

Mond. Feb. 1. Damp. Got to work at "Polly", and wrote nearly 2 pp. Of course the beastly mother of our servant chose this very time to come and say she wants the girl to leave—for a marvel she has been here 10 months. By offer of increased wages, seem to have got over the difficulty. A joke, rather, that I, in my position, should stand trembling for the decision of the gutter-child of fifteen years old!

Tuesd. Feb. 2. Dense fog till afternoon. Wrote 1p., but the thing won't do.

Wed. Feb. 3. Rain. Rescheming the story. Recd Alg's book—"The Scholar of Bygate".

Thursd. Feb. 4. Fine. In afternoon to Museum. There by chance met Joseph Anderson, who introduced me to his brother-in-law, Navarro, husband of the famous Mary. It surprised me to see an insignificant little man, darkish, straight-haired, with regular features—nothing notable. We went and had tea together. Only good thing about the man was his firm hand-grasp.- Wrote to H.G. Smith, to ask some information about Cambridge.

Frid. Feb. 5. Rain. Misery in house. What with this and the bad weather, gave up idea of going to the Nansen reception to-night at the Royal Societies Club. Read the letters of Renan and his sister.

Sat. Feb. 6. Dull, dry. Wrote to my boy. I see from the paper that 900 persons attended the reception last night, so I am not sorry to have stayed away. Reading Hirsch, "Genius and Degeneration [: a Psychological Study]" [1896].

Sund. Feb. 7. Dull. Reading [J.J.] Hissey's "Across England in a Dogcart" [1891].

Mond. Feb. 8. Dull to rain. A new beginning of "Polly". Did 1 p. In evening disturbed by arrival from Bullen of a proof of "The Whirlpool" marked throughout with suggested excisions. On looking through, I find they are on the whole judiciously made, and I have accepted most of them. These will knock out, I should think, some ten pages of matter.- Reply from H.G. Smith, with information desired.

Tuesd. Feb. 9. Fine. Story again out of gear. New scheme.

*   *   *

Wed. June 2. A very long gap, full of miseries and amenities. Somewhere about the 10th Feb., I was driven from home; things having come to an intolerable pass. I spent a night at the Charing Cross Hotel, then went down to Romney, to Harry Hick's. Stayed there about a week. H. examined my chest, and thought I had better see a good doctor. He came up to town with me, and took me to see Pye-Smith, who advised me to go immediately to South Devon. That evening, Wells dined with us at the Hotel Previtali, where I stayed. Next day I dined with Bullen, and the day after went to Budleigh Salterton.

In the meantime, I had called upon Miss Orme, at her house at Tulse Hill. I told her my troubles, and she promised to go to Epsom, and do what she could.

At Budleigh Salterton I lived till last day of May, solely attending to my health. My lodgings were first at Mrs Chown's (opposite Public Rooms) and, for the latter part, next door, at Mrs Waller's. There, in the Easter holidays, little boy Walter came to spend a fortnight, his aunt Margaret with him. He enjoyed himself greatly, and got very brown. We drove one day to Hayes Barton, and then up to Woodbury Castle. Whilst they were still with me Wells and his wife came down on a tandem bicycle, and I have found rooms for them, at the house of Yeats, the gardener, higher up the hill. They stayed a fortnight after W[alter] and M[argaret] had gone, and their company did me a great deal of good. We walked one day to Ladram Bay, and there boated. At length, they left by steamer, to have a walking tour over Dartmoor.

Meanwhile "The Whirlpool" was published and sold better than any of my books hitherto. By the end of May the first edition of 2000 copies was finished.

My reading was concerned with the Ostrogothic rule in Italy. In the 1st vol. of Gregorovius[2] I got hold of a good idea for a historical novel, and worked it out. I obt[aine]d from London the works of Cassiodorus, and read very carefully the 12 books, noting good material. Got also [Johann] Manso's "Geschichte des Ostgoth[ischen] Reiches [in Italien]" [1824], and read it twice. Studied carefully [Robert] Burn's "Ancient Rome [and its neighbourhood]" [1895]. Read a good deal of Dickens, for the little book I am to write. On morning of my departure, I recd from Miss McCarthy a copy of the new vol. of her father's "Hist[ory] of Our Own Times".

Home on afternoon of May 31st. Little Alfred very fat and well.

Tuesd. June 1. Went up to see Pye-Smith. He says I am decidedly better, and that I must now choose a suitable place of abode—high and dry. Went to my tailor's.

Wed. June 2. Fine, close. Pottered about. Enthusiastic letter from Barrie about "The Whirlpool".

435

Thursd. June 3. Close, misty. Reading Gibbon on Justinian.

Frid. June 4. Fine, close. Miss Orme and her sister Beatrice came over from Tulse Hill to tea. Admirable people!

Sat. June 5. Fine, close. Wrote to my boy Walter. Making a rough catalogue of my library, in view of removal.

Sund. June 6. Hot, fine. Reading a little Gibbon.

Mond. June 7. Fine. To keep appointment with W[illiam] Rothenstein at his studio, Glebe Place, Chelsea. He made two drawings of me, one sitting, the other standing—latter I liked best. That remarkable youth Max Beerbohm came in and had lunch with us. Home at 5.30. I am mentioned in a review of Victorian fiction in the [*Daily*] *Chronicle* to-day by Lionel Johnson. Letters from M[argaret] and E[llen].

Tuesd. June 8. Dull, colder. Sent the boy his silver mug, the gift of Dr Zakrzewska and Miss Sprague, which has lain here since its arrival from America. Thinking out my story "The Town Traveller".

Wed. June 9. Dense, cold fog, like November. Wrote nearly 3pp.—a good beginning.

Thursd. June 10. Fine and warm again. Letters from Mother and Walter. Rewrote last ½p., and did 2 more. Reading [Rodolfo] Lanciani's "Ancient Rome [in the Light of Recent Discoveries]" [1888].

Frid. June 11. Fine, hot. Wrote 2pp. in morning. In afternoon to town. Bank, tailor's, hatter's.

Sat. June 12. Very hot. Wrote 3pp. Getting ahead very quickly. Wrote to Walter.

Sund. June 13. Very hot. Finished Lanciani, and read greater part of 3rd vol. of Hodgkin. Wrote to Alg, and to Bertz.

Mond. June 14. Cooler; fine. Wrote 3pp.

Tuesd. June 15. Cooler still. Wrote 3pp. Finished vol. 3 of Hodgkin.

Wed. June 16. Very windy and showers. Wrote 3pp. Reading [A.J.C.] Hare's "[Studies in] Russia" [1885], and Lanciani's "Pagan and Christian Rome" [1893]. Sent Alg £13—a loan for rent.

Thursd. June 17. Gale going on, but fine. Wrote 3½pp.

Frid. June 18. Windy, showery. Wrote 2½pp. Looking through [Johann] Beckmann's "Hist[ory] of Inventions [and Discoveries]" [4 vols., translated 1797-1814].

Sat. June 19. Weather improved, but still windy. Wrote 3pp. Began [J.H.] Middleton's "[Remains of] Ancient Rome" [1892].

Sund. June 20. Dull, windy. Reading Middleton.

Mond. June 21. Finer and warmer, still windy. Wrote 3pp. Middleton.

Tuesd. June 22. So-called "Diamond" Jubilee. Very fine. Thank heaven, possessed my soul in quiet and did 3pp. as usual.- Letter from Wells, one from Nelly.

Wed. June 23. Very hot. Did 3pp.

Thursd. June 24. Heat, ending in thunder. Did 3pp. Wrote to Colles, telling him he may try to sell serial and book rights of this story. Letter from Alg. Paid my rent.

Frid. June 25. Clouded, cooler. Did 3pp. Reading [T.H.] Dyer's "City of Rome" [2nd ed. 1883].

Sat. June 26. Bright, windy. Wrote 3pp. Never got on so quickly with anything. Glanced at a novel called "Elementary Jane" by [R.] Pryce [1897].

Sund. June 27. Dull, hot. Did odds and ends. Read [Georg] Brandes' book on Russia [*Impressions of Russia,* 1890].

Mond. June 28. Fine, hot. Wrote 3pp. Sent off first half of story to Colles. I am going to let him dispose of it as he will, serial and book rights, and see how much he can get.

Tuesd. June 29. Fine, hot. Did 3pp. A letter from farmhouse near Askrigg. Sent it to Alg, for his opinion.

Wed. June 30. Fine, cloudy later, a little rain. Notice of "to let" stuck up before house. Did 3pp. Reading vol. I of Milman's "Latin Christianity" [1854-55].

Thursd. July 1. Very hot. Did 3pp.- Milman.- Letter from Alg.

Frid. July 2. Fine. Did 3pp.

Sat. July 3. Fine. Did 2pp. Miss Collet came.- Violent headache.

Sund. July 4. Dull. Going through vol. 4 of Hodgkin.

Mond. July 5. Fine, windy. Did 3pp.

Tuesd. July 6. Fine. Did 3pp. Disappointed to hear that the rooms at Nappa House, Aysgarth, which I had hoped to get, were taken whilst I was hesitating. Sent off six postcards to other houses in Wensleydale. Great mental disturbance, this, in the middle of my work.

Wed. July 7. Fine, cooler. Bad attack of rheumatism. Did 3pp. Bullen invites me to their "breakfast". Don't think I can go.

Thursd. July 8. Fine. Did 3pp. Recd from Colles £5-17-1, for a story pubd in *The Idler* more than a year ago ["Simple Simon", May 1896].- Wrote to a house at Castle Bolton, trying to secure rooms.

Frid. July 9. Fine. Did 3pp. Finished vol. 4 of Hodgkin's.

Sat. July 10. Very fine. Went off early to town, and visited London Library for first time. Had talk with Wright, the librarian, who began well—saying that he would at once purchase two or three books I asked for, which they hadn't got—Ricci on Ravenna[3], and Augustus, "De Antiquissimis Hymnis". Thence to Paddington, and to Marlow for the Omar dinner. Barrie a new member, but did not come—I think he feared the speech. New acquaintances: Prof. Walter Raleigh of Liverpool—who told me I had met him years ago at Miss Crum's, but I had forgotten it,—Alfred East, and Sir Henry Craik. Also met Sir George Robertson, of Chitral, whom I had casually met once at the Cheshire Cheese, where he was lunching with McCormick, the artist. Talked by the river with Miss Le Quesne, artist, friend of the [Henry] Normans.
  Not a wink of sleep at night, but no worse for it next day. (E. and little boy spent day at Miss Orme's).

Sund. July 11. Fine and hot. Left Marlow at 8.20 and called on Hudson, who is far from well. Lunch with him and then to Worcester Park, to dine with Wells—genial as ever. Home by 11. Found a letter from Mrs Mason of Castle Bolton, definitely letting me her rooms from July 24th to end of August.

Mond. July 12. Windy, fine. Morning given to letter writing. Received the 3rd part (6 sheets) of Lanciani's great map of Rome. Terrible extravagance—30/- with postage. Cannot buy any more just yet.- Parcel from London Library.- Wrote in evening 1½p.—Replied to a correspondent, at Gateshead, called Allhusen, who sends me my portrait to autograph.

Tuesd. July 13. Fine; furious wind. Did 3pp. Reading Ozanam.[4]

Wed. July 14. Hot. Did 3pp., and *finished "The Town Traveller"*.

Thursd. July 15. Very hot. Sent off my MS to Colles.- Reading Leroy-Beaulieu's "The Empire of the Tsars".

Frid. July 16. Hot. Wrote to Rose about my Dickens book. The Series, to be pubd by Blackie, has just been announced in paragraphs.

Sat. July 17. Hot, dull. Getting together notes for the Dickens. Reading Ozanam.

Sund. July 18. Fine, hot. Finished vol. I of Ozanam. Began Beugnot, "Hist[oire] de la Destruction du Paganisme".

Mond. July 19. Dull, close. In evening a thunderstorm of two hours. Beugnot.

Tuesd. July 20. Stormy, more thunder. Beugnot.

Wed. July 21. Stormy, thunder. Glanced through the Eng. translation of Dahn's "Der Kampf um Rom", which deals with my chosen period. A poor, unprofitable book. Can do better than *that*.

Thursd. July 22. Fine, cloudy. Day in town—Brit[ish] Mus[eum] and London Library. In evening to Blackheath to dine with Whale. Guests: Sidney Lee (ed. "National Dict[ionary] of Biog[raph]y"), Clodd, Shorter, a man named West, and Wheatley, the philologist. Lee told me of an oldish literary hack, who one day came to him in great discouragement, and said he should abandon literature. It turned out that he had been reading "New Grub Street".

Frid. July 23. Preparing for departure to-morrow.

Sat. July 24. Terribly hot. Left Epsom by 8.4, and got to King's Cross at 9.35 for the 10 express. Found a roaring multitude; no attention from porters or guards, only by fierce language secured seats in two separate carriages, one for myself, one for E. and Alfred. Perspired all the way to York. There terrific confusion, and with difficulty caught the Northallerton train. Walter and M[argaret] only found us amid the tumult ten minutes after our arrival. The boy came on with us, and we reached Redmire station, in Wensleydale, at 5 o'clock; a trap waiting, to take us up to Mrs Mason's at Bolton Castle.

Sund. July 25. Fine. The place proves satisfactory, though very humble in accommodation. No ventilation in bedrooms, so that we have to leave doors open at night. On the cottage is a grotesque inscription— "Temperance Hotel", which means, it seems, that people can get a cup of tea here. The situation magnificent, looking right across to Penhill, and up and down the Dale.

Mond. July 26. Dull, with showers. I walked to Aysgarth, and there took train for Hawes, where I managed to hire a mail-cart for Alfred. Bought Stanford's guide to N. and E. Ridings.

Tuesd. July 27. Fine. Idled about Apedale Beck. Wrote to Alg.

Wed. July 28. Fine. Up to top of the moors behind us, and had a peep into Swaledale.- Letter from Bullen, who proposes usual royalty for my vol. of short stories [*Human Odds and Ends*], and 75 gu[ine]as on account. Wrote to accept. Note from Harry Hick, who hoped to meet me in London to-day.- Proofs of "Spellbound" from *Eng. Illustrated.*- Reading Whyte Melville's "The Gladiators" [1863].

Went over the Castle, of which one tower is in good preservation, and inhabited (a few rooms below) by a family who show the interior. Queen Mary's room, the state bedroom, kitchens etc. Fine courtyard. Banqueting hall roofless. The dungeon—into which young Walter was afraid to descend. There is a little museum, containing a few interesting local finds—old swords, flints etc, and some curiosities from foreign countries. Amid the queer jumble saw two huge *birches,* said to have been used at Eton College.

*   *   *

Mond. Aug. 2. Days of brilliant sunshine, often severely hot. Do nothing in particular, as a rule, but to-day had a long drive, from 10 o'clock to 4, going through Askrigg to Bainbridge, and back through Aysgarth. At Askrigg saw Mill Gill; not much water coming over the falls, but very beautiful. Delighted with Bainbridge; though the dearth of water has made a mere muddy pool of the Bain just below the bridge. There ate our sandwiches. Young Alfred very good all day, and seemed to enjoy it. This drive cost only seven shillings.

I see from the advts, that Wells's article on my books is in the *Contemporary* this month.⁵—Wrote to Miss Orme.

Thursd. Aug. 5. After some days of terrific heat, a great thunderstorm, with rain.- Not much pleasure here, now; quietness, as usual, lasted only for the first few days of novelty. Constant grumbling and railing at the children for the trouble they give. It sickens me, but I keep stern silence; find it easier to do so than formerly.

Finished "Barnaby Rudge", and began careful reading of Forster's Life of Dickens.

Mond. Aug. 9. Weather still very fine, and not so hot. Had a long walk by myself, to West Burton and back. After ordering dinner at the Black Bull (queer old inn, standing by itself amid the village green) walked about a mile up Waldendale, on the upper road. Capital dinner: cold beef, potatoes and peas, pickles, with stewed plums, cheese cakes and cheese to follow. Talk with naively intelligent fellow, who sold me tobacco in a little druggist's shop.

Tuesd. Aug. 10. Letters from Mrs Travers and Wells—to whom I had written genially about his *Contemporary* article.

Wed. Aug. 11. Cooler, showery. No butcher's meat being obtainable here, (a cart comes only once a week, our last piece went bad) I walked over to Leyburn, and bought some chops etc.

In spite of fine surroundings, a good deal of discomfort here. The garden privy in awful state; it is *never* emptied and only once since we came has dust been thrown in. Bread and cakes admirable; but eggs always boiled hard as stones.

Unable ever to close our bedroom doors at night, as there is no ventilation, and I sometimes feel nervous as I lie awake.

Unfortunately, there is no *man* in the house, and to be given over to the care of women is always dreadful.

Thursd. Aug. 12. Yesterday I saw in a paper at Leyburn that the Bishop of Wakefield [Walsham How] is dead. Did not venture to tell Walter.

Much misery to-day; grumbling, snarling, rage and universal idiocy. What a life! Hardly a day passes without this kind of thing.

Wrote to Alg, asking him to arrange to meet the boy Walter somewhere on our way back, and take him for stay at Willersey.

Mond. Aug. 16. Weather has turned unpleasant; for some days, showery, with cold breezes.- Much trouble with our meat, which breeds livestock a day after it is cooked. Only a part of the general misery, from day to day.

The little child is getting very fat and strong and uproarious. He is called "A'hed"—his own attempt at "Alfred". Seems to me to show great intelligence. For instance, understands a game at hide and seek. Is particularly ready at recognizing pictures of animals—even small woodcuts. A sweet little fellow; comes of his own accord, offering a kiss, for good morning and good night.

Walter troubles me now and then; I seem to perceive in him so much weakness of character. I must not forget that he is still not six years old—a mere baby. And his position in this family of discord is most unfortunate. He and his mother always quarrelling. How *can* he respect her?—It is clear to me that I cannot do better than leave him at Wakefield.- I notice, by the bye, a singular care for, and precision about, his clothing; possibly the result of Wakefield influences.

Am reading—if reading it can be called under these circumstances— Lenormant's "Grande-Grèce".

Tuesd. Aug. 17. A S.W. gale, with bright sunshine. Had to go to Leyburn, to buy meat etc, and took Walter with me. We walked by the lower road, through the woods of Bolton Hall. Fine spot, where the Ure rushes through a deep, precipitous ravine. Walter of course showing his better qualities, as always when alone, for a few hours, with me.

Infamous uproar all day; E.'s behaviour worse than ever. At night I wrote a long letter to Margaret, giving her a detailed account of what I am enduring. This letter she shall preserve, to do me justice some day, if needful.

Wed. Aug. 18. Heavy rain in night and this morning; cleared at 11 for a day of sun and showers. E.'s fury gradually subsiding, and, as usual, she is astonished that I do not forthwith forget the outrages thrown upon me for the last ten days or more.- Wrote to Sturmer.

Sat. Aug. 21. Last few days wild with wind and rain. As result, the water courses very full. We went to Aysgarth to-day, and in the Falls saw a really wonderful sight—the first time I have seen a mountain river in spate.- Of course everything spoilt by E.'s frenzy of ill temper. I merely note the fact, lest anyone reading this should be misled, and imagine a day of real enjoyment.

Tuesd. Aug. 24. A day of all but ceaseless rain. Of course this weather enhances my miseries. Quarrel to-day bet. Edith and landlady's daughter about the washing! I believe, of all our lodging-houses, there was not one where she did not quarrel openly before leaving. Yesterday I gave notice that we should leave on Friday. An interesting detail of to-day's uproar. At dinner time we wanted our tin-opener, which could not be found. E. declared that landlady's daughter took it away with knives from the table a few days ago; the woman angrily denied having done so. When she had left the room, I found the thing; the mistake had been ours. Now Edith *wished to keep the discovery unmentioned,* and broke into fury when I said that of course I must acknowledge the mistake!

I wrote to Miss Orme, telling her that I have made up my mind to spend the winter in Italy. To this plan I shall fiercely adhere.

Wed. Aug. 25. Having recorded what has happened to-day (a crucial instance of E.'s behaviour) I hope to write no more such dreary stuff in my diary.- Little Alfred was playing, just before tea-time, on the stairs leading out of our sitting-room, and he had got hold of my shaving-brush. The end of it came off and rolled down the stairs into the room, where, just then, I was sitting. I paid no attention, but after a lapse of a minute or two, E. came down from above (having heard the object roll) and began to search for the lost end of the brush. Oddly, it could not be found; the thing had mysteriously hidden itself in some corner. As her manner is, E. rapidly passed from annoyance at a futile search to irritation against the person nearest—myself; she asked me if I had taken up the missing object. I replied that I had not, but that I had heard it roll into the room. Her wrath growing, she next roundly accused me of secreting the thing. "There's no knowing how nastiness will show itself", she declared. The search was still vain, and presently we all sat down to tea, - though not till E. had endeavoured to search my pockets. As the meal progressed, her anger reached the virulent stage (I had naturally begged her not to worry about such a trifle,) and at length she said to Walter: "Why, your father jumped up as the thing rolled into the room, and I *saw* him take it up." This was too much. I answered "That is a deliberate lie" and asked Walter whether he thought me capable of lying so on such a subject. The boy, much upset, of course said, "No". At the sight of his tears, E. shouted: "There, that's the second or third time you've made him cry with your ill temper". I was very angry, and told her I would not be accused of lying before my own son*. Thereupon she screamed, with a violent gesture: "*Hold your beastly noise, or you'll have this plate at your head!*"- Hating the odious necessity of what I did, I turned to the boy, and said quietly, "Walter, repeat to me the words your mother has just used". He did so, poor little chap, with tears, and I wrote the sentence at once in my pocket-book. My reason, of course, was that E. invariably denies all her words and actions a day after they have been spoken or performed, and I was determined to allow her no possibility of that in the present monstrous instance.- Still raging, she then addressed herself to Walter, and commiserated him on having such a father, a father unlike all others,- who never bought him a toy (verbatim thus), and who was never in a decent humour,- with much else of the usual kind.

There it is. Decisive, I should think, for ever.

Weather much better to-day. Walter said something this evening that rejoiced me. Looking at some grand sun-lit cumuli, he exclaimed—"They look like mountains in Greece!" I don't know how the idea occurred to him, but it is fine that he should already have that feeling about Greece in his mind.

First sheet of proofs of my vol. of short stories, "Human Odds and Ends."

Frid. Aug. 27. Left Redmire by the 8 o'clock train, and reached King's Cross at 4.20. Beautiful day. At King's Cross, Alg was waiting. We had only a minute's talk, and he and Walter went off to Paddington, on their way to Willersey. Walter, delighted to go, forgot to say goodbye to me, but I was glad to see him so pleased.

At Waterloo I met [James B.] Pinker, the literary agent, and had a talk with him on the journey to Epsom. Wrote this same evening, asking him if he would try to sell American rights of "Human Odds and Ends". Wrote to Sturmer, asking him to lunch with me on Monday.

Sat. Aug. 28. Went to bed last night with bad headache. To-day read half the 1st vol. of Lenormant, making notes. Wrote to Mrs Norman, asking if Norman could give me introductions in Southern Italy.- A temporary servant came. Of course have to keep all my plans secret as yet.

Sund. Aug. 29. Showery. Corrected proofs. Finished reading of Beugnot— interrupted when I went to Yorkshire. Read some chapters of Lenormant, and half vol. 7 of Bingham's "Christian Antiquities".- Wrote to Nelly.

Mond. Aug. 30. Fine and warm. Went to town early, having invited my correspondent, Sturmer, to lunch with me. Found him a genial fellow, well disposed. Called in Henrietta St., saw Lawrence and Hedley Peek; the latter made me promise to go with him to his country place to-morrow and

---

*She bade me speak lower, lest people should hear, and I explained that I had a good mind to call all the people in the house, and ask their opinion of such an insult.

stay over night. Little mind to it. Found a lot of honey, sent here by Harry Hick during my absence, and forwarded to Henrietta St.- Sent Alg £15. A letter from him this morning says that he and Walter got to Willersey on Friday night, the little fellow sleeping for some hours on his lap. Wrote to Blackies, at Glasgow, to get agreement about my Dickens book.

Tuesd. Aug. 31. Showery. In afternoon met Hedley Peek at Lond[on] Bridge, and went with him to his house at Outwood, s[outh] of Redhill. He was cordial, but we are not likely to go further in acquaintance. Read me a lot of his parodies, pubd in the vol. of the Badminton Library called "The Poetry of Sport" [1896], where they are signed "Outwood".

Wed. Sept. 1. Hard rain all day. Working at my Dickens notes, after early return from Peek's.

Thursd. Sept. 2. Fine, windy. Worked at Dickens.

Frid. Sept. 3. Showery. Dickens. Accepted invitation to go next Wed. to the Normans' farm in Hampshire.

Sat. Sept. 4. Fine, windy. Wrote to my boy at Willersey. Dickens.

Sund. Sept. 5. Rain all day. Dickens and Lenormant.

Mond. Sept. 6. Finer. Dickens. Letter from Clodd, praising "The Emancipated", which he has read down at Exmouth in his holiday.- Disclosed my intention of going to Italy. Fury and insult, of course, but quiet afterwards.

Tuesd. Sept. 7. Fine, dull. A day of great misery. Much letter-writing. Man came from Dougharty's, of Brixton, and agreed to remove furniture and books for £4-4. Cost of warehousing to be 5/6 a week.

Wed. Sept. 8. Tolerably fine. Left early for Alton, where Henry Norman met me in his trap, and drove me to his little place (newly purchased) Kitcombe Farm. They are living in a cottage, very comfortably, and planning a larger house on the hillside above. Mrs Norman's baby— Nigel—a few months old. Enjoyed myself. At night, Mrs Norman read aloud two chapters of a novel she is beginning—"The Side-School". As there is no spare room in the cottage, I slept at a farmhouse hard by.

Thursd. Sept. 9. Dull, but fair after much rain in night. Mrs Norman drove me to Selborne, where we went over Gilbert White's house and garden, and the church.- I learnt in talk that L.F. Austin has long been literary secretary to Irving the actor—all whose addresses, speeches etc. he composes. Norman seriously urged that the time had come for a collected edition of my books.- On reaching home this evening, I wrote about this to Bullen. Also to Colles about the US copyright of little Dickens book.

444

Frid. Sept. 10. Fine. Day of letter-writing etc. Infinite labour with arrangements. Yesterday, whilst I was away, Miss Orme came to talk with Edith. Undertook to find rooms for her—three furnished rooms—and engage a nurse-girl. My gratitude to this admirable woman beyond words. What toil and misery she is taking off my hands!

Sat. Sept. 11. Fine. A busy morning in town, buying odds and ends. In afternoon to McCormick's studio, where Roberts met me. Home early in evening.

Sund. Sept. 12. Fine.

Mond. Sept. 13. Dull. Letter-writing. Reading "Edwin Drood". Dined with Wells.

Tuesd. Sept. 14. Day in town. Bought a portmanteau. To Miss Orme, who proposes that Edith and boy should go to live with her, instead of taking lodgings. Terms £50 a quarter. I agreed, and very glad to. Called on J.H. Rose at Balham. Short talk. Received Circular Notes from Bank.

Wed. Sept. 15. Fine. Toiling at packing of books—much exhaustion.

Thursd. Sept. 16. Dull. Finished packing. Inventory of goods stored with Dougharty (302 Brixton Rd)

15 cases of books	Tent in bag, and pole	9 cases of glass,
6 book-cases	Mail-cart	china and sundries
2 bundles of	1 small tin box	brown paper parcels
shelves	1 black handbag	furniture etc.
3 bedsteads	1 black wooden box	
(1 folding)		
1 cot		

Frid. Sept. 17. Fine, but showery. Van came at 8.30, and all furniture cleared by 1.30. Domestic misery to the very end—rage and ill feeling. We all went together by the 2.59 train, I going on to Victoria, E. and Alfred to Tulse Hill. I got to Honeybourne by 10 o'clock, and drove in trap from the inn to Willersey—worn out.

Sat. Sept. 18. Very gloomy and cold. Much talk. Alg hopeful about his short stories. Little Roland a fat, strong boy, in great health; the baby, Alwyn, very tiny, but healthy, and with no facial resemblance to the family.

Sund. Sept. 19. Fine. In afternoon walked over with Alg to our relatives at Broadway.

Mond. Sept. 20. Fine, cold. Left Willersey at 10 o'clock. Drove to Honeybourne with Katie, who was going for the day to Evesham. Got to

Wakefield half an hour late, at 6 o'clock. All well. Enid staying here. Little man very glad to see me—sweet and affectionate. A lot of letters for me; one from George Meredith, inviting me to dine last Saturday. Much talk till late in the evening.

Tuesd. Sept. 21. Windy, but fine. Left Wakefield at 3.15. Bullen to dine with me at Hanell's Hotel, where I stopped the night. Horribly bad dinner. Bullen's talk very depressing; he never has a cheerful word to say about my books.

Wed. Sept. 22. Dull. A few last purchases, and left by the 11 o'clock from Charing Cross. Sturmer came to see me off. Also H. Hick, who travelled with me to Dover. On the steamer met, unexpectedly, with [Amédée] Forestier, who was going for holiday to Burgundy. Smooth passage. Straight on by the Laon line for Basle.

Thursd. Sept. 23. A leaden sky to the top of the Gotthard; then Italian sunshine. From Göschenen, sent Bertz a picture card. Milan by 8.30—dead tired after last sleepless night. Put up at the Hotel Roma—very good and cheap. The family of Russians in the train; a little boy of four or five, with a face of pronounced Kalmuck type; his mother a little of the same, but his father might have been an Englishman. The little chap's inexhaustible strength and good humour for 11 hours' journey.- At Göschenen one hears the first Italian shout: "Venti cinque minuti di fermata".- Snow lying in little heaps near the line, and a good deal on the heights. All the mountain torrents full, leaping from ledge to ledge. Chestnuts laden with fruit. Melons sat in the middle of ordinary fields, and there the fruit ripening on the grass.

Frid. Sept. 24. Fine and hot. Wrote cards to Wakefield and Willersey. The great Cathedral gleaming a wondrous white against the blue.- Left at 10.25 and reached Florence at 6. Impossible to reach Siena same night, so went to the Hôtel di Milano, near station. (Very good).- The bridge of boats over the Pó, parallel with railway, - the old Englishman, from Scotland, who talked good Italian in the train.

Sat. Sept. 25. Very hot indeed. Got up with a sore throat, and left Florence by the 7.23 for Empoli, where I had to wait more than two hours. Then a crawling train brought me to Siena by 1.30, and I went to the Hotel Scala. Greater heat on the journey than I ever knew—unless in America. Throat causing much suffering.

Sund. Sept. 26. Went to bed at 7 last night, and slept, more or less, till 8 this morning. Disturbed by ringing of bells at S. Domenico. Throat better now; cold going to the head. Went to S. Domenico, and saw the head of S. Catherine, shown for benefit of a pilgrimage. Bought a horrid photograph. In spite of triviality of surroundings, an impressive scene. A priest, in front of the shrine, perpetually holding up beads, and bundles of uncertain content, for the saint's blessing—the making form of cross with the object.- Heat unbearable in the sun.- Wrote to Miss Orme and to George Meredith.

Strange and significant contrast. This morning the pilgrims of S. Catherine (chiefly women and children); to-night, the festa of 20th September (postponed on account of the illness of a politician here) to which the whole city flocks into the Piazza. As I write, fireworks are splitting my ears. A gas illumination in the Piazza declares "Roma intangibile". How many Romes there have been!

Interesting to see the wolf and twins on top of columns—the arms of Siena, owing to its foundation as a colony under Augustus.

This afternoon found an excellent room, 3rd floor in Via d. Belle Arti, 18. Splendid view of the Duomo. Terms—100 lire a month, all included except washing; I have no doubt the meals will be admirable. Saw two ladies; one the landlady, Carlotta Gabbrielli, the other (I understood) her sister-in-law, who told me her name was Georgina. Seem delightful people. With them I shall have good practice in Italian, as they speak no tongue but their own.

I notice an inscription on doors in a street: "Il pozzo nero si vuota in questa notte" [literally: the black pit to be emptied tonight]. I presume this means the cesspool. Wonder how often the dread clearance takes place. "Pozzo nero" a fine name!

Mond. Sept. 27. At eleven, moved into my room, with which I am greatly satisfied. Cashed one of my circular notes with Whitby & Co. (Via dei Pellegrini) getting 263 ll. for £10.

From my window a glorious view of the Duomo, and the houses rising to it up the hill-side. This old city has grown through the ages, till it is become as one building, covering in extraordinary agglomeration hill and valley; one thinks the removal of one house would cause everything to fall.

Tuesd. Sept. 28. Sent for a carpenter, to make me a little slant for writing on. Made a beginning at the first chapter of my Dickens, noting the headings. In afternoon walked down to Fontebranda—which would be more enjoyable but for the bad smell from workshops around. Thence to S. Francesco, at opposite side of the town. Gathered some flowers under the walls, and pressed them. Posted to Mother and Walter.

Wed. Sept. 29. A few days ago the papers announced that a little English child had been stolen by an Italian nurse from a family named Young, at La Cava. To-day I see that the child has been discovered at Fuorigrotta, where it was being sent to school by a woman who had undertaken the care of it. The blackguard nurse has disappeared, but I hope will be caught. How one's interest in a thing like this is increased by having children of one's own!

Read Italian all day. My desk has not come yet. A new boarder—young American. Wrote to Miss Collet.

Thursd. Sept. 30. Not quite as hot. My desk arriving, I made a vigorous beginning of work, and wrote 1 1/2 p. Wrote from 9-12; then lunch and an hour's rest; then wrote again from 3-6. This will have to be my day, owing to dinner being at 6.- My cold practically gone, but, as usual, it has left a bad cough.

Frid. Oct. 1. Sky lightly clouded, for first time. Did 2pp., getting on well. The young American here is called Brian O'Dunne. He has been rambling in Europe for two years. Belongs to Florida. Plays the zither.

Sat. Oct. 2. Great thunder-storm last night. To-day gloom. My cough very troublesome. Discontented postcard from E. Wrote 2pp.

Sund. Oct. 3. Cloudy. Rested to-day. Cough getting better. Letter from Nelly, with line from dear little boy, who is enjoying himself greatly with Enid at Wakefield. She sends note from Adele Berger, asking for right to translate "Eve's Ransom". Replied, asking £10. The poor fellow, Allhusen, of Gateshead, sends pitiful letter, saying he has to go at end of October to Australia, probably for life. Wrote with what encouragement I could.

Mond. Oct. 4. Dull. Wrote 2pp. Slow, hard work.

Tuesd. Oct. 5. Heavy rain all day. No sun. Did 2pp.

Wed. Oct. 6. Sunshine again. But cloudy, and cold wind. Walked to the Fort of S. Barbara; fine view. Did 2pp.

Thursd. Oct. 7. Dull still, and coldish. Did 2pp. I go out from 8.30-9 every morning, whilst my room is being done, and sometimes from 12.30 to 2, after lunch. Dare not go out in the evening. Yesterday, and in the night, my cough was very bad. I noticed an unmistakable stain of blood on my handkerchief once.- Well, must get this work done, and then spend more time in open air. Wrote to my boy at Wakefield.

Frid. Oct. 8. Going to take some olive oil every morning; see if it will help me. Bad fit of coughing last night; read from three to four.- Did 2pp.- Letter from Sturmer, mentioning article on me in the *National Review*[6]. One from Mlle Blaze de Bury, asking for copies of *Unclassed* and *Emancipated,* for an article. Suppose I must send them.

Sat. Oct. 9. Cloudy. Feeling much better. Did 2pp. Bought an Italian dictionary.

Sund. Oct. 10. Fine. In morning had a bath in the Via Giovanni Dupré. Afternoon, got weighed by the officer of the dazio at Porta Tufi. Weight 77 1/2 kilos = 170 1/2 lbs. Still losing from my Budleigh Salterton weight. However, I have begun to take olive oil, and I think it does me good. Cough very slight now.- Walked on and saw the Campo Santo, and round through vineyards to Porta Fontebranda.- A [*Daily*] *Chronicle* [of October 6] from Harry Hick, with review of the Life of Tennyson. Reading the paper, I seem to have been months away.

Mond. Oct. 11. Very fine, but cold wind. Did 2pp. Letter from Wells.

Tuesd. Oct. 12. Fine morning, then dull and cold. Did 2pp.

Wed. Oct. 13. West wind. Warmer, but cloudy. Did 2pp. Wrote to Alg.- This evening come half a dozen letters, which have been lying at the P.O.,- in spite of their promise to forward them! Nice management. Called and made complaint. Two letters from Miss Orme, saying that things go fairly well, and that little Alfred is joyous—dear little manny! One from Hudson, one from Katie, one from Bertz.

At another pensione in the street is staying Vincenzo Tateo, an old Garibaldino, nearly blind, but in good health, who has come from Naples to Siena on account of the illness of his old friend Imbriani—paralyzed whilst addressing a meeting a month ago. Tateo seems to be a fine fellow. O'Dunne has seen him, when calling on American friends of his there. One of the proverbs Tateo repeats is interesting:

> Stare a tavola e non mangiare
> Stare a letto e non dormire
> Stare aspettando e non venire
> Sono tre cose da morire.
> [Sitting at a table without eating
> Lying in bed without sleeping
> Waiting for what is not coming
> Are three reasons for dying.]

Last Saturday a great demonstration was held in Rome, to protest against increase of the income tax (richezza mobile). In the Piazza Navona a riot began. It ended in soldiers firing. One man killed, and many wounded.

Thursd. Oct. 14. South wind, dull. Did 2pp. Letter from Wakefield; one from dear little boy.- Gloom in this house. For a year and more the husband of Signora Gabbrielli has been lying paralyzed, dying. To-day he seems near the end. An unfortunate thing for me.- I always come in for such things.

Frid. Oct. 15. Rain in night, fine to-day. Very satisfactory news of little Alfred from Miss Orme. He is weaned at last, poor child, and begins to talk merrily with all and sundry. Did not quite 2pp.

Sat. Oct. 16. Heavy weather. Did only 1p.- Our fellow-boarder, Cappelli, to-day finishes his year's military service. Appears in civil clothes. A good and nice fellow. O'Dunne and I bought a bottle of Marsala, to fête him with.- Poor Signora Carlotta's husband very bad. Gloom and weeping in the household.

Sund. Oct. 17. A gloomy and memorable day. From the morning we understood that Gabbrielli was dying. About three in the afternoon began a violent thunderstorm, which lasted till eight or nine. About six o'clock, whilst we sat at dinner (O'Dunne, Cappelli, and I) the poor fellow expired. Later, as I sat with O'Dunne in his room, which is close to that occupied by the family, we heard of a sudden (amid the roaring thunder) heartbreaking cries of "Addio! Addio! Addio!" Afterwards I learnt that they were then taking the poor Signora Carlotta away from the bedside.- Did not sleep much at night.

Mond. Oct. 18. Fine. Unable to work, so walked with O'Dunne from Porta Ovile to Porta Fontebranda; then into the Public Library, where saw the splendid old MSS, a letter of S. Catherine etc.- At 5 o'clock took place the funeral—24 hrs after death. At Cappelli's suggestion, we put our names among those subscribing for a wreath- "Dagli Amici"—an immense wreath of beautiful flowers, at least six feet in circumference. The other, somewhat smaller, "Dalla Famiglia". As the funeral started, it again thundered and rained. A relief, after all, to think that the poor fellow is no more.

Tuesd. Oct. 19. Very fine. Did 2pp. Paid my subscription to the wreath— *l.* 2.50, and recd a funeral card.

Wed. Oct. 20. Fine. Did 2pp. Letter from Miss Orme, with continued good news.- Yesterday, O'Dunne went out into the country with an Italian acquaintance who [is] said to own villas. He was promised *la caccia.* This proved to be the shooting of small birds—thrushes, finches, etc—in a garden or orchard. There stood a small straw-thatched hut, with a small window. On trees all around hung birds (blinded) singing in cages, as decoys. Aim was taken from within the hut, and great number of birds shot. This not being sport enough, trees are cut down into an umbrella form, and the branches smeared with lime; when the birds alight here, their wings get limed, they fall down, and a man rushes out to kill them with a stick. Moreover they are caught in folding nets, worked by a string, and beaten dead or their necks wrung. This is what is meant when Italians speak of *la caccia!* They can see nothing ignoble in it. Of course, their poverty partly explains the practice, as they eat all the birds thus obtained.

Thursd. Oct. 21. Cold wind. O'Dunne left for Rome. I was told to-day that these people are going to move into a smaller flat on Nov. 1, but that I shall have an equally good room.- Did 2pp.- Letter from Miss McCarthy, saying she wishes a friend of hers [Alfred Lambart], who will pass winter in Rome, to meet me there.

Frid. Oct. 22. Great storm in night. Dull to-day. Rewrote 1p. of yesterday, and did 2 more; the best day yet.

Sat. Oct. 23. Dull. Did 2pp. Recd a copy from Miss Orme of the Oct. *National Review,* with article on my books by Dolman, and another copy from Bullen. The man begins his article by saying that the slow growth of my reputation is one of the literary problems of the time. A partial explanation may be found in this very article, for I see that it was written 3 yrs. ago. He speaks of *Eve's Ransom* as my latest book, and says *The Unclassed* was pubd eleven years ago. So, this thing has probably been lying for 3 yrs. at office of the *National Review,* waiting for publication; and, now that it appears, no one takes the trouble to bring it up to date!- Wrote to Colles.

Sund. Oct. 24. Pouring rain last night. To-day, but little sun. Letter from Alg; he has been in Cumberland.- Talk with Cappelli. He speaks of the increasing power of clericalism. In Siena priests are rich and influential; have obliged shopkeepers to shut up on Sunday.- About the Universities. They are never residential. Students pay a *tassa* of 200 *ll.* a year. If in exam. each year they get a certain number of marks (*voti*)—he says 27 out of a total 30—the *tassa* is remitted. Cheapness of education here explanation of misery among the upper classes, who struggle for employment. Cappelli says that the Contadini in N[orth] are the best off of all.

Wrote to Roberts, and to Bullen.

On the Porta Camollia (the gate looking towards Florence) is written: Cor magis tibi Sena pandit [Siena gives you a warmer welcome]. The *magis* means, in comparison with other cities.

In the evening, set to and did a bit of writing I had promised to Mrs Wood, of Colwyn—about 1000 words of recollections of the old school at Alderley Edge.[7]

Mond. Oct. 25. Cool, but fine sun. Did 2pp. Bought some underclothing.

Extraordinary rains this last week or two along the Adriatic coast. Terrible floods in the flat districts, especially at Ancona. The papers full of calamities.

Tuesd. Oct. 26. Cool morning, and a glorious day. At 2 o'clock, walking in the Lizza, I noticed the shimmering of objects through the hot dry air. Wrote 2pp.

Wed. Oct. 27. Very fine again. Did 2pp. Letter from Miss Orme.- Next Wednesday our people here are going to move to a new flat, and packing is going on with great uproar all day. Shall be most heartily glad when my work is done.- With Cappelli, after dinner, at Caffè Greco.

Thursd. Oct. 28. Again fine. Did 2pp. Letter from the London Syndicate, offering me £12 for a story of 4000 words. I wrote to say that I could not accept less than £20.

Frid. Oct. 29. Fine. In morning did one page. In afternoon, owing to row caused by the removal going on here, I gave it up, and made a sketch of the Duomo from my window—which I have wanted to do all along. Then, to my surprise, I felt able to write again, and by 5.30 had done my second page. How impossible, this, a few years ago! It is strange how much more control I am getting over myself.- Room very bare to-night; only bed and table and wash-stand left.- Letter from Miss Orme. One from Colles, saying he has sold a short story of mine to the *Strand* for 6 gu[ine] as a thousand—a high price. It is a thing called "A Despot on Tour", which I must have sent him at least three years ago, and had wholly forgotten.- Recd from Bullen a copy of "The Emancipated", and gave it to Cappelli.

Sat. Oct. 30. Fine. Suffering much from diarrhoea. Moved at mid-day into the new house, Via Franciosa, 8. A wide view from my windows, but room very cold after the other; aspect north and never any sun. A most blessed thing that I have done so much of my work; must hurry and get away. Wrote 1p.- Recd from Alg *The Review of Reviews*.

Sund. Oct. 31. Fine. Diarrhoea still troublesome. Did 2 pp.- Recd my will from George Whale. Letter from Miss Orme and E[dith]. This house is wretchedly cold and bare. I wondered where the poor old mother of Signorina Georgina put herself of an evening, and to-night, about 7 o'clock, happening to pass the open door of a bedroom, I saw her there lying in bed. What comfortless lives! A few years of youth, and then misery in the corner.- Interesting to me is the man-servant here, called Poldo (Leopoldo). He is just of an age with Signora Carlotta's late husband, and has been in the service of the Gabbrielli family (once rich) practically all his life. Very faithful and affectionate, and will never leave them. I like the man's face, which is curiously full of character. They tell me he is capable of going out late at night if the cat's food has been forgotten.

Mond. Nov. 1. Weather still brilliant. Never a visible cloud. To-day is *Tutti Santi*. Kept like a bank-holiday in England. Everywhere people going about with great wreaths, to be taken to the graves to-morrow; also little lanterns, glass and metal with long stem, for lighting on graves.- Did 2pp.- Letter from O'Dunne, 51 Via Panisperna, Rome. Writes like a very decent fellow.- To-day I exchanged a word with the poor old mother here, who, with a scaldino [hand-warmer] on her lap, was sitting at the front window. It seems a cruel thing to have brought her to a house where there is no sun— she so old and cold. "Ho avuto tanti dispiaceri" [I've had so many sorrows], she keeps saying.- Letter from Mrs Wood, acknowledging receipt of my reminiscences for their school-magazine.

News in paper to-day of three well-known brigands, shot dead by carabinieri, near Grosseto. They were the dread of the Maremma.

At Siena (and here only) they eat to-day a kind of very plain plum-cake, called *Pane coi santi*.

Tuesd. Nov. 2. Fine, but I am suffering much from the cold in this sunless room. To-day is the *Giorno dei morti*.

I was awakened last night by the bells—a terrible sobbing note.- Did 2pp. Wrote to Mrs Norman and her husband.

Two proverbs: Al contadino non far sapere Quanto è buono il cacio colle pere [Don't tell the peasant how delicious cheese is with pears] and: Fatta la legge, trovato l'inganno. [Every law has a loop-hole]

Wed. Nov. 3. Rain all day, and very cold. With aching fingers did my 2pp. Only 2 days more, thank heaven! Note from O'Dunne.

Thursd. Nov. 4. Rain all night and this morning. Then ceased, but no sun. Happily, warmer. Did 2pp. Writing a lot of letters. There came last month's *National Review,* from Wells—the 3rd copy. Letter from Clodd, and one from Miss Collet.- Bought a photograph of Siena.- Wrote to O'Dunne, telling him I shall be in Rome on Monday.

Frid. Nov. 5. Fine again. Did 1 1/2 p. and *finished the book.* A letter from Wakefield. Wrote several letters and cards.

Sat. Nov. 6. Every morning at 6, I hear the *svéglia* [reveille] of the cavalry— who have their barracks at the foot of San Domenico. A bad bugle, or bad bugler; every other note false.- A magnificent day, and, because I was free to enjoy it, of course I have a bad attack of liver, making walking difficult. However, in morning sent off my MS, registered, to Colles; it cost *ll.* 4.75—a heavy expense. Postcards to various people.- Then spent an hour at the Belle Arti, and bought a photograph of a picture by Beccafumi—a Discésa nel Limbo.- In afternoon, to the house of S. Caterina. Every room is made into a chapel, and pictured round—except the little bedroom, a tiny dark cell, where they show a curved slope of bricks on which the saint is said to have laid her head (*la sagra testa,* said the woman who showed me over) when she slept. There, too, in a glass case, are some relics: the lantern she visited the sick with, the top of her wooden staff, a bit of her *cilizio* [hair-shirt], and the *borsa* [bag] in which her head was brought from Rome.- As I left the house, a mother called out to her child: "Caterina!"—Wrote to Clodd.- Recd an invitation from Bassano's, of Bond Street, to sit for photograph. Replied that I would next summer.

Sund. Nov. 7. Signora Carlotta grieved at my coming departure. I, too, sorry to leave the family, though not the place. Suffering much from liver; unable to walk.

Mond. Nov. 8. Left by the 7.15 a.m. Cappelli came with me to the station— a good fellow. A short wait at Chiusi, and reached Rome at about half-past 1, where O'Dunne was looking for me. A beautiful sunrise at Siena, though cold. Descending, we were soon in a thick mist, just such as hung about Trasimenus at time of Roman defeat. Strong contrast bet. the clear, sunny height of Siena, and the cold, wet valleys.

Went to Hôtel Minerva (behind the Pantheon).

Tuesd. Nov. 9. Very warm. Wandering about Rome. Morning with O'Dunne at Colosseum etc.

453

Wed. Nov. 10. Left for Naples by the 1.30 p. m. (Bill at Hotel more than 30 lire—quite enough, considering that I had a very small room, and yesterday did not lunch there. But place very comfortable.)

Fine journey; did not think it would be so mountainous. A good view of Monte Cassino. By when we reached Capua (strange sound at the railway station—"Capua!") a full moon had risen gloriously. Here heard the first of the Neapolitan dialect, women on the platform crying "Acqua da ber'— buon aranci!—uva fresch'"- and paper boys "'u corriera!" ['Drinking water! Good oranges! Fresh grapes! *The Corriere!*] Naples at 6.30, and went, for nearness' sake, to Hôtel Cavour, in the Piazza of the Station. An odd thing; here I found the restaurant closed because of a death in the family! A superstitious man would flee from Italy.

Thursd. Nov. 11. Asked the booksellers, Detken & Co., for an address of an Italian family letting rooms, and they gave me one in the Chiatamone. Came, and took a room at once; 2.50 a day, and, at present, I eat at restaurants. Address: Chiatamone, 40 (II)—Sigra Labriola. A well furnished room, and sunshine for an hour or two in morning; just a glimpse of Somma.

At post found note from Miss Orme, and letter from Miss McCarthy.

Frid. Nov. 12. Cloudy. Heard from Colles that he has recd my MS. Letter from Bertz. In the morning, went to British Consulate, and got my will executed: witnesses, Consul and Vice-Consul. Rolfe (the consul) gave me cards of introduction to people at several towns in Calabria.- Long walk on the glorious Corso Vitt. Emanuele. Dined at my old place in the Toledo— Giardini di Torino. Had some sturgeon. Wrote a lot of letters.- In afternoon an hour at the Museum.

Vesuvius is very active. No fire shows now on the summit, but a long strip of hot lava from somewhere near the bottom of the cone.

Sat. Nov. 13. Scirocco and clouds. Went to the Florio Office in Piliero, and got information about boats to Paola. Also sent off a parcel of books I no longer need to Wakefield. Wrote letters.

Sund. Nov. 14. Scirocco; no sun. Morning at Museum. Sent illustd card to Enid.- The changes in Naples are considerable since I was here last. The old Porto Santa Lucia is now all filled up, and S. Lucia, I suppose, will soon be a street between big houses. The women still do each other's hair as yet, however, and the stalls of shell-fish remain as ever. The great Corso Umberto I has run right through the squalor of the Pendino, making a vast change. Scaffolding is up before the Duomo, for a complete restoration of the façade. Naples seems less lively, even less noisy. The ceaseless street-organs used to be (to me) enjoyable, with their soft notes; now an organ is rarely heard. Before long, I suppose, music will cease in the trattorie.

Mond. Nov. 15. Still scirocco. No appetite, and a little feverish. I have been told to-night by the landlady that her mother is ill—a consequence of an attack of typhoid last year. When am I to get out of this atmosphere of illness and death?- I long for the sea and the mountains. Certainly I shall never lodge again in the Chiatamone.

Wrote to Mrs Norman. H[enry] N[orman] has not let me hear, as he promised, with introduction to [F. Marion] Crawford at Sorrento.

Tuesd. Nov. 16. Left by the Florio boat at 12 o'clock. Before starting had letters from Miss Orme and from Wakefield. At Torre Annunziata lay for 3 hrs taking cargo. The peak of Vesuvius, I saw from here, is now covered with sulphur, which in sunshine has a bright lemon colour. Much filthy smoke from factory chimneys at Torre Ann[unziata].- Dined on board with the officers, I being only 1st class passenger. Dark when I came up on deck again. Just passing bet. Capri and the P[unta] della Campanella. Lights of Capri Marina, and a high revolving lighthouse. Naples glimmering through the dark, far off.

Wed. Nov. 17. Reached Paola before 8 a.m. Lifted through the surf by two men. A fine stretch of pebbly shore. My baggage seized by half a dozen people, and taken to the dogana, where it had to be opened. A woman then put my big portmanteau *on her head,* and climbed with it, resting once, from the Marina to the town. At the dazio the port [manteau] and valise had again to be opened! Then on to a decent little inn, called the Leone, with a view over the bay, flowering oleanders in garden, and laden orange-trees. Had some breakfast. Necessary to hire carriage for Cosenza, as the *corriere* leaves each morning at 5. The driver began by demanding 30 *l.* I got him down to 18 and a mancia—too much, I believe. After breakfast walked about street—wonderfully picturesque. The streaming water-spouts. When the carriage was ready, two well-dressed men came to ask if they might share it with me to Cosenza. I said yes, if they shared the expense, but this discouraged them, and it proved, moreover, that my luggage left no room for other people besides myself. A tussle at last with the porters, who demanded 3 *ll.* for bringing my lugg[age] from Marina. A great crowd listening to the discussion, of course. I got off with 1.30 *l.*— twice too much. We then hitched on behind the carriage a small vehicle to be taken to Cosenza for repair, and at 10 we were off.

Magnificent ascent up the steep mountains; perpetual windings on sides of steep valleys; sun very hot; mists creeping below us when we reached the top. It took about 2 hrs. After half way up began oaks and beeches and bracken (fine autumn tints). I noticed, too, old man's beard, and frequent mulleins. Two crosses near top, indicating murders. Every mile or so a fountain of sweet water, with its blue draped Madonna painted above, and the inscript. Ave Maria. Admirable road. Crossing the top, we looked over a vast landscape, the valley of the Crati. The descent was winding thro' great forests of chestnuts, brown and gold. (Driver told me that in summer the Cosenza people come to Paola for sea-bathing, and always travel in the night.) One cantoniera passed on the mountains, but no village. At foot, we came to the village of San Fili. Rende seen on a hill to the right. Afterwards, struck into the high-road from Naples—so long and straight that I suppose it is the old Rom[an] road by which Alaric marched. Got to Cosenza at 4 o'clock—very dusty, and with a headache. First sight of the hotel (Due Lionetti, recommended by Murray) really alarming—but there seemed to be no choice. Had dinner, and went to bed with my headache.

Thursd. Nov. 18. Fairly good night—in spite of a stench prevailing throughout the house. A terrible hole this—bare and dirty beyond anything I have yet put up with. Too late, I find I ought to have gone to the Albergo Vetere at the top of the town, overlooking the public garden, and with full view of Sila. From the outside, it looks a really decent hotel.

Walked all day. First for geography. The Crati and the Busento meet just at the foot of the hill on which Cosenza stands, bet. town and railway station. On all sides are low hills—except to N., where lies the broad flat valley of the Crati. The hills brown, patched with olives. To E. rises the grand Sila, purpled with sun in afternoon; to W. is the mountain range bet. Crati and Mediterranean—looking so high it seems impossible to cross it in a carriage. The two rivers are now narrow streams, flowing rapidly amid wide, waste beds of sand and shingle—doubtless quite overflowed in winter. At their junction, where Alaric is said to have been buried, the new line of railway (to Pietrafitta) crosses them by iron bridge. Along the river are poplars of rare old gold, and warm plane-trees. Straight N., along the plain, goes the high road by which, no doubt, Alaric marched this way. The rivers have a soft rushing sound. Mingled with it is the clapping noise of the washerwomen, at work all day, their white linen spread on the waste river-beds.

Now, if Cosenza occupies site of Consentia, the story of the slaughter of the captives who dug Alaric's grave is absurd, for the place was in full view of the whole town, at its very entrance.

I have had trouble about the name of the river. At the bookseller's shop here, they assure me it is *Busento*. There are rivers called Basento elsewhere. But all the peasants I asked said *Basenz* or *Basenzio*—until I came to an intelligent old fellow, who said that *Basenzio* was merely the dialectical form, and *Busento* the true one. Now I doubt this. It is very likely a case of a name imposed by literature. Must write for the note from Gibbon.

On the whole, a very pleasant little town. The public garden nicely laid out with acacia walks and fountains. The people nothing like so noisy as the Neapolitans; no importuning by anyone; very little loud gabble going on. Ladies are not seen out of doors. The women of the people have grave, firm faces. In the garden this morning I saw some peasant women, evidently strangers, in a gorgeous costume; a scarlet petticoat, not much below knees, and a blue frock oddly tucked up into knot at the back, imposing white petticoat. About head and shoulders much glittering frippery. The men with them had no peculiarity of dress.

One very interesting thing. All the barbers' shops hang out, as sign, one or two brass basins precisely such as Don Quixote wore for a helmet—of that shape, and with semicircular piece cut out of rim. It quite startled me. I suppose they are to be seen in Spain. I never met them before in Italy.

456

Little wheel traffic in streets. Down by the station one sees the postal diligènza from different places round. A few grand carriages pass—one today with a coronet on panel—quite English style of equipage. The peasantry use mules—and very fat and well treated they look. I suppose these people still have the Bruttii blood in them.

A bit of real humour—I suppose unconscious. A shop in the main street hangs out a glass case full of pistols. Attached to this case, hanging from it, is a placard: "Variato assortimento in corone mortuarie". ["Varied assortment of funeral wreaths".]

Opp. the Prefettura they are building a big new Teatro Garibaldi. On the front are two marble inscriptions; one thus:

20 Sett., 1870
Questa data politica
Dice finita la teocrazia
Negli ordinamenti civili.
Il di che la dirà finita
Moralmente
Sarà la data umana.
[20 September 1870
This political date
marks the end of theocracy
in civil life.
The day which ends its
moral rule will
begin the epoch of humanity.]

The other inscription is a longer triumph over the fall of Papal power.

Among things used to pay off Alaric at Rome, the golden statue of Virtus was melted down. After that, says Zosimus, all valour and honour perished.

Hannibal marched thro' Consentia, on his way to Croton, when leaving Italy.

Frid. Nov. 19. Have slept well, here at Cosenza, in spite of the dreadful house. This morning rose in the dark, had some wretched coffee, and started to catch the 7.10 train. At departure, made acquaintance of a commercial traveller, by name Questa. He has been lying ill for five days, at the Lionetti, with fever, and has suffered much from the neglect of the people. By the bye, his *line* is drugs, and he represents a house at Genoa. We travelled together to Taranto.

A dull, heavy-clouded day. Under such a sky, the country about Metapontum, looking seaward, is wonderfully like certain flat parts of England. Elsewhere, the cactus and agave and the pines destroy this suggestion. I like this great southern plain, so still and dreamy. Everywhere, great bushes of rosemary in flower. At one station, Questa got for me the flowers of a tree called *gaggia* [acacia farnesiana]- very delicate scent.

457

Had lunch at Sibari, where there is a station-hotel. White wine called Moscato dei Saraceni—dry.

On arriving at Taranto, went with Questa in omnibus to the Albergo d'Europa. Finely situated. My windows look, one onto the old town, the other n. across the Mare Piccolo (12m[iles] circumference). But the charge is 3fr. a day; and the eating (à la carte) seems to me indifferent. Questa dined at the Aquila d'Oro, and did much better for less money. I took some oysters with him—tiny and poor.

Questa tells me a good saying: "There are the Italians of the North, and the Itals. of the South—the Nordici and the *Sudici*". [pun on Southerners' and 'dirty people']. The *ritirata* [tattoo] of the marines at 8p.m. A pretty march played about the streets.

Sat. Nov. 20. A little sun, but sky still heavily clouded. At eight o'clock furious firing of cannons from two ships in harbour—to-day, I am told, is the festa of the Queen. Museum, of course, closed; so cannot deliver my letter of introduction to the Director. Walked about among the new buildings landward. A soft, white stone used; great, and often handsome buildings, rapidly encroaching on cultivated land; a ragged edge of olive-orchard and seed-land beyond. The huge Arsenal. Spoke to peasant, who was ploughing. His plough a primordial machine drawn by a little donkey, with whom he was on affect[ionate] terms. He had a long stick, but did not beat the donkey—though it paused every few seconds; simply cried out a remonstrant "Ah!" The furrow a mere scratch in the soil.

Owing to ragged state of outskirts, there are innumerable little boxes of the dazio scattered about—to rob the peasants.

I noticed a sign on a big new house: "Alla Magna Grecia. Stabilimento idroelettropatico"! Well, it is Greek—of a kind.

The man at corner of streets, with picture of a miracle (10th Aug. 97) at the railway station near Loreto. Bought a copy of the story. Each time he mentioned a sacred name, he and crowd raised their hats.

Lunched with Questa at the Aquila d'Oro. Admirable food, and very cheap. At 5 o'clock the two ships in harbour again blazed away with great guns, till both were involved in smoke.

Sund. Nov. 21. Dull morning, and fine afternoon. First of all to the Museum, where I found that the Director (Eduardo Caruso, Soprastante dei Musei e Scavi) was a jovial fellow, speaking English fairly well. He had known [E.A.] Freeman in Sicily, and gave a comical account of him. F., it seems, spoke no foreign tongue, and his daughter used French or German for him; his bullying air and tone awed everybody. The Museum full of interesting things, especially the innumerable miniature busts in stone, thought to be simply portraits.

Asked about the Galaesus. Sig. Caruso had evidently never heard the word in his life (he knows neither Latin nor Greek,) but a man-servant of his said there was a little river flowing into the Mare Piccolo, generally called Gialtrezze, but also, rarely, Galeso. Well, after lunch I set out to find

458

this. Inquiring at the railway station, I was told that the Gialtrezze lay some 3 kil[ometre]s along the shore; the name Galeso they did not know. I inquired of every peasant I met, walking; simply asking: "Come si chiama il fiume qui?" [what is the name of this river?] and pointing forward. Several said "Gialtrezze", and knew no other name; but at length came a railway man, who, to this question, answered straightway "Galeso", and insisted that this was the true name. Subsequently, when I had reached the river itself, a man shooting also replied "Galeso", without hesitation; so I think the matter is certain. Well, this river is hardly half a mile long; it rises amid a jungle of huge reeds, which conceal the source, and flows with a breadth of 15ft or so straight into the sea, between bare land, with a few hoary olives, and a little tillage. Scents of mint and rosemary. The reeds rustled; and on the sea-shore, the tiny wavelets lapped. Grey and green lizards. A boy came along, driving goats, with bells that tinkled. Only one or two little half-ruined white cottages in sight; all else, the wilderness—though railway runs just behind. A fig-tree, shedding last leaves. I sat for half an hour. Gathered some rosemary. On the sea-slope, only bare yellowish crumbling earth, and dead thistles. The afternoon full still and golden.

All the W. shore of Mare Piccolo is covered with huts used by fishermen for the nets, etc—roof-shaped huts; a frame of logs, then thatching, then a thick covering of old ropes—odd effect.

At the station, my inquiries caused amusement, and when I said I should walk, the official repeatedly warned me—"Non c'è novità".

Lenormant says that heaps of murex shells are to be seen at Fontanella on M. Piccolo. At Museum they tell me all that was destroyed, in making the arsenal.

The soft white stone used in new buildings is stone of Lecce.

To-day, Sunday, one sees more women about. They carry mass-books, and keep their eyes down. Those of better class dressed in black.

At the trattorie here, always numbers of officers of the marine.- Common red wine excellent; very light; I drink a whole bottle.

From across M. Piccolo, one sees great diff[erence] bet. old town and new; former, compact of white-washed houses; latter broad roads and yellowish stone.

Mond. Nov. 22. My birthday. A roaring n. wind, blowing the blue sea into white breakers. First went to the pottery shop, where I had yesterday bought 3 little pots for 4½; found them well packed in a hamper, for which I paid 3d. Sent it off by pacco postale.- Then called on English Consul, of whose existence I was ignorant, till the waiter here happened to mention him this morning. He lives in the Palazzo Mandarini, on the Canal. A young fellow, Wilfrid Thesiger (St James's Club, on his card.) Asked me: "Are you the novelist?" and seemed very pleased to meet an Englishman; none come here. I imagine he is utterly ignorant of this country. When I spoke of Metaponto and Sibari, he had to look on the map, to see where these were! Moreover, he talks of *Taránto!* Yet I imagine he must speak some Italian; or how get on at all? Invited me to dine with him at 7.30, and of course I accepted.

459

Went to Museum, and made some drawings of caricature masks and reliefs. Sent cards to Willersey and Wakefield.- Wonderful glass bottles and vases in Museum, perfectly preserved; found in tombs. Age after age represented: Phoenician, Greek, Roman.- Taras, Tarentum, Taranto.

Compare the old pottery, sold for a few soldi, with the fashionable glass and china in the best shops here!

This afternoon walked eastward along shore of the bay. At distance of about a mile, turned from high-road into a cart-road which keeps near the shore; and there presently came across well marked remains of ancient road—clean-cut in the living rock, and with ruts a foot deep. It extends for some twenty yards. Just beyond are great rubbish mounds—the refuse of Taranto, I suppose; and from top of them one has a fine view of the city, with Calabrian hills behind. Gathered some plants, and some land shells.

Dined with Thesiger at 7.30. Found him an admirer of Omar Khayyám; he has a good copy of Fitzgerald. He has lent me "The Land of Manfred [: Prince of Tarentum, and King of Sicily]," [1889] by Janet Ross.

In the *Standard* of 3 days ago, I see my book adv[ertize]d "Human Odds and Ends".

Tuesd. Nov. 23. Glorious sun.- The primitives at Taranto are ploughmen and fishermen; little if any change in these. Watched the fishermen, with their bare terracotta legs, on the rocks below terrace of old town hauling in their great nets—a boy splashing water, to drive fish back into folds till all was gathered up.- Sketched a balcony near there. Bought some little shells in the fish-market (terrible stench). Those empty were said to be *senza frutto*.

Tramontana still blowing. Very cold out of the sun. In afternoon tried to write a sketch for [*Daily*] *Chronicle,* "At the Grave of Alaric", but did not make much of it.[8]

In evening discovered the ruins of the theatre, whence the Tarentines saw the Roman ships. Traces only of foundation, at end of Via Amfiteatro. A beautiful sunset. Kept thinking of Shelley's "the pale purple even". Glow lingered for a long time across the whole w. sky—a grand extent.

I notice that the further south I come, the later people dine. Here the hour is 8, or half-past.- In this place one notices how hard put to it most people are to occupy their time. The dreary empty shops, with men sprawling about on chairs.

Wed. Nov. 24. The always interesting market of earthenware.- Returned his book to Thesiger, and took leave of him.

Again a beautiful sunset; not grand, but very lovely. The afterglow lasts so long—a ruddy flush above soft horizon clouds, which melts by exquisite degrees into dark blue of zenith. Lighthouses (the Cape and one island) suddenly shining clear, pale against the W. sky. The mid-sky a mass of lurid cloud, with sulphur edges—sullen tinted folds. Far and faint—scarcely to be disting[uishe]d from clouds—the Calabrian M[oun]t[ain]s. On the sea, strange curving tracts of white, across the dark rippled water.- The plash of oars in stillness, as a boat creeps along by the rocks.

Thursd. Nov. 25. Left Taranto. The orario [time-table] said the train for Metaponto left at 4.56. At about 3.30, just as I was dressed, the waiter came to tell me that the time was changed to 4.15. I did not believe him, but went off in the carriage provided, and at station found that he was right. A trifle this—time of train changed in middle of month! Cold, dark morning as I started. Reached Metaponto a little after six, and perforce took a room at the station albergo, where I lay till 9. Then breakfasted, and after, with the camerière for guide, set off on foot to see the Tavola dei Paladini. No carriage or horse to be had. Given up, they said, because a foreigner comes only once a hundred years. Moreover, the little museum in house behind station has been transported to Naples.

A walk of 2½ miles or so, by cart-track, over hard ground between fields just being ploughed for grain. In winter, all mud and water; still a few stagnant ponds. Hedges of agave dividing diff[erent] properties. Patches of cactus. Juniper bushes and tamarisks, tall dead thistles, very white, with great seed-heads which show how fine the flower has been. Plovers wheeling and crying all about. Lizards. A dreary bit of country.*

The temple surrounded by a disfiguring wall, ten feet high. No use, for my guide, who had no key to the double iron gate, simply lifted one side off its hinges. Temple very grand. Two parallel rows of columns, one 10, the other 5, and bits of substructure. Plucked some flowers growing there. Noticed with wonder my old friend pennywort thick about feet of columns. A rose-bush. The stone in places greatly eaten, but the capitals grand. A long, hot walk; so did not go further to see the Chiesa di Sansone, which, I understand, only consists of basement stones. Pythag[oras] died at Metap[onto] 497 B.C. They still call the multiplication table—tavola pitagorica.

Ate at station, and lingered about among the eucalyptus grove. A perfect day. Gentle n. wind, and cloudless blue. Queer little settlement of people about the station. Country round dotted with *masserìe* [farm-houses]. Southward, the Calab[rian] M[oun]t[ain]s, and north the low coast-line.

The shore several miles each way from Metapontum, a great plain about 3 miles inland, where the land rises in hillocks. Mostly ploughed. How rich in old days! But, at this season, the limitless brown plain is a weariness to the eye. Towards Sybaris, one crosses a few tracts of wild wood and strangely broken land; esp. a magnificent great wood, with many marshes and dull streams, through the middle of which flows the Sinno (the Siris)— where stood Siris. Here, unfortunately, darkness fell. Reached Cotrone at 10 o'clock, and tumbled into a dirty, shaky old diligence which goes to the Albergo Concordia. Primitive proceedings; no one took my ticket.

Frid. Nov. 26. Cloud and wind. In afternoon a little rain. Walked all around shore by the Strada Regina Margherita; beautiful views n. and s. Point of land projecting into sea. Can see the one column standing on the

---

*Guide said "Non c'è paese"—there is no *town*. Cp. Ulpian: "Qui ex vico ortus est, eam patriam intelligitur habere, cui reipublicae vicus ille respondet." The old attachment of surrounding country to a town—*patria* (paese) (Deriv. of paese).

461

Cape—the Lacinian Promontory. The great walls of castle, and the port—stones from temple of Hera, after g[rea]t earthquake of 1783.

In afternoon called on the Sindaco at the Municipio. He not very civil. I asked him for a permission to view some orange orchards. He evidently thought I had something commercial in view; but scribbled a *permesso*—adding the words "senza nulla toccare" [without touching anything]. With him was a more genial man, who talked to me unintelligibly with a cigar in his mouth. Both fat and looked self-indulgent.

I went to the orchards, which lie on the riv. Esaro (AEsarus), near station—a bit of stagnant green water among high reeds. Beautiful orange-trees and stone pines and huge cactus. Still, the picture is not what I had imagined from reading Lenormant. So often, in Italy, one is repelled by the unlooked-for squalor of things. So here; everything so ragged and dusty and cheerless.

All way bet. town and station, warehouses for oil, wine, oranges and liquorice, window-barred and locked with elaborate padlock. Only the ground floor; about 8ft. high, with great roofs sloping at about 30°—make immense space inside.

Looked into Duomo. Whitewashed, like all these southern churches; to me utterly cold and repellent. A painting of Christ with hideous wounds. There is a miniature copy in bronze of the statue of S. Peter from S. Peter's at Rome, and under it written, that, by order of Leo XIII, 1896, an indulgence of 300 days is given for kissing the toe and saying a prayer.

Talked with several people. If I praised Cotrone, they all answer[ed]—"Yes, but there is no water". Indeed, they are badly off. The river is no river at all. Washer-women wash on the sea-shore.

In one of the bits of garden on the Via Margherita, I asked a gardener the name of a tree. He answered with unintelligible grunt. The universal surliness of gardeners—why?

Life begins in the town about 3 a.m. From then, ceaseless talking in street, with bleating of goats and tinkling of ox-bells. This goat-bleating goes on everywhere, all day.

Sat. Nov. 27. High tramontana. The sea rolling in with white breakers, and dashing over mole. People here wrapped in their great cloaks. Sunshine, however, and I braved the wind. About all day. Sent off a letter to little man at Wakefield, and cards to Clodd, Mrs Norman and Bullen. In afternoon rambled among the hills at back of town, and made sketch of Cotrone from there; then on to the Cemetery, on the way making sketch of castle and harbour. Passed ruined church, thrown down, I hear, by earthquake 3 years ago; old church with Saracen dome,- shown in my first sketch. At Cemetery found a delightful guardian, man who had travelled thro' Europe as servant to a gentleman of Cotrone. Been 9 years at the Cemetery, and has turned it from a waste into a garden. Tremendous geraniums—9 species, he said. Rosemary, splendid roses, and huge bushes of snapdragon, which he called Bocca di leone. Several mortuary chapels around; most of graves marked by a mere wooden cross. As in Greece, skull and cross-bones universal. A fine marble slab to a Lucifero; in Greek style—the scene of parting; a little owl at bottom (civetta) which the guardian said is very common here. Gave me a great bunch of flowers. As I returned, a little lad driving goats asked me for a rose—specially *una rosa*⁹. I gave him one. Then a bigger boy, on a donkey, appropriated the rose. The little lad presently asked me for another flower—modestly saying "Questo piccolo", and was satisfied with a little geranium.

The walk on the hills very interesting. Build a mound of firm sand on sea-shore, and then throw water upon it for some minutes,- and you have these hills in winter. They are simply dried mud; for the most part as bare as the highroad. Of yellowish colour; ridged and furrowed perpendicularly. The surface crackled in minutest way—like mud dried by sun. Here and there great holes, often funnel-shaped, sometimes deep enough to be dangerous. The hills parted by great gulleys and ravines—evidently torrents. In spring, all is covered with deep grass—must be beautiful. From top, made sketch of Lacinian Promontory.- Everywhere growing a flower like a very large daisy, and a sort of hawkweed.

One does not eat well at Cotrone. But I enjoy the immense radishes we have; six in[ches] long, and an inch thick. The wine is very strong. They only put [before] each guest a small decanter, less than a good half-bottle in the north. Temperance of people—a memory of Pythagoras!

A feature of the town are the porticoes lining the chief street and Piazza. Like Bologna.

I passed the Elementary School. Terrific uproar.

It surprises me to see placards hung in front of shops: "Wood hay-rakers".- "Wood binders"—"Wood mowers sold here", with the name of an Eng[lish] firm at Naples below. Why in English?

I find it impossible to understand what has become of the ruins of this city, which once had a circumf[erence] of 12miles. Under ground? It lay, I suppose, on the level ground between shore and hills.

The common type of face here is coarse and bumpkinish—well illustrated by frightful examples in the photographer's window. I see a few fine faces, but not many.

Men greet each other, very often, with a kiss. Strangers, if I ask a question, shake hands with me on leave-taking.

*   *   *

Towards night felt feverish, and had a very bad night, sleepless.

Sund. Nov. 28. Feeling so ill in the morning, that, after a short walk, I decided to send for a doctor. He came at 4 o'clock, said I had caught cold, and must go to bed. I moved into a larger room. Very bad night indeed. This is result of the sketching in the tramontana yesterday—a foolish thing.

Mond. Nov. 29. Fever going on. Doctor came early, and again at evening. A pleasant, kind fellow of my own age, his name Enrico Sculco. (The padrona calls him Scurco.) He amazed me by advising me to eat a *bistecca* with Marsala!! I got out of this—being unable to touch anything but broth.

Moreover, he made me take *two* of my quinine powders together (3 gr[amme]s each) saying that they were very small, and that here it was the custom to give quinine in *dosi forti!* Two hrs. after, I had to take another dose. The result of all this quinine was an extraordinary night—reminding me of De Quincey's opium visions. I saw wonderful pictures; beginning with pictured vases, and sepulchral tablets, and passing on to scenes of ancient City life, crowded streets, processions, armies etc. The remarkable feature was the bright and exquisite colouring of everything. Marvellous detail, such as I could not possibly imagine of myself. Scenes succeeded each other without my ever knowing what would come next. A delight—in spite of my feverish suffering. Lovely faces, on friezes and tombs and vases. Landscape flooded with sunshine.

Tuesd. Nov. 30. Doctor comes twice a day. Has not repeated his *bistecca* suggestion. Told him of my strange night, and he was much impressed,- looked at me oddly.

Uproar out in street. They tell me it is a *"dimostrazione"* agst the "fuocatico"—hearth money. People shouting "Abbasso o' sindaco!" in front of Municipio.

Wed. Dec. 1. Beginning to feel better. There has been a good deal of congestion of that old enemy, the right lung; as usual, it is clearing very soon. Hot poultices, administered by the padrona. The people here, though horribly uncouth, are showing themselves very kind. Two or three of them come together into the room, to look at me and sympathize. The padrona and her servant are alike in a habit of perpetual moaning and groaning. They go about muttering "Ah, Signore! Ah, Cristo!" for no reason in particular. This evening they quarrelled in the kitchen, and the servant—a middle-aged woman, stout and very black-eyed, a pure savage—came to tell me in her terrible dialect all about the *guài* [unpleasant occurrences]— lamenting that she should be so used after having *tanto lavorato* [worked so much], and saying that her relatives were all *freddi morti* [stone dead]. I thought at first she was railing at *me,* for giving trouble, but saw her drift at last.

Twice a day comes the newspaper lad, leaving me *La Tribuna* (which reaches here at 10 p.m., too late for reading that night) and in afternoon the *Don Chisciotte.* Tells me to-day he has a bit of fever, and has taken quinine. Then there is the bright little imp of a lad (about 10 yrs old) who acts as chambermaid. He enters, doffs his cap, asks how I am, and then says "Mi perméttate di fare un po' di pulizia, signore?" which means that he will empty the slops, etc.

The food is very bad; I can hardly swallow anything. Only goats' milk to be had; I take an egg in it. Boiled chicken nothing but rags, so much broth taken out of it.

Thursd. Dec. 2. Much better. Able to eat a little. Had a roasted pigeon— not bad. The chicken broth is tolerable. But the exécrable wine, with its taste of the chemist's shop! Got up for a couple of hours.

My window overlooking the piazza, there is a great noise of voices, day and night—such a noise as in England could only arise from a great excited crowd on some rare occasion. Increased by the porticoes which are in front of ground floor of houses.

My first impressions of people of hotel were unjust. They are filthy and barbarous, but mean well. Their mere appearance, in England, would revolt decent people. Men and women alike expectorate furiously out in the corridor. (This hotel consists of one floor only—a long corridor with rooms on either side, and dining-room at end.) Comical outbreak of padrona's fury, because my milk was brought without egg; and the camerière exclaiming "Un po' di calma!" But the Calabrians do not use much gesticulation, I notice.

An organ, with singing, out in the Piazza. I forgive these people everything as soon as they make music.

The doctor, an excellent fellow. Now (the joke!) is very particular about what I am to eat. He says that it rarely rains here, and that the evil state of the country is due to loss of woods. I suppose, in ancient times, all the coast was wooded—at all events every hill. He has given me a full description of the Capo. The white houses at the end are villinos, belonging to families here; one of them his own. The cape is absolutely bare; not a bush. The earliest mem[orie]s of his childhood are connected with the Colonna, and there, as a boy at liceo, he often practised his lessons in declamation. He now and then takes a spade to dig a little, and always finds something. Some Americans got leave of the proprietor of the soil to excavate not long ago, but when they began to make good discoveries, the govt interfered, claiming Monument as national, and excavations had all to be buried up again. The people of Cotrone makes pilgrimages, often barefoot, to the Madonna del Capo; there they eat and drink, and it ends in orgie—just as in old times!- Doctor often refers to my "visioni", as he calls them.

Frid. Dec. 3. All fever gone. Able to get up. A day of wind and driving rain (from time to time). I read the newspaper—about Dreyfus, and the brutalities in the Parl[iamen]t at Vienna, and the amazing love-correspondence in the *Tribuna*. Wrote up the diary from beg[inning] of my illness.

Towards evening, storm grew violent. High scirocco.

Sat. Dec. 4. Storm all night, and all to-day. Able to get up, and eat in dining-room; but atmospheric conditions make things miserable enough. Doctor called for last time, and gave me prescription for a "cure" of the right lung.[10]

Wrote a letter for Walter's birthday.

The wretchedness of the people in this wild weather, with pelting rain and furious howling scirocco. Objects wretchedly huddled in great capes lurking under the portico opp[osite] my window, and struggling to cross the road. Drearier scene I never knew. Sky a mass of grey cloud; till about 4.30, then suddenly appeared a shimmering of pink cloudlet in a blue space—the beginning of calm, I hope.

465

The habitué at table, whose dishes are ordered for "Don Ferdinando". Hunchbacked over his food; speaking to no one.

Sund. Dec. 5. Wind furious all night. This morning sun, but wind still blowing. In night, I am told, two ships were wrecked in port; one full of pigs—which are scattered all about shore. No men lost.

My newspaper man does not come this morning. For two days, he has had a little fever,- to-day cannot get up, they say. I myself feel inwardly better, but terribly shaky. Shall not regain strength till I get into a better atmosphere.

A wonderful study, the Italian feeding. He knows exactly what his appetite demands. He orders common dishes with laborious detail. He selects and combines from the bill of fare. Generally he eats enormously. He grumbles at the cooking and at the prices. Never shows himself quite content. Is often abusive without limit.

In afternoon wind fell, and sky clouded over. Very doubtful for to-morrow, but think I shall go in any case; this place becomes intolerable. Went out for five minutes, and posted letter to Bertz.

Mond. Dec. 6. Fine and calm. Got away from terrible Cotrone, by the 1.56 train—which of course started 20 m. late. The slow, methodical railway official, coming into carriage, looking round, and murmuring to self "Non manca niente" [Nothing missing]. Astonished to find, at station, an advt of the route from Italy to Harwich, which gives list of N. of England stations, among them Wakefield! At Cotrone they warned me to the end ag[ain]st Catanzaro—so cold and windy.

Pleasant journey along valley of Esaro—mostly a dry channel. Hills on either side, sometimes grassy; much agriculture. Olives generally amid the ploughed fields. Then a tunnel, before descent began towards Catanzaro. Two or three broadish rivers—the banks, as usual, a sort of jungle, very picturesque.

Shepherds, with sheep and goats, idling on the plain by the shore. Very blue sea; white breakers tossing up on shore—result of gale. The lonely shepherds recalling old time.

Towards Catanzaro, inland mountains very beautiful. The plump, rosy man who got in at station, and puzzled me by his healthy appearance; found he was a type of Catanzaro. At entrance to the C[atanzaro] valley, splendid orange orchards—a wonderful sight with the setting sun blazing on them. Full moon rising. Tinted clouds on Sila. The upward valley- line to Catanzaro. Arrived at 6 o'clock, and, after much delay, went up to town in the post cart. Winding ascent of 1/2 hour.

Pop[ulatio]n [?] again descending to shore, to the railway. I read in the newspaper, that a *banco lotto* [lottery office] is given as reward by Govt to *benemeriti della patria* [those who have well deserved of their country], or their represent[ative]s. The law is that 1/12 that fall vacant every year so disposed of, and this proves miserably insufficient.

466

Tuesd. Dec. 7. This Albergo Centrale not very comfortable; cold and sunless; eating very poor.

Found great heap of letters waiting; also typescript of my Dickens to correct, and a copy of [John Holland] Rose's book: "The Rise of Democracy" [in the Victorian Era Series]. Letters from Siga Gabbrielli and Cappelli—with photos of oxen from latter. Day given up to correspondence and typescript. Dull and rainy. Have a slight cold in the head.

Amusing notice on door of my room. Proprietor has found, with *sommo rammàrico* [with extreme regret], that some of his clients go elsewhere to eat, and not to restaurant below. This *tocca il morale* [hurts his personal feelings] of said proprietor, as well as damages the *prestigio della ditta* [prestige of the establishment]. He will do his best to keep up quality of food, etc, and *si onora pregare i suoi rispettabili clienti perchè vogliano benignarsi il ristorante etc.* [begs his honourable clients that they would bestow their kind favours on the restaurant of the house.] Name of Proprietor, Coriolano Paparazzo.

Wed. Dec. 8. Beautiful day. At 10 o'clock, went with my card of introduction to call on Sig. Pasquale Cricelli, the Eng[lish] vice-consul. Found him unable to speak a word of English. He took me to the public gardens, (beautiful, overlooking ravine on east side), then to the Duomo, and the Church of the Immacolata, where there was a great crowd as to-day is the festa of the Immacolata—as much thought of here, said Cricelli, as Christmas. A lively orchestra, of string music, playing loudly in a gallery of the church. Early this morning I heard bagpipes, and they have been sounding all day. Picturesque costumes of Contadine—the same I saw at Cosenza. A very few instances of the Calabrian hat, which is falling out of use. Plenty of fine, even heroic faces, among peasantry. And all so healthy. It delights me to see the healthy, happy children here. Even a beggar, crawling on all fours on pavement, has ruddy face. No uproar, in spite of crowds; people grave and dignified.

Cricelli took me lastly to a chemist's shop, furnished with desks etc of finely carved wood, imitated from 16th cent[ury] work—really a magnificent display. Outside, at street corner, they have a *mostra,* in wrought iron—a sort of griffin, work such as one sees at Siena. Shop full of peasants. The chemist, pointing to a group, called them *Greci.* They come from a village near, and still speak a sort of Greek. They carry babies, and other burdens, on back—not in front.

At another shop, C[ricelli] gave me two silk handk[erchie]fs of Cat[anzaro] manufacture.

Bought 5 oranges for a penny, and ate them, after lunch, looking out over the glorious seaward view. Look right over Squillace, away to Locri.

The town has a ragged appearance. Everywhere building going on. To enter the P.O., you climb over heaps of masonry. One could imagine there had just been a bad earthquake. Painted madonnas over many house-doors.- The tinkling of horse-bells of an evening, as the [carts] climb the long road from station.

467

The two old officers, who dine at same time, but at different tables, and shout from a distance to each other—when they might just as well sit together.

The long, long meals—to kill time.

Teatro delle Varietà: (1) "La Morte di Agolante e la Furia del Conte Orlando". (2) "Una graziosa commedia, Il Castello del diavolo con Pulcinella soldato pauroso". (3) "Nuove duetti e canzoni napoletani" [Variety Theatre: (1) The Death of Agolante and the Madness of Count Orlando. (2) a delightful Comedy, The Devil's Castle with Pulcinella as the Timorous Soldier. (3) New duets and Neapolitan songs.] Theatre will hold 300 people, at hours, 18½ and 21½.

Thursd. Dec. 9. Cloudy; n. wind. At 10 went with Cricelli to the Museum. Fine collection of coins, and a lot of Greek things found at Tiriolo. Arranged to drive from here straight to Squillace to-morrow, if it is fine.- Bought some photographs of costumes—rather dear (15 l. for four—2 coloured). Finished revising the typescript of Dickens and sent it off to Colles.- Letter from O'Dunne.

The buildings here are mostly of rubble, set in cement, with an occasional big stone, and a few courses of Roman bricks. Then, sometimes, faced with stucco. Where no stucco used, the building is covered with big holes, left by the scaffolding.- Rude pictures of Madonna and child over many doors. On poorer houses a great cross scrawled in white plaster.

The scenery around is wonderful. On the n. and w. sides, deep gullies, with torrent bed at bottom; looking dry and hard and barren as a high-road—a little stream trickling in middle. Glorious mountain heights inland. The all but precipitous sides of the hill, on which town stands, planted with figs, olives, vines etc. Everywhere great cactus—never saw it so fine. Palms frequent in private gardens.

Fruits abound. Esp[ecially] apples and oranges. Fichi d'India everywhere. I asked a man for 2 soldi of them to-day, and when he had given me six, and I said I could carry no more, he explained: "Questo per complimento!"- On some of the poor-house balconies one sees immense gourds—nearly 3 ft long—lying on boards to ripen.

The great old Castle, at w[est] of town, which Lenormant says was threatened, has now long disappeared. New buildings in its place. Grand view of Tiriolo from that spot.

The common wine here is excellent. Not to compare with poor stuff at Cotrone.

In evening, director of Museum called, to bring me, from Cricelli, a copy of the Transactions of the Accademia di Catanzaro. I find a useful paper on Cassiodorus. The Director tells me that a great number of coins were stolen from old Museum, and prob[ably] melted down to sell for intrinsic value.

Pouring rain. Passed an hour or two at Caffè, where there was indifferent music. Tone of conversation much better than in corresponding Eng[lish] company. (Of course extreme temperance in drink.) Real *talk,* though never deep; clear reasoning on surface of simple and innocent subjects.

468

Frequent recurrence of such phrases as *ingenio simpatico* and *bella intelligenza*. These people always pay homage to intellect; is it not better (if a pretence) than the Eng[lish] pretence of homage to morality?

The Calabrian peasants seem very interesting. Women who wear these beautiful costumes are certainly not less civilized than Eng[lish] peasants. A good deal more, I think. Cp. their religion with Eng[ish] brutality of Salvation Army etc. The ex-votos in the Church of Immacolata.-

Common and trivial exclamation—"Perdio!" It means no more than "Per Bacco!" A simple relic of heathendom.

I have not yet spoken with a Contadino who did not show understanding of the intellectual attitude. How about the English clown—Wensleydale etc.?

At meal-times, men come into the trattoria selling novels (a great pack tied together), or combs and the like (in box).

I don't think that anything like the fierce egotism of so-called civilized countries will be found here. Hardships of life softened in manifold ways.

Frid. Dec. 10. Cricelli sent a servant early in morning to know if I was going to-day, and at 9 o'clock came himself to see me off. A cloudy, doubtful morning, and luckily I had a closed carriage, instead of an open one. The drive proved terrific: furious rain and wind all the time, after first half hour. We drove down to Catanz[aro] Sala, then along coast a short way, then inland to Squillace, where we arrived about 12. Squillace seems much higher than Catanzaro; to reach it, the road goes inland, behind the hill on which town stands, and then climbs it from the back. Opposite, all the way, is Mons Moscius (now called Coscia di Stalletti), a steep, dark mountain, furrowed with torrent-beds. The river (old Pellena, and now called Fiume di Squillace) swollen by rains, was rushing along the bottom of its deep ravine, the colour of yellow clay. Its bed, heaped with great granite boulders. The valley, in fact, seems to divide two geological systems—the soft stone of the Catanzaro side, and the granite of Squillace. Orange orchards near the sea; higher up, only olives. A great many of the yellow-berried shrubs (name I don't know) growing along the road. Squillace visible all the way, in seemingly inaccessible position. Two great ragged ruins: that of a convent, and, on the topmost height, that of the Norman Castle, with great windows showing the sky through. Difficult to connect Cassiodorus' description—yet possible. Altogether much wilder scenery than Catanzaro.

On arriving could not believe that the Albergo we stopped at was the best—the only one, indeed. A terrible hole. One entered by a filthy kitchen; then came a row of ground-floor rooms, opening out of passage. I was shown into that at the far end. (No upper story). Floor of worn stone, walls of filthy plaster; window impossible to see through—broken, too, in places, and admitting everywhere the fierce wind. Two beds, ready to be made up. Several caricatures (half indecent) from political papers hanging on walls, and an advt of emigrant vessels for New York. Also a wooden crucifix— quaint and ugly and filthy. I had thought of passing a night at Squillace, but could not face these horrors. Ordered some food. Peperoni cut up in oil came as anti-pasto, then a stew of *majale* [pork] and potatoes. Nothing but *majale* to be had in these places—Homeric food. The bread a sort of flat round cake, with hole in middle—consistency of cold pancake. Wine poisonous.

Having eaten, I wandered about the town, in rain and wind. No paving, except a few granite boulders here and there, and occasionally the native rock laid bare. In the steep streets, rain pouring down in a stream. Houses mostly ground-floor only, and squalid beyond description; hardly a decent building. Whole place as if only just recovering from great earthquake—a filthy ruin. On hill-side, huge granite blocks protruding. Climbed to the castle. Norman door still existing; all else ragged ruin. Wild grand view over mountains, and down valley to the sea. Half an hour exhausted me, and I returned to inn.

I noticed that over doorway was written "Osteria Centrale"—and in another place "Albergo Nazionale". When the bill came, it proved a gross fraud. I was charged 5 *ll.* for myself and the two lads—who protested they had not eaten half [what] they were charged with. Paid perforce, and drove away as quickly as possible from the vile hole.

Remember the pig and cat playing together in filthy street—pig scratching cat's back. Black pigs running about everywhere, and hungry dogs.

Women here huddled in wrappers like Indian dhervices—dull yellow stripes on dull red ground—very picturesque. No particular curiosity excited by my walking about; dull, quiet people.

Got to the railway station at 2.30; paid carriage, and sent it away. Then, having asked information, walked a mile along railway, to the tunnel which pierces M. Moscius and here, guided by half a dozen railway men, walked down to the so-called Grotta di Sant'Agazio—a cave about 12 feet high, and running some twenty yards into the hill.* Situated at least 30ft above level of sea; so there must have been changes of level if this was one of Cassiod[orus]'s grottoes for fish. This shows that the shore must have been filling up and rising for ages. Sea formerly rose to the caves, perhaps. A larger cave is called Grotta di San Gregorio, round the point; heavy rain made it impossible for me to go. Conversation with railway men: the jolly, intelligent fellow, and the good-natured simpleton who was addressed as "Brigadiere". Latter amazed at the idea that there were books more than 1000 years old! Big books? As big as a missal? Intelligent fellow exclaiming that races change, but the world goes on for ever. His mirthful delight at name of Cassiodorus. Pointed to the Cascina, further inland on slopes of mountain, called Cascina di Cassiodorio, where also is a Fountain of same name. (Notice the form Cassiodor*io*—not—oro. At the station, the same form was used.)

Murray and Baedeker both say that Squillace is invisible from station. On contrary, there is a fine view of it, and I made a little sketch. At little osteria close by, ate some salami, and drank good wine.

Left by 4.30 train; glad to get out of rain and wind. Remember the lovely

*The yellow turbid river made a vast clean-edged patch on surface of sea. [Gissing's note.]

little sandy bay, with boats, immediately on other side of tunnel which pierces M. Moscius. A boy in train, who comes every morning from Sansostene to Catanzaro to school—no nearer school except elementary. Gave me his card. Afterwards, the Parroco of S. Nicolà at Badolato, who travelled for a few miles and talked—complimenting my Italian. Then, solitude all the way to Reggio. A wild night. Over the mountains, constant lightning; on the sea a grand full moon, occasionally obscured by rain clouds. Gerace (Locri). White waves roaring on shore. Lastly, the mountains of Sicily, faint in moonlight.

No carriage at Reggio station (11pm.). Seized by porters. At Albergo Vittoria, no room to be had; conducted thence to a little place, Albergo Sicilia. Fairly comfortable.

Sat. Dec. 11. Windy and showery in first part, then falling calm. Called at Eng[lish] consulate, but Consul absent, and his Italian wife didn't know when he would be back. Walked the length of the Corso Garibaldi, to the public gardens, and the side of the river. There, a fine building, with handsome portico, looking like a Museum or pict[ure] gallery; inscription "Macèllo" [slaughter-house], and heads of oxen carved on front. Surrounded by lemon orchards, and several tall date-palms—a curious bit of high civilization.

Had lunch here in hotel, alone; no one seems to eat here. Dined at the Vittoria (called Caffè del Genio). Good dinner and cheap; wine excellent. Two poor little girls opened door, near where I sat, and begged for "un pezzo di pane". I threw them my bread, and felt I was behaving brutally.

In morning, a beautiful view of the snows on Etna, glistening on ridges. Sunset, just behind the great mountain, its top always hidden by heavy clouds, and below them, the snow transfigured in a hue of delicate olive-green. After dinner, I sauntered along the Via Plutino—stretching along the shore, with railway line bet. it and sea. Calm, warm night; moon rising. Lights of Messina across the straits, mountain dim. Mood of anger with modern Italians, who ruin all the old associations. These countries ought to be desolate. Over there in Sicily, barbarism trying hard to hold its own— the Mafia at Palermo. The paper talk of the "soppressióne" of persons by them—i.e. the killing.

The train came by, the only quick train to Naples. At crossings of the line, a man stands and blows a horn. Glimpse of letter-waggon, etc.

The one long street, Corso Garibaldi, very dull at night. No caffès, and no bright restaurant. Curiously dead, for a town that looks so large. Pestered by match-boys and newspaper-boys, who act as pimps.

Soft washing of waves along the embankment. Lingered till I was tired out, then back to dreary hotel. Most of the shops close early. People saunter at barber's and chemist's. No vehicles in broad street. But the place is clean and sweet.

Sund. Dec. 12. The touching memorials of those who fell in battle for freedom. At corner of street near my hotel, a stone (set up in 1891) in memory of a young soldier who fell at that spot fighting ag[ain]st soldiers of the Bourbon—"offerse per l'unità della patria sua vita quadrilustre" [sacrificed his life at the age of twenty for the unification of his country]— Aug. 21 1860.

A warm day, showery, with soft wind. Sicily obscured with mist. In mornirg to the Museo Civico, where a rugged Custode (good fellow) showed me over. In front of museum, on level of Via Plutino, the excavation of some Roman thermae—small, prob[ably] private—most interesting. Director told me he had given "sédici anni di vita" [sixteen years of his life] to work of arranging, and lamented that the Museum was still only comunale, not yet taken over by Govt. The little library—2 vo[lumes] only of "Corpus Inscriptionum [Latinarum]". There is a facsimile of the marble tablet treaty bet. Rhegium and Athens. The original was taken by Lord Elgin to London. Two modern pictures struck me: one of a pasture on the heights of Aspromonte—summer sky and herbage, with shepherds and flocks; the other of a tarn and rushing torrent, also high among the mountains, dark and beautiful. The painter dead.

I was asked to sign my name in the book. It consisted only of some 20pp. (mostly Germans), and there, on the very first page, stood the signature "F. Lenormant, Membre de l'Institut de France", small, delicate writing,- and after it that of Prof. Viola. It touched me profoundly. Date, 1882. The Director remembers Lenormant well: "Un bravo giovane". And pasted at beginning of book a bit of paper with a few Greek characters written by Lenormant whilst at Museum.

The stone inscription half in Latin, half in Greek. Beginning "D.M."— ending in Greek characters.

Went to Duomo. Across the whole of the façade, in great letters, is inscribed: "Circumlegentes devenimus Rhegium. Act 28.13".- Sketched the contadino costume, and contadina carrying *botte* [cask] of water on her head.

Every open space here becomes a market-place. Quantities of fruit and vegetables. Cauliflowers more than 1ft. across the top. Everywhere the donkeys of the Contadini tethered by dozen. Grave, good-looking people. No clamour.

Lemons seen about here, chiefly. Nothing like so beautiful as oranges— paler leaves and fruit.

Afternoon, music in public gardens. Military band played. Beethoven— Andante Cantabile; Haydn, quartetto; Rigoletto Atto 1°; Rubinstein, Toreador, and Marcia d'Artiglierìa.

A great part of lower walls of the castle lying shattered—doubtless ever since the great earthquake.

Reflections suggested by these Museums. Myriads of fragments, and all beautiful. What would *our* world leave behind it?

Of course the band in gardens is military. The military discipline seems to be only way of civilizing these people. Courtesy of officers. Contrast boorishness of country folk who—for instance at ticket office—have no idea of forming *queue,* and press before you without shame.

Everywhere on the walls, in red paint, are the names of Crispi and

Tripepi—candidates in recent election for deputato. Just the old Roman style.

Left by the 7.5 express for Naples. Endless time booking my portmanteau. The shouts on the platform: "Linea Catanzaro-Taranto!"—and the man with pillows. "Nolégio guanciali! Si affittano cuscini! Nolégio qui qualunque per correnza" [pillows, cushions and anything wanted for the journey let out on hire]. A notice in the carriage, printed in 4 lang[uage]s (of course 5c. stamp!) warning passengers that in certain tunnels there were scaffoldings. The English ran thus: "Passengers are warned to abstain altogether from protruding head and arms out of the carriage window, there being danger in so doing".

Fellow passengers, the Venetian and the Florentine, who discussed their amorous experiences. Slept very little. At Paola (full moon) bought some càcio-cavallo and bad wine. At Battipaglia cup of coffee. Naples at 7.45, and went to Albergo Ginevra.

Mond. Dec. 13. Warm and fine. I have a room at top, with grand view of Vesuvius. Curious effect. The lower part of mountain is all hidden with mist—as if nothing were there—and above, right up in clouds,- appears top of cone, smoking. Wonderful effect of might.

Called on the Consul, and gave him account of my journey. Decent, but not cordial.

Bought a photog[raph] of Temple of Metapontum. Could get no other photograph of the south. Bought vol. I of Pagano's "Studii sulla Calabria"—to be completed in 10 vols!

Tuesd. Dec. 14. Left by the 8.30 train. A beautiful morning, but soon clouded; and, on arriving at Cassino, found myself in thick, cold mist, which hid everything. Went to an hotel in the town—"Villa Mario Varrone"—very comfortable, and had a good meal. Towards 2 o'clock the mist began to rise, so I ordered a donkey (somaro) and with a lad for a guide started up to the monastery. Wonderful ascent of about 1 hr ½. Received at entrance by a monastic porter, who took my card in to the Prior. In a few minutes, the Prior received me; very courteous. I told him I was getting materials for a historical novel, and he listened with interest. Told me he had been in England this last summer; but of course speaks no English. After showing me a few of the treasures of the library, he passed me over to the Sacristan, who showed me all the little chapels, forming the original monastery (interesting mod[ern] frescoes), and then the church. A wonderfully simple man, telling his stories of old times with perfect intelligence yet with the naïveté of a child. His delight in the treasures of the monastery—in the mosaics and the marbles, and, above all, in the glorious wood-carving of the Choir. Such work as that (walnut wood, 17th cent[ury]) I never saw. The exquisite foliage, the saints thereamid, and the *putti* [angels or. cherubims] on the seats of the choir! My guide kept repeating "Quanto lavoravano allora! Si divertivano, lavorando!" [How much they worked in those days! They enjoyed themselves, working!]

The porphyry pillar, in middle of court, on which stood statue of Apollo;

and the pillars from his temple round outer court of church. It grew dark whilst we were in the church. Guide lit a taper, to keep showing me the beautiful carving. Silence, and dark, and smell of incense, and glorious work all around.

Then I was conducted to my room. Curious oil lamp. Comfortably furnished but no looking-glass. Told, to my alarm, that supper would not be till 1/4 to 8. The glorious landscape from the little window. Sea of mist over the valley of the Garigliano, mountain top rising above. Lights of Cassino just visible, in profound depth. Lights of the train starting for Rome. Lingering sunset over towards Gaeta, where there is, in clear weather, a glimpse of sea.

Sat down to write these notes—after eating a bit of dry bread to stave off hunger.

The supper has been frugal with a vengeance. A plate of lentil porridge with bits of meat in it; a slice of cold brawn; and an apple—decanter of wine, of course. I grow old; this lenten fare does not suit me. Three other guests in the cold, bare room—Italians, besides servants seated at another table.

Have written a letter to dear little boy at Wakefield, and now to bed. The great corridor at night, with two or three hanging lamps—gloomy and echoing to every step. The light of the Middle Ages.

My window here looks over the Liris Valley. The mist still lying everywhere below, but the stars above are very bright. One short row of lights shows the town of Cassino.

Wed. Dec. 15. All round the monastery lies cultivated land, kitchen gardens, and ploughed fields. The trees are oak, ilex and olive—the oaks cov[ere]d with russet foliage. Not far away is the bare cloud-capped height of Monte Cairo, overlooking the monastery.

The geography is this. A spur of hills running westward ends, over Valley of Liris, in a high hill with two crests. On the higher and broader (east) stands the monastery, wooded all round; on the lower, bare and stony, once stood a Temple of Venus. Below both heights is a steep crag, which once had Temple of Janus, and where now is castle—about half height of monastery. Characteristic of hill is the rocky surface. Great rocks everywhere protruding.

In the monastery is a regular Post and Telegraph Office. Posted my letter to Walter.

Walked about this morning for an hour—after cup of coffee and slice of bread. The grand terrace in front of church, overlooking Liris valley— very broad, with great mountains beyond. Round the atrium are granite columns, belonging to old Temple of Apollo. The bronze doors of Church have 36 panels, engraved (once in silver) with possessions of monastery in 11th cent[ury].

Before leaving, bought an album of views (3 *l.*) and gave 5 *l.* to the Monastery. Met the Prior, and took leave of him.- Donkey ready for me at 9.30. Morning dull, but not much mist. Snow on heights eastward. The old road (carriage road made in 1885). Many brambles, and a little old man's beard.

Went to my inn again, ate, and walked about for three hours. Inspected the amphitheatre, and sketched it. Best view of monastery with castle below it, from the bridge over Rapido, at n[orth]end of town. The Rapido a swift and full little river, tinged faint blue with lime. The Amphitheatre covered outside with op[us] reticulatum; the work looks very fine from distance, but the stones are really of anything but reg[ular] diamond shape—often very irregular indeed. Same work inside, only along top. Inside, a mere mound of grassy earth. There remain 5 entrances visible; only one is used.

Beautiful costumes of women; bright shawl, orange stripe on red brown. They say there is no work to be had, and constant emigration—"C'è miseria!" But the people look wonderfully healthy, children too.

The toil, the toil, of that old world! Think of building on these great heights. The old hill-roads mere human Calvaries.

The commonest word in Italian conversation is "mangiare" [to eat]. Heard incessantly.

The wine here like a thin claret.

Dined, and left Cassino by the 5.20. In Rome at 8.30. The three Americans in train. "How long do you think of staying here?"—"To-day's Wednesday, how does Saturday morning strike you?"—"So long?"— "How does Friday strike you? We've got to see Rome." "Well, that gives us one clear day."

Thursd. Dec. 16. At Albergo Tritone. Called on O'Dunne, and with him searched for a room in the northern parts. No success. To bed, tired out.- Letters from several people.

Frid. Dec. 17. Very fine. Found a good room in Via del Boschetto, 41A, on 4th floor. By straining out of window, I can just see Colosseum. Name of people Umiltà. The husband a govt employee. Pay 35 *ll.* a month, and am to have caffè latte at home (extra). Came in after dinner, and heartily glad to be at rest.

Sat. Dec. 18. Wrote to Miss Orme, sending her cheque for £50, and asking her advice about future.- The Italian paper to-day tells me of the death of Alphonse Daudet, which happened yesterday. It is a most remarkable coincidence that he fell down senseless at the dinner table (7.30 p.m.)—thus completing the resemblance of his life to that of Dickens.[11]

Sund. Dec. 19. In morning wrote to Mrs Travers, Miss Sprague, Miss Collet, and two newspaper people who had asked for details of forthcoming work. In afternoon a long walk. From Piazza Navona (with stalls of Xmas toys) to Campo dei Fiori, where I saw the statue of Giordano Bruno—"dove il rogo arse".[12] On to the riverside. Theatre of Marcellus, Portico of Octavia, Isola Tiberina. The e[ast] branch of river—that which flows under Pons Fabricius—is now completely dried, and I suppose will somehow be filled up. Fortuna Virilis, so-called Vesta, S. Maria in

475

Cosmedin, S. George in Velabro, with Arcus Argentarius, and S. Theodore under the Palatine. These places I did not see when I was in Rome before.

Mond. Dec. 20. Very cold. Called on Miss McCarthy's friend, Alf[re]d Lambart, 3 Piazza di Spagna. Found, as I feared, a sort of society man, with no knowledge of Italy. However, he behaved as well as such people can.

Wrote a lot of letters. Sent cheque for £10 to Nelly.- Surprised and pleased to come across a mention of Wells's new book, "The War of the Worlds", in *Messagero* of to-day. Shall send him the paper.

Tuesd. Dec. 21. Cold. In afternoon walked to Porta Maggiore, and saw tomb of Eurysaces. Thence to Santa Croce and the Lateran, where I saw the Baptistry—with the bronze doors which make music on their hinges.

Wed. Dec. 22. Very cold wind. Got a form, at the Bibl[ioteca] Vitt[orio] Emanuele, to be signed at Consulate. Went there, and had talk with unshaven man, the consul, named Franz (Piazza S. Claudio, 96). To call tomorrow morning.- Ordered a pair of trousers at "Old England" in Via Nazionale. Very dear, 27 *ll.*- Letters from Wakefield and Miss Orme. (By the bye, when I spoke to the Consul of my Calabrian journey, he asked "Where is Squillace?")

Thursd. Dec. 23. Got my signature from the Consul, and went to Library. Got ticket of permission to borrow books, that for leave to work in Sala Riservata will be ready on Monday. I had to state on paper what *class* of works I wanted, and was also asked whether I should work there in morning or afternoon!—Find that the headman in the Sala Riservata is a seedy fellow whom I have often seen eating at the Trattoria Toscana, at mid-day.

On the door of the church of Gesù is a printed notice: "Si prega di non sputare in terra, e di non dare elemosine ai poveri nella chiesa" [spitting and alms-giving in church prohibited].- Characteristic!

Frid. Dec. 24. Walked to Porta Pia, and outside walls round to Porta del Popolo. In several places long icicles hanging from walls—very cold indeed.- Note from Alf[re]d Lambart, inviting me to dine on Sunday; accepted.

Sat. Dec. 25. Fine and cold; frost again. Went in morning to S. Maria Maggiore. (Looked in at the Lateran, but found it empty and still.) Great crowd and good singing. Saw the crystal case enclosing the fragments of the Praesepe hoisted onto the High Altar. Amusing to see women and little children with a bit of handkerchief on their heads—obeying the law that they must be covered in church. The great mixed crowd, talking about every sort of affair, with here and there a person kneeling in the midst, or someone conning a mass-book. The incense and the great candles.

At 12, took dinner (by invitation) with my landlord and landlady.

Obliged to eat a great deal too much of very badly cooked food, followed by several glasses of Marsala. Good vulgar folk.

In afternoon to S. Peter's, just in time for Vespers, in Pope's chapel. Beautiful effect of western sunbeams striking across the tribune. Next to me, in the chapel, stood a poor sister of some order, wearing a hideous white bonnet: her ugly face and red nose, and her lips muttering piously. Hope she feels some inward pride, or solace at all events.

Read again the inscription round foot of dome. "Tu es Petrus et super hanc petram edificabo ecclesiam meam et tibi dabo claves regni caelorum." [Thou art Peter, and upon this rock I shall build my church and I shall give unto thee the keys of the kingdom of heaven.]

Gazed at the Stuart monument, with its three portraits. Jacobus III, and his sons, Charles Edward and Henry—"regiae stirpis Stuardiae postremis". [The last scions of the Stuart kings.]

The hideous iron bridge, side by side with the bridge of Hadrian. Ruins view of the Mausoleum.

Home without dinner.

Sund. Dec. 26. Cold very severe. No doubt as a result of it, I have a swollen gland behind the right ear—very painful.- Recd from Colles £23-10 for the story (2 yrs old) called "A Despot on Tour".

Wrote to a Mr. J. Stainer (Folkestone) who has written to me, saying that he was assistant to Father in the year of my birth.

Dined with the Lambarts. The other guest a young fellow (called Burt, I think [see entry for February 7, 1898]) who is Roman correspondent of the *Morning Post*. Detestable type; effeminate in speech; boyish in manner; age cannot be more than 25, I think. He hardly knows any Italian—is taking lessons. What a correspondent for a London paper!

Mond. Dec. 27. Began a wood fire in room to-day, a great improvement. In morning to the Vitt[orio] Em[anuele] Library, where I got an old Ital. transln of Gregory's "Dialogues". Brought home Tosti's "Vita di S. Benedetto".

A lot of letters. One from Miss Orme, giving bad account of state of things. Infinite worry from that vicious idiot. Wrote—but what use?- Wells sends his photograph.

Tuesd. Dec. 28. Library in morning.- In afternoon called Swinton-Hunter, a friend of Sturmer's. Letter from Alg, from Ilfracombe.

Wed. Dec. 29. Not so cold.- Wrote to Don Pasquale, at Catanzaro.- Also to Alg, and Rose, and Dodd, Mead of New York, sending my address.

I dine every evening at a little Trattoria toscana in this street, where they have excellent wine. There is a fat, good-natured mother, a son of about 17, a daughter of 13 or so, and a waiter. The young girl is the very image of the Muse [a blank here] at the Vatican, and often sits in the same attitude, chin on hand, a beautiful head of black hair. Queer old fellows come to eat; two of them addressed as "Cavaliere". They fuss about their food, giving elaborate directions for the cooking of a plate of liver, and freely censuring it when it comes. The hostess explains at length the cost of everything in the market,- "Stia bene", she said to someone departing the other day; and he replied "Si conservi".

Sigra Umiltà brought my lamp to me to-day, asking me to unscrew the top of the oil-hole, which she and Teresa could not do. "Ah!" she exclaimed. "Dio ha fatto gli uomini; e le donne ci ha fatto forse il diavolo!" [God made men and perhaps women were made by the devil!]

Thursd. Dec. 30. Fine, and warmer.- Two wretched letters from Miss Orme. Things going very badly. Wrote severely to E., telling her that she must behave better, or I will take the little child away. Much upset about it.- Letters from Whale and Wells and Miss McCarthy.

Frid. Dec. 31. Have a bad cold—the old story. Miss Orme sends rather better news. Rose and Blackie write in furious haste for proofs of "Dickens", which is to be pubd on Feb. 15th.- In evening came O'Dunne, to offer me ticket for the Pope's Mass to-morrow morning at 8—the 50th anniversary of Leo's first mass. Promised to go if I could; but we shall have to leave in carriage for S. Peter's at 6am.

1898

Sat. Jan. 1. Awake all night. Dared not go to S. Peter's, so, when O'Dunne came at 6, sent him off, and went to bed again. Did not leave home to-day; cold bad. Had mid-day meal with the Umiltà.- Recd about half proofs of "Dickens", and corrected them. Card from Bertz; letters from Mr. Stainer (of Folkestone), Miss Orme and Blackie.

Sund. Jan. 2. Rainy, mild. Cold better. Another lot of proofs. Sent off 1st batch to Blackies, registered. It seems to me that the book reads pretty well.

Mond. Jan. 3. Glorious day. Recd last batch of proofs, corrected, and sent back to Blackie. Also dispatched proofs of whole book to Dodd, Mead & Co.- Letter from Miss Collet.- Invitation from Mrs. Lambart to tea to-morrow.- Morning at the library.

Tuesd. Jan. 4. Fine, colder. Wrote to Rose. Library. Afternoon with Mrs. Lambart; more interesting than I thought. She lent me [Robert] Bridges' poems and a German novel: "Im Liebesrauch" by Heinz Tovote—a man I never heard of.

Wed. Jan. 5. Cold. Library. No letters.

Thursd. Jan. 6. Very cold. Last night and all to-day (Befana) the streets hideous with blowing of tin trumpets, children carrying round effigies.- Library closed, so in morning had a long walk. Forum of Augustus, Forum of Nerva, Colosseum, Porta San Paolo, Aventine, and home by Forum again.-Long letter from Miss Orme, telling of brutal insult and fury. Don't know what to do. Miserable.

Frid. Jan. 7. No sun. Letter from a "Margaret Bernard", of The Liberty, Wells, sending me a card and praise. A man named Trantum, of L'pool, sends a Meredith calendar, composed by himself.- Ed. of *Cosmopolis* asks for a story, which I shall write.

Sat. Jan. 8. In afternoon called on Swinton-Hunter. No idea what he is, but he seems to live luxuriously, and has an Italian secretary, a pleasant fellow.

Sund. Jan. 9. Fine and warm. Long walk in morning. Up the Palatine to S. Sebastiano, which stands on the site of the Temple of Apollo. Then to S. Gregorio, under the Arch of Dolabella. Piazza della Navicella, and by Via Claudia to Colosseum.

Mond. Jan. 10. Fine and warm. Library.

Tuesd. Jan. 11. Fine. Brought from lib. Dahn's two books: "Prokopios von Cäsarea", and "Die Könige der Germanen". No letters.

Wed. Jan. 12. Fine. Called on Baron Lumbroso, but of course he was out. Letter from Bertz. Wrote to him and to Miss Collet. In evening to the Orpheo, with O'Dunne. Very poor. An encore of a singer being refused, the audience made a row, refused to hear the singers still on the programme, and just went away. Oddly Italian, this. English folk would never relinquish part of their money's worth in this way.

Thursd. Jan. 13. Dull. Page-proofs from Blackie. Made the index, and sent it off.- Began Giannone's "Storia del Regno di Napoli" [4 vols, 1723]. Letters from Wells. Baron Lumbroso invites me to dine on Sat[urday].

Frid. Jan. 14. Glorious day. In afternoon to the Lambarts. Get to like the people. Mrs. Lambart very intelligent.- Letter from Nelly, with good news of little man. Postcard from Bertz.- Lambart has been ill, and called on Dr Munthe—of whom I have heard so often. Munthe, I find, lives in the rooms where Keats died.

Sat. Jan. 15. Dinner at the Baron Lumbroso's (Via S. Martino, Macao). A party; some ten people. Among them a Miss Fitzmaurice—Irish; interesting girl (a woman rather) who teaches. On the whole, not interesting evening. The Baroness agreeable, but not very refined. The men wholly uninteresting.- Paid lodgings for next month.

Sund. Jan. 16. Walk in morning out by Porta S. Giovanni. In afternoon, with O'Dunne, to variety concert in V[ia] Due Macelli. Stupid.- Recd "John Bright" [by C.A. Vince] from Blackie [in Victorian Era Series].

Mond. Jan. 17. Library etc.

Tuesd. Jan. 18. Finished as much as I need read of Giannone. Began Marangoni [-Brancuti, author of *Luce e Fango*. 1896]. Trying to think of story for *Cosmopolis*.- Very cold.

Wed. Jan. 19. Cold. In afternoon to leave a card at Baron Lumbroso's. Finished Dahn's "Prokopios".

Thursd. Jan. 20. Cold. Thought out a story for *Cosmopolis*. Working in evening at Dahn's "Könige der Germanen".

Frid. Jan. 21. Touch of bronchitis. Went to bed at mid-day.

Sat. Jan. 22. Not a wink of sleep. Fever and cough. In bed all day.

Sund. Jan. 23. No sleep, but fever gone. Got up. Nelly writes that Colles has sent her cheque for American "Dickens" (£40-3 - out of £50). Good little letter from Walter, written by himself. Usual cheerless news from Miss Orme.

*   *   *

Thursd. Jan. 27. It has evidently been an attack of influenza. Got up a little yesterday for first time. The beastliness of food here has made things worse. A letter from Wells, saying that he and his wife will come at end of Feb[ruary] has decided me to move to a hotel. I shall go to the Minerva. Can't help the expense. I have been trying to do, as a middle-aged invalid, what I did with some inconvenience even as a young and healthy man. The thing is impossible, and I hope I may not have ruined my health.

Justin McCarthy has sent me his new "Life of Gladstone".

Have written to Alg, asking if he could take a house somewhere not too far from London, and let me have two rooms in it.

Invitation this morning from Mrs. Lambart, to lunch to-morrow. Obliged to refuse.

Frid. Jan. 28. Out for first time.

Sat. Jan. 29. Recd from Wells his "War of the Worlds".

Sund. Jan. 30. Very fine day. Morning on the Palatine. Feeling much better.- Reading for the first time "The Last Days of Pompeii" [by Bulwer-Lytton, 1834].

Mond. Jan. 31. Gloom. Called on the Lambarts.

Tuesd. Feb. 1. Fine. Called on Swinton-Hunter, and lent him "War of the Worlds", which Wells has sent me.

Wed. Feb. 2. Fine. In afternoon called Swinton-Hunter, and his friend Severino.- Finished hurried reading of "Die Könige der Germanen". In mornings, going through [Sir W.] Smith's "Dict[ionary] of Eccles[iastical] Antiquities."

Thursd. Feb. 3. Fine, windy. Letter from Alg. Replied.

Frid. Feb. 4. Dull. Got from lib. Savigny's "Hist[ory] of Roman Law in Middle Ages", and an Italian translation of Boethius. Letter from Miss McCarthy.

Sat. Feb. 5. In morning to the Minerva, to make inquiries about rooms. Found I could get no lower terms than 11 lire a day, without wine. This is too much; moreover, the place is kept very hot, which would be dangerous. Wandering rather miserably after that, I chanced upon the Alibert, near

481

Piazza di Spagna. Here they will give complete board (1 bottle of wine) for 9 lire. Wells can have double-bedded room, and complete board for self and wife for 17 lire.- Wrote to Wells about this.

Sund. Feb. 6. Gloomy and windy.

Mond. Feb. 7. With a ticket given by O'Dunne, I went to the Vatican, to the Requiem Mass, for Pio Nono, in the Capella Sistina. Arrived at 9 o'clock, and waited till 10.30 for arrival of the Pope. He entered by the little door to the right of the altar set up in front of Last Judgment; and was seated on a throne on the left of the Chapel. Wore his mitre. Great assembly of foreign Ambassadors. We, the undistinguished crowd, were penned at back of chapel—of course standing,—under the gallery used by women. Much fine singing. I was terribly wearied, and glad to get away at 12 o'clock. Near me stood Lambart, and Hurd, the coresp[ondent] of *Morning Post*. Of course had to be in evening dress—which, by the bye, has become too small for me, and is very uncomfortable. The Pope, at close, spoke the absolution of the grave, a quavering but full voice. Much taking off and putting on of the mitre. Many Cardinals present.

Letter from Miss Orme, strongly recommending a legal separation before I return. Replied consenting to this. She promises the services of her own solicitor.

Tuesd. Feb. 8. Terrible tramontana. Have to go about muffled.

Wed. Feb. 9. Some wind, with bright sun. Read a little of Gregorovius's Roman Diary.

Thursd. Feb. 10. Wind worse than ever. Impossible to walk in the streets, - so bitter. Wrote to Mrs Norman, Miss Collet and Bertz.- Got from lib. Hodgkin's "Theodoric".

Frid. Feb. 11. Wind still blowing. On my way to the lib. this morning, as I passed Via Mazzarino, I saw a little crowd round something on the pavement, and heard a passer-by say: "Si è buttato qui" [He has thrown himself here]. Approaching, I saw an old man lying dead, with a stream of blood from his skull—an old grey-bearded man, decently dressed. His face perfectly placid. They threw a sheet over him, and carried him off in a vehicle. I must look for a report in paper. Seems to have been suicide, from 2nd storey.

Card from Nelly, saying she has received £17-0-9 from L[awrence] & B[ullen], and £6-16-11 from Brit[ish] Produce Supply Association—the remnant of my account there.- Miss Orme writes of four rooms to let in the house of people she knows at Gospel Oak.-

Called at Hôtel Alibert, and gave notice that I should arrive on Monday.

Sat. Feb. 12. Fine, and warmer. Letter from Colles, telling me that Methuen's have finally offered advance of £250, for "Town Traveller", and an American firm [Stokes] £100. Wrote accepting these terms.

I learn from the paper that the suicide of yesterday was a German baron [Baron von Loeper], ill of fever; done in delirium.

Sund. Feb. 13. Yesterday, Lambart sent me tickets for the Pope's Mass at S. Peter's to-day, celebrating the completion of 20th year of his popedom. I reached S. P[eter's] at about 8 o'clock, and found it already crowded. A great queue of cabs and carriages from Ponte S. Angelo; had to alight from my carriage there and walk. Got a place very near to the door by which Pope was to enter—that in right aisle, close to the main entrances. A way barricaded for him all up the nave. He was to have entered at 8.30 but did not appear till an hour later. Rode in his chair above our heads, the flabellum carried on each side of him; with trembling hand gave his benediction. A brass band in the loggia above great doorway struck up, and the people shouted "Viva il papa-re" etc, but with no great enthusiasm. Had an excellent view of the old man's face, which was remarkably complacent—with a little senile moving of the lips.- Did not stop for the Mass. The great organ was hardly audible when it began.

Sent Bertz a picture-card celebrating this occasion.

Mond. Feb. 14. Left my old lodgings in the morning, and went to Hôtel Alibert, where I have a room on the 3rd floor, with morning sun. In evening called at Mrs Lambart's, who told me that Frank Hurd, the *Morning Post* correspondent, has just been adopted by Lord Ronald Gower![1]

Tuesd. Feb. 15. Still rather cold.- Went to Swinton-Hunter's tea-party—a terrible affair. Some score of English women, mostly married to Italians; common and foolish folk. Of course had to talk imbecilities, and was heartily glad to get away.- Recd a copy of my "Dickens" from Blackies.

Wed. Feb. 16. Woke up in the night with a bronchial attack, but it passed before morning. Am taking Scott's Emulsion. To-day being fine and warm, I walked all the morning about the Piazza d'Armi.- Wrote to Blackies, telling them to send four copies of the "Dickens" to Rome, and one to Justin McCarthy, and to send the £30 cheque to Wakefield.- The copy already recd, I sent as present to Mrs Lambart.

Thursd. Feb. 17. Very ill all day—fever and cold. Letters from Miss Collet, and Mrs H. Norman.

Frid. Feb. 18. Took some quinine this morning, and feel better. Card from Sigra Gabbrielli. Wrote to Mrs Norman, Miss Collet and Wells.- Think I have got my *Cosmopolis* story.- Out morning and afternoon on the Pincio. Studied the names of the trees, which in many cases are attached.

Sat. Feb. 19. Rain all day. Vainly struggling still for my story. Cough very bad. Recd from Bertz a newspaper cutting about a new remedy for tuberculosis—called Creosotal. Shall inquire.

Sund. Feb. 20. Finer. Got a small quantity of creosotal, but find it is too thick to take in drops. Wrote to Bertz.

Mond. Feb. 21. Dull. Wrote to Dr von Leyden, of Berlin, asking for advice about use of creosotal. Probably he won't answer. Letter from Bertz, and from Alg, who points out the servant difficulties of our scheme for a joint house. I fear it is fatal. Replied to him.

Tuesd. Feb. 22. Rainy. In afternoon called on Mrs Lambart. She told me that her mother is a Roumanian by birth.- Recd four more copies of "Dickens" from Blackie, and gave one to O'Dunne. Sent one to Bertz.- Got my creosotal mixed with Cod Liver Oil.

Wed. Feb. 23. Rain all day long. Note from Miss Collet, saying that she is delighted with my Dickens.

Thursd. Feb. 24. Showery. In morning showed two people staying here the way to the Capitol. Letters from Miss Orme, and Wells.- News that Zola— whose trial for libelling the generals in the Dreyfus affair ended yesterday— has been sentenced to a year's imprisonment and 3000 francs fine. So far as I understand the matter, France seems sunk in infamy.- Miss Orme has taken 4 unfurnished rooms, for E., from March 19, at 15/- a week. Address: 90 Mansfield Road, N.W. In the house (a relative of landlord) lives Miss Orme's old nurse, a woman who can be thoroughly trusted to keep an eye on E.- Have written to Alg, asking if he will go to London, to see to the moving of furniture from warehouse into the rooms.

Frid. Feb. 25. Dull. Nothing done—except buying some shirts.

Sat. Feb. 26. Fine. In afternoon to the Lambarts'. A card left here by Mr Price, friend of Miss Collet.- Mrs Lambart showed me a cutting from the *Westminster Gazette,* with mention of an article about me in *The Bookbuyer.* Insistence on my days of poverty, and a whole passage of puling (in first person) alleged to be written by me. An infamous forgery[2].- Wrote to Miss Collet, who has sent me an old Diary of her girlhood to read.

Sund. Feb. 27. Very fine. Morning on Palatine. In afternoon called on E.L. Price at the Minerva. He invited me to dine for to-morrow.- Wrote a card to Sturmer about *The Bookbuyer.*

Mond. Feb. 28. Fine morning, then rain. In morning walked over Milvian Bridge, and up the hill on Via Cassia. Dined at Minerva with Price, and his two friends—brothers named Yates, the elder a liberal parson (Thompson Yates). Remarkably pleasant evening. Like Price. Invited him to dine here next Saturday.

Tuesd. March 1. Very fine. Got to work, at last, upon my *Cosmopolis* story—"The Last Illusion"—and wrote 1¼p.- Letter from Alg about our domestic project. One from Miss McCarthy, acknowledging receipt of my "Dickens".

Wed. March 2. Destroyed my writing of yesterday, and did 3pp. of another story, "Mrs Gray's Illusion".- The hotel is invaded by a Swiss "pilgrimage", some 50 people, and, with truly Germanic impudence, the landlord has turned all his regular guests out of the dining-room, and we have to eat in the stuffy little smoking-room! I shall not be able to have Price here to dinner. Must go to a restaurant on Saturday.

Thursd. March 3. Did 3 more pp. Letter from Miss Orme, saying that E.'s behaviour is more outrageous than ever. Replied to her.

Frid. March 4. Weather getting fine and warm. To-day a great festa—the 50th Anniversary of Lo Statuto [the Italian Constitution]. I saw little or nothing of the thing. But in afternoon, as I passed along the Corso, saw three or four Socialists, who had tried to get up a meeting, carried off to police-station. A ludicrous sight: poor, starved little wretches, each one walking between two guardie, with two carabinieri behind him!

Sat. March 5. Fine. In morning walked to see the great statue of Cavour on the "Prati". It stands between the new Palazzo della Giustizzia, which is being built, and a huge shell of an unfinished building, years old. Then round by the Bocca della Verità, and back over Capitol by the Via del Monte Tarpeio, where I have never been before.
Wrote to Alg. Also to E., telling her I am taking lodgings for her.
Read "East Lynne" [by Mrs Henry Wood, 1861]. Not at all a bad book, of its sort.
Dined with Price at the Colonna. Gave him my "Dickens". A good fellow.

Sund. March 6. Fine. Long walk in morning. Tea at Mrs Lambart's.

Mond. March 7. Rainy. Colles sends agreements for "Town Traveller", with Methuen for England, and F. Stokes Co. for U.S. Presses for short stories, and says "Dickens" is going very well.

Tuesd. March 8. Rain. Rose writes, asking me to do a companion vol[ume] on Thackeray. At present the thing seems impossible.- Sturmer sends the *Academy* [of March 5], containing "Mr George Gissing at Home", all taken from that offensive article in the American *Bookbuyer*. Wrote to *Academy,* repudiating the thing [reply published on March 19].- My reputation seems to stir a little at last.
To-day the public funeral of Felice Cavallotti[3], a socialist deputy, killed in a duel outside the Porta Maggiore. Long procession from Monte Citorio, and down the Corso. The unhealthy, and ugly faces of the populace following the bier. An address pasted about the walls by Cavallotti's friends speaks of the duel as a relic of the Middle Ages. In several of the Italian

cities, when the news arrived, people went about shouting, "Abbasso il duello!"

Wed. March 9. Late last night arrived Wells and his wife; I did not see them till this morning. We spent morning together on Pincio.

Letter about "Dickens" from Mrs Laffan, wife of Presid[ent] of Cheltenham College.[4] Replied to her. Refused Rose's suggestion about Thackeray.- Wells has brought *The Outlook,* with excellent notice of "Dickens" by W.E. Henley.[5]

Thursd. March 10. In morning with Wells and Mrs to S. Peter's and Janiculum. Afternoon to call on Mrs Charles Smith (friend of Sw. Hunter) at Palazzo Odescalchi. There introduced to Miss Scott, queer-looking old woman, but intelligent, friend of the Laffans of Cheltenham. Promised to visit her at the Hôtel de Russie.

Frid. March 11. Morning with W.'s to Vatican. Afternoon with them to call on Mrs Lambart.

Sat. March 12. Morning with W.'s to Forum etc. Letter from a man at Stockport [J.B. Oldham] asking biog[raphical] information for a lecture [see the Stockport *Advertiser*, April 1, 1898]. Replied.- After dinner a card was sent in to me, with the name Hornung. It was the novelist (of whom I have read nothing). A man of 30, suffering much from asthma; married to sister of Conan Doyle. Invited us all to call to-morrow evening.

Sund. March 13. In morning to Palatine. Afternoon called on Miss Scott, at the Russie. I gather that she used to write for *Blackwood's.* Interesting old woman.- After dinner to Hornung's—38, Gregoriana—the rooms in which Mary Howitt[6] died. Stayed till 11. Mrs Hornung a large, healthy, good-humoured woman, with wonderfully bright eyes. They have one child.

Miserable stories of James Payn, who, long a confirmed invalid, is now constantly bemoaning his lot with tears.

Mond. March 14. Began a new story for *Cosmopolis,* and worked all morning. Not quite 1p.- Brewster sends the Agreement of Separation. Miss Orme has told him to put a pound a week for household expenses; I must alter this to 25/-.- Wrote to Alg with details of the removal of furniture, which he is to superintend.

Tuesd. March 15. Wrote 1p.- In afternoon to Lambarts', who lent me "Cyrano de Bergerac" [the play by Edmond Rostand, 1897], now being played at Paris, and "Ionica" [anonymous, 1891].

Wed. March 16. Rewrote page 1.- Wrote to my boy at Wakefield, and to Margaret.

Thursd. March 17. Rewrote p.2. Mrs Lambart writes to say that her cousin, who is living with them, has got the chicken-pox, and visits are forbidden. Wrote to Alg, asking him to settle a day with Doughartys.

Frid. March 18. Glorious weather. Wrote 1p. in morning. Afternoon with Wells and wife over Milvian Bridge, and up Via Cassia. On way back, drank a bottle of wine in the little osterià looking from the first ascent of Via Cassia over Rome. A delightful hour. Music of mandoline and guitar.- On returning found a card from man named Croke, - corresp[ondent] of *Daily Telegraph,* living at the Minerva.- After dinner called Mr and Mrs Hornung.

Sat. March 19. Very fine. Did 1p. Afternoon with W[ellse]s to the Medici Gardens, which I had never seen before. Then to Minerva, to call on the journalist Croke. Found him an unscrupulous interviewer, and had a stupid, annoying time; too weak to refuse, and obliged to talk platitudes.

Sund. March 20. Dull. Did 1p. Mrs. Lambart has gone into "retreat" at Trinità dei Monti for a week.- At evening to the Hornungs'.

Mond. March 21. Dull. Did 1p. In afternoon to see Lady Edmund Fitzmaurice, at Hôtel de l'Europe. Sister of Edward Fitzgerald, the mountaineer; not living with her husband. An American; clever but shallow. Introduced to her by Mrs Norman.

Tuesd. March 22. Did nearly 1p., then interrupted by visit from Hornung. Bad attack of lumbago. Had to go to bed dinnerless. Then a night of diarrhoea.

Wed. March 23. Better this morning. Did ½p., and finished my story ["The Ring Finger"]. Posted to *Cosmopolis* [published May 1898].- To lunch with Lady Edmund at the Europe. We took a carriage, and drove out a little beyond the Ponte Nomentano. For first time saw the Anio, and M. Sacer. Walked a mile or so in Campagna, and back to carriage.- Good letter from Alg promising to do everything at Doughartys'.

Thursd. March 24. A new acquaintance at hotel; Mrs Williams, widow with little boy, sister of Mrs Sidney Webb (Beatrice Potter). Unfavourable impression; loud; bullies waiters; forces herself into our conversations.- Weather rainy.- Had Swinton-Hunter and Severino to lunch.

Frid. March 25. Rainy. Morning with W.'s. Pietro in Vincoli and Colosseum. Recd such bad news from Miss Orme, that I telegraphed to her to consult Brewster, and wired to Brewster himself.- Thunder.

Sat. March 26. Great hail-storm in morning, whitening all the streets. With W.'s to S. Angelo, which I went over for first time. Afternoon with Mrs. Williams to Barberini and Medici Gardens. After dinner to a musical party at Hornung's. Only interesting new acquaintance, Mrs. Mallet—who recited a thing of Edward Lear's. Mrs Hornung amazes me by her robust and beautiful health. Her sister, Mrs. Foley, (who lives on a little island beyond Posillipo) also a fine physical type; a little less robust, and more handsome.

Sund. March 27. Morning with W.'s to some churches. Frightful weather, hail, rain, thunder. Posts delayed by storm in English Channel.- Called on Mrs. Lambart.

Mond. March 28. Ceaseless rain. To lunch with Lady Edmund Fitzmaurice. Present: Countess Pasolini, a pleasant woman, speaking good English, and a Signorina Rasponi, of Ravenna, who has done a lot of admirable little drawings of children. In afternoon came Hornung, and talked ad infinitum, as usual.

Tuesd. March 29. Ceaseless rain—or nearly. In morning with Mrs Williams to Vatican Sculpture Galleries.- Read the skit on Wells's "War of the Worlds"—"The War of the Wenuses" [by C.L. Graves and E.V. Lucas, 1898].- Letter from Justin McCarthy, praising my "Dickens".

Wed. March 30. Rainy morning. Afternoon with Mrs. Williams to the Colosseum—warm sun and blue sky for two hours. After dinner, a party at the Caffè Nazionale. Mrs Williams, the Wells', Evans and I. Home at 11 o'clock.

Thursd. March 31. Steady rain.

Frid. Ap. 1. Rain ceaseless. Alg writes that he has finished furnishing of rooms at Mansfield Road. Early this morning Mrs. Williams left for Venice.

Sat. Ap. 2. A fine day at last. We three set out early, drove to P. San Sebastiano, and walked along Via Appia to the Aqueduct of the Villa Quintiliorum, by which we crossed the open country to an osterià, and there had a meal. Thence on to the Ciampino station, and home by train.

Sund. Ap. 3. Dull. Afternoon up to Monte Mario. Letter from Mrs Williams, Grand Hotel, Venice, telling of her safe arrival.

Mond. Ap. 4. Fine. Morning out by Villa Papa Giulio over hill to Acqua Acetosa. Wrote to Alg, Bertz and Hick. E. left Miss Orme's house, for 90 Mansfield Road, last Thursday. Her rent-day is the 19th.

Tuesd. Ap. 5. Very fine. Left Rome with W.'s at 9 o'clock by train to Tivoli. Saw the Cascades, the Temple of Vesta and Villa d'Este; thence walked to the tramway station, outside Porta S. Cróce, where we had lunch at a little trattoria—fried eggs, cheese, fruit and bottle of Tuscan wine, altogether

3 *l*. 05. Then a walk downhill to Hadrian's Villa. Returned to Rome by steam tram.

Wed. Ap. 6. Dull and showery.

Thursd. Ap. 7. With the W[ells]'s and our friend Evans started by train for Albano (9.50). Walked from there, thro' Ariccia, to foot of Monte Cavo. The others ascended to top; I went on to Rocca di Papa, and there awaited them. Lunched well at a trattoria at the end of town. Thence walked on to Frascati, and home by train. The country beautiful with spring flowers: anemones, cyclamen, broom etc. Much butcher's broom. Heard the cuckoo for first time.

Frid. Ap. 8. Hot and fine. In morning to Forum. Dinner with Conan Doyle, the Wells's and the Hornungs, at Trattoria Colonna. Then all together to see moon on Colosseum, and ended evening at Hornungs'.

Sat. Ap. 9. Getting very hot. In evening with Wells's and Evans to Teatro Costanza, and heard "Lohengrin". Had a box too near the stage.- Very pleasant company at hotel just now. Remember the ladies from "Porrth".[7]

Sund. Ap. 10. Hot. News from Colles that 1st part of "Eve's Ransom" has appeared in *Revue de Paris* [on April 1]. In evening to Teatro Nazionale, with Wells's and friend of theirs called Evans—saw "Cavalleria Rusticana" and "Pagliacci". Bad singers and rowdy house.- Called on Mrs. Lambart.

Mond. Ap. 11. In morning with the Lambarts to Vatican Gardens. Afternoon with Wells's on Pincio, for farewell view of Rome.

Tuesd. Ap. 12. Evans left for Perugia at 11 o'clock. At 12 went the Wells's, for Naples. By the 2.30, I and Alfred Turner started north (Turner, the gold medallist—sculpture of R. Academy, for his group "Charity". He also holds the travelling studentship. Nice fellow, rather too soft to do much I fear. He left me at Florence, where he is going to take a studio.).
  Sleepless night in train.

Wed. Ap. 13. In early morning heard "Mantova". In clear dawn, saw Verona. Then the first sunshine struck upon a snow-height in Tyrol— gleaming! The broad entrance to the Brenner pass—crags rising steep from the flat country between them. At Botzen begins the narrowing. Brenner the topmost point. Nowhere so striking as the Gotthard—no engineering feats. Innsbruck a disappointment. Heavy mists on the mountain tops, and the town made ugly by great numbers of big new houses.
  At Ala, the Italian frontier, luggage examined; and again at Kufflein— the German. Miserable evening, after Alps. Reached Munich in wind and rain, and went to the Bamberger Hof. Great difficulty in speaking German. Enjoyed my Munich beer.

489

Thursd. Ap. 14. Left by the 8.25 for Berlin. Rain and wind; after that, a dull day. Striking view of the great Cathedral at Regensburg, its two spires rising above the town. Afterwards, country rather dismal; its flatness only relieved by the pine forests. Much swamp. Berlin at 9 o'clock, where Bertz met me. We ate at a restaurant; then on to his house at Potsdam. Find him looking very old; silvery hair. Yet seems in good health.

Frid. Ap. 15. Evil German bed; no sheet or blanket, but one huge feather pillow to cover one.- Out about 12 with Bertz, to see the river etc. Pleasant, but not beautiful landscape, with little green as yet. A cold wind ruffling the lakes. Went to Sans Souci, and walked all about the gardens; it pleased me very little. Remember the terrace on orange-houses in front of the palace. Slim French Statuary behind the Mausoleum of Emp. Frederick III. In cortile close by, Thorvaldsen's Christ, a fine figure. Inscription on wall of church: Christus unser Frieden. The glaring contrast between these things and the rampant militarism everywhere about.

Ate at the Sans Souci Café. Inscript[ion] on wall: "Trinkt, Brüder, trinkt, bis der letzte sinkt. "[Drink, brothers, drink, till the last of you drops".].

My bedroom window looks right over the Havel, with the Flatow Thurm rising from trees on the far side. Wind driving water into wavelets. A swan, swimming cheerlessly.

The sheer *commonness* of it all, after Italy.

Sat. Ap. 16. Day spent in Berlin. Showery and dull. Hours of walking about streets and parks. Impression of wealth and ambition; little beauty. Feature of the houses, the deep balconies. These new monuments in the Siegesallée of the Tiergarten—the beginning of a great avenue of national statues.- The Goethe statue fine; finer that of Luther, with its groups of reformers.- Immense public buildings. The blatant statue of old William, with the ferocious lions below.- The Maria Kirche, on place where people used to be burnt.- Tired to death after it all.

Sund. Ap. 17. Long walk around Potsdam. Dull sky, but very warm.- My terrible food here at Bertz's—specially the *raw* Westphalian ham at breakfast!

Mond. Ap. 18. Dull. Left Potsdam at 1.28pm. by thro' train for Köln. On straight to Ostende, and thence, at 6am., to Dover. About 11 o'clock reached Hick's house at New Romney, where I passed the night.

Tuesd. Ap. 19. Hicks all well and doing better financially than ever hitherto. Found letter from Alg, saying he is too busy for me to go to Willersey just yet. Proofs of "The Ring Finger" for *Cosmopolis*, which I corrected and sent off.

Wed. Ap. 20. Up to town by early train, and went to Hotel Previtali. Called on Bullen. To tailor's, bootmaker's etc. Astonished to find that I still have more than £200 in bank.

Thursd. Ap. 21. Odds and ends of business.

Frid. Ap. 22. Hard east wind, but it does not affect me. Called on Colles, who is as usual very vague about things. At Grant Richards', got a copy of part II of [William] Rothenstein's "English Portraits", containing Irving and myself. Richards made an astonishing proposition—that I should let him have all the rights in all my work for next 5 years at a price to be determined, said price to be more than I could get from all other sources. Promised to reflect.- In afternoon to the Normans'; met them just coming out, with young Ed[ward] Fitzgerald, and accepted invitation to lunch for Sunday.- On to Rothenstein's studio, in Glebe Place. He tells me the text to my portrait is written by Clement Shorter. Met his young brother, who is just going to the Slade School.- In evening to dine with Mrs Williams, at 152 Oakley St., where she is lodging till she can find a house.

Have recd 2 copies of American edition of my "Dickens", - beautifully done. Wrote to thank Dodd, Mead and Co.

Sat. Ap. 23. In afternoon to see Miss Collet (36 Berkeley Road, Crouch End).

Sund. Ap. 24. In morning to Roberts. Lunched with Mrs Norman. Dined with Sturmer at his club.

Mond. Ap. 25. Went to Ilkley, where Mother and girls and Walter are just ending a fortnight's holiday.

Thursd. Ap. 28. After three days of miserable weather (mist and sleet) we all came to Wakefield. The boy is in excellent health and spirits, and doing well at his lessons.

Frid. Ap. 29. Rain and gloom. Invitation from Authors' Club to be guest of evening. Refused.

Sat. Ap. 30. Same weather. Saw Mr [Matthew Bussey] Hick and Mr Bruce.

Sund. May 1. Sunny. Wrote letters.

Mond. May 2. Returned to London. Previtali Hotel. Dined with Bullen, and met a young Scotchman named Steuart. Bullen far from well. Had to give up his idea of going with me into Sussex.

Tuesd. May 3. In afternoon called on Barrie—out. Then on Mrs. Frederic Harrison, who dissuaded me from going to Midhurst, and advised Frant.

Wed. May 4. Sun and shower. By train to Penshurst. Walked to village, and had lunch at good inn. Lovely place.- Then by train to Frant. Very beautiful; but no suitable lodgings.- Lastly to Tunbridge Wells, where I put up at Temperance Hotel.

Thursd. May 5. Rain all day. Dragged wretchedly about T. Wells. No good. Could not live here. Suddenly decided to go to Dorking. Reached there at 4, and went to Red Lion. Later, took lodgings at 24 Horsham Road, for a week. Have resolved to look for a house here.

Frid. May 6. Fine. Saw a house at Cliftonville, near where I lodged some four years ago. Went over it with the agent and decided to take it for one year—rent £42. Shall have to get a housekeeper. Wrote to Wakefield, to give the news. Sent for books to London Library.

Sat. May 7. Very fine. In afternoon a long walk towards Leith Hill. Letter from Miss Travers, and one from a certain W.H. Brooke (old schoolfellow, he says) begging assistance, very impudently. Also a long type-written letter, very good, about my books, from a man who signs "W.D. Jones", but gives no address. The best letter I ever had from a stranger.

Sund. May 8. Rainy all day. Reading some queer books about Anglo-Israelism, lent me by an old man lodging here—one Mr. Churchill, formerly organist and music teacher. In evening to Parish Church.

Mond. May. 9. Fine. Walked about. Fretting at delay before I can get once more to work.

Tuesd. May 10. Dull and close. Correcting the typescript of "The Town Traveller", for Methuens. Poor rubbish.- Alg writes to borrow £25, once more, to get his family back from Ilfracombe. Alas! Just the money I wanted for my new furniture.

Wed. May 11. Recd from Mrs. Norman her new novel—"The Crook of the Bough". Also copy of *Cosmopolis,* with my story in it—"The Ring Finger".- Ordered carpeting for house.

Thursd. May 12. Up to town in afternoon, and bought, in Little Queen St., a book-case and a revolving writing-chair. Wild expenses these, but I *must* be comfortable. To dine, at Devonshire Club, with George Whale. Present: Clodd, Shorter, Barrie and G.W. Cable. Cable, Barrie's guest in England just now. Going to give public reading of his books at Barrie's house, and elsewhere. Slow, insignificant little man.- Slept at the Craven Hotel.

Frid. May 13. To Shoolbred's, and spent, I fear, about £50 in furniture, crockery etc.- Back to Dorking by 1 o'clock. In afternoon to Meredith's, where I dined, Barrie and Cable being there too.

Sat. May 14. Weather beautiful, after days of much rain. Got a ton of coal into my house. Yesterday at 7, instead of at 2, as promised, my goods arrived from the warehouse in Brixton—books, shelves, writing-table and a chair or two.

492

Sund. May 15. Rain till evening. Pottered about house in the morning, hanging up a few pictures. After tea, walked to Holmwood.

Mond. May. 16. Fine, glorious sunshine from 11 onwards in my front rooms. Waited in vain for my bookcase and writing chair.

Tuesd. May 17. Fine and cloudy. Got a lot of upholstering done. My study almost finished. Bookcase and chair arrived.- A Mrs. Boughton applies for place of housekeeper. Too respectable, I fear. Applied to Miss Orme about her.

Wed. May 18. Furniture from Shoolbred's. Unpacking; misery.

Thursd. May 19. Rain all day. Furniture put into place. Wardrobe and spring mattress had to be hauled up thro' window. Decided to engage Mrs Boughton.- Gladstone died this morning.

Frid. May 20. Terrible day of rain and mist. My temporary servant is to come to-morrow, from 8.30 to 3.30. Slept in the house for first time, and not very well either. New linen sheets grand but uncomfortable.

Sat. May 21. Fine once more. Mrs Grant, the temporary, does very well. In afternoon came Mrs Boughton, and I engaged her. Wages, £18. Very decent woman, I think; widow, with four children. Is to come next Wednesday morning.- Letter from Mrs Wells. They returned from Italy a few days ago, have seen a little of the recent riots[8]; their train north was the last that left Milan. Had meant to return by the Orient line, but at last moment heard there was no berth for them.-

The furnishing of this house (kitchen, study, dining-room, bedroom, servant's room) has cost me, I fear, about £70. Never dreamt of such an outlay of course. Finances getting very low; must work, work.

Sund. May 22. Idling.

Mond. May 23. Very fine till late afternoon, then thunderstorm.

Tuesd. May 24. Fine, and very hot. In afternoon actually got to work, and did 1½p. of a short story—"At Nightfall".

Wed. May 25. Dull and misty. Wrote to Walter. Did 1½p. Mrs. Boughton, the housekeeper, came.

Thursd. May 26. Dull and misty. Finished "At Nightfall" [published in *Lippincott's Monthly Magazine,* May 1900], and made vain attempt to begin another story. Mrs Wells writes to say that the "ladies from Porrth" were at Heatherlea last Saturday, and that Evans will be there next.- My housekeeper dry and distasteful. Strikes the note so hateful to me— sneering at country things in comparison with London. But she cooks well, and seems fairly clean.

Frid. May 27. Fine. Began another story: "The Frank Wooer", and did 1p.

Sat. May 28. Abandoned the story.

Sund. May 29. Fine. By train to Gomshall, had dinner there, and walked up onto the White Downs. Tea at a house at entrance of Ranmore Common, and home through Ranmore.

Mond. May. 30. Dull, ending in rain.

Tuesd. May 31. Dull, showery. Saw with surprise that they have put my sketch "At the Grave of Alaric" into this morning's [*Daily*] *Chronicle*. I sent it to Norman from Taranto, and have heard nothing of it since.- Wrote 1½p. of story—"The Peace-Bringer".

Wed. June. 1. Storm, ending in fine evening. Did 3½pp., and finished "The Peace-Bringer" [published in *The Lady's Realm,* October 1898].

Thursd. June 2. Cloudy to fine. Began another story "The Elixir", and did 4pp.

Frid. June 3. Wrote 1p., finished "The Elixir" [published in *The Idler*, May 1899], and sent three stories off to Colles.- In evening hit upon a possible plot for a play. The idea of making money by a play has grown upon me. We shall see.

Sat. June 4. Dull. Worked all day at the scheme of my play.

Sund. June 5. Fine. In morning, walked to Gomshall and back, about 10 miles. Got the names of my characters.

Mond. June 6. Rainy to fine. In morning wrote out a scheme of my 4 acts, and got all the names. Shall perhaps call play "The Golden Trust". Evening wrote 1½p. of another short story "Fate and the Apothecary". In the middle arrived letter from Miss Orme, saying that E. has been absent from Mansfield Road since Saturday morning, no one knowing where she has gone. Probably to some relative. Replied that, if she does not return speedily, Brewster must be consulted.- Having written this reply, I resumed my work: an impossibility a year or two ago.

Tuesd. June 7. Fine and hot. Wrote 3pp., finishing short story [published in *Literature,* May 6, 1899].- Postcard from Miss Orme, saying that E. returned home yesterday.

Wed. June 8. Mist and drizzle all day. Did little.

Thursd. June 9. Fine, but oppressive. Elaborating play.- Read Pinero's "The Weaker Sex" [1894].

Frid. June 10. Dull, misty. Methuens write to ask if I will undertake introductions to a new edition of Dickens. Referred them for terms to Colles.- Correcting proofs of "The Town Traveller".- Made beginning of the dialogue of my play and wrote 2pp.- Read Gyp's "Le Coeur d'Ariane".[9]

Sat. June 11. Very fine. Cheerful letter from Miss Orme. E.'s behaviour at Mansfield Road has been so bad that her landlord wishes to give me notice. Replied that the lawyer must see her at once, and *settle* something, if possible. Notwithstanding this, made a new beginning of play, and did 3pp.

Sund. June 12. Heavy haze over sky all day; no sun.- Destroyed work of yesterday, and abandoned that play. Struck out a 3 act Comedy—"Clare's Engagement", and wrote 1½p. of it.- In afternoon walked to Wotton.- Reading Gyp's "Le Bonheur de Ginette".

Mond. June 13. To Wotton, and stayed night at Hatch. Heavy cloud over sky, with one little sun gleam in afternoon. Coldish wind. Nightjar in woods at evening.

Tuesd. June 14. Back to Dorking at mid-day. Still same clouded sky; no sun, and bitter wind. Work at a standstill.

Wed. June 15. Faint sunshine. Have re-cast my idea of "The Golden Trust", and rebegan it. Wrote 2½pp.

Thursd. June 16. Sun through hazè all day. Once more destroyed my beginning. Desperate struggle, this.

Frid. June 17. Fine, though hazy. Splitting my head over play.- Learn from Alg, that some days ago E. went to Willersey in pursuit of me, taking poor little Alfred. I don't know how long she stayed. She threatens to give all possible trouble.

Sat. June 18. Very fine and warm. Letter from Miss Orme, saying Brewster is doing his best.- Made new beginning of the play, and did 4pp.

Sund. June 19. Very fine. Did 4pp.- Paid my rent at Mansfield Road.- Reading Dostoievsky's "L'Eternel Mari".

Mond. June 20. Very fine. Did 1½p., and finished Act I.- Wrote to Bullen, telling him of my book to be published by Methuens.

Tuesd. June 21. Fine. Rose with my left hand badly swollen, seemingly result of fly-bite. In evening went to see doctor about it. Lotions etc. No work.

Wed. June 22. Fine. Hand better. Doctor called. Wrote to Wakefield. H. Hick agrees to take Walter in his holiday for 15/- a week. Invitation from

Sir F. and Lady Cook to garden-party at Richmond. Of course shall not go; people unknown to me.- Think I must give up my play. Thinking of another.

Thursd. June 23. Fine. Did nothing. In afternoon came Wells and his wife; delighted with this house.- Letter from Frenchwoman [Gabrielle Fleury], wanting to translate "New Grub Street". Replied to her that Georges Art also thought of doing it.- Invited to lecture on Thackeray, next January, before the Ancoats Brotherhood. Declined.

Frid. June 24. Wild south-west gale, with rain. No work. Paid rates and rent.- Wrote to Grant Richards, referring to his suggestion of 2 months ago, and asking if he could give me £1000 a year for all the rights in all fiction I write during next 5 years—his rights to be 5 years' duration in each instance. Fear there is little chance of favourable reply.

Sat. June 25. Wind and rain. Wasted day.

Sund. June 26. Fine with showers. Idea of another play floating in my mind. Doctor called, and made long examination. Finds a little decided phthisis of right lung, a good deal of emphysema, and a little eczema on the arms—nice state of things altogether.

Mond. June 27. Fine, cloudy. Did nothing.

Tuesd. June 28. Fine. Read [Marcel] Prévost's "Le Jardin Secret" [1897][10].

Wed. June 29. Fine and hot. Reading [Georg] Brandes: "Moderne Geister" [1882].- Letter from Bullen, civilly concerned about my financial worries, but offering no suggestion.

Thursd. June 30. Fine and hot.

Frid. July 1. Fine; rain at sunset.- Eczema still troubling me. Note from the lawyer, Brewster, who is vainly trying to make a settlement of affairs. Sent off my bag to Worcester Park, to Wells's.

Sat. July 2. Fine. By train to Worcester Park. The Pinkers to dine with us.

Sund. July 3. Fine. In morning began to learn bicycle, on hired machine. Tumbles and bruises, but managed to ride a little.

Mond. July 4. Fine. Sore from head to foot, but progress with bicycle. Wells a good and patient teacher[11]. - Yesterday we went to a party at G. Steevens's, the war correspondent, Merton Abbey. Present, Richmond Ritchie, John Collier and wife (d[aughter] of Huxley, and sister of Collier's first wife); d[aughter] of Sir F. Pollock, Hind, editor of *Academy,* Miss

Jane Harrison, the Lecturer on Greek Art, and others. Mrs Steevens an amazing creature, with the voice of a coal-heaver.

Tuesd. July 5. Fine. Learnt to mount and dismount. Aching terribly. Reading Wells's "When the Sleeper Wakes", in proof.

Wed. July 6. Fine. In afternoon came the Marriott-Watsons, on tricycle. To dine , Mr and Mrs Sidney Low.- *A visit from Mlle Edith Fleury*[12], *who wants to translate "New Grub Street".*

Thursd. July 7. Fine. Much progress with bicyle. Dined at the Pinkers'.

Frid. July 8. Fine. Rode in morning with Wells and Mrs W. to Epsom, and ordered a machine, at Hersey's, for £14.

Sat. July 9. Cloudy, but fine. Left Heatherlea at 8am., and with Wells and wife rode all the way home to Dorking, getting here at 10 o'clock. Utterly worn out, but very glad to have achieved this business. Can descend hill with feet on rests. Found Mrs. Boughton all right. The Wells's ate lunch, and rode back home.

Sund. July 10. Dull, and cold wind. In afternoon cycled to Holmwood Station and back; then down thro' Dorking and a mile along Reigate Road, and back home. Very much at ease on the machine.- Wrote to Mlle Fleury.- Thinking about "The Crown of Life".

Mond. July 11. Dull. A little cycling. Grant Richards writes that he is thinking about my proposal.

Tuesd. July 12. Fine and hot. Two hours' cycling. Made cuts in "New Grub St." for Mlle Fleury.

Wed. July 13. Shower in morning, then very fine.

Thursd. July 14. Fine and hot. Send money for W[alter]'s clothing to Wakefield. Wrote to Miss Orme, and to Henry Hick. Thinking out beginning of my book.

Frid. July 15. Terribly hot. Made a beginning of "The Crown of Life".

Sat. July 16. Hot.- New beginning of "Crown". Cycled in evening from 6 to 8.

Sund. July 17. Hot.- Worked all day.

Mond. July 18. Hot. Did 1½p. Ride in evening to Leigh and Betchworth.- Congratulatory letter from F.W.H. Myers about my "Dickens". Replied to him.

Tuesd. July 19. Hot and cloudy. Did 1p.

Wed. July 20. Hot and fine. Heard from 90 Mansfield Road that they insist on E. leaving their house as soon as possible. Of course. Wrote to her that I cannot find her new lodgings. If she gives up the child, she may live where she likes.- Recd 4 copies of "The Whirlpool" from America.

Thursd. July 21. Dull. Wrote 1½p. Reading Meredith's "Modern Love" [1862], and "Le Lys Rouge" by Anatole France [1894].- *Mlle Fleury writes from Suffolk that she will visit me here on the 26th, to talk about "Demos", etc.-* Wrote to Stokes of New York, asking them to send "The Whirlpool" to Dr Zakrzewska and to Martha Barnes.

Frid. July 22. Rainy in afternoon. Did a little more than 1p.

Sat. July 23. Fine. In afternoon to Worcester Park, and back by late train.

Sund. July 24. Fine and hot. In morning wrote 1p. Afternoon cycled to Rusper and back—some 18 miles. Finished "Le Lys Rouge".

Mond. July 25. Dull and close. Letter from Georges Art, in which he complains bitterly that Mlle Fleury has taken from him the chance of translating "New Grub Street". Replied, explaining my innocence in the matter.- Wrote about 1p.

Tuesd. July 26. Fine. *At 11.28 came Mlle Fleury, to spend the day with me; went away by the 8.35.* She has agreed with S[mith] E[lder] & Co. for translation of "New Grub Street" and will publish either in the *Débats* or the *Temps*—both want to get it. Told me of her friendship with Mme de Musset, sister of Alfred; and with Mme Sacher-Masoch. A sweet and intelligent creature, this Mlle Fleury. She brought me a photograph of Mme A. Daudet. I gave her several of my books.

Wed. July 27. Close and dull. Trying vainly to do work. Letter from O'Dunne, who is still in Rome; replied.

Thursd. July 28. Hot.

Frid. July 29. Hot. Walter arrived at Romney for his holiday.

Sat. July 30. Cool and fine. In afternoon cycled to Redhill, and back by Holmwood.

Sund. July 31. Lunched and dined with Mrs Williams, at Holmwood, where she has a cottage for the summer. Met one Laurence (treasurer of Temple) and one Bennet, pleasant man. Magnificent day.

Mond. Aug. 1. Hot. Rode to Shere and back.

Tuesd. Aug. 2. Hot. Suffering from eczema. Went to Epsom, and came back on my new bicycle, cost £14.

Wed. Aug. 3. High wind, hot. Rode back at night, with lamp, from Holmwood.

Thursd. Aug. 4. Wind and heat. Miss Orme writes that E. attacked her landlord and his wife with a stick, and a policeman had to be called. She then went and took lodgings at another house in same road.- Telegraphed to Brewster, to make appointment for to-morrow.

Frid. Aug. 5. Still windy. In morning rode to Betchworth. Brewster asks me to put off my coming to London till he writes again.- Reading Brunetière: "Le Roman Naturaliste" [1883].

Sat. Aug. 6. Storm, clouds gathering. Reading Quinet: "Lettres d'Exil" [1884].

Sund. Aug. 7. Day of heavy rain. Lunched with Bullen at Holmwood.

Mond. Aug. 8. Rainy and cold. Letter from Walter.

Tuesd. Aug. 9. Fine, but cool. In morning to Epsom, to get a new bar on my bicycle—the old one too low.

Wed. Aug. 10. Fine. Wrote beginning of my Preface to "Pickwick".

Thursd. Aug. 11. Fine. Wrote nearly 2pp.

Frid. Aug. 12. Terribly hot. Wrote 1p. In evening to Betchworth.

Sat. Aug. 13. Finished Pref. to "Pickwick"—but must write it again. Heat terrific. In evening to Reigate and home by Leigh.

Sund. Aug. 14. Heat terrible. Lunched at Mrs Williams', to meet Mr Ball.- Heard from H. Hick that Wells is lying ill at *his* house, having come over from Seaford; abcess in kidney. Wrote at once to H.G.

Mond. Aug. 15. Heat. Impossible to do anything.

Tuesd. Aug. 16. Fearful heat.- Reading [E.B.] Lanin's "Russian Characteristics" [1892].

Wed. Aug. 17. Cooler. Went early to London—to tailor's etc. Met mother at King's Cross, and back to Dorking at 5. Mother in excellent health and spirits.

Thursd. Aug. 18. Hot. Did 1½p. of "David Copperfield". Rode to Betchworth. Letter from Mrs. Wells, saying that H.G. is too ill even to write in pencil. Replied to her.

Frid. Aug. 19. Glaring hot. Worked. Sent the usual monthly rent to 90 Mansfield Road, though E. left a fortnight ago.

Sat. Aug. 20. Heat terrific. Worked a little.

Sund. Aug. 21. Same heat. Finished pref. to "David Copperfield"[13].

Mond. Aug. 22. Weather same; little rain at night. Began Pref. to "Dombey".

Tuesd. Aug. 23. Hot. Miss Collet came for afternoon. Did 1p.- Letter from Watts, saying that E.'s furniture was removed last Sat[urday], amid much uproar on her part. She has maliciously destroyed their front garden, tearing up creepers etc.

Wed. Aug. 24. Much cooler. Did 1p. Letter from Halpérine-Kaminsky, of the Lycée Condorcet, saying he is sending me his translation of Tolstoi's "Qu'est-ce que l'art?" and asking my opinion, for publication.

Thursd. Aug. 25. A perfect day. Hear that Wells is just able to get up. Finished Pref. to "Dombey", but must rewrite the last half-page.

Frid. Aug. 26. Dull and misty. Did nothing.

Sat. Aug. 27. Rainy. Went to London, and saw Brewster. He has been able to do nothing except move the furniture from Mansfield Rd to Maple's. E. demands a house of her own, *both* children, and legal separation. She has written an insulting and threatening postcard to Miss Orme, addressed "Bad Eliza Orme".- To tailor's and hatter's, and home at 6 o'clock.- On journey read "Qu'est-ce que l'art?" - Recd copies of "The Town Traveller" from Methuens.

Sund. Aug. 28. Fine, but showery. To Reigate in morning. Wrote letter to Halpérine-Kaminsky about Tolstoi's book.[14]

Mond. Aug. 29. Rainy. Began rewriting of pref. to "Pickwick".- Sent copies of "Town Traveller" to Bertz, Wells, Miss Collet and Justin McCarthy.

Tuesd. Aug. 30. "Pickwick".

Wed. Aug. 31. Finished "Pickwick". Went to London in afternoon, to Maple's Depository. Saw the furniture, and divided into what is to be sold, and what brought to Dorking.

Thursd. Sept. 1. Hot again. Reading Sabatier's Life of S. Francis [of Assisi, 1898]. Also, Pailleron's "Les Faux Ménages" [1869][15].

Frid. Sept. 2. Hot. Furniture came in afternoon. Charges, including removal from Mansfield Road, £8-1-6.

Sat. Sept. 3. Very hot. Arranging furniture. Evening ride to Redhill. Recd Keary's new novel—"The Journalist".- German lady writes for permission to translate "The Schoolmaster's Vision".- Clodd tells me that Andrew Lang praises my "Dickens" in *Longman's* [for September].

Sund. Sept. 4. Hot. To supper at Bullen's.

Mond. Sept. 5. Heat terrible. It is making me ill. Recd from Colles cheque for £214-12-11—Methuen's £250, less deductions for typing, telegrams, commission etc.

Tuesd. Sept. 6. Same heat. Ill with diarrhoea. Grant Richards writes again about my next book.

Wed. Sept. 7. Very unwell. In the afternoon, as I was lying down, the doorbell rang, and Mrs Boughton came up to tell me that E. and the boy were at the door. She had learnt my address from Maples. Happily, there was no scene. I gave her to understand that our parting was final, but that I should not take Alfred away from her as long as she keeps well. The poor little child is now in knickerbockers; he looked bright, but pale; had walked all from the station on this day of terrific heat, but did not seem overtired. I spoke not a word to him, and he hardly looked at me. They had tea, and set off for the station again.- So, this event I have so feared is over. She promises not to come again, but—
Wrote to Grant Richards, promising him option of my next book for immed[iate] payment of £25.

Thursd. Sept. 8. Better. Weather a trifle cooler. Yesterday hottest day of year—94° in shade in London.

Frid. Sept. 9. No change. Idleness.

Sat. Sept. 10. Grant Richards pays £25 for option of 5 years' entire copyright of my next book; terms to be named by me.- Stedman (of Methuens) writes to say that "The Town Traveller" has sold already about 1400 in England, and 1000 for Colonies. He also asks for my next book. I shall make him and Richards bid against each other.

Sund. Sept. 11. Hot and s.w. gale. Reading "Un Amour Idyllique" by [Armand] Charpentier [1894][16].

Mond. Sept. 12. Hot again. Drizzle at evening.

Tuesd. Sept. 13. Hot. No rain yet.

Wed. Sept. 14. Hot.

Thursd. Sept 15. Blazing hot.

Frid. Sept. 16. Terrible heat. Left Dorking by the 7.30 am. and got to New Romney at 11.30. Found Wells recovered, but shaky. He thinks of taking a house at Sandgate. Came back with Walter—journey 3.47 to 8.30, terrible.

Sat. Sept. 17. Heat worse. Impossible to do anything.

Sund. Sept. 18. Happily, morning of rain. Fine evening.

Mond. Sept. 19. Cool. Afternoon of rain, but very light.

Tuesd. Sept. 20. Hot, again. Mother and Walter returned to Wakefield. I saw them off by the 1.30 from King's Cross.

Wed. Sept. 21. Fine, cooler. In afternoon rode to Chilworth. Dined at Bullen's. Methuens write that they think of beginning with "Nickleby", so I must write that preface before getting to my novel.

Thursd. Sept. 22. Foggy. In evening did ½p. of "Nickleby" preface.

Frid. Sept. 23. Fine. Did 1½p. of "Nickleby".- After weeks of misery owing to lack of water supply, the water is at length coming on again.

Sat. Sept. 24. Fine. Finished "Nickleby". Have just got to the end of "La Nouvelle Héloïse" [by J.J. Rousseau].

Sund. Sept. 25. Very fine. Lunched and dined at Bullen's. Sidney Lee and McCormick there. In afternoon walked to Coldharbour.

Mond. Sept. 26. Fine, colder. Thinking over "The Crown of Life".- Reading [Théophile] Gautier's "Fortunio" [1838].

Tuesd. Sept. 27. Fine.

Wed. Sept. 28. Fine. Had Bullen and the Miss Listers to dinner[17].

Thursd. Sept. 29. At evening, and all night, heavy rain.- A leader in [*Daily*] *Chronicle* apropos of letter from a man objecting to Christopher Parish as representative of clerkdom [in *The Town Traveller*].

Frid. Sept. 30. Dull. Correspondence in *Chronicle* on minor clerks, mostly abusive of me.

Sat. Oct. 1. Fine. *Chronicle* correspondence continues.

Sund. Oct. 2. Fine. Dined at Bullen's. In morning a long and glorious ride to Rudgwick. Reading [G.J.] Holyoake's "Sixty Years of an Agitator's Life" [1892].

Mond. Oct. 3. Fine. No *Chronicle* letters.

Tuesd. Oct. 4. Fine, hot. *Chronicle* correspondence resumed. Reading Bourget's "Le Disciple" [1889].

Wed. Oct. 5. Dull, misty. Dined at Bullen's.- Letter to say that Gabrielle will perhaps come over from Paris on Thursday. *Chronicle* still.

Thursd. Oct. 6. Sunless, misty. Gabrielle not able to come till Saturday.- *Chronicle*.[18]

Frid. Oct. 7. Gloom. Reading "Obermann" [by Etienne Pivert de Sénancour, 1804].

Sat. Oct. 8. Gloom; sky breaking at evening; Gabrielle crossed by the Newhaven boat. I met her at E. Croydon—train 40mn late. We got home at 9 o'clock.

Sund. Oct. 9. Bright early, then rain. Talk all day—of the future. G. read me some poems of Victor Hugo; I to her some Tennyson.

Mond. Oct. 10. Misty. In afternoon, walk with G. to the town. Reading aloud at night from Browning.

Tuesd. Oct. 11. Misty. Fine afternoon; walk with G. to Glory Wood. Reading at night.- Colles sends word that [Georges] Art offers 250 fr. for right to translate "The Town Traveller". Accepted it.- Recd copy of "Tony Drum [, a Cockney Boy]" by [Edwin] Pugh, and Clodd's "Tom Tit Tot".

Wed. Oct. 12. Fine. In morning walk with G.- Evening: Tennyson and Poe.

Thursd. Oct. 13. Dull. Walk and talk.

Frid. Oct. 14. Fine. Morning walk with G. to Redlands Wood.

Sat. Oct. 15. The leave-taking: a morning of rain and fog. We left Dorking at 9, but, by mistake, got into the London express, and were carried to London Bridge; when we wanted to stop at E. Croydon. Just, only just, caught the boat-train to Newhaven. G.'s luggage had come to Croydon, meanwhile, but could not be found, so we went on without it. At Newhaven, good-bye. I returned to Croydon, and learnt that luggage was being sent on to Paris.- We have decided that our life together shall begin next spring.

Sund. Oct. 16. Gloom and mist, ending in heavy rain. Reading [Paul] Mariéton's book on George Sand and Musset [*Une Histoire d'Amour,* 1897][19].- Wrote to G.; also to Alg, to Clodd and to Wells.

Mond. Oct. 17. Violent rain and wind. Preparing for "The Crown of Life". Letter from G. and Mme Fleury.

Tuesd. Oct. 18. Gale continues. Made serious beginning of book, and did 3pp.- Wrote to Mme F., and to G.- Reading Michelet's "Les Femmes de la Révolution".

Wed. Oct. 19. Rain. Did 2½pp.

Thursd. Oct. 20. Rainy to fine. My old hours of work: 9-1 and 5-8. Did 3pp. Sent a card to G.- Letters from Margaret and Walter.

Frid. Oct. 21. Dull. Did 2½pp. Letters from G. and Miss Collet.- Colles sends cheque for "The Peace Bringer" in this month's *Lady's Realm.*

Sat. Oct. 22. Gale. Very warm. Did 3pp., finishing Chapter IV. Excellent week's work.

Sund. Oct. 23. Fine. Had a bicycle ride in afternoon; but very muddy.

Mond. Oct. 24. Fine. Wrote 2½pp. Being still pestered by my eczema, I wrote to Dr. T. Robinson, asking for appointment to see him on Wednesday.- Oppressed by hateful talk in the newspapers about war bet. France and England, over contemptible Fashoda business. This would be, to us, a disaster indeed.

Tuesd. Oct. 25. Dull. Wrote 2pp. Letter from G.- Dr Robinson appoints 11 to-morrow.

Wed. Oct. 26. Fine. Pestered by my eczema all night. Went up to see Robinson, and had long talk. He gave me some lotions, and forbade bath! Says I may eat what I like. We shall see. I rather doubt whether this treatment will be any better than the other.

Thursd. Oct. 27. Dull. A ride in afternoon. Did 3pp.

Frid. Oct. 28. Fine. Ride in afternoon. Did 3pp. Reading Mérimée's "Chronique du Règne de Charles IX".

Sat. Oct. 29. Rain. Did 2pp.- Letter from G., who has sold transln of "Our Mr Jupp" to the *Monde Moderne.* They want a sketch of my life, which she has written [published in May 1901]. She says that "Eve's Ransom" appeared in volume the other day (Lévy).- Wrote to her.

Sund. Oct. 30. Wild storm. Reading a little of Victor Hugo's poetry. Wrote to G.

Mond. Oct. 31. Rain and shine. Did 3½pp.

Tuesd. Nov. 1. Brilliant day. In afternoon came [W.M.] Evans. Headache.

Wed. Nov. 2. Great gale. Evans left at 12.30.- In evening wrote 1p.- Letter from G.

Thursd. Nov. 3. Stormy. Mrs Williams came for the afternoon. No work.- Tormented by newspaper threats of war with France. If it breaks out G. and I will go at once to Switzerland.

Frid. Nov. 4. Very fine. Did 3pp. Wrote to G.- Man [Greenough White] writes congratulations from Sewanee, Penn[sylvania]. G. sends a copy of the *Gaulois,* with her translation of my "Two Collectors".

Sat. Nov. 5. Beautiful day. Did 2½pp.

Sund. Nov. 6. Glorious day. Ride in morning to Ockley, and round by Gomshall. Wrote to G., to Wells, and to the man of Sewanee. Going through Carlyle's French Revolution, on Sundays.

Mond. Nov. 7. Fine. Wrote 2½pp.

Tuesd. Nov. 8. Incredible day; warm and clear as summer. Did 2½pp. Reading "Récits des Temps Mérovingiens" [by Augustin Thierry, 1840].

Wed. Nov. 9. Very fine. Rewrote 1p. of yesterday, and did 1½more. Good ride in afternoon. Letter from G., from Nevers, and from Maman. Postcard to G.

Thursd. Nov. 10. Very fine. Wrote 2½pp.- Mlle Blaze de Bury writes for "The Town Traveller", for an article. Sent her a copy.

Frid. Nov. 11. Thick mist all day. Did 3pp.

Sat. Nov. 12. Fog. In afternoon came Clodd, to spend night here.

Sund. Nov. 13. Brilliant day. In morning Clodd and I walked over to Box Hill, to see Meredith. He, far from well, sat with the type-written copy of the dramatization of "The Egoist" on his knees—in which he has little faith. Talked of "big-bottomed" Saxondom, and of *prestige* as an element of victory, with abundant illustration from Napoleonic and other wars.- I left at 11.30, and walked to Dorking station to meet Roberts, back from S. Africa. Clodd came back to lunch. Told Roberts about my private plans.-

Sent letter as usual to G.; postcard from her, at Nevers. She returns to Paris on Monday.

Mond. Nov. 14. Fine. Did 3pp.- Reading Michelet's "La Mer".

Tuesd. Nov. 15. Fog. Did 2pp. Eczema maddening still.

Wed. Nov. 16. Mist and sun. Did 3pp. Letter from O'Dunne. From G.

Thursd. Nov. 17. Fog all day. Did 3pp. Letter from Mrs Williams, saying that she has had scarlet-fever. Whale writes inviting me to Blackheath for night of Omar dinner.

Frid. Nov. 18. Fine. Did 3pp. Sent parcel of books to Mrs Williams.

Sat. Nov. 19. Fine. Did 3pp.

Sund. Nov. 20. Fine. Cycled morning and afternoon—short rides. Finished Carlyle's "Revolution". Wrote to G. and to Mme Fleury.

Mond. Nov. 21. Gabrielle's birthday. Horrid fog and rain; no daylight. Did 3pp. Reading the extravagantly praised "Aylwin" by Theodore Watts. Dull mechanism.

Tuesd. Nov. 22. Very fine and cold. Birthday: age 41. Telegram of congratulations from Justin McCarthy. Letter from G. and Maman. Went up to London, to see Dr Robinson. Have to smear myself with ointment for four days.

Wed. Nov. 23. Ceaseless rain and wind. Rewrote 1p. and did 2 more. Maddening torment of itching all day.

Thursd. Nov. 24. Ceaseless rain. Yesterday a great snowstorm in Midlands and North.- Wrote 2pp.- Sent "Aylwin" to Alg, who has asked me for it.- Irritation perhaps a trifle better than yesterday. Wrote to Miss Collet and Miss McCarthy.

Frid. Nov. 25. Rain and sun. Did only 1p. Eczema terrible, and could not work in evening.

Sat. Nov. 26. Dull. wrote 2pp. Irritation not quite so bad. Wrote to Dr Robinson, to report progress. Card from G.

Sund. Nov. 27. Fine. Pinker came, and agreed to do the business of "The Crown of Life".

Mond. Nov. 28. Thick fog and rain all day. Feeling quite ill with my eczema. No work done.

Tuesd. Nov. 29. Unable to do anything.

Wed. Nov. 30. Fine. Went to London, and got a new prescription from Dr Robinson.- Letter from G.

Thursd. Dec. 1. Cloudy. Prescription successful; much better to-day, but for lack of sleep cannot work yet.

Frid. Dec. 2. Gale. My torment a little diminished. Got to work again; destroyed and rewrote the last 2pp.

Sat. Dec. 3. Gale. Maddened by itching, but eczema getting better. Wrote 2pp.

Sund. Dec. 4. Gale. Things the same. Long letter in French to G.- Reading Michelet's "L'Oiseau".

Mond. Dec. 5. Gale and rain. Did 2pp. Itching the same—a cursed experience.

Tuesd. Dec. 6. Gale and rain. In morning did 1p. Afterwards, racking headache. Hardly ever get a couple of hours continuous sleep at night.

Wed. Dec. 7. Rain in morning, then fine. Did 2pp.- Wrote to Rev. Greenough White, of Sewanee, to acknowledge *Sewanee Review,* with his paper on "The Whirlpool" in it.[20]

Thursd. Dec. 8. Very fine. In afternoon walked up to Ranmore. Did 3pp. Recd a copy of Justin H[untly] McCarthy's "History of the U. States". Copy of *Baltimore Sun,* with review of "Town Traveller", and letter from O'Dunne.

Frid. Dec. 9. Fine. Did 3pp. Good walk in afternoon. Reading "Life of Jerome Cardan" [by W.G. Waters, 1898].- Wrote to Walter, for his birthday to-morrow, and sent him a box of bricks.

Sat. Dec. 10. Fine, but dull. Did 2pp. Postcard from G.

Sund. Dec. 11. Fine, dull. In afternoon walked over to Meredith's. Stayed only quarter of an hour, as Forbes Robertson came to talk over dramatization of "The Egoist".- Wrote to G.

Mond. Dec. 12. Heavy sky. Did 2pp.

Tuesd. Dec. 13. Mist and cold. Did 3pp.- Sent to Wakefield my quarterly £10, and £3-2 for small outlays on Walter.- Reading Michelet's "L'Amour", and Gyp's "Leurs Ames".- Really think the eczema is dying away at last. Troubles me still at night, but not much in day-time.

507

Wed. Dec. 14. Dull. Did 2pp.

Thursd. Dec. 15. Very fine. Did 1p. An hour's ride in morning. Reading [Harold] Frederic's "Gloria Mundi" [1898].

Frid. Dec. 16. Muggy again. Went up to London in morning, and lunched at McCormick's, who took me afterwards to see his brother-in-law in the City, who gave me information about the business of a Russian corn-merchant for my book. Bought presents for Gabrielle and Wakefield.- Evening, Omar dinner. Sat on left of L.F. Austin, the President. Some talk with Frankfort Moore the novelist. Home with Whale to Blackheath.

Sat. Dec. 17. Muggy. Of course not a wink of sleep last night. To lunch at Blackheath came Mrs Clifford. Her stories of early friendship with Kipling, how he read to her "Without Benefit of Clergy"—excitedly seizing her hand at the end.- Home by 7 o'clock. Found parcel from Gabrielle, containing toy for Walter, little present for Mrs Boughton, and Caramels, from Maman, for me. Also photograph of G. at age of 5, and in costume of Mascarille.- Enraged to find here a summons to serve on the Petty Jury at Kingston, on Jan. 3rd.

Sund. Dec. 18. Fine, warm—birds singing as in spring. Wrote to G. and a lot of other letters, among them to Hornung and Miss Barnes.

Mond. Dec. 19. Fine, colder. Did 2pp.

Tuesd. Dec. 20. Fine, frosty. Did 3pp. Eczema greatly better,- George Whale advises me to send the sheriff a doctor's certificate as excuse for non-attendance at Kingston. Wrote to Childcott for one.- Recd circular from a Committee getting up fund for Harold Frederic's widow and four legitimate children. As the youngest of these children is 10, and the eldest 20, I wrote to the Sec[retary, John Stokes,] asking whether anything is to be done to help the other family of young children, whose position is in every way much harder.

Wed. Dec. 21. Foggy. Making up presents in parcels. Did 3pp. Letter from G.- The "Frederic" Secretary replies that there is a separate movement for the aid of the illegitimate family, and that Miss Lyon is going to practise as a Christian Scientist.- Wrote to Miss Collet and Miss Orme.

Thursd. Dec. 22. Very fine. Did 3pp.- Sent off presents to Wakefield and to Paris. Paid Brewster £24—E.'s allowance up to end of this year. Since middle of November it has been raised from 35/- to £2 a week, without my consent. Sent £2-2 to each of the Frederic families.- Reading Daudet's "Soutien de Famille".

Frid. Dec. 23. Very fine. Cycled once more. Did 2pp.

Sat. Dec. 24. Fog. Paid my rent and gave notice of leaving the house. Wrote 2pp.- Present from Miss Collet of "Cranford" [by Mrs Gaskell, 1853].

Sund. Dec. 25. A most wonderful morning. Bright sun, blue sky with little white clouds, clear horizon, warm west breeze. Cycled to Reigate and Leigh. Afternoon, dull. Read "Cranford".

Mond. Dec. 26. Dull. In morning disturbed by receipt of an anonymous letter, hinting that E. has relations with some man. No signature, no address; post-mark "Paddington". Says "you can have the name if you wish". But how? Decided to insert advt in *Daily Mail,* asking writer of letter to let me hear again. Sent letter to Brewster. In evening did 2pp.- Card from G.

Tuesd. Dec. 27. Furious gale all night and to-day, with torrents of rain to-day. Did only 1p.

Wed. Dec. 28. Fine, sunny. Mrs Boughton gone to a funeral. Did 2pp. Letter from G.- Recd from Justin McCarthy his "Modern England".- My advt is in the *Daily Mail* to-day.

Thursd. Dec. 29. Gale and rain in morning. Did 2pp.- Stokes, Frederic's executor, acknowledges the 2 gu[ine]as for the younger children, and says he should like to see me. Ask him for next Sunday. Letter from Walter.

Frid. Dec. 30. Very fine. Did 1½p.

Sat. Dec. 31. Rain all day. Did 1½p. Planned out all the last portion of the book. Reading [Gaston] Boissier's "La Fin du Paganisme" [1891]. See in paper the death of Miss Collet's father[21]; wrote to her.

1899

Sund. Jan. 1. Rain and wind. At lunch time came Stokes. He made it clear to me that Kate Lyon is an admirable woman, who saved Frederic from sheer drinking and has enabled him to do all his work. The three children are in Hampshire, with their governess, who has just been married; money is needed to support them till their mother can do so. The behaviour of the neighbours when the scandal broke out was vile; no one could be got to do any work at the house, for love or money; Stokes (the executor) had to get a commissionaire from London. Mrs Stephen Crane, who lives near, has had the children for four months, since Frederic's breakdown. Stokes showed me the last MS chapter of an unpublished novel "The Market Place". Very small writing; 800 words to quarto page.

Mond. Jan. 2. Snow and sleet and sun. Did 2pp. Letter from Mrs Stephen Crane, thanking me for my cheque for the children; wrote to her. Letter from Miss Collet, about her father's death—quite painless.

Tuesd. Jan. 3. Fine. The Clerk of the Peace at Kingston returns my medic[al] certif[icate], saying it must be verified by a witness. Wrote in reply that I could not do this, now, in time—as Sessions began this morning; and added that I thought my name would have been sufficient guarantee of honourable behaviour.- Perhaps foolish to have written thus.- Did 2pp.

Wed. Jan. 4. Dull. Did 2½pp. Letter from G.- Eczema troublesome again.

Thursd. Jan 5. A wonderful day, cloudless and warm. Did 1½p. In afternoon up to Ranmore.
   Wrote to G.

Frid. Jan. 6. Rain. Did 3pp. Am not fined yet for not attending at Kingston, so suppose my letter was effectual.

Sat. Jan. 7. Rainy. Rewrote a page in earlier part of book. In afternoon to Stokes's, at Purley. Pleasant people; two nice little children. Lot of talk about Frederic; brought away a scrap of his notes for "Gloria Mundi". Home at 8.

Sund. Jan. 8. Lovely day. Letter from G., and wrote to her. In afternoon long walk. Wrote to Thomas Hodgkin, asking if he can direct me to authorities about the economic conditions of 6th cent[ury].

Mond. Jan. 9. Fine. Went to London, and took my MS (the whole book all but 3 Chapters) to Pinker, the agent, to get it type-copied, and set negotiations in train.

Tuesd. Jan. 10. Fine. Eczema bad. Did nearly 2pp.- Worn out with want of sleep.

Wed. Jan. 11. Rain. Notice from the accursed Quarter Sessions that I was fined £2, which can only be got out of by sending an affidavit. Card from G., her father very ill.- Wrote 2pp.

Thursd. Jan. 12. Furious gale. Wrote 2pp. Recd 11 chaps. of typescript from Pinker.- In afternoon swore an affidavit, and sent it to Kingston. Half a guinea thrown away! - Postcard to G.

Frid. Jan. 13. Gale. Did 1p. In evening recd news of death of G.'s father. Telegraphed to her, and wrote.

Sat. Jan. 14. Fine. Wrote 3pp.- Reading the typed copy of "Crown of Life".

Sund. Jan. 15. Rain and gloom. My rascally doctor here has sent bill for £9-14-6. Paid it. Worked over the typed copy.- Wrote to G.

Mond. Jan. 16. Rain. In morning wrote 1p., and *finished "The Crown of Life".*

Tuesd. Jan. 17. Fine. Correcting type. Re-reading "One of Our Conquerors" [by Meredith, 1891]. Wrote to Walter, and to G.

Wed. Jan. 18. Dull, gale. Finished correction of typescript.

Thursd. Jan. 19. Gale and rain. Stedman writes to express delight at my preface to "Pickwick".- Thought out a short story: "A poor Gentleman".- Letter from G. Wrote to her; also to Maman and to René.

Frid. Jan. 20. Gale and rain. Wrote 2½pp. of short story.

Sat. Jan. 21. Gale furious.

Sund. Jan. 22. Decided to go to Wakefield to-morrow.

Mond. Jan. 23 - Sat. Jan. 28. Spent at Wakefield. Frost and fog. The boy very well, and growing fast. Reads very well. Girls better in health, and doing well with their school. Alg was here a week or two ago, in very bad health. Nelly guaranteed to him £150 for the next six months, to enable him to rest. I contributed £50 of this.

Sat. Jan. 28. On way home, called at Miss Collet's, and had tea and supper. Dorking at midnight. Persuaded by Madge, have given up meat. Shall see the result in a few weeks.

Sund. Jan. 29. Fog. Reading Mérimée's "Une Correspondance Inédite".

Mond. Jan. 30. Dull. Trying vainly to get a short story, better than "A Poor Gentleman".

Tuesd. Jan. 31. Misty. Cycle ride in morning. Read Stevenson's "Inland Voyage" [1878], and "Travels with [a] Donkey [in the Cévennes]" [1879].

Wed. Feb. 1. Misty. Gravely troubled about the practical difficulties of next spring. Long letter from G. Unable to do any work.- Feeling of hollowness from my diet.

Thursd. Feb. 2. Went to see Miss Orme, to talk of anonymous letter. On to town, and tried to see Watts, E.'s former landlord, who is a private detective. Had to leave a note for him. Back at 5.

Frid. Feb. 3. Wonderful day of sun. Resumed my short story and did 2pp. Reading "Harry Richmond" [by Meredith, 1870].

Sat. Feb. 4. Gloom and wind. Finished "A Poor Gentleman" [published in the *Pall Mall Magazine,* October 1899].

Sund. Feb.5. Gloom. Read Gyp's "Tante Joujou". Wrote to Wells, and to G. Sent to Wakefield 10/- for girls' subscription to Parents' Union.

*   *   *

Tuesd. Feb. 21. A week's illness (sore throat) and small harassments. Since then have written Preface to "Bleak House", and begun that to "Oliver Twist". Weather wonderfully bright and mild; the other day, sent G. my first primrose from garden.

Wed. Feb. 22. Wonderful day of sunshine. Did 1p. In morning cycled to Leatherhead. Burnt a great mass of old papers.

Thursd. Feb. 23. A day like June. Finished "Oliver". Wrote to G.

*   *   *

A long hiatus. First part of it occupied with illness. Bad influenza, followed by relapse with pleurisy. Slow recovery; great weakness.

However, went on with my arrangements (all writing at an end) and on

Sat. March 22 [Doubtless a mistake for April 22] said good-bye to

Dorking. Mrs. Boughton remained to see the furniture removed to warehouse. (F. Kendall, High Street.) I am to pay 2/6 a week. Insured for £100.

Travelled to Willersey, where Madge and Walter are spending holiday.

Mond. May 1. Left Willersey, and came to Lewes. Put up at the White Hart, to wait till Gabrielle sends for me to Rouen. Found 2 postcards from her, proposing that I should go on Wednesday, the day she and Maman arrive there.

Tuesd. May 2. Idling. Telegram to put off my going till Saturday.

Wed. May 3. East wind. Reading "Hard Cash" [by Charles Reade, 1863]. Great difficulty in getting through the day.

Thursd. May 4. Bright sun and east wind. Card from G. They arrived at Rouen yesterday.

Frid. May 5. Same wind. In evening, as I sat at dinner, who should come in but [William] Rothenstein and a friend, who proved to be Walter Sickert.[1] Sickert lives at Dieppe, and has come over for a day with R. at Newhaven.

Sat. May 6. Brilliant sun, but same terrible wind. Sea roughish. Left by 11.30 boat, and had to roll about before Dieppe for an hour, waiting tide. Did not feel ill for a moment. Reached Rouen at 7 o'clock, and found G. and Maman at the Hôtel de Paris. Have a room next to theirs, looking over the quays.

Sund. May 7. Fine morning, but bitter wind. With G. and Maman went to Cathedral. The tomb with "Hic jacet cor Ricardi regis Anglorum".- Our fright over Maman's absence at lunch-time, she having left us to return by herself. Inquiry at pharmacies!- In the evening, our ceremony. Dear Maman's emotion, and G.'s sweet dignity.

Mond. May 8. Same wind. We saw Maman off to Paris at 3.30, then waited for our train at 4.50. Visited Joan of Arc's tower. Reached Fécamp about seven, and were met by vehicle. Beautiful drive of 12 kilom. to S. Pierre en Port. Just dark. Admirable hotel—Les Terrasses; glorious sea-view. Terms 5.50fr. a day each.

Tuesd. May 9. Suddenly, perfect weather, calm and warm. Spent day on shore, sitting and talking. There are two twaddling Englishmen here, no one else. Food excellent; perfect order and cleanliness.

Wed. May 10. Weather the same. Walks and talks.

Thursd. May 11. All day, though sky clear, masses of mist kept sweeping from the sea. At night, perfect and lovely calm. Our talk in the silence, after dinner. A few notes of the nightingale.- Sent card to Bertz.

*   *   *

Tuesd. May 16. Mostly fine weather. Ordered for 6 months the *Weekly Times*. Yesterday, posted to Stedman my Preface to "Nicholas Nickleby".

Thursd. May 18. Ordered *Athenaeum* for 13 weeks.

Mond. May 21. Two days of rain and storm; now fine again.- The Flora of the region seems identical with that of England. Spring flowers abundant. Bright yellow fields of colza. The enclosed farm-yards and orchards.

Sat. June 3. We came yesterday to Paris from Veules (near S. Valéry) where we had spent a week. Country much less interesting than at S. Pierre, but a good beach. Interesting little village of Sotteville-sur-Mer, close by. The hotel not very good; rooms small. We regretted S. Pierre with its beautiful views and walks. Maman delighted to see us. A tropical railway journey.
    Found here cheque for £9 from *Literature* for "Fate and the Apothecary". Spent this morning in writing letters, and in correcting proof of Pref. to "Nickleby".

Mond. June 5. Thought out a story "The Scrupulous Father".

Tuesd. June 6. Very hot. In morning, wrote 1p.- In afternoon G. and I called upon her aunt Pauline. In evening we dined with Mme Lardin de Musset, sister of Alfred. She lives on 4th floor, near Madeleine; we spent evening in her bedroom—the red-draped bed a handsome piece of furniture in corner. In a niche of the dining-room a fine bust of Alfred. Portraits of him as child (one of him and Paul, together, as young boys.) Though about 80, Mme de Musset has no infirmities; very clear of speech and firm of mind. She said to me that I had not disappointed her expectation. (G. is a dear friend of hers.) She had seen Balzac, but did not know him well; at times he was *bavard*.- Thus, my first dinner in Paris is on the date of my marriage with G.- the 6th of the month.
Wed. June 7. In morning, rewrote my first page, and a little more.

Thursd. June 8. Wrote 1p. and ½.

Frid. June 9. Wrote 1½p. In evening Miss Ward (Mlle Miss) dined here. Weather cooler.

Sat. June 10. Finished my story. Recd cheque for £15 odd from Colles, for "The Elixir" in *Idler*. Also says he has sold "At Nightfall" in America [to *Lippincott's Magazine*] for $65, and hopes to sell in England. Letter from Miss McCarthy, saying that the "Reminiscences" have been found at Fécamp. Her father has undergone successful operation for cataract.

Frid. June 16. Began my Pref. to "Old Curiosity Shop", and wrote 1p.- Yesterday received at last the 2 vo[lumes] of McCarthy's "Reminiscences",

514

which have been in some ridiculous way detained at Fécamp, though fully addressed to S. Pierre en Port. Wrote to McC[arthy] about them. Sent Pinker my story "The Scrupulous Father" [published in the *Cornhill Magazine,* February 1901, and the New York *Truth,* December 1900].

Mond. June 19. Finished Pref. to "Old Curiosity Shop".

Tuesd. June 20. Began Pref. to "Martin Chuzzlewit".

Frid. June 23. Finished "Chuzzlewit". Sent cheque for £11-17-8 to Nellie— W[alter]'s money.

Mond. June 26. Finished Pref. to "Barnaby Rudge".

Thursd. June 29. Began my book of travel "By the Ionian Sea".

Frid. June 30. Finished 3rd chapter.

Tuesd. July 4. Finished 5th chapter. Wrote to Bullen to ask for last year's accounts.

Wed. July 5. In afternoon with G. to call on Mme Herwegh, widow of Georg Herwegh, who, at age of 82, still supports herself by giving lessons. She gave us reminiscences of Heine—who, it seems, looked much like a banker, and talked in a rather doleful, drawling voice. Fine portrait of Herwegh in the poor little room.

Sat. July 8. Have written 7 chaps.- At last received payment from S.E.R. Co. for my books which they lost - £2-14-9.

Tuesd. July 11. Sent Pinker the first 9 chaps.- In evening had letter from him, in which he tells me that the typescript of "Crown of Life", going to America, was wrecked a month ago on the liner "Paris", and only a few days ago dispatched again. He has had infinite trouble to recover it from hands of authorities, when saved from the wreck. It is slightly stained with sea-water.

*   *   *

Frid. July 28. It is about ten days since we left Paris. We went first of all to Samoens, in the valley of the Giffre, and there (at the Hôtel des Glaciers) spent a week. Elevation is about 750m. Glorious scenery, but a damp situation. Made an excursion one day to Sixt, at the valley head, where is a good hotel in an old monastery—very little frequented. Saw the great curved mountain side, covered with cascades, which is called Fer à Cheval. From Samoens we travelled to Trient, in one day, leaving at 5am., and getting to Trient at 10pm. Had arranged for rooms at Hôtel des Glaciers, but were badly served in this matter; so next morning changed to the Hôtel des Alpes, where we are very comfortable (4fr. a day). Elevation 1300ft. Fine railway journey from Annemasse to Martigny, along south shore of Lake of Geneva: exquisite light. A long stop at Evian, whence we looked across to Lausanne. Beautiful position of St Gingolf, a little further on. From Martigny a drive of four hours up the great mountain to the Col de la Forclaz, when night fell; then down steep descent, for 300m., to village of Trient.

In front of the hotel a roaring torrent, coming down from the Glacier de Trient—the last glacier eastward of the Mont Blanc range. The glacier itself gleaming up against the sky.

To-day resumed work on "By the Ionian Sea", and wrote 1p.

Sat. July 29. Wrote a little more than 1p. Letter from Miss Collet, who has been for a holiday to Christiania.

The peasants are getting in their hay from the mountain slopes below the fir woods. They make huge bundles in a canvas wrapper, and carry them home on their heads.- The miserable little wooden cottages.

Here the flowers are all English. Abundant harebells. Wild thyme and mint. Corn cockles.

Sund. July 30. Wrote 1p. Weather glorious all these days.

Tuesd. Aug. 1. In afternoon walked up to the pass called La Forclaz. Two hotels there; one the Isselaz, the other Hôtel de la Fougère. Fine view over Trient valley.- Constant going of carriages, mostly with English people, from Martigny to Chamonix, by way of the Tête Noire.

Sat. Aug. 5. Left hotel at 7am., and ascended the Col de Balme. Took me a little more than 3 hours. At first, steep winding path through beautiful fir wood; afterwards, open mountain side, and melting snow in the nooks. At the top, a poor hotel. Magnificent view of Valley of Chamonix—of Mt Blanc the best that can be had, I should think. Frontier of France and Switzerland marked by a stone near hotel.- Rested two hours, and descended by 2.30. The Alpine rose is faded; could only find one flower. Height of the Col, 2300m.

At our hotel here is a certain M. Bovet, professor of French at Univy of Rome. Talk with him.

Wed. Aug. 9. Rain yesterday and to-day. This morning finished "By the Ionian Sea"—something less than 35 MS pages.

Sund. Aug. 13. Receiving proofs of "The Crown of Life". To-day sent Pinker second half of Calabrian MS.

In afternoon climbed to the village of *Les Jeurs*. Footpath turns off to left, up hill, just before the Tête Noire hotel. Winding climb of 20 minutes, often by precipices; then a level path through the village, which consists of a score of little chalets, dotted over mountain side. (The wooden tiles on roofs, held down by big stones.) Remember the wooden barn partly filled with new hay—exquisite scent. Opposite great rugged-topped mountain, stony, grey, covered with fire [illegible], and furrowed with torrent-ravines; deep down, invisible in narrow ravine, the Eau Noire, flowing with soft, just audible murmur, to join the Trient. To left, in Chamonix direction, valley closed by the double-peaked Buet, glaciers on its sides; to right, Fin Haut, seeming to cling on the midside of its great mountain, with white torrents leaping past it into profound gorge. Its white hotels and church tower. Exquisite soft haze. Ceaseless sound of chirping grasshoppers. About the village, little plots of corn or vegetables, with stone barriers to prevent earth slipping down mountain. Great ribs of rock everywhere protruding. The grass (after hay harvest) a brilliant emerald.- Only one or two women to be seen. Profound quiet. Everywhere wild thyme growing and ferns, with the myrtilles—bilberries?

Wed. Aug. 16. Finished correcting proofs of "Crown of Life". My best book yet for style. Began short story, "Humplebee" [published in the *Anglo-Saxon Review,* March 1900].

Mond. Aug. 21. M. and Mme Bovet left; G. and I accompanied them on their walk to Salvan, as far as first village. Mme Bovet took with her "The Nether World", which she is reading. Excellent people. Bovet is only 29 years old; I took him for 38. Like these people very much. They waited 6 years to be married, owing to opposition of Mme Bovet's mother, who still refuses to see Bovet. Their home at Lausanne. Theodore David, the sculptor, is doing a bust of an old woman in the village—very good.

Remember the church carillon.

Recd and corrected typescript of second half of "By the Ionian Sea".- G. and I have been photographed among the rocks by M. Laperrière, a Paris photographer who is staying here. Going to send Bertz a copy.

*　　*　　*

Aug. 30. Left Trient at 7.30am. for Martigny, driving over the Forclaz. Then by train to Berne. Passing saw Chillon, Montreux etc. Passed night at Berne—Hôtel de la Croix Fédérale.

Aug. 31. By 8am. train to Lucerne, and thence by boat, on lake of Four Cantons, to Flüelen. Thence by train to Airolo, to Hôtel Lombardi. Second-class pension, 5 francs.

Sept. 1. Walking about the country. The picturesque villages of Valle and Madrano. The difficult patois.

My delight in speaking Italian again.

Sept. 2. Walked to Brugnasco, half way to the Val di Piora. Rain this afternoon.

*　　*　　*

517

Sat. Sept. 9. Left Airolo, for Locarno. Yesterday, G. and I went up to Piora, a very severe climb of about 3½hrs. Through Brugnasco and Altanca, then up the gorge with waterfalls to the Val Piora, which is filled by the Lago Pitoni. Lombardi's Hotel stands just on edge of lake—no other houses. There we lunched. After lunch, splendid sunshine suddenly changed to violent storm; with hail which covered mountains like snow. We started back, and at Altanca had to shelter from violent downpour. On descent to Airolo from Brugnasco, all but lost the difficult path, and at the moment when night was falling! Might have been very serious.

Sund. Sept. 10. The Pension here very bad; we evidently ought to have gone to the Villa Righetti, which has a fine view (here none at all) and a large garden full of vines. It is custom at the Italian lakes for pensionnaires to help themselves to grapes in garden; hardly any in our garden here.- G. and I climbed up to the Madonna del Sasso (to-day is Nome di Maria.) Grand view of head of lake, which, by the bye, is being gradually filled up by the Ticino and the Maggia.

Sat. Sept. 16. Yesterday, we left the Villa Muralto, because of bad food, and moved to Hôtel Belvedere, high up the hill, where food is excellent. Bedroom looking onto mountain at the back, with terraced vines, and the Madonna del Sasso white in moonlight—also the shining white little stations of the Cross.- Walk last evening up mountain to Orselina and Brione.- Vain attempt to appoint meeting with M. D'Arcis[2] at Cannobio; he telegraphs this morning that he can't come.

Sund. Sept. 17. Glorious day. The garden here is very picturesque; in the middle a great magnolia, giving broad shade; then a lot of palmetti, agaves and flowering shrubs unknown to me. Many pergolas, heavy with fruit, and also pomegranates and a few lemon bushes. Bamboos. Peaches abundant. Every road about here on the mountain side is bordered with vineyards, and peaches can often be picked up, fallen from trees.

Remember a good *mot* of the man Simone, at Villa Muralto: "Le bon air vaut mieux que la bonne nourriture"—excellent, considering the meanness of his *pension.*

At sunset, the group of mountains at head of lake turn to warm colour, almost that of rose petals, with shadows of deep violet. The other mountains about the lake are entirely covered with verdure, a soft, deep green.

Tuesd. Sept. 19. G. and I took the 8 o'clock boat to Brissago. Thence walked to Cannobio, and up to the Badia, where we spent afternoon with the Recordon family.[3] The beautiful chestnut woods. Back at 7 o'clock.

Sat. Sept. 23. Left Locarno early, in heavy rain and cloud. Travelled to Lucerne, and spent night there, Hôtel Monopol.

Sund. Sept. 24. Day at Lucerne; dull, but no rain. Travelled to Paris by night express.

Mond. Sept. 25. Back at 13 Rue de Siam. Hope to get soon to work.

Wed. Sept. 27. Recd from Pinker cheque for £254-9-4—balance, after deductions, of advance English and American royalties on "Crown of Life". See that £1-9-9 is charged for salvage of the typescript wrecked on its way to America.- Sent cheque for £20 to Wakefield (2 quarters of Walter); also, cheque to London Lib[rar]y, and to Dr Lett. Ordered *Athenaeum* for 6 months.

Frid. Sept. 29. Began a new novel—name uncertain. Did about 1½p.

Sat. Sept. 30. Did 2½pp.

Sund. Oct. 1. Rain all day. Made a new beginning of my book (The Coming Man) and did 2pp. Reading the "Proverbes et Comédies" by Alfred de Musset.

Mond. Oct. 2. Nearly 3pp.

Tuesd. Oct. 3. 1½p. Wrote to Mrs Boughton, asking her to go to Dorking and sell furniture at the warehouse.

Wed. Oct. 4. Rewrote 1p. and did 1 more.

Thursd. Oct. 5. Great struggles with beginning of book. Wrote 4 pages. Have to destroy 1st chap.- Letter from Harold E. Gorst who says he is starting a weekly like the *Saturday* and wants articles from me. Replied, asking terms.

Frid. Oct. 6. Did 3pp.

Sat. Oct. 7. Did 2½pp.

Sund. Oct. 8. Did 2pp. In afternoon to call upon Mme Sacher-Masoch, the repudiated wife of the novelist, who married another woman in Heligoland. Has a son in business in London.

Mond. Oct. 9. Fine weather just now. Did 3pp.

Tuesd. Oct. 10. Did 2pp.

Wed. Oct. 11. Our servant, Louise, down with diphtheria, sent to hospital. Work stopped.- As Gorst offers only 30/- a column, replied that I couldn't write for him.- Card from Mrs Boughton, saying that, on Monday, she sold furniture to Sanford of Dorking, and had it removed yesterday morning.

Thursd. Oct. 12. No work. Recd Sanford's cheque for £16. Sent her expenses to Mrs Boughton.

Frid. Oct. 13. Had to make a new beginning of my book.

Sund. Oct. 15. Work hopeless during absence of servant. As Gorst has written again, offering £2-2 for column of 740 words I decided to do him an article. Began "Tyrtaeus" apropos of Swinburne's sonnet urging to war with the Transvaal.

Mond. Oct. 16. Finished "Tyrtaeus" and sent it off [published in the *Review of the Week,* November 4, 1899]. Louise has come back, and I once more began "The Coming Man".

Tuesd. Oct. 17. Did 2pp. Last night, young Sacher-Masoch called. Son of the novelist—about four and twenty.

Wed. Oct. 18. Did 2pp.

Thursd. Oct 19. Did 2pp.

Frid. Oct. 20. Did 2pp. In afternoon generally walk in the Bois.

Sat. Oct. 21. Did 2pp. Recd to-day proof of my article "Tyrtaeus". Also cheque for £9, payment with Colles's deduction, for Preface to "Pickwick". Yesterday came copies of "The Crown of Life". Sent presentations to Ibsen and to Tolstoi, also Bertz's copy.

Sund. Oct. 22. Wrote a lot of letters, and sent off copies of book to Miss Collet, Meredith, Justin McCarthy.

Mond. Oct. 23. Wrote 2pp. "Crown of Life" to Wakefield.

Tuesd. Oct. 24. Wrote 2½pp. Bad sore throat.

Wed. Oct. 25. Did 2pp. Robert Eustache and wife to dine. Didn't go out all day, because of throat. Note from Miss Collet, who is in Paris and wishes to call.

Thursd. Oct. 26. Did 2½pp. Letter from Shorter, offering £20 for a short story for his "Illustrated Newspaper for the Home" [*The Sphere*], first part of which is to appear in January. Shall do it. Cold the same.

Frid. Oct. 27. Did 2pp. In afternoon Miss Collet called.

Sat. Oct. 28. Did 2pp. Out for first time after my cold. See that poor old Grant Allen died last Wednesday—after horrible sufferings. I saw him last at an Omar dinner.

Sund. Oct. 29. A day of visiting, with G. First to Mlle [Chevalier] de la Petite Rivière, who is translating "The Whirlpool" [no record of publication]. Then to a Polish couple, musician and his wife, pleasant artistic people. Then to the Funck Brentanos—mother and daughter delightful women. Lastly to Mlle Read.[4]

Mond. Oct. 30. Did 1½p. In afternoon to Miss Collet, 28 Avenue de Friedland. She leaves for England on Wednesday.

Tuesd. Oct. 31. Wrote 2½pp.

Wed. Nov. 1. Did only 1p.

Thursd. Nov. 2. Did 2pp. Reading Balzac's "Mercadet" [1851-53].

Frid. Nov. 3. Did 3pp. Letter from Miss Collet, saying her copy of "The Crown of Life" has not reached her. Another loss in the post!

Sat. Nov. 4. Did only 1p. Reading [Victorien] Sardou's "Nos Intimes" [1861].

Sund. Nov. 5. In afternoon visits to Mme Edmond Saglio (wife of director of Musée de Cluny, where she lives) and the Augustin Monods. Afterwards called on [Théodore] David, the sculptor, Avenue de l'Observatoire.

Mond. Nov. 6. Did 2pp. Began Tolstoi's "La Guerre et la Paix".

Tuesd. Nov. 7. Did 2pp. Sent Methuen my Pref. to "Bleak House". Wrote reply to a letter from Clodd. Letter at night from Thomas Hardy, speaking with approval of my *Review of the Week* article.

Wed. Nov. 8. Did 3pp. Wrote to Hardy.

Thursd. No. 9. Did 2pp. Mme Sacher-Masoch to lunch. Alg writes that Chatto & Windus have bought his "Secret of the North Sea" for £55.

Frid.Nov. 10. Did 2pp. Wrote to Pinker about his proposed transfer of my books from L[awrence] & B[ullen] to Methuens.

Wed. Nov. 15. Days of disorder. Decided to put aside all I have written of "The Coming Man", for the present, and to begin an entirely new novel. Did 1p.

Sund. Nov. 19. Alas, alas! Once again a new beginning. Book to be called, perhaps "Oracles". Did 2pp.

Mond. Nov. 20. Did 3pp.

Tuesd. Nov. 21. G.'s birthday. Did nearly 4pp.

Wed. Nov. 22. My birthday. G. gave me a scarf-pin set with Roman coin. Did 3pp.

Thursd. Nov. 23. Did 1½p. Thinking of calling my book, not "Oracles", but "Among the Prophets".

Frid. Nov. 24. Did 1p.

Sat. Nov. 25. Did 3pp.

Tuesd. Nov. 28. Once again rebegan "Among the Prophets". Did 3pp. To-day recd copies of "The Crown of Life" from America.

Wed. Nov. 29. Had to interrupt work to write a short story for Shorter's new paper. Did 2pp. of "Snapshall's Romance". Sent American copies of "Crown of Life" to Miss Collet and Clodd, and gave one to Miss Ward.

Thursd. Nov. 30. Nearly finished "Snapshall", but found it useless. To dine at Mme de Musset's. Home at 1am.

Frid. Dec. 1. Up at usual hour, and rewrote the whole of "Snapshall", 4pp. [published as "Snapshall's Youngest" in *The Sphere,* February 17, 1900]. A good day's work.

1900

Feb. 14. For two months and a half have ceased to chronicle. A week ago I finished my novel, "Among the Prophets"; and have now sent it to be typewritten by a sister of Miss Ward at Birmingham. Yesterday and to-day wrote the Preface to "Sketches by Boz". Feeling much depressed by the S. African war, with its hateful motives, and ceaseless disasters. Reading very little. My novel is poor stuff, and I wish I could afford to destroy it—but I am sore pressed for money. Have had to stand guarantee to Alg for £100 with the Wakefield and Barnsby Bank.- Mother and Nelly have been very ill with influenza.- A week ago G. and I went to the Théâtre Français, and saw 3 pieces: "Le Passant" (Coppée)—"Le Bonhomme Jadis" (Murger) and "On ne badine pas avec l'amour". Tickets given us by Mme de Musset.

Mond. Feb. 19. Finished all my Dickens prefaces—Christmas Books being the last.

Tuesd. Feb. 20. Heard from Pinker that "By the Ionian Sea" is accepted by the *Fortnightly*. Serial rights 120 guineas.

*   *   *

Wed. March 14. Finished a short story—"The House of Cobwebs" [published in the *Argosy,* August 1900].

Tuesd. March 27. Finished a short story—"The Pig and Whistle" [published in the *Graphic,* Christmas 1904].

*   *   *

Sat. Ap. 21. On Ap. 2 I left Paris, to pass a month or so in England. Arriving in London, spent the night at Clodd's. Next days, saw Pinker, and on to Wakefield. Mother just recovering from bad influenza. Stayed at Wakefield some nine days. Cheerless weather, and, of course, had caught a bad cold. Then to Lincoln where I spent five days—Saracen's Head—and took many notes. Then to St Neots for a couple of days. Went over to Huntingdon, saw Cromwell's House and Hinchin[g]brook[e]—from outside. Weather meanwhile had suddenly changed to warmth and brightness of summer. Returned to London, and put up at Clodd's. Last night met Miss Collet at Writers' Club; then to join Clodd at Whitefriars' Club, Anderton's Hotel, Fleet St. Gilbert Parker in chair—a metallic, vulgar man. Caught a glimpse of Silas Hocking—an elderly man, very commonplace.- My cold nearly gone, but left eyelid badly swollen since I left Lincoln.

*　　*　　*

May 1, Tuesday. After a couple of days at Sandgate, with Wells (who showed me the foundations of the house he is building) I travelled to Newhaven, spent the night there, and to-day crossed to France. Found all well at home.- The first part of "By the Ionian Sea" appears in the new *Fortnightly.*

May 4. Since arriving, have had a sharp attack of intercostal rheumatism. In bed for two days.

Thursday, May 10. Began short story—"The Rash Miss Tomalin".- Card from Wells, from Amiens. He is cycling from Boulogne to Paris.

Sat. May 12. Finished story and sent to Pinker [published as "A Daughter of the Lodge" in the *Illustrated London News,* August 17, 1901].

*　　*　　*

Frid. May 25. Having let the flat to Exhibitioners for June, we left Paris for St Honoré-les-Bains (Nièvre) where we have taken the Villa des Roses for the whole summer—rent about £50. Left Gare de Lyon at 10.30, evening, and reached Vandenesse at 8 in morning, whence an hour's drive to St Honoré. Found the villa very nice. Large garden, in which we have use of all vegetables and fruit.

*　　*　　*

May 28, Monday. Made a beginning of "The Coming Man", and wrote about half a page.

Tuesd. May 29. Made a new beginning, and did 2pp. Weather magnificent.

Wed. May 30. Did 2pp. Better work, I think, than I have done since "New Grub Street". This place suits me well. I have a little bedroom for study, with a view of trees and hills. Blessed tranquillity without and within the house. Weather to-day cooler, tending to rain.

Thursd. May 31. Did 2pp. Yesterday received from Wells photographs of myself, taken when I was there. Wrote to Mrs Wells. Also to Roberts, who is at Veytaux, in Switzerland.

Frid. June 1. Did 2pp. Rain, clearing at evening. Pinker writes that Smith & Elder will not take over my books from Bullen. Chapman & Hall offer £130 for 7 years' right of the "Ionian Sea" volume. Accepted.

524

Sat. June 2. Did 1 1/2 p. In afternoon went over the Château de la Montagne.

Sund. June 3. Had to write for Methuen a page of Intr. to "Master Humphrey's Clock".

Mond. June 4. Destroyed Sat.'s work. Did 3pp.

Tuesd. June 5. Did 2pp.- All about here the acacia grows as a woodland tree (but is not indigenous, as I fancied). It is just bursting into bloom, and the country is white with it.

Wed. June 6. Did 2pp.- Recd Clodd's Memoir of Grant Allen.- The lovely nights here. Strange sounds: ceaseless voice of grasshoppers (grillons)—the hoot of toads, far-sounding—the cry of owls—often loud clamour of frogs. The road bordered with acacias, now in full flower, lading air with exquisite scent.

Thursd. June 7. In morning read "Grant Allen" and wrote to Clodd. Afternoon did 1p.

Frid. June 8. Did 2pp.

Sat. June 9. Did 1 1/2p. Saw in paper death of Stephen Crane, and wrote about it to Mrs Crane, via H.G. Wells.

Sund. June 10. Read Bk 20 of "Odyssey".

Mond. June 11. Did 1 1/2p. Recd Wells's new novel—"Love and Mr Lewisham".

Tuesd. June 12. Did 2pp. Very hot weather, with high south wind, which has blown for three or four days.

Wed. June 13. Rewrote 1p. of yesterday, and did 2 more—a good day. Heavy rain after the dry, windy heat. Our garden begins to yield small strawberries and a few cherries. The roses are magnificent.

Thursd. June 14. Did 2pp.

Frid. June 15. Did 1 1/2p. Pinker sends cheque of £21-3 for American publicn (*Truth*) of "The Scrupulous Father"[1]. He thinks it might be well to hold over "Among the Prophets", and I shall do so.

Sat. June 16. Did 1 1/2p. Working hard and well—no time for reading, except papers.

Sund. June 17. Read Bk 21 of the "Odyssey". Circular from Shorter, saying that some friends of Clodd are going to give him present on his 60th birthday, and asking for subscription. Gladly sent a guinea[2]. Wrote to Walter, and sent Nelly quarterly cheque. Wrote to Pinker, deciding to hold over "Among the Prophets".

Mond. June 18. Did 2pp. Letter from [William Leonard] Courtney, of *Fortnightly,* saying he wants "By the Ionian Sea" to make a nice volume, and asking if I can suggest an illustrator. Replied, mentioning Forestier and McCormick.

Tuesd. June 19. Did 2pp. Extremely hot.

Wed. June 20. Did 2pp. Pinker writes that he has sold "The House of Cobwebs" to *The Argosy* for 5 gu[ine]as a thousand words.

Thursd. June 21. Poor day; not in tune. Did ½p. Sleep badly, don't know why.

Frid. June 22. Did 1 1/2p. In afternoon walked with G. to village of Mont up the hills. Letter from Nelly this morning. They have advertized for a family to take Walter during the summer.

Sat. June 23. Did 2pp.

Sund. June 24. With G. to the top of the Vieille Montagne, whence there are grand views. We ate our lunch on the old stronghold at the summit, among the trees. Then it began to rain, and we had to walk back in it.- Letter from Pinker, saying that he has sold "Pig and Whistle" to the *Graphic,* at 5 gu[ine]as a thousand words.

Mond. June 25. Did 2pp. Wrote to Pinker.

Tuesd. June 26. Did 2pp.

Wed. June 27. Did 1/2p.

Thursd. June 28. Only 1/2p., and decided that I must go back to make some changes.

Frid. June 29. Couple of pp. rewritten in back chapter. Ready to proceed again.

Sat. June 30. Did 1 1/2p.

Sund. July 1. Finished Bk 22 of "Odyssey". I had asked Pinker to get me a copy of map of Gaul pubd by Murray. Now he sends it, with news that Murray, hearing it was for me, wished to give it me. Wrote thanks to John. Sent cheque to Dorking. Card to Nellie, who is deciding about Walter's summer holiday.- Weather very hot.

Mond. July 2. Very hot, ending in storm. Did 2pp.

Tuesd. July 3. Did 1 1/2p. Invitation to Omar Dinner for July 23rd—alas! Wrote to Wells about his book.

Wed. July 4. Did 2pp.

Thursd. July 5. Did 2pp.

Frid. July 6. Did rather more than 2pp. Showery.

Sat. July 7. Did 2pp. A good week.

Sund. July 8. Read part of Bk 23 of "Odyssey". Horrible news from China—massacres at Pekin[3] etc. Wrote to Miss Collet—and to Hudson.

Mond. July 9. Did about 1p.

Tuesd. July 10. Did 1 1/2p. To my great surprise, a note from *Ouida,* from Lucca, praising "Ionian Sea" and wondering how I understood the dialects!

Wed. July 11. Did 2pp. Wrote reply to Ouida.- Recd from London vol. I of Holm's "Hist[ory] of Greece" [4 vols., 1898] (with postage 6/9).

Thursd. July 12. Did 2pp. Corrected proof of "Pig and Whistle" for *Graphic.*

Frid. July 13. Did 2½pp. Visit from René and his friend Bourre, who stay till Sunday evening.

Sat. July 14. Bad news from Wakefield. Seven boys at the school have had measles, also Nelly and Walter—W. lightly. School broken up till after summer. Madge nursing, and well, also mother. Wrote to them.- Did 2pp.

Sund. July 15. René and M. Bourre left us.

Mond. July 16. Did 2pp.

Tuesd. July 17. Did 1p. Heat extreme. I write in shirt and trousers, and, even so, perspire.

Wed. July 18. Did 1p. Nelly has been suffering severely from toothache since her measles. Walter up and well. Wrote to Nelly. Letter from E. Walter-Madge, Treasury, Calcutta, asking for autograph.

Thursd. July 19. Did 2pp. The heat extreme. Hear it is terrible in London.

527

Frid. July 20. Did 3pp. Letter from Walter.

Sat. July 21. Did only 1/2p. Day of cloud and thunder, but no rain.

Sund. July 22. Read a little Homer. Hot. Recd. demand for income tax. Filled up return and sent.

Mond. July 23. Did 1p.

Tuesd. July 24. Did 1p. Sent Nellie cheque for £8-2-4—boy's clothing account, and payment for his holiday to come at the Hatfields', Harrogate (15/- a week).

Wed. July 25. Did 1 1/2p. Heat very great again. Letter from Hudson.

Thursd. July 26. Heat crushing. Did 1p.

Frid. July 27. Rewrote p[age] of yesterday. Futile storm at night, no rain.

Sat. July 28. Did 1p. Heat so severe that I sit in vest and drawers, with bare feet, yet can scarce do anything.

Sund. July 29. At last storm with a good deal of rain; much cooler. Read 24th "Odyssey". Finding that the *Athenaeum* this week omits my name from the Rochester edn of Dickens in "The New Publishing Season", I wrote to ask Methuen if he or the paper was responsible. *Athenaeum* omitted my name from the Dickens under head of "New Books" when "Pickwick" appeared—though they mentioned Kitton. This seems to me deliberate, and is to me inexplicable.

Mond. July 30. Bright and cool. Did 2 1/2pp.

Tuesd. July 31. Warm again. Did 2pp. Recd demand for £13-8 income tax—on last three years. I have never been asked to pay till this year.

Wed. Aug. 1. Rewrote 1p. and did another. Recd Aug. no. of *The Argosy,* with "The House of Cobwebs".

Thursd. Aug. 2. Did 1p. Miss Ward arrived, to spend a month here.

Frid. Aug. 3. Did 2pp. Letter from Methuen. Says he has written to a friend of his on *Athenaeum* staff about my affair.

Sat. Aug. 4. No work.

Sund. Aug. 5. Attack of lumbago. Wrote to Walter (at Harrogate—c/o Mrs Hatfield, Cringletie), Mother at Grasmere with girls, and Bertz.

Mond. Aug. 6. Did 1p. Recd from Wells the Italian translation of his "Invisible Man". Weather cloudy and damp!

Tuesd. Aug. 7. No work. Rain, rain.

Wed. Aug. 8. Did 1p. Methuen writes that his *Athenaeum* correspondent declares there is no animus whatever against me. Of course! Replied to him, very quietly, just letting him see my opinion was unchanged.

Thursd. Aug. 9. Did 2pp. Weather fine again.

Frid. Aug. 10. Rewrote 1p. of yesterday, and did 1 more. Feeling better. Reading George Sand's Lettres à Musset et à Sainte-Beuve.

Sat. Aug. 11. Did 2pp.

Sund. Aug. 12. Read some Plato. Fine.

Mond. Aug. 13. Wrote 2pp. Getting hotter again.

Tuesd. Aug. 14. Did 1 1/4p.

*   *   *

Frid. Aug. 17. Days of inability to work. Frightfully nervous; to-day got to work again, and did 1p.- René came, to stay for fortnight. Have just read a novel "Le [Roman d'un] Petit Vieux", by Mme Lescot [1900]—an example of commonplace, but not ill written, French fiction.[4]

Sat. Aug. 18. Did 2pp.

Sund. Aug. 19. Drive in donkey-cart. Read some Plato. Wrote to Walter at Harrogate.

Mond. Aug. 20. Did 2pp.

Tuesd. Aug. 21. Did 2pp. Getting on much better in this cooler weather. Difficulties with Chapman & Hall about volume of "Ionian Sea". I find they want to buy whole 7 years' copyright (America as well as England) for £130. Have sent protest to Pinker.

Wed. Aug. 22. Did 1 1/2p.

Thursd. Aug. 23. Misery. No work.

Frid. Aug. 24. Did 1 1/2p. Mme de Musset came to stay here for three weeks.

Sat. Aug. 25. Did 1p. In afternoon the donkey-cart.- "Trollope".

Sund. Aug. 26. Having been troubled for some time with an eruption on right side of forehead, went to see Dr Cornoy, who prescribed a daily bath and waters at the Etablissement.- Recd from Pinker £46-17-8, the second half payment from *Fortnightly* for "Ionian Sea".

Mond. Aug. 27. Did 2pp.

Tuesd. Aug. 28. Did 2pp. Weather very rainy.

Wed. Aug. 29. Did 1p. and *finished "The Coming Man"*. In afternoon, excursion in donkey-cart.

Thursd. Aug. 30. Dispatched MS to Pinker. To-day, Gabrielle has finished her translation of "The Odd Women", and sends it to the *Revue des Deux Mondes,* for Brunetière's decision.[5]

Frid. Aug. 31. Idling.

Sat. Sept. 1. Wrote first draught of pref. to "An Author at Grass".

Sund. Sept. 2. Bad toothache. No reading. Wrote to Walter and Miss Collet.

Mond. Sept. 3. Rewrote my Preface—much better.

Tuesd. Sept 4. Did 1¼p.

Wed. Sept. 5. Went with Miss Ward to Autun—Gabrielle not being able to get away on account of Mme de Musset. We drove to Remilly station, and got to Autun at 10.30. Déjeuner, good and cheap, at Hôtel de la Poste. Saw the Cathedral, the beautiful Renaissance fountain close by it, the Museum in the building occupied by the Société Eduenne—these before eating. Museum surprising by its extent, and admirably arranged. M. Bulliot, who has explored the Mont Beuvray, proving it to be the site of Bibracte (and not Autun, as used to be thought) has given most of his discoveries to this Museum, in the Salle du Beuvray.

After eating, walked a mile or so up the hill beyond town to Couhard, where is the pyramidal tomb called of Divitiacus. Most beautiful view. The wooded hills, and the town with Cathedral spire—the Bishop's Palace and the Seminaries etc. Picturesque village of Couhard, with its stream, and the odd little huts built along it for washing, one in front of each cottage.

Thence to the Museum in Rue St Nicolas (the Abbaye de St Martin), where we saw fragments of tomb of Brunhilda. On to the two Roman gates—Porte St André and Porte d'Arroux, latter named from river. Rested on bridge over river, looking up at the great gate.

Back to St Honoré at about 10 o'clock. Day of perfect weather—not a cloud, but never too hot. Must mention the Statue of Divitiacus at end of the beautiful Promenade des Marbres.

Thursd. Sept. 6. Wrote to Ouida and to Bertz. Also to Editor of *Les Débats* [De Nolèche] about "New Grub Street", which he delays to publish.

Frid. Sept. 7. Did 1p.

Sat. Sept. 8. Did 1p. In afternoon came typoscripts of half "The Coming Man". Began to correct.

Sund. Sept. 9. Finished typos. Read some Shakespeare.

Mond. Sept 10. Did 1½p.

Tuesd. Sept. 11. Did 2pp.

Wed. Sept. 12. Did 1p. Letter from Walter.

Thursd. Sept. 13. Did ½p. Recd £33-1-6 for "House of Cobwebs" in *Argosy.*

Frid. Sept. 14. Did ½p. Pinker writes about "The Coming Man". Will try to get it into weekly edn of *Times.*

Sat. Sept. 15. Did 1½p.

Sund. Sept. 16. Finished correction of typoscript of "The Coming Man". Letter from a Mr Macdonell, in enthusiastic praise of "Ionian Sea".

Mond. Sept. 17. Did 1p. Sent off typoscript to Pinker. Wrote to Mr Macdonell. Letter from Nelly, who has been cycling from Broadway to Oxford, with Alg.-

Tuesd. Sept. 18. Did 1½p.

Wed. Sept. 19. We were to have gone with Miss Ward to-day to the Beuvray. But storm came on in the night, and all day it has been cloudy. Did 1p.

Thursd. Sept. 20. Rain all day. Did 1½p.

Frid. Sept. 21. Did 1½p. Miss Ward left us, going back to Paris. Have just read [Ruskin's] "Unto this Last" [1862].

Sat. Sept. 22. Did ½p.

Sund. Sept. 23. Shakespeare.

Mond. Sept. 24. Did 1p.

Tuesd. Sept. 25. Did 1p. Grundy writes acknowledging mistake in his map of Gaul [published by John Murray in 1899], saying it was fault of exposer.

Wed. Sept. 26. Did 1p.

Thursd. Sept. 27. Did ½p. Mme de Musset left us. Wrote to Nelly, sending the quarter's cheque.

Frid. Sept. 28. Did 1½p.

Sat. Sept. 29. Did 1p.

Sund. Sept. 30. Pinker sends cheque for £89-4-3—half payment for book rights of "Ionian Sea", and payment from *Graphic* for "Pig and Whistle". Bad rheumatism and headache. Early to bed.

Mond. Oct. 1. No work. Ill.

Tuesd. Oct. 2. Recovered. Had to rewrite the page of Saturday.

Wed. Oct. 3. Did a little more than 1p. Ouida sends more Musolina cuttings.

Thursd. Oct. 4. Did 1¼p.

Frid. Oct. 5. Did 1p. Wrote to my furniture man at Dorking asking if he could undertake removal of all my things to Paris.

Sat. Oct. 6. Did 1p. Pinker writes that Bullen wants to sell my books to Heinemann, who alone will offer the price he wants. At Pinker's advice (and in accordance with my own antipathy) I refuse Heinemann.

Sund. Oct. 7. Did little or nothing.

Mond. Oct. 8. A day of holiday. G. and I drove to Château Chinon, spent the day there, and back to dinner by another route. Weather perfect; cloudless sky, and sun not too hot. Situation of the little town on its hillside very picturesque. A fair going on, chiefly for the sale of pigs, which lay in great numbers about the streets. Climbed to the hill-top, where are a few remains of the castle foundations. Beautiful view into the deep valley of the Yonne, the river hidden amid rocks and woods, but its flow just audible afar. On the southern horizon, the summit of Mont Beuvray. Drive cost 15 francs.

Tuesd. Oct. 9. Did 1p. Weather magnificent.

Wed. Oct. 10. In morning did 1/2p. In afternoon, M. Purdet conducted G. and me to see the so-called druidical stones up near the village of Mont.

Thursd. Oct. 11. Did 1p. Finished "Autumn".

Frid. Oct. 12. Did 1 1/2p. Wrote to congratulate [Henry] Norman on his election as Liberal M.P. for Wolverhampton.

Sat. Oct. 13. Did 1p.

Sund. Oct. 14. Nothing.

Mond. Oct. 15. Long walk with G.

Tuesd. Oct. 16. Did 1p.

Wed. Oct. 17. Rain. Did 1p. Sent to bank for 600 francs.

Thursd. Oct. 18. Rain. Did 1p.

Frid. Oct. 19. Thick fog all day. Did 1p. Have great faith in this little book!

Sat. Oct. 20. Did 1p.

Sund. Oct. 21. Translated some lines of "Odyssey" into verse, for my book [Winter XV]. Weather turned bitterly cold.

Mond. Oct. 22. Frozen, but working. Did 1p. Sent Pref. of "Barnaby Rudge" to Methuen.

Tuesd. Oct. 23. Did about 1/2p., and *finished "An Author at Grass"*. In style, it is better than anything I have yet done.

Wed. Oct. 24. Wrote to Miss Collet and to Bertz.

Thursd. Oct. 25. Sent "Author at Grass" to Pinker. Exquisite autumn weather. Recd copy of a novel "Jenny of the Villa" from a Mrs [C.H.] Radford, at Plymouth.[6]—Our servant, Louise, has been called away by mother's illness. The usual misery after her departure.

Frid. Oct. 26. Confusion, but managing to think over the next novel.

*   *   *

Wed. Nov. 21. Gabrielle's birthday—32. We left St Honoré about three weeks ago, and went to stay for a week at Chasnay (Fourchambault), with the Eustaches. Very pleasant time. Then for a fortnight to Tazières, close by, with the Saglios—Alfred Saglio there for a day or two. Made acquaintance of Col[onel] St Clair, brother-in-law of Mme Eustache, who was over from Portsmouth for a short time at Chasnay. Several times at Nevers, where I came to know G.'s uncles, aunts and cousins[7]. At Tazières read a good deal of Sainte-Beuve[8]. On Mond. Nov. 19th returned to Paris. Thinking of bringing my books over from Dorking. René no longer lives with us, and I shall have his room for a study. Weather miserable for several days—gloom and rain. At Tazières corrected the typoscript of "An Author at Grass".

* * *

Tuesd. Dec. 25. I suppose the first Christmas Day in my life on which I worked. Began "A Vanquished Roman", after long labour at the scheme, and did more than a page.- Things here in wild disorder, on account of R[ené]'s frantic proceedings. I have his old room as a study, but it is still full of cumber. Marvellous that I can work at all—a sort of despair drives me. Nothing from Pinker yet about my novel.

Wed. Dec. 26. Did about 1p.

Thursd. Dec. 27. Rebegan the book, and did 1p.

Frid. Dec. 28. Wrote 2pp. Went into town, and bought a bookcase (90 francs) at Scherf's, 35 Rue d'Aboukir.

Sat. Dec. 29. Did 1p. My bookcase set up, but gives me little pleasure, here in this dreary flat.

Sund. Dec. 30. Did 1p.- An unknown person, (Miss) L.M. Burton, sends me as a present an etching of Mason's "Young Anglers"; also some fairy tales (MS) of her own writing[9], and a long letter about my books. Replied. Hamlin Garland writes from Chicago, requesting autograph.[10] Replied. Ouida writes about the brigand. Replied. Northern Syndicate asks for article of 2500 words on Dickens's Homes and Haunts, for £6-6. Promised it for payment on delivery of MS.[11] Wrote to Clodd.

Mond. Dec. 31. A little more than 1p.

1901

Jan 1. Did 1½p.

Wed. Jan. 2. Did 1½p. Recd Methuen's cheque for Pref. to "Bleak House", but not for "Oliver Twist", though it was published a fortnight ago. Went to see the agents of my Portsmouth removers, Messrs Johnson, 37 Rue d'Hauteville.

Thursd. Jan. 3. Did 1p. Pinker writes that Holt of America offers £150 for right of "The Coming Man". Good news.

Frid. Jan. 4. Day at the Bib[liothèque] Nat[ionale]. Read Sidon[ius] Apoll[inaris], and got some good notes.

Sat. Jan. 5. Did ½p. Weather frosty.

*   *   *

Wed. Jan. 23. A long interruption. A fortnight ago my books arrived from Dorking, all safe. But the dampness of the books gave me a bad cold, from which I am only just recovering. My room is finished, and comfortable. I have bought two book-cases (Scherf) which cover one of the walls. Hope to get to work again soon, but am still very weak.

The newspaper this morning tells me that *Queen Victoria died* last night, at Osborne, at 6.30. The end has been certain for several days. Wrote to Walter and to Mother.

Frid. Jan. 25. Pinker writes that Chap[man] & Hall offer £350 for 7 years rights of new novel. At same time, Holt objects to spring publication, and, if it is insisted upon, withdraws offer of £150 in advance of royalties, and will only pay £100. Of course I accept this, as I cannot wait till autumn.- Methuen writes proposing an edition of "The Town Traveller" in their Sixpenny Novelists, with royalty of ½d per copy. Refer him to Colles.[1]

Mond. Jan. 28. Got to work on my article on Dickens's Homes and Haunts, and did 1p.

Wed. Jan. 30. Finished the article. Pinker sends agreement with C[hapman] & H[all] for novel. They pay half the £350 at once, and half on publication, which is to be before 1st of May.

Frid. Feb. 1. Resumed work on Roman novel, and wrote a few lines.

Sat. Feb. 2. Did 1p.- Funeral of Victoria.

Sund. Feb. 3. Rain all day. Did 1p.

Mond. Feb. 4. Did 1p.

Tuesd. Feb. 5. Did 1½p.

Wed. Feb. 6. Vile weather all this time, cold and dark; my cough very troublesome. Did 1¼p.

Thursd. Feb. 7. Frost. Did 1p.

Frid. Feb. 8. Frost. In morning wrote 1p., but in evening had to destroy both that and the preceding; rewrote one of them.

Sat. Feb. 9. Did 1½p. Frost.

Sund. Feb. 10. Did 1½p.

Mond. Feb. 11. Rewrote ½p. of yesterday, and did 1½p. more. Letter from Wells, from Schweizerhof at Lucerne, where he and wife are passing two days before going on to Italy.

Tuesd. Feb. 12. Did 1½p. Still frost.

Wed. Feb. 13. Did ½p.

Thursd. Feb. 14. Did 1p. Cold very severe. G. saw de Nolèche, who promises that translation of "New Grub Street" shall begin in the *Débats* next week. So, at last!- Recd cheque for £6-6 for my article on Dickens's Homes and Haunts.

Frid. Feb. 15. Did 1p. Cold terrible.- Pinker sends cheque for £157-10— first half (minus commission) of C[hapman] & H[all]'s payment for new novel. He says they have some beautiful illustrations for "Ionian Sea", which are to be sent for my opinion.

Sat. Feb. 16. Wrote 1p.

Sund. Feb. 17. Recd the oil sketches [by Leo de Littrow] and pen drawings made from my own sketches to illustrate "By the Ionian Sea". They don't seem to me *very* good, but I dare say they will be pleasing in the book. Wrote to Whale, Miss Collet and Madge.

Mond. Feb. 18. Did 1p. Returned to Pinker the drawings.

Tuesd. Feb. 19. Did 1p.

Wed. Feb. 20. Did 1p.

Thursd. Feb. 21. Rewrote the last 1½p. To-day begins publn of "New Grub Street" in *Les Débats.*

Frid. Feb. 22. Déjeuner with Delaborde. After all, "New Grub Street" only begins *to-day.* No writing. G. sent money to S[mith], E[lder] & Co.[2]

Sat. Feb. 23. Bad cold again. Reading Tacitus. No work.

Sund. Feb. 24. Complete proofs of "By the Ionian Sea" arrive. Pass day in correcting. Fine type.

Mond. Feb. 25. Still correcting proofs.

Tuesd. Feb. 26. Not able to do much, but thought about my book.

Wed. Feb. 27. Wrote ½p. Weather milder.

Thursd. Feb. 28. Rain all day. Wrote 1p.

Frid. March 1. Rainy, but warm. Did 1¼p.

Sat. March 2. Correcting type-copy of novel for America.

Sund. March 3. Correcting. Weather improved. Hit on new name for novel—"Our Friend the Charlatan".

Mond. March 4. Idling.

Tuesd. March 5. Idling. Bought Wells's "Tales of Time and Space".- Invitation from Percy Fitzgerald to join a club called the Boz; no subscription; 2 dinners a year, attendance optional. Accepted.[3]

Wed. March 6. Did 1p. News from Wells (from Genoa) that he will be here to dine with us on Friday.

Thursd. March 7. Did 1p.

Frid. March 8. Sent typoscript of "Charlatan" to Henry Holt & Co., New York.- Wells and wife came to dine with us. Good evening.

Sat. March 9. G. and I went to have tea and dine with the Wells's at the Grand Hotel.

Sund. March 10. Wells's went home. Weather dark and cold. Work out of the question.

*   *   *

Wed. March 13. Finished correction of proofs of half "Our Friend", and returned to Chapman.

Frid. March 15. G. down with influenza. C[hapman] & H[all] write asking for parag[raph]s about my two books to insert in their advt lists. Wrote and sent.- Reading Bourget's "Drame de Famille".

Sund. March 17. Resumed writing, and did 1½p. Letter to Bertz. Weather getting warmer.

Mond. March 18. Wrote 2pp.—a good day. Weather warmer, but dark and wet.

Tuesd. March 19. Did 2pp.

Wed. March 20. Did 1½p. Hideous weather; day after day, rain and gloom.

Thursd. March 21. Did 1½pp. Sent to Chapman & Hall corrected proofs of "Ionian Sea", with proofs of woodcuts, for which I have indicated place in text. Pinker writes that he has sold "*A Charming Family*" to *Illust[rated] Lond[on] News* for 5 gu[ine]as a thousand [published on May 4, 1901].

Frid. March 22. Cold. Did 1p.

*   *   *

Wed. Ap. 3. Long bout of influenza. Able to do nothing but correcting proofs of "Our Friend the Charlatan". This morning did a feeble beginning of work again.

Sat. Ap. 6. Startled to receive letter from Madge, asking if I could at once take Walter away, and send him to school. He is too difficult for them to manage. M. suggests a school at Bakewell; 20 gu[ine]as a term. This is very serious. Wrote to Miss Collet, asking her advice, and to M. asking if she could possibly keep W. to end of summer.

I got resolutely to work, and did ¾p. Yesterday finished proofs of "Charlatan" and "Ionian Sea". To-day have received some more coloured illustrations for "Ionian Sea"—very good.

Sund. Ap. 7. Sudden outbreak of summer warmth. Wrote about 1p. Returned coloured sketches to Chap[man] & Hall.

Mond. Ap. 8. Wrote 1½p.

Tuesd. Ap. 9. Wrote 1p.

Wed. Ap. 10. In night, attack of rheumatism in left side, severe pain.- Letter from Wakefield, saying Walter can stay with them to end of summer term.

Letter of good advice from Miss Collet.- Did 1p.- Corrected proofs of Pref. to "Barnaby Rudge".

Thursd. Ap. 11. Did 1p.

Frid. Ap. 12. Wrote 1p. Note from Chap[man] & Hall asking for suggestion for cover of "Ionian Sea". I can only say that it ought to be of olive green.- Miss Collet sends information about the Rawlings School at Quorn, which seems as if it would do for Walter.

Sat. Ap. 13. Weather still vile. Did 1p. Blackies write to offer me £35 for my rights in vol. on Dickens, which they can dispose of to the Gresham Publishing Co., to be used in a new edition of Dickens's novels. Replied, asking for fuller information.

Sund. Ap. 14. Rain, rain. Did 1p., and rewrote 1.

Mond. Ap. 15. Rain and wind. Did 1p.

Tuesd. Ap. 16. Tempest and sun. Did 1p.

Wed. Ap. 17. Did 1p.

Thursd. Ap. 18. Blackies write offer £50 for all rights in my "Charles Dickens"—i.e. right to continue to pub[lish] it in the Victorian Era Series, as well as to dispose of it to Gresham Co. Replied accepting.- Proofs of "Charming Family".- In afternoon with G. to the Bois.- Did only ½p.

Frid. Ap. 19. Did 1p. Weather again fine.

*   *   *

Frid. Ap. 26. After a week of idleness, went to consult doctor about my condition—Dr Chauffard, Bd St Germain. He tells the old story: emphysema, chronic bronchitis, and moist spot on right lung. Prescribes fiery punctures, and hypodermic injections. For the treatment, went to see Dr Lorrin, Avenue Kléber, who began punctures at once. Chauffard says that the seaside would be dangerous for me just now—I much wonder if he is right. Advises summer at St Honoré or in high mountains.

1902

Archachon, Ap. 7. Yesterday chanced to open the first vol[ume] of my Diary, and found it such strange and moving reading that I have gone on, hour after hour.- Who knows whether I may not still live a few years; and if so, I shall be sorry not to have a continuous record of my life. So I resolve to begin journalizing once more, after all but a year of intermission.

Soon after the last entry, I went to England, chiefly to sit for my portrait for *Literature*.[1] Gabrielle went with me, and we stayed with the Wells's at Spade House, Sandgate; and with the Pinkers at Worcester Park. As I seemed to be getting good, I stayed on for a month at Sandgate; G. returned to Paris. Hick then persuaded me into seeing Pye Smith, who took a discouraging view of my chest-disease, and advised a Sanatorium. Against my better judgment I went to Dr Jane Walker's newly opened Sanatorium, at Nayland, Suffolk, and stayed there till August. Then I joined G. and her mother at a villa at Couhard, Autun, where we remained for a month or two. Place very damp, and did me much harm. After that we were guests [of the Saglios] at Tazières till end of November. I then went up to Paris, and saw Chauffard, who shook his head and advised the winter at Arcachon. To Arcachon I went. G. came and spent a week with me, then back to Tazières, and soon to Paris.

Not much work done this last year. However, at Autun I revised and lengthened "An Author at Grass", which Pinker sold to the *Fortnightly Review*.[2] I wrote a "David Copperfield" preface for a new American edition [published by George Sproul in 1903], and an article "Dickens in Memory" for a special number of *Literature* [December 21, 1901]—both these at Tazières. Then I undertook for Chapman & Hall an abridgement of Forster's Dickens, and got it finished by January of this year. At Arcachon have also written a couple of short stories—"Miss Rodney's Leisure" [published in *T.P.'S Weekly,* Christmas 1903] and "Christopherson" [published in *The Illustrated London News,* September 20, 1902]. Pinker is just now paying a short visit to United States.

"Our Friend the Charlatan" and "By the Ionian Sea" came out in May of last year, and were brilliantly reviewed. Not much sale though, I think, for either—the old story.

Tuesd. Ap. 8. Troubled all the winter by insomnia. A couple of days ago tried spending the morning down by the shore, instead of on the chaise longue, as always; result, 6 hours of good sleep, which continues.

Spent yesterday and to-day in reading my old Diary. Mr Radcliffe (English clergyman of Arcachon) called in morning, during my absence, and left me the *Spectator.* Letter from Miss Orme, with good news of little Alfred, in Cornwall.[3]

540

I am staying here at Villa Souvenir in the Ville d'Hiver—badly managed and decayed house, the mistress, Mlle Gatineau, deaf as a post, and at the mercy of insolent servants. All my days have been passed on chaise longue in the galerie de cure, where, somehow, I have managed to write now and then. Companions two young Frenchmen—Cognat, a Normalien [student in a training college], and Anthier, in business; a few weeks ago came another, Farronault, a commercial traveller. Never have I lived so long in the company of blackguards. Cognat is an educated peasant; Anthier only to be described as a cad. Impossible to give an idea of the filthiness of their minds and the grossness of their talk. They are petty, envious, malicious; always jeering or sneering at someone or other.[4] [half a line crossed out]

I am paying 8 francs a day.

Wed. Ap. 9. Cheerless weather; not at all springlike. Down to shore for an hour or two. Loitering time away; no reading.

Thursd. Ap. 10. Grey sky; a little rain. In afternoon to the shore. Reading idly in "Country Month by Month" [by J.A. Owen and G.S. Boulger]—a book which often makes me *ache* with thoughts of England. Card from G.

Frid. Ap. 11. Sunshine in mid hours of the day. In afternoon to Radcliffe's. Idleness. In the past week quite unable to fix my thoughts on anything. Great disappointment about "An Author at Grass", which Courtney promised to begin in the Ap. number of *Fortnightly*. I fear now that it will not even begin in May.

Sat. Ap. 12. Fine. In morning a long walk. Afternoon and evening, usual chaise longue, reading Gregorovius. Receive no letters nowadays.

Sund. Ap. 13. Fine morning, grey after. In morning to [Le] Moulleau and back. When I came here I could not have walked half this distance; but it makes me cough a good deal. Gregorovius. No letter.

Mond. Ap. 14. Gloom and heavy rain. Thank goodness, at last recd proofs of first section of "An Author at Grass". Corrected and returned, with a line to Courtney (Ed. *Fortnightly*).- Recd copy of Hudson's book "El Ombú", and read. Of course less interesting than his natural history work.- Letter from G. Miserable story of René. Decided that we go for a year or so to the pays basque. We shall leave Paris (I hope, for ever) in June. A piece of good news is that *La Rue des Meurt-de-faim* [New Grub Street] is accepted for vol[ume] publication by the *Revue Blanche* people. They pay G. 300f. for first edn, and another 300 if there is a second. They ask, also, for other volumes by me.

Tuesd. Ap. 15. Fine morning, later dull and cold. A wretched April, this. Went to Andap's (English Bank) to leave a cheque for cashing.- Gregorovius.

Wed. Ap. 16. Fine. Letter from G. She has seen de Nolèche, of the *Débats,* who says that many people have asked him when "La Rue des Meurt-de-Faim" is going to appear as a volume.- Letter from Nelly.- Wrote to Miss Orme and Miss Collet.

Thursd. Ap. 17. Very fine. In afternoon, with a party of three, in voiture à sable (20fr.) to the Pointe du Sud. The modern forest uninteresting; the natural forest beautiful with undergrowth.- Great hawthorns (some in flower), and bracken. Wild boars said to be common. Men and women (in breeches) working at getting resin from the pines; their lonely *cabanes* at long intervals. The huge sand-hills along shore.- Home for dinner, less tired than I expected.

Frid. Ap. 18. Fine. Mr Radcliffe brought me a batch of *Blackwoods,* which occupied the day. Wrote to Nelly (who is with mother at Leyburn,) and to Walter (who is with Madge, at Broadway.) Also to Hudson, acknowledging his book.- Feel that my excursion of yesterday did me good.

Sat. Ap. 19. Fine, close. Recd from Pinker cheque for £68-3-7, a/c up to March 25th.

Sund. Ap. 20. Fine, warm. In morning to shore. Mooned over Blackwoods.

Mond. Ap. 21. Hot day. Did a little packing.

Tuesd. Ap. 22. Day of rain. Letter from G., which decided me to go to Pension Larréa, at S. Jean de Luz, instead of Hotel, as I had meant. Called in afternoon to say good-bye to Radcliffe, but he was not at home.

Wed. Ap. 23. Fine. Farewell visit to Festal [his Arcachon doctor], who made thorough exam[inatio]n, and is to write to Dr Chauffard. His fee 100 francs—astonishingly little.

Thursd. Ap. 24. With great gladness, said good-bye to Arcachon. Took the 7.42am. train, and reached S. Jean de Luz at mid-day. To the Pension Larréa (42, Quai, Ciboure) recommended by the Mlles Batézat to Gabrielle. Quaint, decent house; a good bedroom; pension, 6f. a day. No one else here at present, of which I am glad.- Greatly delighted with first view of town and neighbourhood. On the journey, the first view of the great breakers rolling in at Bidart, very fine. In afternoon, walked about a good deal, and without fatigue. Sent cards to Madge, Nelly, Miss Orme and G.- Very fine day. The country a mass of spring flowers. After dull winter among the pines, the mountain and shore refresh my eyes.

Frid. Ap. 25. Fine, hot. Walked morning and afternoon, seeing town and shore. Can do nothing towards finding a house till I have seen the Mlles Batézat, who are absent just now.- Wrote to Cognat.

Sat. Ap. 26. Dull, heavy. Can get no sleep yet. A nightingale sings all night behind the house. Read a little Gregorovius; out of sorts.

Sund. Ap. 27. Fine, with showers; close morning, then cold.- Appeal from a Sister of Mercy, of Skiberarn, Co. Cork, for some of my books for a library to be used by the poor. Judicious! - Walked a good deal. Each day feel a little stronger. Instituted reform, by which I hope to feel better. Dinner to be very light—no soup, no meat or vegetables. Cannot gain much weight thus, but sleep I must.

Acacias overhanging the sea shore just breaking into flower.

Mond. Ap. 28. Cloudy and showery. In morning took a drive, by Urrugne and base of La Rhune and through Ascain home. At Ascain made inquiries, but the place did not at all attract me, and seems impossible as abode. Drive cost 10f. - far too much.- Letter from A[rthur] Waugh, the new Manager of Chap[man] & Hall, saying that he is sending me proofs of my Forster. Letter from G.

Tuesd. Ap. 29. A day of wild wind and rain; clearing towards 5 o'clock, but cold. If my proofs had come, I could have used the time, which, as it is, I have wasted.

Wed. Ap. 30. Still windy, but no rain. Recd complete set of slip-proofs of my Forster, and began to correct. Also recd Gregorovius' "Hadrian", second-hand from Mudie's. Ordered from Mudie's the *Spectator* and *Blackwood's* (this second hand) until end of year.- In afternoon to see Mlles Batézat, very pleasant and anxious to be of help. Went into S. Jean, and saw a villa which seemed likely—Villa Catalina. Wrote to the owner about it—a Miss Watson at Pau.

Impossible to account in any way for some of our dreams. Last night I saw a corpse lying on a bed, and understood that it was Matthew Arnold. Just as he was about to be put into his coffin, I saw a movement of his hand, and cried out—"He is not dead". And he began to raise himself, and sat up, completely recovered.

Thursd. May 1. Wretched day—rain, fog, north wind. All morning worked at proofs of Forster. In afternoon went to see the Batézats, for half an hour; back straight. Letter from Walter and from Madge at Broadway.- Recd copy of new *Fortnightly,* containing first part of "Author at Grass".

Frid. May 2. Fine, at last, and not too hot. Letter from Miss Orme, and from Bertz. Wrote to Madge at Wakefield. Reading Gregorovius' "Hadrian".

Sat. May 3. Heavy clouds, little sun. "Hadrian". Wrote to Miss Orme and to Madge.

Sund. May 4. To bed last night at 8 o'clock, and had much refreshing sleep.- To-day rain and wind; the breakers very fine. Reading still at "Hadrian" - a poor book, badly translated.

Mond. May 5. Fine, but cold still. Useless house-visiting, all too big.- Cheque from Pinker. £23-2-9, for "Riding-Whip" with deductions [published in the *Illustrated London News,* March 22 and 29, 1902].

Tuesd. May 6. At 3am. a slight shock of earthquake. I was roused from a doze by what sounded like a great sudden rush of wind through the house— doors, windows and walls shook. But I did not think of earthquake until I heard talk of it this morning.- Letter from Nellie, proposing that Walter shall go to Norwich Grammar School in the autumn; replied approving.- This afternoon went to see Mr Genty [formerly professor of classics in a collège]—friend of Mlles Batézat—and with him to look at the Villa Olaberrieta, on top of hill, half a mile out of town. A lovely place, but too far, and too exposed to see winds, and doubtless too dear.

Wed. May 7. Morning rather fine; then getting worse till night, when came storm of cold wind and rain. At 8 o'clock this morning our little street was strewn with yellow iris and other plants and leaves, and presently came by a long procession, chanting. It was the Rogation ceremony—first time I have seen it.- Went to examine an apartment to let on the Place de la Mairie. Rather suitable,- Letter from Roberts, praising "Author at Grass". Wrote to G.- Recd *Blackwood* and *Spectator* from Mudie's.

Thursd. May 8. Storm in night; thunder and lightning. To-day, bitter north wind; snow on La Rhune— very beautiful in sunshine. Afternoon to hear music in the Place—Ascension to-day. Sent illustrated post-cards to Gabrielle. Wrote to Roberts.- Feeling vast improvement of health.

Frid. May 9. Another day of wild wind and storm. Did nothing.

Sat. May 10. Hard rain all day, and not a gleam of sun. Went to say good-bye to the Mlles Batézat, and got from library Loti's "Matelot" [1893].

Sund. May 11. Fine, but windy. Finished "Matelot". Recd a proof of my article on Dickens's Homes written I don't know how long ago for the Northern Newspaper Syndicate.

Mond. May 12. Weather slowly improving. Got from lib[rary] "Les Traditions au Pays Basque" [anonymous, 1899]—newspapers full of the great eruption at Martinique; supposed annihilation of town of St Pierre, with all shipping in the port.- Went to see the rooms again at Mme Lannes', Place de la Mairie and decided to take them. Rent for 6 months, f. 1200, with right to prolong for a second 6 months, at f.300.

Tuesd. May 13. Finer but still cloudy. Letters from Madge and from Walter. Worked a little.

Wed. May 14. Fine, but still the northerly wind. In afternoon called on the Gentys. Reading "Ramuntcho" [by Pierre Loti, 1897]. Letter from Alg. Terrible weather in England.

Thursd. May 15. Dull and rainy.

Frid. May 16. Towards evening, weather calm and bright.- Spent day over [William] Watson's Poems, which I have just received from bookseller.- Letter from J.W. Fell, who is seemingly strong and well after fearful winter at Halifax. In his case the Sanatorium cure seems to have been genuine.[5] To-day signed lease of Mme Lannes' rooms.

Sat. May 17. Fine, but doubtful now and then. Recd proofs of illustrations for my Forster.

Sund. May 18. Last night and all to-day violent N.W. gale. Frequent sunshine, broken by furious storms of rain and hail, obscuring everything. The sea very high; surf breaking grandly over the breakwaters.- Idleness.

Mond. May 19. The gale still furious as ever—having already blown, without a moment's interruption, for 48 hours. Four ships have taken refuge to the harbour. Did my packing to-day, but nothing else, unable to go out on account of the wind and every now and then, wild rain.

Tuesd. May 20. Had meant to leave to-day, but a letter from G. in morning spoke of vile weather at Paris. Decided to wait two days more. Went to Mme Lannes', and there saw a servant (Marianne Curutchague) whom, after much talk, I engaged from July 1 at 30f. a month.- Got from lib[rary] "L'Abbé Constantin" ([Ludovic] Halévy, [1882]).- In afternoon walked to Socoa; not quite fine yet, and in evening rain and wind began again.- Sleeping very well lately.

Wed. May 21. Sunshine, but very cold north wind (in night, terrific rain). In morning walked a little; the rest of the day did not venture to go out. Having nothing to read, and nothing to do, passed the day in utter idleness—heaven knows, indeed, how the hours have gone by. And how often in my life have I spent such a day as this,- blank, wearisome, wasted! A sort of destiny of idleness and wasted time seems to oppress a great part of my life. Each time a day such as this comes, I make a resolve that it shall never happen again. But circumstances are too strong for me. Indeed, the only way in which I could avoid this miserable folly of barren hours would be to live always in reach of a large library—the impossible thing for me, now and ever.

Thursd. May 22. Fine. Left S. J[ean] de L[uz] by 1.44 train. Bordeaux to dinner. Walked about streets a little. Night at Hotel Commercial, opp[osite] station.

Frid. May 23. Fog and drizzle at Bordeaux. Left by 8.28. Paris at 5.30. Fine on arriving.

Sat. May 24. Fine.

Sund. May 25. Fine. Went to see Miss Ward.

*   *   *

Sat. May 31. Weather rainy and stormy, day after day. Finished correction of proofs etc of my "Forster".

*   *   *

Tuesd. July 1. A month of disorder and weariness. Having decided to take a cheap flat as pied à terre at Paris, decided at length for Boulogne, 6 rue de Billancourt, 4th floor, to the right. Decent little place; rent only 675fr. On Saturday last did the removal.- Gabrielle's mother going to stay with Miss Ward, rue de la Pompe. Weather hot, but I bore the toil better than I expected [a whole line crossed out]. Things are now straight here—except the books, just thrown onto the shelves.

Excitement about King Ed[ward]'s illness, happening the day before what was to be coronation day, Thursday last.[6] Passed many hours, otherwise intolerable, reading [John] Forster's "[Life and Adventures of Oliver] Goldsmith" [1848]. Corrected proofs of "Summer" (Author at Grass) for *Fortnightly*. Pinker has settled for publicn of volume by Constables, who pay £100 in advance, and 20% royalty.

Last week appeared G.'s translation of "New Grub Street" - La Rue des Meurt-de-Faim, pub[lished]d by the *Revue Blanche*. Went with her to the office, to inscribe copies for critics etc.

Wed. July 2. Travelled from Paris by the 9.29am., and reached St Jean de Luz at 9.52 at night. Easy journey, in first class. Found all in good readiness at Ciboure.

*   *   *

Thursd. July 10. Got to work upon my new novel "Will Warburton" and did ½p.

Frid. July 11. Rewrote yesterday's work.

Sat. July 12. Wrote 1½p. Weather delightful.

Sund. July 13. Wrote ½p., and finished chap. I.- Saw from *Athenaeum* that Hudson has received a Gov[ernment] pension.- Greatly rejoiced. Don't know the sum. Received from him the Spanish Dictionary and Grammar he has bought for me; at once wrote to send money (8/10) and to congratulate.- In afternoon went all through the Sp[anish] Grammar, and in evening read a page of "Don Quixote", in the little 4 vol[ume] edition I bought years ago, looking forward to a day when I might learn Spanish.

Mond. July 14. Wrote 1p.

Tuesd. July 15. Wrote 1p. Finished Chap. I of "Don Quixote". A great thing to be really achieving this old ambition.

Wed. July 16. Wrote 1p., finishing Chap. 2.- Recd Roberts's new novel "Immortal Youth".- Weather bad; gloom and wild wind and rain—perhaps result of renewed eruptions in Martinique.

Thursd. July 17. Wrote ¾p.

Frid. July 18. Wrote 1p.

Sta. July 19. Wrote nothing. Recd request from editor to review for the *Times* a signed article on Dickens, by Swinburne, in *Quarterly*.

Sund. July 20. Began article on Swinburne.

Mond. July 21. Finished article, and posted.[7] In the 3rd Chap. of "Quixote". Weather very rainy, and now and then decidedly cool. Fine waves breaking over the breakwater in the bay this afternoon.

Tuesd. July 22. Fine. Did 1p., having to return to Chap. 2.

Wed. July 23. Did 1p. Gabrielle went to Bayonne.

Thursd. July 24. Did 1p.

Frid. July 25. Did 1p.- In afternoon to see Mr Ford, retired Indian, at his house above the Ascain road, where he lives with consumptive son. Nice fellow. Played on the pianola. Magnificent day, but hot.

Sat. July 26. Did 1p.

Sund. July 27. Letter-writing.

Mond. July 28. Did ½p. To see Miss Acklom, at St Jean de Luz.

Tuesd. July 29. Did about 1p.

*   *   *

Sat. Aug. 9. Coronation of Ed[ward] VII.- Yesterday and to-day wrote for the *Times* a review of Kitton's "Life of Dickens".[8]

Sund. Aug. 10. Recd from *Times* cheque for £4-4, for my notice a fortnight ago, of Swinburne's *Quarterly* article on Dickens.

Mond. Aug. 11. Got to work again, after a week, on my novel, and did ½p. Been reading in my Latin Anthologia lately. Have recd Wells's new story, "The Sea Lady". Done 17 chap[ter]s of "Don Quixote", which I now read very easily.- Roberts tells me that Hudson's pension is £150.

*   *   *

Mond. Aug. 18. By early train to Irun, over the Spanish border. Thence by train to Fuenterabbia. Very picturesque; the projecting roofs in carved wood, the draperied balconies etc. Old ivy-covered castle of Charles V. Some old dwelling houses falling into ruin. Crossed the Bidassoa to Hendaye, and thence back by train. Very hot.

*   *   *

Sat. Sept 20. Up very early, to catch 6 o'clock train to Bayonne, going to S. Jean Pied de Port. But at station found that time of train had been changed to 5.30. Decided to go to Sare, and just caught the diligence. Very fine, warm autumn day. By Ascain and St Pé, a very round about road—in all 2½ hours. Follows the Nivelle, which rises somewhere near the Rhune. At Sare had déjeuner at primitive hotel. Ham and eggs—the only good dish obtainable in mountains. Offered "côtelettes de cochon". Drank cider. Then I called on Mr [Wentworth] Webster, long English Chap[lain] at St Jean de Luz. Has given life to study of Basque. Little white old man, very deaf, very pleasant and bright; speaks of his ruined health, but looks very well. Said he knew me well by name; had not read my books, but always read the notices of them.

Sare, little village with several very large houses, lies in a great basin, hills all round, itself on a hill. Protected from North by the Rhune—position which allows of a few vineyards. Culture mostly maize; little else, for Basques are pastoral, not agricultural.

Impressions of the day. The two pollarded planes giving shade before every door. Green-painted bench before each house. White, cool houses; open verandahs and balconies. Great square many-windowed towers of churches, built on arches. In churchyard at Sare, marble stone to Count Stolberg—Stolberg of Holstein 1800-1834. The priest teaching children catechism in Basque. The pelote-wall in each village.- Brown green of burnt grass on mountains; fresh and often vivid green of grass below—just been cut for second crop of hay, carried on carts by the fine fallow cows and oxen, with sheepskins on heads.- Maize tied up.- The little Nivelle rippling over stones. Hedges of hazel etc, with convolvulus, ferns and yellow autumn flowers—fleabane, agrimony etc. The jingling bells on horses of diligence—maddened by flies and stamping ceaselessly at halts. Long halt at St Pé. Seats for 2 on box, for 6 inside. From St Jean de L[uz] to Sare, 1.50f. each.-

Day of imperceptible south wind, with wonderful clearness. Slight haze. Landscape soft and luminous.

I came back all the way by diligence. Gabrielle walked by the shorter mountain road from Sare to Ascain, doing it in ½ h[ou]r less than diligence.

*　　　*　　　*

November 1. Third part of "Author at Grass" appears in *Fortnightly.* Have corrected all proofs of the volume for Constables, to appear early next year.- Am writing "Will Warburton", which, after more than 50pp. finished, I had to begin all over again about a fortnight ago. Do only one page a day. Think of the old days, when I have done as many as 10!

Nov. 8. Left in carriage at 8.30 in morning, with the Gentys, for an excursion into Spain. Clouded sky all day, and very windy, but no rain. Went up over the shoulder of the Rhune, and then down the long winding road to Vera, where we ate our own provisions at the fonda.

The fine old bridge, three-arched, of grey stone, covered with little ferns, ivy etc. On one side two refuges, deep and pointed. In one of them, the wall covered with fruiting ivy and spleenwort; a fig-tree with few leaves and figs, growing up from between stones over the water.- The Bidassoa, dark green and here still, between banks of maize-fields, the maize stalks light brown. A blue kingfisher flashed by.- Mountains all around; in front the compact little village, with great church high-towering above; brown tile roofs and white houses, with galleries or wooden balconies, where vines hang. Beyond, the high, bare Rhune, craggy and red with ferns.- Autumn foliage (chestnuts etc.) reflected in the dark stream.- The ox-cart, solid wheels, woven branches, full of bracken.

At 3.30 started on the drive home, down valley of the Bidassoa. Scenery grand. Narrow gorge; abrupt windings; river rushing, or still; grey crags, high and wild; great mountain sides, with bracken. The valley broadened, bet. dark mountains cov[ere]d with oak, autumn yellow, and green meadows below. Little farms, with piles of dead bracken, collected for litter. Every few yards, a douanier's hut. At Behobia crossed into France, the little town becoming Béhobie. Then over the hill to Urrugne, and home by 6.30.

At the fonda, the sheet of popes' portraits, from St Peter, on the wall. Black-haired girls. In church, Virgin of Seven Sorrows, the saints etc. dressed in real clothing.

[on inside of back-cover]

Paid into Bank
1896 Jan.

	£. s. d.		L[awrence] &
	6. 6.-	(Alg's cheque)	B[ullen] "[Human]
Jan. 20	25. -.-	(Dodd Mead)	Odds & Ends" £78-15
Feb. 12	29. 8.3	(L[awrence] & B[ullen]))	Colles "Despot" 23-10
March 2	25. 4	(Lane)	Blackie 30- 0
April 23	75.12	(Shorter)	L[awrence] &
Aug. 30	20. 0	(Cosmopolis)	B[ullen] royalties
	14.16	(Bullen)	Circular note 10- 0
	19. 0.9	(Colles)	

Alfred's Birthday Jan. 20th 1896
Walter's Birthday Dec. 10th 1891
"Whirlpool" finished p. 37. Dec. 18, 1896. translated into French.
"Town Traveller" begun June 9th '97 (translated into French)
"Dickens" begun 30 Sept. '97
Begun "Crown of Life" July 15 '98
"Our Mr Jupp" translated into French.
"Eve's Ransom" translated into French.
"Ionian Sea" begun 29 June '99.
"Charlatan" begun Oct. 1 1899.
"Odd Women" translated by G. into French
"Author at Grass" begun 1st Sept. 1900.
"Veranilda" begun Dec. 25 1900.
"Will Warburton" begun July 10, 1902.
Article on Realism May 19, '95.
Ionian Sea tour begins Nov. 17, 1897.
"At the Grave of Alaric" *Chronicle* 31 May, 1898.
Sat to Elliott & Fry May 7 '95.
Sat to Mendelssohn Nov. 5. '95.
Delete bottom of p. 30 and top of p. 31 [this, on the original, corresponds to the entry for August 9, 1896]
Gab's birthday Nov. 21
G.'s birthday Nov. 22
Reading Hodgkin's "Italy and her Invaders" p. 7 June 28 '95

Notes

Abbreviations:

CPB : *George Gissing's Commonplace Book* (New York, 1962).
GCH : *Gissing : The Critical Heritage* (London and Boston, 1972).

1888

1 *Margaret and Other Poems,* by an East Anglian, i.e., Thomas Waller Gissing, London, Simpkin, Marshall, and Co., 1855.
2 W.M. Phelps and J. Forbes-Robertson, *The Life and Work of Samuel Phelps* [the Victorian actor], 1886.
3 His reply to Miss Scott, in imperfect condition, is in the Carl H. Pforzheimer Library, New York.
4 *Hortus Inclusus* : Messages from the Wood to the Garden, sent in happy days to the sister ladies of the Thwaite, Coniston [Mary and Susie Beever], ed. A. Fleming, Orpington, 1887.
5 "Two Philanthropic Novelists: Mr Walter Besant and Mr George Gissing", *Murray's Magazine,* April 1888, pp. 506-18. Reprinted in *GCH.*
6 Emily Jane Pfeiffer, *née* Davis (1827-90), poetess. *Women and Work: an Essay* was published in 1887.
7 In a letter of April 8, 1888 to his brother Algernon, Gissing wondered who this Sowerby could be. Perhaps a relative of J.E. Sowerby who illustrated T.W. Gissing's *The Ferns and Fern Allies of Wakefield* (1862). Wakefield *was* the original of Dunfield.
8 Mary Adelaide Walker, *Eastern Life and Scenery, with Excursions into Asia Minor, Mytilene, Crete, and Roumania* (2 vols., 1886).
9 '"Robert Elsmere" and the Battle of Belief', *Nineteenth Century,* May 1888, pp. 766-88. Gladstone's notes held by the British Museum contain extracts from The *Unclassed* and *Thyrza.* He also commented favourably on *In the Year of Jubilee* (1894).
10 The licensed victualling trade was at a critical moment in its history. Since the early seventies there had been a dispute as to whether or not brewers and publicans ought to be compensated for the withdrawal of their licences. The United Kingdom Alliance was strongly against compensation and it organised demonstrations which were at their height in the Spring of 1888.
11 This album of press-cuttings is in the Yale University Library.
12 The manuscript has been either lost or destroyed.
13 Frederick III (1831-1888), king of Prussia and Emperor of Germany, reigned only a few months after the death of William I early in 1888. The 'young savage' was William II (1859-1941) who reigned until Germany's defeat in 1918.
14 In 1888 Smith Elder sold to W.H. Smith 422 copies in quires of the one-volume

edition printed and published anonymously in 1886. Cancel title-pages and a new binding were used. There is no record of this state of the one-volume edition in *The English Catalogue*.

15 Stewart Headlam was the head of a group of clergymen of the Church of England who, in the 1870s, tried to create a socialist movement in Great Britain.

16 Henry King, *Savage London: Lights and Shadows of Riverside Character and Queer Life in London Dens* (Sampson, Low, 1888).

17 Perhaps H.J. Latham, author of *God in Business* (Nisbet, 1889).

18 The strike resulted from the depression in the match trade. It was deplored in some quarters that English consumers did not sufficiently buy English. Over £300,000 was spent on foreign matches in 1888, and this seriously affected sales of Bryant and May's products. Arthur Morrison refers to the problem in his novel *A Child of the Jago* (1896).

19 Ellen Gissing proposed to George that the whole family should spend their holiday at Seascale, on the Cumbrian coast, where they used to go before Thomas Gissing's death.

20 John Gibson Lockhart (1794-1854). Gissing doubtless refers to his Life of Scott.

21 Probably the wife of the photographer mentioned in the entry for 22 August 1888.

22 In 1869. See two of his letters written at the time in *Letters of George Gissing to his Family*, pp. 2-4.

23 Some iron churches dated back to the early days of the Industrial Revolution. John Wilkinson, a pioneering ironmaster, had such a staunch belief in iron that he had not only built the first iron bridge over the Severn, but also an iron chapel for Wesleyans. He was buried in an iron coffin.

24 Two photographs of Gissing taken that day are in the editor's collection.

25 George Crabbe (1754-1832), the Aldeburgh poet, author of *The Village*, an antipastoral in reaction to work like Goldsmith's *The Deserted Village*. Gissing expanded this remark on Crabbe in a letter to Ellen of 30 August 1888 (*Letters of George Gissing to his Family*, pp. 221-22).

26 Edwin Austin Abbey (1852-1911), illustrated the works of Shakespeare and painted 'The Quest of the Grail' and 'The Coronation of King Edward VII'. James Millet (1846-1903) was a landscape painter of the Swiss School, who stayed in Paris from 1883 to 1896.

27 Louise Caroline Alberta (1848-1939), princess of Great Britain and Ireland, Duchess of Argyll, the sixth child and fourth daughter of Queen Victoria. She was endowed with literary and artistic tastes.

28 Mrs Ashton Wentworth Dilke (Mary Dilke), author of *Women's Suffrage* (1885), whose husband translated Turgenev's *Virgin Soil*.

29 Achille Bazaine (1811-88), Field-Marshal who commanded French troops in the Crimean War, in Mexico, then in Lorraine during the Franco-Prussian War. He was sentenced to death but had his sentence commuted. He escaped from prison and died in Madrid.

30 Georges Ohnet (1848-1918), French playwright and novelist, best remembered for his novel *Le Maître de Forges* (1882).

31 Catulle Mendès (1841-1909), French poet, playwright and novelist, a member of the Parnassian school of poetry, *La Première Maîtresse* was published in 1887.

32 The Whitechapel murders had begun 31 August, on which day a woman was found murdered in the backyard of a house in Whitechapel. In October the police began to receive postcards and letters signed 'Jack the Ripper'. The murders continued until 1889, but their perpetrator was never brought to justice. In a recent book, *The Identity of Jack the Ripper* (1970), Donald

McCormick reported that Walter Sickert and George Gissing were both suggested as suspects.

33 Louise Michel (1830-1905), French Revolutionist. In the Franco-Prussian War she ministered to the wounded and took part in armed sorties from Paris. After fighting at the barricades during the uprising of the Commune, she was sentenced to deportation for life, but was pardoned under the general amnesty of 1880.

34 The Eiffel Tower was designed by Gustave Eiffel (1832-1923) for the Universal Exhibition held in Paris in 1889. When Gissing saw it it reached to about one third of its completed height (300 metres).

35 Directory named after Sébastien Bottin (1764-1853), a French administrator.

36 Emile Gaboriau (1835-73), French novelist, one of the pioneers of the detective novel, the author of *Monsieur Lecoq*.

37 "Down with the thieves!" The 'thieves' were of course the députés, the French M.P.'s.

38 The unabbreviated advertisement would have read: 'Georges A.'A. Ne vis plus depuis votre départ. Meurs d'envie de vous revoir. Eprouve profond chagrin. Suis tous les jours marche du navire. Attends impatiemment de vos nouvelles. Bien triste. Donnez adresse et détails du voyage.' [Georges A.A. Have been pining away since you left. Am longing to see you again. Feel very miserable. Follow every day vessel's route. Impatiently awaiting news. Am very sad. Give address and details of voyage.]

39 Jean Eugène Baffier (1851-1921), French sculptor, a pupil of Aimé Millet. He produced busts, terra cotta figurines and bronze statues.

40 Eutrope Bouret (1833-1906), French sculptor, pupil of Buhot. Among his works are 'Psyché au tribunal de Vénus', and a bust of Alexis Bouvier, the popular novelist, over his tomb in the Père La Chaise cemetery.

41 The abolition of the commercial treáty between Italy and France in 1886 was an attempt on the part of Italy to protect herself against the competition of French products.

42 Perhaps Luigi Mariani, author of *Studii storici*, Naples, 1871.

43 'Arciconfraternita' merely means 'confraternita maggiore, principale'.

44 Edward John Trelawny (1792-1881), Shelley's friend, author of *The Adventures of a Younger Son* (1831) and of *Records of Shelley, Byron and the Author* (1858).

45 Henry Reeve edited the *Edinburgh Review* from April 1855 to October 1895.

46 Pasquale Stanislao Mancini (1817-1888), Italian jurist and statesman who served in turn as minister of public instruction, justice and foreign affairs. He published a number of works on jurisprudence.

1889

1 Tillotson and Son were a newspaper syndicate publishing the works they commissioned in seven newspapers, in particular the *Bolton Evening News*. See Frank Singleton, *Tillotsons 1850-1950: Centenary of a Family Business* (Bolton and London, 1950).

2 'Mr John Morley and Progressive Radicalism', by W.H. Mallock, *Quarterly Review*, January 1889, pp. 249-80.

3 A second-hand copy of the three-volume edition which Roberts had sent to Mlle Le Breton on his behalf.

4 This was never written but, somehow, the words cling together in the short story entitled 'The Muse of the Halls' which is concerned with Music Hall life (Christmas 1893 number of *The English Illustrated Magazine*).

5 Georges Boulanger (1837-91), French general. As war minister he came to be accepted by the mob as the man destined to give France its revenge for the disasters of 1870. In 1889 he became an open menace to the parliamentary republic, and was tried and condemned *in absentia* in October. He committed suicide in Brussels on September 30, 1891.

6 Jean-François Raffaëlli (1850-1924), French portrait and landscape painter, etcher and sculptor. He also illustrated books.

7 Emile Montégut (1825-95), literary critic on the *Revue des Deux Mondes* from 1857 to 1890. He translated Shakespeare's works and Macaulay's *History of England*.

8 The quotation reached the printers in time to be on the title-page of the first edition.- Ernest Renan (1823-92), philologist and historian, had made himself known by his studies on the origins of Christianity, in which he applied the method of the historian to the Biblical narrative. Jules Claretie (1840-1913) wrote historical plays and comedies of manners.

9 Noël Kolbac (1859- ?). A pseudonym. Novelist and playwright. Author of *Le Sang, roman magique* (1888) and *Spécialité pour divorces,* comédie-bouffe en un acte (1888).

10 Published in the *Bolton Evening News,* December 28, 1889, p. 2, and reprinted in *Selections Autobiographical and Imaginative from the Works of George Gissing,* ed. A.C. Gissing (1929).

11 See an interesting account of his thoughts on that day in *CPB,* pp. 22-23.

12 Published in Ch. VII of Morley Roberts' *The Private Life of Henry Maitland* and in Edward Clodd's *Memories,* Ch. XV.

13 Thomas Woolner (1825-92), sculptor and poet, and a member of the Pre-Raphaelite brotherhood. His poem first appeared in *The Germ* in January 1850, then was expanded in the 1860s.

14 *Allibone's Dictionary of Authors—Supplement* (Philadelphia, 1891), I, p. 675.

15 Articles on the English Society of Authors, Walt Whitman, Schopenhauer and popular culture among others. See Gissing's letter to Bertz of July 7.1889, in *The Letters of George Gissing to Eduard Bertz,* pp. 63-64.

16 Henry Romeike founded a press-cutting agency in 1881.

17 Frederika Bremer (1801-65), Swedish novelist whose strongly ethical interest and quiet humour are reminiscent of Jane Austen's manner. *Hertha* was published in 1856.

18 His thoughts on death penalty are recorded in *CPB,* pp. 24-25. The occasion was the condemnation of Mrs. Maybrick. See in the Notable British Trial Series *The Trial of Mrs. Maybrick,* edited by H.B. Irving (1927).

19 See note 21 for 1888.

20 Georg Julius Robert Schweichel (1821-1907) published a great number of novels from the 1860's to the 1890's. He also wrote a narrative about his travels in Italy.

21 "The Nether World", September 1889, pp. 370-80. Farrar succeeded in writing ten pages on the book without mentioning once its author's name. Reprinted in part in *GCH.*

22 Henry Thomas Buckle (1821-62), the author of the *History of Civilization in England.*

23 Frank Brangwyn (1867-1943), painter and engraver. He worked for a time with

William Morris, making drawings for tapestries.

24 Thomas Stirling Lee (1856-1916), one of the founders of the New English Art Club and the International Exhibition of Painters, Etchers and Sculptors.

25 John Caird (1820-98), principal of the University of Glasgow and author of *An Introduction to the Philosophy of Religion* (1880) or his brother Edward Caird (1835-1908) who also published a number of works on philosophy and religion.

26 See his notes from Ribot's *L'Hérédité psychologique* in *CPB*, pp. 59-62.

27 Heinrich Schliemann (1822-90), the famous German archaeologist who excavated Troy, Tiryns, and Mycenae.

28 Reprinted in translation in *GCH*.

29 Avlona, nowadays Valona, is a correction, as is the sentence in brackets. What Gissing had written originally is illegible. The portion of the coast he mentions is now part of the Albanian territory.

30 Matilde Serao (1856-1927), Italian realistic novelist of Neapolitan life, influenced by Flaubert and Zola. Her novels include *Fantasy, The Conquest of Rome, The Ballet-Dancer,* and *Farewell Love.*

31 *Sebetia, Schizzi napoletani* appeared in three parts in 1884-95. Amilcare Lauria (1854-1931) used the pen-name of Sebetius.

1890

1 Wilhelm Wendlandt, "Das literarisches Markt", *Deutsche Presse,* December 8, 1889, pp. 394-98.

2 *Demos* had been published anonymously in 1886. Tauchnitz did not bring out *The Nether World.*

3 Salvatore Farina (1846-1918), popular Sardinian novelist who has been called the Italian Dickens.- Francesco Mastriani (1819-91), Neapolitan novelist whose life was one of destitution. His works, sentimental or realistic, found some favour in the Mezzogiorno.- Gaetani has not been identified.

4 According to A.C. Young, Hugo Fink probably worked for the zoological station founded by Dr Dohen, a German naturalist, in 1872, as a centre for the study of the plant and animal life of the Mediterranean Sea area.

5 Malwida von Meysenbug (1816-1903), German authoress of aristocratic origin who was in deep sympathy with the movement for the unification of Italy. Her *Memoirs of an Idealist* appeared in 1876.

6 *The Speaker* (1890-1907), continued as *The Nation* (1907-1931), edited by T. Wemyss Reid until 1899.

7 Thomas Holcroft (1745-1809), actor, novelist and playwright, a friend of Thomas Paine and William Godwin.

8 William Henry Edwards, *A Voyage Up the River Amazon,* including a residence at Para, New York, 1847. Edwards was an American who wrote on butterflies in the 1860s and 1870s.

9 He wanted to know "what term of office is required in a Govt office if a man wishes to resign his place" (letter to Algernon, June 1, 1890). Evans has not been identified.

10 Very likely the Oxford Music Hall, to which Gissing refers in his scrap-book (Carl H. Pforzheimer Library).

11 "The Bronze-caster—a Study from Life" appeared in *Macmillan's Magazine* for

January 1891 and the other articles in *Murray's Magazine* between January and June 1891.

12 Taken by G. and J. Hall, of Wakefield. A copy of this portrait is in the editor's collection.

13 Augustine Birrell (1850-1933), essayist and politician, best remembered by his *Obiter Dicta* (1884, 1887 and 1924). He entered Parliament as a Liberal in 1889.- Osborne Morgan (1826-1897), Q.C., J.P., M.P. (Liberal). He held a number of political posts, carrying through the House of Commons the Married Women's Property Act (1882), of which Gissing had just been writing in ch. XXVI of *New Grub Street,* and an Act abolishing corporal punishment in the Army.

14 The Bampton Lectures are delivered at Oxford annually, the cost being defrayed out of the proceeds of the estate left for the purpose by the Rev. John Bampton, of Trinity College, who died in 1751.

1891

1 See "The Revision of *Thyrza*", by C.J. Francis, *Gissing Newsletter,* October 1971, pp. 7-9.

2 An amusing extract is transcribed in *CPB,* p. 48. Richard Bentley (1662-1742), classical scholar and theologian, figures in Swift's *Battle of Books* and in Pope's *Dunciad.*

3 *An Introduction to the Study of English Rhythms,* by Harold Dingwall Bateson.

4 Frederick Dolman published "The Social Reformer in Fiction" (*Westminster Review,* May 1892, pp. 528-37) in which the three novels published by Smith, Elder in inexpensive editions, *Demos, A Life's Morning* and *The Nether World,* figured prominently.

5 Review by Louis Frederic Austin, in the number for May 2, 1891. Reprinted in *GCH.*

6 A commentary (May 2, 1891) and a review proper (May 9, 1891). Both are reprinted in *GCH.*

7 Both novels were published in Harper's Franklin Square Library, in 1886 and 1889 respectively.

8 The hot discussion about *New Grub Street* began on June 1, 1891 with a eulogy of the novel by Walter Besant. On July 1, 1891, Andrew Lang rebutted Besant's views and Besant replied. (Their controversy is reprinted in *GCH.*) In the August number of *The Author* were printed anonymous protests of two writers who sided with Besant.

9 The *Saturday Review* for October 17, 1891 wrote of the first one-volume edition of *Thyrza:* "Mr Gissing is supposed to be the photographer of the London poor, and in the course of pushing with his camera up slums and courts in the East End we have seen him taken to task for his cynicism and his excess of realism. To ourselves it does not appear that the author of such a book as *Thyrza* deserves any reproof of this kind. Our warning to him would rather be to avoid anything like an excess of sentiment or a too rose-coloured view of the society he describes."

10 He made copious notes from the book in *CPB,* p. 31.

1892

1 There is no record of any publication in book form by H.Vanwyke in the) British Museum catalogue.

2 The serialization of *New Grub Street* as *Ein Mann des Tages* covered the period December 29, 1891-April 30, 1892.

3 This new monthly was edited by Henry Hyde Champion. Roberts's article appeared in the May 1892 number. Reprinted in *GCH*.

4 "Figaro's Coming Man: Mr Algernon Gissing", *London Figaro*, April 27, 1892, pp. 3-4.

5 The first American edition of the book is that of the AMS Press (1968).

6 *Mr and Mrs Bancroft On and Off the Stage,* written by themselves, 2 vols., 1888.

7 Reprinted in *GCH*.

8 *Times,* July 1, 1892, p. 18. Reprinted in *GCH*.

9 Sir Henry Stafford Northcote (1846-1911), second son of Sir Stafford Northcote (Earl of Iddesleigh), leader of the House of Commons. He was Conservative M.P. for Exeter from 1880 to 1899.

10 No record of any publication in volume form by this correspondent.

11 She published a novel, *A New Race Diplomatist* (Lippincott Company), in 1900.

12 "Why I don't Write Plays. XV: Mr George Gissing", *Pall Mall Gazette,* September 10, 1892, p. 3. Gissing's answer was part of an enquiry made by William Archer into the reasons why so many leading novelists did not write for the stage.

13 In fact Bentley's ledgers show that his loss amounted to only £23.16.5.

14 William's letters to George are now held by the Berg Collection of the New York Public Library.

15 Under the auspices of the Royal Society of Musicians. See "Concerts", *Athenaeum,* November 26, 1892, p. 748.

1893

1 "At the annual meeting of the Ex[eter] Lit[erary] Socy, a man who looked and spoke like a plumber said: 'I'm not a very old gentleman, but' etc'". *CPB,* p. 42.

2 The paragraph appeared in the *Athenaeum* for March 25, 1893, p. 379.

3 There is no record of this memoir having been written and published.

4 The *National Observer* (1890-97), which had originated in the *Scots Observer* in 1888, was edited by W.E. Henley until March 1894.

5 Clara E. Collet, "George Gissing's Novels: A First Impression", *Charity Organization Review,* October 1891, pp. 375-80.

6 *The Athenaeum,* May 27, 1893, p. 67. Reprinted in *GCH*.

7 *Pall Mall Gazette,* May 29, 1893, p. 4. Reprinted in *GCH*.

8 Appendix I, "Tennyson—and After ?", pp. 325-31.

9 Probably Charles Stewart (1840-1916), solicitor in London from 1872 onwards, member of the Council of the Law Society, and author of two volumes of reminiscences and essays.

10 Gissing noted an amusing extract in his *Commonplace Book,* p. 42: "Where

Trelawny describes how he thrashed an usher at school, he says: 'The sweat dropped from his brows like drops of rain from the eaves of a pigsty." He used this again in *Will Warburton* (1905), p. 38.

11 In a series of paragraphs about Gissing Zangwill wrote: "Gissing has this supreme distinction: he is the only man of the age who has never been paragraphed—not even mendaciously. His movements are a mystery, his style of dress is known only to his tailor. Shakespearean in his range of character, he is Shakespearean also in his incorporeality. But unlike Shakespeare, he has not kept his personality out of his books—and in so doing he has missed being the Shakespeare of our day." *Pall Mall Magazine,* July 1893, p. 442.

12 *Illustrated London News,* August 5, 1893, p. 155. Reprinted in *GCH.*

13 Works by Chateaubriand—*Atala, René* and *Les Natchez.*

14 Clara Collet collaborated to Charles Booth's *Life and Labour of the People in London.* See Ruth M. Adams, "George Gissing and Clara Collet", *Nineteenth Century Fiction,* June 1956, pp. 72-77, and on Charles Booth and his family, Belinda Norman-Butler, *Victorian Aspirations,* the Life and Labour of Charles and Mary Booth (London, 1972).

15 Photograph reproduced for instance in the *Sketch,* January 9, 1895, p. 517.

16 Probably *Grammont: Memoirs,* by Anthony Hamilton, reissued in 1890.

17 Jean Jules Jusserand (1855-1932), diplomat and man of letters, was like Taine, Chevrillon, Siegfried and many others, a distinguished French analyst of English and American literature and history.

18 Thomas Bailey Aldrich (1836-1907), a New England writer who edited the *Atlantic Monthly* from 1881 to 1890. He wrote poems, plays, novels and short stories. His best known work is *The Story of a Bad Boy* (1870).

19 "London's Street Music", *Echo,* September 19, 1893, p. 1. The passage quoted ('Do you know that music . . . foul hands') occurs in Ch. IX, 'A Golden Prospect'.

20 'His sympathy with the suffering is less superficial, more discriminating, and more poignant than Mr Besant's. Perhaps that is the reason why his work, which repels at first, grips the reader so much more from its warm humanity and its breathing reality. However unpleasant the atmosphere, his men and women live before you with hot blood and throbbing veins. Mr Besant's characters are too often only lay figures.' N.O.B., 'Mr Walter Besant', *Echo,* 2 October 1893, p. 1.

21 The Miners' Federation brought out 300,000 men in a strike which lasted nearly four months, and ended in the resumption of work at the old rates and the establishment of a Conciliation Board for the future regulation of wages.

22 Article signed N.O.B., *Echo,* 16 October 1893, p. 1. Reprinted in *GCH.*

23 Kershaw Thorpe Best, author of *An Etymological Manual.*—Francis Gribble (1862-1946) was a minor novelist and journalist who published, in quick succession, *Red Spell, The Things that Matter, The Lower Life* and *Only an Angel* in 1895-97. He often contributed to the *Fortnightly Review* and was the original editor of Phil May's Annual.- *Funny Folks,* a popular weekly, which appeared from 12 December 1874 to 28 April 1894.

1 His letter appeared in the *National Observer* for January 27, 1894, p. 271. It was concerned with the grammatical errors made by a character in *Appassionata*, a novel by Elsa D'Esterre-Keeling.

2 Half the cost of printing of *The Odd Women*—the one-volume English edition and the colonial edition were printed from American type. Lawrence & Bullen published their one-volume edition in March 1894.

3 *Charicles; or, Illustrations of the Private Life of the Ancient Greeks*, by Wilhelm Adolf Becker (1796-1846), published in 1840. The story is set in the fourth century before Christ.

4 Ada Rehan (1860-1916), American actress. According to *Who Was Who*, during the seasons of 1875-78 she enacted nearly two hundred different characters in Shakespeare's plays. In 1879 she was engaged by Augustine Daly for his New York Theatre, playing from then on under his management in London, Berlin, Paris as well as in America. She created a *furore* with her impersonations of Viola, Rosalind and other Shakespearean heroines.

5 "Mr George Gissing", *Pearson's Weekly,* June 30, 1894, p. 787.

6 The publication of novels in three-volume form had become the general practice since Walter Scott's publishers had set the fashion. Now that the circulating libraries—Mudie's and Smith's prominent among them—no longer found profitable a system of which they were the main supporters, the system quickly collapsed. English publishers henceforth issued novels straightaway in one volume which was meant to be *bought* by the public. On this important question, see Royal A. Gettmann, *A Victorian Publisher,* a Study of the Bentley Papers (Cambridge, 1960) and Guinevere L. Griest, *Mudie's Circulating Library and the Victorian Novel* (Newton Abbott, 1971).- Gissing did not write a volume of essays, *The Private Papers of Henry Ryecroft*, until 1900-01.

7 The paragraph on Gissing is in the *Echo* for Monday, July 23, 1894, p. 1.

8 "Literary Gossip", *Athenaeum,* August 4, 1894, p. 163. The paragraph gave some account of Cecil Roberts's life—"one of hard work and adventure such as falls to the lot of few men, for besides many years at sea both before the mast and as an officer, he was gold and tin mining in Queensland, pearl fishing in the Louisades, seal fishing in Behring's Sea, and exploring with Dr. Schrader's expedition up the Augusta River, New Guinea." Cecil Roberts was the author of *Adrift in America* and several short stories written in collaboration with his brother Morley.

9 Augustus J.C. Hare, *The Story of Two Noble Lives,* being memorials of Charlotte, Countess Canning, and Louisa, Marchioness of Waterford, 3 vols., 1893.

10 Martha Somerville, *Personal Recollections from early life to old age, of Mary Somerville*. With selections from her correspondence, by her daughter (1873).

11 Clara Collet found the title "prettyish", but Gissing replied that she was mistaken as to his intentions—that the title was "satirical, and in keeping with the tone of the book".

12 Augustus J.C. Hare, *Sussex* (London, 1894), pp. 115-16. The quotation ("At the lowest point . . . couch grass is burning") is from Ch. XLI ("The Living") of *Thyrza*.

13 Published in *Lloyd's Weekly Newspaper* (September 15, 1895) and reprinted in *George Gissing: Essays and Fiction*, ed. P. Coustillas (Baltimore, 1970).

14 A photograph of Gissing in this outfit can be seen in Jacob Korg's *George Gissing: A Critical Biography* (1963).

15 Paul Margueritte (1860-1918), French realistic novelist, author of the once famous four-volume saga *Une Epoque* dealing with the Franco-Prussian war of 1870-71. In collaboration with his brother Victor (1866-1942), he wrote many novels advocating the emancipation of woman and international amity.

16 Doubtless some work of Thomas Randolph (1605-35), poet and playwright, who addressed several poems to Ben Jonson.

17 Emile Bergerat (1845-1923), prolific writer of novels, dramas and criticism.

18 George Edwardes (1852-1915) first entered into management with John Hollingshead at the Gaiety Theatre in 1885, and was at various times manager of the Duke of York's, Empire, Garrick, Comedy and Criterion Theatres. He married Julia Gwynne, the actress, whom Gissing had known in the early 1880s.

19 Robert Harborough Sherard (1861-1943), novelist and critic whose production extends from 1880 to 1930. He was the author of such novels as *A Bartered Honour* (1883), *The American Marquis* (1888), *After the Fault* (1906), and wrote lives of Wilde, Zola, Daudet and Maupassant. He translated and edited Pierre Loti.

20 Yetta Blaze de Bury had heard of Gissing through the wife of Francis Warre Cornish, Vice-Provost of Eton College from 1893 to 1916. Mrs Blanche Cornish was the daughter of the Hon. W. Ritchie, Legal Member of the Council in India.

1895

1 *The Times,* December 27, 1894, p. 3. "If foreign judgment in matters literary really might pass as an indication of the opinion of posterity, the author of 'Demos' and of 'New Grub Street', Mr George Gissing, ought to-day to be content with his lot, for in a lecture given this afternoon [Dec. 26] by Mlle Yetta Blaze de Bury he and his work were the sole theme . . . [She] has attempted to show how completely his impulse as an artist was conditioned by his scientific convictions, or rather his philosophy of life, taken, whether he willed it or not, from the Darwinian storehouse to which, for such men as Mr Gissing, Professor Huxley has been the incomparable guide."

2 L.F. Austin, "A Study in Drab", *Sketch,* January 9, 1895, p. 517. Reprinted in *GCH.*

3 No portrait was used by the editor. Only some gossip on Gissing appeared in the issue for March 27, 1895, p. 23.

4 Photographs of the novelist taken that day are to be found in *George Gissing: Essays and Fiction* (1970) and in Jacob Korg's *George Gissing* (1963).

5 Walter Besant's paragraph in the *Author* for January 1, p. 208, had been quoted by the *Daily Chronicle* of the next day, p. 3, and this had led to correspondence from Jerome on January 3 and Shorter on January 4 about Gissing's contributions to their journals.

6 It was a review of *In the Year of Jubilee,* January 26, 1895, p. 98. Reprinted in *GCH.*

7 For some unknown reason the project never materialized.

8 Both the *Spectator's* review of *In the Year of Jubilee* (February 9, 1895, pp. 205-6) and the letter to Morley Roberts are reprinted in *GCH.* The contemplated survey of Gissing's work did not appear in the *Fortnightly Review.*

9 Vol. I, p. 6 of the Supplement. Reproduced in *George Gissing: Essays and Fiction* (1970).

10 Gissing's six sketches for Jerome were published in *To-day* from May 4 to June 8, 1895 as a series entitled "Nobodies at Home".

11 The cutting in Gissing's papers at Yale is dated April 13, 1895 but the title of the journal has been partly cut out. Perhaps the journal was the [*New York Commercial*] *Advertizer*.

12 A photograph of Gissing taken that day can be seen in Edward Clodd's *Memories* (1916).

13 Arsène Houssaye (1815-1896), French novelist, historian and playwright. He was the author of a pungent satire, *L'Histoire du 41ème fauteuil de l'Académie Française*.

14 The stanzas have been printed several times—in Edward Clodd's *Memories*, in Morley Roberts's *The Private Life of Henry Maitland* and in *The Letters of George Gissing to Edward Clodd*.

15 Edward Henry Palmer, *The Desert of the Exodus*, Journeys on foot undertaken in connection with the ordnance survey of Sinai and the Palestine Exploration Fund (Cambridge, 1871). Sir Walter Besant wrote *The Life and Achievements of E.H. Palmer* as well as a book on Jerusalem in collaboration with him.

16 The Omar Khayyám Club was founded on October 13, 1892 by Frederic Hudson, C.K. Shorter and George Whale. It included 59 members who met three times a year. See *The Book of the Omar Khayyám Club 1892-1910* (London, 1910).

17 Either William Luker, portrait and landscape painter whose works were exhibited regularly from 1852 to 1889 or his son William, born in London in 1867, a member of the Royal Society of British Artists.

18 "Londoners at Home", *Quarterly Review*, July 1895, pp. 59-82. A long review-article of *London of To-Day*, by Charles Eyre Pascoe (1894) and of volumes V and VI of Charles Booth's *Life and Labour of the People in London* (1895).

19 Elizabeth Matthew, the wife of Sir James John Trevor Lawrence (1831-1913), of Burford, Dorking, former Conservative M.P. for the Reigate Division of Surrey.

20 Henry Parkman Sturgis, a son of the well-known American-born London financier.

21 Published in the *Colophon*, Part 18 [1934]. He overlooked some of his earnings, especially for the first ten years of his career.- In the present entry, he had first written "nearly" in the place of "more than".

22 Peter Alfred Taylor (1819-91), radical politician, M.P. for Leicester from 1862 until his retirement in 1884. His wife, Clementia, was a daughter of John Doughty of Brockdish, Norfolk. Taylor edited a volume of Mazzini's work in 1875.

23 The substance of Gissing's reply did not appear in *To-Day*, but in the *Idler* for April 1896 in an article by Burgin entitled "How Authors Work", pp. 344-48.

24 A photograph taken that day can be seen in *George Gissing and H.G. Wells* (1961).

25 There is no record of publication.

26 "Mr Gissing First and Last", *Daily Chronicle*, December 2, 1895, p. 3. Reprinted in *GCH*.- No review of *The Unclassed* could be traced in the *Northern Figaro*.

1 Giovanni Verga (1840-1922), Italian novelist, dramatist and writer of short stories. He described life at the lower level of society in Sicily. His best known work is *Cavalleria Rusticana* (1880).

2 The copy with Gissing's revision is held by the Alexander Turnbull Library, Wellington, New Zealand. See the Harvester Press edition of *Isabel Clarendon* (1969) edited by P. Coustillas.

3 See *CPB*, p. 26, where Gissing transcribed this statement of Spencer's: "There is no political alchemy by which you can get golden conduct out of leaden instincts." He commented: "Precisely. And the whole answer to Socialism is: that if Society were ready for pure Socialism, *it would not be* such as it is now."

4 Based on his American experiences in the Tennessee community of Rugby founded by Thomas Hughes.

5 "Our Learned Fellow-Townsman" appeared in the *New York Times* on March 20, 1896.

6 *Born in Exile,* of which A. & C. Black published a yellowback at 2s. in 1896, was never issued by Lawrence & Bullen.

7 His only book to all appearances.

8 The wife of John Michael Gordon Biddulph (afterwards Lord Biddulph) (1869-1949). J.P., D.L., Director of Martins Bank.

9 Harold Frederic took a photograph of Gissing and Whale at the station. It was reproduced in the New York *Bookman*, April 1898, p. 99, and in *George Whale 1849-1925* (London, 1926).

10 Rosalind Ellicott, educated at the Royal Academy of Music under Frederick Westlake and Thomas Wingham, became an A.R.A.M. in 1896. Among her works are an overture (Gloucester Festival), 1886, and a choral ballad, "Henry of Navarre", 1894. She died in 1924.

11 (Sir) William Henry Hadow (1859-1937) edited Shakespeare and Tennyson and was the author of many works on music like *The Oxford History of Music* (1901-1905), *Richard Wagner, Studies in Modern Music,* etc.

12 G.B. Burgin's account of this party confirms that Gissing felt ill at ease in it. "George Gissing. Some Personal Impressions and Opinions", *Bookman,* January 1915, pp. 120-21.

13 The aim of Toynbee Hall, founded in 1885, was to improve the cultural level of the East-Enders. Another attempt of the same kind was the People's Palace, initiated by Walter Besant.

14 Gissing merely gave the date and place of his birth, and a list of his publications in volume form from *The Unclassed* (1884) to *Eve's Ransom* (1895).

15 William Morris (1834-1896), poet, novelist, art craftsman and socialist leader, author of *News from Nowhere* (1891). Gissing had him in mind when he created the character of Westlake in *Demos* (1886).

16 'Woman's Kingdom: "The Odd Women" and its influence in England'. A cutting is among Gissing's papers at Yale; the title of the newspaper (probably 7 November 1896) has been cut out.

1897

1 It appeared in the number for 22 January 1897, p.1.

2 Ferdinand Gregorovius (1821-91), German historian, author of a *History of Rome in the Middle Ages* (1859-73) and of *Lucrece Borgia* (1874).

3 Corrado Ricci, who published three books on Ravenna between 1878 and 1889.

4 Antoine Frédéric Ozanam (1813-53), French writer and historian, author of works on Dante. He was one of the first Roman Catholics to realize the importance of the "social question".

5 "The Novels of Mr George Gissing", *Contemporary Review,* August 1897, pp. 192-201. Reprinted in *GCH.*

6 Frederick Dolman, "George Gissing's Novels", *National Review,* October 1897, pp. 258-66. Reprinted in *GCH.*

7 "The Old School", *Dinglewood Magazine,* December 1897, pp. 2-4. Reprinted in *George Gissing at Alderley Edge,* by P. Coustillas (London, 1969).

8 The sketch appeared in the *Daily Chronicle* on May 31, 1898, p. 6, and was reprinted in *Selections Autobiographical and Imaginative,* ed. A.C. Gissing (1929).

9 Above this sentence Gissing wrote in brackets "architect?" to remind himself that the bigger boy had taken it for granted that he was an architect. See *By the Ionian Sea,* Ch. 8.

10 Gissing clearly appears on Dr. Enrico Sculco's agenda, which has been preserved by his son, Dr. Silvio Sculco. He was called upon twice a day from Nov. 28 to Dec. 2, once on the 3rd and again once on the 4th. Dr. Sculco's fee amounted to 24 lire. I am indebted to Dr. Francesco Badolato for this information.

11 Gissing compared Dickens and Daudet at some length in chapter XI of *Charles Dickens, A Critical Study* (1898), the book he had recently written at Siena. Among other resemblances, he noted their attitude to the people, their 'enjoyment of the virtues and happiness of simple domestic life' and their humour. Both novelists died suddenly.

12 Giordano Bruno (1548-1600), Italian philosopher who fought scholastics and Aristotelian logic. He was burnt alive in Rome and his statue was erected "where the pyre burned".

1898

1 Lord Ronald Sutherland Gower (1845-1916), sculptor and author of publications mainly on the fine arts. The Shakespeare Monument at Stratford is by him.

2 The *Westminster Gazette* of February 17, 1898, p.10, commented on an article by John Northern Hilliard, "The Author of *The Whirlpool*", which accompanied a review of the novel by Hamlin Garland (*Book Buyer,* February 1898, pp. 38-42). Gissing was made to declare: "If my stories are pessimistic, it is only because my life is such. My environments were sordid, the people were sordid, and my work is but a reflection of it all. Sadness? My books are full of it. The world is full of it [. . .] Ah, the toil for the 'weib und kind', how it fashions men's lives! Mine has been but the common lot. No use saying much about it. I

find my little happiness in the fields in summer, and am content when I think of the toiling millions, twelve miles away, who never see a blue sky, or feel the earth yield beneath their feet."

3 Felice Cavallotti (1842-98), politician and writer. He played an important part in the unification of Italy. He was killed on March 6 in a duel against F. Macola, editor of the *Gazzetta di Venezia.*

4 The Rev. Robert Stuart de Courcy Laffan who was principal of Cheltenham College from 1895 to 1899.

5, "Charles Dickens", *Outlook,* 134-35. Reprinted in GCH.

6 Writer of children's books, and translator of Andersen.

7 Probably F. and A. Steel, of Perth, Scotland. See *George Gissing and H.G. Wells* (1961), p. 98.

8 There was an outbreak of violent popular agitation in Milan in May 1898. The Crispi Cabinet reacted strongly and tried to reduce the freedom of the Press as well as the rights of combination. But the electorate disapproved of this policy, sending 33 socialist deputies to Parliament. On 29 July 1900 the anarchist, Bresci, was to assassinate King Umberto I to avenge the victims of the Milan uprising.

9 Gyp, pseudonym of Sybille Marie-Antoinette de Riquetti de Mirabeau (1850-1932), prolific writer of political and social novels. She satirized Society life and was nationalist in a passionate and narrow-minded fashion.

10 Marcel Prévost (1862-1941), French novelist who reacted against naturalism and whose novels are largely concerned with female psychology. His best known works are *Les Demi-Vierges* (1894) and *Les Vierges Fortes* (1900).

11 See Wells's own reminiscences in his *Experiment in Autobiography* (1934).

12 Gissing crossed out "Edith" after Mlle Fleury became "Gabrielle" to him, so as to avoid using the first name of his second wife. See *The Letters of George Gissing to Gabrielle Fleury* (1964), p. 30.

13 Of all the Dickens introductions that he wrote only six were published by the time the Rochester edition was discontinued by Methuen—those to *The Pickwick Papers* (1899), *Bleak House, Nicholas Nickleby* and *Oliver Twist* (1900), *Barnaby Rudge,* and *The Old Curiosity Shop* together with *Master Humphrey's Clock* (1901). They were collected in 1924-25 in *Critical Studies of the Works of Charles Dickens* and in *The Immortal Dickens,* together with the introductions to *Dombey and Son, Martin Chuzzlewit* and *Sketches by Boz.* The introductions to *David Copperfield* and to the Christmas Books have disappeared. See *Gissing's Writings on Dickens,* by P. Coustillas (Enitharmon Press, 1969).

14 The article which Halpérine-Kaminsky contemplated writing could not be located.

15 Edouard Pailleron (1834-99), poet and playwright. He is best remembered by *Le Monde où l'on s'ennuie* (1868), a satirical comedy of manners.

16 Armand Charpentier (1864-1949), French novelist. He was a disciple of the Goncourt brothers and Zola and his novels—the work of an anti-clerical and pacifist writer—have a markedly naturalistic tendency.

17 Edith and Alys Lister were friends of A.H. Bullen's. The former was a writer who published verse under the pseudonym of E.M. Martin and stories and articles under a variety of other names. See *Frank Sidgwick's Diary and Other Material Relating to A.H. Bullen* (Oxford, Blackwell, 1975).

18 The leading article which started off the discussion (*Daily Chronicle,* 29 September 1898, p.4) and an article summing up the controversy (*Speaker,* 8 October 1898, p.429) are reprinted in *GCH.*

19 Paul Mariéton (1862-1911), poet and novelist. Founder and editor of the *Revue Félibréenne*.

20 "A Novelist of the Hour", *Sewanee Review*, July 1898, pp.360-70. Reprinted in *Collected Articles on George Gissing*, ed. P. Coustillas (1968).

21 Collet Dobson Collet had died on the previous Wednesday at the age of eighty-five. In the middle of the century he had taken an active part in the agitation for the repeal of the taxes on the press. At the time of his death his *History of the Taxes on Knowledge* was appearing in the *Weekly Times*.

1899

1 See Rothenstein's recollections of that occasion in his *Memories* (1934, vol. I, p. 304).

2 Mme D'Arcis was, with the Choisys and the Bovets, one of Gabrielle's Swiss friends. She lived at 136, Chêne Bougeries, Geneva. Letters written by Gabrielle in April 1904 are dated from that address.

3 Mme Recordon was the proprietress of the Villa Badia at Cannobio, on the Italian shore of Lago Maggiore. Gabrielle and Mme Fleury had been staying there on holiday a few years before.

4 Louise Read was the executrix of Barbey d'Aurevilly (1808-89), the aristocratic poet and novelist.

1900

1 In a letter to Pinker of June 17, 1900 Gissing referred to a cheque for £21.0.3.

2 On the ceremony, see *The Sphere*, July 14, 1900, p. 56.

3 The massacres in China were one aspect of the struggle between modernists and traditionalists. The Yihetuan secret society, called the Boxers in the West because their symbol was a closed fist, besieged the foreign legations in Peking. The European reaction to these events was spectacular. By August an army of 20,000 foreign troops had relieved the legations.

4 Mme Lescot, a minor novelist now altogether forgotten, wrote stories with titles which convey something of the atmosphere of the period: *Fêlures d'âme, Mariages d'aujourd'hui, Vaines promesses*, etc.

5 Gabrielle's translation was not published, but the manuscript has been preserved.

6 *Jenny of the Villa*, published by Edward Arnold in 1900, is the only novel by the author in the British Museum.

7 Details on Gabrielle's relatives can be found in *The Letters of George Gissing to Gabrielle Fleury* (1964).

8 Further reading of Sainte-Beuve in 1901 led to the addition of a section on Port-Royal (Autumn VIII) in *An Author at Grass*, retitled *The Private Papers of Henry Ryecroft*.

9 There is no record of any publication in volume form by Miss L.M. Burton.
10 Hamlin Garland (1860-1940), the American novelist, who had reviewed *The Whirlpool* in the *Book Buyer* of February 1898.
11 The article on Dickens's homes and haunts appeared in the *Nottinghamshire Guardian*, August 16, 1902, p.8. It was reprinted in *Homes and Haunts of Famous Authors* (London, 1906).

1901

1 The projected sixpenny reprint of *The Town Traveller* was published by Methuen in March 1902.
2 The serialization of *New Grub Street* as *La Rue des Meurt-de-Faim* in the *Journal des Débats* lasted until June 3, 1901. Gabrielle paid £10.10s. to Smith, Elder for translation rights. As Gissing had sold the entire copyright of the book, none of this money went back to him.
3 See P. Coustillas, *Gissing's Writings on Dickens* (1969), p.12.

1902

1 The portraits taken on that occasion by Elliott & Fry are those reproduced in the 1927 volume of family letters and in the 1935 edition of *Workers in the Dawn*. (The portrait in the latter is mistakenly dated 1895). Besides Gissing's portrait *Literature* published an article on his works by Morley Roberts (July 20, 1901, p. 52), which is reprinted in *GCH*.
2 "An Author at Grass" was serialized in the *Fortnightly Review* in four instalments—May, August, November 1902 and February 1903.
3 Edith Gissing was by now confined in a lunatic asylum, and Alfred was living with a farming family at Mabe, near Falmouth, in Cornwall.
4 See the entry in *CPB*, p. 65.
5 J.W. Fell was, like Miss Rachel White, one of the fellow patients at the Nayland Sanatorium with whom he kept in touch. He lived at Plane Trees, New Pelton, Halifax.
6 There had been huge preparations for the coronation of the King. Troops and many eminent people had arrived from all parts of the Empire. The news published on the morning of the 24th June that the King was seriously ill and that surgeons had had to operate for perityphlitis caused great surprise and emotion. As Gissing noted in due course. the coronation took place on 9th August.
7 Published under the title "Mr Swinburne on Dickens" in the *Times Literary Supplement* for July 25, 1902, p. 219. Reprinted in P. Coustillas's *Gissing's Writings on Dickens* (1969).
8 Published under the title "Mr Kitton's Life of Dickens" in the *Times Literary Supplement* for August 15, 1902, p.243. Reprinted in P. Coustillas's *Gissing's Writings on Dickens* (1969).

WHO'S WHO in GISSING's DIARY

A

A. See GISSING, ALGERNON.

AGABY, Miss. Musician. Gissing became acquainted with her through the Gaussens in 1884; he refers to a concert she gave in April 1885 in a letter of same month to his brother.

ALG. Algernon Gissing, George's brother. See under GISSING.

ALLEN, GRANT (1848-99). Scientist and writer, and sometime professor of mental and moral philosophy in Jamaica. He wrote a number of scientific works, but was known to the general public by his pot-boiling novels. His story *The Woman Who Did* (1895), on the problem of free union, created a sensation.

ALLHUSEN, E.L. A correspondent of Gissing and a collector of his works. His name is connected with a famous association copy of *Workers in the Dawn*.

ANDERSON, CHARLES (1826-1893). Vicar of St. John's, Limehouse. He corresponded with a number of men of letters. His acquaintance with Gissing began in May 1887 shortly after the publication of *Thyrza*. He introduced Gissing to Edward Clodd. See Edward Clodd's *Memories* (1916) and *The Letters of George Gissing to Edward Clodd,* ed. P. Coustillas (1973).

ANDERSON, JOSEPH. American journalist on the Boston *Evening Transcript.* He wrote on Gissing's life and works on several occasions in the 1890s. He was the brother of Mary Anderson, the actress.

ANDERSON, MARY (1859-1940). Actress. Sister of Joseph Anderson, the journalist. She stayed occasionally in Broadway, Worcestershire, where Algernon Gissing lived for a time. She was the model for the heroine of Mrs Humphry Ward's first novel, *Miss Bretherton,* and published two volumes of reminiscences.

ART, GEORGES. French critic and translator who contributed to the *Revue Bleue* at the turn of the century. Besides Gissing he translated Balfour, John Morley and R.L. Stevenson.

ASH, CONNIE (1865-?). A friend of the Gissing sisters with whom Gissing fell in love in the summer of 1890. His correspondence shows that his sisters did their best to persuade him that she would make a bad housewife, unsuitable for him.

ATKINSON, CHARLES MILNER (1854-1920). Stipendiary magistrate for Leeds from 1894, and J.P. for the West Riding of Yorkshire. His publications on legal matters and his study of Jeremy Bentham were posterior to Gissing's death.

AUSTIN, ALFRED (1835-1913). Journalist and Poet Laureate. A tory, he was editor of *The National Review* and in that capacity published three short stories by Gissing. Lord Salisbury made him Poet Laureate, and he shortly afterwards published an unfortunate ode celebrating the Jameson Raid.

AUSTIN, LOUIS FREDERIC (1852-1905). Literary journalist. He was a regular contributor to the *Illustrated London News* and the *Sketch,* an active member of the Omar Khayyám Club and a skilful writer of *vers de société.*

B

BAIN, NISBET (1854-1909). He was in business in the City, then in 1883 became assistant librarian in the British Museum. He published a great number of translations from the Russian, the Hungarian, and the Scandinavian languages, as well as historical works.

BAINTON, GEORGE. A Coventry clergyman with literary interests, compiler of *The Art of Authorship,* a book in which he printed without permission a number of letters from contemporary authors.

BARING-GOULD, SABINE (1834-1924). Novelist and writer of religious and miscellaneous works. Living in Devon he made an extensive use of the antiquities and folklore of that county. *Mehalah* (1880) and *The Gaverocks: a Tale of the Cornish Coast* (1887) are among his best known novels.

BARNARD, FREDERIC (1846-1896). Illustrator and genre painter. He worked for such reviews as *Good Words, Once a Week,* the *Illustrated London News* and *Punch.* His illustrations of the Household Edition of Dickens's works were particularly successful.

BARNES, MARTHA (1858-1946). A pupil of Gissing's at the Waltham High School, near Boston. She resumed her relations with him in 1895 and they corresponded for some years. See the article by P.M. Stone on Gissing and Miss Barnes in the *Waltham News Tribune,* November 17, 1953, p. 9.

BARRIE, Sir JAMES (1860-1937). Dramatist and novelist. The son of a weaver, he worked as a journalist in Nottingham and moved to London in 1885. During the next fifteen years he wrote stories exploiting a sentimental image of life in Scotland. Afterwards, he became a successful playwright.

BASHKIRTSEFF, MARIE (1860-84). Russian diarist whose Journal, written in French and published posthumously in 1887, attained a wide popularity. Gissing read it with keen appreciation.

BATEMAN, Sir ALFRED EDMUND (1844-1929). Board of Trade official. He played an important part in many international commercial negotiations and exhibitions between the 1870's and the end of the First World War.

BECKE, GEORGE LOUIS (1848-1913). Author of many books with the Pacific as a background, in particular *By Reef and Palm* (1894), *The Ebbing of the Tide* (1896), and *Pacific Tales* (1897).

BEDFORD FAMILY. Tom and Mary were the elder Mrs Gissing's nephew and niece, and consequently George's cousins. They lived in Broadway, Worcestershire. Mary married one Austin Williams in 1894. Gissing had no close relations with them.

BEERBOHM, Sir MAX (1872-1956). Critic, essayist and caricaturist. He was a sharp, witty satirist of literary mannerisms and social pretences, and he had already earned himself a reputation by the time of Gissing's death.

BEESLY, EDWARD SPENCER (1831-1915). Positivist leader and professor of history at University College, London, from 1860 to 1893. He translated two of Auguste Comte's works. It was through him that Gissing became a contributor to *Vyestnik Evropy* in 1881-82.

BENTLEY, GEORGE (1828-1895). Publisher and editor of *Temple Bar*. He prided himself on giving good, moral books to the British public. His philistinism made relations with Gissing difficult in the mid-eighties.

BERGER, ADELE. German writer who translated *New Grub Street* under the title *Ein Mann des Tages*.

BERTZ, EDUARD (1853-1931). Man of letters. A socialist exile, he became acquainted with Gissing late in 1878, lived for some years in London, migrated to America where he became a member of Thomas Hughes's Tennessee community and in 1884 returned to Germany. He corresponded regularly with Gissing and wrote occasional articles on his work. See *The Letters of George Gissing to Eduard Bertz* (1961).

BESANT, ANNIE (1847-1933). Socialist and theosophist. After separating from her husband, the Rev. Frank Besant in 1873, she associated with Bradlaugh as freethinker and radical, then joined the Fabian Society in 1885, and transferred her interest to theosophy a few years later.

BESANT, Sir WALTER (1836-1901). Historian, social reformer and novelist. He began to write novels in collaboration with James Rice (1844-82), then continued on his own with philanthropic stories like *All Sorts and Conditions of Men* and *The Children of Gibeon*. He was instrumental in the foundation of the People's Palace and the Society of Authors.

BINKS, JOHN. A friend of Gissing's father. Like him he was associated with the Mechanics' Institute. Gissing called on him occasionally when he was in Wakefield.

BLACK, CLEMENTINA. A novelist and journalist who wrote on labour and feminist problems. She was a contributor to the *Illustrated London News* in the 1890s.

BLACK, JOHN GEORGE. A fellow student of Gissing's at Owens College. He was involved in the affair which led to his friend's expulsion. They saw a good deal of each other in the early 1880s, and resumed relations in 1895 for a time. Gissing was also in touch with Black's sister in 1893.

BOSHER, Mr and Mrs. Brother-in-law and sister-in-law of Gissing. Bosher married Susan Underwood, sister of Edith. He was a pawnbroker in Fulham Palace Road, London.

BOUGHTON, Mrs. Gissing's housekeeper at 7 Clifton Terrace, Dorking (1898-99).

BOVET, ERNEST (1870- ?). Professor at the University of Rome (1897-1901), then at the University of Zurich (1901-21). He contributed many articles to the *Semaine Littéraire* and the *Bibliothèque Universelle,* and was the editor of *Wissen und Leben.* He became Swiss Secretary for the League of Nations.

BREWSTER, S.N.P. Solicitor whose chambers were at 11 New Inn, Strand, W.C. He failed to arrange a divorce between Gissing and his second wife.

BROUGHTON, RHODA (1840-1920). Novelist. Her earlier work won her a reputation for audacity of which the late Victorian and Edwardian age deprived her. Among her best known novels are *Cometh up as a Flower* (1867) and *Doctor Cupid* (1886). Her popularity was at its highest in the 1870s and 1880s.

BRUCE, SAMUEL. A friend of Gissing's father at Wakefield. He collaborated with him in creating the local Mechanics' Institute. Gissing visited him occasionally when he happened to be in Wakefield.

BRYAN, CHARLES. Gissing's landlord when he lived at 1 St. Leonard's Terrace, Exeter.

BRYCE, JAMES (1838-1922). Politician and historian. He held a number of political and diplomatic posts from Gladstone's third ministry to the First World War, and wrote books on the Holy Roman Empire, Transcaucasia and South Africa among others.

BULLEN, ARTHUR HENRY (1857-1920). Scholar and publisher. He edited and published many authors of the Elizabethan and Jacobean period. As partner in the firm of Lawrence & Bullen he was Gissing's main publisher during the years 1892-97.

BURGIN, GEORGE B. (1856-1944). Novelist, critic and journalist. He was sub-editor of the *Idler* until 1899 and Secretary of the Authors' Club from 1915 to 1917. He published over ninety novels from 1894 to 1938.

BURNS, JOHN (1858-1943). Trade unionist and politician. An early member of the Social Democratic Federation, he played a prominent part in the London open air agitation in 1887 and in the Dock Strike of 1889. He became an M.P. in 1892 and occupied government posts from 1905 to 1914. He had started in life as a miner.

BURROWS, HERBERT. Socialist leader, member of the Social Democratic Federation. He was a minor political figure from the mid-eighties to the First World War.

BURY, YETTA BLAZE DE (1845-1902). Author. She was the daughter of Henry Blaze, Baron de Bury, and Rose Stuart who were also writers. She wrote in both French and English. Her projected articles on Gissing never seem to have been written. She did not include him in her *Romanciers anglais contemporains* (1900).

C

CABLE, GEORGE WASHINGTON (1844-1925). American novelist, author of stories of the old society of Louisiana.

CAINE, Sir HALL (1853-1931). Novelist. He was a Manxman and a friend of D.G. Rossetti. His widely popular novels, which include *The Deemster* (1887) and *The Bondman* (1890), were usually set in the Isle of Man.

CARTER, MARY E., later Mrs Stevenson. Novelist, a cousin of Dora Carter of Wakefield, who was a friend of Ellen Gissing. Her works include *Mrs Severn* (1890) and *Mrs Elphinstone of Drum* (1893) as well as various writings of a religious nature. She published extracts from Gissing's letters to her in *T.P.'s Weekly,* December 27, 1912, p. 864.

CHALMERS, ANDREW. Unitarian minister in Wakefield, author of *Transylvanian Recollections: Sketches of Hungarian Travel and History* (1880) and *Red Cross Romance* (1893).

CHAMPION, HENRY HYDE (1859-1928). Man of letters and politician. He served in the Army during the Afghan War and as adjutant at Portsmouth, then became a leading element of the Social Democratic Federation, was tried for sedition after the Trafalgar Square Riots in 1886 and won the London Dock Strike in 1889. Four years later, he migrated to Australia, became a leader-writer on *The Age* (Melbourne) and founded the Book-Lovers' Library. He reviewed Gissing's later books in *The Book Lover.*

CHEVALIER, ALBERT (1861-1923). Comedian. He was for many years associated with the Kendals, A.W. Pinero, the Bancrofts etc. In the mid-nineties he made himself a name with his famous coster-songs. He wrote over a hundred sketches, monologues and plays.

CLIFFORD, Mrs WILLIAM KINGDON (1853-1929). Prolific novelist and playwright whose production extended from the mid-eighties to her death. She was a close if prejudiced analyst of woman's mind. Her husband (1845-79), who was professor of applied mathematics at University College, London, is well known for his philosophical treatises.

CLODD, EDWARD (1840-1930). Scientist, man of letters and Secretary of the London Joint Stock Bank. An agnostic, he was an intelligent popularizer of the work of Darwin, Spencer and Huxley, and was on friendly terms with many writers of his time.

COLLES, WILLIAM MORRIS (1855-1926). Literary agent. Originally a barrister, he founded the Authors' Syndicate in 1890, of which he was the managing director. He was Gissing's agent from 1893 to 1898 and continued to do transactions for him even after Gissing turned to James B. Pinker.

COLLET, CLARA ELIZABETH (1860-1948). M.A., Labour correspondent of the Board of Trade, collaborator of Charles Booth in his gigantic work on the London poor. She was one of Gissing's close friends for the last ten years of his life.

COLLIER, JOHN (1850-1934). Painter. He studied art at the Slade School, and in Paris and Munich. He published several volumes on art and contributed to periodicals, mainly articles on artistic subjects.

COLVIN, Sir SIDNEY (1845-1927). Man of letters and keeper of the prints and drawings at the British Museum. He contributed widely to periodicals on the history and criticism of art, and he published a number of biographies and literary studies, on Landor and Keats among others.

CONWAY, MONCURE (1832-1907). Author. A Unitarian minister, he had to give up his career because of his sermons against slavery. He wrote books on Carlyle, Emerson, Hawthorne and Thomas Paine.

COOK, Sir FREDERICK LUCAS (1844-1920). M.P. from 1895 to 1906; head of Cook, Son & Co., warehousemen, St. Paul's.

COOKSON-CRACKANTHORPE. Montague Hughes Crackanthorpe, K.C., of 20 Rutland Gate, S.W., and Newbiggin Hall, Westmorland. He assumed by royal license the name of Crackanthorpe in lieu of Cookson on succeeding to the Newbiggin estate in 1888. Gissing gave lessons to his sons in the 1880's.

CORELLI, MARIE (1854-1924). Prolific and best-selling novelist, whose first story, *A Romance of Two Worlds* (1886), was an instant success. Her stories were marred by their magniloquent and portentous tone.

CORNWALL, BARRY. Pseudonym of Bryan Waller Procter (1787-1874). Poet born at Leeds. He was a schoolfellow of Peel and Byron, and joined the circle of Leigh Hunt and Charles Lamb. His wife survived him until March 1888.

COURTNEY, WILLIAM LEONARD (1850-1928). Journalist and critic. He was at various periods editor of *Murray's Magazine,* of the *Fortnightly Review,* a member of the editorial staff of the *Daily Telegraph* and a director of Chapman & Hall. He wrote philosophical and literary works.

CRACKANTHORPE, HUBERT (1865-96). Short-story writer, author of *Wreckage, Sentimental Studies* and the posthumous *Last Studies.* He drowned himself in the Seine when his career was only starting.

CRAIK, Sir HENRY (1846-1927). Secretary of the Scotch Education Department, Whitehall, from 1885 to 1904, and man of letters. He published a Life of, and Selections from, Swift, as well as books on Scotland and India.

CRANE, STEPHEN (1871-1900). American writer who depicted the New York slums in *Maggie* and made his name with his Civil War novel, *The Red Badge of Courage.* He served as war correspondent in Cuba and Greece, and spent the last few years of his life in England.

CRAWFORD, FRANCIS MARION (1854-1909). Popular American novelist who from 1883 onwards lived mainly at Sorrento. His novels, of which Gissing read a few, are set in a variety of countries—Italy, Germany, Turkey, the East as well as England and America.

CRAWFURD, OSWALD (1834-1909). Novelist and man of letters. After a number of years in the Foreign Office, he turned to literature, wrote travel narratives and novels, and contributed to many reviews.

CRUM, Miss. Walter Grahame's aunt.

CURTIS, Miss, of 13 Church Street, Eastbourne. Gissing probably met her during his stay in that town in February 1888. She was one of the several young women with whom he thought he was in love between Nell's death and his second marriage.

D

DAVEY, Lord (1833-1907). Q.C. in 1875; M.P. for Christchurch in 1880-85; Solicitor General and knighted in 1886; M.P. for Stockton-on-Tees in 1888-92; Lord Justice of Appeal and Privy Councillor in 1893. He became Baron Davey of Fernhurst in 1894.

DAVID, THEODORE (1869-1902). Sculptor and draughtsman. He was born in Lausanne and died in Paris.

DAVIDSON, JOHN (1857-1909). Poet and dramatist. With his *Fleet Street Eclogues,* he made himself a reputation as a poet of city life. It was this aspect of his work which Gissing appreciated. The two men corresponded and met occasionally in the mid-nineties.

DELABORDE, ELIE MIRIAM (1839-1913). French pianist and composer, under whom Gabrielle Fleury studied. He gave concerts throughout Europe. From 1873 onwards he taught music at the Conservatoire de Paris.

DILKE, CHARLES (1843-1911). Politician and writer. He was a Member of Parliament and Under-Secretary of State for Foreign Affairs. His second wife was the widow of Mark Pattison. His personal honour and morality were brought into question by a divorce case in which he was co-respondent.

DIXON, ELLA NORA HEPWORTH. Novelist and journalist. Daughter of William Hepworth Dixon, editor of the *Athenaeum.* She edited *The Englishwoman,* an illustrated magazine, March 1895-December 1899.

DOBSON, HENRY AUSTIN (1840-1921). Poet and critic. As a poet he was a skilful practitioner of light verse, imitations, parodies and translations. As a critic he concentrated on the literary history of the 18th century, with works on Goldsmith, Walpole, Hogarth and Richardson.

DOLMAN, FREDERICK (1867-?). Journalist. He was on the staff of a number of journals and took an active share in the local government of London. He wrote on Gissing's works sympathetically on several occasions.

DOWIE, MENIE MURIEL. See NORMAN, Mrs HENRY.

DOYLE, Sir ARTHUR CONAN (1859-1930). Novelist and controversialist, who achieved world fame with his Sherlock Holmes stories. He met Gissing in Rome in 1898, but the two writers seem to have had little interest in each other's works.

DUNNE, BRIAN BORU. American journalist whom Gissing met for the first time in Siena in 1897. He was on the staff of the *Baltimore Sun,* and corresponded with the novelist after his return to America. See *George Gissing and H.G. Wells* (1961).

E

E. Edith Gissing, *née* Underwood; the novelist's second wife.

EAST, Sir ALFRED (1849-1913). Painter. Knighted in 1910. He became President of the Royal Society of British Artists.

ELSON, LOUIS CHARLES (1848-1920). Music critic, lecturer, author and teacher, of Boston. He was on the staff of the *Boston Advertiser* from 1886 until his death, and was known and appreciated throughout the States and Canada. Gissing became acquainted with him in Boston in 1876.

EUSTACHE, ROBERT (1853-1927). A relative of Gabrielle Fleury, living at the Château du Chasnay, at Fourchambault, near Nevers. He was a landowner with artistic tastes who wrote verse and painted pictures. He married his cousin Gabrielle Crawshay in 1899. They had one daughter, Denise Eustache-Le Mallier, the present owner of the Château du Chasnay.

EVANS, W.M. A friend of the Wellses. According to Royal A. Gettmann, he was on the staff of the *Monitor,* the Roman Catholic journal, and he later became secretary of Newman House.

F

FARRAR, FREDERICK WILLIAM (1831-1905). Novelist, sermon and theological writer. He taught at Harrow and was headmaster of Marlborough School, then became Canon of Westminster, Archdeacon of Westminster and Dean of Canterbury. He wrote stories for boys reflecting the ideas of Thomas Arnold on education.

FITZGERALD, EDWARD ARTHUR (1871-1931). Mountaineer and author of *Climbs in the New Zealand Alps* (1896) and *The Highest Andes* (1899). He was first married to Jeanne de Rothiacob, then, in 1903, to Ménie Muriel Dowie, formerly Mrs Henry Norman.

FITZGERALD, PERCY HETHERINGTON (1834-1925). Editor, biographer and novelist, mainly remembered for his activities as a Dickensian. He was a friend of John Foster.

FLEURY, GABRIELLE MARIE EDITH (1868-1954). Gissing's third "wife". She was the daughter of Auguste Fleury, head cashier of the Docks and Warehouses Company at Marseille. See introduction to *The Letters of George Gissing to Gabrielle Fleury* (1964).

FORBES-ROBERTSON, Sir JOHNSTON (1853-1937). Theatrical manager from 1896 to his death. He had been a pupil of Phelps, and for a time the leading actor at Bancroft's and Hare's Theatres.

FORESTIER, AMEDEE (1854-1930). French black and white artist who worked principally for the *Illustrated London News*. He illustrated novels by Besant, Seton Merriman, Anthony Hope and many others. Like Gissing, he was a member of the Omar Khayyám Club.

FREDERIC, HAROLD (1856-1898). American journalist and novelist. He was the London correspondent of the *New York Times,* and met Gissing at a dinner of the Omar Khayyám Club. His greatest success was *The Damnation of Theron Ware (Illumination)* in 1896.

FREEMAN, EDWARD AUGUSTUS (1823-1892). Historian. His main work was the six-volume *History of the Norman Conquest of England* (1867-79). Gissing read a number of his works in the 1890s and walked in his footsteps in Calabria.

FUNCK-BRENTANO, THEODORE (1830-1906). French philosopher and sociologist born in Luxemburg. He founded the Collège libre des sciences morales. Gabrielle Fleury was a friend of his wife and daughter. Theodore's son, Frantz (1862-1947) made a distinguished career as a historian.

G

G. Gabrielle Fleury, the novelist's third "wife".

GARRISON, FRANK. The son of William Lloyd Garrison (1805-79), the poet and anti-slavery leader, who befriended Gissing during his stay in Boston. He followed the novelist's growing reputation in America in the 1890's.

GAUSSEN FAMILY. It consisted, among other members, of Mrs Gaussen—a friend of Gissing's and an admirer of his works from 1884 onwards—, her husband, David, their son James, to whom Gissing gave lessons, and their daughter Ella. They lived at Broughton Hall, Lechlade, Gloucestershire, and spent the Season in London.

GILDER, RICHARD WATSON (1844-1909). American editor and poet. He was assitant editor of *Scribner's Monthly,* then editor of the *Century,* and brought out a number of volumes of prose. He was abroad in the mid-nineties.

GISSING, ALFRED CHARLES (1896-1975). The novelist's younger son. Like his brother Walter he was educated at Gresham's School, Holt, Norfolk. Between the wars he wrote a number of articles about and edited several books by his father. He also published a biography of Holman Hunt. From the end of the second world war to his death he lived in Switzerland.

GISSING, ALGERNON (1860-1937). Gissing's younger brother. Like George and William, he was educated at Wakefield, then at Lindow Grove School, Alderley Edge, Cheshire. Although he was trained as a solicitor, he opted for a literary career in the 1880's, writing some thirty books, mainly novels. He married Catherine Baseley in 1887. His project of writing a biography of his brother as a counterblast to Roberts's *Private Life of Henry Maitland* never materialized.

GISSING, CATHERINE (KATIE), *née* Baseley (1859-1937). Algernon Gissing's wife, They had five children Enid, Roland, Alwyn, Katharine and Margaret. She suffered much from the straightened circumstances of her household.

GISSING, EDITH, *née* Underwood (1867-1917). The novelist's second wife and the daughter of a working sculptor. She was committed to a lunatic asylum in 1902 and died at Fisherton House, Salisbury, on February 27, 1917, of organic brain disease.

GISSING, ELLEN (1867-1938). Gissing's younger sister. Until after his death, she lived in Wakefield, Yorkshire, where she kept for years a preparatory school with her sister Margaret. She wrote two articles of reminiscences about George in the *Nineteenth Century and After* (1927) and *Blackwood's Magazine* (1929) as well as some religious books.

GISSING, MARGARET (1863-1930). George's sister. She was educated at Wakefield, was governess for a time and founded a preparatory school with her sister Ellen. George described her as "always in poor health" and "rather bitterly religious".

GISSING, MARGARET BEDFORD (1832-1913). The novelist's mother. She was the daughter of a Droitwich solicitor, a competent housewife, but her eldest son deplored her lack of interest in intellectual matters.

GISSING, MARIANNE HELEN, *née* HARRISON (1858-1888). The novelist's first wife, whom he met in the streets of Manchester in the winter of 1875-76. They married in October 1879 and separated in 1883.

GISSING, THOMAS WALLER (1829-1870). The novelist's father. A Suffolk man who settled as a pharmaceutical chemist in Wakefield. A Liberal in politics he became municipal councillor of the town, wrote occasionally for the *Wakefield Free Press*, and published two booklets on the local flora and three slender volumes of verse.

GISSING, WALTER (1891-1916). The author's elder son. He was trained as an architect and worked for the Society for the Protection of Ancient Buildings. He was killed at Gommecourt, in the battle of the Somme, on July 1, 1916. He could not be identified.

GISSING, WILLIAM (1859-1880). Brother of the novelist. After leaving Lindow Grove School, at Alderley Edge, he worked in a Manchester bank for a time, then for health reasons, had to live on music lessons at Didsbury. He died of consumption.

GORST, HAROLD E. (1868-?) Son of the Rt. Hon. Sir John Gorst (1835-1916), the politician. He was the editor of the short-lived *Review of the Week*, wrote the volume on Disraeli in the "Victorian Era Series" and various other books. See his own recollections, *Much of Life is Laughter* (1936).

GOSSE, EDMUND (1849-1928). Critic, verse writer and essayist. His work on Ibsen, whom he translated, was instrumental in introducing the "new drama" to England. His criticism was urbane, but often inaccurate. He wrote occasional articles on Gissing's works and helped H.G. Wells to secure a pension on the Civil List for Gissing's two sons.

GRAHAM, R. CUNNINGHAME (1852-1936). Politician and man of letters. He took a prominent part in the episode of "Bloody Sunday" in Trafalgar Square on November 13, 1887. An M.P. from 1886 to 1892 he turned to literature in the mid-nineties.

GRAHAME, WALTER (1872-?). A private pupil Gissing had taken in July 1884. Grahame was a cousin of Anthony Hope Hawkins (1863-1933), the author of *The Prisoner of Zenda* and other romances. He was also related to Kenneth Grahame (1859-1932), author of *The Wind in the Willows*.

H

HALPERINE-KAMINSKY, ILIA (1858-1936). Russian writer, who was naturalized French in 1890. He translated many Russian authors into French (e.g. Tolstoi) and French writers into Russian (e.g. Daudet, Dumas fils, Zola and Sardou).

HAMLYN, Mrs, *née* SELOUS. Daughter of Frederick Selous, the big-game hunter. She eloped with Morley Roberts in 1893 and married him in 1896 after her husband's death. She died in 1911. See Storm Jameson, *Morley Roberts: The Last Eminent Victorian* (London, 1961).

HARDY, THOMAS (1840-1928). Novelist. He was occasionally in touch with Gissing from 1886 to 1903. See P. Coustillas, "Some Unpublished Letters from Gissing to Hardy", *English Literature in Transition,* 1966, IX, no. 4, pp. 197-209.

HARRISON, AUSTIN (1873-1928). Author. He had Gissing as a tutor in the 1880's, and later wrote on him on several occasions. He was editor of the *English Review* and published a number of works on political and social questions, as well as a volume on his father, Frederic Harrison.

HARRISON, BERNARD (1871-1956). A son of Frederic Harrison, the man of letters and Positivist leader, and the elder brother of Austin Harrison. Gissing had him as a regular pupil from 1880 to 1884, then again for a short period late in 1887. He became a landscape painter and was converted to Roman Catholicism.

HARRISON, EDGAR E. A printer living in Gunnersbury. He had occupied 7K Cornwall Residences before Gissing. He was a member of the well-known firm of printers, Harrison and Sons, 59 Pall Mall, S.W.

HARRISON, FREDERIC (1831-1923). Man of letters and Positivist leader. He befriended Gissing after the publication of *Workers in the Dawn* and employed him as tutor for his two eldest sons, Austin and Bernard. He had two other sons, Godfrey and René.

HARRISON, JANE ELLEN (1850-1928). Greek scholar. Vice-President of the Hellenic Society, 1889-96; lecturer in classical archaeology at Newnham College, Cambridge. She published many works on Greek art and literature.

HARTE, WALTER BLACKBURN. Sub-editor of the *New England Magazine* (Boston), and author of *Meditations in Motley* (Boston, 1894).

HARTLEY, ALFRED (1855-1933). English painter and etcher. His works were on show in the great London exhibitions from 1885 onwards. He was awarded a bronze medal at the 1889 Universal Exhibition. Gissing was in touch with him in the late 1880's and 1890's.

HEADLAM, Rev. STEWART (1847-1924). Clergyman and Christian socialist, who played a significant part in the socialist movement from the 1870s to the foundation of the Labour Party. He was an active Fabian and prominent on the London School Board, and published a number of books on religious, theatrical and political subjects.

HENLEY, WILLIAM ERNEST (1849-1903). Poet, playwright, critic and journalist. He was editor of the *Scots* (afterwards) *National Observer*, and was looked up to by a group of young men including Kipling and Morrison. He was a staunch imperialist and an advocate of everything English.

HERWEGH, GEORG (1817-1875). German socialist poet who spent most of his life in exile. His social hymn *Mann der Arbeit, aufgewacht!* has remained one of the war-songs of the socialist movement. His widow, who lived in Paris, was a friend of Gabrielle Fleury.

HICK FAMILY. The members of it mentioned here are Matthew Bussey Hick, the pharmaceutical chemist who sold his shop to Gissing's father; his son Henry, a schoolfellow of the novelist and a doctor, who renewed acquaintance with him in 1895 (see *Henry Hick's Recollections of George Gissing,* ed. P. Coustillas, 1973); and Ethel, a sister of Henry, who lived with her father in Wakefield.

HILLIARD, JOHN NORTHERN. American journalist who reviewed a number of Gissing's later works, and offended him by publishing a pseudo-interview of him in the February 1898 *Book Buyer.*

HIND, C. LEWIS (1862-1927). Writer. Author of many artistic and literary publications. He was editor of the *Pall Mall Budget* (1893-95), then of the *Academy* (1896-1903). His book *More Authors and I* (1922) contains an interesting chapter on Gissing.

HOCKING, SILAS KITTO (1850-1935). Novelist. He was ordained in 1870 but resigned the pastorate in 1896. He was on two occasions an unsuccessful candidate for Parliament. His literary production amounts to some fifty novels.

HODGKIN, THOMAS (1831-1913). Historian and banker. He was a devoted and active member of the Quaker community and a public-spirited citizen of Newcastle.

His main work, which covers ground trodden by Gibbon, was *Italy and her Invaders* (1879-1899).

HODGSON BURNETT, Mrs (1849-1924). Novelist and dramatist. She reached fame and fortune with *Little Lord Fauntleroy* (1886), which she dramatized herself. It brought her over £20,000.

HODGSON, WILLIAM SCOTT (1864- ?) Self-taught seascape painter in oil, pastel and water-colour. He was formerly chairman of Thomas Hodgson Ltd, lace manufacturers of Nottingham. He married Emily Humphreys, whom Gissing censured heavily.

HOPE, ANTHONY (ANTHONY HOPE HAWKINS) (1863-1933). Novelist. He made his mark with *The Prisoner of Zenda,* set in imaginary Ruritania, and added the corresponding epithet to the language. Besides other successful though slight romances, he wrote plays and a chatty volume of *Memories and Notes* (1927).

HORNUNG, ERNEST WILLIAM (1866-1921). Novelist and journalist. After two years in Australia in 1884-86, he turned to literature for good and achieved his greatest success with *The Amateur Cracksman* and *Mr Justice Raffles.* He met Gissing in Rome in 1898 and wrote an article on him at his death (*Week's Survey,* January 9, 1904).

HUDSON, WILLIAM HENRY (1841-1922). Naturalist and writer of South American origin. He wrote a number of books about birds which were praised but little read until *Green Mansions* (1904), by its success, helped to create interest in his earlier works. He corresponded with Gissing for some fifteen years.

HUGHES, THOMAS (1822-1896). Novelist and miscellaneous writer. He was the author of *Tom Brown's School-Days* and like Charles Kingsley, a Christian Socialist. He founded a short-lived community at Rugby, Tennessee, which Eduard Bertz, a member, depicted in his story *Das Sabinergut* (1896).

HUNTER, WILLIAM ALEXANDER (1844-98). Lawyer and professor of Roman law at University College, London. He was editor of the *Weekly Dispatch* for five years.

I

IMAGE, SELWYN (1849-1930). Artist. He attended the Slade School, Oxford, under Ruskin, and became Slade Professor of Fine Art, Oxford (1910-1916).

J

JACOBSEN, JENS PETER (1847-1885). Danish writer, mainly known for his novels *Marie Grubbe* (1876) and *Niels Lyhne* (1880). They are impressionistic pictures of life which introduced decadent sensibility into northern literature.

JAY, Rev. OSBORNE. Vicar of Holy Trinity, Shoreditch, author of three books describing his philanthropic work, *Life in Darkest London* (1891), *The Social*

Problem (1893) and *A Story of Shoreditch* (1896). He was a friend of Arthur Morrison in whose *A Child of the Jago* he appears as Father Sturt.

JEROME, JEROME K. (1859-1927). Novelist and playwright whose greatest success was *Three Men in a Boat* (1889). He was editor of two reviews, the *Idler* and *To-Day,* in which Gissing's name appeared frequently.

JOLLY FAMILY. Relatives of John Shortridge, a Yorkshireman married to a Capri woman, whom Gissing met during his first stay in Italy. The Jollys, who lived in Acton, near London, welcomed Gissing on his first visit, but they soon gave him the cold shoulder, perhaps after hearing of his past.

K

KATIE. See GISSING, Catherine.

KEARY, CHARLES FRANCIS (1848-1917). Novelist and writer on history and philosophy. He was for some years on the staff of the British Museum, then turned to writing, never enjoying more than a *succès d'estime.*

L

LANE, JOHN (1854-1925). Publisher. Joint-founder with Elkin Matthews of the Bodley Head publishing firm in 1887. The partnership was dissolved in 1894 and the *Yellow Book* launched by Lane in the same year. Gissing contributed "A Foolish Virgin" at Lane's request.

LANG, ANDREW (1844-1912). Historian, poet, anthropologist and journalist. The catholicity of his interests led him to dissipate his energies in too many fields. His crabbed character was not incompatible with a sanguine view of life.

LAWRENCE, HARRY W. Publisher and A.H. Bullen's partner in the firm of Lawrence & Bullen. Frank Swinnerton's *Background with Chorus* contains some details about his personality.

LEAF, Dr. WALTER (1852-1927). Greek scholar and banker. He married the daughter of J.A. Symonds. His publications include a *Companion to the Iliad* and a translation of Homer's poem.

LE BRETON, FANNY. French translator who worked for Hachette, the Paris publishing firm. She translated *Demos* (1890, 2 vols.), using the pseudonym of Hephell.

LEE, Sir SIDNEY (1859-1926). Man of letters. He published a number of books on the times of Shakespeare, a biography of Queen Victoria, and edited the *Dictionary of National Biography.*

LEE, VERNON, pseudonym of VIOLET PAGET (1853-1935). English essayist and novelist. She wrote studies of art and life (especially in Italy), essays and sketches.

LINTON, Mrs LYNN (1822-98). Novelist and short-story writer. She took part in contemporary controversies over Darwinism and woman's emancipation.

LITTROW, LEO VON, or DE (1860- ?). Marine painter born in Trieste. He worked in Munich, Vienna, Fiume and Abbazia, and exhibited his works in Germany and Austria from 1880 onwards. Gissing was moderately pleased with his illustrations for *By the Ionian Sea.*

LOW, SIDNEY (1857-1932). Author and journalist. He was sub-editor of the *St. James's Gazette* under Frederick Greenwood whom he succeeded as editor in 1888 for a decade. He was afterwards literary editor of the *Standard* (1904-05). His publications include historical works and a Life of De Quincey.

LOWNDES, Mrs MARIE ADELAIDE (1848-1947). Novelist and playwright. She was acquainted with many important people of her time and her diary, published in part, is especially valuable.

LUSHINGTON FAMILY. Vernon Lushington (1832-1912), J.P., Q.C., was Secretary to the Admiralty from 1869 to 1877 and Judge of the County Courts for Surrey and Berkshire from 1877 to 1900. Gissing gave lessons to his daughters in the early 1880's. One of them, Kitty, married Leopold James Maxse, proprietor of the rightist *National Review* from 1893 to 1929, a journal which published several of Gissing's short stories.

M

MAARTENS, MAARTEN. Pseudonym of Joost van der Poorten-Schwartz (1858-1915). Dutch novelist writing in English. His satirical stories usually deal with his own countrymen and are critical of manners and motives.

McCARTHY, JUSTIN (1830-1912). Novelist, politician and historian. He was leader writer on the *Daily News* from 1870 onwards, and M.P. for some twenty years. He wrote a *History of our Own Times* covering the whole Victorian period. He corresponded with Gissing, and so did his daughter.

McCARTHY, JUSTIN HUNTLY (1860-1936). Dramatist, novelist and historian. Son of Justin McCarthy, M.P., mentioned above.

McCORMICK, ARTHUR DAVID (1860-1943). Painter and engraver. From 1889 he exhibited his works at the Royal Academy and at the Royal Institute of Painters, of which he was a member. Gissing made his acquaintance through Morley Roberts, and he met him several times in the 1890's.

McILVAINE, CLARENCE W. A member of the firm Osgood, McIlvaine & Co., which published the works of Thomas Hardy. Gissing met him at Hardy's in 1895.

MARRIOTT-WATSON, HENRY BRERETON (1863-1921). Australian novelist who settled in London in 1885. Early in his career he did a good deal of journalism for the *Pall Mall Gazette,* the *National Observer* and *Black and White.* He was a friend of H.G. Wells and Stephen Crane.

MASSINGHAM, HENRY WILLIAM (1860-1924). Journalist. He was in turn on the staff of many newspapers and journals, especially the *Star*, the *Daily Chronicle*, the *Daily News* and the *Nation* which he edited from 1907 to 1923. He published volumes on *The London Daily Press, Labour and Protection*, and many articles in the magazines.

MEREDITH, GEORGE (1828-1909). Novelist and poet. Gissing made his acquaintance in 1884 when Meredith was manuscript reader for Chapman & Hall. They met again in 1895 and until he left England for good Gissing was an occasional visitor at Boxhill. They kept up a desultory correspondence.

METHUEN, Sir ALGERNON (1856-1924). Publisher. He changed his name from Stedman to Methuen in 1899, ten years after founding the firm of Methuen & Co. He published a number of popular authors: Kipling, Belloc, Chesterton, Anthony Hope and Stevenson among others. Gissing reproached him with failing to recognise the distinctive character of his works, and with not having published *The Crown of Life* at the opportune moment.

MEYNELL, ALICE (1847-1922). Poet, essayist and critic. A Roman Catholic, she married Wilfred Meynell in 1877, and their home was visited by many literary friends like Tennyson, Coventry Patmore, Meredith and Francis Thompson, whom the Meynells rescued from destitution and drug-addiction.

MONKHOUSE, ALLAN NOBLE (1858-1936). Journalist, novelist and playwright. As a writer on the *Manchester Guardian* and a contributor to the *Manchester Quarterly* he often wrote on Gissing's works (see *GCH*). He wrote a number of novels and plays which were appreciated by a small but enthusiastic following.

MONOD, AUGUSTIN (1859-1913). Latin scholar and pedagogist. He taught in the Lycée at Orléans and in the Lycée Montaigne in Paris. He was the author of some ephemeral publications.

MOORE, FRANKFORT (1855-1931). Irish novelist who wrote a number of stories set in the eighteenth century and introducing historical characters like Samuel Johnson, Burke and Sheridan.

MOORE, GEORGE (1852-1933). Novelist and playwright. Gissing rather jealously watched his career as a realist from the mid-eighties to the mid-nineties. They both wanted, though in different ways, to free English fiction from the repressive moralism of the Victorian age.

MORISON, COTTER (1832-1888). Biographer. He wrote lives of Gibbon and Macaulay, but his best work was his *Life of St. Bernard* (1863). His last book, *The Service of Man* (1887) was written from the Positivist point of view.

MORLEY, JOHN (1838-1923). Politician and man of letters. He was twice Chief Secretary for Ireland, then Secretary of State for India, and Lord President of the Council. Gissing became acquainted with him through Frederic Harrison in 1880 and contributed articles on Social Democracy for the *Pall Mall Gazette*, then under his editorship.

MORRISON, ARTHUR (1863-1945). Novelist and art collector. His lower-class stories of the nineties, in which there have been revivals of interest in the inter-war period and in the 1970's, show a severe objectivity of treatment which earned itself the name of "new realism".

MUSSET, HERMINE LARDIN DE (1819-1905). Alfred de Musset's sister, and a friend of Gabrielle Fleury's. She married a M. Lardin, but when she became a widow, resumed using her maiden name in tribute to her brother.

MYERS, FREDERIC WILLIAM HENRY (1843-1901). Inspector of Schools and President of the Society for Psychical Research. He published several volumes of poems as well as monographs on Wordsworth and Shelley.

N

NANSEN, Dr. FRIDTJOF (1861-1930). Explorer and author. He made a memorable North Pole Expedition in which he reached the highest latitude ever attained until then' (1893-96) and visited England shortly afterwards.

NELLIE, sometimes NELL. Gissing's sister, Ellen.

NEVILL, Lady DOROTHY (1826-1913). Daughter of Horatio Walpole, third Earl of Orford. She published a number of volumes of recollections from 1906 until her death.

NICOLL, Sir WILLIAM ROBERTSON (1851-1923). Journalist and man of letters. He was editor of the *Bookman* and the *Expositor*. He published a great number of literary and religious works. Gissing appears in his volume of essays *A Bookman's Letters* (1913).

NORMAN, Mrs HENRY (1867-1945). Novelist and traveller. She divorced Henry Norman and married Edward Fitzgerald, the mountaineer, in 1903. She had a great admiration for Gissing's works.

NORMAN, Sir HENRY (1858-1939). Journalist. He was on the editorial staff of the *Pall Mall Gazette* for seven years, then (when Gissing knew him) literary editor of the *Daily Chronicle*. Like his first wife, Ménie Muriel Dowie, the novelist, he was a great admirer of Gissing's work.

NORRIS, WILLIAM EDWARD (1847-1925). Novelist. He was trained as a barrister but never practised. He published an average of one novel a year from the nineties to his death.

O

O'DUNNE. See DUNNE.

O'RELL, MAX. Pseudonym of BLOUET, LEON PAUL (1848-1903). Author, traveller and lecturer. He was correspondent of the *New York Journal* and several French newspapers. He wrote many books which were first published in France, then translated by his wife into English.

ORME, ELIZA. (1848- ?) A Conveyancer who had offices in Chancery Lane. She was a niece of the first Mrs Coventry Patmore (*née* Emily Andrews), the "Angel in the house" of Patmore's poem. The Orme family numbered the Tennysons, the Rossettis and Holman Hunt among their friends. Like Clara Collet, Miss Orme greatly helped Gissing to solve the difficulties consequent upon his separation from his second wife.

OTTMANN, VICTOR (1869- ?). Publisher. His firm and his journal, *Das litterarische Echo,* were short-lived. He published the German translation of *Demos.*

OUIDA (1839-1908). Pseudonym of Marie-Louise De La Ramée. Her forty-five novels are chiefly concerned with fashionable life. She was an eccentric, temperamental person and lived most of her life in Italy.

P

PAGET, WALTER. English painter and illustrator, brother of Sidney E. Paget (1861-1908), who is better known. Besides Gissing's *Eve's Ransom,* Walter Paget illustrated the works of Scott and Stevenson.

PARKER, Sir GILBERT (1862-1932). Miscellaneous writer and lecturer. He travelled extensively, published poems, plays, travel narratives and novels.

PAYN, JAMES (1830-1898). Novelist, editor and publisher's reader. He edited *Chambers Journal* from 1858 to 1874 and the *Cornhill Magazine* from 1883 to 1896, read manuscripts for Smith, Elder & Co., and published a large number of novels.

PEEK, HEDLEY. Man of letters, editor of the *Encyclopaedia of Sport* (1897) and author of a novel and a collection of short stories.

PEMBERTON, Sir MAX (1863-1950). Novelist and journalist. He became editor of *Chums* in 1892, then of *Cassell's Magazine* (1896-1906). He is best remembered for his exciting adventure stories, and has left a useful, if chatty, volume of recollections, *Sixty Years Ago and After* (1936).

PINERO, Sir ARTHUR WING (1855-1934). Dramatist. He played an important part in the revival of the theatre at the end of the century. His most noteworthy plays are *Sweet Lavender* (1888), *The Second Mrs Tanqueray* (1893) and *The Notorious Mrs Ebbsmith* (1895).

PINKER, JAMES B. (1863-1922). Literary agent. Before becoming one of the main agents, he had been editor of *Black and White* and *Pearson's Magazine,* also manuscript reader of a publishing house.

PLITT. A German friend of the Edgar Harrisons, who, like them, lived at Gunnersbury. Gissing went with him to France and Italy in 1888. He is frequently referred to in *The Letters of George Gissing to Eduard Bertz* (1961).

POLLOCK, Sir FREDERICK (1845-1937). P.C. and K.C.; published many books on jurisprudence matters.

PROCTER, Mrs. See CORNWALL, BARRY.

PYE-SMITH, PHILIP HENRY (1839-1914). Consulting physician to Guy's Hospital and lung specialist. Gissing sought his advice in 1897 and again in 1901 before his stay at the Nayland Sanatorium. He had serious doubts as to his professional skill.

R

RALEIGH, Sir WALTER (1861-1922). Professor of English literature in Liverpool, Glasgow and London successively. He published a number of works on the English novel, Stevenson, Milton, Wordsworth, Shakespeare and Johnson.

REUTER, GABRIELE (1859-1941). Novelist. She wrote novels about female emancipation, the best known of them being *Aus guter Familie* which is concerned with the subject treated by Gissing in *The Odd Women.*

RICHARDS, THOMAS FRANKLIN GRANT (1872-1948). Publisher. He had just begun his adventurous career, which he related in his *Author Hunting,* when he got in touch with Gissing about the publication of *The Crown of Life.*

RICHARDSON, Sir BENJAMIN WARD (1828-1896). An authority on hygiene and a born raconteur. See Edward Clodd's *Memories,* pp. 271-73, which are worth comparing with Gissing's recollections.

RITCHIE, Mrs RICHMOND (1837-1919). Anne Isabella, elder daughter of Thackeray, author of a number of novels and collections of essays. She married Richmond Ritchie, K.C.B., in 1877. Gissing met her several times in the late 1880's, and her husband in 1898.

ROBERTS, MORLEY (1857-1942). Novelist. He was educated at Owens College, Manchester, where he became Gissing's lifelong friend. From the 1890s to the 1930s he wrote occasional articles on Gissing's life and works, but his main contribution was the fictionalized biography *The Private Life of Henry Maitland* (1912). He married Mrs Hamlyn in 1896.

ROBERTSON, Sir GEORGE (1852-1910). Educated at the Westminster Hospital Medical School, he took part in many military expeditions in the 1880's and 1890's. He was severely wounded at the siege of Chitral in March-April 1895.

ROBINSON, FREDERICK WILLIAM (1830-1901). Novelist and editor. Writer of special articles for the *Graphic, Black and White, Belgravia* and other journals. He wrote novels almost continually from 1851 to 1901.

ROCKETT. Gissing's landlord at 24 Prospect Park, Exeter, in 1891. Some scathing remarks about him and his family are to be found in the novelist's *Commonplace Book.*

ROSE, JOHN HOLLAND (1855-1942). Historian. He was a fellow student of Gissing's at Owens College and became a fellow of Christ's College. He taught at Cambridge University from 1911-19 and published many books, in particular on the Napoleonic period.

ROTHENSTEIN, Sir WILLIAM (1872-1945). Painter and Principal of the Royal College of Art. He made 750 portrait drawings and 135 lithographs from 1889 to 1925. He was still little known in Gissing's lifetime. He was knighted in 1931.

ROVETTA, GEROLAMO (1851-1910). Italian novelist and dramatist who attempted to give a realistic picture of society in his country. His work includes *Il Primo Amante* (1892), *La Baraonda (1894)* and *L'Idolo* (1898).

RUTHERFORD, MARK. Pseudonym of William Hale White (1831-1913). Educated with a view to becoming an independent minister, he entered the Civil Service, ending his career as assistant director of contracts at the Admiralty. His work consists in autobiographical writings, novels and criticism.

S

SACHER-MASOCH, AURORA VON (1845- ?). Wife of the celebrated Austrian novelist, Leopold von Sacher-Masoch (1836-95), from whose name "masochism" is derived. His divorced wife was a friend of Gabrielle Fleury's.

SAGLIO FAMILY. The Saglios of Tazières, a château close to the château du Chasnay, at Fourchambault, consisted of Alfred Saglio, owner of the foundry at Fourchambault, his wife and their children Joseph and Marie (c. 1860-1909). They were cultured people, living a leisurely life punctuated by journeys to Switzerland. See Denise le Mallier, *Le Roman des Dufaud* (1971) and *The Letters of George Gissing to Gabrielle Fleury* (1964).

SARCEY, FRANCISQUE (1827-1899). French critic and lecturer. He was dramatic critic on *Le Temps* from 1867 to his death, and achieved considerable success as a lecturer in France, England, Belgium and Holland.

SCHREINER, OLIVE (1855-1920). South African novelist who achieved her greatest success with *The Story of an African Farm* in 1883. She was a free-thinker interested in politics, especially in woman's place in society.

SERGEANT, EMILY FRANCES (1851-1904). She wrote over ninety novels and tales and was most successful in drawing the middle-class provincial non-conformist home.

SHARP, WILLIAM (1855-1905). Biographer, novelist and poet. He wrote lives of Shelley, Heine, Rossetti and Browning. A notable part of his work appeared under the female pseudonym of "Fiona Macleod".

SHORTER, CLEMENT KING (1857-1926). Journalist and critic, editor of such journals as the *Illustrated London News,* the *English Illustrated Magazine,* the *Sketch* and the *Sphere,* to all of which Gissing contributed. He wrote a number of books on the Brontës, George Borrow and other literary figures.

SHORTRIDGE, JOHN WOOD. A Yorkshire man living at Massa Lubrense, near Sorrento, whom Gissing met during his first Italian trip. They corresponded casually until Gissing's death.

SICHEL, EDITH (1862-1914). Writer of studies in French social and artistic history, and of articles on literature and art. Her philanthropic activities led her to interest herself in Gissing's early works. His letters to her are in the Berg Collection of the New York Public Library.

SLADEN, DOUGLAS (1856-1947). Critic and miscellaneous writer. He also wrote novels, studies of Australian poets and travel narratives.

SMITH, ALFRED JOHN (c. 1856-1895). A fellow-student of Gissing's at Owens College, where he studied science. They corresponded regularly until his— apparently self-inflicted—death in 1895. His existence seems to have been a pathetic one.

SMITH, GEORGE (1824-1901). Publisher. A member of the firm Smith, Elder & Co. He published the works of Charlotte Brontë, Thackeray, Ruskin, Matthew Arnold, Browning etc, and was the founder of the *Dictionary of National Biography*. Gissing was sharply critical of him in his *CPB*.

SMITH, HENRY GIBSON (c. 1856-1931). Brother of A.J. Smith and fellow-student of Gissing's at Owens College. He entered holy orders in 1881 and was rector of Halewood from 1891 to 1902, then Vicar of Allerton, near Liverpool, from 1902 to 1919. Gissing corresponded with him occasionally in the 1890's, but was on more intimate terms with his brother Alfred John.

SMITH, WILLIAM. Son of the Rev. Benton Smith (1845-1896), the Universalist minister who obtained for Gissing a post as teacher in the High School of Waltham, Mass., in January and February 1877.

SPRAGUE, Miss. A relative of the Rev. Benton Smith, the Waltham Universalist minister, and a friend of Dr. Zakrzewska. She helped Gissing to get a post as teacher at Waltham in 1877.

STANNARD, WILLIE. (1868- ?). One of Gissing's cousins, who frequently saw him in the few years after his return from America, when he had an active interest in political and social affairs. As the present diary shows, the two young men corresponded in 1889.

STEAD, WILLIAM THOMAS (1849-1912). Journalist. He was editor of the *Pall Mall Gazette* from 1883 to 1889 and founded the *Review of Reviews* in the following year. He was a militant pacifist and strongly opposed the war with the Transvaal. He published a number of books on topical and political questions.

STEDMAN. See METHUEN.

STEEVENS, GEORGE WARRINGTON (1870-1900). Scholar, journalist, man of letters and war correspondent. He worked for many journals, the *Pall Mall Budget*, the *National Review*, the *New Review*, the *Daily Mail*, etc.

STEINITZ, CLARA (1852- ?). Wife of Berlin publisher Heinrich Steinitz. She translated *Demos* for "Ottmanns Bücherschatz-Bibliothek".

STURMER, HERBERT HEATON. Writer, author of *Some Poitevin Protestants in London* and other volumes. He corresponded fairly regularly with Gissing from

1896 to 1899 and met him several times. See his article on the novelist in the *Week's Survey,* January 9, 1904, pp. 173-74.

SUMMERS, WILLIAM (1853-1893). A fellow-student of Gissing's, together with his brother Alfred, at Owens College, where he was an exceptionally bright student. He was liberal M.P. for Huddersfield from 1880 to his death, except for a few months in 1885. See his obituary in the *Times,* January 2, 1893, p.5.

SYMONDS, JOHN ADDINGTON (1840-93). Art historian, critic and poet. He published a number of works on Italian art and literature which were familiar to Gissing, and played an important role as a popularizer of Italian culture in England.

T

TENNYSON, Lord ALFRED (1809-92), the great Victorian poet. Gissing was encouraged to admire him by his father, and retained an interest in his work to the end, even though he recognized that the man was disappointing and his work more remarkable for its manner than for its matter.

THORNYCROFT, Sir WILLIAM HAMO (1850-1925). Sculptor, son of the sculptor Thomas Thornycroft and Mary Thornycroft, herself a sculptor.

TINCKAM, C.W. Gissing's landlord in his Brixton period. He was on the staff of Sampson, Low, the publishers, and passed on to him anything he came across in the press about his work.

TRAILL, HENRY DUFF (1842-1900). Journalist and critic. He wrote various biographical studies and was the first editor of *Literature* (from 1897 until his death), the ancestor of the *Times Literary Supplement.*

TRAVERS FAMILY, of Dorney House, Weybridge. They invited Gissing and sent him many presents in the mid-nineties. They were genuine admirers of his works.

TURNER, ALFRED (1874-1940). Sculptor educated in London and Paris. He began his artistic studies at the City and Guilds School of Art, entered the Royal Academy School in 1894 at the age of twenty. He won the British Institute scholarship and the Gold Medal and travelling studentship of the Royal Academy. Among his many public works is the King Edward Memorial.

U

UNDERWOOD FAMILY. The family of Gissing's second wife, Edith. The other children were Susan (Mrs Bosher), Flossie (Mrs Lloyd), George and James. See also under GISSING, EDITH.

UNWIN, T. FISHER (1848-1935). Publisher. He founded the publishing house which bore his name in 1882 and published Gissing's *Sleeping Fires* in his Autonym Series. He was a Liberal and sat on many committees whose aim was the promotion of international peace and cooperation.

W

WALKLEY, ARTHUR BINGHAM (1855-1926). Dramatic critic of the *Times*. He published a number of books on contemporary drama and encouraged the revival of the theatre after its prolonged decline in the nineteenth century.

WARD, ALICE (1859-1936). Journalist living in Paris, correspondent of the *Author*. She wrote under the pseudonym of Alys Hallard. From 1897 to 1922 she translated works by Pierre de Coulevain, René Doumic, Gyp and others. She was a friend of Gabrielle Fleury's.

WATSON, Sir WILLIAM (1858-1935). Poet. His essential gift was his turn for epigrammatic terseness in his poems commemorating other poets. He was associated with the *Yellow Book*.

WATT, ALEXANDER POLLOCK (1834-1914). Literary agent. He was the originator of the concept of the literary agent. Gissing asked him to sell *Born in Exile*, but as he was only moderately pleased with the result of his efforts, he then turned to W.M. Colles.

WATTS-DUNTON, WALTER THEODORE (1832-1914). Critic and novelist. He was a regular contributor to the *Athenaeum* for many years, and scored a success with his mediocre novel *Aylwin* (1898). He befriended Swinburne in his declining health.

WAUGH, ARTHUR (1866-1943). Publisher, critic and journalist. He was in succession London correspondent of the New York *Critic* (1893-97), literary adviser to Kegan Paul & Co. (1895-1902), managing director, then chairman of Chapman & Hall until the Second World War. He edited Dickens, Milton, Tennyson, Arnold, Lamb and George Herbert.

WELLS, HERBERT GEORGE (1866-1946). Novelist, reformer and controversialist. He was a devoted, if sometimes impatient, friend of Gissing's, but damaged the novelist's reputation and behaved tactlessly to his relatives after his death.

WHALE, GEORGE (1849-1925). Solicitor and author. A rationalist, he was one of the founders of the Omar Khayyám Club, and played an active part in local government. He wrote a volume on *Greater London and its Government* and many articles and essays, in particular on Samuel Johnson.

WHEATLEY, HENRY BENJAMIN (1837-1917). British scholar, author of many books on literary and topographical subjects. When Gissing met him he was treasurer of the Early English Text Society.

WILLIAMS, Mrs ROSALIND, *née* POTTER (1865-1948). The youngest daughter of Richard and Laurencina Potter, and sister of Beatrice Webb (1858-1943), the Fabian Socialist. She married Dyson Williams, a barrister, in the mid-eighties, and became a widow shortly afterwards. She remarried about 1900 and became Mrs George Dobbs.

WISE, THOMAS JAMES (1859-1937). Bibliographer and forger. He began collecting at the age of seventeen and gradually amassed the collection named the

Ashley Library from his house in North London. He made a business of faking first edition pamphlets, and his credit as a bibliographer was seriously damaged by the discovery of this in 1934.

WOOD, JAMES (1834-1908). Gissing's principal when he was a student at Lindow Grove School, Alderley Edge, Cheshire. He afterwards transferred his school to Colwyn Bay. Gissing corresponded occasionally with him, as well as with his son Stanley. See P. Coustillas, *George Gissing at Alderley Edge* (1969).

WOOD, Sir HENRY TRUEMAN (1845-1929). He was in succession Secretary, Treasurer and Chairman of the Council of the Royal Society of Arts, and he was officially connected with a number of exhibitions in England and abroad.

WOODS, MARGARET L. (1856-1945). Novelist and poet. She was a daughter of the Dean of Westminster, and the wife of Henry George Woods, President of Trinity College, Oxford. She made her name with her novel *A Village Tragedy* (1887), which Gissing greatly admired.

Z

ZAKRZEWSKA, Dr. One of the people who befriended Gissing in Boston in the winter of 1876-77. She introduced him to Lloyd Garrison. Beside an important medical practice she had a clinic in the town. On Saturday evenings she held literary gatherings in her home which young Gissing attended.

ZANGWILL, ISRAEL (1864-1926). Novelist and Zionist. After a few years' teaching, he turned to journalism and novel-writing. His work includes *Children of the Ghetto, Ghetto Tragedies* and *Dreamers of the Ghetto.* He paid a tribute to Gissing in *To-Day*, February 3, 1904, pp. 433-34.

ZANGWILL, LOUIS (1869-1938). Man of letters. Brother of Israel Zangwill. He was a journalist until the publication of his first book under the pseudonym of Z.Z. Gissing liked his novels.

ZAPP, ARTHUR. Prolific novelist and playwright with whom Eduard Bertz was acquainted. Gissing read a number of his works.

Index

I. Gissing's Writings

"Among the Heather", 353.
"Among the Prophets", 521-23, 525-26.
"At a Week's Notice", 254.
"At Eventide", 385-86.
"At High Pressure", 389.
"At Nightfall", 493, 514, 563.
"At the Grave of Alaric", 460, 494, 550.
"An Author at Grass", 530-34, 540-41, 543-44, 546, 549-50, 565-66. See also *The Private Papers of Henry Ryecroft.*

Barnaby Rudge, Introduction to, 515, 533, 539, 564.
"Beggar's Nurse, The", 386.
"Benedict's Household". See *The Whirlpool.*
Bleak House, Introduction to, 512, 521, 535, 564.
Born in Exile ("Godwin Peak"), 3, 6, 8, 241-51, 253, 263, 265-69, 271-74, 276-78, 280, 298, 329, 366, 411, 557, 562, 589.
By the Ionian Sea, 11, 515-17, 523-24, 526-27, 529-32, 536-40, 550, 563, 581.

"Calamity at Tooting, A", 371-72, 374.
"Capitalist, A", 311-12, 328-29, 331, 333-34.
"Casual Acquaintance, A", 261, 263-64.
Charles Dickens, a Critical Study, 448-54, 467-68, 478-81, 483-86, 488, 491, 497, 501, 539, 550, 563-64.

"Charming Family, A", 538-39.
Christmas Books, Introduction to, 523, 564.
"Christmas on the Capitol", 119, 127, 142-43, 155, 169, 185, 554.
"Christopherson", 540.
"Clare's Engagement", 495.
"Clement Dorricott", 31, 34.
"Coming Man, The". See *Our Friend the Charlatan.*
"Common Lot, The", 398-99.
"Comrades in Arms", 324-25, 329.
"Conspiracy of Kindness, A", 255.
"Conversion, A", 389.
Critical Studies of the Works of Charles Dickens, 564.
Crown of Life, The, 497-98, 502, 504-11, 515-17, 519-22, 550, 582, 585.

"Daughter of the Lodge, A", 524.
David Copperfield, Introducution to, 499, 500, 564 (Rochester edition); 540 (Autograph edition).
"Day of Silence, The", 313, 320-23, 391.
Demos, 6, 15, 24, 27, 29, 30, 32, 50, 101, 138, 144, 151, 158, 166, 185, 201, 205, 212-14, 221, 225, 251-52, 254, 261, 266, 270, 278, 281, 327, 394, 498, 551, 555-56, 562, 580, 584, 587.
Denzil Quarrier ("The Radical Candidate"), 257-64, 268-73, 275, 278, 296, 307, 328, 347, 366, 368.
"Despot on Tour, A", 377, 389, 452, 477, 550.
"Dickens in Memory", 540.
Dombey and Son, Introduction to, 500, 564.
"Domestic Appeal for Reticence in Art, The", 273.
"Drug in the Market, A", 360.

591

"Elixir, The", 494, 514.

Emancipated, The ("The Puritan"), 144-60, 166-68, 210-14, 216, 219, 220, 229, 249, 268, 287, 289-91, 307, 312, 318, 323-25, 347, 355, 366, 371, 444, 448, 452.

"Enchantress, The", 373-74, 376.

Eve's Ransom, 339-43, 347-49, 351, 356, 359, 361-66, 370, 372-73, 389, 411, 424, 448, 451, 489, 504, 550, 561.

"Ewe Lamb, The", 392.

"Fate and the Apothecary", 494, 514.

"Fate of Humphrey Snell, The", 350-51, 360, 389-90.

"Firebrand, The", 377.

"Fleet-footed Hester", 310-12.

"Flowing Tide, The". See "The Salt of the Earth".

"Foolish Virgin, The", 391-93, 397, 419, 580.

"For Art's Sake", 271-72.

Forster's Life of Dickens Abridged, 540, 543, 545-46.

"Frank Wooer, The", 494.

"Freak of Nature, A", 351, 365, 371.

"Free Woman, A", 389.

"Friend in Need, The", 360.

"Gentle Bagman, The", 365.

"Girl's Wild Oats, A", 302.

"Godwin Peak". See *Born in Exile*.

"Golden Trust, The", 494-96.

"Hapless Boaster, The", 406.

"Head Mistress, The", 168-69, 201, 211.

"Hilda Wolff", 224-26.

"His Brother's Keeper", 311, 342, 368.

"Homes and Haunts of Dickens, The", 534-36, 544, 566.

"Honeymoon, The", 324, 338.

"House of Cobwebs, The", 523, 526, 528, 531.

"How a Misfortune Made a Philosopher", 302-03.

Human Odds and Ends, 390, 440, 443, 460, 550.

"Humplebee", 517.

Immortal Dickens, The, 564.

"In Honour Bound", 325, 341.

"In No-Man's Land", 389.

"Inspiration, An", 352, 368.

"Insurgents, The", 17-21.

"In the Cause of Humanity", 292.

In the Year of Jubilee ("Miss Lord of Camberwell", "Nancy Lord"), 8, 309, 314-22, 326-32, 335, 338, 341-42, 344-47, 349, 351, 355-56, 359-60, 362-63, 366, 368, 383, 385, 394, 559-60.

"Invincible Curate, The", 385.

"Iron Gods, The", 292-300, 302, 309-11.

Isabel Clarendon, 3, 15, 296, 402, 562.

"Jack in Office", 264.

"Joseph", 405.

"Justice and the Vagabond, The", 377.

"Last Illusion, The", 484.

"Laughing Doctor, The", 266.

"Letty Coe", 252, 369.

Life's Morning, A, 14, 15, 17, 24, 25, 26, 30, 31, 37, 43, 71, 109, 143, 225, 239, 245, 292, 556.

"Light on the Tower, The", 392, 397.
"Little Woman from Lancashire, The", 388.
"Lodger in Maze Pond, A", 312, 328-29, 331, 347, 363-64, 368.
"Lord Dunfield", 388.
"Lou and Liz", 301-02, 304, 310.

"Magnanimous Debtor, The", 391.
"Manfred: a Reminiscence", 168.
"Man of Letters, A", 213, 216-20.
"Marian Dane", 21.
Martin Chuzzlewit, Introduction to, 515, 564.
"Master Humphrey's Clock", Introduction to, 525, 564 .
"Medicine Man, The", 385.
"Merely Temporary", 371.
"Merry Wooing, A", 352.
"Midsummer Madness, A", 313, 324.
"Minstrel of the Byways, A" ("A Shrewd Investment"), 295-97.
"Miss Lord of Camberwell". See In the Year of Jubilee.
"Miss Rodney's Leisure", 540.
"Mrs. Cray's Illusion", 485.
"Muse of the Halls, The", 316-17, 324, 554.

"Nancy Lord". See In the Year of Jubilee.
Nether World, The, 7, 13, 15, 24-37, 39, 41, 42, 45, 46, 118, 121, 123, 126-7, 129-30, 132, 136, 138-40, 142, 144, 146-48, 153, 155-56, 165-66, 201, 210, 213, 225, 248, 251-52, 254, 261, 290, 300, 314, 517, 554-56.
New Grub Street, 3, 5, 6, 7, 8, 227-32, 235, 237-40, 242-46, 248, 253,

256, 258-59, 270, 272-73, 275, 284, 289, 309, 312, 353, 366, 427, 439, 496-98, 524, 531, 536-37, 541-42, 546, 556-57, 566.
Nicholas Nickleby, Introduction to, 502, 514, 564.
"Nobodies at Home", 561.
"No Character to Lose", 282.

Odd Women, The, 8, 283-86, 289-96, 299-302, 305-07, 309, 311, 316, 328, 334, 355, 366, 368, 390, 404, 428, 530, 550, 557-59, 562, 565.
Old Curiosity Shop, The, Introduction to, 514-15, 564.
"Old Maid's Triumph, An", 385.
"Old School, The", 451, 563.
Oliver Twist, Introduction to, 512, 535, 564.
"One of the Luckless", 405.
"One Way of Happiness", 405-06.
"Oracles". See "Among the Prophets".
Our Friend the Charlatan ("The Coming Man"), 519-21, 524-31, 535, 537-38, 540, 550.
"Our Learned Fellow-townsman", 376, 562.
"Our Mr. Jupp", 313-14, 331, 504, 550.
"Out of Fashion", 389.

"Parent's Feelings, A", 388.
"Patron of the Drum and Fife, The", 376-77.
Paying Guest, The, 8, 378-80, 390, 392-94, 399-401, 413.
"Peace-Bringer, The", 494, 504.
"Pessimist of Plato Road, The", 323, 343, 352.
"Philanthropist, The", 395.
"Phoebe", 246, 258.

593

Pickwick, Introduction to, 499, 500, 511, 520, 528, 564.
"Pig and Whistle, The", 523, 526-27, 532.
"Pilgrim Pedagogues, The", 311.
"Place of Realism in Fiction, The", 373, 378, 550.
"Poet's Portmanteau, The", 323, 361.
"Polly Brill". See *The Town Traveller.*
"Poor Gentleman, A", 511-12.
Private Papers of Henry Ryecroft, The, 5, 6, 11, 14, 559, 565, See also "An Author at Grass".
"Prize Lodger, The", 394.
"Profitable Weakness, A", 385.
"Puritan, The". See *The Emancipated.*

"Radical Candidate, The". See *Denzil Quarrier.*
"Rash Miss Tomalin, The". See "A Daughter of the Lodge".
"Raw Material", 385.
"Raymond Peak". See *Born in Exile.*
"Revolt", 223.
"Riding-Whip, The", 544.
"Ring Finger, The", 486-87, 490, 492.

"Salt of the Earth, The", 351, 355-56, 368.
"Schoolmaster's Vision, The", 396, 501.
"Scrupulous Father, The", 514-15, 525.
"Shrewd Investment, A". See "A Minstrel of the Byways".
"Simple Simon", 349, 438.

Sketches by Boz, Introduction to, 523, 564.
Sleeping Fires, 360-67, 372, 396, 399, 402, 410.
"Snapshall's Youngest", 522.
"Son of the Soil, A", 389.
"Song of Sixpence, A", 385.
"Spellbound", 12, 405, 440.
"Spendthrift, The", 371-73.
"Storm-Birds", 221-23.

"Their Pretty Way", 349, 559.
Thyrza, 8, 27, 31, 45, 50, 122, 124, 144, 156, 222-23, 235, 238, 241, 245-46, 258, 313, 316, 346, 349, 353, 554, 556, 558-59.
"Tout of Yarmouth Bridge, The", 385.
Town Traveller, The ("Polly Brill"), 6, 433-34, 436-38, 482, 485, 492, 495, 500-03, 505, 507, 535, 550, 566.
"Transplanted", 388.
"Twin Souls", 412.
"Two Collectors", 386, 505.
"Tyrant's Apology, The", 350-51, 377.
"Tyrtaeus", 520.

Unclassed, The, 3, 4, 28, 34, 143, 296, 355, 386-87, 389-90, 394-95, 412, 448, 451, 561.
"Under an Umbrella", 311, 320, 322, 326, 332.

"Vanquished Roman, A" (*Veranilda*), 534-39, 550.
"Victim of Circumstances, A", 261, 289, 291, 293.
"Victor Yule", 226-27.

"Well-Meaning Man, A", 385.
Whirlpool, The, 8, 409-14, 416,
420-35, 498, 507, 520, 550, 563,
565-66.
"Why I don't Write Plays?", 284,
557.
Will Warburton, 546-50, 558.
"Woman-Queller, The", 337.
Workers in the Dawn, 3, 7, 416,
566-67, 5777.

"Yorkshire Lass, A", 412, 414.

II. Persons

A. See Gissing, Algernon.
Abbey, E.A., 41, 552.
Acklom, Miss, 547.
Addison, Joseph, 155-58; *Tatler,* 21,
34, 148-49, 232-33.
Aeschylus, 189, 292.
Agaby, Miss, 34, 35, 145, 567.
Aicard, Jean, 372.
Ainscough ("Rivington Pyke", 413,
562.
Ainslie, Noel, 13.
Ainsworth, W.F., 322.
Alaric, 456-57, 460.
Alden, Stanley, 14.
Alderson, Charles, 153, 156.
Aldrich, T.B., 315, 558.
Alexander VII, 108.
Alexander, Dr., 371.
Alg. See Gissing, Algernon.
Allen, Grant, 12, 240, 244, 306,
374-75, 383, 397, 425, 433, 520,
525, 567.
Allhusen, E.L., 438, 448, 567.
Allibone, 154, 554.
Altick, Richard D., 1.
Amedeo, Prince, 204-05.

Amos, 294.
Ampère, J.-J., 168.
Anacreon, 201, 261, 353.
Andersen, H.C., 248, 401.
Anderson, Charles, 25, 244-46, 567.
Anderson, Joseph, 409-11, 415, 417,
432, 434, 567.
Anderson, Mary, 409, 434, 567.
Andrea del Sarto, 56, 89, 104, 116-
17, 125.
Anstey, F., 266, 300, 339, 343.
Anthier, 541.
Antoninus Pius, 104.
Apelles, 97.
Apollonius Rhodius, 181.
Appleton's, 364.
Aristophanes, 145-46, 148, 170,
180-81, 183-85, 232, 259.
Arlidge, J.T., 288.
Armour, 415.
Armstrong, W., 421.
Arnold, Edward, 302, 304, 310.
Arnold, Matthew, 378. 543.
Arrowsmith, 382.
Art, Georges, 389, 391, 411, 424,
434, 496, 498, 503, 567.
Ash, Connie, and family, 13, 223,
567.
Atkinson, C.M., 370, 567.
Augustine, St, 295.
Augustus (emperor), 56, 90, 93, 100,
121, 447.
Augustus, 438.
Austin, Alfred, 326, 400, 568.
Austin, L.F., 323, 374, 376, 379,
444, 508, 556, 560, 568 .

Bachelor, Albert, 324.
Bacon, Francis, 155, 244, 391, 394.
Baedeker, 19, 46-48, 53, 60, 65, 74,
79, 82, 83, 85, 88, 94, 96, 97, 106,
113, 120, 122, 137, 156, 168, 175,
177, 197, 403, 470.

Baffier, Eugène, 55, 553.
Bagram, Miss, 35.
Bain, Nisbet, 414, 568.
Bainton, George, 42-44, 216, 568.
Balestier, Wolcott, 410.
Ball, Mr., 499.
Ballantyne, S., 386.
Balzac, Honoré de, 20, 21, 50, 133,
    136, 140, 262, 281-82, 333, 423,
    514, 521.
Banazzo, 130.
Bancroft, Squire and Marie, 278,
    557.
Banks, Mrs. Linnaeus, 3.
Banks, W.S., 412.
Barcock, Mrs. (nurse), 401-03.
Baring-Gould, Sabine, 27, 268, 278,
    339, 355, 568.
Barker, E.H., 410.
Barkley, H., 312.
Barnard, Frederic, 343, 348, 352,
    354-55, 357, 390, 568.
Barnes, Martha, 364, 373, 396, 413,
    420, 498, 508, 568.
Barnes, Mr. (teacher), 377.
Barnes, William, 388.
Barras, Paul, 387.
Barrett; C.R.B., 353.
Barrett, Frank, 428.
Barrie, James, 340, 342, 413, 415,
    427-29, 432, 435, 438, 491-92, 568.
Barrie, Mrs. James, 432.
Baseley, May, 218-19, 223, 377, 428.
Bashkirtseff, Marie, 219-20, 568.
Bassano (photographer), 453.
Bately, Dr., 381.
Bateman, A.E., 415, 568.
Bateson, Harold, 242, 556.
Batézat, Mlles, 542-44.
Batterham, Dr., 330, 332.
Bazaine, Achille, 44, 552.
Beaumont, Dr., 390, 393, 401, 416,
    430, 432.
Beaumont and Fletcher, 17, 265.

Beccafumi, 453.
Becke, G.L., 426, 569.
Becker, W.A., 334, 559.
Beckmann, Johann, 436.
Bede, Cuthbert, 66.
Bedells, Mrs., 284, 557.
Bedford, Tom and Mary, 41, 42,
    288, 320, 353, 377, 569.
Beerbohm, Max, 436, 569.
Beesly, E.S., 147, 569.
Bell & Co., 347, 355.
Bellini, Giovanni, 130, 132, 134,
    135, 140.
Benington, Mr., 370.
Bennet, Mr., 498.
Benson, E.F., 344.
Bentley, George, 159, 569. See also
    Bentley & Son.
Bentley, Richard, 167. See also
    Bentley & Son.
Bentley, Richard, 241, 556.
Bentley & Son, 4, 31, 160, 166-68,
    210, 212, 249, 252, 257, 264, 287,
    289-90, 557. See also Bentley,
    George and Bentley, Richard.
Berger, Adele, 270, 272, 278, 448,
    569.
Bergerat, Emile, 353, 560.
Bergson, Philip, 313.
Bernard, Margaret, 479.
Bernini, Pietro, 108-09.
Bertz, Eduard, 11, 34, 36, 44, 47, 48,
    53, 57, 66, 677, 82, 88, 90, 105,
    108-09, 113, 116, 123-24, 127,
    135-36, 138, 140, 142, 146, 148,
    150, 152-53, 155-56, 158-59,
    164-65, 169-70, 176, 182, 185, 188,
    190, 195, 201, 210, 212, 216-17,
    220-22, 225-26, 229-30, 234, 238,
    240-42, 244-47, 250-53, 255-60,
    264-65, 270-71, 273-74, 277-79,
    283, 291-92, 295, 301-03, 306-07,
    313, 318-19, 321, 323-24, 327,
    332-33, 339-40, 348-49, 355,

358-60, 363-65, 369, 371, 373-74,
377-78, 380, 385, 389, 394, 396-97,
399, 400, 404, 408, 410-12, 418,
423-24, 428, 436, 446, 449, 454,
466, 479-80, 482-84, 488, 490, 500,
513, 517, 520, 528, 531, 533, 538,
543, 554, 569, 579.
Besant, Annie, 35, 569.
Besant, Walter, 24, 26, 235, 274,
282, 290, 294, 318, 354, 359-61,
391, 551, 556, 558, 560, 562, 569.
Besant and Rice, 271.
Best, K.T., 322, 558.
Beugnot, 439, 443.
Bias, 96.
Biddulph, Mrs. J.M., 413, 562.
Bieman, Neville, 430.
Bingham, Joseph, 443.
Binks, Mr. and Mrs. John, 370, 569.
Bird, Isabella L., 421-22.
Birrell, Mr. and Mrs. Augustine,
231, 556.
Bishop, Mrs. I.L., 406.
Björnson, B., 286, 351.
Black, A. & C., 265-67, 269, 271,
274, 276-77, 298, 411, 562.
Black, Annie, 309-10, 312, 327, 570.
Black, Clementina, 35, 569.
Black, John George, 391, 394-95,
569.
Black, William, 342, 424.
Blackett. See Hurst & Blackett.
Blackie, 439, 444, 478-80, 483-84,
539, 550.
Blackmore, R.D., 345.
Blackwood, 233, 240-41, 262, 272,
289, 291, 293, 297, 368.
Blouet, Mme, 433.
Blundun, Rev., 267.
Blunt, Lady Anne, 336.
Boethius, 481.
Boissier, Gaston, 413, 509.
Bolitho, Miss (landlady), 269-70.
Bonghi, 122.

Booth (Wakefield family), 370.
Booth, Charles, 232, 313, 558, 572.
Borrow, George, 306-07, 414, 430.
Bosher, Mr. and Mrs., 284-85, 287,
570, 588.
Boswell, James, 148-51, 212, 272.
Botticelli, A., 62.
Bötticher, Carl, 190.
Boughton, Mrs. (housekeeper), 493,
497, 501, 508-09, 519, 570.
Bouilhet, L., 51.
Boulanger, General, 124, 131, 554.
Bouret, E., 55, 553.
Bourget, Paul, 25, 27, 138, 167, 169,
393, 503, 538.
Bourre, M., 527.
Bovet, M. and Mme E., 516-17, 565,
570.
Bowden, Mr., 357.
Boyd, A.K.H., 293.
Bradley, Miss, 104.
Brandes, Georg, 437, 496.
Brangwyn, Frank, 167, 554.
Bremer, Frederika, 159, 554.
Brewer, Mrs. (landlady), 332, 367.
Brewster, S.N.P., 486-87, 494-96,
499, 500, 508-09, 570.
Bridges, Robert, 394, 479.
Briggs, Asa, 7.
Bright, John, 480.
Brodribb, William, 373.
Brontë, Charlotte, 33, 141, 400, 426,
433.
Brook, George, 407.
Brooke, Sir James (Raja of
Sarawak), 316-17.
Brooke, W.H., 492.
Broughton, Rhoda, 11, 22, 570.
Brown, Dr., 271.
Brown, H.F., 362.
Brown, Miss (landlady), 22.
Browne, Sir Thomas, 385.
Browning, Elizabeth Barrett, 115-16.
Browning, Robert, 38, 216, 229,
256, 313-14, 503.

Bruce, Mr. and Mrs. Samuel, 159, 219, 223, 367, 372, 408, 415, 429, 491, 570.
Brunelleschi, F., 117.
Brunetière, Ferdinand, 499, 530.
Bruno, Giordano, 201, 475, 563.
Brutus, 65.
Bryan, Charles, 254, 282, 288, 290, 293, 300, 304, 307-08, 570.
Bryce, James, 322, 392, 414, 570.
Buchanan, Robert, 356.
Buck, A.H., 167.
Buckle, H.T., 131, 167, 554.
Buckley, Mrs., 303.
Bullen, A.H., 7, 260-62, 268, 273, 277, 284, 287-91, 293, 295-97, 299-302, 309, 311, 316, 323-24, 328-30, 334-35, 338-39, 342, 346-48, 352-53, 355, 359-64, 380, 382, 386, 390-91, 394-95, 402-03, 412, 423-24, 430, 433-34, 438, 440, 444, 446, 451-52, 462, 490-91, 495-96, 499, 501-03, 515, 524, 532, 550, 564, 570. See also Lawrence & Bullen.
Bulliot, M., 530.
Bullock-Webster, Mrs., 239, 245.
Bulwer-Lytton, 481.
Bunn, Mr. and Mrs., 380-82.
Bunyan, John, 40.
Burgin, G.B., 391, 420, 561-62, 570.
Burn, Robert, 435.
Burney, Fanny, 10.
Burns, John, 35, 570.
Burns, Robert, 155-56, 402, 427.
Burrows, Herbert, 35, 570.
Burton, Miss L.M., 534, 566.
Burton, Sir Richard, 364, 378.
Burton, Robert, 259.
Bury, Yetta Blaze de, 355, 359, 448, 505, 560, 571.
Busselli (landlord), 79, 80.
Butcher, S.H., 311.
Butler, Samuel, 256.

Byron, Lord, 23, 92, 224, 397-98, 426.

Cable, G.W., 492, 571.
Caecilia Metella, 87, 100.
Caesar, 65, 90, 93.
Caine, Hall, 11, 22, 343, 571.
Caird, Professor, 169, 555.
Caligula, 91, 100.
Campbell, J.D., 350.
Canning, Lady Charlotte, 343-44, 559.
Canova, A., 106.
Canton, William, 398.
Cappelli, 449-53, 467.
Caravaggio, 88.
Carlyle, Thomas, 9, 38, 39, 152, 256, 318-19, 336, 396, 505-06.
Carnegie, Andrew, 341.
Carpaccio, 132.
Carpenter, Mrs., 333.
Carpenter, W.B., 167.
Carracci, Annibale, 51, 82, 83, 89.
Carter, Dora and family, 38, 40, 217, 225, 255, 302, 571.
Carter, Mary E., 34-36, 38, 144, 147-48, 571.
Caruso, Eduardo, 458.
Casaubon, Isaac, 251.
Cassell, 5, 6, 367, 372, 378, 389, 393-94, 399.
Cassiodorus, 435, 468-70.
Catherine, St, 446-47, 450.
Catullus, 362, 395.
Cavallotti, Felice, 485, 564.
Cavour, 485.
Cervantes, 59, 547-48.
Chalmers, Andrew, 367, 370-71, 408, 571.
Champion, H.H., 303, 322, 325, 399, 557, 571.
Chapman, George, 7. See also Chapman & Hall.

598

Chapman & Hall, 4, 213, 354, 379, 400, 524, 529, 535-36, 538-40, 543.
Charpentier, Armand, 501, 564.
Chateaubriand, A. de, 48, 558.
Chatto & Windus, 253, 255, 521.
Chaucer, Geoffrey, 243-44, 327.
Chauffard, Dr., 539-40, 542.
Cherbuliez, Victor, 392, 425.
Chesneau, E., 313.
Chevalier, Albert, 301, 571.
Chevalier de la Petite Rivière, Mlle, 520.
Chevreul, Eugène, 44.
Childcott, Dr., 508.
Chopin, Frédéric, 48, 50.
Chown, Mrs. (landlady), 435.
Christie (stockbroker), 170.
Church, Alfred, 373.
Churchill, Mr., 492.
Cicero, 45, 65, 99, 148-49, 295.
Cima da Conegliano, 140.
Cimabue, Giovanni, 117.
Clarétie, Jules, 140, 554.
Claude (Lorrain), 71, 89.
Claudius, 121.
Cleobulus, 96.
Clifford, Mrs. W.K., 508, 571.
Clodd, Amy and Edith, 426.
Clodd, Edward, 14, 342, 371, 373-76, 379, 383-84, 397-98, 400, 426, 432-33, 439, 444, 453, 462, 492, 501, 503-05, 521-23, 525, 534, 554, 561, 567, 571.
Clodd, Mrs. Edward, 426.
Cognat, 541-42.
Cole, Mr and Miss, 239.
Coleridge, E.H., 384.
Coleridge, J.T., 344.
Coleridge, S.T., 148, 250, 350, 384.
Colles, W.M., 6, 7, 316, 319-22, 327-29, 331-32, 334-35, 342, 348-49, 352-53, 360, 363, 365, 371, 374, 376, 382, 389, 391, 405, 411, 415, 423-24, 434, 437-38, 444,

451-54, 468, 477, 481-82, 485, 489, 491, 494-95, 501, 503-04, 514, 520, 535, 550, 571, 589.
Collet, Clara E., 9, 14, 273, 304-06, 309-26, 328-31, 334, 336-39, 341, 345, 348, 350, 354-57, 359, 361-62, 365, 367, 369, 371-74, 376-80, 382-85, 388-92, 394, 396-97, 399-402, 404-06, 408, 411, 414, 416-17, 419-21, 423, 425, 428, 430, 432-35, 437, 447, 453, 475, 479-80, 482-84, 491, 500, 504, 506, 508-10, 512, 516, 520-23, 527, 530, 533, 536, 538-39, 542, 557-59, 572.
Collet, C.D., 509-10, 565.
Collier, John, 400, 496, 572.
Collier, Mrs. John, 496.
Collins, William, 138.
Colvin, Sidney, 427, 572.
Commodus, 91, 121.
Condorcet, 58.
Conington, John, 233.
Constable & Co., 7, 546, 549.
Constantine, 121.
Constantine (Prince), 176.
Conway, Moncure, 395, 572.
Cook, Sir F. and Lady, 496, 572.
Cook, Harry, 379.
Cookson-Crackanthorpe, 21, 572.
Cooper, Fenimore, 229, 234-35.
Coppée, François, 404, 523.
Corelli, Marie, 22, 572.
Cornish, Mrs. (landlady), 236.
Cornish, Mrs. Blanche, 355, 560.
Cornish, C.J., 380.
Cornoy, Dr., 530.
Cornwall, Barry, 388, 572.
Corregio, 48, 104.
Couldridge, Mrs. (landlady), 292.
Courtney, W.L., 395, 526, 541, 572.
Couture, Thomas, 52.
Cowley, Abraham, 238.
Cowper, William, 275, 429.
Cox, Sir G.W., 391.

Crabbe, George, 40, 363, 365, 371, 552.
Crackanthorpe, Hubert, 420, 572 .
Craig, Mrs. (landlady), 286.
Craik, G.L., 219.
Craik, Sir Henry., 438, 572.
Crane, Stephen, 525, 572.
Crane, Mrs. Stephen, 510, 525.
Crawford, F.M., 12, 226, 252, 292, 298, 302, 342, 423, 455, 573.
Crawfurd, Oswald, 354, 573.
Credi, Lorenzo di, 125.
Cricelli, Pasquale, 467-69, 477.
Crispi, F., 132, 137, 472.
Crockett, S.R., 371.
Croke, 487.
Cromwell, Oliver, 217, 256, 523.
Crum, Miss, 17, 26, 31, 37, 438, 573.
Cunningham, 416.
Currie, 407.
Curutchague, Marianne (servant), 545.
Curtis, Miss, 12, 27, 28, 573.
Cust, Henry, 379.

Dabb, Mrs. (landlady), 415.
Dabb, Mr., 417.
Dahn, Felix, 439, 480-81.
Dante, 15, 71, 102, 125, 166.
Danton, G., 55.
D'Arcis, M. and Mme, 518, 565.
Darwin, Charles, 170, 244, 251.
Daudet, Alphonse, 25, 27-29, 33-35, 37-38, 46-47, 49, 52, 133, 150, 262-63, 295-96, 334, 357, 373, 404, 475, 508, 563.
Daudet, Mme A., 498.
Daudet, Ernest, 44.
Daudet, Léon, 351, 387.
Davey, Lord, 420, 573.
David, Theodore, 517, 521, 573.
Davidson, John, 311, 316-17, 319,

334-35, 344, 351-52, 356, 397, 399-400, 404, 426-27, 573.
De Bourcard, F., 205.
Defoe, Daniel, 402-03.
Dekker, Thomas, 17, 150.
Delaborde, Elie, 537, 573.
Deland, Mary, 357.
De La Rue (landlord), 160, 164.
Democritus, 170.
De Nolèche, 531, 536, 542.
De Quincey, Thomas, 145, 242, 247, 274, 298-99, 361, 464.
Diana, Benito, 140.
Dickens, Charles, 17, 18, 20, 22, 36, 152, 430, 435, 439-40, 444-45, 447, 475, 495, 523, 528, 534-36, 539-40, 543-48, 563-66. See also in I, *Charles Dickens, a Critical Study* and Dickens titles.
Diggle, J.W., 344.
Dilke, Charles, 387, 573.
Dilke, Mrs. Ashton, 43, 552.
Diogenes Laertius, 274, 371.
Disraeli, Benjamin, 290.
Disraeli, Isaac, 246-47.
Dixon, Ella N.H., 362-63, 573.
Dixon, W.H., 154.
Dobbs, Mrs. See Williams, Rosalind.
Dobson, H.A., 243, 323, 415, 573.
Dodd, Mead & Co., 389, 392, 400, 477, 479, 491, 550.
Dolci, Carlo, 88, 89, 104, 117.
Dolman, Frederick, 4, 243, 450, 556, 563, 573.
Domenichino, 89, 101, 105.
Domitian, 121.
Donne, John, 397.
Dostoievsky, F., 26, 36, 46, 227, 262-63, 269-70, 281, 327, 433, 495.
Dow, Gerard, 48.
Dowden, Edward, 257.
Dowie, Ménie, Muriel. See Norman, Mrs. Henry.

Doyle, Arthur Conan, 427, 486, 489, 574.
Dreyfus, Alfred, 465, 484.
Droz, Gustave, 233.
Du Camp, Maxime, 349.
Duff, Grant, 387.
Dumas, Alexandre, 370.
Du Maurier, George, 409.
Dunn, 280.
Dunne, Brian Boru, 447-50, 452-53, 468, 475, 478-80, 482, 484, 498, 506-07, 574.
Dürer, A., 51, 105.
Duruy, Victor, 121.
Dyer, T.H., 437.

E. See Gissing, Edith.
Eardley, Frank, 382.
East, Sir Alfred, 438, 574.
Easterbrook, Thyrza (servant), 263, 266, 268.
Eastlake, Lady, 416.
Ecclesiasticus, 424.
Eckenstein, Lina, 416.
Edgeworth, Maria, 271, 354, 356.
Edward VII, 546, 548, 566.
Edwardes, Mr. and Mrs. George, 354, 560.
Edwards, Nelly (servant), 255, 262-63.
Edwards, W.H., 218, 555.
Egerton, George, 360.
Eiffel, Gustave, 46, 52, 553.
Elgin, Lord, 472.
Eliot, George, 3.
Ellen (servant), 290-91, 295-96.
Ellicott, Mrs., 414.
Ellicott, Rosalind, 414, 562.
Elliott & Fry (photographers), 372-74, 376, 550, 566.
Elliott, Mrs. Frances, 402.
Ellis, Alfred (photographer), 314, 372-73.

Ellis, Havelock, 232.
Elson, Louis, C., 403, 574.
Elston, Mrs. (landlady), 250, 302, 338.
Elyard, S. John, 143.
Emerson, R.W., 421.
Ensor, R.C., 2.
Epicurus, 96.
Epimenides, 96, 274.
Erasmus, 365.
Ernst, Herzog, 153.
Erroll, Henry, 28.
Escott, T.H.S., 398.
Euripides, 26, 71, 86, 99, 250, 313.
Eurysaces, 476.
Eustache, M. and Mme Robert, 520, 533-34, 574.
Evans (Algernon Gissing's friend), 218, 555.
Evans, W.M., 488-89, 493, 505, 574.
Evelyn, John, 10.

Farina, Salvatore, 201-02, 555.
Farrar, F.W., 165-66, 181, 554, 574.
Farronault, 541.
Faustina, 104-05, 124.
Fell, J.W., 545, 566.
Fennessey, Mr. and Mrs., 169-70, 324-25.
Fenno, R.F. & Co, 412.
Festal, Dr., 542.
Feuillet, Mme Octave, 352.
Finck, H.T., 424.
Fink, Hugo, 203, 205-06, 208, 555.
Fisher, Ernest E., 280, 306.
Fisher Unwin. See Unwin, T. Fisher.
Fitzgerald, Edward, 232, 396, 413, 415, 460, 491.
Fitzgerald, E.A., 415, 487, 574.
Fitzgerald, Percy H., 537, 574.
Fitzmaurice, Lady Edmund, 487-88.
Fitzmaurice, Miss, 480.

Flaubert, Gustave, 232.
Fletcher, John, 265.
Fleury, Auguste, 511, 575.
Fleury, Mme A., 504-06, 508, 511, 513-14, 540, 546, 565.
Fleury, Gabrielle, 9, 12, 14, 496-98, 503-15, 517-18, 520-23, 526, 530, 532-33, 536-47, 549-50, 564-66, 575, 578, 583.
Fleury, René, 511, 527, 529, 534, 541.
Flossie (servant), 282.
Foley, Mrs., 488.
Forbes-Robertson, Sir J., 507, 575.
Ford, Mr., 547.
Forestier, Amédée, 379, 446, 526, 575.
Forster, John, 20, 151, 240, 440, 540, 543, 545-46.
Forster, W.E., 2, 3.
Fra Angelico, 92, 97, 125, 294.
France, Anatole, 498.
Francia, 104.
François I, 48.
Franz (consul), 476.
Fraser, Bishop, 344.
Frazer, Sir J.G., 422.
Frederiç, Harold, 410, 413-14, 424, 508-10, 562, 575.
'Frederick III, 32, 45, 490, 551.
Freeman, E.A., 166-67, 373, 387, 389, 391-92, 416, 421, 458, 575.
Fremantle, Hon. C., 164.
Fricke, 207.
Frith, Henry, 251.
Froude, J.A., 276, 318-19, 365.
Funck-Brentano, Theodore and family, 521, 575.

G. See Fleury, Gabrielle.
Gabbrielli family, 447, 449-50, 452-53, 467, 487.
Gaboriau, Emile, 47, 553.

Gaetani, Carlo, 201, 555.
Galba, 121.
Galileo, 118, 121.
Galton, Sir Francis, 422.
Gambetta, Léon, 47.
Gardner, Mrs. (landlady), 329.
Gargiulo, Giacomo, 79.
Garibaldi, G., 51, 65, 91, 129, 457, 471.
Garland, Hamlin, 534, 563, 566.
Garofalo, 104.
Garrison, Frank, 389, 575.
Garrison, William Lloyd, 575, 590.
Gaskell, Elizabeth, 3, 331, 509.
Gasquet, F.A., 386.
Gatineau, Mlle, 541.
Gaussen, Mrs. David, 28, 33-35, 38, 46, 152, 157-58, 167, 210-11, 240, 567, 575.
Gaussen, Ella, 27, 34, 38, 41, 145-46, 218, 231, 272-73, 275, 340, 575.
Gaussen, James, 211, 575.
Gautier, Théophile, 49-51, 138, 502.
Genty, M. and Mme, 544-45, 549.
Géricault, Théodore, 52.
Ghirlandaio, 117, 125.
Giannone, Pietro, 480.
Gibbon, Edward, 99, 237-38, 256, 280, 293-94, 322, 369, 377-78, 384, 392, 436, 456.
Gilbert and Sullivan, 162, 232, 317-18.
Gilder, R.W., 348, 575.
Gill, Miss, 365.
Gillman, James, 148.
Giorgione, 91, 130.
Giovanni da San Giovanni, 116.
Giovanni da Udine, 99.
Gissing, Alfred (son), 401, 403-05, 417, 419, 422-24, 427, 430, 435, 438-42, 445, 449, 478, 495, 498, 501, 540, 550, 566, 575, 577.
Gissing, Algernon (brother), 9, 10,

20, 21, 25, 32, 34, 36-44, 53, 54,
57, 58, 71, 75, 80, 88, 113, 121,
123-24, 131, 142-43, 145-49, 151-
55, 157-60, 163, 165-68, 170, 179-
80, 183, 195, 203, 205, 210-14,
216-21, 224-26, 230-31, 233, 236-
42, 244-45, 247-51, 253, 255-58,
260-68, 270-72, 274-81, 283-93,
297-98, 300-02, 304, 306-07,
309-10, 312, 315-16, 319-25,
327-28, 331, 333-34, 336-43, 346,
349-52, 354-57, 359-65, 371-73,
376-79, 381, 383, 385-87, 389,
391-99, 401, 404-05, 408-11,
413-14, 416, 420-22, 424, 428,
431-34, 436-37, 440-41, 443-46,
449, 451-52, 460, 477, 481, 484-88,
490, 492, 495, 504, 506, 511, 521,
523, 531, 545, 550, 557, 576.
Gissing, Alwyn (nephew), 445.
Gissing, Captain, R.N., 232.
Gissing, Catherine (sister-in-law),
21, 32, 38, 41, 46, 71, 81, 82, 121,
123, 139, 142, 152, 170, 189, 195,
203, 236-37, 262, 270, 276, 285,
287-88, 304, 306, 308, 324, 327,
334-35, 353, 364, 376, 385, 397,
445, 449, 576.
Gissing, Edith (wife), 8, 13, 226-42,
245, 247-49, 254, 256-59, 262-83,
285, 287-90, 292, 296, 298, 300-01,
303-08, 310-15, 317, 319, 321-22,
325, 327, 330, 336-39, 344-47,
349-52, 356-58, 362, 370-71, 377,
380-82, 384-86, 389-90, 397,
400-05, 408, 413, 416, 419 , 422,
424, 429-30, 438-45, 448, 452, 478,
484-85, 488, 494-95, 498-501,
508-09, 512, 566, 576.
Gissing, Ellen (sister), 10, 18, 24, 26,
30, 32, 35-43, 45-48, 53, 56, 67,
71, 77, 80, 90, 101, 103, 109, 111,
113, 115, 118, 120-22, 124, 127,
130-32, 136, 139-41, 143-47, 149,
151-54, 156, 158, 160, 162, 164-65,
167, 169, 170, 186, 188-90, 195,
201, 210-20, 222-28, 230, 234, 236-
38, 241, 243, 245, 247-49, 252-53,
256, 259-61, 263, 266-69, 272-73,
275, 277-78, 281-84, 287-88, 293,
297, 301-02, 305, 312, 315, 319,
321-22, 324-26, 334-39, 341-42,
345, 348-49, 351, 353, 355-57, 359,
361, 364-65, 372-73, 376-78, 380,
384, 394, 397-98, 400, 403, 409-16,
419-20, 422-25, 427, 433, 436-37,
443, 448, 476, 480-82, 491, 511-12,
515, 523, 526-28, 531-32, 542, 544,
552, 576.
Gissing, Enid (niece), 71, 142, 224,
287-88, 306, 320-21, 335, 346,
353-54, 393, 446, 448, 454.
Gissing family at Agbrigg and
Wakefield, 171, 172, 185, 235,
243, 290, 307, 319, 323, 360, 399,
407-08, 426, 446, 449, 453, 455,
460, 476, 492, 495, 507-08, 519-20.
Gissing, George (of West Croydon),
281.
Gissing, Margaret (sister), 31, 32,
36, 38-43, 47, 55, 67, 101, 103,
121, 143, 145, 148, 153, 155, 158-
67, 169-70, 188, 205, 211, 213-17,
220, 222-25, 228, 230, 238, 241-42,
245, 249-52, 263, 267, 275-76, 278-
83, 286, 301-02, 313-14, 328, 339,
344, 357, 363, 384, 388, 394-95,
397, 399, 403, 407-09, 415-17, 419,
422, 424, 429, 435-36, 439, 441,
486, 491, 504, 511-13, 527-28,
536, 538, 542-43, 545, 576.
Gissing, Margaret Bedford (mother),
17, 19, 28, 32, 34, 38, 39, 41, 44,
47, 58, 62, 67, 90, 109, 136, 148,
152, 156, 158-59, 163, 166-68, 175-
76, 191, 194-95, 207, 210, 214,
220, 223-24, 230, 236, 239, 242,
244, 249, 251-52, 254, 259, 262-65,

269-70, 277, 283-84, 287-901,
301-07, 309-10, 317-18, 322, 324,
344-45, 354-55, 357, 363, 367, 376,
378, 380, 396-97, 401, 411, 415,
420, 422-23, 429, 436, 447, 491,
499, 502, 523, 527-28, 535, 542,
576.
Gissing, Marianne Helen (wife), 13,
22, 23, 576.
Gissing, Robert Foulsham
(grandfather), 338.
Gissing, Roland (nephew), 373, 376,
445.
Gissing, Thomas Waller (father), 23,
26, 34, 94, 338, 408, 410, 551-52,
569-70, 576.
Gissing, Walter (son), 263-70, 272-
73, 275-79, 281-82, 285, 287, 289-
94, 296-97, 301, 303, 305-08, 311-
13, 315, 317-18, 321-26, 328-34,
337-45, 347, 349-51, 353, 355-60,
367, 370-72, 380-84, 386, 388-89,
392-97, 400-05, 407-14, 416-25,
427-30, 432-36, 439-44, 446-49,
462, 465, 474, 480-81, 486, 491,
493, 495, 497-99, 502, 504, 507-09,
511, 513, 515, 519, 526-31, 535,
538-39, 542-45, 550, 575-77.
Gissing, William (brother), 291, 370,
397, 557, 576.
Gladstone, W.E., 28, 106, 111, 481,
493, 551.
Goethe, J.W., 11, 40, 42, 47, 52, 53,
56, 93, 101, 271-74, 364, 490.
Gogol, N., 26.
Goldsmith, Oliver, 38, 151, 156, 240,
546.
Goncourt, E. and J., 28-30, 351.
Gorst, Harold E., 519-20, 576.
Gosse, Edmund, 11, 242, 244, 290,
299, 302, 306, 379, 395, 414-15,
577.
Goudeau, Emile, 158.
Gower, Lord Ronald S., 483, 563.

Graham, Charles, 143.
Graham, J.W., 258.
Graham, R. Cunninghame, 35, 577.
Grahame, Alexander, 19.
Grahame, John, 17, 19.
Grahame, Walter, 13, 17-20, 26,
28-31, 33, 37, 38, 53, 54, 67, 77,
81, 82, 104, 120, 127, 152-53,
157-58, 165-66, 169, 189, 201, 214,
216, 227-28, 233, 236-37, 246, 248,
255, 257-60, 291, 299, 300, 354,
369, 577.
Grammont, P. de, 314, 558.
Grand, Sarah, 147.
Grant, Mrs. (servant), 493.
Graves, C.L., 488.
Gray, Asa, 234.
Gray, Thomas, 242-43.
Green, J.R., 218, 391.
Gregorovius, 435, 482, 541, 543-44,
563.
Gregory, 477.
Gresham Publishing Co., 539.
Greuze, J.-B., 52, 55.
Gribble, Francis, 322, 558.
Griest, Guinevere L., 1.
Groening, Miss, 394.
Gründl, Signora (landlady), 122,124,
126-27, 131, 136, 138.
Grundy, George, 532.
Gruter, Jan , 119.
Guasco, F.E., 119.
Guercino, 89, 91, 105.
Guido, 87, 89, 91.
Guizot, F., 257.
Gwynne Julia, 354, 560.
Gyp, 495, 507, 512, 564.

Habakkuk, 294.
Häberle, Frau (landlady), 60, 190,
195.
Häberle, Laurence, 201, 205-08, 210,
218.

Hachette, 47, 48, 50.
Hadow, W.H., 414, 562.
Hadrian, 179, 477, 543-44.
Haendel, G.F., 292.
Haggard, Rider, 318.
Halévy, Ludovic, 545.
Hall, Jane (in fact Jane Hall Waller, grandmother), 338.
Hall, Mr. and Mrs., 38, 40, 159, 224, 552, 556.
Hallam, Henry, 253.
Halpérine-Kaminsky, Ilia, 500, 564, 577.
Hamel, Miss, 374.
Hamerton, P.G., 433.
Hamilton, Mr., 327.
Hamlyn, Mrs., 170, 324, 577.
Hand, Miss, 28.
Hannibal, 457.
Hansen, Captain, 209.
Hardy, Thomas, 3, 24, 28, 155, 225-26, 230, 236, 247, 249, 262, 269, 280, 285-86, 331, 340-41, 346, 360, 379-80, 386-88, 393, 521, 577.
Hardy, Mrs. Thomas, 387-88, 426.
Hare, A.J.C., 312-13, 343, 346, 349, 428, 436, 559.
Hare, A.W., 85.
Harmsworth, 2.
Harper's, 155, 251-52, 556.
Harrison, Austin, 1, 147, 167, 420, 577.
Harrison, Bernard, 17, 18, 145, 149, 376, 420, 577.
Harrison, Edgar E., 21, 25, 27, 29, 37, 43, 80, 116, 121, 143, 149, 168, 211, 217-18, 234-35, 577, 584.
Harrison, Frederic, 17, 147, 149, 181, 249, 393, 414, 420, 427, 577, 582.
Harrison, Mrs. Frederic, 146-47, 244-45, 249, 289, 419-20, 491.
Harrison, Godfrey, 147.
Harrison, Jane Ellen, 497, 578.

Harrison, Marianne Helen. See Gissing, Marianne Helen.
Harrison, René, 147.
Harte, Bret, 274, 280.
Harte, W.B., 289, 292, 294, 364-65, 367, 578.
Hartley, Alfred, 144, 149-50, 168-69, 185, 211, 213, 229, 231-32, 275, 301-02, 324, 332, 367, 432, 578.
Harwood, Miss, 210.
Hatfield family, 528.
Haweis, H.R., 272.
Hawthorne, N., 30, 40, 67.
Haydon, B.R., 253.
Hayward, A., 273.
Headlam, Rev. Stewart, 32, 33, 35, 168, 552, 578.
Heine, Heinrich, 24, 49, 50, 152, 213, 265, 515.
Heinemann, 47, 391, 532.
Heinemann & Balestier, 264, 268, 278, 296, 300, 368.
Heinzen, 400.
Henderson, Dr., 257, 263-65, 267, 277, 301, 307.
Henley, W.E., 311, 319, 486, 557, 578.
Henry & Co., 353-54.
Herodian, 237.
Herrick, Robert, 148, 265.
Herwegh, Georg, 515, 578.
Hesiod, 232-33.
Hick, Ethel, 220, 337, 578.
Hick, Henry, 372, 376-77, 389-90, 396, 400, 412, 422, 427, 435, 440, 444, 446, 449, 488, 490, 495, 497, 499, 540, 578.
Hick, Matthew Bussey, 159, 220, 256, 259, 367, 371, 491, 578.
Hill, W.K., 354.
Hilliard, J.N., 372, 409, 563, 578.
Hind, C. Lewis, 496, 578.
Hirsch, William, 434.
Hissey, J.J., 434.

605

Hocking, Silas Kitto, 523, 578.
Hodgkin, Thomas, 378-79, 389-90, 436-38, 482, 510, 550, 578.
Hodgson, Miss (landlady), 38.
Hodgson Burnett, Mrs., 415, 579.
Hodgson, Mr. and Mrs. W.S., 161-62, 579.
Hoffmann, H., 348, 350.
Hogarth, D.G., 409.
Holbein, Hans, 323.
Holcroft, Thomas, 217, 555.
Holm, Adolf, 527.
Holt & Co., 535, 537.
Holyoake, G.J., 503.
Homer, 40, 42, 181, 242-43, 245, 261, 266, 279, 292-95, 341-42, 525-28, 533.
Hooker, Richard, 232.
Hope, Anthony, 353-54, 361, 367, 577, 579.
Horace, 26, 86, 90, 93, 97, 98, 105-06, 110, 113, 120-21, 123, 246, 267, 277, 414.
Hornung, E.W., 486-89, 579.
Hornung, Mrs. E.W., 486-89, 508.
Horsley, J.W., 26.
Houghton Mifflin, 347.
Houssaye, Arsène, 373, 561.
How, Walsham, 441.
Howard, John, 154.
Howells, W.D., 138, 320.
Howitt, Mary, 486, 564.
Hudson, W.H., 144, 147, 149, 168-70, 185, 210, 225, 243, 299-301, 310-12, 319-20, 324, 337, 342, 391, 400, 414, 430, 438, 449, 527-28, 541-42, 547-48, 579.
Hughes, Thomas, 315, 562, 569, 579.
Hugo, Victor, 158, 162-65, 503, 505.
Humbert I, 68.
Hungerford, Mrs., 227.
Hunt, Holman, 375.
Hunt, Leigh, 154-55.

Hunt, W.C., 315.
Hunter, W.A., 43, 579.
Huntingtower, Lady, 375.
Hurd, Frank, 477, 482-83.
Hurst & Blackett, 20, 21, 25, 142, 147-48, 205, 286, 297, 316, 319, 359, 365, 392-93, 395, 414.
Hutchinson, 424.
Hutton, Laurence, 26.
Hutton, R.H., 376.
Huxley, T.H., 254, 362, 397-99, 496.
Huysmans, J.K., 394.

Ibsen, H., 11, 30-32, 168, 256-58, 260, 273, 520.
Image, Selwyn, 433, 579.
Imbriani, 449.
Ingram, J.H., 402-03.
Ingres, D., 48.
Innes & Co., 351-53, 355, 360, 370.
Irving, Henry, 444, 491.
Irving, Washington, 38, 39.
Ison, Miss, 394.

Jackson, Rev., 209.
Jacobsen, J.P., 11, 156-57, 211-13, 579.
James II and III, 106, 477.
James, Henry, 33, 257, 276, 282, 285, 310, 413.
Jameson, Mrs., 403.
Japp, A.H., 361.
Jarmey (sexton), 338.
Jay, Rev. Osborne, 314-15, 357, 367, 378, 425, 579-80.
Jebb, J. Gladwyn, 424.
Jebb, R.C., 37, 241.
Jefferies, Richard, 235, 279.
Jerome, Jerome K., 5, 319-20, 332, 356-57, 360-61, 366-67, 560-61, 580.
Jessopp, A., 315.

Johnson, Lionel, 360, 436.
Johnson, Samuel, 218-19, 238, 335-36, 429.
Jolly, Dr. and Mrs., 81, 144, 149, 156, 211, 580.
Jones, A.H., 169.
Jones, W., 408.
Jones, W.D., 492.
Jonson, Ben, 148, 246, 275, 424, 427.
Josephus, 351-53.
Jugurtha, 107.
Julia Domna, 104-05.
Julian the Apostate, 99, 237.
Jusserand, J.J., 314, 558.
Justinian, 436.

Kant, E., 274, 334.
Kate or Katie. See Gissing, Catherine.
Keary, C.F., 11, 397, 399-402, 425-26, 501, 580.
Keats, John, 84, 85, 480.
Kebbel, T.E., 365.
Keble, John, 344.
Keer, Isabella, 306-07, 309, 311, 377-78.
Kegan, Paul, 375.
Keith, Dr. G.S., 406.
Kemble, Fanny, 396.
Kennedy, Benjamin, 387.
Kernahan, Coulson, 351.
King, Mrs. (charwoman), 38, 41, 44, 132, 139, 142, 146, 156-57, 163, 165-66, 201, 205, 210, 218, 236.
King, Henry, 34, 552.
Kinglake, A.W., 217.
Kingsley, Charles, 158-59, 171, 182, 189, 201, 402.
Kingsley, Henry, 289, 357.
Kipling, Rudyard, 11, 279, 285, 310, 340, 410, 427, 508.
Kitton, F.G., 528, 548, 566.

Knight, E.F., 359.
Knight, Joseph, 305.
Knott, G.H., 248.
Kolbac, Noël, 140, 554.
Kroker, Ernst, 125, 390.
Krout, Mary, 428.
Kuhe, Wilhelm, 423.

Labriola, Signora (landlady), 454.
Laffan, Rev. R.S. and Mrs. 486, 564.
Lamartine, A. de, 353.
Lamb, Charles, 159, 223, 275.
Lambart, Alfred, 450, 476-77, 480-84.
Lambart, Mrs. A., 477, 479-81, 483-89.
Lanciani, R., 436, 438.
Landor, W.S., 145, 170, 231, 285.
Landseer, Sir E.H., 23.
Lane (manager of 7K), 21, 28, 34, 121, 314.
Lane, John, 356, 383, 391, 550, 580.
Lang, Andrew, 5, 414-15, 501, 556, 580.
Lang family, 159, 250, 252.
Langhorne, J. and W., 216.
Lanin, E.B., 499.
Lannes, Mme (landlady), 544-45.
Laperrière (photographer), 517.
Larmath, M.H., 327.
La Spagna, 106.
Latham, H., 34, 552; 367.
Laurence (treasurer of the Temple), 498.
Lauria, Amilcare, 194, 196, 201, 555.
Lawrence, Lady Elizabeth, 385, 561.
Lawrence, Harry W., 6, 7, 323, 347-48, 352-53, 364, 370-72, 397, 411-12, 443, 580. See also Lawrence & Bullen.
Lawrence & Bullen, 4, 6, 13, 257,

259, 262-65, 270, 272, 279, 281, 283, 286, 297, 300-01, 307, 312, 318, 329, 334, 351, 366, 368, 383, 397, 408, 412, 482, 521, 550, 558, 562. See also Lawrence, H.W. and Bullen, A.H.

Layard, Sir A.H., 317-18.

Lea, Miss, 419.

Leaf, Dr. Walter, 413-14, 580.

Lear, Edward, 356, 488.

Le Breton, Fanny, 24, 29, 47, 48, 50, 52, 53, 56, 101, 122, 158, 213, 554, 580.

Lee, Jonas, 257, 378.

Lee, Sidney, 439, 502, 580.

Lee, T.S., 168, 555.

Lee, Vernon, 27, 28, 384, 580.

Le Gallienne, Richard, 352.

Legouvé, Ernest, 172.

Leighton, Frederick, 116.

Lemaître, Jules, 52.

Lenormant, François, 176, 441, 443-44, 459, 462, 468, 472.

Leo XIII, 120, 195, 478, 482-83.

Leonardo da Vinci, 47, 50, 51, 53, 99, 104.

Leoncavallo, Ruggero, 489.

Leopardi, Alessandro, 105.

Leopardi, Giacomo, 65, 166.

Le Quesne, Miss, 438.

Le Roux, Hugues, 438.

Leroy-Beaulieu, Anatole, 438.

Lescot, Mme, 529, 565.

Leslie, G., 428.

Lessing, G.E., 274.

Lester, E., 227.

Lett, Dr., 519.

Levy, Amy, 276.

Lewis, Dr. J. King, 269, 287.

Liddon, H.P., 157.

Linton, Mrs. Lynn, 22, 228, 581.

Lippi, Lippino, 117.

Lippincott's, 154.

Lister, Edith and Alys, 502, 564.

Littrow, Leo von, or de, 536, 581.

Lizzie (servant), 324.

Lizzy (aunt), 143.

Lloyd, Mr. and Mrs., 284, 588.

Lockhart, J.G., 36, 402, 427, 552.

Locking, Leonora, 432.

Lombroso, 385.

Longfellow, H.W., 67.

Longman, 255, 257, 375.

Lorrain, Dr., 539.

Loti, Pierre, 383, 544-45.

Louise, Princess, 41, 552.

Louise (servant), 519-20, 533.

Low, Sidney, 399, 497, 581.

Lowndes, Mrs. M.A., 433, 581.

Lowther Clarke family, 281.

Lucas, E.V., 488.

Lucian, 185, 188-89, 229, 238.

Lucretius, 274-75, 278.

Lucullus, 65.

Luker, William, 383, 561.

Lumbroso, Baron and Baroness, 480.

Lushington family, 145, 581.

Lushington, Kitty, 112, 420, 581.

Luther, 490.

Lyell, Charles, 239-40.

Lyon, Kate, 508, 510.

Lysander, 259.

Maartens, Maarten, 413, 581.

Macaulay, Lord, 255-56, 356.

McCarthy, Dr., 22.

McCarthy, Justin, 414, 435, 450, 481, 483, 488, 500, 506, 509, 514-15, 520, 581.

McCarthy, Justin Huntly, 507, 581.

McCarthy, Miss, 435, 450, 454, 476, 478, 481, 485, 506, 514, 581.

McCormick, A.D., 167, 230, 235, 322, 342, 438, 445, 502, 508, 526, 581.

Macdonald, F.W., 232.

608

Macdonnell, James, 232.
Macdonnell, Mr., 531.
McIlvaine, C.W., 387-88, 391, 393, 581.
Mackail, J.W., 421, 427.
Mackenzie (of "Funny Folks"), 322.
Maclaren, Ian, 395.
McLennan, Malcolm, 415.
Macmillan, 264, 296, 328, 368, 375-76, 400.
MacWhirter, 371.
Maddison, Lena, 40.
Maddison, Margaret, 224.
Madge. See Gissing, Margaret.
Mahaffy, J.P., 34, 371.
Malbranc, Dr. 207, 211.
Malet, Lucas, 267, 275.
Mallet, Mrs., 488.
Malot, Hector, 37.
Maman. See Fleury, Mme A.
Mancini. P.S., 111, 553.
Manso, Johann, 435.
Mantegazza, Paolo, 283.
Mantle, Mrs. (servant), 395-96, 400.
Marangoni-Brancuti, 480.
Maratta, Carlo, 83, 88, 89, 99.
Margaret (servant), 263, 267-68, 272, 277.
Marghieri, Alberto, 65.
Margueritte, Paul, 353, 560.
Mariani, 65, 553.
Mariéton, Paul, 504, 565.
Marionello, 203, 208.
Marlow, Christopher, 313.
Marriott-Watson, H.B., 497, 581.
Marston, Philip, 170.
Martial, 238-39, 241, 256, 386.
Marvell, Andrew, 279.
Masaniello (Tomaso Aniello), 202.
Mascagni, Pietro, 489.
Mason (artist), 534.
Mason, Mrs. (landlady), 438-39.
Maspéro, Gaston, 277.
Massey, Miss (landlady), 162, 165.

Massingham, H.W., 348-49, 396, 582.
Masson, David, 242.
Mastriani, Francesco, 201, 555.
Mather, Sir Herbert, 395.
Matsys, Quentin, 89.
Maupassant, G. de, 33, 35, 36, 310-11.
Maxse, Mrs. L.T. See Lushington, Kitty.
Maybrick, Mrs., 554.
Medhurst, Annie (servant), 363, 367, 381, 400, 406.
Melani, Alfredo, 99, 100, 103.
Menandros, 96.
Mendelssohn, Felix, 50, 51.
Mendelssohn (photographer), 393, 395-97, 550.
Mendès, Catulle, 45, 552.
Menzies, Dr., 139-40.
Meredith, George, 288, 334, 378-80, 385-88, 397, 400, 410, 430, 432, 446-47, 479, 492, 498, 505, 507, 511-12, 520, 582.
Meredith, Marie Eveleen, 388.
Meredith, William, 387.
Mérimée, Prosper, 504, 512.
Merivale, Charles, 378-79.
Methuen, Sir Algernon, 501, 511, 514, 528-29, 582. See also Methuen & Co.
Methuen & Co., 5, 6, 334-35, 361, 363, 365, 482, 485, 492, 495, 500-02, 521, 525, 533, 535, 566. See also Methuen, Sir Algernon.
Meynell, Wilfred and Alice, 410, 582.
Meysenbug, Malwida von, 210, 555.
Michel, Louise, 45, 553.
Michelangelo, 83, 87, 91, 93, 94, 97, 99, 111, 120-21, 289, 334.
Michelet, Jules, 50, 402, 504, 506-07.
Middleton, J.H., 437.

Mill, John Stuart, 280.
Millais, John Everett, 116.
Miller (accountant), 186, 188-91.
Miller, Ellen E., 324.
Miller, Hugh, 240.
Millet, James, 41, 552.
Milman, H.H., 437.
Milton, John, 118, 238, 242, 379.
Mitford, E.L., 318.
Mollo, Ernesto, 200, 202, 205-06, 208.
Mommsen, Theodor, 387.
Monkhouse, A.N., 399, 582.
Monod, Augustin, 521, 582.
Montaigne, Michel de, 238.
Montalembert, 376-78.
Montégut, Emile, 138, 554.
Montgomery, Florence, 384.
Montrésor, F.F., 384.
Moore, Frankfort, 508, 582.
Moore, George, 10, 27, 356, 396, 420, 582.
More, Hannah, 66.
Morgan, Osborne, 231, 556.
Morison, Cotter, 375, 387, 582.
Morley, John, 124, 147, 375-76, 400, 553, 582.
Morris, Mowbray, 264.
Morris, William, 423, 562.
Morrison, Arthur, 10, 356, 430, 552, 580, 583.
Mounet, Paul, 46.
Mounet-Sully, J., 52.
Mudie's, 301, 341, 343, 349, 361, 363, 402, 543-44, 559.
Müller, Karl, 176.
Mundall (dentist), 271.
Munthe, Axel, 167, 480.
Murat, Joachim, 78.
Murger, Henri, 18, 19, 49, 51, 214, 523.
Murray (guide-book), 88, 89, 92, 94, 103, 105, 456, 470.
Murray, John III, 411.

Murray, John IV, 526.
Musset, Alfred de, 48, 498, 504, 514, 519, 523, 529-30.
Musset, Hermine Lardin de, 498, 514, 522-23, 529, 532, 583.
Myers, F.W.H., 246, 414, 497, 583.

Nahum, 294.
Nansen, Dr. F., 433-34, 583.
Navarro, Antonio F., 434.
Nell. See Gissing, Marianne Helen.
Nellie, sometimes Nell. See Gissing, Ellen.
Nero, 62, 64, 88.
Neuville, A. de, 51.
Nevill, Lady Dorothy, 425, 583.
Newman, F.W., 170, 369.
Newman, J.H., 302.
Nicholls, Rev. A.B., 400.
Nicoll, W. Robertson, 232, 348-49, 379, 583.
Nordau, Max, 365.
Norman, Mrs. Henry, 13, 281, 364-66, 372-73, 377, 382, 391, 395-96, 398-400, 410, 420, 429, 431-33, 438, 443-44, 452, 455, 462, 482-83, 487, 491-92, 583.
Norman, (Sir) Henry, 373, 379-80, 438, 443-44, 452, 455, 491, 494, 533, 583.
Norman, Nigel, 444.
Norris, W.E., 427, 583.
Northcliffe, Lord, 2.
Northcote, Sir Stafford, 280, 557.

O'Dunne. See Dunne, Brian Boru.
Ohnet, Georges, 44, 552.
Oldham, J.B., 486.
Oliphant, Kingston, 426.
Oliphant, Laurence, 291, 344.
Oliphant, Margaret, 291, 336, 423.
Oliver, J.W., 400.

Omar Khayyám, 403, 460.
Orcagna, Andrea, 117.
O'Rell, Max, 433, 583.
Orf, 59, 60, 108-09.
Oriani, 204.
Orme, Beatrice, 436.
Orme, Eliza, 348, 352-53, 390,
    435-36, 438, 440, 442, 445, 447,
    449-52, 454-55, 475-79, 481-82,
    484-88, 493-95, 497, 499, 500, 508,
    512, 540, 542-43, 584.
Ortmans, F., 411-12, 479.
Ottmann, Victor, 266, 273, 278-79,
    584.
Ouida, 139, 258, 527, 531-32, 534,
    584.
Ovid, 160-62, 164-65, 168, 395, 414.
Owen, J.A., 397.
Owen and Boulger, 541.
Ozanam, A.F., 438-39, 563.

Pagano, José, 473.
Paget, Walter, 357, 584.
Pailleron, Edouard, 500, 564.
Palgrave, F.T., 38, 39, 72.
Palgrave, W.G., 325-26.
Palma Vecchio, 89, 128, 130.
Palmer, E.H., 378, 561.
Panagópoulos, Alexandre, 193-96.
Paparazzo, Coriolano, 467.
Parigory, Constantin, 175, 184-85,
    188-91.
Parker, Gilbert, 405, 523, 584.
Pascal, Blaise, 58.
Pasolini, Countess, 488.
Pater, Walter, 50.
Patmore, Coventry, 397.
Pattison, Mark, 242, 251.
Pattison, Mrs. Mark, 387.
Pauli, Reinhold, 314.
Pauline (G. Fleury's aunt), 514.
Payn, James, 6, 37, 40-42, 232, 253,
    362, 486, 584.

Pearce, J.H., 362.
Pearson, C.H., 401.
Pearson, Karl, 283-84, 292.
Peek, Francis, 403.
Peek, Hedley, 443-44, 584.
Pellico, Silvio, 65, 69.
Pemberton Max, 367, 379, 389, 392,
    584.
Penni, Francesco, 99.
Pepys, Samuel, 10, 40.
Persius, 395.
Perugino, 106, 117, 125.
Peruzzi, Baldassare, 99.
Petherick, E.A., 264.
Pfeiffer, Emily, 26, 551.
Phelps, Samuel, 24, 191, 551.
Philip II, 237.
Phillips, Mrs. (nurse), 262-67.
Phillips, Mrs. (of Brampford
    Speke), 267, 272, 275, 306-07.
Pinero, A.W., 32, 149, 395, 494,
    584.
Pinker, James, B., 6, 7, 443, 496-97,
    506, 511, 515-16, 519, 521, 523-26,
    529-36, 538, 540, 542, 544, 546,
    565, 572, 584.
Pintoricchio, 105.
Pio IX, 195.
Pittacus, 96.
Plato, 185-86, 189-90, 224, 261, 529.
Pliny, 168, 238, 373, 385.
Plitt, 24-26, 41, 43-49, 51, 53-61, 65,
    67-69, 71, 81, 82, 124, 136-37, 140,
    148-51, 153, 155, 157-58, 167-68,
    175, 181, 584.
Plotina, 104-05.
Plutarch, 216, 218, 259, 338-43,
    422-23.
Poe, Edgar, 67, 402-03, 503.
Pollock, Sir Frederick, 496, 584.
Pope, Alexander, 143, 219, 238.
Porcia, 65.
Porter, Henry, 169.
Poseilippos, 96.
Powles, Louis D., 316.

Poynter, Edward, 98.
Praxiteles, 86, 100.
Prescott, W.H., 237.
Press, Miss (landlady), 251.
Pressensé, E. de, 316.
Prével, Jules, 52.
Prévost, Marcel, 496, 564.
Price, E.L., 484-85.
Procter, Mrs., 388.
Prothero, R.E., 343, 384.
Pryce, R., 437.
Pugh, Edwin, 503.
Punshon, Morley, 232-33.
Purdet, M., 533.
Pye-Smith, Dr., 435, 540, 585.
Pythagoras, 193, 461, 463.

Quatrefages, Armand de, 264, 556.
Questa, 457-58.
Quilter, Harry, 28.
Quinet, Edgar, 499.

Rabelais, François, 256.
Rachel, 50.
Racine, Jean, 47, 50.
Radcliffe, Rev., 540-42.
Radford, Mrs. C.H., 533, 565.
Rae, John, 395.
Raffaelli, J.F., 135, 554.
Raimondi, Marcantonio, 105.
Raleigh, Sir Walter, 244.
Raleigh, Sir Walter (professor), 438, 585.
Randolph, Thomas, 353, 560.
Raphael, 23, 42, 53, 82, 83, 89, 92, 94, 98, 99, 101, 104, 106 ,126.
Rasponi, Signorina, 488.
Raymond, Mme Xavier, 56.
Read, Louise, 521, 565.
Reade, Charles, 297, 330, 513.
Recordon family, 518, 565.

Reeve, Mr. and Mrs. Henry, 101, 553.
Rehan, Ada, 336, 559.
Rembrandt, 48, 54, 55.
Renan, Ernest, 140, 289, 434, 554.
Repplier, Agnes, 350.
Reusch, F.H., 234.
Reuter, Gabriele, 212, 585.
Reynolds, Sir Joshua, 106.
Ribot, Théodule, 170, 555.
Ricci, C., 438, 563.
Richards, T.F. Grant, 433, 491, 496-97, 501, 585.
Richardson, Sir B.W., 374-75, 585.
Ritchie, Emily, 167.
Ritchie, Richmond, 496, 585.
Ritchie, Mrs. Richmond, 167, 398, 585.
Roberts, Cecil, 261, 343, 559.
Roberts, Morley, 3, 9, 18-22, 24-27, 29-31, 34-36, 39, 41-43, 45, 47, 53, 57, 58, 66, 82, 90, 97, 104, 120, 122, 124, 127, 131, 139, 142-51, 153, 155-57, 159, 164, 166-70, 172, 178, 189, 195-96, 201, 204, 207, 210-13, 216, 218-23, 225-37, 239-41, 243, 245-51, 253, 255-62, 264-66, 269-73, 275-79, 284-86, 288, 291-92, 294-96, 298-99, 301, 303-04, 307, 309-11, 314, 316-17, 319-20, 322, 324-25, 330, 332, 337, 342-44, 348, 355-56, 360-61, 363-65, 372, 377-78, 384, 391-93, 399, 400, 405, 409-10, 412, 419, 421, 423, 430, 433, 445, 451, 491, 505, 524, 544, 547, 554-57, 559-61, 566, 576-77, 585.
Robertson, F.W., 257.
Robertson, Sir George, 438, 585.
Robin, M., 164.
Robinson, Dr., 504, 506-07.
Robinson, F.W., 5, 224, 415, 585.
Rochefort, Henri, 432.
Rockett, C.J. and family, 236, 239, 242-43, 251-53, 255, 585.

612

Rolfe, Neville (consul), 454, 473.
Romanes, G.J., 248, 426.
Romano, Giulio, 98, 99, 104.
Romberg, 164.
Romeike, Henry, 155-56, 554.
Rosa, Salvator, 89.
Rose, J.H., 430, 432, 439, 445, 467,
  477-79, 485-86, 585.
Rosny, J.H., 433.
Ross, Janet, 460.
Rossetti, D.G., 305.
Rostand, Edmond, 486.
Rothenstein, William, 436, 491, 513,
  565, 586.
Rottimaler, Mme, 312.
Rousseau, J.-J., 48, 502.
Rovetta, Gerolamo, 352, 355, 586.
Rowe, Miss (landlady), 288, 290.
Rubens, P.P., 51, 54, 55, 116.
Runciman, John, 374.
Ruskin, John, 25, 89, 114-17,127-28,
  130-31, 137, 189, 375, 531, 551.
Russell (photographer), 359-60, 362,
  364.
Rutherford, Mark, 3, 410, 412, 586.

Sabatier, Paul, 500.
Sacher-Masoch, Aurora von, 498,
  519, 521, 586; her son, 520.
Saglio, Alfred and family, 533, 540,
  586.
Saglio, M. and Mme Edmond, 521.
St Clair, Colonel, 534.
Saint-Pierre, B. de, 66.
Sainte-Beuve, Charles, 529, 534,
  565.
Sallust, 26.
Sampson, Mrs., 390.
Sand, George, 18-20, 31, 38, 44, 48,
  49, 136, 261, 334, 422, 504, 529.
Sarah (servant), 21.
Sarcey, Francisque, 46, 48, 56, 57,
  133, 135, 586.

Sardou, Victorien, 521.
Savigny, Friedrich, 481.
Savonarola, Girolamo, 120.
Schiller, F. von, 272.
Schliemann, Heinrich, 178, 190, 555.
Schopenhauer, Arthur, 334, 374.
Schreiner, Olive, 147, 586.
Schweichel, Georg, 165, 554.
Scott, Miss, 486.
Scott, Miss E.F., 25, 26, 551.
Scott, Walter, 22, 29, 219-22, 257,
  289. 552.
Scott-Stevenson, Mrs., 321.
Scribe, Eugène, 172.
Sculco, Dr. Enrico, 463-65, 563.
Seeley, J.R., 364-65.
Sénancour, E. Pivert de, 503.
Septimius Severus, 104.
Serao, Matilde, 194, 351-54, 356,
  359, 555.
Sergeant, E.F. Adeline, 227, 427,
  586.
Severino, 481, 487.
Severn, Joseph, 85.
Shailer, Mrs., 41, 42, 247, 289, 320.
Shakespeare, William, 20, 41, 106,
  142-43, 170, 265, 275, 286, 294,
  297, 313, 325-26, 334, 336, 340-42,
  531.
Sharp, William, 216, 379, 586.
Shaw, G.B., 321.
Sheffield, Mr. 371.
Shelley, P.B., 84, 159, 414, 460.
Sherard, R.H., 354, 357, 560.
Sherlock, Mrs. (landlady), 22, 23.
Shorter, C.K., 5, 300, 310-13,
  315-17, 322-25, 327-29, 337-38,
  340-41, 343, 348, 353, 357, 359-61,
  365, 370, 374, 376-79, 381-82, 386,
  390-92, 396-97, 400, 406, 413, 426,
  432-33, 439, 491-92, 520, 522, 525,
  550, 560, 586.
Shortridge, J.W. and family, 75-81,
  88, 97, 132, 144, 180-81, 189,
  197-208, 211, 213, 586 .

Shortridge, Nellie, 144.
Sichel, Edith, 13, 26, 153, 155-56, 159, 166-67, 169-71, 175, 181, 189, 195, 219-20, 231, 551, 587.
Sickert, Walter, 513.
Sidgwick, Henry, 334.
Sidonius Apollinaris, 535.
Sienkiewicz, Henryk, 433.
Simone (landlord), 518.
Skeat, W.W., 425.
Sladen, Douglas, 355, 587.
Slater, J.H., 377.
Smiles, Samuel, 2, 411.
Smith (Oxford don), 31.
Smith, Adam, 395.
Smith, A.J., 13, 39, 139, 142, 153, 155, 185, 217, 233, 239, 243, 247, 256, 261, 270-71, 274, 313-14, 319, 325, 331, 352-53, 376, 587.
Smith, Archdeacon, 158.
Smith, Mrs. Charles, 486.
Smith, Elder, 4, 6, 17, 25, 37, 45-48, 53, 58, 118, 121, 143, 146, 212, 222-23, 225, 232, 235, 238, 243-44, 251, 253, 259, 262, 360, 498, 524, 537, 566. See also Smith, George.
Smith, George, 7, 25, 587. See also Smith, Elder.
Smith, H.G., 376, 434, 587.
Smith, Sir W., 481.
Smith, Watson, 325.
Smith, William, 403, 587.
Socrates, 71, 179.
Sodoma, 104.
Solon, 95.
Somerville, Mary, 344, 559.
Sophia, Princess, 176.
Sophocles, 37, 38, 52, 54, 111-12, 190-91, 193.
Southey, Robert, 217, 257.
Sowerby, W.C., 26, 551.
Sparkes, Janet (servant), 392-93, 395.
Spencer, Herbert, 396, 403, 562.

Spenser, Edmund, 275.
Sprague, Miss, 395-96, 400, 402-03, 410, 415, 433, 436, 475, 587.
Sproul, George, 540.
Squire, Mrs. (landlady), 382.
Stainer, J., 477, 479.
Stamer, W.J.A., 167.
Stanford, 204.
Stanley, Dean A.P., 343, 364.
Stanley, Sir H.M., 187.
Stannard, Willie (cousin), 118, 120, 123, 132, 195-96, 587.
Statter, Dr., 370.
Stead, W.T., 340, 587.
Stedman. See Methuen, Sir Algernon.
Steel, F. and A., 564.
Steele, Richard, 243- Tatler, 21, 34, 148-49, 232-33.
Steevens, G.W., 496, 587.
Steevens, Mrs. G.W., 497.
Steinitz, Clara, 138, 150, 166, 587.
Steinitz, Mr., 281, 587.
Stendhal, 138.
Stephen, Sir J.F., 328.
Stephen, Leslie, 242.
Stephens, W.R.W., 392.
Stepniak, 283.
Sterne, Laurence, 243.
Steuart, J., 261, 491.
Stevens (undertaker), 22.
Stevenson, R.L., 33, 278, 313, 362, 367, 374, 394, 399, 414, 512.
Stevenson and Osbourne, 393, 395.
Stewart, Charles, 307, 557.
Stokes Co., 483, 485, 498.
Stokes, John, 508-10.
Stolberg, Count, 548.
Street, G.S., 365.
Stuart, Charles Edward and Henry, 106, 477.
Sturgis, H.P., 388, 561.
Sturmer, H.H., 404, 423, 442-43, 446, 448, 477, 484-85, 491, 587-88.

614

Sudermann, Hermann, 380, 383.
Suetonius, 238.
Summers, Alfred, 294, 588.
Summers, William, 280, 294, 303, 588.
Sutton, Dr. C.S., 210.
Swan, Bradleigh, 109.
Swift, Benjamin, 429.
Swift, Jonathan, 242, 402, 406-07.
Swinburne, A.C., 34, 356, 427, 520, 547-48, 566.
Swinton-Hunter, 477, 479, 481, 483, 486-87.
Symonds, J.A., 114, 127, 133, 138-39, 289, 362, 409, 588.

Tacitus, 537.
Taine, Hippolyte, 109, 138, 166, 405.
Tasso, Torquato, 77.
Tateo, Vincenzo, 449.
Tauchnitz, 201, 205, 253, 256, 555.
Taylor, Isaac, 154, 327.
Taylor, Jeremy, 255.
Taylor, Miss, 386.
Taylor, Mrs. P., 390, 561.
Taylor, Tom, 253.
Temple, F., 233.
Tennyson, Alfred, 23, 86, 99, 217, 229, 286, 290, 325, 388, 416, 420, 428, 449, 503, 557, 588.
Tennyson, Lady, 419.
Tessandier, Aimée, 50.
Thackeray, F. St. John, 386.
Thackeray, W.M., 17, 28, 38, 485-86, 496.
Thalberg, S., 70.
Theocritus, 181.
Thesiger, Wilfrid (consul), 459-60.
Thierry, Mme, 415.
Thierry, Augustin, 505.
Thompson family, 152.
Thomson, Edith, 392.

Thomson, James, 242.
Thomson, Joseph, 335.
Thornborough, Mrs., 27.
Thornbury, G.W., 313.
Thornycroft, Sir W.H., 415, 427, 588.
Thorvaldsen, B., 490.
Thucydides, 17, 18, 26.
Tiberius, 79, 91, 93, 100.
Tillotson's, 118-19, 127, 142-43, 155, 185, 553.
Tinckam, C.W., 304-10, 326, 330-31, 337-39, 345, 351, 354, 373, 392, 404, 406, 425, 588.
Tinckam, Mrs. C.W., 308-10, 392.
Tintoretto, 129, 134, 138.
Titian, 56, 71, 89, 124, 126, 130.
Titus, 88, 121.
Tobit, 406.
Tolstoi, Leo, 36, 37, 249, 296, 343, 395, 500, 520-21.
Tosti, 205.
Tosti, Luigi, 477.
Tovote, Heinz, 479.
Towlson White, 76.
Tozer, H.F., 320, 372.
Traill, H.D., 243, 272, 588.
Traille, Bernard, 284.
Trajan, 104.
Trantum, Mr., 479.
Travers, Mrs., 13, 377-78, 389, 393-94, 396-98, 406-07, 409-11, 414, 427, 432, 440, 475, 588.
Travers, Rosalind, 13, 367, 372, 377, 384, 413, 492.
Trelawny, E.J., 84, 307, 553, 557-58.
Tripepi, 473.
Tristram, H.D., 321-22.
Trollope, Anthony, 530.
Turgenev, Ivan, 18, 33, 35, 36, 170, 211, 295, 385.
Turner, Alfred, 489, 588.
Turner, William, 187, 204, 334, 384.
Tylor, E.B., 265.

Umilta family, 475-76, 478-79.
Underwood, Edith. See Gissing, Edith.
Underwood, Florence (Flossie, later Mrs Lloyd), 233, 238, 588.
Underwood, George, 244, 588.
Underwood, James, 229-30, 235.
Unwin, T. Fisher, 5, 6, 360-61, 365-67, 372, 402, 588.
Usedom, A. von, 207-08.

Vandermirden, Mrs. Victoria (in fact, Von der Meden), 336, 377.
Van Dyck, 51, 57, 88.
Van Lennep, 317-18.
Van Ostade, 55.
Vanwyke, H., 269, 557.
Vasari, G., 87, 117, 294.
Velasquez, 421.
Verga, Giovanni, 399, 562.
Vergil, 18, 45, 93, 199, 233.
Verney family, 385, 388.
Veronese, 91, 135.
Vic. See Vandermirden, Mrs. V.
Victor Emmanuel (son of Humbert I), 68.
Victor Emmanuel II, 119.
Victor, Wilhelm, 429.
Victoria (Queen), 535-36.
Vieusseux, André, 392.
Vince, C.A., 480.
Viola, Professor, 472.
Virginia (servant), 206, 208.
Voltaire, 50.
Volterra, Daniele da, 106.
Von Leyden, Dr., 484.
Von Loeper, Baron, 482-83.
Von Thielmann, 426.

Wagner, Richard, 489.
Walker, Dr. Jane, 540.
Walker, Mr. and Mrs., 169.

Walker, Mary Adelaide, 27, 551.
Walkley, A.B., 395, 589.
Wallace, A.R., 248.
Wallace, Professor, 169.
Waller, Edmund, 297.
Waller, Mrs. (landlady), 435.
Walter, M., 208.
Walter-Madge, E., 527.
Walters, Alan, 350.
Walton, Isaac, 239.
Ward, Alice, 514, 522-23, 528, 530-31, 546, 589.
Ward, Lock, 6, 357, 361-62.
Ward, Mrs. Humphry, 28, 252, 428, 551.
Ward, Mrs. Waller, 312.
Waterbury, Jennie, 284, 557.
Waterford, Lady Louisa, 343-44, 559.
Waters, W.G., 507.
Waterton, Charles, 42.
Watson, Miss, 543.
Watson, William, 376, 387, 396, 545, 589.
Watt, A.P., 6, 253, 255-57, 263-66, 277, 360, 400, 589.
Watts landlord), 500, 512.
Watts, G.F., 116.
Watts-Dunton, W.T., 379, 506, 589.
Waugh, Arthur, 543, 589.
Webb, Beatrice, 12, 487.
Webster, Wentworth, 548.
Wells, Amy, 427.
Wells, Catherine, 429, 432, 481, 486-88, 493, 496-97, 499, 524, 536-37.
Wells, H.G., 3, 12, 402, 427-30, 432, 435, 437-38, 440, 445, 449, 453, 476-78, 480-84, 486-89, 496-97, 499, 500, 502, 504-05, 512, 524-25, 527-28, 536-37, 540, 548, 564, 574, 577, 589.
Wesley, Jessie (landlady), 245.
West, 439.

Whale, George, 348, 365, 374, 379, 396, 399, 405, 411-12, 414, 427, 439, 452, 478, 492, 506, 508, 536, 562, 589.
Whately, Archbishop, 297.
Wheatley, H.B., 439, 589.
White, Arnold, 24.
White, Gilbert, 444.
White, Greenough, 505, 507.
White, Rachel, 566.
Whitman, Walt, 24, 208.
Whyte-Melville, G.J., 440.
Wicksteed, P.H., 170.
Widgery, W.H., 354.
Wieland, C., 229, 238.
Wilde, Oscar, 310, 375.
Wilkins, W.W., 373.
William I, 24, 490, 551.
William II, 32, 551.
Williams, Austin, 42, 353, 569.
Williams, Mary Bedford. See Bedford, Mary.
Williams, Raymond, 1, 2.
Williams, Mrs. Rosalind, 12, 487-88, 491, 498-99, 505-06, 589.
Wilmot, Blanche, 367.
Wilson, Dr., 119, 121.
Wilson, Mrs. Robert, 410.
Wise, T.J., 400, 589-90.
Wood, Dr., 76.
Wood, Dr. Frank, 367, 370-71, 408.
Wood, James, 201, 370, 401, 407-08, 590.
Wood, Mrs. James, 451-52.

Wood, Mrs. Henry, 11, 485.
Wood, Sir Henry T., 375, 590.
Wood, J.G., 268.
Wood, Stanley, 404, 407, 590.
Woods, Margaret L., 17, 104, 590.
Woodward, Llewellyn, 2.
Woolf, Joseph, 399.
Woolner, Thomas, 150, 554.
Wordsworth, Christopher, 259.
Wordsworth, William, 40, 85, 147, 246.
Wright (librarian), 438.
Wright, W.A., 396.
Wright, Thomas, 316-17.

Xenophon, 299, 300-01, 306-07.

Yates, Thompson, 484.
Yeats (gardener), 435.
Younghusband, F.E., 430.

Zakrzewska, Dr., 389, 395-96, 400-03, 407, 436, 498, 590.
Zangwill, Israel, 309, 363-64, 379, 414-15, 420, 558, 590.
Zangwill, Louis, 416, 590.
Zapp, Arthur, 271, 590.
Zola, Emile, 54, 133, 308, 310-13, 317, 403-05, 411-12, 415, 484.
Zosimus, 457.

617